THE RELIGIONS
OF CANADIANS

THE RELIGIONS OF CANADIANS

EDITED BY JAMIE S. SCOTT

UNIVERSITY OF TORONTO PRESS

7685350 04

www.utppublishing.com

Library and Archives Canada Cataloguing in Publication

The religions of Canadians / edited by Jamie S. Scott.

Includes bibliographical references and index.
Also issued in electronic format.
ISBN 978-1-4426-0516-9

1. Religions. 2. Canada—Religion. 3. Religious pluralism—Canada. I. Scott, Jamie S.

BL80.3.R44 2012   200   C2011–908515–1

We welcome comments and suggestions regarding any aspect of our publications—please feel free
to contact us at news@utphighereducation.com or visit our Internet site at www.utppublishing.com.

North America
5201 Dufferin Street
North York, Ontario, Canada, M3H 5T8

2250 Military Road
Tonawanda, New York, USA, 14150

ORDERS PHONE: 1–800–565–9523
ORDERS FAX: 1–800–221–9985
ORDERS E-MAIL: utpbooks@utpress.utoronto.ca

UK, Ireland, and continental Europe
NBN International
Estover Road, Plymouth, PL6 7PY, UK
ORDERS PHONE: 44 (0) 1752 202301
ORDERS FAX: 44 (0) 1752 202333
ORDERS E-MAIL: enquiries@nbninternational.com

The University of Toronto Press acknowledges the financial support for its publishing activities
of the Government of Canada through the Canada Book Fund.

Typesetting: Em Dash Design

Printed in Canada

For Josh, Nick, and Emily

Contents

Acknowledgements

||||||||||||||||||||||||||||||||||||||||||||||||||||||||||||||||||||||||||||||||||||||||||||||||||||||||||||||||||||||||||||||||||||||||||||

Two decades have passed between the conception and the appearance of *The Religions of Canadians*, so a great many people have helped to bring the book to the light of day. I first thought of the project in Palmerston North, New Zealand, in 1992. I was on sabbatical leave from my academic home base at York University in Toronto, conducting research on Christian missions in the South Pacific, and was invited to give a talk at Massey University on the state of Religious Studies as a scholarly field in Canada. As a "thank-you," my hosts Peter Donovan and Bronwyn Elsmore presented me with a copy of a book they had recently published titled *The Religions of New Zealanders*. The book brings together essays on the variety of religious traditions that have taken root in New Zealand's social and cultural landscape, dedicating separate chapters by different authors to disparate traditions. For a number of reasons, it seemed obvious that Canadians might enjoy a similar sort of volume, so it is to Peter and Bronwyn that my first thanks go for planting the idea for *The Religions of Canadians*. This idea remained dormant for a long while, though, as I finished other research. Then, in 1994, out came Jacob Neusner's *World Religions in America*, which followed more or less the same rubric as *The Religions of New Zealanders*. The time had come to start the ball rolling in earnest for *The Religions of Canadians*. It took over two years to round up a complement of suitably qualified colleagues, and then almost five more years until we had first drafts of most of the material, all of which was reworked in an effort to achieve balance and continuity of content and style across the diverse chapters.

During this time, some contributors dropped out of the project and were replaced by others, in two or three cases necessitating the radical rewriting of chapters. My second vote of thanks, therefore, goes to those colleagues who stuck with *The Religions of Canadians* from my initial invitation to contribute to the book through all the revising to eventual publication, as well as to those colleagues who joined us late and were willing to undertake the difficult task of bringing to maturity the half-hatched work of others. Third, I must express my gratitude to the University of Newcastle, New South Wales, Australia, in particular Terry Lovat, Pro Vice-Chancellor (Education & Arts), and Stephen Webb, Director of the Research Institute of the Advanced Study for Humanity (now the Australian Institute for Social Inclusion and Wellbeing), for appointing me Visiting Research Professor of Interdisciplinary Studies, 2008–2009, which allowed me to commit myself full-time to the final completion of the manuscript.

Fourth, I would like to recognize the influence of dozens of students who have taken my York University course "The Religions of Canadians" over the last two years. They have read much of the manuscript as part of their course material and the book is stronger for their feedback. Fifth, thanks go to the folks at the University of Toronto Press and their affiliates, especially Michael Harrison, for their encouragement, wisdom, and efficiency throughout the production and publishing process, as well as the anonymous manuscript readers for their many insightful and constructive comments. Sixth, due credit appears with photographs, but I would like to single out my York University colleague Candace Iron for special thanks: when we lacked pictures, she went out and took some, with remarkable results. Last but not least, of course, it is a delight to say "thank you" to Josh, Nick, and Emily for the countless ways, visible and invisible, that they have supported me throughout the long gestation of *The Religions of Canadians*.

Jamie S. Scott

Director, Graduate Program in Interdisciplinary Studies

York University, Toronto

Religions and the
Making of Canada

JAMIE S. SCOTT, YORK UNIVERSITY

||||||||||||||||||||||||||||||||||||||||||||||||||||||||||||||||||||||||||||||||||||||||||||||||||||||||||||||||||

S
ome years ago, T. Sher Singh, an occasional columnist for the
Toronto Star from Guelph, Ontario, wrote an "op-ed" piece on the
coincidence of several sacred festivals occurring over a two-week
period in the spring—the birthday of Hindu Lord Rama; Christian
Easter; the Muslim Feast of Sacrifice; the birthday of Jain Lord Mahavira;
Jewish Passover; Sikh Baisakhi; and Saka, the Buddhist New Year. This
coincidence of sacred festivals may not be all that unusual. But a more
searching set of questions underlies the prominence given to Singh's
piece in the opinion and editorial pages of the newspaper: why did
Singh and the editors of the *Toronto Star* think that a topic of this sort
would be of interest to their readership? What kind of readership would
be able to make sense of such a motley array of religious events, any-
way? And more critically, why does this coincidence of sacred festivals
merit "op-ed" commentary, rather than simply remaining a matter for
the newspaper's section on religion, or perhaps the local news pages or
what's-on notices?

To a large degree, we may answer these questions by invoking the
intertwined lexicons of constitutional equality and legitimated multiculturalism that began to saturate the atmosphere of everyday life in Canada

in the last decades of the twentieth century.[1] Legislated on 17 April 1982, Canada's Charter of Rights and Freedoms includes extensive protections and guarantees for various kinds of rights and freedoms. Under "Fundamental Freedoms," the Charter lists "freedom of conscience and religion," "freedom of thought, belief, opinion and expression, including freedom of the press," "freedom of peaceful assembly," and "freedom of association," all of which play roles in individual and collective spiritual life.[2] After being delayed to allow provincial governments time to bring their own legislation into line with the Charter, section 15 dealing with "Equality Rights" took effect three years later, on 17 April 1985. This section includes religion among a number of social and cultural identifiers safeguarded in law: "Every individual is equal before and under the law and has the right to the equal protection and equal benefit of the law without discrimination and, in particular, without discrimination based on race, national or ethnic origin, colour, religion, sex, age or mental or physical disability," though this subsection "does not preclude any law, program or activity that has as its object the amelioration of conditions of disadvantaged individuals or groups including those that are disadvantaged because of race, national or ethnic origin, colour, religion, sex, age or mental or physical disability."[3]

The Canadian Multiculturalism Act passed into law on 21 July 1988, gaining royal assent after all political parties constituting Canada's federal Parliament supported the adoption of the legislation. The act takes its cue from the Charter of Rights and Freedoms, reiterating that "the Constitution of Canada provides ... that everyone has the freedom of conscience, religion, thought, belief, opinion, expression, peaceful assembly and association and guarantees those rights and freedoms equally to male and female persons."[4] Once again including religion among various kinds of individual and collective identifiers, it goes on to state that "Canada is a party ... to the *International Covenant on Civil and Political Rights,* which Covenant provides that persons belonging to ethnic, religious or linguistic minorities shall not be denied the right to enjoy their own culture, to profess and practise their own religion or

---

1   What follows owes something to my essay "Religion, Literature and Canadian Cultural Identities," *Literature and Theology* 16, no. 2 (2002): 1–14.

2   Charter of Rights and Freedoms, Department of Justice Canada, accessed 11 January 2012 from http://laws.justice.gc.ca/eng/charter/.

3   Ibid., 3–4.

4   Canadian Multiculturalism Act, Department of Justice Canada, accessed 11 January 2012 from http://laws-lois.justice.gc.ca/eng/acts/c-18.7/.

to use their own language," and that "the Government of Canada recognizes the diversity of Canadians as regards race, national or ethnic origin, colour and religion as a fundamental characteristic of Canadian society and is committed to a policy of multiculturalism designed to preserve and enhance the multicultural heritage of Canadians while working to achieve the equality of all Canadians in the economic, social, cultural and political life of Canada."[5] The act then requires the Canadian federal government to both "recognize and promote the understanding that multiculturalism reflects the cultural and racial diversity of Canadian society and acknowledges the freedom of all members of Canadian society to preserve, enhance and share their cultural heritage," and "recognize and promote the understanding that multiculturalism is a fundamental characteristic of the Canadian heritage and identity and that it provides an invaluable resource in the shaping of Canada's future."[6] In this respect, the policy of multiculturalism does not just encourage communities of different ethnic backgrounds to maintain the ways of life and customs of their countries of origin; it also lays a legal foundation for public subsidizing of varieties of ethnic heritage with tax dollars—or perhaps with lottery money, which you might say serves as a kind of voluntary tax.

At the heart of this multiculturalist agenda lies what Canadian social philosopher Charles Taylor has called a "politics of recognition." For Taylor, religious diversity is a key aspect of such politics; in his words, " ... it is reasonable to suppose that cultures that have provided the horizon of meaning for large numbers of human beings, of diverse characters and temperaments, over a long period of time—that have, in other words, articulated their sense of the good, the holy, the admirable— are almost certain to have something that deserves our admiration and respect, even if it is accompanied by much that we have to abhor and reject."[7] In this spirit, where Americans have historically taken pride in the United States as a melting pot of constituent immigrant legacies, Canadians have preferred to speak of their country in less reductionist ways; first in terms of English and French Canada, and now as a mosaic—or perhaps a shifting kaleidoscope—of social and cultural

---

5   Ibid., 2.

6   Ibid., 3.

7   Charles Taylor, *Multiculturalism and the Politics of Recognition* (Princeton: Princeton University Press, 1992), 72–73.

identities.[8] This mosaic includes the various and vying beliefs and practices of the world's religions, as immigrant devotees have come to embody and express them across Canada over the decades. In turn, the more nuanced cultivation of diversity and difference in Canada's social and cultural life requires Canadians to continually assess and re-assess their appreciation of individual and collective religious beliefs and practices, especially when it comes to balancing the rights and responsibilities of new immigrant communities against the power and privilege of more established religious groups.

The legislative linkage between the Canadian Multiculturalism Act and the Charter of Rights and Freedoms marks what Will Kymlicka and Wayne Norman have identified as "a growing awareness of the importance of certain interests that had typically been ignored by liberal theories of justice; *e.g.* interests in recognition, identity, language, and cultural membership."[9] Despite this insight, however, the policies associated with the act have attracted their naysayers. Such doubters hail from disparate quarters, but their arguments mostly share a common concern: "how to show respect for diversity in a pluralistic society without at the same time damaging or eroding the bonds and virtues of citizenship."[10] Wary that too much emphasis on social and cultural diversity risks undermining the stability and identity of Canada as a distinctive people constituting a unified nation, skeptics about the country's multicultural agenda often refer to Neil Bissoondath's book, *Selling Illusions: The Cult of Multiculturalism in Canada,* first published in 1994, as a representative statement of the key aspects of their position. A Canadian of East Indian Trinidadian origin who publishes in English and lives in Quebec, Bissoondath offended the leaders of visible minority and liberal white communities alike with his description of multicultural Canada as "a zoo of exoticism."[11] His book

---

8   Commonly associated with the Canadian ideal of multiculturalism, the image of the mosaic was coined in 1922 by an American travel writer, Victoria Hayward, who describes the varied "[c]hurch architecture" of the Prairies as "a mosaic of vast dimensions and great breadth" (Victoria Hayward, *Romantic Canada* [Toronto: Macmillan and Company, 1922], 187). John Murray Gibbon popularized the image in *Canadian Mosaic: The Making of a Northern Nation* (Toronto: McClelland and Stewart, 1938), and as Augie Fleras and John Leonard Elliott note, it has since become "ingrained in Canadian society" (in *The Challenge of Diversity: Multiculturalism in Canada* [Scarborough, ON: Nelson Canada, 1992], 64). On the figures of mosaic and kaleidoscope, see Janice Kulyk Keefer, "From Mosaic to Kaleidoscope," *Books in Canada* 20, no. 6 (1991): 13–16.

9   Will Kymlicka and Wayne Norman, eds., *Citizenship in Diverse Societies* (New York: Oxford University Press, 2000), 5.

10   Ibid.

11   Neil Bissoondath, *Selling Illusions: The Cult of Multiculturalism in Canada*, rev. ed. (Toronto: Penguin Books Canada, 2002), 211.

claims that, far from advancing "a factual and clearminded view of our neighbours," Canada's multicultural policies depend on "stereotype, ensuring that ethnic groups will preserve their distinctiveness in a gentle and insidious form of cultural apartheid," thus leading "an already divided country down the path to further social divisiveness."[12]

Such skeptical critiques of Canada's multicultural policies assume a particular shape in the realm of the religious. On the one hand, the skeptic will admit, keeping company with Canadians of similar religious background may well help newcomers of different ethnic origins to adapt more comfortably to life in Canada, since familiar values will continue to shape everyday life, cushion the shock of the new, and provide shelter from discrimination, whether real or perceived. On the other hand, the skeptic will reply, such associations run the more undesirable risk of creating ghettoes of religious minorities made up mostly of relative newcomers to Canada. When marginalized in this way, the skeptic's argument goes, recent immigrants will inevitably experience frustration in their efforts to integrate into society and culture at large—or worse, they will find themselves subtly and silently excluded.

At the same time, the lines distinguishing religious from ethnic heritage are often difficult to identify. While Canada's Charter of Rights and Freedoms and the Canadian Multiculturalism Act may offer formal redress against religious prejudice and encourage social and cultural diversity, today's media often include stories about religious leaders who claim to repesent local, regional, or even nationwide discomfort with perceived systemic prejudices against particular minority beliefs and practices. Such declared discomfort may pertain to all manner of issues, some purely domestic in nature, others involving overseas connections; some having to do with individual behaviours, others with collective activities. A random list of easily conceivable instances from the religious traditions discussed at length in the chapters that follow might include: a Roman Catholic, Irish Canadian priest in the Maritimes condemning all abortion, regardless of circumstances; a sermon decrying homosexuality by a Pentecostal Christian, Korean Canadian minister in Vancouver; an Orthodox Jewish Canadian rabbi rallying the support of Montrealers for Israel's tactics in Gaza; a Muslim, Pakistani Canadian imam advocating the right of schoolgirls to wear the hijab in Regina's city soccer leagues; a Hindu, East African Canadian Brahmin giving his blessing to marriages

---

12 Ibid., 191.

arranged for teenagers in regional Toronto; a Buddhist, Myanmarese Canadian monk vowing to immolate himself on Parliament Hill unless the federal government expresses official support for Aung San Suu Kyi; a Sikh Canadian Granthi insisting that baptized males do not have to wear helmets when riding motorcycles around Winnipeg; or a Baha'i, Iranian Canadian elder in Calgary justifying the faith's refusal to promote women to its highest administrative ranks. We might find many examples, both historical and imaginable. What is more, it is an unwelcome irony that those skeptical of multiculturalism sometimes garner further support for their position by referring to the history of encounter, conflict, and occasional accommodation between Canada's Aboriginal and non-Aboriginal communities.[13] In chapter 1, we see how the non-Aboriginal majority's "that's not the way we do things now" approach has for decades confronted Aboriginal peoples; in other chapters, we sometimes read about newcomers hearing "that's not the way we do things here" from groups with a more established presence upon Canada's religious landscape, regardless of whether such newcomers belong to a mainstream or a marginal religious community.

Mindful of these ambiguities, *The Religions of Canadians* attempts to trace the efforts of Canada's different spiritual constituencies to negotiate the often-rocky terrain between slavish perpetuation of the religious ways of "over there" and "back then" and creative adaptation of inherited beliefs and practices to the social and cultural demands of a new life in a new world. This negotiation includes the efforts of Aboriginal peoples, for whom "over there" and "back then" assume equally important, if obviously different significance, usually having to do with claims to traditional lands and natural resources appropriated by colonizing Europeans. The words "tradition" and "traditional" carry numerous meanings, of course. References to Aboriginal lands as "traditional" convey some sense of what the historian of religions Mircea Eliade (1907–86) called mythic time—that is, life *in illo tempore,* "in that time," the time of oral narratives, the time of the ancients, before the historical record of imperial

---

13 Various terms have been and continue to be used to refer to the earliest inhabitants of North, Central, and South America, including "Aboriginal," "Amerindian," "Indian," "Indigenous," and "Native." In recent decades, "First Nations" has gained wide usage in Canada, but not in the United States or elsewhere. Except where specific Canadian communities are alluded to, as in the chapter on Bahá'ís, we use "Aboriginal" throughout *The Religions of Canadians,* partly because the last long-form Canadian census of 2001 uses this term in its statistical record of the way Canadians identify their religious affiliations, and partly because many of the spiritual traditions of Canada's first peoples transcend modern national boundaries, as shown in Chapter 1, "Aboriginals."

conquest and colonial settlement.[14] On the other hand, celebrated historian of Christianity Jaroslav Pelikan (1923–2006) draws an important distinction between "tradition" and "traditionalism." Discussing his book *The Vindication of Tradition,* Pelikan called "tradition" the living faith of dead people, and "traditionalism" the dead faith of living people.[15] In this context, to talk of Aboriginal lands as traditional is to perpetuate their significance as part of the living faith of dead people.

In perhaps the most helpful study of these notions, American sociologist Edward Shils (1910–95) draws directly upon the roots of the word "tradition" in the Latin verb *tradere,* which means "to transmit." Shils defines tradition as "anything that is transmitted or handed down from the past to the present," across the generations, including religious beliefs and practices.[16] As Shils points out, though, in certain intellectual circles the modern stress on "empirical science" and "rationality of judgement" has brought the notion of tradition into disrepute.[17] For many European Enlightenment thinkers and their heirs, "tradition embodies all that is obstructive of the growth and application of science and reason to the affairs of human beings."[18] In some ways, this viewpoint echoes Pelikan's "traditionalism," with its sense of the way authoritarian resistance to individual and collective freedoms may accompany religious dogma and hollow ritualism. On the other hand, as Shils stresses, "the appreciation of the accomplishments of the past and of the institutions especially impregnated with tradition, as well as the desirability of regarding patterns inherited from the past as valid guides, is one of the major patterns of human thought."[19] On occasion, such appreciation may even involve what social and cultural historians Eric J. Hobsbawm and Terence O. Ranger have called "the invention of tradition," that is, the fabrication and development of "a set of practices normally governed by overtly or tacitly accepted rules and of a ritual or symbolic nature, which seek to inculcate certain values and norms of behaviour by repetition, which automatically

---

14 Mircea Eliade, *The Myth of the Eternal Return or, Cosmos and History,* trans. Willard R. Trask (Princeton: Princeton University Press, 1954), 20.

15 From an interview with Jaroslav Pelikan appearing in *US News & World Report,* 26 July 1989. For a fuller discussion of these issues, see Jaroslav Pelikan, *The Vindication of Tradition* (New Haven: Yale University Press, 1984).

16 Edward Shils, *Tradition* (Chicago: University of Chicago Press, 1981), 12.

17 Ibid., 4.

18 Ibid., 7.

19 Ibid., 21.

implies continuity with the past."[20] Such innovations include both "'traditions' actually invented, constructed and formally instituted, and those emerging in a less easily traceable manner within a brief and dateable period—a matter of few years perhaps—and establishing themselves with great rapidity."[21] These latter perspectives, less suspicious than the former, reflect Pelikan's notion of "tradition."

A kind of stock-taking of the role and status of the religious in Canada's founding, development, and ongoing formation, *The Religions of Canadians* identifies and examines the many ways in which the Canadian heirs of different religious legacies strive to keep alive the beliefs and practices of these traditions and to avoid the dead letter of traditionalism. Put another way, the chapters that follow may be read as extended accounts about religions on the move in the making of Canada, though over the centuries many different factors have propelled such movements. In some cases, religious mobility has originated in European imperial conquest, colonial settlement, and the accompanying phenomena. As we see in the second and third chapters of *The Religions of Canadians,* it was under such conditions that French and English adventurers founded the earliest Roman Catholic and Protestant Christian congregations in *la Nouvelle-France* and Nova Scotia in the sixteenth and seventeenth centuries. Associated missions extended this Christian presence westwards and northwards; most notably Roman Catholics in the sixteenth and nineteenth centuries and evangelical Protestants in the eighteenth, nineteenth, and twentieth centuries. The European Christian legacy is everywhere to be seen in today's Canada; churches and chapels of all denominations continue to dominate the landscapes of the majority of communities—urban, suburban, rural, and remote, from coast to coast to coast. Christians have continued to find a home in Canada, though they are as likely to migrate from Africa, the Caribbean, Central and South America, Eastern Europe, or East and South Asia as from Great Britain, Ireland, or other parts of Western Europe. Though 16.2 per cent of Canadians declared themselves to be of "no religion" in the country's last long-form census in 2001, 72.5 per cent self-identified as Catholic Christian or as belonging to a Protestant Christian denomination. Other Christian groups included several Orthodox churches and the Church of Jesus Christ of Latter-day

---

20   Eric J. Hobsbawm and Terence O. Ranger, eds., *The Invention of Tradition* (Cambridge: Cambridge University Press, 1983), 1 (emphasis added).

21   Ibid., 1.

Saints, whose members are commonly known as Mormons; together, these groups total another 1.8 per cent of Canadians.[22]

As the other chapters of *The Religions of Canadians* reveal, however, recent decades have seen varieties of not only Christian, but also Jewish, Muslim, Hindu, Buddhist, Sikh, and Baha'i communities begin to feature prominently upon Canada's social and cultural landscapes, albeit in far fewer numbers to date. Though they do not directly have to do with the centuries of Europe's high imperial and colonial ambition, the reasons that members of these communities move to Canada vary widely. Changes in economic, social, or political circumstances have obliged—or perhaps enticed—individuals, families, and even whole communities from all parts of the globe to seek more secure and prosperous lives for themselves in Canada. Sometimes, political oppression or religious persecution has driven people from their homelands: Jews have fled the shock and aftershock of recurrent anti-Semitism in Europe, and to a greater or lesser degree various Christians, Muslims, Hindus, Buddhists, Sikhs, and Bahá'is have sought refuge in Canada from discrimination in their countries of origin. On other occasions, Canada has welcomed the survivors of catastrophe. Such events may be of human making, like the Vietnam War (1955–75) and the Iran-Iraq War (1980–88), or the protracted, internecine conflicts in Cambodia (1970–75), Eritrea (1972–81), Ethiopia (1974–91), Lebanon (1975–90), Nigeria (1967–70), Sri Lanka (1983–2009), Somalia (1991–present), Sudan (1983–2005), and the former Yugoslavia (1991–95), all of which were to a large extent fuelled by a toxic mix of ethnic and religious antagonisms. In other instances, disasters may be of nature's making, like the tsunami that swept over Buddhists, Christians, Hindus, and Muslims alike from Indonesia to Sri Lanka (2004), or the earthquake that devastated predominantly Catholic Haiti (2010).

More generally, from the 1960s to the present day, the intertwined processes of decolonizing development and transnational globalization have contributed to the movement and mutation of religions across continents and oceans, producing diaspora communities linked in complex networks of shifting economic interdependence and social and political influence. In Canada, the availability and sophistication of modern transportation and information technologies has enabled local and regional

---

22 Statistics Canada, accessed 27 June 2011 from http://www12.statcan.ca/english/census01/
    products/highlight/Religion/Page.cfm?Lang=E&Geo=PR&View=1a&Code=01&Table=1&Star
    tRec=1&Sort=2&B1=Canada&B2=1. Here and for all future references to the 2001 census, see
    Appendices A and B.

religious communities to raise national and even worldwide fund-raising drives for building grand places of worship and for recruiting clerics and other professionals to staff them. Following models established by Christian institutions, Jewish synagogues, Muslim mosques, Hindu and Buddhist temples, Sikh *gurdwaras,* and Baha'i houses of worship and attendant facilities have come to provide not just liturgical, ritual, and other formal religious services, but also economic assistance and educational and social programs.

From chapter to chapter, *The Religions of Canadians* tries to capture these diverse aspects of religions on the move, at once shaping and being shaped by fresh challenges and new horizons in the making of Canada. With the exception of Chapter 1, which discusses Aboriginal traditions, each chapter tells the story of a religious community, albeit in many cases a complicated story involving a number of different ethnic groups, sometimes stretching over many centuries, and taking us to several different regions of the world as well as many parts of Canada. Mindful of these complexities, each chapter is divided into five sections. An introductory statement and a summary afterword form bookends for three longer sections. To establish context, the first longer section provides the essential elements of a religious tradition, outlining its history, geography, doctrines, and rituals. Exploring similarities and differences between classical and Canadian forms of the tradition, a second section then traces the ways in which its adherents have come to Canadian shores and the ways in which setting up a new home in a new land has perpetuated, transformed, or occasionally led to the abandoning of inherited beliefs and practices. A third section visits two or three contemporary communities, describing what the tradition looks like in the here and now and suggesting likely directions of future development within Canada and in relation to the tradition's global constituency. The three main sections of Chapter 1 mirror rather than mimic the other chapters. The first section outlines the religious life of Canada's Aboriginal communities before the arrival of Europeans; the second describes the effects of colonial and imperial hegemony upon important Pan-Indian traditions maintained by Aboriginal Canadians; and the third, how Aboriginal Canadian peoples continue to transform their religious heritage amidst the challenges of the contemporary world. A glossary of key terms, a list of key dates, a bibliography of key readings, a directory of key websites, and a list of key questions for critical reflection close out each chapter. Throughout *The Religions of Canadians,* photographs illustrate the stories told.

The Religions of Canadians espouses no single methodological or theoretical paradigm, still less any particular understanding of "religion." The
English word "religion" comes from the Latin *religio,* which scholars generally assume to be related to the verb *religare,* meaning "to bind." In this
sense, to be religious is to be bound or committed to a certain perspective on the origins and purpose of life and the appropriate way to live it.
But more expansive definitions of the religious are legion, some positive
and constructive, others unsympathetic or reductive. Famously, for social
theorist Karl Marx (1818–83), for instance, "[r]eligion is the sigh of the
oppressed creature, the heart of a heartless world, and the soul of soulless
conditions ... the opium of the people," while sociologist Emil Durkheim
(1858–1917) writes of religion as "a unified system of beliefs and practices relative to sacred things."[23] By contrast, philosopher Alfred North
Whitehead (1861–1947) proposed that "[r]eligion is what the individual
does with his own solitariness."[24] For Whitehead, "[c]ollective enthusi-
asms, revivals, institutions, churches, rituals, bibles, codes of behaviour,
are the trappings of religion, its passing forms."[25] In more recent years,
anthropologist Clifford Geertz (1926–2006) advanced a multifaceted and
much-quoted definition of religion as "a system of symbols which acts to
establish powerful, pervasive, and long-lasting moods and motivations
in men by formulating conceptions of a general order of existence and
clothing these conceptions with such an aura of factuality that the moods
and motivations seem uniquely realistic."[26]

At certain points in *The Religions of Canadians,* a particular understanding of the religious will come to mind, while other points might signal
different ones. That said, though, much of the writing in this book pre-
sumes a working—though again, not absolute—distinction between the
religious on the one hand and the sacred, spiritual, or holy on the other.[27]
In his celebrated study *The Idea of the Holy,* historian of religions Rudolf
Otto (1869–1937) associates these latter terms with a "non-rational" human

---

23 Karl Marx, "A Contribution to the Critique of Hegel's Philosophy of Right: Introduction [1844],"
    in *Writings of the Young Marx on Philosophy and Society,* intro. Lucio Colletti, trans. Rodney
    Livingstone and Gregor Benton (Harmondsworth: Penguin, 1975), 244; Emile Durkheim, *The
    Elementary Forms of Religious Life,* trans. and intro. Karen E. Fields (New York: The Free Press,
    1995), 44.

24 Alfred North Whitehead, *Religion in the Making* (New York: Macmillan, 1926), 17.

25 Ibid.

26 Clifford Geertz, *The Interpretation of Cultures: Selected Essay* (New York: Basic Books, 1973), 90.

27 What follows elaborates upon ideas expressed in my essay "Religion and Postcolonial
    Literatures," in *Cambridge History of Postcolonial Literature,* ed. Ato Quayson (Cambridge:
    Cambridge University Press, 2012), 764.

susceptibility to the "uncanny," "numinous," or "wholly other."[28] Identifying the uncanny, numinous or wholly other as *mysterium tremendum,* meaning "frightening mystery," and *mysterium fascinans,* meaning "fascinating mystery," Otto writes: "The daemonic-divine object may appear to the mind an object of horror and dread, but at the same time it is no less something that allures with a potent charm, and the creature, who trembles before it, utterly cowed and cast down, has always at the same time the impulse to turn to it, nay even to make it somehow his own."[29] Later commentators on religion have tended to collapse Otto's categories into the phrase *mysterium tremendum et fascinans,* thus conjuring a radically ambiguous sense of the sacred, spiritual, or holy as an at once "frightful and fascinating mystery."[30] Following Otto, such writers recognize that we associate this non-rational or "first-order" susceptibility with a variety of phenomena, ranging from ghouls and ghosts to goddesses and God almighty.

On the other hand, scholars often reserve the term "religious" for more rational, systematic, "second-order" articulations of this rudimentary, yet radically ambiguous human susceptibility. In other words, we articulate our experience of the sacred, spiritual, or holy in the practical and theoretical lexicons of what Ninian Smart (1927–2001) identifies as the visible and tangible "dimensions" of the religious—that is, myths, doctrines, ethics, rituals, institutions, and material manifestations in nature and culture.[31] In this respect, *The Religions of Canadians* assumes that such a distinction usually locates a personal sense of inward conviction about the meanings and ends of religion at the centre of a phenomenology of these outward expressions of the sacred, spiritual, or holy. Smart calls this sense of conviction the "experiential" dimension of religion.[32] When we are analyzing the various forms and expressions of the religious, this experiential dimension allows us to distinguish the committed "insider" from the uncommitted "outsider." Though by no means definitive, the insider's perspective is nonetheless crucial to any attempt to fathom what

---

28 Rudolf Otto, *The Idea of the Holy: An Inquiry into the Non-Rational Factor in the Idea of the Divine,* trans. John W. Harvey (London: Oxford University Press, 1958), *passim.* Notice that Otto invokes the category "non-rational," meaning that our susceptibility to the numinous may not be satisfactorily explained either in terms of a philosophy of reason or in terms of a psychology of the irrational.

29 Otto, *The Idea of the Holy,* 13, 31.

30 Ninian Smart, *Philosophers and Religious Truth* (London: SCM Press, 1964), 132.

31 Ninian Smart, *Secular Education and the Logic of Religion* (New York: Humanities Press, 1968), 104.

32 Ibid., 104.

the American pragmatist philosopher William James (1842–1910) called "the full fact" of any religious phenomenon, meaning not only its visible and tangible manifestations, but also the motivations and intentions of participating adherents.[33] Accordingly, each of the contributors to *The Religions of Canadians* says something about their personal relation to the tradition they are discussing. In some cases, a contributor might be a practising member of the tradition as well as a scholarly commentator on it; in other cases, more the latter than the former; and in one or two instances, an uncommitted, though empathetic outsider.

At the same time, other commentators have argued that the very notion of religion—and hence of particular religions—originates as an ideological construct of Western Enlightenment rationalism. For such commentators, there is no such thing as "Christianity," "Judaism," "Islam," "Hinduism," "Buddhism," "Sikhism," or "Baha'i," only Christians, Jews, Muslims, Hindus, Buddhists, Sikhs and Bahá'is living in particular times and in particular places, their everyday existence shaped by myriad influences, some of inward origin, others imposed from without. While it is certainly possible to identify as religious the sort of persistent predominance of motive and intention in patterns of behaviour and expression that philosopher of religion Paul Tillich (1886–1965) called "ultimate concern," it is also the case that on any given day in any given place, an adherent of a given tradition may or may not attribute to religion the urge to act in a certain way or the expression of a given opinion.[34] In other words, religions are mobile in another sense, too. What counts and what does not count as Christian, Jewish, Muslim, Hindu, Buddhist, Sikh, or Baha'i changes from time to time and from place to place.

All in all, then, *The Religions of Canadians* adopts the spirit of sociologist Max Weber (1864–1920), who resisted the temptation of trying to define religion, arguing that "the essence of religion is not even our concern, as we make it our task to study the conditions and effects of a particular type of social behavior."[35] In an effort to more fully appreciate the wide variety of beliefs and practices that constitute the religious landscape of Canada, the chapters that follow blur and blend historiographical, phenomenological, and sociological approaches in a version of what Geertz

---

33 William James, *The Varieties of Religious Experience: A Study in Human Nature,* vol. 15 of *The Works of William James,* ed. Frederick Burkhardt and Fredson Bowers (Cambridge, MA: Harvard University Press, 1985), 393.

34 Paul Tillich, *Dynamics of Faith* (New York: Harper and Row, 1957), 5.

35 Max Weber, *The Sociology of Religion,* trans. Ephraim Fischoff (Boston: Beacon Press, 1963), 1.

called "thick description."[36] Adopting this mixed methodological stance, *The Religions of Canadians* does two jobs at once. We introduce readers to the religions of the world *and*, looking through the lens of religion, we trace the complex processes that constitute the making of Canada. Put another way, *The Religions of Canadians* explores the world's religions from a Canadian point of view by locating the religions of Canadians within a global context. Though challenging, this double act has benefits. As with other books on the world's religions, readers are invited to look through the small end of the analytical telescope at the religious big picture—to leap, say, into the nineteenth-century world of colonial Christian missionaries, or into Hindu culture and society in medieval India. At the same time, though, *The Religions of Canadians* turns the telescope around and invites readers to learn about the unfamiliar by focusing upon the familiar—to encounter Islam on a visit to a Sunni mosque in Edmonton, Alberta, for instance, or to envision Buddhist chanting by journeying to a Tibetan monastery in rural Cape Breton, Nova Scotia.

In turn, *The Religions of Canadians* differs in a crucial respect from both other books about the world's religions and other books about religion in Canada. In several cases, we deliberately spend a *dis*proportionate amount of time on certain religious traditions and the communities of Canadians practising them—disproportionate, that is, relative to the size of the Canadian community and the length of time the tradition has been represented in Canada. Most books exploring the world's religions dedicate about an equal number of pages to Aboriginal American and African religions, Judaism, Christianity, Islam, Hinduism, Buddhism, and the religious traditions of China, Japan, and Korea. For demographic reasons, Christian traditions predominate in other books about religion in Canada: as already indicated, Catholics and Protestants taken together still account for roughly four out of five Canadians self-identifying as religious in the 2001 federal census. Both these formats usually grant only a few paragraphs to smaller groups like Sikhs or Bahá'is. In *The Religions of Canadians,* by contrast, the Sikh and Baha'i traditions enjoy more or less equal time with Catholics and Protestants, and we plan for future editions of the book to include accounts of as yet under-researched traditions like Daoists, Jains, Jehovah's Witnesses, Mormons, Orthodox Christians, Parsees, Rastafarians, and others. We hope that future editions will also feature fuller discussions of some of the New Religious Movements explored

---

36 Clifford Geertz, *The Interpretation of Cultures: Selected Essay* (New York: Basic Books, 1973), 5.

briefly in this edition's closing, "Afterword: New Religious Movements and the Religions of Canadians Going Forward."

Most colleges and universities across Canada offer a course on world religions at the first- or second-year level. For the most part, this large constituency of mainly younger Canadians uses course kits assembled by the instructor or a textbook put together in the United States or the United Kingdom. There has been no text specifically designed for Canadian students, focusing on Canadian aspects of the history, doctrine, ethics, rituals, and institutional life of the religions of the world, and bringing peculiarly Canadian perspectives to bear on these materials. My own experience teaching an introductory course on world religions for over 20 years at York University, Toronto, tells me of the need for such a book in Canada. Changing demographics across the country, especially in the major urban centres, now mean that university classes are made up mostly of younger Canadians from a wide array of ethnic, social, and cultural backgrounds. Frequently feeling distanced from the habits and opinions of older family members and their forebears, these students wonder about family origins and how their antecedents came to be in Canada. In particular, these younger Canadians often query inherited values and customs, a legacy in which religion has invariably played a big role. At the same time, although these younger Canadians share common experiences in everyday life—especially the pervasive presence of globalized popular culture at school, in the workplace, and at the mall—they nonetheless represent a profusion of various and vying social and cultural traditions. Put all these things together and it is not too hard to appreciate how younger Canadians might sometimes feel they have little in common either with older family members *or* with peers from their own communities, let alone those from different backgrounds.

Appreciating the role of the religious in the making of contemporary Canada goes a long way to helping us understand what values and customs different communities share and do *not* share with each other, and how and why such things are so. In its widest reach, however, *The Religions of Canadians* challenges the commonly held misconception that religion is a thing of the past. Since the Enlightenment, proponents of the so-called secularization hypothesis have long asserted that human reason—consistently applied not only in the black-and-white calculations of hard science, but also to the less cut-and-dried arrangements of economic, social, political, and cultural life—systematically reveals the inauthenticity of religion and of the efforts of the religious to explain the ambiguities and unruliness of human history. This attitude persisted well into the second half of the twentieth century. In 1959, for example, sociologist C. Wright Mills (1916–62) felt quite confident prophesying the passing of the sacred:

> Once the world was filled with the sacred—in thought, practice, and institutional form. After the Reformation and the Renaissance, the forces of modernization swept across the globe and secularization, a corollary historical process, loosened the dominance of the sacred. In due course, the sacred shall disappear altogether except, possibly, in the private realm.[37]

Far from witnessing the end of religion, however, the late capitalist West, including Canada, has for some decades been undergoing what some scholars have called the process of "desecularization." Once a radical secularist himself, for instance, sociologist Peter L. Berger has completely reversed his position:

> The world today, with some exceptions ... is as furiously religious as it ever was, and in some places more so than ever. This means that a whole body of literature by historians and social scientists loosely labeled "secularization theory" is essentially mistaken.[38]

Indeed, other commentators have taken this argument still further, writing not just of desecularization, but in more constructive terms of the "re-enchantment of the world" and the "persistence of faith."[39] As we move towards the middle decades of the twenty-first century, there is no sign of these trends abating. As *The Religions of Canadians* reveals, new and established religious ideas and practices enjoy a lively presence upon Canada's social and cultural landscape, belying such assumptions about the passing of religion and the triumph of the modern. Other national readerships have long had access to books addressing a good many of these concerns and their implications for the conduct of everyday life; *The Religions of New Zealanders* and *World Religions in America: An Introduction* are two

---

37 C. Wright Mills, *The Sociological Imagination* (Oxford: Oxford University Press, 1959), 32–33.

38 Peter L. Berger, ed., *The Desecularization of the World: Resurgent Religion and World Politics* (Washington, DC: Ethics and Public Policy Center, 1999), 2.

39 Morris Berman, *The Reenchantment of the World* (Ithaca: Cornell University Press, 1981); Jonathan Sacks, *The Persistence of Faith: Religion, Morality and Society in a Secular Age* (New York: Continuum, 2005).

good examples.[40] Now there is an equivalent for Canadian readers. We hope you enjoy learning about the religions of Canadians as much as we have enjoyed researching and writing *The Religions of Canadians.*

FURTHER READINGS

Bibby, Reginald W. *Unknown Gods: The Ongoing Story of Religion in Canada.* Toronto: Stoddart, 1993.

Bissoondath, Neil. *Selling Illusions: The Cult of Multiculturalism in Canada.* Toronto: Penguin Books Canada, 1994; revised 2002.

Bramadat, Paul, and David Seljak, eds. *Religion and Ethnicity in Canada.* Toronto: Pearson, 2005.

Bramadat, Paul, and David Seljak, eds. *Christianity and Ethnicity in Canada.* Toronto: University of Toronto Press, 2008.

Choquette, Robert. *Canada's Religions: An Historical Introduction.* Ottawa: University of Ottawa Press, 2004.

Pals, Daniel L. *Seven Theories of Religion.* New York: Oxford University Press, 1996.

Stausberg, Michael. *Contemporary Theories of Religion: A Critical Companion.* New York: Routledge, 2009.

Sweet, Lois. *God in the Classroom: The Controversial Issue of Religion in Canada's Schools.* Toronto: McClelland and Stewart, 1997.

Taylor, Charles, et al. *Multiculturalism: Examining the Politics of Recognition.* Princeton: Princeton University Press, 1994.

---

40 Peter Donovan, ed., *The Religions of New Zealanders* (Palmerston North: Dunmore Press, 1990); Jacob Neusner, ed., *World Religions in America: An Introduction* (Louisville, KY: Westminster John Knox Press, 2000).

ONE

Aboriginals

JORDAN PAPER, UNIVERSITY OF VICTORIA

||||||||||||||||||||||||||||||||||||||||||||||||||||||||||||||||||||||||||||||||||||||||||||||||||||||||||||||||||||||

T raditionally, the sacred permeated every aspect of everyday life for the Aboriginal peoples of the Americas. The coming of Europeans, however, entailed severe challenges to traditional Aboriginal ways. Invading North America from the sixteenth to eighteenth centuries, Spanish, French, English, and other colonizers brought disease and warfare, eventually forcing the indigenous inhabitants onto reserves. The threat of starvation compelled most Aboriginal people on reserves to become Christians, while their traditional religious rituals were criminalized. In Canada, Aboriginal children were removed from their homes to residential schools where many were physically and some sexually abused by Christian clergy. Still, large numbers of Aboriginal people maintained their spiritual beliefs and ritual practices surreptitiously. The last residential schools closed in the 1970s and 1980s, and Aboriginal youth began to agitate politically against centuries of oppression and abuse. This activism brought a revival of Aboriginal culture, including renewed interest in traditional spirituality and the wisdom of Aboriginal elders. The revitalization of Aboriginal religions continues to the present day. What follows explores this complicated story using the methods of religio-ecology and ethno-hermeneutics. The chapter draws upon relevant scholarly literature and four decades of personal involvement with some of the traditions discussed.

THE HERITAGE

In order to appreciate the spiritual traditions of the Aboriginal peoples of the Americas, one must move away from models of understanding usually associated with the study of Western religions. First, traditional Aboriginal spirituality was not separable from other dimensions of their culture; every feature of life, every activity was imbued with its spiritual aspects. The sacred consisted of the animals, the plants, earth, sea, sky, and the ancestors, and since the natural world and the numinous were one, every individual lived and breathed in the midst of the sacred. Gathering food, building structures, playing games, going to war—all involved rituals that linked the individual to the sacred. Religion and spirituality were so much a part of everyday life that there were no words for them in Aboriginal languages.

Second, the idea of proselytizing or converting people to one's own religion would not have made sense to Aboriginal peoples. It was recognized that one's spiritual traditions differed to varying degrees from the traditions of others, but such differences made one's own traditions neither better nor worse. Since Aboriginal traditions included no concept of salvation, there was no inclination to bring others into one's own tradition. An exception might occur when someone captured in a raid was offered the opportunity to be adopted into their captor's community. Many rituals were clan-oriented, and only those who were members of the clan could take part; thus, outsiders could not be brought in save through adoption. Various traditions had adjunct ritual societies, which captives were invited to join and into which they were initiated, automatically making that captive part of the tradition into which he or she had been adopted. But such rituals were additional to the rituals the initiate already practiced; they did not replace them.

Third, persecution because of religion was inconceivable to Aboriginal peoples. The notion that there is a single or ultimate truth was alien to their traditions. As we shall see, Aboriginal religious understanding was based on individual experiences. Thus, no-one could say that another person's understanding was wrong, let alone punish that person for the form their spiritual understanding took or for the kinds of rituals they practised. Likewise, and fourth, other spiritual traditions were not considered bad or undesirable. Individuals were expected to follow the traditions of their families, groups, clans, and culture, including the traditions of other communities, for when individuals found the rituals of other traditions appealing they would add them to their own. In some cases, raids brought another tradition's sacred artifacts as prizes, which then became especially sacred to those who had captured them. In other words, the spiritual traditions discussed in this chapter were held in mutual respect by all Aboriginal peoples, whatever their local affiliations. Religion was never conceived of negatively, whether it came from another individual or another tradition.

When French, Spanish, English, and Russian settlers arrived in the northern half of the North American continent from the 1500s to the 1700s, they encountered many Aboriginal cultures speaking hundreds of different languages. Although each culture had its distinct modes of spirituality, all but the far northern Inuit shared certain common features. Most common were the use of **tobacco** as a sacred offering, found in both North and South America, and the **Spirit Lodge**, disdainfully known in English by the secular term "Sweat Lodge" and found as far south as in the Mayan culture of Central America. Aboriginal peoples also shared an understanding of sacred space as defined by the deified Four Directions or Four Winds; a belief in the efficacy of various kinds of ritual power, or **medicine**; and a belief that the deities brought insight to humans in ceremonial songs and dances. It is often said that Aboriginal people pray through their bodies by dancing.

In terms of the geography of today's Canada, these traditions fell into several religio-ecological regions. In the far north were the Inuit, who are more properly described as a circumpolar people, as their culture and language extends from Siberia through Alaska, Canada, and Greenland (for this reason, their religion is not discussed in this chapter). South of the Inuit, throughout the area drained by the MacKenzie River, were Athapaskan-speaking cultures (Dené), who lived a semi-nomadic gathering-hunting lifestyle. Less than a thousand years ago, some of these people migrated to the south-western part of North America and became known as the Navajo and Apache (Diné). A similar lifestyle was found among Algonkian-speaking cultures, from present-day eastern Canada through the northern part of the Great Lakes region and across to the Prairies. In the arable area of southern Ontario, Iroquoian-speaking peoples lived in palisaded villages composed of large, matrilineal, matrilocal clan dwellings, some as large as a modern football field and surrounded by gardens. After the Spanish-introduced horse reached the northern Prairies, Algonkian- and Siouan-speaking peoples were comfortably able to live full-time on the Prairies, following the vast bison herds. Several different foraging cultures lived between the Rocky and Cascade mountains. Along the west coast of present-day British Columbia and up the river valleys that drained into the Pacific Ocean lived peoples who also spoke many different languages, yet shared such common cultural features as large, plank **longhouses** and an economy based on fish and sea mammals. Many of these traditions extended south of the present-day border with the United States. Further south, the economies were based on agriculture; here, more complex socio-political systems developed, with larger populations living in towns and even cities.

The arrival of Europeans at first led to trade in furs, increasing the material wealth of Aboriginal peoples. But these contacts also led to a massive loss of life from smallpox, influenza, and other communicable diseases, to which Aboriginal peoples had developed no immunity. Perhaps 90 per cent of the population died, leading to massive cultural disruption. At the same time, the fur trade allied different Aboriginal peoples to competing European powers and brought them into their wars. For example, the Wyandot (Hurons), an Iroquoian-speaking people living in the southern part of Georgian Bay, Ontario, were allied to the French, while the Haudenosaunee (Iroquois), living south of the Great Lakes, were allied to the English. The English equipped the Haudenosaunee with firearms and they forcibly displaced the Wyandot. The Algonkian-speaking peoples (Anishinaabek) north of the Great Lakes, who were allied to the Wyandot, were then armed by the French. The Anishinaabek moved south and displaced the Haudenosaunee. Also, various Aboriginal peoples sought to monopolize trade with Europeans. The Haudenosaunee were thus motivated to move northwards and the Great Lakes Anishinaabek to move westwards, forcing Siouan-speaking peoples further west, where many discovered the horse and developed a new lifestyle on the Prairies. This lifestyle, celebrated today by Hollywood and pulp-fiction writers, became the archetypal Aboriginal way for non-Aboriginal North Americans, even though it lasted only a century.

When Europeans began to colonize North America, they forced the indigenous inhabitants—already considerably decimated by diseases brought by the Europeans, and by warfare associated with the fur trade— onto smaller and smaller reserves. In Canada, competing Christian missionary societies, working hand in hand with agents of government, assumed positions of authority on these reserves. In 1876, these arrangements were given the force of law in the first Indian Act, which was designed to encourage Aboriginal peoples to break with their own traditions and to assimilate to European Canadian ways. Many Aboriginal people converted to Christianity, but often only for fear of starving. Aboriginal religious rituals were criminalized and people were jailed for taking part in them, especially dancing. Children were forcibly removed from their parents to residential schools, where many aspects of indigenous culture, language, and religion were forbidden on pain of physical punishment. Many children were sexually abused by the Christian clergy. Still, Aboriginal traditions continued to be practised in secret.

In principle, Aboriginal religious practices were no longer illegal after the revisions to the Indian Act in 1951, but persecution continued well into the 1970s. When the Canadian Charter of Rights and Freedoms was assented to in 1982, no cabinet minister was willing to allow that freedom of religion applied to the practice of Aboriginal religions. Already in the early 1970s, however, Aboriginal youth had begun political action aimed at ending repression. Interest in traditional religion revived, as the young sought the wisdom of Aboriginal elders, many of whom had been ostracized from their communities by Christian missionaries. This recovery of traditional knowledge and revitalization of Aboriginal spirituality has continued throughout the Americas to the present day.

PAN-INDIAN RELIGION

Some scholars speak of **Pan-Indian** religious understanding and ritual life. Despite local and regional differences, Aboriginal Canadian traditions share a fundamental ideology with virtually all Aboriginal traditions in the Americas. This theological foundation allows for the sharing of rituals. In the Pan-Indian understanding, the whole natural world is perceived as numinous. The cosmos is understood in relation to a sacred centre, which infuses all rituals, wherever and whenever they are carried out. Offerings are made to the spiritual forces in all directions: Sky and Earth, and the Four Directions or Four Winds—four being the sacred number in virtually all Aboriginal traditions. Sky and Earth are perceived as the primal parents, and the spiritual forces are identified with animals, colours, and all manner of other associations, which vary from culture to culture, and even from clan to clan. Sun and maleness are identified with Sky, and Moon and femaleness with Earth. Among the Four Directions or Four Winds and their associations, West Wind is identified with Thunder.

In Aboriginal religious traditions, every wild plant and animal is simultaneously natural and spiritual. Most plants and animals are valued for their sustenance of humans. Since sustenance is understood to be a female role, they are perceived as primarily female. Aboriginal cultures are predominantly egalitarian, yet some Western interpreters have incorrectly assumed that each species of animal is ruled by a male, and that only that ruler is numinous. But in Aboriginal societies, leaders are chosen for specific activities, and adherence to their authority is voluntary. As well, the sexes are understood to be equal and complementary to each other.

Unlike the rest of nature, humans are understood to be weak; we are dependent on plants and animals in order to survive, but wild plants and animals do not need humans to live. It is understood that each individual must develop a special relationship with one or more spiritual entities in order to maintain their lives. These spiritual entities are most commonly animal spirits, although some who are more spiritually attuned may have relationships with weather and other powerful spirits. Those particularly proficient in these relationships will name infants in order to pass on the protection of these spiritual entities. The children keep these names until they have begun to develop such relationships themselves, and then each child takes a new name.

In many Aboriginal traditions, these relationships between individual humans and the spirits are obtained through fasting, often known as vision questing. Children begin by fasting for a day, reaching the traditional fasting length of four days or longer in adolescence. For young women, the first major fast is at the time of menarche (first menstruation). For males, there is no similar physiologically marked change, but the first major fast will take place during adolescence. During these fasts, individuals isolate themselves from others and abstain from food, drink, and sleep. In the resulting visions, individuals will obtain not only spirit guardians, but also wisdom for their communities, theological understanding, and sacred songs and rituals. Thus, aside from the above common generalities, spiritual understanding is individualistic within the possibility of cultural understandings.

In the Northwest Coast traditions, names, songs, and ritual prerogatives are also obtained through bilateral inheritance. Among Six Nations traditionalists, they are also obtained through membership in matrilineal clans. But for the Anishinaabek and Blackfeet, they are obtained on an entirely individual basis through fasting and other forms of spiritual questing. All spirits are understood as relations, and they are reverently addressed as Grandmother and Grandfather. In the Northwest Coast traditions, humans may be reincarnated as fish and sea mammal spirits. In northern Aboriginal American traditions, all individuals are expected to function with the assistance of guardian spirits for the benefit of their group. As with any talent, some people show more aptitude than others. So, traditionally, certain individuals may be sought to lead raiding parties because of a strong relationship with spirits useful for martial activities; others may be sought out to lead hunting parties; and others again for healing particular illnesses, and so forth.

When Aboriginal peoples hunt and gather wild plants and animals, they treat them with the respect that is due to powerful, numinous beings. Rituals are performed before and after these activities. A hunted animal is asked to give its life so humans may live. After it allows itself to be killed, it is treated with great respect and special rituals, so that others of its kind will give themselves again and again. Similarly, plants are spoken to; the need for each plant is explained, and a gift, usually tobacco, is given in exchange for the gift the plant makes of itself. For the horticultural Six Nations, Earth itself is appealed to at planting time for the gift of her children, Corn, Beans, and Squash; on harvesting, celebrations are held to honour these gifts. Except among the Northwest Coast peoples, tobacco is the most common ritual gift; it is offered directly to Earth or Water, or onto Fire, or shared through smoking. Before rituals begin, the place of offering, the ritual objects, and all persons involved are spiritually purified with other sacred plants. Depending on the locale, sweetgrass, cedar leaves, and sage are used.

Aboriginal religious traditions include shared ritual elements. One of these rituals is called by the Anishinaabek "Spirit Lodge," which, as we have noted, westerners often disdainfully term "Sweat Lodge." The Spirit Lodge is an intense communal experience that engenders a mild trance and the experience of rebirth, renewal, and healing, in the more holistic sense. Potent symbolism involved in the rituals includes the conjoining of the primal parents, Sky and Earth. A canopy of skins or bark (now canvas and blankets) stretched over a dome-shaped framework represents the cosmos above the earth. Before the Anishinaabek and Blackfeet were forced into permanent houses on reserves, the canopied structure served as a typical dwelling, the familiar wigwam. Prior to reserve life, Six Nations longhouses contained small rooms that were used for the same ritual. On the Northwest Coast, small earth and wood structures were built for this purpose. Elsewhere in North America, various Aboriginal cultures used small caves dug into river banks or dressed, stone structures, like those of the Mayans.

For the Spirit Lodge ritual, rocks are heated to high temperatures, replicating the union of Sky and Earth. Called "Grandfathers," the red-hot rocks are then brought into the pitch-dark structure and plunged into a central hole symbolizing the vagina of Earth. Sacred water is sprinkled on the rocks, symbolizing the fertilizing rain and creating live steam. The ritual can last for many hours and may involve the singing of sacred songs, cleansing oneself through confession to those present, sharing experiences, and healing. When the ritual is completed, the participants crawl out through the narrow opening, hot and soaked with sweat, reborn to the world and their waiting friends and relatives, like infants from the womb. This sense of rebirth is central to several Spirit Lodge ritual functions: it may rejuvenate relations among ritual leaders before major ceremonies; it may help in healing the ill; it may renew spiritual strength before a challenging task; or it may regenerate a sense of community among people brought together in an intimate, intense setting, at once physical and spiritual. This last function characterizes Pan-Indian gatherings, as well as gatherings of people from different religious backgrounds, such as Aboriginal traditionalists and Christian clergy.

A second, widely practiced ritual has more explicit Pan-Indian purposes, since one of its functions has to do with rituals of adoption, or "the making of relatives." Aboriginal people have engaged in long-distance trade from at least as far back as we can trace their history. For thousands of years copper was mined along the shores and islands of Lake Superior, and worked into beautiful objects traded throughout the watersheds of the Mississippi, Missouri, and Ohio rivers. Beautiful shells from the Atlantic and Pacific shores were similarly traded, as were mica, fine stone tools, and other objects. A thousand years ago, an urban mercantile centre developed just east of present-day St. Louis, as large as any city in Europe at that time. This centre served as the hub for a vast trading network, based on the canoe, which covered the Missouri, Mississippi, Ohio, and St. Lawrence river basins, as well as the Great Lakes.

Rituals of adoption were needed if traders were to move between cultures and among societies that at times were ritual enemies. Hitherto strangers or enemies might thus become relations. From well over 2,000 years ago until about 500 CE, an unusually shaped, one-piece pipe was often used in these rituals throughout the drainage areas of the northern Mississippi and Ohio rivers and the Great Lakes. The rituals involving this pipe would thus enable strangers to traverse large territories. This one-piece pipe was gradually replaced by the two-piece ritual pipe that continues to be used today. The bowl and stem of this pipe are separate, and the separation and joining of these two pieces carries symbolic and religious significance. Often referred to as the "Sacred Pipe," this ritual object assumed many stylistic variations and became common throughout much of North America, from the sub-Arctic to the Gulf of Mexico, and from the Atlantic coast to the Rocky Mountains. In this large area, while some Aboriginal cultures also used pipe shapes unique to their traditions, all used this two-piece pipe for rituals when people of different cultures came together. European explorers quickly came to understand the usefulness of the Sacred Pipe when travelling through various Aboriginal territories.

Usually made of red or black stone, the bowl of the Sacred Pipe represents the female Earth, and the stem, commonly made of reed or of wood, represents maleness. The two pieces of the pipe are kept separate save when ritually used. At this time, the two pieces are conjoined: the male stem is inserted into the female bowl, replicating cosmic creation, as does the Spirit Lodge ritual. Once purified in the smoke of sacred plants, the pipe is joined together and filled in a ritual manner with sacred tobacco or substitutes (bearberry leaves, for example). Offered first to the six sacred directions (Sky, Earth, and the Four Directions or Four Winds), the pipe is then shared among the circle of participants in a sunwise direction. Females and males sit on opposite sides of the circle and face each other, thus completing the human circle. The participants will smoke the pipe differently depending on their visions or ritual prerogatives. After the pipe has made a full round of the circle, it is taken apart with thanks to the spirit realm, thus completing the ceremony. The Sacred Pipe allows for a double communion: a communion between the human smoker and the spiritual recipients of the tobacco smoke-offering, and a communion between all those sharing the same pipe.

The spiritual power of Sacred Pipe and Spirit Lodge rituals allows for Aboriginal people of different traditions to share in the same religious experience. Because these Pan-Indian rituals are at once integral to a number of different traditions, they are commonly practiced in intertribal contexts. Chief among these occasions are rituals known as "powwows."

When Aboriginal peoples in both the United States and Canada were forbidden to practise their religion on pain of incarceration, they developed these nominally secular intertribal celebrations. Seeing powwows as non-religious festivals which attracted tourist dollars, the churches, police, and military authorities in nearby non-Aboriginal communities did not oppose them. But many of the dances, the drumming, and such dance paraphernalia as eagle feathers had deep religious roots. Visions and dreams determined participation in some of the dances, notably women's "jingle dances." When Aboriginal religious traditions began to revitalize in the 1970s, some of the powwows reverted to their religious basis. Aboriginal participants once again began openly to practice Spirit Lodge and Sacred Pipe ceremonies as part of these powwows.

The only modern mode of Pan-Indian religion is the Native American Church. At the beginning of the reserve period in the southern Prairies, a new religion spread northwards. This new religion involved elements of meso-American religious practices as in Mexico and throughout much of South America, vision questing is done using psychoactive plants rather than fasting. These plants allow for rituals that engender visions in a short period and in a communal setting. The North American workweek made it difficult to participate in traditional ceremonies, however, as these rituals typically lasted four days or longer. Therefore, an all-night ritual was created that used the traditional northern Mexican peyote—a sacred, psychoactive cactus—as well as other sacred objects, like a water drum and a ritual fan. North American Aboriginal people found that this new religious ritual fit their increasingly modern lifestyle.

The adherents of this new religion organized on the model of Protestant churches. The first incorporation was in Oklahoma in 1914 under the name "First-Born Church of Christ." Eventually, the name was changed to "Native American Church," which was incorporated in a number of states. Some forms of the Church use the Bible and other Christian elements. Although legal acceptance was difficult and uneven, the Native American Church became the first Aboriginal religion to be recognized in the United States, and peyote has relatively recently become legal for religious use in Canada. Recent estimates place the number of adherents in the United States and Canada at 250,000, the majority of whom also participate in other forms of Aboriginal religion. As a Pan-Indian mode of religion which emphasizes the direct experience of the numinous in a communal ritual context, the Native American Church is the first major, successful Pan-Indian religious adaptation to the post-reserve context.

In all of these religious traditions, women and men are equal participants, although they may have different, complementary roles. For example, during rituals, men and women often sit separately, though opposite each other, either as two halves of a circle or while facing each other across two sides of a ritual structure. Men and women have their own drums, Sacred Pipes, and Spirit Lodges, and to some degree they enjoy their own rituals.

In many traditions, as we have noted, menarche is a major marker in a female's life, characterized by important rituals and communal celebrations. Traditionally, women would seclude themselves to varying degrees during menstruation, because they were understood to be particularly spiritually powerful during that time—so powerful that they could overwhelm the spiritual power of males. Menstruation was understood to be a time of physical and spiritual renewal, when women bonded more intimately with Earth and Moon, to whom they are physically and spiritually attuned. It should be noted that many Western observers, imbued with the Christian doctrine of original sin and Eve's role in the Fall of Man, incorrectly applied related notions of pollution to these Aboriginal rituals—mistakenly assuming that women were considered spiritually inferior in Aboriginal traditions, as they often have been in Western monotheistic traditions.

ABORIGINAL CANADIAN RELIGIONS

To exemplify the diversity and continuity of Aboriginal Canadian religions, let us now focus more closely on four living traditions. The Anishinaabek (Ojibwe, Odawa, and Potowatami) of the central and western Great Lakes region represent former hunter-gatherer traditions. The Haudenosaunee, the Six Nations people, traditionally a horticultural-hunting culture, continue their religious tradition in the eastern Great Lakes region. The Niitsitapi ("Blackfoot Nation": Kainai, Siksika, and Piikani), who were living on the Prairies before the arrival of the horse, remain in their homeland to the east of the Rocky Mountains. Along the west coast (Northwest Coast traditions), a number of different peoples share several common features in their ritual life; let the Kwakwaka'wakw (Kwakiutl) represent them. Remember, too, that none of these four general groupings of Aboriginal traditions are exclusively Canadian; all may be found on both sides of the border with the United States, which in some cases actually splits Aboriginal reserves.

Anishinaabe Religion

Peoples speaking various Algonkian dialects may be found across Canada from the Atlantic to the Rocky Mountains, between the Inuit and Dené to the north and the Six Nations to the south. The Anishinaabek (the plural form of Anishinaabe) speak the closely connected Ojibwe, Odawa, and Potawatomi dialects of the Algonkian language family, and their religious traditions have experienced major revitalization in recent decades. Some Anishinaabe rituals are similar to those practiced by Aboriginal peoples to their north and west, whose Cree language is also closely related to theirs. The Anishinaabek presently reside on reserves in Ontario, southeastern Manitoba, north-eastern Minnesota, and northern Wisconsin and Michigan—that is, in the general area surrounding the Great Lakes. Many also live in cities, notably Toronto and the twin cities of Minneapolis-St. Paul.

The practices of the traditional Anishinaabe religion included Pan-Indian rituals and spiritual understandings, as well as Dream Dance drum rituals, hunting and healing rituals, and a number of circumpolar rituals. The latter involved particular practices associated with Bear; a form of divination called pyroscapulamancy in which heat is applied to scapulae—a ritual that continued into the twentieth century only among the Algonkian-speaking cultures of present-day Labrador; and the **shaking tent** ritual, which is similar to the Lakota Yuwipi and Inuit shamanistic binding rituals. In the shaking tent ritual, a specialist is tied up and placed in a very small teepee. After a performance of drumming and singing by those assisting, voices of spirits can be heard entering the now-shaking structure. With the help of these spirits, information important to the community or to particular individuals is ascertained. At the end of the ritual, the specialist leaves the structure unbound.

The Midéwiwin has also been important in the survival of Anishinaabe religion. It arose as a *cultus,* that is, as a religious option into which adherents are initiated in addition to the normative religion of the culture. The relationship of the Midéwiwin to the Anishinaabe religion in general is somewhat analogous to the relationship of Masonry to Protestant Christianity. Persons who are considered by the community to be upright and working for the good of society may be invited to join through an initiation ceremony. There are four degrees of initiation (or eight in some modes), and they involve rituals symbolizing death and resurrection through the exercise of spiritual power. While the roots of the Midéwiwin lie deeply in the past, the present form seems to have taken shape by the seventeenth century. At that time, an Anishinaabe trading town arose at

Only the lower part of the frame of this early-twentieth-century Anishinaabe Midéwiwin Initiation Lodge is covered with brush. It is similar to those used today in Ontario and Manitoba.
PHOTO BY FRANCES DENSMORE.

the south-western end of Lake Superior, where the West meets the Great Lakes transportation network. The Anishinaabek had led a semi-nomadic existence prior to the height of the fur trade, moving in a seasonal round between various modes of subsistence. As the scale of trade increased, settlements were established for part of the year. This development also follows the dispersion of the Wyandot among the Anishinaabek after the attacks by the Haudenosaunee. The Midéwiwin rituals incorporated the Wyandot drum and longhouse with traditional Anishinaabe shamanistic practices. This synthesis gave many Anishinaabek a religious means for coping with the political and economic upheavals of this period, as well as the ravages caused by the epidemic diseases introduced by Europeans. The importance of the Midéwiwin continued until the Anishinaabek were forced onto reserves, where these and other traditional rituals were forbidden by the Christian missionaries whose persecution was backed by the full force of provincial, state, and national law.

As the practice of traditional Aboriginal religion was reaching its low point in the late 1960s, the Black Power movement in the United States stimulated a similar Red Power movement among Aboriginal people. In 1968, to protect Aboriginal people in the Minneapolis-St. Paul area who were subject to vicious racist attacks, several Anishinaabek formed the American Indian Movement (AIM). At first an urban development, these young Aboriginals came into contact with Siouan Lakota elders and religious

"An Algonkian Medicine Ceremony," mid-nineteenth century, by Seth Eastman. Interior of a Midéwiwin Ceremonial Lodge, which today would be covered by canvas. ILLUSTRATION BY SETH EASTMAN.

leaders to their west. These elders and AIM formed an alliance to protect Aboriginal traditionalists and their religious practices, which led to the Second Battle of Wounded Knee in 1973. There, young Aboriginals armed with a few .22 calibre rimfire rifles and other light weapons confronted the military might of the United States army for several weeks. This standoff was followed by a march on Washington and the Native People's Caravan march to Ottawa in 1974. These activities raised awareness of the plight of Aboriginal people among the general population and marked the beginnings of equal rights for Aboriginal peoples. The leaders of AIM also had profound effects on the revitalization of Aboriginal religious traditions.

One of the spiritual leaders of the Second Battle of Wounded Knee was Leonard Crow Dog (born 1945). Though still a young man, Crow Dog had been raised to be a traditionalist ritual leader. He conducted many Lakota rituals, including the Thirst (Sun) Dance and the Ghost Dance. As the Anishinaabe leaders participated in these rituals, they began to seek out the rituals of their own heritage. One of the founders of AIM, Eddie Benton-Banai (born 1934), contacted Anishinaabe elders who had continued their traditions—particularly the Midéwiwin—in secret. Benton began the revitalization of the Midéwiwin in north-western Wisconsin, its original centre, and was a founder of St. Paul's Red School House, a native-way school based on Midéwiwin teachings. This revitalization spread to nearby reserves in Canada.

Benton attracted other Aboriginal religious revivalists. In the early 1970s, Jim Dumont, who had studied Christian theology at the University of Toronto, and his wife Edna Manitowabi (born 1945) were searching for their Aboriginal religious roots. They found Eddie Benton, who helped them to bring the Midéwiwin to eastern Ontario. Christian missionaries still in de facto control of many reserves resisted this revival of Aboriginal rituals, and young men and women who wanted to re-establish their traditions had to leave. They founded a community south-east of Sudbury where traditional fasting, Spirit Lodge, and Midéwiwin rituals could take place. Working with Art Solomon (1914–97), who served under Christian ministers as an unpaid prison chaplain to Aboriginals, young Aboriginals from this Sudbury community began to visit Aboriginal inmates of Ontario prisons, where decades of repression had created a disproportionately large Aboriginal population. Renewed interest in their religious heritage spread among young Anishinaabek and traditional rituals were once again practised openly on the reserves. With that, Christian missionary control of the reserves was broken. The Midéwiwin now has four large meetings a year, one for each season. These meetings rotate among reserves in Wisconsin, Michigan, Manitoba, and Ontario. They are attended by Anishinaabek from all over the Great Lakes region for four busy days of ceremonies, initiations, teachings, and socializing.

After the Native People's Caravan march to Ottawa in 1974, Vern Harper (born 1936), a Great Plains Cree raised in Toronto and one of the leaders of the Canadian AIM, began to seek spiritual training like Benton had. Together with his former wife, Pauline Shirt (also a Cree elder), Harper founded the Wandering Spirit Survival School (1977), a native-way school within the Toronto District School Board. In 1989, the school was renamed the First Nations School of Toronto. Given the urban Aboriginal demography, the school's curriculum contains elements of Pan-Indian ceremonies, the Midéwiwin, and the Six Nations Longhouse Religion.

As well as the native-way school, Anishinaabek in Toronto enjoy a number of religious supports, including an Aboriginal centre where annual elders' conferences continue to introduce urban Aboriginal Canadians to their own traditions. Toronto also offers men's and women's residences for Aboriginal people striving to put their lives back together, many of them residential school survivors. Various forms of assistance are available at these residences, including traditional spiritual healing. At Anishnawbe Health Toronto, Toronto's Aboriginal people may find traditional healing circles, often led by members of the Midéwiwin, as well as Western forms of medicine. Harper himself has also been serving as a chaplain to Aboriginal inmates at a men's prison for many years, and he leads Spirit Lodge rituals for urbanites and conducts spiritual healings in the Toronto and Guelph areas.

Not all Aboriginal traditionalists are involved with the Midéwiwin *cultus*, however. When the Christian missionaries lost control of the reserves, other forms of traditional Anishinaabe religion were revived, such as the shaking tent ritual. Wikiwemikong on Manitoulin Island, by the north shore of Lake Superior, is the largest unceded reserve in Canada. Its health centre comprises two joined halves: a Western-style medical clinic and a structure for traditional Anishinaabe healing ceremonies. As well, the Catholic Church on Manitoulin Island and the nearby, Jesuit-run Anishinaabe Spiritual Centre have incorporated Anishinaabe religious symbolism into their ritual and social life, including during Mass. The Second Vatican Council (1960–65) made this liberalization possible. Wikiwemikong holds an annual music festival, too. The Three Fires Society—the secular branch of the Midéwiwin—sponsors the festival, which is held in celebration of the three traditions of the Ojibwe, Odawa, and Potawatomi.

Six Nations: The Longhouse Religion

Many centuries ago, five Iroquoian-speaking cultures of the Finger Lakes region in present-day upstate New York confederated under an oral constitution, which subsequently became a model for the early formation of the United States of America. They were later joined by another Iroquoian-speaking people from the south-eastern part of the continent. This Six Nations confederacy is composed of the Cayuga, Mohawk, Oneida, Onondaga, Seneca, and Tuscarora. The Six Nations, who were allied first with the Dutch and then with the English, dominated the fur trade. Their warriors took control of the entire area, mediating between European fur traders and other Aboriginal groups. As allies of the English, they first fought against the French and their Aboriginal allies, and then most sided with the English in the American War of Independence (1775–83). The success of the colonists against the English led to the downfall of the Six Nations as a major power. When the English army secured the area north of the Great Lakes, many of the Six Nations fled there with them, forming the core of the Six Nations reserve near Brantford in southwestern Ontario, which is there to this day. Those that remained found their traditional territories opened to colonization and their traditional lifestyle eroding.

Today, Six Nations people live on reserves on both sides of Lake Ontario and on the large Seneca reserve in the mountains bordering Pennsylvania. One reserve is split by several borders: Akwesasne (St. Regis reserve outside Cornwall, Ontario) lies in Ontario, Quebec, and New York.

Prior to the formation of the United States, the Six Nations lived a typical horticultural-hunting lifestyle. Women controlled the large matrilineal and matrilocal clan dwellings. As clan heads, the **clan mothers** appointed male leaders (called chiefs by Europeans) who met in a council to decide such external matters as war, trade policy, and alliances. If the clan mothers did not approve of these policies, they possessed the power to replace the chiefs, who in effect served as spokesmen for the clan mothers. Women gardened and maintained households; men served as warriors, hunters, and long-distance traders.

A rich ritual life permeated both female and male activities. The loss of territory, and of military and political power, robbed the men of their traditional way of life to a greater extent than the women. Males became dysfunctional, throwing the balance of everyday life into jeopardy, a pattern which would recur on many reserves. European colonists flooded traditional Six Nations territory with liquor, and by the late eighteenth century, alcoholism and despair had become serious social and personal problems among Six Nations men. Ganeodiyo (Handsome Lake, died 1816), a Seneca, suffered from this common malaise. Near death, he experienced a series of visions that resulted not only in a personal transformation but also in the revitalization of Six Nations life; Ganeodiyo's subsequent leadership caused major changes in Aboriginal culture and society as it spread among the people. Under Quaker Christian tutelage, he transformed the large dwellings of the Six Nations clan lifestyle, anchored by female-dominated horticulture, to the European model of the nuclear family, living in small cabins and centred on a male-dominated agronomy. Strong-willed women who objected were persecuted as witches.

But these changes allowed Six Nations ceremonial life to flourish once again, as Ganeodiyo's followers developed a semi-institutional religion that has continued to the present day among the Six Nations people. The new religion included such traditional medicine societies as the **False Faces**. Quaker Christian teachings transformed Sky of the Sky-Earth cosmic pair found in normative Iroquoian religion into an omnipotent "creator" god. This new religion is called the Longhouse Religion, as most rituals take place in long, rectangular structures reminiscent of traditional clan dwellings. More than two centuries old, the Longhouse Religion continues today, outdating all other forms of modified Aboriginal religion in northern North America. Longhouses may be found on all of the major Six Nations reserves, along with Christian churches. Participation in Longhouse ceremonies tends to be restricted to those belonging to the appropriate clans, based on maternal lineage. A reconstructed ceremonial Longhouse can be visited at the Woodland Cultural Centre on the Six Nations Reserve in Brantford, Ontario.

It was among Mohawk followers of the Longhouse Religion at Akwesasne that one of the first modern demonstrations against the Canadian federal government's violation of treaties with Aboriginal nations took place. In 1969, the border crossing on reserve land between New York and Ontario was blockaded over the government's plan to expand the crossing by taking Mohawk land without permission. The protest was led by traditionalists like Ernie Benedict (1918–2011), and was influential on the activities of the AIM. Over the violent objections of assimilationists, the traditionalists at Akwesasne created their own school using their own language, as well as a newspaper, *Akwesasne Notes,* which quickly gained a continent-wide circulation. Traditional religious practices and socio-cultural roles, including the position of clan mother, were also revived. Later, in 1990, the Mohawk Warriors Society at the Kanesatake reserve led protests against the illegal expansion of a golf course onto a sacred burial ground at Oka, just outside Montreal. This protest escalated into a military confrontation that lasted for months and gained worldwide press coverage.

Straddling the international border, Akwesasne was also one of the first reserves to have a casino. On the United States side, this casino attracted organized crime, and smuggling soon became an issue on the reserve, exacerbated by differing interpretations of an early international treaty. The Longhouse traditionalists were opposed to these activities and increasingly found themselves subject to extreme violence. After decades of turbulence, in 1993, a group led by a traditional elder named Tom Porter left the reserve and purchased land in their traditional territory in the Mohawk Valley of New York, where they hoped to practice their traditional religion and lifestyle in peace.

The Longhouse Religion enjoys a rich ritual life based on the Cycle of Thanksgiving. There are ceremonial dances throughout the year, most honouring the gifts on which human lives depend in each season: Maple (maple syrup); planting the Three Sisters (Corn, Beans, and Squash); Strawberry, Green Beans, Green (fresh) Corn, and Harvest (dried corn).

Other dances honour weather and cosmic spirits, such as the Thunders, Sun, and Moon. One dance honours the dead, who have always been important in the Haudenosaunee traditions. As in many cultures around the world, the Midwinter Ceremony is the most elaborate. Held at winter solstice, this ceremony includes a year-renewal ritual known as the "Stirring of the Ashes." This ritual also involves such healing societies as the False Face Society, one of several ritual associations into which Longhouse members may be invited to be initiated.

Niitsitapi Religion

The Niitsitapi (Blackfoot Confederacy) comprise three closely related traditions: the Siksika (Blackfeet), Kainai (Blood), and Piikani (Peigan), split into north and south variants. They are Algonkian-speaking peoples who once lived on the Prairies, using dog-pulled travois for transportation before adopting the horse—in contrast to the Algonkian-speaking Great Plains Cree, who adopted horses when they moved to live full-time on the Prairies. With the use of horses, the Niitsitapi became a powerful nation; their traditional territory was bounded by the North Saskatchewan River to the north, the Yellowstone River to the south, the confluence of the North and South Saskatchewan Rivers to the east, and the Continental Divide to the west. Their economy was very much dependent on the bison, although they also hunted other animals in the eastern part of the Rocky Mountains. The adoption of horses enabled the Niitsitapi to follow the migrating bison herds more easily, and they became feared mounted warriors. Wealth for Niitsitapi was based on herds of horses that were gained through raiding other Great Plains peoples.

The horse also allowed this essentially nomadic people to carry larger collections of ritual objects than they could have with dogs. These collections are called medicine bundles, and they are key elements of the rich Niitsitapi ritual tradition. Their religion includes such Pan-Indian modalities as the Sacred Pipe and Spirit Lodge, along with fasting for visions. Like other Great Plains traditions, initiations into age-graded and gender-specific ritual societies were an important aspect of Niitsitapi religion, and the most important ceremonies were part of an annual gathering called **Okan** (known in non-Aboriginal literature as the "Sun Dance"). Okan is a year-renewal ritual that takes place in early summer, when there is enough grass for the many horses needed to bring large numbers of people to the ceremony. All the ritual societies play significant roles at this time, as do the keepers of the **sacred bundles** and pipes.

Sacred bundles are kept by married couples; part of their prescribed ritual life is to care for the bundle. Keeping the bundles involves daily rituals and various ritual injunctions regarding diet, sexual activities, and other practices. Bundles are passed from couple to couple and are opened in elaborate rituals as required by the community, or as called for on great ritual occasions like the Okan. The bundles contain collections of sacred objects wrapped in hides and cloth. These objects may include pipes, drums, rattles, specially shaped stones, and ritual apparel; all are emblematic of and gifts from sacred beings. Certain myths, songs, dances, and rituals are associated with each of the objects in a sacred bundle. These associations are far more important than the objects themselves, some of which are periodically renewed.

The Okan can only take place if, at some point in the preceding year, a highly respected woman has vowed to Sun to put on the ceremony. She is then called the "Sacred Woman." Nowadays, the vow is usually given when a woman is requesting Sun's aid for a seriously ill member of the family. Between the making of the vow and the Okan ceremonies, the woman and her husband live a ritually prescribed life. When all the people have gathered together at the Okan grounds, the Sacred Woman's Lodge is raised, where she fasts during the four days of the ceremony. During this time, the Sacred Woman's husband engages in a series of Spirit Lodges. The Sacred Woman wears a special, sacred headdress, which is kept with the important Beaver bundle (the keepers of the Beaver bundle function as the head priests in the ritual). A special, arbour-like, circular structure is ritually constructed, where "dancers" who have pledged their participation dance in place for the four days of the ritual, abstaining from food and drink. The dancers, who have offered themselves in this way for the well-being of the community, often experience visions. Towards the end of the four days, the dancers may have themselves pierced in self-sacrifice to the spirits, again as an offering for the welfare of the community. Skewers are either inserted through their chests and tied to the central sacred pole, or inserted through their backs and tied to bison skulls. They then either dance in place, leaning back from the pole, or drag the skulls until the flesh is torn and they are freed. Such dancing often induces visions, too, which are understood as gifts from the spirits.

From the late nineteenth century until the late twentieth century, the Canadian federal government tried to put an end to Niitsitapi religious practices, especially Okan ceremonies. By the late 1960s, old couples often found it hard to recruit younger couples to take on the ritual responsi-bilities of caring for the sacred bundles, and some ritually transferred them to the Alberta Provincial Museum. Since then, a few of these bun-dles have been repatriated to the communities. In other cases, elders have been more fortunate, among them the late Piikani couple Joe (1909–99) and Josephine (born 1917) Crowshoe, whose lives span virtually the entire twentieth century. As keepers of the Thunder bundle and of bundles cen-tral to Okan, the Crowshoes struggled to maintain their Niitsitapi religion, often practising in secret. Josephine served as a Sacred Woman, and their children are now keeping bundles and continuing their religious traditions. In 1991, the Crowshoes were together awarded the Order of Canada—an indication of the government's new understanding that, in the Niitsitapi traditions, married couples carry on the traditions together. Ironically, however, the couple was rewarded for helping to save Niitsitapi religion by a government that had spent a century trying to eradicate it.

Some Niitsitapi families have been able to retain aspects of their tra-ditional lifestyle through ranching. Having been masters of the horse in pre-reserve times, these Aboriginal ranchers find modern ranching suit-able for maintaining this aspect of their culture. But for the most part, the Niitsitapi still struggle to maintain their traditional religious lifestyle. For many years, they tried to stop the damming of the Oldman River in south-western Alberta, and were ultimately unsuccessful. The river is sacred to the Niitsitapi; Oldman is their name for Coyote, the culture-hero deity of many of the Great Plains Aboriginal traditions (non-Aboriginal observ-ers sometimes refer to Coyote as a trickster figure). Neither the Canadian federal government nor the Albertan provincial government has acknowl-edged Niitsitapi concerns about profaning the sacred river.

Another example of the Canadian government's disrespect for Niitsitapi religious traditions has to do with the transporting of sacred bundles. Like many Aboriginal peoples, the Niitsitapi community is split by the international border between Canada and the United States. The United States government has passed regulations allowing the Niitsitapi to take their sacred artifacts back and forth across the border so that they are able to fully participate in community rituals. The Canadian government has failed to pass similar laws, and so the Niitsitapi run the risk of having their sacred bundles and other ceremonial objects con-fiscated when they return to Canada. Travelling only a few kilometres across the border may result in the loss of sacred eagle feathers or other essential ritual items.

Kwakwaka'wakw Religion

Kwakwaka'wakw rituals are typical of many Northwest Coast traditions; their traditional territory included the north and north-eastern shores of Vancouver Island, the mainland shore across the Strait of Georgia, and several inland areas contiguous to these shores. Today the Kwakwaka'wakw are restricted to a few small reserves; the government of British Columbia has a history of resistance to land claims negotiations with the many Aboriginal groups within their jurisdiction. Before the coming of Europeans—first Russians, then the Spanish and the English—the Aboriginal peoples of the north-west coast of North America, from northern California up through the Alaskan panhandle, lived in coastal or riverside villages surrounded by dense rainforests of monumental cedar. Their clan longhouses were supported by posts and walled with planks from these giant trees, and their oceangoing crafts were also hewn from them.

Blessed with abundant fish and sea mammals, and prolific plants and trees, Northwest Coast Aboriginal peoples enjoyed a rich ceremonial life. Contrary to the other traditions discussed in this chapter, these groups are not egalitarian; their cultures feature complex, hierarchical clan structures with bilateral inheritance (from both mother and father). This inheritance includes not only social status but also rights to fishing and hunting grounds (important to subsistence) as well as ceremonial prerogatives associated with dances, masks, songs, and names. In addition, rights to names come from visions, initiations, and talent, along with inheritance.

The Northwest Coast traditions have many rituals, but most important is the one called **potlatch**. The term comes from "patshatl," which means "to give" in Chinook, the pidgin trade language formerly used along the coast. The potlatch is usually held in the winter, a time for lengthy ceremonials in many traditions around the world. Replete with feasting, ceremonial speeches, singing, and dancing, and using a rich array of elaborately decorated masks, costumes, drums, rattles, backdrop screens, and copper plaques, the most important aspect of the potlatch is to give away one's riches. As in all the Aboriginal-American traditions, prestige comes not from the accumulation of goods, which is understood as selfish and immoral, but through the giving away of possessions. The clan head gives away his or her accumulated wealth, though it is understood that the clan itself is the true giver of these blessings. The greater the wealth given away, the greater the resultant prestige and power. The potlatch marks events central to the lives of these people: birth, marriage, death, and the giving of names and ceremonial rights. The recitation of these lifetime markers

"Masked dancers—Qagyuhl (Kwakwaka'wakw)." Staged photograph at Alert Bay, BC, early twentieth century. PHOTO BY EDWARD S. CURTIS.

in the course of the potlatch helps to maintain social structures and to perpetuate cultural memory.

The coming of Europeans and the resultant fur trade led at first to an enhancement of this ceremonial life. Like other Northwest Coast Aboriginal peoples, the Kwakwaka'wakw boasted a long tradition of carving cedar poles and planks, and the availability of steel chisels and axes led to an elaboration of this tradition. Villages were full of carved house-posts (poles celebrating the complex clan relationships with the spirit realm), funerary posts (with the remains of important persons placed in boxes atop the poles), and decorated house-fronts. The wealth attendant on the fur trade resulted in ever greater potlatch giveaways. But the Europeans also brought smallpox, which decimated many villages; and firearms, which led to greater losses of life during traditional raiding.

Colonization came later to the west coast of Canada, but it was more devastating for the Aboriginal peoples who lived there. Even after British Columbia joined the Canadian Confederation in 1871, the government continued to refuse to recognize Aboriginal rights and would sign no treaties with the Aboriginal peoples. Reduced to reserves barely large enough for their houses, Aboriginal people were often exploited as servants and cheap labour for fish-canning factories. Missionaries and government agents placed in charge of the reserves were particularly incensed by the potlatch. It was thought of as un-Christian, and it was criticized for distracting Aboriginal workers from their jobs, poorly paid though they were. Protestant missionaries and government officials in particular looked upon the unconditional giveaways as contrary to the Calvinist ethic of accumulated wealth as a sign of grace.

In the late nineteenth century, the first laws against all Aboriginal ceremonials were passed; colloquially, these laws were known as the pot-latch laws. In 1921, a Kwakwaka'wakw potlatch was held at Village Island, after which 45 persons were arrested for participating. Participation was deemed to include dancing, making speeches, and giving away gifts. Of those arrested, 20 were imprisoned and three were remanded subsequent to appeals. Twenty-two others had their sentences suspended on the con-dition that they handed over all their ceremonial accoutrements to William M. Halliday (1866–?), the Indian Agent in Alert Bay, who tried the cases.

These ritual items were subsequently delivered to the British Columbia Provincial Museum (now the Royal British Columbia Museum); the National Museum of Man (now the Museum of Civilization) in Ottawa; and the Royal Ontario Museum in Toronto. Some objects ended up in the per-sonal collection of Duncan Campbell Scott (1862–1947), the Superintendent General of Indian Affairs at that time. Others items were sold by Halliday to the United States collector George G. Heye (1874–1957), whose collection was relatively recently taken over by the Smithsonian Institution, forming the core of the new Museum of the American Indian in Washington, DC. After these events, potlatch ceremonies were held in secret, for social and cultural traditions could not be maintained without them.

In 1951, the so-called potlatch laws were dropped from a revised fed-eral Indian Act, but not specifically repealed. The following year, Mungo Martin (1879–1962) hosted the first public potlatch for over three decades in Victoria. In 1966, a traditional longhouse or Big House was erected at Alert Bay for holding potlatches, and the first on this site was hosted by Mr. and Mrs. James Knox. Since then, hundreds of potlatches have taken place, hosted by many families. The Alert Bay Big House was built adjacent to the former residential school, and this juxtaposition visually illus-trates an important shift in Northwest Coast Aboriginal fortunes: from cultural and religious repression to cultural and religious revitalization. Many Northwest Coast Aboriginal communities have since built ceremo-nial Big Houses and resurrected many of their religious ritual practices.

Encouraged by these developments, the Kwakwaka'wakw more urgently sought the return of their confiscated ceremonial objects from the museums to which they had been sent by Halliday. Eventually, the

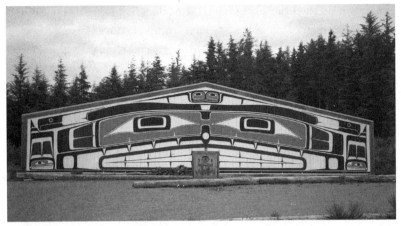

Contemporary Kwakwaka'wakw (Kwakiutl) "Big House" at Alert Bay, BC, for potlatch ceremonies.
PHOTO BY JORDAN PAPER. REPRINTED BY PERMISSION. © 2007, JORDAN PAPER.

authorities agreed to return the sacred objects on the condition that the Kwakwaka'wakw construct museums to house them. In 1979, a traditional structure was built at Cape Mudge; it is called the Kwakiutl Museum. The following year, the Big House at Alert Bay was converted into a museum with attached offices, theatre, and gift shop; it is called the U'mista Cultural Centre. To replace it, an even larger Big House was built for the potlatch and other ceremonies in 2000. Many of the confiscated items were then repatriated by the National Museum of Civilization and the Royal Ontario Museum.

In spite of the return of the potlatch, many serious problems remain for the Kwakwaka'wakw and other Northwest Coast Aboriginal communities. In particular, Aboriginal groups residing in British Columbia face unresolved issues about treaty negotiation, especially land rights and resource ownership. The Kwakwaka'wakw, for example, have poor access to fishing, their only source of income, and their sacred sites remain unprotected. These unresolved issues make it far more difficult for the Kwakwaka'wakw to live according to their religious tradition than for groups in some other parts of Canada and the United States.

Similar conditions prevent other Aboriginal peoples on the Northwest Coast from more fully returning to their traditions. The status of the whale serves as a good example of these difficulties. For some of these communities, both in Canada and in contiguous parts of the United States, religious life centres on Whale; whales figure importantly in these cultures, not only as a resource but as a deity. Typical of gathering traditions worldwide, the primary source of subsistence is simultaneously a primary deity, as is Bison on the Prairies. In 1999, the Makah, whose homeland is just across the narrow Strait of Juan de Fuca from Vancouver Island, received permission from both international and national regulatory agencies to take two whales every year for ceremonial purposes. Without Whale, the Makah cannot revive their traditional religious life. However, when the Makah went to take the whale, there was a furious uproar. Non-Aboriginal environmentalists in powerboats harassed the Makah in their traditional paddleboats and picketed their small reserve with signs, one among them reading, "Save the whales, Kill the Indians." Later, the Canadian federal government refused similar permission to other Aboriginal groups on Vancouver Island with similar religious requirements.

All in all, by the late 1960s Aboriginal religious traditions in Canada had reached a low point. A century of Christian missions on the reserves had undermined traditional beliefs and practices, and the residential school system—funded by the federal government and managed mainly by Roman Catholic, Anglican, and United Church clergy—had alienated generations of Aboriginal children from the ways of their forebears. Some Aboriginal leaders have spoken of these and other policies of assimilation as a coordinated form of attempted cultural genocide. On the other hand, while many Aboriginals had nominally become Christian, significant numbers of Aboriginal elders continued to secretly teach their traditional ways.

Disillusioned by the cultural malaise of the middle-aged generation, who suffer from widespread alcoholism, drug abuse, and suicide, many Aboriginal youths have looked for a way out. Many have also taken their own lives; in some cases, suicide among adolescents on reserves was so rampant that coroners spoke of suicide epidemics. But other young Aboriginal people sought out their elders and began to cultivate traditional religious beliefs and practices. A renaissance of Aboriginal religion was in the making. Devout Christian Aboriginals argued against the paternalism of the churches, and increasing numbers of Aboriginal ministers appeared in the vanguard of Protestant movements for liberation from restrictions on Aboriginal ways. Notably, Stan McKay, a Cree from Manitoba, served as the Moderator of the United Church of Canada from 1992 to 1994.

Christian missionizing among Aboriginal peoples generally included negative, racist attitudes towards Aboriginals themselves and the disparaging of every aspect of Aboriginal culture as the work of Satan. Despite these challenges to Aboriginal practices, a major revitalization of traditional religions has since taken place in each of the four Aboriginal groupings we have discussed. Revival of traditional ways began at different times and proceeded at different speeds. For the Haudenosaunee, it occurred at the beginning of the nineteenth century, while the Kwakwaka'wakw began to recover their traditional religion after the law criminalizing Aboriginal religions was dropped in 1951. For the Anishinaabek, religious revitalization rapidly expanded through the 1970s, while the Niitsitapi have experienced a slower process that did not reach fruition until the late 1980s.

Longhouse Religion represented the earliest conscious modifications to traditional ways, thanks in large part to the ability of the Six Nations to adapt to rapidly changing socio-economic conditions. First, Longhouse society moved from a horticultural-hunting milieu to an agricultural one. Then, in the second half of the twentieth century, Six Nations culture was flexible enough to accommodate a modern industrial economy; Mohawk high-steel workers built most of the skyscrapers in New York City throughout the twentieth century. In another context, many Niitsitapi found that by focusing on ranching they could maintain important aspects of their traditional lifestyle, and the Okan ceremonies expressed their determination to continue the annual ritual gatherings of pre-contact times. By contrast, the Northwest Coast Aboriginal peoples in British Columbia have struggled with adapting to modern economies. If these groups were allowed sufficient access to and control over traditional maritime resources, they would recover not only the economic base they enjoyed in pre-contact times, but also the powerful blessings of their traditional sea spirits. For the Anishinaabek, the semi-institutionalized Midéwiwin offers spiritual benefits, particularly for those who live in cities. The intense four-day ritual experience of the Midéwiwin cycle, which occurs in four annual ceremonies that rotate among rural reserves throughout the Great Lakes area, allows a periodic return to the natural world, the traditional realm of Anishinaabe numinous beings.

AFTERWORD

In the main, the most important remaining issues for Aboriginal Canadian cultures and societies have to do with government policies and procedures, at both the provincial and federal levels. The leaders of Canada's Aboriginal peoples continually express the desire to be free from governmental control. A viable economic base is essential for this independence. With regard to religion per se, the primary problem has been a lack of recognition by the government and the courts. Canada's legal courts understand religion from a fundamentally Christian framework; hence, religion is expected to entail houses of worship, for example, which are specific for religious activities and for those activities only. A legal system rooted in Christian values and expectations also tends to stress the importance of written sacred texts over other kinds of sacred objects. It is not inclined to respect natural materials kept in medicine bundles as sacred objects, or to show much concern for protecting natural geographical sites as sacred places when non-Aboriginal economic requirements dictate otherwise.

Finally, non-Aboriginal culture tends to understand Aboriginal religious traditions from ersatz sources, not from Aboriginal elders. For example, popular New Age writers sometimes create fantasies about Aboriginal religions that are often completely unrelated to actual lived traditions. Aboriginal elders disown these fantasies, but their popularity often persists, spurred, it seems, by little more than the desire to make money. In some cases, serious misunderstandings have arisen from such New Age paradigms, prompting environmentalist groups to vociferously attack real Aboriginal cultures and religious practices. Greenpeace has been at the forefront in seeking an end to ritual activities that are essential to the continuation of certain Aboriginal religious traditions, such as the ritual hunting of whales for non-commercial ceremonial feasts. Non-Aboriginal cultures no longer seem to understand that hunting in and of itself can be a religious act, a communion between supplicating humans and powerful spirits who give themselves so that humans may live. In spite of these many serious roadblocks, however, the Aboriginal religious renaissance continues in the twenty-first century.

KEY TERMS

Clan Mother	A woman designated as the leader of one of the matrilineal clans of the Six Nations people. She appoints a man to speak for her.
False Faces	One of the healing societies of the Six Nations people involving the ritual wearing of sacred masks. Now an aspect of Longhouse Religion, membership requires invitation and initiation.
Longhouse	A structure for ceremonies of the Iroquoian traditions, replicating the matrilineal-clan longhouse dwellings of traditional times. The traditional religion of the Six Nations people is known as the Longhouse Religion. For ceremonial gatherings, Northwest Coast Aboriginal peoples erect Big Houses, reproducing the ancient designs of traditional times.

Medicine	An English-language word often used to designate any aspect of traditional Aboriginal culture that is both sacred and powerful. It is often related to holistic healing in the broadest sense—to make whole again that which is broken or out of balance.
Okan	The major ritual complex of the Niitsitapi (Blackfoot Nation) involving the gathering of the people in the early summer, usually called the "Sun Dance" by those not of the tradition.
Pan-Indian	Any aspect of Aboriginal culture that is shared among a large number of traditions, including religious rituals found in urban Aboriginal centres, universities, prisons, and so on.
Potlatch	The major ceremonial complex of the Northwest Coast Aboriginal traditions, involving a major giveaway as part of the ritual, along with dances and oratory.
Sacred Bundle	Among Great Plains Aboriginal traditions, a complex of sacred items usually wrapped in cloths and/or hides.
Shaking Tent	An Anishinaabe ritual in which a powerful healer enters a small, teepee-like structure that shakes after it has been entered by the spirits whom she or he calls into the structure.
Spirit Lodge	An Anishinaabe term for the Pan-Indian structure that is filled with heated stones for the heat purification ceremonies that accompany many important events in Aboriginal religious traditions.
Tobacco	One of the four sacred plants of Pan-Indian religion. The other sacred plants are cedar, sage, and sweetgrass.

KEY DATES

1649 CE	The Wyandot are forced from their Georgian Bay homeland by the Haudenosaunee; some merge with the Anishinaabek.
1778	Captain Cook reaches Nootka Sound on Vancouver Island. The Spanish had reached the southern part of the island in 1774, and the Russians were already established in Alaska.
1784	Joseph Brant, an Anglican, leads his Six Nations followers to settle on the Grand River in southern Ontario.
1799–1800	Ganeodiyo (Handsome Lake) has a series of three visions that eventually leads to the establishment of the Longhouse Religion.
1876	Passage of the Indian Act, which was designed to assimilate Canada's Aboriginal population by destroying their culture and religion.

1921	Arrest of 45 Kwakwaka'wakw by the Indian Agent in Alert Bay for participating in a potlatch.
1951	Dropping of the criminalization of Aboriginal religious practices from the Indian Act.
1970	Blue Quills, near St. Paul, Alberta, becomes the first school in Canada to be controlled by an Indian Band.
1974	Native People's Caravan march to Ottawa.
1985	Passage of Bill C-31, ending the official policy of assimilation.
1996	The last federally run residential school closes at Gordon, Saskatchewan.

KEY READINGS

Benton-Banai, Edward. *The Mishomis Book: The Voice of the Ojibway*. St. Paul: Indian Country Press, 1979.

Bringhurst, Robert. *A Story as Sharp as a Knife: The Classical Haida Mythtellers and Their World*. Vancouver: Douglas and McIntyre, 1999.

Brown, Jennifer S.H., and Robert Brightman. *"The Orders of the Dreamed": George Nelson on Cree and Northern Ojibwa Religion and Myth, 1823*. Winnipeg: University of Manitoba Press, 1988.

Geyshick, Ron. *Te Bwe Win (Truth)*. Toronto: Summerhill Press, 1989.

Helm, June. *Prophecy and Power among Dogrib Indians*. Lincoln: University of Nebraska Press, 1994.

Hungry Wolf, Beverly. *The Ways of My Grandmothers*. New York: William Morrow, 1980.

Paper, Jordan. *Offering Smoke: The Sacred Pipe and Native American Religion*. Moscow, ID: University of Idaho Press, 1988.

Paper, Jordan. *Through the Earth Darkly: Female Spirituality in Comparative Perspective*. New York: Continuum, 1997.

Paper, Jordan. *Native North American Religious Traditions: Dancing for Life*. New York: Praeger, 2007.

Smith, Theresa S. *The Island of the Anishnabeg: Thunderers and Water Monsters in the Traditional Ojibwe Life-World*. Moscow, ID: University of Idaho Press, 1995.

Tooker, Elizabeth. *The Iroquois Ceremonial of Midwinter*. Syracuse: Syracuse University Press, 1970.

KEY WEBSITES

http://www.turtle-island.com [Aboriginal American broadcast and video productions]

http://www.afn.ca [Assembly of First Nations]

http://www.haudenosauneeconfederacy.ca [Haudenosaunee Confederacy]

http://www.blackfeetnation.com [Blackfeet Nation]

http://www.firstnationsnt.ca/ [Industry Canada's First Nations on SchoolNet]

http://www.three-fires.net/tfn/index.htm [Midéwiwin]

KEY QUESTIONS FOR CRITICAL REFLECTION

1. Does the term "supernatural" have any meaning in the Aboriginal Canadian understanding of life?

2. How do we understand the dichotomy between the secular and the sacred when every aspect of one's surroundings is numinous?

3. Why did European Americans set out to utterly destroy Aboriginal Canadian cultures and religions?

4. How can modified Aboriginal Canadian religious traditions fit within an urban setting?

5. Who leads rituals in religious traditions that are egalitarian?

TWO

Catholic Christians

TERENCE J. FAY, UNIVERSITY OF TORONTO

n the age of European exploration, Catholic nations took early control of the North American continent. Spain colonized the southern regions of what are now Mexico, Arizona, New Mexico, California, Louisiana, and Florida, and converted the Aboriginal peoples of those areas to the Catholic faith. Spanish-Dominican, Franciscan, and Jesuit missionaries in great numbers landed in the south to spread the Catholic faith. With Spain firmly in control of the southern regions, Jacques Cartier (1491–1557) and Samuel de Champlain (*ca.* 1567–1635) landed in the northern regions of the continent and claimed them for the French flag and for the Catholic religion. French-Franciscan and Jesuit missionaries evangelized the northern regions with the same spiritual intensity as their brethren in the southern regions. It seemed inevitable that the Catholicism of both Spain and France would bind North America into the Catholic fold.

Then, in the seventeenth century, English Puritans and dissenters landed on the North American shores of the Atlantic coast. They brought with them a variety of Protestant faiths and founded several English colonies, which soon became densely populated. These colonies flourished and expanded to the interior, especially after the American War of Independence (1776). From these latecomers to North America emerged a strong, Christian faith built upon the spirituality of John Calvin, and this came to exercise a great influence upon the religious, social, and economic life of the increasingly powerful United States of America. Nevertheless, in Mexico and Canada, Catholics remained firm in their faith, but on the periphery of the American Protestant powerhouse.

THE HERITAGE

According to Catholic teaching, and for Christian historians like me, the Christian tradition began with the history of Israel in the Hebrew Bible, or **Old Testament**. Sometime between 6 and 4 BCE at Bethlehem in Judea, Jesus was born into this tradition, the son of a Nazarene carpenter, Joseph, and his young wife, Mary. Recounted in the **New Testament Gospels** of Matthew (1:1–18) and Luke (1:26–35), the Catholic doctrine of the virgin birth expresses the miracle of Jesus' conception by the Holy Spirit. Jesus began his public ministry at the age of 30 and gained 12 Jewish **disciples** as his first followers, with Peter being chief among them. After three years of itinerant teaching, Jesus incurred the enmity of the Jewish religious authorities and their Roman overlords. He was crucified in Jerusalem at the time of the Jewish Passover. According to Christian scripture, he rose from the dead three days later. Christians commemorate the crucifixion of Jesus on Good Friday after 40 days of fasting, penance, and prayer known as Lent, and then celebrate his resurrection at **Easter**.

For his Jewish followers, the crucifixion and resurrection of Jesus expressed his willingness to practice what he preached at all costs, confirming his status as the Messiah or **Christ** of biblical prophecy. After Jesus departed this world, the first Jewish Christians met in Jerusalem, led initially by James, the brother of Jesus. They attended synagogue on Saturday, and on Sunday they commemorated the Jewish Passover supper of Jesus, known by Christians as the "Last Supper." This ritual was later institutionalized as the Catholic **sacrament** of the Eucharist. The Acts of the Apostles (1:9–11) describes how, 40 days after Easter, the risen Jesus appeared to his followers to comfort and encourage them, then ascended into heaven, promising that he would return. The Feast of the Ascension marks these events. The Feast of Pentecost follows ten days later, marking the descent of the Holy Spirit upon Jewish Christians in Jerusalem and the start of the Christian Church's mission, as narrated in Acts (2:1–31).

In these early years, the **apostles** Peter (*ca.* 1–67) and Paul (*ca.* 5–67), a Jewish convert, travelled around the Roman Empire preaching the message of Jesus to Jewish communities. In 70 CE, the Roman military destroyed the Second Temple in Jerusalem, obliterating the Jewish-Christian fellowship and forcing them to disperse. Jewish-Christian communities developed in the cities of the Mediterranean and the Middle East. The centre of Christian worship shifted to Rome, where Peter and Paul had been martyred in about 67 CE in an act of Roman persecution. In the diaspora, Jewish Christianity attracted gentile adherents and was transformed into Greco-Roman Christianity. Politically, economically, and legally their world was Roman, but culturally it was Greek. As Peter and Paul had carried the gospel to the west, the apostle Thomas (died 72) carried the gospel east to the Syrians, Persians, and Indians. In a sacramental imitation of the baptism of Jesus in the River Jordan by John, newcomers were baptized into these Christian communities.

As they awaited the return of the risen Jesus, early Christian communities followed his teachings about the kingdom of God. Jesus summed up the Ten Commandments of Jewish scripture by instructing his followers to love God with all of their hearts, minds, and souls, and to love their neighbours as themselves. Preparing for the return of Jesus, Christian communities began to develop an institutional life, structured around bishops, presbyters, and deacons. Reflecting on the intense religious experience of Jesus, Greek-Christian thinkers created the theology of the **Trinity** at the councils of Nicaea (325) and Constantinople (381). Later, at the councils of Ephesus (431) and Chalcedon (451), theologians formulated the doctrine of the **hypostatic union**, which states that the one person of Christ unites human and divine natures and recognizes Mary as the bearer of God. These intellectual clarifications produced the **Nicene Creed** (325), which helped to liturgically unite scattered Christian communities. By the end of the fourth century, prompted by the Alexandrian theologian Athanasius (*ca.* 297–373), Christian leaders had also agreed upon the canon of the New Testament, to which they added the Hebrew scriptures to form the Christian Bible.

These theological and canonical developments went hand in hand with the adoption of Christianity as the religion of the Roman Empire. In 313, Constantine's Edict of Milan granted toleration to all religions, including Christianity, and the emperor provided land and money in restitution for Christian property confiscated during persecutions under such predecessors as Nero (37–68), Decius (*ca.* 201–251), and Diocletian (244–311).

On the traditional site of the apostle Peter's crucifixion, the basilica of St. John Lateran was consecrated as the cathedral church of Rome in 324. Constantine (*ca.* 272–337) united the eastern and western empires after decades of civil war, and in 330 moved the capital from Rome to Constantinople, formerly the Greek colony of Byzantium. Tensions between east and west existed, however. The Petrine doctrine promulgated by Pope Leo I (*ca.* 400–61; reigned 440–461) asserted that the apostle Peter handed on primacy to the bishop of Rome over all other bishops. When Leo intervened to determine the outcome of the Council of Chalcedon (451), his doctrine gained acceptance from most other Christian Churches. The Roman Church's spiritual influence grew. The great fourth-century theologian Augustine (354–430) wrote *City of God* justifying the Church's spiritual authority over all earthly powers. Exercising this civil leadership in 455, Pope Leo I confronted Attila the Hun and the Vandal armies and avoided the complete destruction of Rome. During the ninth and tenth centuries, the Eastern and Western Churches differed over questions of western jurisdiction, eastern iconoclasm, the long hair and beards of eastern monks, western unleavened bread, and the use of the word *filioque* in the creed. As one of the two original patriarchal sees, Rome maintained it was first among equals, which Constantinople became less likely to grant as the centuries wore on.

The Lombard invasions of the sixth century and the rise of Islam in the seventh sealed the decline of the western empire's great urban centres, and monks began to restructure Christian life around their monasteries in the countryside. Originating in the Egyptian desert during the third and fourth centuries with ascetics such as Anthony (*ca.* 251–356) and Pachomius (*ca.* 290–347), monasticism spread through the efforts of Basil (died 379) in the east and Benedict (480–547) in the west, both of whom supplied rules for the communities they founded. Through the centuries, Benedictine monasteries became rural centres of learning, hospitality, and communal devotions. Embracing poverty, chastity, and obedience, monks and nuns formed communities supported by their own labour. The papacy of Gregory the Great (*ca.* 540–604; reigned 590–604) epitomizes this period of change, as Europe and the Church made the transition from the urban culture of ancient Rome to the agrarian world of medieval feudalism. Gregory made peace with the Lombards, and missionaries like Augustine of Canterbury, who evangelized the English, took Christianity to the furthest reaches of Europe. Equally influential as a practical theologian, Gregory's *Pastoral Rule* served as a handbook of spiritual responsibilities and administrative duties for medieval bishops.

In 732, near Tours, France, Charles Martel (*ca.* 688–741) halted the advance of the Muslim Moors on Europe, and on **Christmas** Day, 800, Pope Leo III (750–816; reigned 795–816) crowned Charlemagne (*ca.* 742–814) as the Holy Roman Emperor at St. Peter's Basilica in Rome to seal the alliance between Church and state. This alliance confirmed the Catholic Church as the spiritual and moral guide for Christians and the state as their earthly protector, but at the same time alienated the Byzantine emperor by ignoring his jurisdiction. The Holy Roman Emperors insisted that monasteries follow the Benedictine Rule, and—starting in the tenth century—the Cluny Reform. The noble, Romanesque architecture of this Carolingian renaissance communicated the spiritual loftiness of monastic life centred on the work of the liturgy and prayerful study. In 1054, however, tensions between east and west escalated into mutual excommunication between Pope Leo IX (1002–54; reigned 1049–54) and Patriarch Michael Cerularius (1043–59). In 1024, the Venetian crusade captured Constantinople, resulting in what is known as the **Great Schism**. Over the centuries, parts of some Eastern Churches re-established contact with the Church of Rome, the most obvious examples being the Ukrainian, the Syro-Malabar, and the Maronite Churches. In 1965, after the Second Vatican Council (1962–65), Pope Paul VI (1897–1978; reigned 1963–78) and Patriarch Athenagoras I of Constantinople (1886–1972; reigned 1948–72) officially removed the schism between the Eastern and Western Churches.

The medieval period was a time of power and glory for the Catholic Church. To bring divine worship to cities emerging across Europe and without churches, Dominican and Franciscan friars preached on street corners and in market places. Eventually the parish system was restored under diocesan direction, and the religious orders continued to offer the comfort of regular services. The faithful prayed together, reciting "Our Father," "Hail Mary," and the "Apostles' Creed," as well as the Ten Commandments, the sacraments, capital sins, and cardinal virtues. The construction of urban churches, most notably the magnificent gothic cathedrals that still dominate many European vistas, provided employment for skilled workers, while unskilled peasants earned a livelihood working on the monastic properties. The enthusiastic devout established a network of shrines and sacred sites across Europe, and pilgrimages to these places offered fellowship and community, as the *Canterbury Tales* of the English poet Geoffrey Chaucer (*ca.* 1343–1400) reveals. Intellectual life thrived, and universities were founded at Oxford, Paris, Cologne, Pavia, and Edinburgh, many of which boasted new hospitals—as did the larger monasteries and abbeys.

The elegant lines of the epic *Divine Comedy* by Dante Alighieri (1265–1321) seem to capture the visual essence of the Italian poet's journey towards the divine. The English anchoress Julian of Norwich (*ca.* 1342–1417) wrote strikingly of "Mother Jesus" in the meditative *Revelations of Divine Love* (1393). In philosophy and theology, the Franciscan Bonaventure (*ca.* 1217–74) gave mystical illumination to Christian thought in works like *The Mind's Road to God* (1259), while the Dominican Thomas Aquinas (1225–74) systematized Christian theology in the *Summa Theologiae* (1265–74), which ranks as one of the greatest achievements of medieval **Scholasticism**.

At the same time, however, various moral and spiritual shortcomings compromised these triumphs. Early in the medieval period, the reforming Pope Gregory VII (*ca.* 1015–85; reigned 1073–85) was determined to free the Church from the encroachment of the imperial government in Europe. In 1075, he forbade the **lay investiture** of clerical offices, as well as clerical concubinage. But the Holy Roman Emperor Henry IV (1050–1106; reigned 1084–1105) continued to invest bishops, so Gregory excommunicated and deposed him. Threatened by the breakup of his realm, Henry in 1077 made the famous pilgrimage to Canossa in the Alps, where the Pope was lodging on his way to Germany. The emperor spent three days at the castle gates asking forgiveness. When forgiveness was extended, Henry returned to Germany, only to meddle in Church affairs again. Though the Catholic Church and the Holy Roman Empire settled this controversy over lay investiture at the Concordat of Worms (1122), other struggles between the papacy and earthly rulers continued to further delineate the powers of civil and ecclesial realms. Between 1309 and 1377, rival ecclesial and political interests obliged a succession of seven French popes to take refuge in Avignon in southern France, in the shadow of the French crown. Domestic wars, the Black Death, and an autocratic governance exerted financial pressure on the papacy. Experiencing a kind of spiritual stasis, the Catholic Church suffered two and then three rival claimants to the papal throne in a period known as the Great Western Schism (1378–1417). In 1414, this conundrum was solved at the Council of Constance, which pressured rival claimants to resign, and three years later appointed Martin V Pope (*ca.* 1368–1431; reigned 1417–31), who restored papal sovereignty.

Periodic efforts by the populace to recover the spirituality of earlier times took many forms. In *The Imitation of Christ* (*ca.* 1418–27), Thomas à Kempis (1380–1471), a member of the Dutch Brethren of the Common Life, preached a communitarian existence of prayerful devotion, as does the fourteenth-century *Devotio Moderna* of the Beguines. In Italy, diocesan priests chose to live a common life of prayer, working among the needy and the sick. In a similar fashion, the members of the Oratory of Divine Love, founded in Genoa in 1497 by the layman Hector Vernazza, lived a devout life in community. In England, John Wycliffe (*ca.* 1329–84) argued for limitations on papal power, while John Huss (*ca.* 1372–1415) uttered a similar call in Bohemia, as did the Dominican Savonarola (1452–98) in Florence. At the same time, the fifteenth-century **Renaissance** created a great appetite for classical and Christian wisdom. Spreading to France, Holland, Germany, and England in the sixteenth century, this Italian cultural awakening included a progressive, liberating, and religious revival. Rather than relying upon the sacraments of the Church, some scholars sought personal encounters with God through the scriptures. In 1516, Erasmus of Rotterdam (1466–1536) published a highly regarded Greek edition of the New Testament. About the same time, the German Augustinian monk Martin Luther (1483–1546) found warrants in scripture to justify debate over a number of Church practices. Prompted by the way the Dominican friar Johan Tetzel (1465–1519) huckstered ecclesiastical certificates known as "indulgences" for the remission of temporal punishment, Luther posted his *Ninety-Five Theses* on the door of Wittenberg Cathedral in 1517, thus precipitating the Protestant Reformation.

Inspired by Paul, Luther's later writings disseminated the three basic principles of Protestant salvation: justification by faith, grace, and scripture. Since the vast majority of German-speaking Christians could not understand the Catholic Church's standard Latin edition of the Bible, known as the *Vulgate,* Luther translated the scriptures into German. He also insisted · that baptism and the Eucharist alone were true sacraments, since in his view only they were indicated in the scriptures. These contentions raised new questions for Catholic theologians. Between 1545 and 1563, Catholic bishops and theologians gathered in a series of meetings known as the Council of Trent to address these issues. They reflected on current, spiritual problems and formulated an updated theology and Church discipline. To the questions Luther raised about justification, the council taught that works are part of the Christian act of faith, that the sacraments mediate grace, and that the scriptures are understood in the context of Catholic Church tradition. Church teachings guide the Christian conscience, and the seven Catholic sacraments and the Latin *Vulgate* were part of the Church's teachings. In matters of Church discipline, bishops were instructed to live in their dioceses, and priests in their parishes. Priests were to be well-educated at the seminary and preach weekly in their parishes. The changes had the effect of enlivening spiritual commitment, harmonizing liturgical practice, and unifying Church administration under the direction of the diocese and the Holy See.

If the new energy of Trent and its updating of the Catholic Church provided an informed and capable clergy, Catholic spirituality became more meditative, too. The depth and commitment of this Catholic renewal appears especially in Spain in writings like *The Way of Perfection* (1566) and *The Interior Castle* (1577) by Teresa of Avila (1515–82); *The Ascent of Mount Carmel* (1579) and *The Dark Night of the Soul* (1585) by John of the Cross (1542–91); and *On Prayer* (1544) and *Sinner's Guide* (1567) by Louis of Granada (1505–88). Spain was also the home of Ignatius of Loyola (1491–1556), a Spanish soldier who was converted and underwent a year-long retreat in a cave at Manresa. Ignatius elaborates upon this profound experience in his *Spiritual Exercises* (1522–24), which demands personal commitment in the name of Jesus Christ to the service of the Catholic Church. At the University of Paris, Ignatius gathered around him theological students such as Francis Xavier (1506–52) and Peter Faber (1506–46) and founded the Society of Jesus or Jesuits. In 1540, Pope Paul III (1468–1549; reigned 1534–49) approved the Jesuits as a new order for apostolic work. Heartened by the reforms of the Council of Trent, Jesuit missionaries preached the gospel first in Europe, then overseas in such diverse places as Ethiopia, India, China, Japan, and North and South America.

The Council of Trent formed Catholic attitudes and at the same time delineated differences between Catholics and Protestants. Religious sectarianism grew on both sides. At the same time, an explosion of scientific knowledge and colonial expansion overtook Europe from the sixteenth to nineteenth centuries. The ideas of Nicolas Copernicus (1473–1543), Galileo Galilei (1564–1642), and Isaac Newton (1643–1727) challenged the traditional concept of the geocentric universe as found in the scriptures and in the writings of Aristotle and Ptolemy, arguing instead for the heliocentric universe as we now understand it. Later, evolutionary theory, most famously associated with Charles Darwin's *On the Origin of Species* (1859), brought into question the biblical account of creation as then understood in Christian tradition. European expansion extended Catholic horizons in other ways, as the voyages of Christopher Columbus (*ca.* 1451–1506) and other explorers revolutionized world geography, and Catholic missions exported European learning and values to Africa, Asia, and South and North America. Nor were the missionaries themselves naïve about the cultures they encountered. The Italian Jesuit Matteo Ricci (1552–1610) learned Mandarin perfectly, taught mathematics and astronomy, became an advisor to the Chinese emperor, inculturated the gospel into Chinese culture, and waited patiently for Chinese interest in Christian salvation to develop. Robert de Nobili (1577–1656) landed in India, adopted a Brahmin life style, learned Sanskrit, published books in Tamil, and established Christian communities among the Hindu upper castes. Alexandre de Rhodes (1591–1660) quickly assimilated into Vietnamese culture, fashioned a Vietnamese alphabet that is still in use, and trained indigenous catechists to evangelize their people.

The rationalistic philosophy of the eighteenth-century **Enlightenment** and its political outcomes affected the Catholic Church. To secularize civil society, the Austrian, Portuguese, Spanish, and French governments made the Church a department of the state. Political and military pressure from the Bourbon kings in France, Spain, and Portugal caused the Holy See to suppress the Jesuits in 1773, and about 800 colleges and 1,000 mission stations around the world were closed. In 1789, the French Revolution burst upon Europe like a bomb. In the name of liberty, fraternity, and equality, clergy were forced by oath to choose between the French Republic and Catholicism, and revolutionaries seized Church property, suppressed religious life, and closed convents and monasteries. They forbade worship, forced priests and nuns to abjure their calling or be killed, and drove between 30,000 and 40,000 clergy into exile. The revolutionary spirit radiated out to the cities of Holland, Germany, Italy, and Austria. Enlightenment philosophers looked disparagingly upon Catholic clergy in anticipation of a secular world based on the authority of the nation state. Ironically, however, the French Emperor Napoleon Bonaparte (1769–1821) recognized the political value of religious freedom and gave Christians some breathing space, and for his part, Pope Pius VII (1742–1823; reigned 1800–23) recognized the need for the Catholic Church to adjust to the Enlightenment ideals of the French state. In the "Concordat of 1801," the papacy and the French government agreed to freedom of worship, equality of religions, government selection of bishops with papal approval, and clerical salaries to compensate for loss of property.

Following the French Revolution and the Napoleonic Wars, a great desire to reclaim religious life swept across Europe. French works like *Réflexions sur l'état de l'Église* (1808) by Hugo-Félicité de Lamennais (1782–1854) and *Du pape* (1819) by Joseph Marie de Maistre (1753–1821) spearheaded a romantic upsurge of Roman Catholic revival. This movement restored the authority of the Pope and prompted the recovery of

St. Peter's Square, Vatican City, looking down from the roof of St. Peter's Basilica.

Catholic orders. The Dominicans, Franciscans, Jesuits, Benedictines, and Redemptorists revived, and the Missionary Oblates of Mary Immaculate, the Missionaries of Our Lady of Africa of Algeria (*Pères Blancs* or "White Fathers"), and other congregations were founded to communicate the new **Ultramontane** enthusiasm of loyalty to the spiritual leadership of the Holy See. Once again, Catholic missionaries set out for Africa and Asia to preach the gospel. In 1846, the election of 54-year-old Giovanni Mastai-Ferretti (1792–1878) to the papacy marked the popular highpoint of this devotional revival, and as Pope Pius IX (1792–1878; reigned 1846–78) he came to personally symbolize the renewed leadership of Rome in the Catholic world. In 1850, the Pope directed that the Roman liturgy be imitated in all Latin Rite Churches. He encouraged pilgrimages to the Holy See and veneration of Roman martyrs, and he appointed bishops around the world who upheld Ultramontane spirituality. Papal *nuncios* and apostolic delegates were reappointed to Catholic nations. Bishops established national seminaries in Rome, so that their seminarians might study theology and receive the *Romanità*. Religious congregations moved their headquarters to Rome for easy communication. In 1854, the papacy declared the doctrine of the Immaculate Conception, and in 1864 the *Syllabus of Errors*. Pius IX crowned his career by presiding over the First Vatican Council (1869–70), which promulgated the definition of papal infallibility, the culmination of the Ultramontane movement.

This papal conservatism dominated the Catholic Church for almost 100 years. At the same time, important precedents were set for a greater degree of social engagement. Pope Leo XIII (1810–1903; reigned 1878–1903) issued *Rerum novarum* (1891) and Pope Pius XI (1857–1939; reigned 1922–39) promulgated *Quadragesimo anno* (1931), which warned against materialist interpretations of human existence, whether from right or left, and decried the capitalist exploitation of workers, urging employers and nation states to protect workers' rights as a Christian duty. Finally, in the aftermath of World War II and the decline of European colonial power, a new spirit of reform swept through the Catholic Church. Several factors urged changes, among them being the realization that centuries of Christian anti-Semitism had paved the way for Germany's National Socialist Party to perpetrate the mass murder of Jews in the Holocaust. A second factor was demographics, in that larger numbers of Catholics lived in Africa, Asia, and the Americas than in the Church's traditional centres in Europe. Surprising conservative Catholics, the 77-year-old Pope John XXIII (1881–1963; reigned 1958–63) called an ecumenical council. In the fall of 1962, 2,460 bishops from around the world filled Saint Peter's Basilica in Rome for the Second Vatican Council (1962–65), 42 per cent of them from Africa, Asia, and Latin America.

Before the first session of the council, the Canadian Cardinal Paul-Émile Léger wrote to John XXIII to stress the need for a genuine *aggiornamento* of Catholic institutions. Léger asked that the Church not restore dead structures of the past, but that it put itself at the service of humanity. Under the guidance of theological experts like Karl Rahner (1904–84), Henri de Lubac (1896–1991), and Yves Congar (1904–1995), the council issued decrees promoting vernacular liturgy, scriptural and catechetical renewal, increased collegiality and lay involvement among the bishops, and religious freedom and interfaith dialogue. The council also argued that Christian revelation is found primarily in the local church. Balancing tradition and modernity, episcopal collegiality prevailed for a time over papal absolutism, and the Catholic Church accepted itself as historical. After the council, Liberation theology emerged in the writings of theologians like Gustavo Gutiérrez (born 1928) and Juan-Luis Segundo (1925–96). This practical theology arose from the current economic thought that Christians should exercise a preferential option for the poor in developing societies, especially in Latin America. The council left some important questions for the future, notably the importance of deliberative synods, the status of women in the governing structures of the Church, and the balance of power between local churches and the Roman curia. On these and other issues, tensions between restorationists and post-modernizers continue to animate Catholics. North American feminist theologians like

Rosemary Radford Ruether (born 1936) and Elizabeth Fiorenza (born 1938) have criticized the Catholic hierarchy as patriarchal, even as lay congregations like *Opus dei* (Latin for "Work of God"), founded in 1928 by the Spanish priest Josemaria Escriva (1902–75), exert a strong conservative influence on Catholic Church policy. With over 80,000 members in 80 countries, *Opus dei* teaches that the work of the layperson in the eyes of God is as important as that of the priest. In 2002, Pope John Paul II (1920–2005; reigned 1978–2005) beatified Josemaria Escriva as a saint of the Catholic Church.

THE MAKING OF A CANADIAN CATHOLIC COMMUNITY

Catholics are the largest religious group in Canada, representing 43.2 per cent of the population, according to the last long census of 2001. For over 400 years, various Catholic groups have been migrating to Canada; today they include French Canadians, Scots, Irish, Germans, Ukrainians, Poles, Italians, and more recent immigrants from Africa, South America, East and South Asia, and the Caribbean. About 43 per cent of Aboriginal Canadians are also Catholics. From the beginning, Aboriginal Canadian Christianity has been profoundly interlinked with French Catholicism. Encouraged by the explorer Samuel de Champlain, Aboriginal Canadian Catholicism began in 1604 with the baptism of the first Mi'kmaq and Malecite neophytes in the French colony of Acadia, which today spans parts of eastern Quebec and the Maritime provinces in Canada, and parts of New England in the United States. In 1611, Jesuits Pierre Biard (*ca.* 1567–1622) and Énemond Massé (*ca.* 1574–1646) began a methodical program of Christian instruction. At Port Royal the two priests studied the Aboriginal Canadian languages, translated a catechism, and educated neophytes in their own tongue. After 1615, Récollet priests settled along the St. Lawrence River and carried the gospel to the Montagnais and the Algonquin. In 1625, the Jesuits arrived to reinforce the Récollets in the valley of the St. Lawrence River, fanning out to evangelize the Montagnais to the north and the Huron to the west. In 1635, the Jesuits opened a *collège* in Quebec to educate French and Aboriginal children. In 1639, under Marie de l'Incarnation (1566–1618), the Ursuline Sisters opened a school for both Aboriginal Canadian and French girls in Quebec, and the first Augustines de la Miséricorde de Jesus arrived to care for the sick of both nations at Hôtel-Dieu de Québec and in the nearby Aboriginal Canadian community of Sillery. Similar institutions were established in Montreal (Ville Marie), where Jeanne Mance (1606–73) founded a hospital in 1642, and Marguerite Bourgeoys (1620–1700) founded a school for both French and Aboriginal girls in 1658.

Between 1639 and 1649, Jesuit missionaries carried the gospel further into the interior of Huronia. In 1634, Jean de Brébeuf (1593–1649) and his companions founded a mission at Ste Marie-among-the-Hurons on the Wye River, near modern-day Midland, Ontario, and their exploits are recorded in the voluminous *Jesuit Relations*. Acculturating to Aboriginal Canadian ways, the missionaries learned how to travel by canoe, carry heavy bundles over portages, eat Huron food, and live in longhouses. Brébeuf oversaw the composition of a Huron grammar and dictionary, and composed Canada's first Christmas carol, *Jesus Ahatonhia*. By 1649, the Jesuits had baptized over 5,000 Hurons, but wars between the Hurons and their historic rivals, the Iroquois, brought a sudden end to the mission. Five Jesuits were killed, including Brébeuf, and in 1930 they were canonized along with three other companions by Pope Pius XI. The reconstructed residence at Ste Marie-among-the-Hurons and the shrine on the hill above it testify to the service of these martyrs to the Huron people. The survivors made their way back to Quebec where the Catholic religion continued to put down deep roots among the Aboriginal Canadians. The figure of Kateri Tekakwitha (1656–80) epitomizes this Aboriginal Canadian devotion. In 1679, the young Mohawk convert took a vow of chastity and assumed a life of strict asceticism. She is loved and honoured by the Aboriginal community, and in 1980 she was beatified by Pope John Paul II. Shrines in the Aboriginal community of Kahnawake, just outside Montreal, and near Tekakwitha's birthplace at Wading River, New York State, celebrate her sanctity.

The early history of the Catholic French Canadians is closely tied to that of the Aboriginals. Ministering to both nations, the missionaries travelled with the French trappers, traders, and merchants who fanned out west from Acadia and the heights of Quebec, establishing fur stations on the riverbanks at Kingston, Niagara, and Michilimackinac, and then extending this network south down the Mississippi River to New Orleans. In the seventeenth century, a second generation of settlers developed the long, narrow river lots on the south shore of the St. Lawrence River towards Montreal, and then down the Richelieu River and other tributaries flowing into the St. Lawrence. These *habitants* cut timber, built churches, and formed new communities. In 1659, François de Laval (1623–1708) became

Quebec's first bishop. He organized the parish system, and in 1663 he founded the *Séminaire de Québec,* ensuring a steady supply of locally born, well-educated *curés,* who tended the parishes in mobile rotation. The settlers funded their upkeep with tithes paid to the seminary, and any money left over was shared among the parishes according to need. In the eighteenth century, new families arranged a second line of lots along the same riverbanks, helping to consolidate the dispersed population. By 1670, the French Canadians numbered about 7,000; by 1754, through natural increase, the population had grown to about 55,000, scattered among 100 or so parishes and with an equal number of Aboriginal Canadians. Laval encouraged the settlers to resist the temptations of colonial life; he criticized cards, horseracing, and dancing, for example, and campaigned ceaselessly against the sale of alcohol to Aboriginal Canadians. Under his successor, Jean-Baptiste Saint-Vallier (1653–1727), these attitudes hardened into a more stringent regimen, strongly influenced by rigorist teachings. Saint-Vallier also abandoned Laval's itinerant pastoral model, establishing resident clergy in the parishes.

In 1760, the British conquest of New France brought French Canadians under Anglican-Protestant control. The British military considered the risk of revolt to be high among the Catholic Acadians of Nova Scotia, and between 1755 and 1762 they extinguished the community by deportation. But Quebec's French Canadians were more fortunate. The terms of surrender were benign and granted freedom of worship, and in 1766 Jean-Olivier Briand (1715–94) was accepted as the "superintendent" of the Catholics in Quebec, though his future ecclesial appointments were subject to British scrutiny. In 1774, to ensure the loyalty of French Canadians for the anticipated conflict with the American colonies, the English government passed the Quebec Act, which granted peacetime rights for French language, laws, and tithes. Prompted by the growing number of Protestant loyalists coming north in the aftermath of the American War of Independence (1775–83), England passed the Canadian Constitution Act in 1791, dividing British North America into Protestant Upper Canada and Catholic Lower Canada, and conceding the rights of land, government, and religious practice. During the War of 1812, the Bishop of Quebec, Joseph-Octave Plessis (1763–1825), encouraged French Canadians to support the English cause and gained credibility for Catholicism in Lower Canada. As a reward for French Canadian loyalty to the English crown during the war, Plessis was granted the title of Bishop of Quebec, the Catholic diocese was expanded to five dioceses, and Canadian Catholics were recognized in law. Later, the

British Act of Union (1840) threatened to place Lower Canada under the effective control of predominantly Protestant Upper Canada. Seeing an advantage in a difficult situation, Quebec accepted the opportunity offered. The French Canadians thus interpreted the first Education Act (1841) of the unified Province of Canada, which called for Christian schooling in Canada East (Lower Canada) and Canada West (Upper Canada), as the legal licence for both Catholic and Protestant school systems.

In Europe, following the French Revolution and Napoleonic Wars, the Ultramontane-inspired Catholic revival saw missionary orders renew their evangelizing efforts among the Aboriginal peoples of Canada. The Sisters of the Presentation arrived in 1833; the Christian Brothers in 1837; Oblates in 1841; Jesuits in 1842; Basilians in 1852; and Resurrectionists in 1857. The Jesuits opened the Collège-Ste-Marie in Quebec, renewed their former missionary stations at Walpole Island and Wikiwemikong, and opened new stations at Fort William and Nipigon. As in the seventeenth century, the missionaries lived in the Aboriginal Canadian communities and learned the languages and cultures. They compiled dictionaries and grammars in Ojibwa and Cree, preached, taught, and wrote catechisms, journals, and hymnals. In response to a request from Bishop Joseph-Norbert Provencher of Saint Boniface (1787–1853), the Grey Nuns in 1844 set up a hospital for Aboriginal, Métis, and non-Aboriginal settler Canadians at the Red River settlement in modern-day Manitoba. The following year the Oblates arrived in the Hudson Bay territories, and between 1845 and 1900 they sent 273 priests and brothers to the western and north-western regions of Canada to evangelize Aboriginal and Métis communities. In 1858, the Sisters of Saint Anne set up a mission on Vancouver Island. In 1886, the Sisters of Providence were ministering to the less fortunate in western and north-western Canada, and in 1896 they were joined by the Sisters of the Child Jesus. These congregations founded, financed, and staffed numerous Catholic institutions, including churches, schools, and hospitals. Though some Catholic missions were successful, others were not so welcome; controversy surrounds the residential schools in particular. By 1931, there were 44 Catholic residential schools, most of them run by the Oblates; in 1991, the order issued a formal apology for the physical and sexual abuse that was experienced by Aboriginal Canadian children at these schools. Though these abuses are generally considered a dark part of the history of Catholicism in Canada, Catholicism has also provided many Aboriginal Canadians with literacy skills and the avenue for the religious expression of sincere devotion. The pilgrimage site at Lac

Pilgrims attend the blessing of Lac Ste. Anne, Alberta, where Plains Indians once gathered for Sun Dance ceremonies and which now serves as a sacred site for Aboriginal North American Catholics.
PHOTO BY YIWAHIKANAK.

Ste Anne in northern Alberta is a good example. In 1887, the Oblate priest Jean-Marie Lestanc established a shrine at the mission in order to honour Ste Anne, the grandmother of Jesus. Two years later, a pilgrimage to the shrine started. Once a Sun Dance site known to the Great Plains Cree as "Spirit Lake," Lac Ste. Anne now receives over 20,000 pilgrims every summer, the vast majority of them being Aboriginal North Americans.

At the same time, the centre of French Canadian Catholic vitality moved from Quebec to Montreal, where Bishop Ignace Bourget (1799–1885) cultivated the Ultramontane spirit of revival to confirm French Canadians in a spiritual adherence to Catholic liturgy, theology, and devotions. In 1875, Bourget initiated Montreal's Cathedral of Saint-Jacques, which embodied this vision. Bourget modelled the cathedral after St. Peter's Basilica in Rome, giving concrete form to a conviction that French Canadians were destined to carry Catholicism to the rest of North America. The mass-marketing of religious literature reaffirmed bonds between Quebec and Rome, while Bourget's newspapers, *Les mélanges religieux* and *The True Witness*, kept the laity continually mindful of feast days and parish news, and argued the moral and spiritual merits of the *Syllabus of Errors*. Pilgrimages to old shrines like Notre-Dame-de-Bonsecours in Montreal

Statues of Montreal's 13 patron saints crown the façade of the Cathédrale Marie-Reine-du-Monde (Cathedral of Mary, Queen of the World). Originally dedicated to Saint Jacques (Saint James), the cathedral is modelled after St. Peter's Basilica in Rome to cement the conviction that French Canadians were destined to spread Catholicism in North America. PHOTO BY ROBERT B. MERKIN. REPRINTED BY PERMISSION. © 2008, ROBERT B. MERKIN, http://vleeptronz.blogspot.com.

and Notre-Dame-des-Victoires in Quebec revived, and new shrines were constructed. Founded in 1883, Notre-Dame-du-Cap became the most popular Catholic pilgrimage centre in North America once word spread that its statue of the Virgin Mary had twice granted miracles. Bourget's zeal carried over into public education, social programs, and politics as well. In 1875, the Quebec Assembly responded to clerical pressure and granted bishops control of the Catholic school system. Further buoyed by Pope Leo XIII's emphasis upon social questions as the nineteenth century drew to a close, Quebec's Catholics enjoyed the highest level of institutional benefits for the infirm and the indigent in all of Canada, thanks in large part to the efforts of hundreds of religious women who ran homes and services for orphans, prostitutes, unwed mothers, the sick, the aged, the abandoned, the incarcerated, the mentally and physically handicapped, and the dying.

In 1933, the Jesuit *École sociale populaire*'s *Programme de restoration sociale* gave fresh impetus to the Church's involvement in social issues by helping to support Catholic trades unions. This involvement continued until the 1960s, when the unions were secularized along with other French Canadian social and cultural institutions, including schools, during *La révolution tranquille* ("The Quiet Revolution").

Although they continue to make up a large portion of Canada's Catholic population, the French were only the beginning of an influx of Catholic migrants to Canada. During the eighteenth century, Irish immigrants from Wexford and Waterford landed in Newfoundland to work in the fishing industry, and by the beginning of the nineteenth century over 30,000 Irish Catholics were living in the colony. Though they constituted the majority, British Penal Laws forced them to practise their faith covertly. In 1783, the British softened these laws and allowed Catholics to build chapels administered by resident clerics and practise their faith openly. In 1784, in response to a request from the Irish congregation in St. John's, the Holy See appointed the Irish Franciscan James Louis O'Donel (1737–1811) to oversee these developments, and in 1796 he became the British colony's first vicar apostolic (missionary bishop). Like Quebec's Bishop Plessis, with whom he maintained close relations, O'Donel recognized the value of diplomacy. A disciplined ascetic with rigorist leanings, his insistence on obedience to the British crown gained further important concessions for Newfoundland's Catholics, including the right to their own cemeteries, legal recognition of Catholic marriages, and government support for Catholic education. The successors of O'Donel continued his policies, and in 1829 Thomas Scallan (1765–1830), the third bishop of St. John's, led the celebrations that marked the British government's passing of the Catholic Emancipation Act, which enabled the election of Catholics to Newfoundland's first House of Assembly in 1832.

The improved status of Newfoundland's Catholics raised tensions with Protestants, and the accession of the Ultramontane vicar apostolic Michael Anthony Fleming (1792–1850) in 1830 hardly eased these tensions. He invited the Sisters of the Presentation of the Blessed Virgin Mary and the Sisters of Mercy to open schools that would mould the future mothers of Catholic families, while he himself supervised a school for boys. He argued that Catholics should stop trying to ingratiate themselves with Protestants; rather, he felt they should seriously concern themselves with their devotions, education, and mutual care. In 1839, Fleming started construction on the Basilica of St. John the Baptist on the site of a former British garrison overlooking the city. Symbolizing the strength and endurance of the colony's Irish Catholics, the massive cathedral was the largest church in North America. Soon after, Newfoundland politics began to harden along decidedly denominational lines. In 1843, for example, public funding for education was divided proportionally between Protestant and Roman Catholic school boards. Seeing this progress, Rome established Fleming as the first resident bishop of the Newfoundland diocese in 1847.

A number of Newfoundland's Irish Catholics sought better lives by migrating to Halifax, Nova Scotia, and Saint John, New Brunswick, but the largest migration of Irish Catholics to British North America occurred in Lower and Upper Canada between 1815 and 1845. Many sought work in canal construction, lumbering, and farming along the Ottawa Valley and the Eastern Townships of Quebec. Others formed English-speaking enclaves in Quebec and Montreal. Still others ventured further into Upper Canada, some establishing rural Catholic communities, others interspersing with Protestant neighbours. A few of these immigrants ran small businesses or did clerical work, but the majority took labouring jobs. Alexander Macdonell (1762–1840) was consecrated the Bishop of Kingston in 1826 and played a key role in forging the Irish Catholics of Bytown, Kingston, Peterborough, Perth, Toronto, and London into a community of over 52,000, or 16 per cent of Upper Canada's population. Later, between 1846 and 1850, a further 230,000 immigrants sought refuge from the Great Famine ravaging Ireland. These new Irish migrants settled throughout Canada, taking farming, trades, merchandising, manufacturing, and labouring work.

Being neither Protestant like most English-speakers, nor French-speaking like most Catholics, the Irish Catholics often found themselves caught in a double bind, especially on the question of separate schools. But the community prospered, often exercising an important influence on Canada's development. In Montreal, Thomas D'Arcy McGee (1825–68) drew upon Irish support to win a seat in the new House of Commons, having championed the educational rights of religious minorities, a policy which was written into the British North America Act governing the Confederation of the new Dominion of Canada in 1867. In Toronto, the first Catholic bishop, Michael Power (1804–47), infused the predominantly Irish congregation with a Roman zeal that had dominated his own training at the *Séminaire de Québec*. During the 1850s, Power's successor, the French Ultramontane Armand de Charbonnel, risked the ire of the Protestant majority—especially Irish Protestants—by making frequent appeals to Irish Catholic nationalists to agitate for a separate school system in Canada West. His genuine interest in Catholic education is reflected in the establishment of St Michael's College and the recruitment of Basilian Fathers, Christian Brothers, and the Sisters of Saint Joseph to teach in Catholic schools. Less controversially, de Charbonnel presided over the completion of St Michael's Cathedral; encouraged the founding of voluntary benevolent organizations like the St. Vincent de Paul Society (1850) and the Young Men's Saint Patrick's Association (1855); and confirmed Toronto's Catholic community in its loyalty to the Holy See. He encouraged such traditional spiritual practices as the family recitation of the rosary, the Stations of the Cross, and holy week services and pilgrimages. By the 1870s, a full 70 per cent of Toronto's Irish Catholics regularly attended mass on Sunday.

Other Catholic groups immigrated to Canada from Scotland, Germany, Ukraine, Poland, Hungary, Italy, and Portugal, transforming the predominantly French and Irish Canadian Church into a truly multicultural institution. The Scots were among the first to arrive in substantial numbers at about the same time as the Irish. The first wave of Gaelic-speaking Highlanders landed between 1770 and 1815, settling in Prince Edward Island, Cape Breton, and eastern Nova Scotia, as well as in south-eastern Upper Canada. Between 1815 and 1840, a second, more impoverished wave of Highlanders settled in the vicinities of Antigonish, Charlottetown, and Kingston. The Scots built schools and churches, and sought their own Gaelic-speaking clergy. Hoping to cultivate uniformity according to French Canadian standards among Canada's Catholics, the visiting Bishop Plessis was scandalized that Scottish priests failed to wear the soutane on their rounds, making them indistinguishable from Protestant clergy. Still, he was touched by the liveliness of the Scottish faith, which was single-minded in its nurturing of family life, pursuit of education for its children, and its unswerving conviction that salvation came through the sacramental system of the Catholic Church. By 1840, the existence of three Scottish bishops—Alexander Macdonell of Kingston (1762–1840), Angus Bernard MacEachern of Charlottetown (1759–1835), and William Fraser of Antigonish (1778–1851)—represented a strong challenge to French Canadian leadership. In 1853, to provide higher education for Scottish Catholics, Bishop Colin F. McKinnon (1810–79) founded Nova Scotia's St. Francis Xavier College, which continues today as a free-standing Catholic university. In 1897, the college granted its first degrees to four women through the affiliated Mount St Bernard College, making it the first Catholic institution in North America to do so. Despite differences in temperament and tradition, Irish and Scottish Catholics from the Atlantic provinces went on to supply most of the English-speaking bishops for Winnipeg, Regina, Saskatoon, Calgary, Edmonton, Vancouver, and Victoria, offering a significant contrast to

French Canadian religious culture and adding the first elements of pluralism to Catholicism in Canada.

In the middle of the nineteenth century, Germans migrating to Canada included Catholics among their numbers. The first Catholics were located in Waterloo County in Canada West in the 1840s, and in 1848 Bishop Michael Power of Toronto asked the Jesuits to care for the 12,000 German Catholic settlers in the area of Maryhill, Ontario. In 1852, with two other priests and a brother, the Austrian Jesuit Father John Holzer (died 1888) moved the Catholic mission centre from Maryhill to Guelph. They founded a school for boys, the Loretto Sisters founded one for girls, and the Sisters of St. Joseph opened St. Joseph's Hospital for the sick and the aged. From Guelph, the Jesuit priests made regular pastoral visits to 56 mission stations on the Bruce Peninsula. They gathered Catholics at centrally located farms to teach catechism and minister the sacraments. Both clergy and laity planned the construction of parish churches for the future. In 1866, two Resurrectionist Fathers, Eugene and Louis Funcken (died 1888 and 1890), opened St. Jerome's College in Berlin (renamed "Kitchener" during World War I) in south-western Ontario. The languages of instruction were German and English, so that the door was left open for Irish as well as German students. In the spirit of friendship, Lutheran, Anglican, and Mennonite students from Waterloo County were also welcomed into St. Jerome's.

German-speaking Catholics also settled in the Canadian Midwest. In 1886, a group immigrated to Canada from Josephstal, near Odessa on the Black Sea, and settled St. Joseph's Colony, west of Regina. Unhappy with the homestead system used in the Canadian west, St. Joseph's colonists chose a large tract of land, laid out a village site in the Russian *dorf* style, and founded a German-speaking Catholic community. The parish church and school were placed at the centre of the community, and homes and farms were arranged around it. Other German Catholics arrived, including ten families and seven single men from Bavaria, who established a small community south of Josephstal. Forty-three other families from the Dnieper region bought a site near Josephstal and built a church, school, and homes at the rural hamlet of Rastadt and Katharinental. German Protestants from the Black Sea also settled in the area and shared in the life of these new Catholic Canadians.

More German Catholics came from the United States in 1903. About 8,000 German Americans trekked from the American Midwest to found St. Peter's Colony east of Saskatoon. A German-American land company had taken out options on 50 townships—about 1,800 square miles of rich soil—and then encouraged Germans from the American Midwest to claim quarter-sections of 160 acres at $10 each. Within a few years these homesteads were occupied, parish churches and private schools were built, and German Canadian villages were formed. The heart of the colony was St. Peter's Priory, which was founded by Benedictine Fathers from Cluny, Illinois, and St. John's, Minnesota. In 1921, the Holy See declared St. Peter's an abbacy and the abbot also served as bishop for the 36 German Catholic parishes in the area. The abbey printed a German-language newspaper, *St. Peter's Bote,* with an English edition called the *Prairie Messenger,* which is still widely read throughout Western Canada. Also in 1921, the abbey opened St. Peter's College as a Catholic high school for boys; in 1925, it became affiliated with the University of Saskatchewan, and in 1972 it began to offer university courses. Métis, French Canadian, Irish, English, and German Protestant families interspersed among the German Catholic majority of St. Peter's.

Ukrainian Catholics have also played a significant role in the Canadian Church. Eighty per cent of the 100,000 Ukrainians who arrived in Canada in the late nineteenth and early twentieth centuries were Catholic. While Ukrainian Orthodox Christians came mostly from Bukovina and the eastern Ukraine, the majority of Ukrainian Catholics came from Galicia and Carpatho-Ukraine. Taking advantage of the newly completed Canadian Pacific Railway, the Ukrainians joined other settlers hoping to make a new life by farming the Canadian Prairies. The Empress Maria Theresa of Austria (1740–80) labelled the Ukrainian Catholics as Greek Catholics, one of the 20 Eastern Churches in union with Rome, so that they would not be confused with her Latin Catholics to the west. At the Union of Brest in 1596, the Ukrainians recognized the spiritual leadership of the Holy See but maintained their Byzantine liturgy, ecclesial traditions, and married priests. In 1894, at the request of the North American bishops, Pope Leo XIII forbade married priests from migrating to North America, depriving Ukrainian Catholics access to needed clergy. Resisting the efforts of Archbishop Adélard Langevin (1855–1915) of Saint Boniface to incorporate them within the Latin Church, the Ukrainian community persevered in their religious traditions by erecting wayside crosses, constructing eastern-style churches, and organizing their own devotions in accordance with Byzantine Church practices. After consultation, Langevin changed his mind, and by 1902 celibate clergy began to arrive from Lviv. In 1912, Pope Pius X (1835–1914; reigned 1903–14) appointed Nykyta Budka (1877–1949) as the first bishop of 128,000 Ukrainian Catholics. The Canadian Latin Church began to actively recruit Ukrainian-speaking clergy, supply funds for Eastern Catholics, and support Budka's newspaper, *Canadian Ruthenian / Canadian Ukrainian*, first published in 1911. The Catholic Church Extension Society contributed money for the construction of churches and schools. Budka enjoyed the support of 47 priests and maintained eastern liturgies in 229 parishes and mission stations. The Ukrainian Catholics eventually created five Byzantine Catholic dioceses, or eparchies, in the Canadian cities of Winnipeg, Edmonton, New Westminster, Saskatoon, and Toronto. After losing some Ukrainians in the formation of the Ukrainian Orthodox Church in 1918, Ukrainian Catholics helped to soften the edges of French- and Irish-Canadian religious tensions and led the Canadian Church towards multiculturalism. By the end of the twentieth century, the Ukrainian Catholic Church numbered 200,000 members scattered across Canada in 350 parishes.

Ukrainians were not the only immigrants to Canada from Eastern Europe. Before World War I, some 110,000 Polish Catholics arrived from Galicia. Fleeing the *Kulturkampf* of Germany's Otto von Bismarck (1815–98), they settled at Berlin; at Barry's Bay and Wilno in eastern Ontario; and on homestead farms in Western Canada. Polish neighbourhoods also emerged in Montreal, Toronto, Hamilton, and Winnipeg. In 1898, Archbishop Langevin founded Holy Ghost parish to serve Winnipeg's North End, which included Poles, Ukrainians, Germans, and Slovaks. Though the familiar Latin liturgy was a comfort to the Polish Catholics, the German sermons of the Oblate priests reminded them of Bismarck's *Kulturkampf* and demanded their protest. In 1902, Langevin confirmed the Polish Oblate priest Jan Kulawy (1872–1941) as pastor, and Germans, Ukrainians, and Slovaks sought help to form their own parishes. Also in 1902, the Holy Ghost Fraternal Society of Winnipeg was established to offer insurance benefits to Polish Catholics as protection against sickness and unemployment. Religious festivals, feast days, and social events reinforced the Polish Catholic identity, and Polish newspapers provided useful information on homesteading, employment, and the Canadian way of life. After World War I, more than 50,000 new Polish immigrants joined the community, which then numbered in excess of 145,000. By 1929, Polish Catholics had established 33 parishes and 157 missions across the country and were assimilating more easily into Canadian culture than Ukrainian Catholics had.

Southern Europe has also provided Canada with large numbers of immigrant Catholics. Italians comprise the largest group, with over 95 per cent being Catholic. By the 1890s, several hundred Italian Catholic labourers were working in Montreal, Toronto, and British Columbia's Okanagan region. In 1908, the diocese of Toronto reconsecrated the Irish Church of St. Patrick as Our Lady of Carmel, the first parish church for Italian Catholics. During the first three decades of the twentieth century, direct Italian immigration to Canada numbered almost 150,000, with the majority arriving before World War I. Settling mainly in urban centres, Italian workers accepted employment on the railways, in construction, and building urban roads and sewers. Priests from several orders served these immigrants—in Montreal, principally Servites, but Franciscans in Toronto—as well as Carmelite nuns. In 1934, Toronto's Italian community sponsored a Good Friday procession, which continues to this day. It winds its way around the Italian neighbourhood south of College Street, starting and ending at the Church of St. Francis Assisi. The elaborately costumed actors play the roles of Jesus Christ, Judas Iscariot, Mary Magdalene, Jewish pharisees, the Roman procurator Pontius Pilate, and imperial soldiers.

As in the Ukrainian, Polish, and German communities, education developed into a bone of contention between the ecclesiastical hierarchy and Italian Catholics, though in a different way. In 1939, Archbishop James McGuigan of Toronto (1894–1974) discovered that Fascist propaganda had permeated the classes in Italian language and culture taught in some Catholic parish halls and churches. But that same year, as Europe edged towards World War II—when Italian Fascists sided with Nazi Germany against the Western allies—the Italian consul, to McGuigan's great relief, withdrew funding for the school program and the issue died a natural death. In the three decades following the war, Italy ranked second only to Great Britain as a source for Canadian immigrants, with over 500,000 settling in Montreal, Toronto, Ottawa, Hamilton, Guelph, Windsor, Thunder Bay, Winnipeg, Edmonton, and Vancouver. Following the migration chains of relatives and village friends, many of these newer Italian migrants continued in the employment patterns of their predecessors, but others worked as gardeners, operated trucking firms, and opened bakeries, barbers, fruit and vegetable stores, and shoe repair shops. As well, many Italian women worked in the needle trade and garment industry.

The Catholic hierarchy responded to this influx of new congregants in several ways. The clergy were bolstered by the Scalabrini Fathers, who specialized in ministering to immigrant Italians, and overtures were also made to Rome's *Ufficio Centrale per l'Emigrazione* to provide secular priests. By the early 1970s, 60 priests served 250,000 Italian Catholics in more than 30

Toronto parishes. At the same time, relations between the Italian Catholic community and the ecclesiastical hierarchy were not always as smooth as could be hoped. To begin with, overcrowding was a problem; a number of parishes were divided between Italian-speaking and English-speaking Catholics. While the older, more established Irish and Scottish congregations worshipped in the sanctuary, Italian parishioners were forced to hold their services in church basements or auditoriums, making them feel less than equal. These tensions increased after the Second Vatican Council, when English-speaking Catholics were often keen to adopt the vernacular liturgy: Italian-speaking congregants just as often preferred the traditional Latin, fearing that different masses said in English and in Italian would perpetuate their second-class status.

In the late nineteenth century, most Italian immigrants came from northern Italy, but this trend shifted over the course of the twentieth century, with the majority having roots in southern Italy. These newcomers practised a popular form of Catholicism unfamiliar to the French and Irish Canadian hierarchy, and it was equally scorned by many Italian-speaking priests who came from northern Italy. Small shrines containing a few candles and plastic, religious statues of Jesus, the Virgin Mary, and local Italian saints found places in Toronto homes and gardens, just as they had in the rural villages of southern Italy. But festivals in honour of patron saints were the main source of unease. These festivals, which continue today, begin with the Good Friday procession and last through the summer. Organized by religious social clubs, the festivals include colourful processions featuring lavishly dressed statues of the Madonna and patron saints, brass bands, competitive sports, banquets and dances, and sometimes fireworks. Participants put on their finest clothes, and the festivals function as social events, reuniting extended kinship ties and providing joyous displays of popular religious enthusiasm. The clergy were uncomfortable about the use of the mass to sanctify what they considered secular celebrations. But by the 1970s the tensions had begun to ease. In 1970, the creation of an Italian Pastoral Commission gave the community a greater say in Church matters, and taking their cue from Coadjutor Archbishop Philip Pocock (1906–78), the clergy publicly urged a greater spirit of charity among the different ethnic constituencies of Toronto's Catholic Church. In 1993, 62 saints' processions received the blessing of the clergy. The Italian community in Canada now numbers over 1.25 million and is ranked seventh in size among Canadian ethnic groups, with nearly 500,000 Italian Canadians in Toronto. Family values remain central to this community, and receiving the sacraments of the Catholic Church remains part of Italian family life.

The Portuguese have also contributed to the vibrancy of Catholic life in Canada. After World War II, the Canadian and Portuguese governments signed agreements allowing Portuguese workers into Canada for railway, construction, and farm work. In the 1950s, nearly 20,000 Portuguese arrived, almost 90 per cent of whom were Catholic. Most immigrants came from the Azores, in particular the island of Sao Miguel. In the following two decades, family sponsorship programs and chain migration boosted the Portuguese community in Canada to 140,000, the vast majority of whom settled in Toronto and Montreal. Many young men also came to Canada to escape military service in Portugal's African colonial wars. As in the other nations of southern Europe, the festivals of the Catholic saints play an important part in the life of the Portuguese Roman Catholic community. These festivals are marked with processions, public prayers and offerings, competitive sports, and family get-togethers. In 1963, Madeiran Portuguese rented a farm in Orangeville, Ontario, to mark their ten years of residency in Canada with a celebration of the feast of *Nossa Senhora do Monte*. This festival, an important religious and social event in Madeira, is now held every year in Madeira Park, south of Sutton, Ontario. In 1966, under the guidance of Father Alberto Cunha, Azorean immigrants brought the Christ of Miracles festival to Toronto. Celebrants decorate a statue of the Christ of Miracles with flowers and fine clothes, and process with it through the streets of Toronto, starting from St. Mary's Church on the corner of Adelaide and Bathurst streets. Portuguese Catholics hold festivals in Montreal, Winnipeg, and Vancouver, with Portuguese-speaking priests presiding over these events. In 1968, Cunha launched *O Jornal Portugues*. The Canadian community of Portuguese Catholics now numbers over 350,000.

During the 1950s, Quebec students and politicians were chafed under the autocratic methods of the regime of Maurice Duplessis (1890–1959) and were preparing themselves for radical social and political change. Historian Michael Gauvreau has argued convincingly that Catholic Youth organizations, which included students, workers, and farmers, demanded the democratization of the province in support of liberal ideals.[1] *La révolution tranquille* came to fulfillment during the premiership

---

1   See Gauvreau, *The Catholic Origins of Québec's Quiet Revolution, 1931–1970* (Montreal: McGill-Queen's University Press, 2005).

A chalice for holding Holy Water and a Roman Missal, which contains scriptural texts, prayers, and liturgical rubrics for the celebration of the Mass in the Catholic Church, alongside a crucifix and an altar candle. PHOTO BY LIMA. REPRINTED UNDER THE TERMS OF THE CC-BY-SA LICENSE AGREEMENT.

of Jean Lesage (1912–80), who was elected in 1960. Social services were removed from the hands of the Church and new, university-trained civil servants took control. In five years, hospitals, schools, unions, and social services were secularized. Accepting the need for change, Quebec clergy remained acquiescent, seeking only to help bring about a peaceful outcome to the adaptations facing them. Yet soon after the province of Quebec was secularized, many Quebecois ceased attending church and spent their Sundays attending other activities.

The structural collapse of Catholicism in Quebec was felt throughout the Catholic world. Sensing both a crack in the ecclesiastical edifice and a paradigm shift in world culture, Pope John XXIII called for an ecumenical council to shed light on the diminishment of Christian life. More than 2,400 bishops travelled to St. Peter's Basilica in Rome to convene the Second Vatican Council. At the suggestion of the bishops, the agenda prepared by the Roman curia was put aside and the bishops prepared their own. The creators of the new agenda declared that the gathering in Rome would be a pastoral council, concerned less with dogmatic definitions or condemnations than with spiritual renewal in an *aggiornamento* or "bringing-up-to-date" of the Catholic Church. Unanimously approved, the documents which emerged from the council were constructive and optimistic in tone, recommending conciliar relations among the bishops and subsidiarity in the hierarchical structure of the Church. The council declared that revelation begins at the local level, and it encouraged dialogue with other Christians and with non-Christians. Most important for the faithful, the council pronounced that the sacred liturgy and the Bible would henceforth be written in vernacular languages. Canadian clerics like Paul-Émile Léger (1904–91) played an active role in the council, and they returned to implement the recommendations in their Canadian dioceses. English and French were integrated into the sacred liturgy; women were hired at Catholic universities and diocesan offices; and opportunities were sought for interfaith dialogue. The Canadian Catholic Church became a significant member of the Canadian Council of Churches.

The Second Vatican Council and the liberal social politics of the third quarter of the twentieth century heralded other changes for Catholics in Canada—from American Charismatic Catholicism to the sexual revolution and the movement for women's liberation. American Charismatic Catholicism arrived from the University of Notre Dame, South Bend, Indiana. Led by Catherine de Hueck Doherty (1899–1985), Catholic community members at Combermere, Ontario, were among the first to welcome the new movement. This enthusiasm spread from Halifax to Vancouver, introducing Catholic Canadians to the sort of experiential religion more normally associated with Protestant Pentecostal Christians, including speaking in tongues, prophecy, praying over others, and being slain in the spirit. Like their Protestant counterparts, Charismatic Catholics desired the freedom of Bible spirituality without the traditional structures of Catholic devotional life.

In the 1970s and 1980s, the widespread calls among Western liberals for sexual freedom and women's liberation affected Catholic life in Canada as well as in the United States. Among other factors, public recognition of the domestic abuse of women and children, as well as the inequities that often faced homosexuals, not only in their daily lives but also in law, added further weight and urgency to these calls. Catholics in Canada had to deal with these issues. Historically, families and employers did their best to avoid such abuses becoming public in order to save appearances, or even to protect abusers. Families maintained appearances so that their daughters would be married into good homes and their sons launched into respectable careers, and likewise, employers maintained the appearance that they served the public without blemish. Among the professions exposed for abusing those entrusted to their care were the Catholic clergy. The figures of abuse within the clergy are 1 or 2 per cent—smaller than that of abuses committed in families, and about the same as clergy in other religions. Like other institutions and professionals, the Church is working to improve its process of identifying and removing abusers from office. Over four decades, its reluctance to act quickly has meant that the Catholic Church in North America has paid hundreds of millions of dollars in reparations and counselling services for victims. Although the Catholic Church was slow to act, it is now adamant in its aim to halt further sexual abuse at all levels.

RECENT TRENDS IN THE CATHOLIC COMMUNITY

The immigrant Catholic communities we have met so far—the Irish, the Scots, the Ukrainians, the Poles, the Italians, and the Portuguese—exemplify the intrinsically pluralistic character of Canadian Catholicism. Over the years, other Catholic ethnic groups have also played parts in weaving the intricate tapestry of an international Canadian Church: Hungarians, Croatians, Lithuanians, Belgians, newcomers from Latin America and the Caribbean islands, Africans, and Asians—including Goan, Keralite, Tamil, Filipino, Vietnamese, Chinese, and Korean Catholics. These ethnic groups contribute to the multicultural complexity of Canadian Catholicism. In 1967, Canada revised its immigration policy to a point system that decreased the importance of family sponsorship and increased the importance of qualified persons, easing access to many Asians, Africans, and South Americans. In this section, we shall focus upon Canada's Filipino, Chinese, and Tamil Catholics.

The Spanish colonized the Philippines in the sixteenth century, and Catholic missionaries evangelized the indigenous people. In 1898, at the end of the Spanish-American War, the Philippines were ceded to the United States. At all levels, Filipino culture continued to be strongly shaped by Spanish Catholic beliefs and practices, but gained an overlay of American liberal democratic ideals and a familiarity with the English language. In the 1970s and 1980s, Ferdinand (1917–89) and Imelda (born 1929) Marcos succeeded in establishing and maintaining autocratic authority over the Philippines, despite Catholic opposition led by Archbishop Jaime Sin of Manila (1928–2005). During these decades, many Filipinos fled the Marcos dictatorship and set out for Canada in the hopes of economic security and a better family life. Filipino immigration to Canada has followed the chain migration pattern. Funded by a member of her family, an older sister might come to Canada as a nurse, for example; and then, once she has become a Canadian resident, she might sponsor her siblings and parents and provide for their initial settlement. Filipinos in Canada are 82 per cent Catholic.

Chinese contact with Christianity began in 1582, when Matteo Ricci and Michele Ruggieri (1543–1607) entered China wearing purple silk gowns with the blue border of scholars. After gifting two clocks to the emperor in 1601, they were allowed to travel to Beijing and live there. Ricci and his Jesuit colleagues became astronomers and mathematicians to the Chinese Imperial Government. Having learned Mandarin and other dialects, they translated the Catholic catechism and the Decalogue into Mandarin and made converts among the Mandarin intellectual class. The evangelization of the Chinese élites continued until the middle of the eighteenth century, when the Jesuits withdrew. Evangelical work was not renewed until the middle of the nineteenth century, though British and American Protestant missions far outnumbered their Catholic counterparts—especially the China Inland Mission, founded in 1865. Many Chinese who were flee-ing the chaos that accompanied the fall of the last Qing emperor and the establishment of the Republic of China sought work in British Columbia and likely professed the Catholic faith. After a notorious head tax failed to discourage Chinese migration, targeted Canadian legislation passed in 1923 permitted only diplomats, professionals, and students to come from China. In the 1930s and 1940s, civil war between Chinese Nationalists and Chinese Communists increased pressure to allow more immigrants, espe-cially when Chinese Christians suffered persecution at the hands of the Communists, who defeated the Nationalists in 1949. Likewise, when the British revealed their intention to hand over Hong Kong to the Chinese communist government in 1997, many Westernized Chinese made plans to leave. Chinese immigration to Canada from Taiwan, Hong Kong, and mainland China increased significantly in the 1990s and in the first years of the new millennium. Of the Chinese who have come to Canada, about 21 per cent are Christian, and of these about 12 per cent are Catholic. The British presence in Hong Kong meant that many Chinese from the col-ony were proficient in English, which eased the challenges of building a new life in Canada.

In contrast to the sixteenth-century beginnings of Filipino Christianity and the seventeenth-century beginnings of Chinese Christianity, Tamils trace their Catholicism back to the apostle Thomas or his disciples, who, tradition has it, evangelized southern India in the first century of the

Christian era. Just as American ideals and education came to permeate Filipino life, Tamil culture came under Western influences in somewhat analogous ways. In the sixteenth century, the Portuguese introduced the beliefs and practices of European Catholicism along the Coromandel Coast of south-west India and Ceylon (now Sri Lanka). Over 200 years later, in 1815, the British took control of Ceylon, and in 1858 the establishment of the British Raj in India introduced their educational ideas and the parliamentary system of government throughout South Asia. Like Filipinos and Hong Kong Chinese, Tamil Catholics have mixed cultural roots, with a strong overlay of Western ideas and Anglophone customs. Tamils are predominately Hindu, with only 12 to 15 per cent being Christian. The first Tamils arrived in Canada in the late 1960s, but beginning in 1983, greater numbers of Sri Lankan Tamil Catholics sought refuge in Canada from the discrimination and violence associated with the civil war between Hindu Tamils and Buddhist Sinhalese. Usually well-schooled in English and wearing Western dress, the first Tamil immigrants assimilated readily into Canadian society. Tamils arriving in Canada after 1983 represented more of a cross-section of Tamil society and culture. They frequently speak Tamil and are steeped in South Asian culture; for example, the women often wear *saris.*

There are significant similarities and differences among the ways Filipino, Chinese, and Tamil immigrants have adapted their Catholicism to life in Canada. Filipino marriage customs illustrate the inclusive nature of their culture, in which American, Spanish, and Chinese *mestizos* freely intermarry. Filipinos come from an egalitarian society where women and men have equal access to education, and marriage partners share in the decision-making. Often the women in Filipino families end up being the family accountants. In Canada, Filipino families hope to have a say in the selection of marriage partners for their children. The Filipino family is child-centred and older children are expected to help their younger siblings. In Canada, Filipinos continue their traditions of tolerance and inclusivity. Twenty per cent of Filipinas marry non-Filipinos, and Filipinos fit easily into existing Catholic parish structures across the country. The small number of Filipino clergy in Canada work in mixed parishes rather than in separate Filipino parishes. At the same time, Filipinos preserve certain aspects of Spanish traditions. They actively participate in parish liturgy, but at weddings they practise the Filipino customs of lighting candles, offering coins, and presenting the veil and the cords. Filipinos venerate Santo Nino, and on Holy Thursday and Good Friday they delight in singing the Pabasa in Tagalog. On All Saints Day and All Souls Day, families gather at the cemetery to spend the day praying, singing, and honouring their deceased relatives. Toronto's Filipino Catholics also enjoy summer pilgrimages to the Martyrs' Shrine at Ste Marie-among-the-Hurons, where they offer prayers for family and friends.

Since Christian scholars educated only the Mandarin élites in Christian beliefs and practices, the vast majority of the Chinese population continued their traditional Chinese ways. Chinese customs are well-established and strongly adhered to when it comes to marriage. Marriages of mixed religion or mixed ethnicity are rarely welcomed; Chinese Catholic parents prefer their children to marry Chinese Catholics in a Catholic ceremony, believing that partners of the same religion and common culture share more personal bonds uniting them. That said, parents will usually accept the choices of their children. Like other Chinese parents, Chinese Catholics believe that after the marriage it is necessary for both families to pull together, especially when it comes to accepting new in-laws, so that all may work to smooth over any misunderstandings that may occur.

Like the Chinese, Tamil tradition gives priority to close-knit families and tends to be exclusive in its marriage customs. Sometimes taking advantage of web-based matchmaking services, Canadian Tamils—including Tamil Catholics—arrange the marriages of their children within their class and caste, and pay a suitable dowry to the groom's family. A young Tamil has a moral obligation to provide the dowry for his sisters. Tamils prefer to marry second cousins or sponsor a partner from home to strengthen family bonds. Traditionally, the husband governs the family while his wife plays a subordinate role, not even calling her husband by his first name. A Tamil woman's self-image is based on her *dharma,* or traditional duty, as a loyal wife, homemaker, and mother. Traditionally, her personal satisfaction comes from fulfilling these life-roles rather than pursuing career aspirations for herself. But this tradition does not mean that Tamil women do not exercise authority; their influence over the daily life of the family can be all-pervasive, if comparatively unobtrusive. On the other hand, in Canada these customs are softened as in many younger couples both partners work and share family responsibilities. Like Filipinos and Chinese, Tamils treasure family life more than single life; they see their children as gifts from God.

The conservatism of Tamil cultural and social traditions permeates the lives of Tamil Catholics. Unlike Filipinos, they tend to seek out parishes that provide the liturgy in vernacular Tamil. Great importance is attached to religious customs and ritual devotions. During Christmastime most Tamils, including Hindus, celebrate religious events in their homes as part of the season. Tamil Catholics have one Toronto parish in their own language, but three centres of worship, including St. Boniface Church in Scarborough and the Tamil Catholic Cultural Centre in Mississauga. In Montreal, Tamils have the Saint-Iréné community at Notre Dame de la Délivrance on rue Delisle. During Easter Holy Week, the communities conduct an evening vigil on Maundy Thursday, and on Good Friday they read the Johannine Passion and observe the communal Stations of the Cross. Carnatic singing, *Bharata Natyam* dance, and instrumental music provide cultural continuity and spiritual inspiration. Like Filipinos, many Tamil Catholics make summer pilgrimages to the martyrs' shrine at Ste Marie-among-the-Hurons. Offering candles before the relics of the seventeenth-century Jesuit missionaries killed for their faith, they write short prayers for friends and family in Canada and Sri Lanka, both in English and in Sanskrit.

Filipinos, Chinese, and Tamils share intense interest in the education of their children and the retention of their culture. In Canada, 30 per cent of Filipinos speak Tagalog. They read Filipino newspapers, listen to Filipino radio, and sing in Filipino choral groups. A government heritage program has made language instruction available along with lectures in Filipino culture and history. They wear traditional dress at formal events like weddings, with the women in butterfly-sleeve frocks and the men in *barong tagalog*. Traditional food is served on such ceremonial occasions—dishes of spring rolls, fish, seafood, rice, roast pig (lechon), vegetables, and puto. Independence Day celebrations include Aboriginal dances like the *Tininkling*, the *Pandango*, and the *Maglalatik*. Likewise, recent Tamil arrivals maintain a strong sense of cultural nationalism. Tamil Catholics send their children to Catholic schools, which educate them in Canadian culture, while also taking advantage of heritage programs, which teach the children the Tamil language, Carnatic vocal skills, and *Bharata natyam* dance. Tamil newspapers and magazines, Tamil radio, and Tamil videos are all popular in Canada, and Sri Lankan musicians and artists tour communities across Canada to keep the Tamil language and culture alive.

Of the three cultures, the Chinese place the highest emphasis on education for their children. In China, many Chinese attend Catholic schools that have a high reputation across Asia. When arriving in Canada, Chinese newcomers similarly search out the best schools before establishing their family homes. Parents emphasize the value of education to their children along with the need for them to respect their elders. The children who have their primary education in China have a chance of retaining their Chinese language and culture after they come to Canada. Sometimes, young Chinese Canadians who are educated in Canada have a difficult time absorbing the Chinese culture and languages, which have become foreign to them. Many Canadian-born Chinese students find it hard to relate to Hong Kong-born students and the Hong Kong culture of their forebears, and many believe the latter to be irrelevant for them in Canada. To compensate, over 50 Chinese language schools exist in Vancouver and Toronto to increase familiarity with Chinese languages and culture. Traditional practices are encouraged, like celebrating the Chinese New Year, eating moon cake at Chung Chau, and remembering the deceased at Ching Ming and Chung Yeung. Over 17 per cent of Chinese Canadians have completed university—twice the percentage of European Canadians.

Having made the transition to Canada, Filipinos are actively involved in political and social outreach. In 1981, Dr. Conrado Santos (born 1934) was elected to the Manitoba provincial legislature, and in 1988, Dr. Rey Pagtakhan (born 1935) won a seat representing Manitoba in the Canadian Parliament, and has served as a federal cabinet member. Alex Chiu, a Chinese Filipino, has served as a councillor in Markham. Filipino volunteers are heavily involved not only in their own social organizations, but also in more broadly based community organizations. To raise funds, they sponsor traditional dinners, encouraging their children to become involved in the entertainment, which includes ceremonial dress, traditional dances, and choral presentations. At the same time, Filipino Catholics often work with other community church groups, helping to organize religious festivals for All Saints Day, Christmas, and Holy Week. By contrast, at least among older Tamil immigrants, there is less attention to establishing a strong social and cultural presence in Canada and more concern for family members still caught in the aftermath of the civil war in Sri Lanka, which ended in 2009. In some quarters, a lack of fluency in English poses barriers to the formation of links with the larger social and political community in Canada. The exclusive marriage customs also reinforce the strong internal ties of the Tamil community. The Church's liturgy and devotions tend to strengthen Tamil family bonds, rather than establish ties between the Tamil community and other Catholic groups. Novenas, Charismatic prayer groups, passion plays, and pilgrimages to Marian shrines all play a part in maintaining Tamil kinship ties. Tamil Catholics also raise funds for the

Church in Sri Lanka to help support Catholic orphanages and human rights organizations working with war victims.

The picture of Chinese Catholics offers another variation. With the emergence of a Chinese Canadian middle class in Canada, Chinese Catholics lend their support to groups lobbying for human rights issues that affect the Chinese Canadian community as a whole. In Scarborough, Ontario, for example, one such group successfully fended off protests that the purchase of homes by Chinese newcomers was causing real estate prices to rise. In another context, the Chinese Canadian Knights of Columbus have developed interests in mass media and have worked with the Catholic Salt + Light Television station, founded in 2003 and based in Toronto, to produce five television episodes for Chinese Catholics. The Knights also teach Chinese newcomers the whys and wherefores of volunteer work in Canada. This re-education is necessitated by the fact that such work was impossible in China, where Catholics were jailed for volunteering for the Church. Thus, it often comes as a pleasant surprise that in Canada it is safe to volunteer for community work.

For Filipino, Chinese, and Tamil Catholics, the paschal mysteries surrounding the death and resurrection of Jesus Christ provide meaning and inspiration as they strive to make the transition from "back then" and "over there" to a new life in Canada. All three groups value education and enjoy strong family ties. Their children attend Catholic schools and learn religion in the Canadian context. Filipino Catholics are rooted in an egalitarian society and practise social and political outreach in Canada. By contrast, Chinese and Tamil Catholics continue the traditions of patriarchal societies and remain focused on their respective cultures. Yet many Chinese Catholics have been Westernized by the legacy of the Catholic schools they and their forebears attended in China; know English; and are familiar with Western religious practices. They accept the value of a Westernized religious tradition. Similarly, having been partially Westernized by Catholic practices and Catholic education, Catholic Tamils assimilate to established Canadian ways more easily than their Buddhist compatriots. Though Filipinos, Tamils, and Chinese alike are in transition from inherited traditions to Canadian culture, all three groups bring new energy to Catholicism in Canada. Indeed, the Catholic Church sometimes furnishes unlikely connections between the three communities. For instance, Tamil Catholic priest Father Gaspar Raj Jegath (born 1966) directs Radio Veritas, a radio station based in the Philippines, which regularly reports on the situation in Sri Lanka for Tamils living overseas.

AFTERWORD

The history of the various ethnic Catholics in Canada can be envisioned in three developmental stages: Gallicanism, Romanism, and Canadianism. The spirit of Gallicanism began to unfold with the arrival of the French laity and Catholic clergy on the northern shores of North America. Gallican spirituality was a particular branch of French Catholicism rooted as far back as the thirteenth century, which manifested itself in a strong commitment to Catholicism, but with a stiff resistance to papal intervention in France. This spirituality was later affirmed by the Pragmatic Sanction of Bourges (1438) and formulated in the seventeenth century by the faculty of the University of Paris under four points: (1) papal respect for French canons and customs; (2) acceptance of limited papal intervention in France; (3) papal authority being subject to conciliar supremacy; and (4) acceptance of papal primacy with the rejection of the unilateral exercise of papal infallibility. Gallican spirituality moulded a very strong, mystical, and militant Catholicism. This crusading spirituality motivated lay missionaries as they penetrated up the St. Lawrence, bringing Christianity to the Aboriginal fur traders at Montreal; and inspired the Jesuit missionaries plying the upper reaches of the Ottawa River and the Great Lakes to bring the gospel to Aboriginal peoples. Clerical and lay missionaries willingly endured the hardships of learning the languages, eating the food, living the Aboriginal lifestyle, and giving their lives in service of their community.

The second developmental stage of the Catholic Church in Canada began in the nineteenth century when the Holy See in Rome guided the growth and expansion of Canadian diocesan, parochial, and missionary enterprises. After two centuries of missionary zeal, the Roman Congregation for the Propagation of the Faith wished to bring order to the chaos by establishing the traditional backbone of Catholic order: the Canadian hierarchy. As a reward for loyalty during the War of American Independence and the War of 1812, the British Government, which hitherto had referred to the leader of Quebec's Catholics as "the superintendent of the Romish church in Canada," recognized Joseph-Octave Plessis as "Roman Catholic Bishop of Quebec."[2] After the long wait for recognition and considering the needs of his geographically huge diocese,

---

2   See, for example, Adam Shortt and Arthur G. Doughty, eds., *Canada and Its Provinces: A History of the Canadian People and Their Institutions*, vol. 11 (Toronto: Printed by T. & A. Constable at the Edinburgh University Press for the Publishers' Association of Canada, 1913–1917), 40.

Bishop Plessis petitioned the Holy See and the British colonial office that he be named the Catholic archbishop of Quebec and that five bishops be appointed to assist him in the cities cropping up across the vast expanse of Canada, from Charlottetown in Prince Edward Island to Saint Boniface in Manitoba. The Holy See immediately approved Plessis' request, but the British Colonial Office did not. A compromise was worked out that eventually allowed auxiliary bishops to be appointed to augment the Catholic episcopal organization in Canada. The practice of appointing new bishops across Canada to serve isolated faith communities was repeated again and again until, by the twentieth century, it had generated an established episcopacy of 70 sees. As the episcopacy served to Romanize the Canadian Catholic Church, Ultramontane religious congregations—notably the Oblates, Jesuits, Basilians, Lorettos, Grey Sisters, Sisters of Notre Dame, Sisters of St. Joseph, Sisters of St. Ann, and Sisters of Providence—sent missionaries to Canadian cities and to the northern and western regions of Canada. Following Roman standards, the priests, brothers, and sisters built schools, hospitals, and a Catholic social network to care for the poor, for orphans, and for the aged.

The third developmental stage of the Catholic tradition in Canada came with the endeavour to Canadianize Roman practices. Canadian bishops, theologians, clerics, and laity had embraced Roman traditions while at the same time adjusting them to Canadian needs. For instance, Catholic schools were always central to the thinking of Canadian Catholics, and thus Catholics lobbied for adequate funding to foster Catholic schools in the Canadian provinces. Catholics insisted on schools that taught religion but, at the same time, moved towards accepting the educational requirements of each province. For example, Catholic school boards following Canadian customs did not insist on the gender segregation of European schools and accommodated them to various provincial curricula. During the interwar period, when the economy seemed unable to support working people, Catholics developed Canadian social and economic responses to the Great Depression of the 1930s. The Antigonish Movement at St. Francis Xavier University advocated co-operatives, continuing education, and democratic participation in civil life. In Quebec, French Canadians developed a response to hard times that included a combination of Catholic social thought, New Deal Keynesianism, and Quebec nationalism. In Ontario, Henry Somerville (1889–1953), as editor of the *The Catholic Register*, taught Canadian Catholic social justice to the clergy and laity. In the Canadian West, Father Eugene Cullinane (1907–97) showed that Catholicism and the Co-operative Commonwealth Federation (CCF) shared many common goals of social thought, and that the social teachings of the CCF should not be condemned. The teaching and nursing religious orders adhered to Canadian professional requirements and upgraded their credentials to become fully qualified. In 1943, a key step in Canadianization was taken when the bishops formed the Canadian Catholic Conference to guide the multicultural Canadian Church on such issues as medical care, higher education, refugees, and the CCF.

Canadian Catholics have thus anchored themselves in Canadian life over 400 years. They moved from the pioneering stages of Gallican spirituality in the seventeenth and eighteenth centuries to the embrace of Roman standards in the nineteenth century, and finally to accommodate Catholic teaching and practice to the multicultural religious and intellectual environment in twentieth-century Canada. Reflecting Canadian multiculturalism, Canadian bishops have included among their parishioners French Canadians, Irish, Scots, Germans, Poles, Hungarians, Italians, Portuguese, and many from smaller ethnicity groups. Not surprisingly, the Archdiocese of Toronto reflects Canadian multiculturalism still more vividly, containing within its jurisdiction Eastern parishes of the Coptic, Ethiopian, Malankara, Maronite, Syrian, Melkite, Albanian, Byelorussian, Bulgarian, Greek, Russian, Ruthenian, Chaldean, Armenian, Syro-Malabar, Ukrainian, Slovak, Yugoslav, and Romanian Byzantine Churches. These Catholic ethnic groups reveal how Canadian Catholic theology and practice is formed—and will continue to be formed—in the Canadian atmosphere of multiculturalism.

KEY TERMS

Aggiornamento	Authored by John XXIII, means "bringing-up-to-date," denotes the spirit of renewal that permeated the Second Vatican Council.
Apostle	"A messenger," a term applied to those who first spread the teachings of Jesus.
Christ	"One anointed by God" (Greek, after the Hebrew "messiah"), a title the disciples gave to Jesus in the belief that He fulfilled Jewish prophecy.
Christmas	The Christian festival celebrating the traditional birthday of Jesus, in Bethlehem, Judea, sometime between 6 and 4 BCE.
Disciple	"A pupil," the term applied to the early followers of Jesus.

Easter	The Christian festival celebrating the day of Jesus' resurrection on Easter Sunday, three days after His crucifixion on Good Friday.
Enlightenment	The intellectual movement, beginning in eighteenth-century Northern Europe, that gave pre-eminence to science and reason in all areas of social and cultural life, including religion.
Gospel	"Good news," a term applied to the first four books of the New Testament (Matthew, Mark, Luke, and John), which contain the good news of Jesus' life, death, and resurrection.
Great Schism	In 1054, the official break, through mutual excommunication, between the Roman Catholic Church and the Eastern Orthodox Church.
Hypostatic Union	The Christian doctrine that Jesus Christ has two natures (human and divine) united in one person.
Lay Investiture	The right claimed by European kings to invest bishops with ring and crosier.
New Testament	The 27 books added by Christians to the Hebrew Bible (Old Testament) to form the canon of Christian scriptures.
Nicene Creed	Statement of essential Christian beliefs formulated at the Council of Constantinople, which amplified the earlier Apostles' Creed and is recited in the Catholic Eucharistic liturgy.
Old Testament	What Christians call the Hebrew Bible.
Renaissance	The revival of classical learning and biblical scholarship in fifteenth-century Italy, which spread to Northern Europe in the sixteenth and seventeenth centuries.
Sacraments	In Catholic teaching, seven liturgical signs giving God's grace: baptism, penance, confirmation, Eucharist, ordination, matrimony, and the anointing of the sick.
Scholasticism	The term explaining the use of Greek reason to formulate medieval systematic theology, of which Thomas Aquinas was the most celebrated exponent.
Trinity	In Christian doctrine, the union of three persons (Father, Son, and Holy Spirit) in one godhead.
Ultramontane	A movement of Catholic spiritual renewal, meaning "beyond the mountains [Alps]," which began in France in the seventeenth century and was renewed in the nineteenth century. Nineteenth century Ultramontanists called for personal loyalty to the Pope and strict adherence to the norms of the Church in Rome.

KEY DATES

ca. **30 CE**	Death of Jesus.
ca. **65**	Deaths of the apostles Peter and Paul in Rome.
313	Constantine's Edict of Milan legalizes Christianity.
325–451	Church Councils of Nicaea, Constantinople, Ephesus, and Chalcedon.
800	On Christmas Day, Pope Leo III crowned Charlemagne Holy Roman Emperor.
1054	Break between Rome and Constantinople.
1122	Concordat of Worms.
1274	Death of Thomas Aquinas (*Summa Theologiae*).
1563	Council of Trent concludes.
1600s	French Catholic missions to Aboriginal Canadian settlements.
1749–1914	German immigration to Halifax, Lunenburg, Waterloo County, and Western Canada.
1750s	Irish immigration to Newfoundland.
1755–62	British deportations of Acadians.
1770s	Scottish immigration to Nova Scotia and Prince Edward Island.
1774	Quebec Act guarantees Catholic freedom of worship.
1829	Catholic Emancipation Act passed by the British Parliament.
1830–1950s	Renewed Ultramontane spirituality inspires Canadian Catholics.
1845	Oblates begin missions to western Aboriginal Canadians.
1870	First Vatican Council concludes.
1870s	Polish immigration to Renfrew and Waterloo Counties, Ontario, and Western Canada.
1890s	Ukrainian immigration to Ontario and Western Canada.
1890s–1914	First Italian immigration to Montreal, Toronto, and Vancouver.
1950s–1970s	Second Italian immigration.
1960s–present	Portuguese, Filipino, Tamil, Chinese, and other ethnic Catholic immigration to Canada.
1965	Second Vatican Council concludes.

KEY READINGS

Canadian Catholic Historical Association. *Historical Studies.* Toronto: Canadian Catholic Historical Association, 1933–2002.

Canadian Historical Association. *Canada's Ethnic Group Series.* Ottawa: Canadian Historical Association, 1980–2002.

Choquette, Robert. *The Oblate Assault on Canada's Northwest.* Ottawa: University of Ottawa Press, 1995.

Fay, Terence J. *A History of Canadian Catholics: Gallicanism, Romanism, and Canadianism.* Montreal: McGill-Queen's University Press, 2002.

Fay, Terence J. *The New Faces of Canadian Catholics: The Asians.* Toronto: Novalis, 2009.

Gauvreau, Michael. *The Catholic Origins of Québec's Quiet Revolution, 1931–1970.* Montreal: McGill-Queen's University Press, 2005.

Greer, Allan, ed. and intro. *The Jesuit Relations: Native and Missionaries in Seventeenth-Century North America.* New York: Bedford/St. Martin's, 2000.

Jenkins, Philip. *Pedophiles and Priests.* Toronto: Oxford University Press, 2001.

Magocsi, Paul Robert, ed. *Encyclopedia of Canada's Peoples.* Toronto: University of Toronto Press, 1999.

Murphy, Terrence, and Roberto Perin. *A Concise History of Christianity in Canada.* Toronto: Oxford University Press, 1996.

Voisine, Nive, and Jean Hamelin, eds. *Les Ultramontains canadiens-français.* Montreal: Boréal Express, 1985.

KEY WEBSITES

http://www.newadvent.org/cathen/ [*Catholic Encyclopedia*]

http://www.umanitoba.ca/colleges/st_pauls/ccha/index2.html [Canadian Catholic Historical Association]

http://www.cha-shc.ca [Canadian Historical Association]

http://www.catholicanada.com/directory.html [Catholic Canada Directory]

http://www.ewtn.com/vnews/headlines.asp [EWTN Newslink; includes Catholic World News and Vatican Information Service]

http://www.biographi.ca/index-e.html [Dictionary of Canadian Biography]

http://www.zenit.org [Vatican News Agency]

http://www.cccb.ca/site/index.php?lang=eng [Canadian Conference of Catholic Bishops]

KEY QUESTIONS FOR CRITICAL REFLECTION

1. What does Canadianization of the Catholic Church mean? Is this the same thing as nationalizing or Protestantizing the Church?

2. Should the Irish and French Canadian Catholics be expected to share Christian unity in the same Church at the same time?

3. Should Filipino, Tamil, Chinese, or other so-called ethnic Catholics be encouraged to remain Filipino, Tamil, Chinese, or any other kind of ethnic Catholics, or should they be expected to become Canadian Catholics?

4. How do Canadian Catholics of European heritage welcome Asian, African, and Caribbean Catholics into their churches?

5. Has the relationship between the Canadian Catholic Church and the Holy See in Rome changed over the years, and what is the nature of this relationship today?

THREE

Protestant Christians

C.T. MCINTIRE, UNIVERSITY OF TORONTO

||||||||||||||||||||||||||||||||||||||||||||||||||||||||||||||||||||||||||||||||||||||||||||||||||||||||||||||||||||||||||||||||||

P rotestants are a variety of Christians who, like all Christians, attach themselves to Jesus Christ, the one whom they confess died, was buried, and rose again according to the scriptures. They trace their roots for the most part to what is often called the European Reformation of the sixteenth century, a movement marked above all by the rejection of the papacy, the affirmation of the primacy of the Bible in matters of faith, and the assertion of the priesthood of all believers.

In Canada, Protestants represent by far the most diverse and complex religious group. During the nineteenth century and most of the twenti-eth century, they were also the most numerous, and they remained the most numerous in most regions of Canada through the early twenty-first century. They have by some measures—ecclesiastical, social, economic, political, educational, and in the realm of the arts—dominated the life of Canada for most of its history. Being Protestant means much more than going to church; it entails a way of life, a culture. On the world scale, they belong to the trans-Atlantic Protestant mega-region that spans the northern regions of both Europe and North America, ranging from the eastern border of Estonia and Latvia with Russia to the western coast of Alaska opposite Siberian Russia. They are co-religionists of expansive new Protestant movements in Latin American, China, India, sub-Saharan Africa, and elsewhere in the twenty-first century.

The very existence of Protestants in Canada is marked by paradox. Most Protestants in Canada in the twenty-first century probably do not think of themselves as Protestants. The very term can appear strange to them. Some who say they are Protestants appear in the reports of Statistics Canada as if they are not, and others who say they are not Protestants appear prominently in the reports as if they are. They comprise a class of people easily distinguished from others, yet they nearly defy attempts to understand them as a religious group at all. They first arrived in the territory we call Canada during the sixteenth century, yet they are commonly discussed as latecomers. In an era when considerably smaller Canadian populations of Muslims, Hindus, Buddhists, Chinese popular religionists, and Aboriginal religionists attract attention, they are habitually overlooked. In spite of their historical dominance, they welcome invisibility, present an image of embarrassment, tolerate their belittlement by others, and quietly suffer neglect by scholars of religion. Since the late twentieth century, Canadian Protestants themselves have seemed bent on contributing to their own demise.

THE HERITAGE

The paradox of Protestants in Canada is compounded by Protestant history. The conventional story that has inspired Protestants for centuries locates their beginning in what people often call "The Reformation" of the sixteenth century in Europe. According to this account, "The Reformation" began on 31 October 1517 when Martin Luther (1483–1546), a learned but troubled monk, posted *Ninety-Five Theses* on the castle door in Wittenberg, Saxony, Germany, focused on God's forgiveness of sin and attacking perceived abuses of Christianity within the papal Catholic Church. Luther led a long line of remarkable people associated with Protestant movements—Ulrich Zwingli (1484–1531) and Conrad Grebel (*ca.* 1498–1526) of Zurich; Martin Bucer (1491–1551) of Strasbourg; John Calvin (1509–64) of Geneva; Thomas Cranmer (1489–1556) of Canterbury; John Knox (*ca.* 1510–72) of Edinburgh; and Menno Simons (1496–1561) of Friesland. These leaders mounted heartfelt criticisms of the Roman Pope, papal doctrine, and priestly corruption. As a consequence of their actions and challenges, a new array of churches and religious allegiances called Protestant emerged in Europe.

A statue of Martin Luther stands in the market square, Wittenberg, Germany, with the church where Luther preached in the background. PHOTO BY MICHAEL SANDER. REPRINTED UNDER THE TERMS OF THE CC-BY-SA LICENSE.

A wider canvassing of the history of Protestants allows us to recognize the merits of this conventional account, but leads us to elaborate a more complicated story. We may be sure that significant Protestant movements did emerge out of the rupture with the papal Catholic Church in Europe in the sixteenth century, and they undoubtedly did reject the papacy, key Catholic teachings, and church corruption. The leaders were important. But major movements that count as Protestant occurred well before the sixteenth century, and other major Protestant movements arose after the sixteenth century. No Protestant movements were merely the work of well-known figures. Indeed, all were driven by ordinary people. Moreover, the aim of the earliest leaders was simply to reform certain matters in the church, and it was not until tensions become irresolvable that the breaks with the papal Catholic Church occurred and became permanent.

Protestant history entails not just *The* Reformation, but many reformations; not one distinctive period, but several; not only big leaders, but also movements of whole peoples that mattered. It is a mark of Protestants that reformation is never final, and no one movement of reformation suffices for all. Protestants expect reformation to recur, they exhort themselves repeatedly to reformation, and they embrace new reformation as no surprise. Protestants proclaim and embody a cyclic interpretation of history that requires the repeated removal of impurities in the present, the return to the sources at the beginning, and the reconstruction of things for the future according to the way they were intended to be from the beginning. Two sayings arose among Protestants that capture the meaning of reformation: *post tenebras lux*—after darkness, light; and *ecclesia reformata semper reformanda*—the church reformed is always reforming.

On the global scale, the Protestant division with Catholics was a regional event. It took place within the small world of Latin Christianity in papal Europe. Protestants maintained near total disregard for the rest of Christianity—the Eastern Orthodox and Oriental Orthodox Churches in Eastern Europe, Asia, and Africa. They defined themselves against Catholics obedient to the Pope, and constructed their practices, institutions, discourse, and beliefs in opposition to the Church of Rome. Both papal Catholics and new Protestants felt confined within their small home terrain and desired to enlarge their territories beyond Western Europe. The Portuguese ventured south along the Atlantic coast of Africa throughout the fifteenth century, and the Spanish, Portuguese, and English journeyed west across the Atlantic Ocean from the 1490s onward, followed soon after by the French and later the Dutch. Their efforts were most assuredly attempts to reach India and China, thwart Islam, expand markets, seek fish, and multiply power, but they were also designed to exalt Catholic or Protestant Christianity. Both Protestants and Catholics successfully extended their reach across the globe over the centuries, entangling with each other as well as with the Orthodox Churches in the process.

The emergence of Protestants, however, starts much earlier than the sixteenth century. Three major strains of Protestants begin their stories in the twenty-first century with reformation movements that originated well before the sixteenth century. **Waldensians** continue to describe themselves as "a Protestant religious community that for the last 800 years has survived and prospered, despite repeated attempts at repression and extermination during the first five hundred years."[1] Waldensians trace their history to a movement that began in Lyons in France in the 1170s, linked to Peter Valdo (*ca.* 1140–1218). Likewise, the Moravian Church in America identifies itself as "a Protestant denomination with more than five hundred years of history."[2] Moravians, Czech Brethren, and other Czech Protestants find their origins in a movement dating from about 1400, linked to Jan Hus (*ca.* 1369–1415) of Prague. A third line of Protestants identifies with a movement in England dating from the 1370s, associated with John Wycliffe (*ca.* 1328–84) of Oxford. The followers of Wycliffe bore the name Lollards, and later folded into the Anglican movement of the sixteenth century. Anglican Evangelicals in the 1870s founded two theological colleges: Wycliffe Hall in Oxford, England, and Wycliffe College in Toronto, Ontario, both designed to remember and continue their heritage. In addition to these earliest Protestants, French Protestants make the point that, even in the sixteenth century, the Protestant movement in France did not start with Luther in Germany in 1517, but with Jacques Lefevre d'Etaples (*ca.* 1455–1536) in Paris in 1512.

The Protestant movements begun before Luther are matched by major new strains of Protestantism begun well after the sixteenth century. In the seventeenth century, **Baptists**, Congregationalists, Quakers, **Independents**, and Unitarians diverged from the Church of England, as did **Methodists** in the eighteenth century. Movements in the nineteenth century in England and the United States produced more new Protestants, including Plymouth Brethren, the Salvation Army, Disciples of Christ, and Holiness groups, while movements in the twentieth and twenty-first centuries generated massive numbers of new Protestants in the form of Pentecostals and indigenous Independent churches across the world. By contrast with what came later, it quickly became evident that the Lutheran and Anglican versions of the reformation movement had stayed closer to the Catholic Church in liturgy and practice than subsequent Protestant expressions.

Within this longer timeline, we can relativize the understanding of the sixteenth century that is privileged by the traditional account of "The

---

1   "Luoghi Storici Valdesi, Tavola Valdesi, Comitato per i Luoghi Storici delle Valli Valdesi," accessed 27 June 2011 from http://www.valdesi.org/ENindex.html.

2   "Good Shepherd Moravian Church, Calgary, Alberta: A Protestant Church of the Moravian Denomination Serving North-West Calgary," accessed 27 June 2011 from http://www.goodshepherdmoravian.org/moravian.html.

Reformation." It becomes, instead, the period when certain hugely important Protestant movements began: Lutherans, **Anglicans**, Zwinglians, Calvinists, Anabaptists, Mennonites, and **Presbyterians,** as well as **Huguenots.** These movements exhibited virtually the same beliefs, practices, and behaviours that the Waldensians, Lollards, and Hussites had already promoted for generations. Like Valdo, Wycliffe, and Hus, they rejected the Pope and elevated the Bible; and they possessed the same religious authenticity, piety, and fidelity. They combated corruption and irreligion in their day, as did their predecessors. They also experienced the same calamities of excommunication, execution, and religious war that had already befallen the earlier reformers.

Yet, the sixteenth-century reformation movements remain central, even if they were not the first or the last strains of Protestants. The traditional story actually singles out not the first Protestants, or the beginning of Protestantism, but those Protestants who were colossally successful—and the beginnings, from there, of the escalation of Protestantism into a world movement. The sixteenth-century movements renovated the whole of the religious, social, political, and cultural worlds within which they arose. The enormous scale of their results derived directly from their relationships with the ruling powers. Unlike earlier and later strains of Protestants, sixteenth-century Protestants achieved exceptional alliances with the ruling authorities and notables of the kingdoms and cities where they flourished, and brought significant numbers of kings, queens, nobles, and wealthy burghers into their movements. These wielders of power adopted, protected, and favoured Protestantism, and enabled the movement to succeed. In like manner, the earlier reformation peoples also thrived when civic rulers and notables supported them, but when the powerful withdrew support or opposed them, they had to flee, or migrate, or burrow underground. That they survived at all is a marvel. The sixteenth-century movements likewise prospered when they enjoyed sustained political support, but faltered when they did not.

Rulers gave their support to the upstart movements for complex reasons that varied according to the case. Civic support depended as much on the exigencies of nation-building, fear of approaching Islamic Ottoman Turks, resistance to papal power, the self-interest of markets and finance, and international conflict, as it did on matters of doctrine, devotion to God, forgiveness of sin, and the desire for salvation. Time and again during the sixteenth century, when facilitated by the strategic support of civic authorities, Protestant reform groups transformed the whole of church, society, and culture. The most monumental results occurred in Germany, Scandinavia, the Baltic, the Swiss cantons, England, Scotland, France, and the Netherlands. Anabaptists, who theologically renounced alliance with civic authority, briefly transformed Münster, Germany, with civic support. Conversely, important Protestant movements in Poland, Bavaria, Austria, Hungary, Italy, Spain, and Portugal collapsed when the civic authorities abandoned, opposed, or destroyed them.

In theological terms, Protestants explained their involvement in church and society in much the same manner as the Roman Catholics they overturned. They mirrored their Catholic opponents, as well as the Eastern Orthodox and Oriental Orthodox Churches, in their conviction that the Christian religion is not to be confined to a compartment of life or to what goes on in church. Protestants continued to understand that the teachings of Jesus Christ ought properly to infuse the whole of life and animate a way of life. From the 1500s onward, Protestant explorers, fishers, merchants, settlers, political figures, and missionaries from the new Protestant regions perpetuated the familiar patterns of Christian society when they entered North America, South America, Asia, Africa, and Oceania. After long migrations across Europe to Russia, Anabaptists, beginning in 1789, constructed a Mennonite commonwealth that functioned like a Christian state within the Russian empire under Orthodox czars, where even they melded religion, politics, farming, taxation, economics, arts, and society into one, just like the papal Catholic and new Protestant societies they left behind.

The name Protestant apparently first surfaced in 1529 when a group of German princes and representatives of imperial cities objected to the decision by the Diet of Speyer of the Holy Roman Empire to stop the spread of Luther's teachings. The term soon proved useful to refer to a great variety of new religious movements on the continent. In time, the term served to cover the movements of reformation against the papal church that originated before as well as after the sixteenth century.

In practice, Protestant groups usually call themselves by specialized names that denote their connection with some identifying feature: a leader, a theology, a polity, a practice, a culture, an ethnicity, a church denomination. The list of names seems nearly endless: Waldensians, Hussites, Moravians, Huguenots, Zwinglians, Calvinists, Anabaptists, Anglicans, Hutterites, Baptists, Presbyterians, Independents, Pentecostals, Pietists, Evangelicals, Fundamentalists, Africa Methodist Episcopal Zionists, Dutch Reformed, members of the United Church of Canada, brothers and sisters of the True Light Church, and so on. Countless Protestants in the twenty-first century go by no name at all. They merely think of themselves as belonging to some local church or local assembly. The power of these names, or of having no name, generates the remarkable paradox that huge numbers of Protestants do not think of themselves as Protestants. Anglicans, for instance, tend to regard themselves as "a third way" and deny that they are Protestants, as do Pentecostals for different reasons. Many successors of the Anabaptists wonder why they should be classed as Protestants, since both Roman Catholics and Protestants persecuted them in the sixteenth century. Masses of twenty-first-century Independent Christians in China, Africa, India, Latin America, and North America never think about the matter, even while they remain historically traceable to Protestant forebears. In the twenty-first century, the term Protestant remains useful for historical reasons to cover all of these groups, even when they or people talking about them hesitate to apply the term. Others, notably Old Catholics in the Netherlands, Germany, and North America, derived from a nineteenth-century separation from Roman Catholics, do not call themselves Protestants, and neither do members of the Philippine Independent Church that separated from Rome in the twentieth century. But by allying with Anglicans and Episcopalians, both groups began to slip under the Protestant canopy. Jehovah's Witnesses, Mormons, Christian Scientists, and the Church of Scientology emerged from Protestant sources, but adherents to those movements came to think of themselves—and be thought of by others—as definitely not Protestant.

There are two marks that have perhaps distinguished Protestants the most from other Christians over the ages. The first mark is ecclesiastical and doctrinal: Protestants reject the Roman Pope, the papal church, and papal teaching, and seek to reform the church and life on a new basis. The second mark is historical: no matter what their group, Protestants can trace the history of how they or their predecessors separated from the Roman Pope and the papal Catholic Church, and they testify how they sought, and continue to seek, to reform the church and life. In telling their histories, they also distinguish themselves from the Oriental Orthodox and the Eastern Orthodox strains of Christians who never came under the Roman Pope and who trace their histories directly to the earliest period of Christianity. These traditions include the Eastern Orthodox churches of Greece, Serbia, Ukraine, Russia, and adjacent regions, centred on Constantinople, and the Oriental Orthodox churches of Egypt, Ethiopia, Eritrea, Syria, Armenia, Persia, and India. Members of the

Assyrian Church of the East, with roots in Mesopotamia and Persia, are not received as Protestants, but Anglicans in particular have developed long-standing fraternal relations with them.

Two doctrines have stood out above all among Protestants: the authority of the Bible and the priesthood of all believers. As expressions of these doctrines, Protestants have tended to honour three symbols articulated in the sixteenth century that indicate the source of the reformation they continually seek. These symbols are often called the reformation principles: *sola gratia*—by grace alone; *sola fide*—by faith alone; and *sola scriptura*—by scripture alone. First, Protestants exalted the primacy of the authority of the Bible as the written Word of God—*sola scriptura*. They intended by this assertion to deny the authority of the Roman Pope and the papal Catholic Church to determine right belief, right practice, and right living. No matter how differently the various groups might circumscribe what they mean, they continue to place the Bible first.

Second, Protestants affirmed the doctrine of the priesthood of all believers. When they overthrew the Pope, they overthrew priests as well. They converted popular antipathy to priests into the removal of the priestly class. They denied that clergy, including above all the Roman Pope, control access to God and the means of salvation. They affirmed instead that every person enjoys direct, immediate access to God and salvation. They confessed that salvation comes by God's grace alone—*sole gratia*—and a person receives salvation through Jesus Christ by faith alone—*sola fide*. For Protestants, Jesus Christ is the only mediator between God and the people. Nothing intervenes—not priests, not saints, especially not Mary, not the Pope. Protestants uniformly reconstructed the church as the people of God. They saw themselves as a new kind of people—literate, self-directed, responsible to God, free to act, ready to decide. They elevated the laity and empowered ordinary people in church, family, and society. Domestic worship and individual acts of worship with scripture and prayer became normal, together with transformed moral practice. Lay religion became paramount.

These two signature doctrines combined to guarantee that Protestants would produce differing and even conflicting understandings of God's message. Protestants claimed the competence as believers to read and respond to the Bible for themselves, and different readers understood the Bible differently. Waldensians, for instance, bore persecution because they insisted on following the Bible in ways contrary to papal teaching. Baptists renounce the baptism of infants and restrict baptism to believing adults because of their reading of the Bible, while Presbyterians instruct parents to bring their newborn babies to baptism because of their reading of the Bible. Pentecostals tie their experience of speaking in tongues under the power of the Holy Spirit to the Bible, where they find the experience of tongues reported and promised to others, while those who reject such glossolalia do so because of the Bible.

By separating from the centralizing authority of the Roman Pope, Protestants set themselves on a course of institutional and intellectual differentiation, creating a seemingly limitless diversity of structures, practices, and theologies. Movements towards church union did little to alter this long-term tendency. By the end of the nineteenth century, the term **denomination** emerged to signify distinctive ecclesiastical connections among Christians who espoused similar beliefs, observed common practices, and recited shared histories. As the logic of Protestant difference worked itself out, the number of denominations increased exponentially. By the year 1900, the number of denominations in the world, almost all of them Protestant, reached perhaps 1,900. By the year 2000, the number surpassed 30,000.

The Protestant commitment to the Bible and the priesthood of all believers generated certain typical activities. First, for the benefit of a wider population, Protestants translated the scriptures into the languages of the people. The Waldensians put portions of the Bible into Provençal; Wycliffe produced the Bible in English; Hussites rendered the Bible in Czech; Luther translated the Bible into German, and so on. The King James translation of the Bible authorized by James I (1566–1625) in 1611 dominated English-speaking Protestant practice for 350 years, until a host of new translations took over in the late twentieth century. By the year 2000, translators, chiefly Protestants, had put all or part of the Bible into about half of the world's 6,900 or so languages and were planning to at least begin translations into the remaining languages by 2025.

Second, Protestants created an entire culture of the written and spoken word, centred on the Word of God. Their public worship gave pre-eminence to verbal acts, especially reading the Bible, prayer, song, and sermons. They favoured clergy who preached well. They appointed lay preachers, evangelists, catechists, teachers, and missionaries to spread the message. When they altered church interiors or built new church buildings, they positioned the preaching site—the pulpit—at the front, either in the centre or off to one side and on a higher level than the other church furnishings. They installed long rows of seats—the pews—facing the pulpit, and transformed the people into audiences. They produced written confessions of faith and catechisms as testimonies to what they understood the Bible to say. To enable people to read the Bible and to prepare their leaders, they promoted education. They educated their children at home, and created schools, colleges, seminaries, universities, and, beginning in the nineteenth century, Sunday schools. Protestants adopted the new technology of printing from moveable type, and powered its spread by publishing and distributing tracts, devotional readings, sermons, books, newspapers, and, above all, Bibles in vast numbers. In the twentieth century, they again adopted the new technologies, successively mastering radio, television, and the Internet as platforms for preaching, education, and evangelism into the twenty-first century.

Third, Protestants simplified just about everything connected with church, family, and their common life. Their lives became austere. They gave rise to the cliché that Protestants feel awkward if they have too much fun. They discarded beliefs and usages they regarded as superstitious and idolatrous, and eliminated others not commanded or warranted by scripture. They abolished devotion to the Virgin Mary, prayer to the saints, holy relics, miraculous healing, processions, pilgrimages, religious feasts, kneeling as a devotional posture, the sign of the cross, prayer for the dead, mandatory celibacy, and the very notion of ritual. They removed crucifixes, altars, and images, and minimized art. Waves of iconoclasm swept periodically over Protestant regions, leaving behind spare interiors at home and at church. They put an end to penance, indulgences, and confession. They abolished Purgatory. Only the French Revolution of 1789 matched the magnitude of the Protestant oppression of monks and nuns, the suppression of monasticism, the destruction of monasteries, and the confiscation of monastic and ecclesiastical wealth.

From the Waldensians onward, Protestants universally rejected the claim Roman Catholics made for the Mass, that the actions of the priest transformed the substance of bread and wine into the substance of the body and blood of Jesus Christ. Protestants retained what Roman Catholics called the Mass, but changed its meaning and role among their people. They continued to observe this liturgical meal as a **sacrament**, or in some communities as an ordinance, but without salvific power, and maintained its biblical tie with the last supper that Jesus Christ shared with His disciples before His crucifixion. They could not, however, agree on what alternative meaning to find in it. Instead of the Mass, they called it the Lord's Supper, Holy Communion, the Eucharist, or simply communion, according to their competing theologies. They positioned it less centrally and observed it infrequently. Against Roman Catholics, who permitted laypeople to partake only of the bread, they extended both elements of the meal—bread and wine, or in anti-alcohol circles, grape juice—to the laity. They also retained baptism as a sacrament, or at least an ordinance, but denied it any salvific power. They discarded the five remaining sacraments observed by Roman Catholics, Eastern Orthodox Christians, and Oriental Orthodox Christians, but nearly all Protestants kept the functions of the five discarded rituals, sometimes under new names—confirmation (or joining the church), marriage, penance (or repentance), ordination of clergy (or setting apart), and anointing of the sick and dying (or prayers for healing).

Generally, Protestants had less to do in church or for religious exercises than Catholic congregations did. As compensation, they added music, and the people began to sing as congregations and families. They sang hymns and psalms, and eventually gospel songs and choruses, and choirs sang chorales, anthems, spirituals, and gospel music. They had less reason to go to church, since nothing happened there as significant as the substantial presence of Jesus Christ in the Mass. Depending on the time and culture, they relied instead on persuasion, social pressure, legal coercion, and voluntary decision to maintain attendance in Protestant churches. In the nineteenth and twentieth centuries, many Protestants revived some lost practices. Anglicans, for instance, resumed frequent Eucharists and founded sisterhoods and monastic orders, while Pentecostals reclaimed miracles of healing, Protestant pilgrimages to the Holy Land became common, and Evangelical missionaries who had been killed for their faith became veritable saints. Theological criticism of Roman Catholics abated as well. After Roman Catholics revised their teachings and practices during the Second Vatican Council (1962–65), Protestants across the wide spectrum of denominations entered into dialogue with Roman Catholics in order to clarify and mitigate their historical differences. Roman Catholics faced the accusation that the Second Vatican Council had made their church, and even their Mass, too Protestant.

If Protestants had less to do in church, they had more to do in the rest of their lives; they had constructed new ways of life. Whereas previously only monks had religious vocations, now Protestants validated the occupations of daily life as religious vocations. They turned every beneficial pursuit in society, politics, and the economy into a calling to love and serve God and neighbour. They established countless organizations for social, economic, and cultural purposes. They elevated the place of family among ordinary people. Their clergy married and had children. Protestants surely appeared among all social classes and were engaged in just about any line of work, but just as surely they became preponderant in the middle classes and among the wealth-creating occupations, especially trade, finance, industry, the stock market, technology, and science. No nuanced answer has yet emerged to explain the extraordinary, coincidental correlation between the world map of Protestants and the map of the wealthiest countries in the world. Granted that every human community contains a generous supply of hard work, intelligence, and goodwill, as well as greed, exploitation, and self-centredness, and granted that there are exceptions, it nonetheless appears that certain societies stand out for their combination of historically Protestant identities and exceptional economic well-being: Great Britain, The Netherlands, Germany, Switzerland, Sweden, Norway, Denmark, Finland, the United States, Canada, Australia, New Zealand, and South Africa. Protestants have been among the first to congratulate or condemn these countries for this result, and to articulate theological justifications of capitalism on one side or theologies of social justice, socialism, or even communism on the other. Protestants have also borne the responsibility, or blame, for generating secularizing tendencies that have marginalized Christian religion within the modern world, and for producing the class of people who claim to have "no religion" at all.

From the very beginning, Protestants acted to fulfill the mandate from Jesus Christ that they found in the Bible at Mark 16, Matthew 28, and Acts of the Apostles 1: "Go ye into all the world, and preach the gospel to every creature." Waldensians, Lollards, and Hussites began the process with their itinerant preachers and group migrations. From the sixteenth century onward, and especially in the nineteenth century, Protestants of all sorts spread their religion by every means available—migration, settlement, trade, fishing, empire, war, and the search for resources, as well as missions and evangelism. By the twenty-first century, Protestants had crisscrossed the globe and established their presence in virtually every country of the world. In 2000, the list of the countries with the six largest Protestant populations in the world contained some surprises. They were, in order, the United States, China, Germany, India, Nigeria, and Great Britain. Canadian Protestants may place well down the list in size, but they would rank high on another scale: the impact of Protestants on Canada has been enormous.

THE MAKING OF A CANADIAN PROTESTANT COMMUNITY

Protestant Christians of Canada fit neatly into the usual treatment of Canadian religions. According to the conventional story, "English" stands for Protestant and "French" for Roman Catholic. The story says that Roman Catholics arrived first and Protestants came second. It goes on to say that when the British conquered the French at the Plains of Abraham in Quebec City in 1759, English Protestants gained dominance over French Roman Catholics. The conventional story features big leaders, famous clergy, official acts, big events, missions, and written documents. Like the conventional story of "The Reformation" of the sixteenth century, much is plausible in this account. But closer examination discloses that this story also misses the complexity of the history of Protestants in Canada. The need for revision becomes apparent when the focus shifts away from traditional subjects—the clergy, big names, churches, missions, official acts, and certain written documents—to include the laity, ordinary people, life outside church, lived religion, unofficial practices, oral traditions, other documents, and new readings of familiar texts.

The picture that emerges depicts two subjects, usually kept apart, advancing hand in hand: the construction of the New World in Canada and the construction of a Protestant presence in Canada. From the sixteenth century onward, the Protestant movement in Canada proceeded as an expression of the Protestant movement in Europe during the same period. When we reconsider the Canadian story, we notice immediately that neither the French nor the English were the first Christians to arrive in what we call Canada. The first Christians were Norse mariners connected with a Norse colony in Greenland. Leif Eriksson (*ca.* 970–1020) and his crew arrived in the region we know as Newfoundland and Labrador around the year 1000. Norse people built settlements on Newfoundland's north peninsula, one of which was L'Anse aux Meadows, rediscovered in 1960. They maintained settlements off and on for perhaps 350 years. The first Norse settlers were neither Roman Catholic nor Protestant, but Christians, before the sharp lines were drawn between Latin Catholics and Greek Orthodox Christians after 1054.

Hence, when the next Christians arrived in 1497, they were not first, but second, long after the Norse—and neither were they French. They were English, with at least one Italian among them, and they were not Protestant, but Catholic. Giovanni Caboto (*ca.* 1450–99), known as John Cabot, led an English crew out of Bristol, England, financed by English merchants and authorized by the English King Henry VII (1457–1509) well before England renounced the Pope. Cabot and crew landed at Newfoundland, plausibly on Bonavista Peninsula, and claimed it for England. Other English journeys followed, but no sustained English project for Canada took shape at that time. The English acted in response to the Portuguese, who had reached Africa's Cape of Good Hope by 1488, and the Spanish, who with Christopher Columbus (*ca.* 1451–1506)—also an Italian—had reached the Americas in 1492. Both Portugal and Spain were Catholic powers. In 1493 and 1494, in an act of presumption that seemed normal, and without regard for other countries, Pope Alexander VI (1431–1503; reigned 1492–1503) brokered the Treaty of Tordesillas that divided the world outside Europe between Portugal and Spain. The English project behind Cabot ignored the treaty and reflected the selective disregard of papal authority that had been common in England since at least the early 1300s, the same anti-papal ethos that issued in Protestantism.

The Spanish did not reach Canada, but the Portuguese did—as Catholics, in annual journeys from 1499 to 1502, and they claimed the land for Portugal. They were officially the third Christians to arrive in Canada, possibly culminating in a Portuguese settlement at Ingonish or Mira Bay on Cape Breton Island, sometime between 1521 and 1526. The Portuguese left their mark on Atlantic Canada with place names like Labrador and Portugal Cove, but they lost official interest in the north, and Spain never tried, leaving Northern America to England and France, if they wanted it. And thus the French, with their official expeditions, were the fourth to come to the Canadian region, and at the time they were Catholic as well. In 1524, on the authority of the French king, Francis I (1494–1547), a French crew reached Newfoundland, led by another Italian, Giovanni da Verrazzano (1485–1528). Then Jacques Cartier (1491–1557) and his crews, presumed to be Catholics, made three official voyages to the region between 1534 and 1543, and they claimed the land for France.

The French voyages, however, further disarrange the conventional story. The official French expeditions were not simply Catholic. They also included Protestants, either as leaders, participants, or both. Thus, the first Protestants to enter the region that became Canada were French, not English. French Protestants were fundamental to the founding of Canada, and they are invariably overlooked. The French investigation of Northern America occurred during the very years when the Protestant movement emerged in France. New Protestants surfaced in France by the late 1520s, and between the 1530s and 1550s, Protestant communities proliferated and flourished in France. French Protestants, known as Huguenots, included people of all ranks of society—nobles, royalty, peasants, artisans, and seamen, as well as merchants, teachers, officials, and others—who converted to the reformed religion in huge numbers. Important Protestant populations developed on the French Atlantic coast and in the south of France. In 1562, civil war erupted between the entrenched Roman Catholics and the increasingly powerful Protestants, and continued for 30 years. France very nearly became Protestant.

Cartier's first voyage, in 1534, had a Protestant as its sponsor: Philippe de Chabot (*ca.* 1492–1543), Seigneur de Brion, governor of Normandy and Burgundy. On the second voyage, from 1535 to 1536, Cartier and his crew spent the winter in Stadacona, located on the St. Lawrence River at the future site of Quebec City. On his third journey, in 1541, Cartier brought a large group of settlers whom Francis I placed under the authority of a Protestant noble, Jean François de la Rocque (*ca.* 1500–60), Sieur de Roberval. La Rocque de Roberval's patron was Marguerite d'Angoulême (1492–1549), the Protestant sister of the king. La Rocque de Roberval's commission from Francis I appointed him General Lieutenant of Canada and authorized him to construct "towns and forts, temples and churches." Temple was the name given to French Protestant places of worship.

In 1541, the settlers established a village on the St. Lawrence River at Cap Rouge, west of the future site of Quebec. The actual site was rediscovered in 2005. They named it Charlesbourg-Royal and later France-Roi. Cap Rouge was the first official French settlement in the New World, a priority generally omitted from the Canadian narrative. During the first year, Cartier led the community, but for the second year La Rocque de Roberval himself lived there and headed the settlement, replacing Cartier who returned to France. La Rocque de Roberval was the first documented Protestant to live in Canada. There were likely other Protestants among the settlers and sailors, including Cartier's second in command, Jean Alfonce (1484–1544/1549), who was from La Rochelle and perhaps a Protestant. While it lasted, the settlement depended on beneficial interaction with the Aboriginal peoples. It disbanded in 1543.

Between 1555 and 1565, as tensions with Catholics back in France increased, French Protestants, seeking other outlets, established Huguenot colonies to the south in Brazil, Florida, and Carolina. These lasted until they were crushed by the Catholic Portuguese and Spanish. When the Edict of Nantes, proclaimed by Henry IV in 1598, gave the Huguenots relative religious freedom, Huguenots continued to lead or participate in what transpired in the Canadian region. From 1598 to 1603, Troilus de Mesgouez de la Roche (*ca.* 1536–1606) sponsored and for a time headed a settlement on Sable Island, off the coast of Nova Scotia. La Roche displayed Protestant sympathies and had fought on the Huguenot side against the Catholic League in France. Henry IV (1553–1610), a Protestant who ostensibly converted to the Catholic Church, but who retained his Huguenot sympathies, authorized the settlement. The settlement may have included other Protestants. In 1600 another French group settled at Tadoussac on the St. Lawrence River at the mouth of the Saguenay River, east of the future Quebec. Two Huguenots, Pierre Du Gua (*ca.* 1558–1628), Sieur de Monts, and Pierre Chauvin de Tonnetuit (*ca.* 1575–1603), led the settlement. There apparently was a Huguenot minister among them, the first French Protestant minister—indeed the first Protestant minister of any kind—in the Canadian region. Tadoussac, from its founding in 1600, became the oldest continuously inhabited French settlement in Canada, a priority in continuity largely forgotten except at Tadoussac.

In 1604, Pierre du Gua again led a settlement that included Roman Catholics and Huguenots, this time on Île Sainte Croix in the Sainte Croix River between what later became New Brunswick and Maine, near the Bay of Fundy. The colony resettled at Port-Royal across the bay in the future Nova Scotia in 1605. Jean de Biencourt de Poutrincourt (1557–1615), Baron de Saint-Just, a Huguenot, participated in and then led the community. The settlement at Quebec in 1608, under Samuel de Champlain (*ca.* 1570–1635), included both Catholic and Protestant settlers. Champlain most likely grew up Protestant, and he married a Protestant, Hélène Boullé (1598–1654). Although, like Henry IV, both Champlain and Boullé ostensibly converted to the Roman Catholic Church, they remained sympathetic to Protestants throughout their extraordinary careers. Port-Royal and Quebec became the two most successful French settlements—one at the heart of Atlantic Acadia, and the other along the St. Lawrence River at the heart of New France. Both included Protestants from the beginning.

In the French villages, starting with Charlesbourg-Royal/France-Roi at Cap Rouge in 1541–43, and Tadoussac in 1600, the Protestants among the settlers no doubt practiced lay religion and lay morality. The work of La Rocque de Roberval at Cap Rouge offers a glimpse of Huguenot practice. Their religious expression involved individual devotions, domestic worship, and common worship. They prayed, sang, told stories from the Bible, affirmed their reliance on Divine providence, and practised Huguenot morality in their common lives. At Tadoussac, the Huguenot pastor conducted services of worship and other observances according to the emerging Reformed Protestant practice. It is plausible that the first Protestant contact with Aboriginal people occurred at one of these villages, possibly at Tadoussac, followed by Sainte-Croix, Port-Royal, and Quebec.

Meanwhile, the English resumed their official involvement in the region of Canada, but now as Protestants, no longer as Roman Catholics. The Anglican reformation began in the 1530s under Henry VIII (1491–1547), continued under Edward VI (1537–53) until 1553, lapsed under Queen Mary (1516–58), a Roman Catholic, and resumed with vigour under Queen Elizabeth (1533–1603) starting in 1558. In the 1570s, 80 years after Cabot, the English finally sent an official party to investigate the Canadian region. Martin Frobisher (1535/1539–94) led three voyages between 1576 and 1578. On the second voyage in 1577, Frobisher, upon returning safely to Frobisher Bay near the Arctic Ocean, conducted the first recorded Protestant service in Canada. On his third journey, Frobisher's party included an Anglican minister, Robert Wolfall, who in 1578 celebrated the first recorded Anglican service of Holy Communion in Canada, on shore at Frobisher Bay, near Iqaluit. He is also the first known Church of England minister in the Canadian region. As described by Frobisher in 1578, the men on board English ships heard Morning Prayer and Evening Prayer from the Anglican Book of Common Prayer, first published in 1549 and revised in 1559. Humphrey Gilbert (1539–83) and John Davis (ca. 1550–1605) followed with a voyage to Canada in 1583. Leaders and crews were Protestants. Gilbert entered St. John's harbour in Newfoundland and straightaway claimed the land for England. He declared that henceforth all worship in the region would conform to the Book of Common Prayer, and instituted regular use of the Anglican Prayer Book in the lands that became Canada.

The first official English settlement in Canada began in 1610 at Cupers Cove, later known as Cupids Harbour, on the Avalon Peninsula in eastern Newfoundland. It was an Anglican settlement led by John Guy (died ca. 1629) from Bristol, who held a commission from James I. Significant and sustained Anglican contact with Aboriginal peoples began with this settlement, if not before. Cupers Cove followed upon two previous official Anglican settlements outside Canada: a short-lived venture on Roanoke Island in 1585, and the permanent success at Jamestown, Virginia, in 1607. In 1613, a fleet of Protestants from Jamestown sacked the French settlement at Port-Royal in an effort to assert English Protestant control of the north Atlantic coast, but the French quickly restored their position in the region.

The reference to Cupers Cove opens up a surprising vista on a deeper level of the emergence of Protestants in Canada. A lively world of fishers unfolds outside official records, overlooked by the standard religious accounts. The people of Cupers Cove survived by fishing on the Grand Banks off the coast of Newfoundland. Ever since 1497, if not before, when John Cabot and his crew reported an abundance of cod in Newfoundland waters, fishers from European Atlantic ports made the journey across the ocean once or twice a year in increasingly large numbers. They created a massive international fishery throughout the 1500s, involving Basque, French, Portuguese, and Spanish as well as English fishers. The number of vessels was staggering, with hundreds of ships and many hundreds of fishers, a vastly greater number of people than all the official expeditions put together. Time and again, the official explorers encountered European fishing vessels already anchored in the harbours they fancied themselves to be discovering. The great majority of vessels caught cod, but many hunted whales, and fur trading developed as a sideline.

The indications are that the fishers developed long-standing seasonal land stations and semi-settlements for drying their cod. They sometimes wintered over. After about 1560, French and English fishers gradually displaced the Portuguese, Spanish, and Basques, who withdrew from the Newfoundland fishery. French fishers came from the French Atlantic coast and frequented the south, west, and north coasts of Newfoundland— including the site later called Placentia—as well as the St. Lawrence River, including Tadoussac. English fishers came from the southwest of England and attached themselves to the eastern shore of Newfoundland, especially around the Avalon Peninsula, at sites later named Trinity Bay, Conception Bay, Harbour Grace, Hibb's Hole, Cupers Cove (later Cupids), Ferryland, and, above all, St. John's. Some people who are connected with those places in the early twenty-first century claim to trace their lineages to fishers in the 1500s.

The earliest fishers from any country were Catholics. But starting in the late 1550s, as the Protestantization of England proceeded under Queen Elizabeth I, the English fishers from any port would have been Protestant—formally Anglicans, and possibly including at least a few Separatist Protestants. Humphrey Gilbert met with English fisher settlers at St. John's harbour in Newfoundland in 1583 when he declared the region to be Anglican. There may have been English Protestant fishers earlier still, perhaps during the late 1540s and early 1550s when religious reform flowed thoroughly through the population of ordinary English people, sanctioned by the government of Edward VI. After about 1580, Dutch fishers appeared on the Grand Banks; by then, they would have included Reformed Protestants as well as Catholics. To this activity may be added the exploits of Peter Easton (*ca.* 1570–1620), a successful privateer under Queen Elizabeth I, and later a pirate. He frequented the eastern shore of Newfoundland from about 1600 with his crews, and established a semi-settlement at Harbour Grace in about 1610, with another one later at Ferryland. Easton and his men were Anglicans.

From the late 1550s onward, it is likely that French fishers, like French settlers, included Protestants along with Roman Catholics. By the end of the 1550s, La Rochelle on the French Atlantic coast had developed into a city with a Protestant majority, and La Rochelle was by then the largest port providing men and ships for Canadian fishing grounds. Fishers, sailors, shipmasters, and ship pilots as well as shipping merchants and suppliers were counted among the La Rochelle Protestants. There may have been Protestants on the fishing ships as early as the 1540s, about the same time as Cartier and La Rocque de Roberval's settlement at Cap Rouge.

Little is known about the life and culture of the fishers on board their ships or in their seasonal land stations and semi-settlements. Fishing voyages, like official expeditions, were Christian undertakings, whether Protestant or Roman Catholic. The fishers and mariners lived side by side with death and the unknown on a daily basis, and no atheists were among them. Catholic crews, such as the sailors with Christopher Columbus, raised the crucifix, marked the daily offices, and recited the Salve in appeal to the Virgin Mary. Protestant fishers and mariners trusted in divine providence, and, by contrast with Roman Catholics, availed themselves of simple prayers to God, songs, and stories of the Bible. We might call this fisher Protestantism, or mariner Protestantism, with leadership in religion and the common life supplied by shipmasters. The English fishers in their land stations and semi-settlements no doubt lived as Protestants, well before the official Anglican settlement at Cupers Cove in 1610. Whether English or French, official or fisher, regular Protestant interaction with Aboriginal peoples in Newfoundland may also be dated before Cupers Cove, from at least 1560–1600, if not earlier, and was of constant necessity thereafter.

English fishers knowingly played a role in the struggles over religion back home. Starting in about 1560—when the Spanish, Portuguese, and Basques, all Roman Catholic, began to withdraw from Newfoundland fishing, leaving it to the English and French—the English fishers played a strategic role in Protestant England's difficult relations with Catholic

Spain. Certainly from 1603, after the end of the war between the English and Spanish, if not earlier, Protestant English fishers found themselves trans-shipping dried cod via Protestant England to the Iberian Peninsula for Catholic consumption during meatless fast days. Within England, the economic importance of Newfoundland fishing weighed heavily in the typically Anglican move to mitigate the break with papal Catholic tradition. At issue were the 160 fish days per year. The Church of England retained the Catholic practices of eating fish instead of meat during Lent, on Wednesdays, and on Fridays or Saturdays, and the Protestant British Parliament enforced the practice with fish laws promulgated from the 1560s to the 1680s.

With the establishment of Quebec in 1608, Huguenots continued to arrive in New France. They became prominent among merchants, in the army, and in various crafts, and they dominated trade between New France and the French Atlantic regions. Some marriageable Huguenot women from La Rochelle were included among those sent over by royal authority to offset the overabundance of men in New France. Two Huguenots, Guillaume de Caen and Emery de Caen, received a monopoly in the fur trade from the French crown in 1621, and most of the crews of their ships were Huguenot. Emery served twice as Governor of New France during the 1620s and 1630s. Louis, Thomas, and David Kirke (*ca.* 1597–1654), French Protestants in the service of England, captured Tadoussac in 1628 and Quebec in 1629, and stayed in charge until the areas reverted to France by treaty in 1632. David Kirke became Proprietary Governor of Newfoundland in 1637 by appointment from the English king, Charles I (1600–49).

Nonetheless, Huguenots soon found their freedom impeded in New France, in spite of the freedom provided by the Edict of Nantes of 1598. In a move to impose the traditional form of the unity of religion and society, in 1627 the charter of the new Compagnie des Cent-Associés, reinforced by subsequent regulations, established the Roman Catholic Church as the religion of New France. At this time, French authorities began to formally block Huguenots from coming to New France. Huguenots who were already there had to hide their identities by practising as Roman Catholics, as well as marrying and having their children baptized in the Catholic Church. It became even more difficult for them when, in 1685, Louis XIV (1638–1715) abolished the freedoms conceded to Protestants by the Edict of Nantes in 1598. The authorities needed what the Huguenots contributed to New France, however, and closed their eyes to who they

Canterbury Cathedral, seat of the Archbishop of Canterbury, head of the Church of England.

really were. Many more arrived after the death of Louis XIV in 1715. As lay Protestants without publically recognized pastors and religious practice, the Huguenots gave expression to their religion within their families and through the very work they did, and some worshipped privately in house churches. After the British defeated the French on the Plains of Abraham in 1759, they instituted Protestant services of public worship, and some Huguenots resurfaced next to the British participants.

Throughout the long stretch of the seventeenth and eighteenth centuries, the English jostled with the French for control of the Atlantic regions of Canada and the St. Lawrence valley. Lands and settlements changed hands several times, and the area's religion changed as well. When the British captured Port-Royal in 1710, for instance, they converted the French-Catholic chapel into a Church of England site. The Church of England occupied the position of the established church wherever the English Crown took control. Beyond the Atlantic region and New France, the Protestant English took every opportunity to extend their presence across the vast expanse of what became Canada. The Royal Charter of the Hudson's Bay Company in 1670 gave the trading company both economic monopoly and political jurisdiction in the north and north-west, as well as the authority to provide Anglican clergy throughout the vast central region known as Rupert's Land. Like the French, the English intended to maintain the traditional structure of the unity of religion and society. On the Pacific side of the continent, Captain James Cook (1728–79) landed on Vancouver Island at Nootka Sound in 1778, and claimed the entire region for Protestant Britain.

International treaties and the laws of the British Parliament fixed the main lines of the religious map of Canada. Protestants secured domination in Canada by war, diplomacy, and legislation—even as, paradoxically, the same events guaranteed the perpetuation of, and freedom for, an immense Roman Catholic presence in Canada. The Treaty of Utrecht in 1713 gave the Protestant English control of Acadia, Newfoundland, and Rupert's Land, and the Treaty of Paris in 1763 gave them control of New France. That left the Catholic French with the islands of St. Pierre and Miquelon to safeguard their presence on the Grand Banks. In spite of persistent anti-Catholicism in Britain, the British Parliament carried through to fulfill promises made to French Catholics. The Quebec Act of 1774 legislated religious freedom for Roman Catholics in Canada, while the Constitutional Act of 1791 continued and expanded Catholic freedom. It created a division in Canada, arrayed along the St. Lawrence River between Lower Canada and Upper Canada. The first was predominately French and Catholic, centred on the city of Quebec, and the second predominately British and Protestant, positioned well to the west towards Niagara and soon centred on the new town of York, later renamed Toronto. The purpose was to mitigate the results of the British conquest of the French and enable French Catholics in Lower Canada to run their own affairs separate from Upper Canada. The contrast with the legal restrictions that at the same time were maintained against Roman Catholics in England was stark.

In 1783, the second Treaty of Paris recognized the independence of the mostly Protestant United States of America and established the southern boundary of Canada. The Nootka Conventions with Catholic Spain, completed by 1794, removed the Spanish from Vancouver Island and opened the way for a Protestant advance on the Pacific coast. The Hudson's Bay Company absorbed the North West Company in 1821, and connected with Protestant British interests on Vancouver Island. The Oregon Treaty between Britain and the United States in 1846, as well as the purchase of Alaska by the United States from Russia in 1867, determined the western boundary of Canada and put a stop to American Protestant advance as well as Russian Orthodox expansion. By means of these agreements, Protestant rule prevailed from the

Atlantic to the Pacific and from the American border to the Arctic, from sea to sea to sea. It could easily have been otherwise. Catholic Spain, Catholic Portugal, Catholic France, Orthodox Russia (by the eighteenth century), and (after 1783) the Protestant United States all contended with Protestant Britain for a position in North America. Canada could easily have emerged Roman Catholic, or even Orthodox or American Protestant.

During the 1600s, Anglican settlements expanded in number and size in Newfoundland and Nova Scotia. Anglicans in these regions were the first to be engaged in the task that eventually faced all Protestants arriving in the New World: they created formal ecclesiastical structures. In 1699, following upon generations of lay religion and domestic religion, Anglicans laid out the first Church of England parish in Canada with the founding of the Church of St. John the Baptist in St. John's, Newfoundland. The Society for the Propagation of the Gospel in Foreign Parts, the Anglican mission agency created in England in 1701, entered Newfoundland in 1703 and began to support church expansion. The oldest Anglican ecclesiastical building still in use in the twenty-first century, St. Paul's in Halifax, Nova Scotia, went up in 1750. In 1787, the Church of England established the first Anglican diocese outside of Great Britain, Ireland, and the Channel Islands, and this diocese covered all of what became eastern Canada. It is not certain when the first Aboriginal people became Protestant, but indigenous Anglicans date their formal connection with the Church of England to at least the ministry of Rev. Thomas Wood among the Mi'kmaq in Nova Scotia, beginning in 1753. Wood went on to translate the Apostle's Creed, the Lord's Prayer, and portions of the Bible into Mi'kmaq, and compile a Mi'kmaq grammar dictionary.

Huguenots and Anglicans were the first Protestants in Canada, but in the 1600s and especially in the 1700s, Protestants of other traditions also appeared. Like Huguenots and Anglicans, the appearance of new varieties of Protestants depended on many factors: settlement, international politics, war, trade, and the search for resources as well as missions, witness, and religious conversion. All of these Protestant newcomers interacted with Aboriginal peoples. In spite of strenuous efforts to the contrary, the emerging presence of diverse Protestant denominations, coupled with the continuing presence of Roman Catholics, further undermined the traditional unity of religion and society. The Protestant tendency to proliferate difference begat the multireligious society that came to characterize Canada by the year 1800, and created the prototype of the pluralist society that Canada has become in the twenty-first century.

Some early instances of Protestant diversity illustrate this point. A Welsh settlement lasted briefly at New Cambriol, Newfoundland, in 1617, with settlers connected with the Church of Wales. In 1619 Danish Lutherans, led by Jens Munk, a layperson, and Rasmus Jensen, the first Lutheran pastor in Canada, settled for a year at the mouth of the Churchill River on the shores of Hudson Bay. They claimed the land for Denmark and conducted the first Lutheran services in Canada. In 1621, William Alexander obtained a charter from James I to found a Scottish colony near Port-Royal. The settlers, who were attached to the Church of Scotland (which was by then Presbyterian), made two attempts at settlement: one in 1622–23 and another from 1629–32. They called the site Charles Fort, and the area New Scotland. When the British took control of Acadia from the French in 1713, they translated the Presbyterian name into Latin as Nova Scotia. Meanwhile, Congregationalists reached Newfoundland by the 1640s, and Quakers seem to have been at St. John's, Newfoundland, as early as 1659.

The pluralist trend continued through the 1700s. Large numbers of Scottish and Irish Presbyterians entered Nova Scotia after 1713. When the British founded Halifax in 1749, Anglicans and Presbyterians swelled the population. Nonetheless, Protestants remained heavily outnumbered by Acadian Catholics. To secure Protestant hegemony, the British promoted the immigration of peoples they called "Foreign Protestants." Between 1750 and 1752, they welcomed shiploads of Lutherans from Germany and Montbéliard, and Calvinists from Germany and Switzerland. German Calvinists organized St. Andrew's Presbyterian Church in Lunenburg in 1753, the Presbyterian congregation with the longest continuous history in Canada. The first ongoing Lutheran congregation in Canada, St. George's Lutheran Church in Halifax, began in 1756 as a chapel within St. Paul's Anglican Church. When these measures to Protestantize the region proved insufficient, the British undertook the forced removal of Acadian French Catholics, whose loyalty they doubted. From 1755 to 1762, the British expelled more than 10,000 Acadian Catholics from Canada and gave their land to Protestants, notably to Congregationalist farmers drawn by the promise of land from New England in the United States.

Diversity among Canadian Protestants multiplied elsewhere. Scottish Presbyterians served in the British army, and in 1759, when the British conquered New France, Scottish soldiers, led by the Church of Scotland's army chaplain, founded St. Andrew's Presbyterian Church in Quebec City, the first Presbyterian church in the region. On the Prairies in 1812, Thomas Douglas, Earl of Selkirk (1771–1820), set up the Red River Colony at the site that became Winnipeg. The settlement included Scottish and Irish Presbyterians, Anglicans, and Swiss Reformed. Moravians, who honoured the Czech heritage of Jan Hus, established settlements in Labrador, beginning with Hopedale in 1752 (restored in 1782), then Nain in 1771, and Okak in 1776. Most Inuit in the region became Moravians. Quaker settlements began outside Newfoundland in the 1780s and 1790s. The earliest Baptists appeared in Nova Scotia in the early 1760s, and in 1763 they formed the first Baptist church in Canada at Sackville, in what later became New Brunswick. The first Methodists can be dated to 1766 in Newfoundland, a product of the ministry of Laurence Coughlan, a Church of England cleric initially supported by the Society for the Propagation of the Gospel. The first Methodist chapel in Canada was built at Conception Bay in 1768. From the 1780s on, German Mennonites migrated from Pennsylvania into Upper Canada. During the American Revolutionary War and after American independence in 1783, many thousands of Protestants who remained loyal to the British Crown migrated into Nova Scotia and Upper Canada. Most of these Loyalists were Anglicans, but many were Baptists and Methodists. Most were white, but thousands among the Anglicans, Baptists, and Methodists were black. David Campbell, a freed slave from South Carolina, was a leading Baptist preacher among them. Thousands more Loyalists were Anglican Mohawks who migrated from New York to the Niagara region.

From the beginning, the British, like the French, had simply assumed that they would recreate in Canada the patterns they knew in their mother country. They established the Church of England as the religion of Canada. The British Crown, as Head of the Church of England, governed Canada, and the British Parliament, a Protestant body, legislated for Canada. By the Constitution Act of 1791, Parliament set aside a substantial portion of public lands, called the Clergy Reserves, as an endowment to fund "Protestant clergy," understood to mean Anglican clergy. But there were significant differences in the Canadian Protestant approach from that of the mother country. During the nineteenth century, missions and ministry among Aboriginal peoples, unknown in the home country, became a central task of virtually every Protestant denomination, and helped define what it meant to be Protestant in Canada. Roman Catholics and non-Anglican Protestants operated under a regime of religious freedom not found in Great Britain. Large numbers of immigrants built up the Anglican population throughout the nineteenth century, but they also multiplied the number and variety of other Protestants, especially Methodists and Presbyterians. Non-Anglicans asserted themselves against Anglican hegemony. The government's strategy at first was to co-opt them into the establishment. In 1828, Parliament included Church of Scotland ministers among the Protestant clergy funded by the Clergy Reserves, and the authorities added Methodist ministers in 1840. The government terminated the Clergy Reserves in 1854, formally ending the religious establishment, although the clergy already funded by the Clergy Reserves continued to receive their payments until they died.

An informal Protestant establishment carried on, however. In 1867, Nova Scotia, New Brunswick, Quebec, and Ontario joined together as provinces to create a new nation, the Confederation of Canada, under the Protestant British Crown. Quebec as a province replaced Lower Canada, which had been known as Canada East since 1841, while Ontario replaced Upper Canada, which had been called Canada West from the same date. Anglicans, Presbyterians, and Methodists, as well as Congregationalists, Baptists, and other Protestants, in spite of conflicts among themselves, conjointly asserted the Protestant identity of the new nation. Simultaneously, they accommodated the Roman Catholic identity of Quebec, formally a province, as a kind of nation within the nation. When the United States of America strenuously opposed the formation of a large British monarchy on their northern border, an Anglican politician, Leonard Tilley (1818–96), solved Britain's diplomatic problem. He pointed to Psalms 72:8 in the King James Version of the Bible: "He shall have dominion also from sea to sea." He suggested that Canada instantiated the extension of the rule of God envisioned by the Psalmist. The new nation became the Dominion of Canada, rather than the Kingdom of Canada, and Canadians proudly called their country "His Dominion." The name lasted until 1982, after which the 1 July date marked Canada Day instead of Dominion Day.

With scarcely a pause, from 1867 onward the new Canada became an empire that moved westward across the continent, mirroring the expansion of the American empire to the south and colonizing Aboriginal peoples. The westward movement linked up with an eastward movement from the Pacific coast. Protestant settlers had gravitated to Vancouver Island as early as 1843, and had stimulated the creation of two Anglican crown colonies: Vancouver Island in 1849 and British Columbia in 1858. One by one, the new nation carved out provinces and territories, from Manitoba and the Northwest Territories in 1870, to a new British Columbia in 1871, to Saskatchewan and Alberta in 1905. This imperial movement benefited from new waves of migration from eastern Canada and immigration from outside Canada. Offers of land in the Prairies by Canadian agents attracted

Danish Lutherans as well as several branches of Mennonites from Russia, Prussia, Poland, and Banat. Hutterites, originally from Central and Eastern Europe, migrated from the Dakotas and Montana in the United States. Before 1860, the Underground Railroad from the United States delivered a significant number of former black slaves to what became Ontario, including Baptists, Methodists, and Methodist Episcopalians. Many more Protestants than Roman Catholics and Orthodox groups moved onto the enlarged platform produced by the creation of Canada.

The waves of Protestant immigrants continued into the twentieth century: Lutherans from the Baltic region, Scandinavia, and Iceland; Pentecostals, Holiness, Nazarenes, the Church of God, and the Disciples of Christ from the United States; Salvation Army from Great Britain; Protestants from Greece; and Christian Reformed and Free Christian Reformed from the Netherlands. Black Anglicans came in large numbers from the Caribbean. Protestants gained significantly when Newfoundland, the original bastion of Protestant settlement, united with Canada in 1949. Protestants dominated all of Canada outside Quebec and New Brunswick. In 1967, revisions to the Immigration Act opened the way for waves of new people from outside Europe to enter Canada: they came from Asia, Africa, Oceania, Latin America, and the Caribbean. Large numbers of these immigrants were Protestants, and they redrew the Canadian Protestant landscape. Notable among them were Chinese Independents, Korean Presbyterians, Japanese Anglicans, Mar Thoma Christians from India, Presbyterians from Ghana, and Haitian, Hispanic, and Brazilian Pentecostals.

During the nineteenth and twentieth centuries, the great majority of Aboriginal peoples became Christian. Most became Protestants, brought into Christianity largely by other Aboriginal peoples. Newly created Protestant mission societies and church mission boards, parallel with several Catholic religious orders, initiated new work among Aboriginal peoples. Aboriginal converts in turn became missionaries, evangelists, teachers, and pastors in their own right. Whole Aboriginal groups, settlements, and villages became Christian. The greatest share of Aboriginal peoples became Anglicans and the next-largest share became Roman Catholics, while others became Moravians, Methodists, Presbyterians, Baptists, and, in the twentieth century, United Church and Pentecostals. In the process of becoming Christians, the Aboriginal peoples invariably changed the religion into something that was their own.

In tandem with the Canadian government, starting in the 1870s, Protestants and Roman Catholics used residential schools to deepen and perpetuate the new identity of Aboriginal peoples as Christians and Canadians. Aboriginal children lived at these schools, detached from their families and peoples, where teachers and administrators all too often induced them to give up their Aboriginal culture and assimilate into English Canadian or French Canadian culture. Many children at these schools were sexually and physically abused. It took decades before Protestant and Roman Catholic authorities acknowledged that abuses had been committed, and that their programs of assimilation had caused harm. The United Church in 1986, Anglicans in 1993, and Presbyterians in 1994 offered formal apologies to Aboriginal peoples. Simultaneously, the vast majority of Aboriginal Christians, in spite of the harm caused to them by residential schools, reaffirmed their Christian identities.

Canadian Protestants found it easy to diversify by division. They split over doctrine, power, leadership, behaviour, morals, and practices. They also divided over language, ethnicity, tradition, time of migration, and property. There were, for instance, 7 Methodist denominations in Canada before 1874, 14 Presbyterian bodies before 1875, and some 20 Mennonite denominations in the twentieth century. In the city of Toronto during the 1980s, Protestant churches with origins in Kerala, India, were affiliated with six different denominations.

Protestants also undertook considerable efforts to achieve Protestant union. Soon after Confederation in 1867, Protestants felt the need for a church to reflect the immenseness of the new nation. Methodists achieved church union in 1874 and 1884; Presbyterians did the same in 1875; Anglicans established a nationwide General Synod in 1893; Congregationalists united in 1906; local mergers beginning in 1908 produced Local Union Churches throughout Canada; and a chain of regional Baptist Conferences extended across Canada by 1911. In 1925, Methodists, Congregationalists, most Presbyterians, and the Local Union Churches merged to create the **United Church of Canada**. Their aim was to fulfill the prayer of Jesus "that they all may be one" (John 17:21) and to offer healing to the nation as what they first hoped would be the national church. By 2000, the Canadian Council of Churches and the Evangelical Fellowship of Canada, as organizations of interdenominational co-operation, contained within their combined memberships the vast majority of Canadian Protestants. Paradoxically, however, while important church unions did occur, the number of distinct Protestant denominations in Canada has continued to increase, from perhaps 50 around the year 1900 to around 460 by 2000, and a projected 725 by 2025. The Canadian experience

Rural communities of all Protestant denominations across Canada raised funds to build white woodframe and clapboard places of worship like this United Church in Economy, Nova Scotia.
PHOTO BY CANDACE IRON. REPRINTED BY PERMISSION. © CANDACE IRON.

mirrored world trends towards both increased union and increased diversity.

Protestant groups new to Canada, whatever the period, tended to replicate a common pattern. Like Anglicans before them, they at first tried to reinstall their former life in the new land, but soon had to reinvent their traditions, practices, and structures to fit the new encounters and circumstances they found in Canada. Their Protestant ways changed, sometimes imperceptibly, sometimes deliberately, because they were in Canada. They re-narrated their histories to tie themselves to their origins, and to position themselves as the natural destination of all that went before. Protestants ceased to live as a diaspora from elsewhere and became indigenous to Canada. They became Canadian Protestants.

Some of the changes made in Canada came to characterize Protestant practice. Protestants of all varieties, including Anglicans, made their churches serve as more than just places of worship on Sunday. They expanded their churches into centres of cultural, educational, artistic, social, and even economic life. They created numerous devices for financing their endeavours: enhanced giving, pew rents, financial pledges, every member canvasses, offering envelopes, book sales, strawberry festivals, and eventually substantial endowments in stocks and bonds instead of land. They took time to elaborate connecting institutions similar to what they had known at home—dioceses, presbyteries, synods, general assemblies, general synods, conferences, and yearly meetings—but even these familiar devices underwent change. Anglicans, for instance, pioneered the admission of the laity to their diocesan synods and gave them the vote. Gradually, nearly all Protestant churches removed themselves from foreign rule to become self-governing, self-financing, and self-propagating.

When there were no ministers, when ministers were in short supply, or when new needs arose, Protestants appointed lay readers, lay evangelists, and lay workers, supplemented by itinerant preachers. At first, their ministers came from the old country or the United States. Eventually most groups trained their clergy in Canada. At first, these clergy members were all men. Women ministers first appeared in the nineteenth century among Holiness groups, before there were women ministers in Europe. Starting in the 1960s, women clergy became commonplace, and in some denominations they promised to eventually outnumber men.

Protestants also constructed whole settlements, towns, and cities as Protestant locations. The rhythm of the week in these places centred on Sunday, both at home and in public life. Newcomers of any variety, like Huguenots before them, at first emphasized domestic religion and assembled in house churches. Even though men might legally have been the heads of these families, women tended to exercise immediate religious authority over the children and the home, and frequently in the house churches as well. As soon as Protestants organized public churches, their worship followed a Protestant template, and looked and sounded remarkably similar across groups (except among Quakers). For non-anglophone immigrant traditions, language invariably became a site of contention, and the shift to English in worship provided a gauge of their adaptation to Canada. Their earliest buildings tended towards simple neoclassicism in style, while their constructions from the nineteenth century to the 1960s almost universally adopted organic Gothic style, or occasionally Romanesque style, no matter what the region or denomination. After about 1960, the architecture swiftly diversified beyond echoes of previous styles throughout Canada.

All versions of Protestants constructed or cooperated with organizations for social care, care of the poor and hungry, mutual aid, moral concern, evangelism, missions, and public action. At the same time, Protestants who engaged in commerce, business, banking, and manufacturing powered the economy and led the development of Canada into one of the most prosperous countries in the world. After Confederation, politicians who were Protestants animated parties across the political spectrum with Protestant expressions of varying types of social ethics. Protestants dominated the

Conservative and Reformed parties towards the right as well as the Liberal Party in the centre, and the New Democratic Party towards the left. The Canadian health care system, praised as a model for the world for its inclusive and caring embrace of all Canadians, was the product of a movement led by Tommy Douglas (1904–86), a Baptist minister and politician. In the 1980s and 1990s, Protestants initiated public acceptance of homosexual members and, later, homosexual partnerships and marriage.

Protestants stressed the importance of education for the young. They established schools and academies, and eventually colleges, seminaries, and universities throughout Canada. Protestant or Roman Catholic origins lie behind virtually all colleges and universities founded in Canada before the 1960s, as well as some institutions founded since then. Protestant and Roman Catholic school systems quickly spread across the nation, embodying a de facto dual establishment, with both systems funded by the public treasury. The school system in Newfoundland, for instance, accommodated schools of several religious connections within the common frame of government funding and maintenance of standards: Anglican, United Church, Salvation Army, Seventh-day Adventist, and Pentecostal as well as Roman Catholic. In Quebec, Protestant schools received special standing in the provincial system.

In the late twentieth century, the vast majority of Protestant schools committed unprecedented acts of self-immolation. Protestant schools eradicated their Protestant character and history, put on what they called a secular identity, and transmuted into what became referred to as "public schools." Protestant schools in both Newfoundland and Quebec lost their standing in the 1990s as a result of provincial legislation. By contrast, Roman Catholic schools almost universally retained their identity and maintained their position in the public sphere. From about 1970, Protestants allied with Jews, Muslims, Buddhists, Sikhs, Hindus, and practitioners of Aboriginal spirituality in a campaign to move the public school system towards a pluralist model, away from a monolithic secularist model.

Movements parallel with the experience of Protestant schools occurred within Protestant universities and colleges, but mostly at earlier times, and with a twist. In Ontario, for instance, the Arts sections of the University of Trinity College (Anglican) and Victoria University (Methodist/United Church) blended into the University of Toronto as a presumably secular edifice. In the 1970s, however, the Divinity and Theological divisions of Trinity and Victoria began to receive government funding under terms that maintained their independent Protestant identities within the orbit of the University of Toronto. By contrast, Catholic universities have in most cases succeeded in maintaining their Catholic heritage. For instance, like the Protestant institutions, the University of St. Michael's College was embraced within the secular university framework, but still managed to maintain the Catholic identity of the Arts Faculty as well as the Theological Faculty.

Within the larger environment of Canada, French Protestants stand out as the exception that clarifies the rule of Protestant history. The Huguenots in New France began in ways that resemble the initial experiences of others who came later, and they might have carried these on. But the power of the state in New France overwhelmed them, and, unique in Canadian history, Protestants in French regions lost public worship, went into exile, and virtually disappeared from public life. It took new migration and new missions in the nineteenth century to produce a new French Protestant presence in Quebec. A French Reformed denomination did not appear until the 1980s. *L'église réformée du Québec,* inaugurated in 1988, rediscovered the history of the earliest Huguenots in New France, and deliberately reinterpreted French Protestant history in Canada in order to connect the new denomination with those Huguenot beginnings. Their narrative also located the beginning of French Protestantism in Europe—not with Luther in Germany in 1517, or Calvin in Geneva in 1536, but with Jacques Lefevre d'Etaples in Paris in 1512. In the early twenty-first century, francophone Pentecostals from Haiti, Africa, and Oceania became the ones to swell the ranks of French Protestants in Quebec, rather than the French Reformed.

The Canadian census of 1871, the first conducted after the founding of the Dominion of Canada in 1867, revealed that Protestants outnumbered Roman Catholics 57 per cent to 41 per cent. Nationally, the four largest Protestants groups were, in order, Methodists, Presbyterians, Anglicans, and Baptists. Protestants remained the national majority in Canada during the census of 1961. Thereafter the Protestant numbers went into free fall as the population of Canada ballooned. The 2001 census revealed a radically altered national picture: driven chiefly by large-scale immigration from historically Roman Catholic regions—Italy, Portugal, Poland, the Philippines, Latin America, Haiti, Vietnam, and others—Roman Catholics retained about 43 per cent of the population nationally, while Protestants dropped to about 32 per cent. This figure represented the combined share of those listed in the census as "Protestants" and those listed as "Christians, not included elsewhere," virtually all of whom were Protestants.

It is also significant that the people claiming to follow "no religion" in the 2001 census amounted to about 16 per cent. Many of these were Chinese immigrants who had arrived since the 1960s, and for whom the census category "religion" made no sense, but who practiced what others regarded as religions, including Chinese popular religion, Buddhism, Taoism, Confucianism, and Falun Gong. But many others claiming "no religion" may be understood as former Protestants. These ex-Protestants were of two kinds. One kind, when asked by pollsters, said they were "spiritual" and "believe in God," but were "not religious," while another kind claimed they were agnostic, atheist, humanist, or "secular," and "not religious." Both sets had surely drifted from their Protestant heritage, but they nonetheless retained Protestant characteristics in their ethic, culture, memory, and habit, and in the wider world continued to react like Protestants. Understood in this way, the combination of Protestants and Protestant-like ex-Protestants outnumbered all religions nationally except Roman Catholics, and approached the Roman Catholic percentage.

The 2001 census offered a rather different picture at close range. The ensemble of Protestants outnumbered all other groups in seven provinces and territories, all outside the original New France: Newfoundland, Nova Scotia, Ontario, Manitoba, Saskatchewan, Alberta, and Nunavut. In British Columbia and the Northwest Territories, Protestants and the ex-Protestants portion of the "no religionists" still predominated. Viewed at still closer range, various groups were especially noticeable in certain regions: Baptists in the Maritime provinces; Mennonites and Lutherans in the three Prairie provinces; Anglicans in the three northern territories as well as in Newfoundland, Nova Scotia, and Ontario; Presbyterians in Prince Edward Island; Salvation Army in Newfoundland; and Pentecostals in the northern territories. In Quebec, the effects of the near annihilation of French Protestants by New France continued to be felt, with Protestants showing a very small minority. The United Church appeared significantly distributed across more regions than any other Protestant body. Anglicans were the second-most widely distributed, while Independents and Pentecostals noticeably increased their numbers and distribution throughout Canada. Remarkably, in other words, as of the 2001 census, the legacy of Protestant and Roman Catholic beginnings in Canada, and the relationships achieved early on in each region throughout Canada, still generally defined the look of Canada's religious map.

Beginning in the 1960s, and continuing into the twenty-first century, Canadian Protestants engaged in the process of remaking themselves. It was at this time that they initiated the greatest changes in Protestant history since the sixteenth century. The people who disliked these changes and reminded Protestants of their heritage and traditions were made to appear hopelessly bigoted and reactionary. Women moved into greater prominence, with significant numbers of women ordained as clergy and appointed to governing bodies of Protestant churches. Congregations became more multi-ethnic and multicultural. Worship and music changed as most traditions created new worship styles, new worship books, new liturgies, new hymnals, and new music. New creeds and new statements of faith appeared in most traditions, and often across traditions. New church buildings broke with Gothic, Romanesque, and Classical idioms to create original architecture expressive of new understandings of community and worship. Laypeople became more engaged in leading worship, less passive, more participatory, and less like an audience. Social manners in church became informal, casual clothes more acceptable, and social classes more confused—or, perhaps, more people became bourgeois.

Paradoxically, at the same time, the clergy across traditions adopted high ecclesiastical dress that distanced them from their congregations. Preaching gave way to more frequent celebration of the Eucharist in many traditions. Protestants found new ways to infuse their lives with spirituality, contemplation, and mysticism. Social justice and the environment moved to the top of most Protestant agendas. Sexual issues pushed out theological questions as Protestants across the theological spectrum contested gender roles, sexual freedom, divorce, abortion, sexual harassment, abuse of Aboriginal children in residential schools, homosexuality, same-sex marriage, and clergy and bishops in same-sex partnerships. Venues for education multiplied. Pedagogy became less centred on authority. Protestants emerged predominant among religious groups using public media, including newsprint, radio, television, and the Internet. Differences within each denomination became more significant than differences between denominations. People with similar leanings within different denominations felt close to each other. Cross-denominational identities trumped denominational identities; for example, charismatic, spiritual, liturgical, evangelical, Catholic, fundamentalist, radical, liberal, conservative, feminist, progressive, liberationist, green, and postmodern.

Most remarkably, the great bulk of Protestants lost their memory of what had made them Protestant in the first place. New Independent churches showed little interest in their Protestant roots. Historic Protestants began to find the Roman Pope appealing. Pope John Paul II (1920–2005;

reigned 1978–2005) and Mother Teresa (1910–97) became religious models for Protestants. Ecumenical Protestant *rapprochement* with Roman Catholics became universal. Conservative Protestants began to count Roman Catholics as allies in theology and morality, especially on sexual issues. Anglicans, the United Church, Presbyterians, and even Baptists adopted worship styles noticeably similar to Roman Catholics. The historic Protestants entered into formal dialogue with Roman Catholics, and so did Pentecostals. In 1997, the Canadian Council of Churches, the stronghold of Protestants and Orthodox Churches, enrolled the Canadian Conference of Catholic Bishops among its members, an act exceptional on the world scale.

In the aggregate, beginning in the 1960s, Canadian society came to lose its predominantly Protestant hue. Some present indications suggest that Canada might become a secular society in which the traditional religions would wither away. The number of people claiming "no religion" would become an unstoppable force, and allegiance to this-worldly affairs and humanity-as-such, what might be called "secular religion," would govern the common life. However, other markers suggest that what Canada has transformed into is not a secular society, but a multireligious and pluralist society. Traditional religions have not collapsed; Roman Catholics have maintained their strength; and devotees of other world religions have increased in number and impact. Protestants have not simply declined, but have changed their configuration, and many of the "no religionists" have turned out to be ex-Protestants still attached to religion after all.

Strengthened by their diversity, and no longer hegemonic, Protestants continue to occupy their places in Canada next to a multitude of other religious groups, and seek new ways to infuse the whole of their lives with the teachings of Jesus Christ. Almost anywhere in Canada—whether in megalopolitan Toronto, post-rural, semi-suburban Stony Plain, Alberta, or Iqaluit near the Arctic Circle—Protestants continue to offer an ever-modifying selection of church communities motivated to serve the spiritual, moral, and civic well-being of Canadians in the pluralist society that Canada has become.

RECENT TRENDS IN THE PROTESTANT COMMUNITY

A close look at two local Protestant communities in Canada serves well to indicate both the variety of Protestant experience and significant recent trends among Protestants in the twentieth century. St. James' Cathedral, on King Street at Church Street in Toronto, Ontario, is an Anglican community that dates back to 1793. First Baptist Church, on Huron Street at D'Arcy Street in Toronto, is a Baptist community that originated in the 1820s. The heritage of St. James arises directly from the Protestant reformation of the sixteenth century in England, while the heritage of First Baptist comes from the new reformation in the seventeenth century in England that produced new Protestants apart from the Church of England. These two communities exemplify two ways of being Protestant over the long term. They have coexisted within Toronto for all these many generations with little communication between them. They could hardly seem more different. Yet, as Protestants, they have a surprising amount in common.

St. James' Cathedral traces its beginning to the moment in 1793 when residents gathered for the first-known service of public worship in the newly founded town of York in Upper Canada. York became Toronto in 1834, while Upper Canada became Canada West in 1841 and then Ontario in 1867. The service was Morning Prayer, and it was conducted by a lay British soldier using the Anglican Book of Common Prayer as revised in 1662. After their defeat in the American Revolution in 1781, and the creation of Upper Canada in 1791, the British established York as a Protestant city and the capital of the new region within their still-expanding overseas empire. The people were British, Protestant, and white. They were immigrants from the mother country, migrants from the Maritimes and Lower Canada, and Loyalist refugees from the United States. People from all ranks of society gathered for regular services of public worship led by laypeople. They met in homes and public buildings. As a matter of course, the Church of England functioned as the religion of Upper Canada, and Protestant convictions, morals, and habits shaped the government, commerce, family, and social life. The Church of England remained strongly attached to the sixteenth-century Protestant movement in England through the Book of Common Prayer instead of the Mass, and the Archbishop of Canterbury and the English Crown instead of the Pope.

In 1797, the civic authorities established the Parish of St. James at York, lodged within the Diocese of Quebec, and designated six acres of Crown land in the centre of town for parish use. The first permanent cleric arrived in 1800, and the first church building—a simple, wooden, neo-classical structure—opened on King Street at the corner of Church Street in 1807. The arrival of John Strachan (1778–1867) in 1812 as the church's second cleric gave St. James and the future Toronto a powerful figure in church and society. With the creation of the Diocese of Toronto in 1839, hived off from the Diocese of Quebec, Strachan became the first Bishop of Toronto and St. James became the pro-cathedral. Parishioners built three further church buildings on the same site, in each case after fire destroyed the previous one. The new buildings of 1833 and 1839, both in stone, continued the neo-classical tradition, while for the building of 1853 they chose brick and stone and followed the new trend to Gothic.

The First Baptist Church of Toronto finds its origins among a population of runaway black slaves who fled the United States for the legal freedom of British soil in Upper Canada after the War of 1812 (1812–15). Their founding story tells of a growing number of blacks who met in homes or outdoors for worship led by laypeople. They identified with each other as a suffering people, and valued their community as a caring family and source of spiritual strength. They practised their Baptist religion, which they had brought from the United States. As Baptists, they stressed religious conversion, baptism of adult believers, voluntary assembly in autonomous congregations, and independence from the state. These Baptist traits starkly distinguished them from Anglicans. As Baptists, they celebrated their roots in a seventeenth-century Protestant movement in England that produced large numbers of local congregations opposed to the Pope, as well as to the Church of England.

The particulars of their early history are difficult to ascertain, since runaway black slaves left fewer written records than white Anglican rulers. Over the years, First Baptist has published three different dates of their origin. All three dates continue to show up in various venues. A strong oral tradition tells of the founding of the church in 1826, when Washington Christian (*ca.* 1776–1850), an energetic preacher, became the first pastor. Christian, an ex-slave, was ordained by the Abyssinian Baptist Church in Harlem, New York City. After operating for a year as a house church under his leadership, the First Baptist congregation moved into rented space at St. George's Masonic Lodge. The second founding date, published for many years, is 1834, the year the congregation began to worship in a rented building on March Street, later known as Lombard Street, south of Richmond Street. The congregation swelled during the 1830s, drawing on new waves of ex-slaves from the United States via the Underground Railroad, and white Baptist immigrants from Great Britain and the United States. An American visitor to the church on March Street in 1837 observed that the congregation included an equal number of blacks and whites under the ministry of a black pastor.

The third founding date that is sometimes cited for First Baptist Church is 1841. In that year, the congregation received a gift of land from a sympathetic white British landowner and was able to build a church in the new Gothic style on Queen Street, near the corner of Victoria Street. The area was considered removed from the epicentre of Toronto around St. James' Cathedral, barely six streets away. The white members of the congregation soon switched to a new Baptist church that had opened on Bond Street, and First Baptist resumed life as a black congregation. It went by the name First Coloured Calvinistic Baptist Church, and sometimes Queen Street Coloured Baptist Church. During the 1850s, enlarged by a further influx of fugitive slaves, the church split over disagreements about property and ministry. For over a decade, a second black Baptist congregation met on Teraulay Street, north of Queen Street (later co-opted by an extension of Bay Street).

In the twenty-first century, St. James and First Baptist vividly maintain the marks and memories of their origins. St. James continues to be faithful to the Anglican tradition as both a thriving downtown parish and the esteemed cathedral of the largest diocese in Canada. The church relishes its position as the first church of any kind in Toronto, and thinks of itself as the mother church of the diocese. It actively pursues its role as a great civic institution within the city, the province, and the country, and has hosted Queen Elizabeth II, the Queen Mother, Prince Charles and Princess Diana, and other members of the royal family when they have visited Toronto.

St. James lost its standing as pro-cathedral in 1883, when the diocese established St. Albans Cathedral outside the town centre. When that project eventually failed, St. James resumed its dual status as parish and pro-cathedral in 1935. From that moment on, the people and clergy deliberately embellished the building, the music, and the worship. Before long, they and everyone else called St. James simply "the Cathedral, the beautiful downtown Cathedral." The depopulation of the historic city centre in the twentieth century left the church walled in by warehouses, manufacturing buildings, and dilapidated housing. Decades of tedious manoeuvreing got the surrounding land cleared and converted into St. James Park by 1980. Since then, the Cathedral, with its majestic presence and imposing spire, has stood visually stunning amid land that matches the grant from the Crown 200 years earlier. Paradoxically, St. James enjoys a more prominent position and reputation in the city and region in the twenty-first century than at any time since the earliest days of York, and it has a significant national and international reputation.

Whites with British names still predominate on St. James' parish list in the early twenty-first century, but immigrants from other cultures are evident, including blacks from the British Caribbean. In social terms, St. James parishioners have from the beginning displayed a traditional Anglican distribution of people across the ranks of society, governed by wealthy members of the ruling class. Since the late twentieth century, the parishioners have presented the solid look of the middle and upper-middle classes, weighted towards banking, management, and commerce. Single people of all ages form the majority; children are few; many are retired; and women outnumber men. Most parishioners live far from the church, dispersed throughout the city and the suburbs. The number living in the neighbourhoods nearby is markedly increasing as the downtown becomes repopulated. In 2000, Sunday attendance ran about 550, well below the figure of 1,200 common before 1920. The new figure indicates less a simple decline than a reconfiguration of the services of worship and other activities within the total ministry of the cathedral. The combination of regular services, special services, parish groups, concerts, lectures, diocesan events, public events, lunch programs for homeless people, health care, and tours mounted by the Cathedral pushed the number who use the premises annually to roughly 60,000, by far the highest number of any church in the diocese, and not very different from the totals in 1920. St. James, as part of the Anglican Church of Canada, participates in an enormous network of other churches, including the global Anglican Communion, the Canadian Council of Churches, and the World Council of Churches; and bilateral dialogues with other traditions, including the Roman Catholic Church.

Likewise, First Baptist remains devoted to its original principles, and the adherence to Baptist distinctives has continued unchanged over the generations. The church delights in its history as the mother church of Baptists in the city, and as a black church. The people tell and retell their founding story derived from the connection with the Underground Railway, a rousing tale of liberation from suffering and pilgrimage from slavery to the Promised Land. The church occupies a position of eminence as the oldest continuing black institution in the city, and enjoys an immense reputation in the province and across Canada. As Toronto expanded, the congregation followed westward shifts in the black population away from the historic centre. From the first building in 1841 at Queen and Victoria Streets, the church moved west to a new Gothic-style building on University Avenue at Edward Street, completed in 1905. The name became University Avenue Baptist Church. Here the congregation began the tradition of claiming 1826 as the founding date, instead of the usual 1841 or 1834.

By the early 1940s, the name First Baptist Church took hold, and the primacy of the church in Toronto Baptist history received recognition. After 50 years on University Avenue, the congregation sold the property to Shell Oil Company (who demolished the church) and in 1955 moved west again to the new edge of central Toronto. They built a fine red-brick church at 101 Huron Street, on the corner of Huron Street and D'Arcy Street, moderate in size and subdued Gothic in style. The architecture reflected a Protestant template widely used in the suburbs in the 1950s. The new site, in the neighbourhood of Dundas Street and Spadina Avenue, sat in the middle of the greatest concentration of blacks in the city at the time. It was also a major Jewish area. Very soon, in the 1960s, both blacks and Jews moved away, replaced by Chinese. The black Baptists soon found themselves on a side street in the middle of the largest Chinatown in Eastern Canada, far from the new areas of black concentration farther north, and invisible to the rest of the city.

The First Baptist congregation remains almost entirely black in the early twenty-first century. Over the generations, the predominance of fugitive slaves gave way to several waves of blacks from Nova Scotia who traced their heritage to the black Loyalists from the 1780s. People of Nova Scotian heritage make up 80 per cent of the congregation. The remaining members are newer immigrants from various Caribbean nations, the United States, and several African countries, as well as a few whites, Chinese, and others. In 2000, the baptized membership numbered about 140, and Sunday attendance ranged from 125 to 150. The figure is lower than it was in the peak period from the 1960s to the early 1990s, but as large as or larger than most other periods since 1826. In social terms, most of the people live well up the social ladder among the broad middle classes, long removed from the poverty of ex-slavery in the early years, and with fewer links to the occupations of manual labour, railroad work, domestic service, and the trades common in the twentieth century before the 1960s. Most members are married; there are few families with young children; and women outnumber men. They live scattered across Toronto and the suburbs, and almost no one lives near the church.

Until 1966, First Baptist maintained membership in the Amherstburg Regular Missionary Baptist Association—pronounced "Amusburg"—an alliance of black Baptist congregations in Ontario. Simultaneously, since 1929, the church has belonged to the white-dominated, but multi-ethnic Convention of Baptists of Ontario and Quebec. While vigorously preserving its local autonomy, the church connects via the Convention to national and global Christianity, including Canadian Baptist Ministries, the Baptist World Alliance, the Canadian Council of Churches, the World Council of Churches, and various bilateral ecumenical relationships including the Baptist-Roman Catholic dialogue, and, unlike St. James, the Evangelical Fellowship of Canada. Members of First Baptist circulate locally through events and groups in other churches nearby. These include the black congregation of the British Methodist Episcopal Church, with whom First Baptist has had a relationship since the mid-nineteenth century, and St. George's Anglican Church, which for many years included a large black minority and sometimes a gospel choir.

Snapshots of the two churches, taken in the early twenty-first century, reveal two experiences of what it is like to be a Protestant church. Things surely change right after the snapshots are taken, just as they were changing right up to that one moment in time. The two churches have turned out to be both remarkably different and remarkably similar. The snapshot of First Baptist finds that the focal point of the week is the 11:00 a.m. service of worship on Sunday morning. It is the only service available on Sunday. The church dropped the evening or late afternoon Sunday service in the 1970s. The Evening Prayer Service meets on Wednesdays at 7 p.m., the only weekday service. To reach their church, congregants must pass through the busy streets of Chinatown, fully open for business on Sunday mornings, reflecting the "no religion" report of many Chinese. Members enter from Huron Street through a side door that leads to the back of the congregation. Male and female ushers welcome them and hand out the church bulletin containing the order of service, the announcements, and some news. People stand at the back or sit in the pews, chatting and laughing with each other, and they all know each other. The people are well-dressed, the men in suits and the women in dresses, with many women wearing hats.

The worship space of First Baptist is rectangular, with wooden pews from the 1950s arranged in rows on either side of the centre aisle facing the platform in front. The pulpit rises high up on the front left, large enough for the pastor to move about while preaching, and it holds the open Bible. A small lectern stands on the platform at the right, used for announcements and special music. The choir sits on either side at the back of the platform. An electronic organ is hidden behind the choir to the right. A smaller electronic organ sits on the floor to the right, in front of the pews. The electric guitarist sits in a chair on the floor, at the front and to the left. At the far front of the church, in a recessed space behind the platform, is the baptismal pool. It is the focal point of the interior. The pool is large, with room for the pastor to stand with an adult believer and thrust the believer backward, fully robed, under the water in baptism. The walls of the church are bare. The glass in the Gothicized windows is lightly coloured and translucent.

Breaking this Protestant simplicity are three paintings. On the side wall at the back, opposite the entry, hangs *Ascension of the Black Christ*, a huge oil painting, arresting in its theme and magnificent in its depiction, signed by Hector Whistler (1905–76) and dated 1954. It represents Jesus Christ ascending into heaven above the front of a church, praised by the faithful reaching after Him from a long, external staircase, and awaited by the angels. Jesus is black, His hair is short, and the people and angels are black. A second oil painting is fastened high on the front wall above the platform. The artist, J. Loxton Rawbon (1855–1942), gave it to the congregation in 1934. Jesus is praying in Gethsemane before His betrayal to the authorities who crucified Him. This Jesus is white and His hair is long.

A detail from Hector Whistler's painting *Ascension of the Black Christ* (1954), which hangs opposite the main entrance to First Baptist Church of Toronto. PHOTO BY CANDACE IRON. REPRINTED BY PERMISSION OF THE FIRST BAPTIST CHURCH OF TORONTO. © CANDACE IRON/FIRST BAPTIST CHURCH OF TORONTO.

He wears a purple robe, His face serene, His image idealized, the event romanticized. A third painting, occupying the centre of attention, is a mural on the recessed wall of the baptismal pool. The scene was not the Jordan River in the Holy Land where Jesus received baptism, but a deep blue lake in an evergreen forest on the Canadian Shield in Ontario. The water in the lake looks cold. Baptisms here are Canadian. There are no people in the mural; the setting awaits the next believer's baptism.

The snapshot of St. James reveals four services to choose from on Sunday—three services of Eucharist in the morning and a Choral Evensong in the afternoon. Weekdays offer four services daily, Monday to Friday— two Eucharists, Morning Prayer, and Evening Prayer. A Eucharist is the sole service on Saturday. The 11:00 a.m. Eucharist on Sunday is the centrepiece; of all these services it is the best attended, the most looked after, and the most protected. Parishioners enter at the back, either from King Street under the spire or from Church Street into a narthex. The neighbourhood is nearly empty, the businesses being closed on Sunday mornings. The bells in the tower ring and the huge clock in the tower strikes the hour. Male and female ushers greet people at the door, hand them a portfolio of papers containing the service bulletin, the weekly announcements and news, and notices of concerts and diocesan events. The ushers then lead them to the nineteenth-century pews aligned in rows facing front around a centre aisle, and shut the pew doors behind them. The church is moderately full and no one talks. The atmosphere is serious. The space is huge. The ceiling is very high. Most people are well dressed, but no women wear hats, and some people wear casual clothes.

The large, royal arms of Queen Victoria, mounted above the centre aisle at the back, dominate the interior space. There are no paintings or murals as such in the church, but sculptures and bas reliefs of wood and stone abound. An icon, small in size, can be found in a side chapel. The lower walls are plain, but the tall windows on the upper walls along both sides of the nave and around the apse in front hold a stunning array of stained glass from the late nineteenth and early twentieth centuries. They depict the story behind St. James' Cathedral, a straight line drawn from the beginnings of the Christian Church at Pentecost, through the sixteenth-century Reformation in England, to the arrival of the British in Canada, and culminating in the Cathedral under Bishop Strachan.

On a sunny morning, the interior colours of St. James are splendid. Tattered military flags are positioned on the sidewalls, signalling the Cathedral's historic connections with the British Empire. Brass and stone plaques here and there remember prominent parishioners or those killed in the war. Two front-side chapels and one elaborate chapel at the back add complexity. A pulpit large enough for the preacher to stand in rises up high on the left at the front, and a large, brass eagle lectern holding the open Bible stands on a raised level at the right. A simple cross is mounted on the wall behind the pulpit. The front opens into an enormous chancel, with oak choir pews positioned on each side at a right angle to the parishioners. A magnificent pipe organ console is visible at the back left of the chancel. A massive array of organ pipes is mounted high on the wall at the back of the nave above the entry, and other pipes are mounted on both sides near the front. The focal point of the front is the long, stone altar at the back of the chancel. A very long, white, linen covering runs the length of the altar, and the dressings of the altar change colour with the liturgical seasons. The throne of the Bishop of Toronto sits to the left of the altar. The whole of the front is marked off from the people by a low, wide stairway and stone railing. Parishioners have ample room to walk forward and mount the steps during the Eucharist.

The arrangement and atmosphere of First Baptist and St. James match the way their people worship. Both maintain highly ordered services that control spontaneity. The 11:00 a.m. service is the centrepiece at both churches. Both are one and a half hours long, and the difference in the content of these services displays their difference in style, theology, liturgy, and emphasis. St. James follows one of the approved Anglican worship books, either the revised Canadian Book of Common Prayer from 1962 or the Canadian Book of Alternative Services from 1985. The Common English Lectionary provides a three-year cycle of scripture readings, with four passages from the Bible designated for each Sunday. The scripture readings as well as the prayers, sermon, and music reflect the preset focus of the day. By contrast, First Baptist glories in freedom of worship. The pastor and a worship committee create the service of worship Sunday by Sunday, working a few weeks ahead, selecting a theme for the day, with Bible readings, hymns, and a sermon topic to fit. The weekly services nonetheless repeat a familiar pattern.

Both churches continue to use their high pulpits at the 11:00 a.m. service, but they differ over the role of preaching. At First Baptist, the sermon remains central. The sermon is substantial, no less than 30 minutes long, not scripted, and delivered as a piece of oratory by the pastor. It includes biblical exposition, meaningful stories, some humour, and devotional reflection. The theology is conservative, even Evangelical, although some members are uncomfortable with that term, calling it sectarian. At St. James, the sermon was once central and long, but since the 1950s the Eucharist has gradually displaced the sermon as the focal point and expanded to fill the time available. The sermon has shrunk to ten minutes of well-written and well-read text, with several preachers taking turns. The message tends towards the theologically liberal, while the liturgy remains tenaciously conservative. The two churches have diverged over prayer as well. At First Baptist, a long, extemporized prayer spoken oratorically by the pastor remains crucial. At St. James, laypeople offer the prayer, known as intercessions, following the pattern of the prayer book, and the prayer is scripted, short, and read aloud by different people on a rota.

Music is significant at the 11:00 a.m. service in both churches. The people sing and so do their choirs. St. James continues to use the Canadian Anglican hymnbook of 1938 and looks unfavourably on new hymns. The clergy chant the words of the Eucharist, and the organ dominates. For more than a century, the 11:00 a.m. service at St. James featured the Cathedral Choir of Men and Boys, founded in 1898 to replace the original choir of women and men. Long-standing political and theological pressure finally forced the Cathedral to create three other choirs involving women, as well as, for a while in 2000, a choir of girls. In the early twenty-first century the choir of men and boys gave way to a choir of men and women composed entirely of professional singers. The choirs stress excellence and sing a repertoire of music ranging from the earliest available music of the church to new, classical-genre compositions. The choir processes in measured, solemn steps, followed by the clergy. First Baptist previously used the same formal Canadian Baptist hymnal of 1936 that is found in white Baptist churches, but has now switched to an informal, non-denominational American book of hymns and gospel songs, supplemented by new gospel choruses introduced in the service bulletin. The music has become more rhythmic, and the floor organ and electric guitar have added beat and liveliness. The church features a 15-minute Praise Time just before the 11:00 a.m. service. The church's three choirs all include women and men. The Senior Choir, previously the Morning Choir, was established in 1920, and concentrates on anthems. The Singing Disciples use the church as a base for spreading gospel music throughout the region. Voices of Joy, at first a youth choir, later became a gospel choir for all ages. When these last two choirs process and sing, they sway, even dance, and raise and move their arms in praise to God in a style that draws on American black gospel culture.

Each church places one of the two sacred rituals recognized by Protestants at the centre of its identity. For the Anglicans they are two sacraments; for the Baptists, two ordinances. Baptism reigns at First Baptist, while the Eucharist is central at St. James. The baptismal pool at First Baptist occupies the central position precisely because the insistence on the baptism of adults by immersion and the rejection of the baptism of infants so largely defines the Baptist identity. Mandatory adult baptism sets them apart from the Anglicans at St. James, as well as from Roman Catholics, Orthodox groups, and most other Protestants. At St. James, baptism of newborns is the norm, with adult baptism practised for new converts. At First Baptist, the rule is adult conversion, adult belief, adult baptism, and adult membership. Each person must individually make a public statement of commitment to Christ in front of the pastor, deacons, and congregation, and then follow Christ through the waters of baptism to seal their union with Christ and receive membership in the church. At St. James, there is a Parish list instead of formal membership, and any baptized person gets on the Parish list simply by signing up, no questions asked.

At St. James, the communion table was the focal point of the interior starting from the very beginning when the building opened in 1853. Holy Communion occurred only once a month, while morning worship without communion was the primary Sunday service. After the Catholic-influenced liturgical movement arrived in Toronto in the 1950s, the Eucharist steadily took over until it became the norm, celebrated every Sunday and every day of the week. The communion table made of wood became an altar made of stone, which was huge and received colourful dressings. Before the 1960s, the altar at St. James stood against the wall; thus, during the Eucharist, the clergy faced the altar with their backs to the people, approaching Almighty God on their behalf. After the 1960s, they pulled the altar slightly away from the wall, moved around to the other side, and faced the gathered community, approaching God together with the people. The behaviour of the people changed accordingly. Before the end of the 1950s, most people coming to worship on a Sunday that offered Holy Communion left before communion began, in keeping with the teaching that no one should receive the bread and wine unworthily. But since about 1960, virtually everyone moves forward as a group to receive communion, even though their saintliness is no greater than that of previous parishioners. Parishioners kneel at the railing in front of the altar, receive a flat, white wafer of unleavened bread, and drink a sip of wine from a silver chalice. At First Baptist, the communion is an individual act and infrequent. The people remain in the pews. Each person first takes a tiny cube of white bread from a tray passed by an usher, and then takes a tiny, individual plastic cup of grape juice from another tray. Only baptized adult members of the church receive, hence no children participate. From the 1980s, children at St. James began to receive the bread and wine along with adults, in recognition of their union with the body of Christ by virtue of their baptism, and without the formal preparation or confirmation that used to be required.

The people of the two churches give different reasons when they explain why they go to their church instead of any other. For the people of First Baptist, the church is family, and the family is historically black, even when some members are not. They call each other Sister and Brother. A significant number of people have remained deeply loyal members for a very long time and know the stories of one another's lives. They freely give money to support the church, whose very existence depends on their regular, sacrificial, voluntary giving; First Baptist receives no endowment. As church members, they lunch together at the church each Sunday after morning worship. They look after each other in times of sickness or mourning. They support each other financially when a need is known. Beginning in 1995, they turned outward as a family and, in co-operation with the Chinese Gospel Church a block away, began to feed, clothe, and give shelter to people in the downtown who were homeless and hungry. They maintain a high rate of participation in a network of church organizations and committees during the week. The oldest of these associations is the Tolliver Missionary Circle, the principal group for women members of the congregation, founded in 1926 to support missions and ministry. The Wednesday Evening Prayer Service is a time to give testimonies of the working of God in their lives and a time to pray for each other and the needs of the world. They desire to protect family values, and speak out against homosexual practices and homosexual marriage. Over the generations, they have steadily become more politically and socially conservative.

Many people have also come to St. James for a very long time. There is also a large network of groups meeting throughout the week, of which the most significant is also the chief women's organization, the York Group, successor to the Women's Auxiliary founded in the 1880s. Indeed, the women of St. James have over the generations maintained what is virtually a church within the church. Many parishioners know each other well. Many pushed the Cathedral to make the transition from the politically conservative practice of *noblesse oblige* in relation to "those less fortunate than ourselves" to the more caring and politically progressive motivation of social justice for the poor. The new ethic characterizes the Cathedral's ministry to the people rendered systemically homeless and hungry by Canadian society. It also drives the Cathedral's public acceptance of gays and lesbians within its congregations and groups, and its newer ministries of health and wellness. Yet, in contrast with First Baptist, especially since the age of old wealth has passed away, the draw of St. James is not family and mutual support. St. James captivates the vast majority of participants, including those animated by social justice, by virtue of its character as a cathedral. They love the Cathedral because of the building, music, and liturgy, which reveal the beauty of holiness and evoke feelings of awe. A large portion of people who frequent St. James enjoy a style of church attendance characterized by anonymity; they slip into the service and slip out again. Many parishioners support St. James generously with their money, but the great majority of annual income comes from the endowment. The Cathedral maintains its operations largely through the mechanism of a multimillion-dollar portfolio of investments in stocks and bonds bequeathed by the wealthy of former times. Superficially, St. James can appear more like a religious corporation with a large staff than a caring religious community.

AFTERWORD

The two communities of St. James and First Baptist indicate where to look in order to glimpse the future of Protestants in Canada. The pastor and congregation of First Baptist embrace a mission statement that commits them to becoming even more intentionally a gospel people, more deeply rooted in the biblical story. They aim to fully be a community of Christ's disciples faithful to God, to each other, and to the world. As a move in this direction, several motivated members committed themselves to further Bible training in an evening diploma program at Tyndale College and Seminary, a conservative Evangelical institution in Toronto. The church has less to do with McMaster Divinity College in Hamilton, Ontario, the regional Baptist seminary historically favoured by the Baptist Convention. For a while, the church's website carried devotional reflections by a long-standing member of the congregation who was an early participant in the training program. The pastor preaches sermons encouraging a deeper spiritual life, a personal relationship with Jesus Christ, and richer knowledge of the Bible.

The people of First Baptist are aware that being black and being family are not synonymous with being Christ's disciples. Yet, the experience of black slavery and black liberation, the pilgrimage to the Promised Land, and the record of the church as the source of spiritual guidance still give the church its story, even for members whose story is different. Every year the people celebrate the anniversary of their beginning, and over the years they have greatly heightened the significance of their black inheritance. They have celebrated an annual black history event since the 1980s, and during the church's 175th anniversary in 2001 they created the Black Heritage Room, prominently located in the overflow alcove at the front-left of the church. The people of First Baptist have begun to wonder whether another move would be beneficial, perhaps leaving the centre of Toronto for one of five or six new areas of black concentration farther west and north. But they have also considered renewing the church as a multicultural Baptist congregation devoted to Jesus Christ in downtown Toronto, actively engaged in evangelizing the immediate neighbourhood. They wonder whether disconnecting themselves from their black story risks the loss of their identity and whether they can successfully navigate the transmission to a new story that incorporates the old with the new.

St. James' Cathedral had found its future mission by the 1980s. It was then that the people and the clergy completed the long process of transforming the church into a cathedral of a certain kind, one marked by the beauty and excellence of the building, liturgy, and music. St. James achieved a secure identity, a stable source of parishioners, and a significant endowment. The present challenge is to maintain the traditional appeal of the beauty and excellence of the Cathedral's building, liturgy, and music in an epoch when most Anglicans have moved on to other concerns. Anglicans in Canada have generated new liturgies, new music, new structures, new theology, new social ethics, and new missions. The wider Canadian world has given greater weight to spirituality, community, justice, and adaptation, expressed in multicultural modes. St. James offers to link up with these new directions by offering a community of exploration, reconciliation, pilgrimage, dialogue, and social action. By 2001, an uproar from the wider citizenry of Toronto blocked corporate-style plans to erect a condominium tower on cathedral land behind the apse of historic St. James. People not attached to the Cathedral objected that the gigantic tower would diminish the Cathedral's magnificence, desecrate an ancient cemetery, misuse heritage land, destroy the historic Parish House, and undermine the Cathedral's ministry. By 2009, St. James made a U-turn, building instead on a parking lot a low-rise, multimillion dollar, open, glass Cathedral Centre designed to renew and extend the heritage Parish House and enhance the reach of the cathedral's ministry into the community.

In the twenty-first century, the people of both St. James' Cathedral and First Baptist Church tend not to think of themselves as Protestants. Indeed, they tend to not even know they are Protestants. To the Anglicans, Roman Catholics look surprisingly similar to themselves in liturgy and devotion; and St. James has mounted an Orthodox icon in one of the side chapels, hinting at the appeal of Orthodox spirituality. To the Baptists, Roman Catholics seem more and more like companions in support of traditional morality and theology, and the Orthodox seem remarkably spiritual. Both communities focus on their particularities. Since at least the 1970s, the people of St. James, along with Anglicans elsewhere, have thought of themselves as simply Anglicans. They have reclaimed their Catholic roots from before the Protestant movement of the sixteenth century, and their ecumenical roots from early Christianity. The people of First Baptist, when asked, likewise think of themselves as simply Baptists. In conversation, members are able to speak vividly of their personal commitment to Christ, their life of prayer, and their distinctive Baptist theology. They identify themselves ever more strongly with the earliest Christian communities referenced in the Bible.

Yet, upon closer examination, both churches still exhibit the historical marks of their Protestant characters. They still strongly tie themselves to their respective movements of reformation in the sixteenth and seventeenth centuries. They still steer their common life according to the Protestant inventions: in the one case, the Anglican Book of Common Prayer and its successors; in the other case, the principles and practices called Baptist. They still speak in Protestant idioms and operate within historically Protestant structures. They still profess that Jesus Christ animates their lives above all, according to the scriptures. They still profess the desire for continual renewal and reform. They settled centuries ago some questions that Roman Catholics still struggle with, such as whether to continue to ban clergy from marrying or exclude laypeople from receiving the cup in communion. They have both moved on, against the protests of Roman Catholics and Orthodox groups, to ordain women as ministers.

And, of course, as Protestants, they both still reject the super-authority of the Pope of Rome.

From such apparently common motivations, and in the face of so many common experiences and shared tendencies, First Baptist and St. James maintain their historic differences with each other. The two churches still feed that ongoing characteristic of Protestants throughout Canada and the world: they differentiate without an end in sight. In stark contrast with Roman Catholics, who in some sense hold together under the Roman Pope and who absorb a relatively wide range of difference within, Protestant Christians produce an ever-enlarging diversity so remarkable that it surpasses the imagination.

Both First Baptist and St. James know full well the power of the burgeoning new Protestant movements of Pentecostals and Independents expanding across the Toronto megalopolis, across Canada, and across the world. Both communities are also fully aware of the growth of the religion of "no religion," with its totally secular commitment to this world only. Between the pull of secular "no religion" on one side and the vitality of the new Protestant movements on the other, First Baptist and St. James make their way into the future. At the same time, the examples of the two communities suggest something basic about the future of Protestants in Canada. The future turns not on the achievement of some universal strategy or grand design, but on the spiritual well-being and shared commitments within each local community. Some communities will disappear, others will achieve a kind of steady state, still others will renew and expand, and new communities never seen before will no doubt continue to emerge. Judging from the stories of St. James' Cathedral and First Baptist Church in Toronto, Protestant Christians appear likely to carry on with their missions and ministries in Canada in ways that are quite unforeseen.

KEY TERMS

Anglicans   Adherents of the churches in communion with the Archbishop of Canterbury, historically related to the separation of the Church of England from the papacy in the sixteenth century, as well as to the continuity of Christianity in England since the earliest Christian period. Anglicans were the second Protestants to arrive in Canada, and until 1854 they were virtually the state church.

Baptists   Products of a seventeenth-century movement of reform away from the Church of England that stressed congregational autonomy, freedom from the state, and the baptism of adult believers versus infant baptism as practiced by Anglicans, other Protestants, Roman Catholics, and Orthodox Churches. Baptists have been present in Canada since the eighteenth century.

Denomination   A boundary-defined, ecclesiastical connection among like-minded local churches or assemblies who share a common history, mutually recognize each other as committed to the same things, and, in at least some sense, accept each other's jurisdiction in matters of the church.

Huguenots   French Protestants who trace their origins to a movement of reform dating from 1512 in Paris. Huguenots renounced the papacy, produced a Reformed Church separate from the Catholic Church of France, and were the first Protestants to arrive in Canada.

Independents   Churches and other assemblies of Christians who profess not to belong to a denomination, and who stress instead the authority of local assemblies and their freedom to construct their own beliefs and practices in response to their own experience of the Bible. The first Independents appeared in England in the seventeenth century. Since the 1960s, new Independents have proliferated explosively in Canada and worldwide.

Methodists   Protestants whose roots lie in a movement of spirituality, piety, and moral reform within the Church of England in the eighteenth century. Methodists eventually organized separate chapels, churches, and denominations, and spread worldwide. They came to Canada in the late eighteenth century and merged into the United Church of Canada in 1925.

Presbyterians   Members of churches historically related to reform movements in sixteenth-century Scotland and England, associated with similar movements in Switzerland and Holland. Presbyterians renounced the papal Catholic Church and established local congregations connected with each other by presbyteries. Their churches are governed jointly by laypeople and clergy, without bishops. Most Presbyterians merged into the United Church in 1925.

Protestants	Christians who can trace the history of how they or their antecedents became separate from the Catholic Church in communion with the Pope of Rome, and who do not regard themselves as either Catholic or Orthodox, in the sense of Eastern Orthodox, Oriental Orthodox, or the Assyrian Church of the East. Amid myriad differences, Protestants tend to agree on the primacy of the Bible and the priesthood of all believers, and stress the simplicity and directness of a life aligned with God.
Sacraments	Also called ordinances, sacraments are mandatory Christian rituals by which tangible, visible things either become or represent a spiritual reality and provide a means of divine grace. In contrast with Roman Catholics and Orthodox, who recognize seven sacraments, Protestants recognize only two: baptism with water in the name of the Trinity; and communion with bread and wine, or grape juice, variously called the Lord's Supper, Eucharist, communion, or Holy Communion.
United Church of Canada	A nationwide Protestant denomination formed in 1925 by the union of Methodists, most Presbyterians, Congregationalists, and Local Union Churches, producing the largest and most widespread Protestant denomination in the country.
Waldensians	Understood as the first Protestants, connected with a movement of reform in the late twelfth century in Lyons, France, and named after Peter Valdo. Waldensians elevated the authority of the Bible, condemned the papacy, and denied the intervention of priests as necessary for salvation, resulting in their separation from the Catholic Church of Rome. Their descendants concentrated in southern France and northern Italy.

KEY DATES

1170s	First Protestants, the Waldensians in France.
ca. **1400**	Hussite movement in the Czech region; Lollards in England starting from the 1370s.
1517–40s	Lutherans, Zwinglians, Anglicans, Anabaptists, and Mennonites in Western Europe.

1534	Huguenot Philippe de Chabot sponsors Jacques Cartier; Huguenot Jean François de la Rocque, Sieur de Roberval, heads a settlement including Catholics and Protestants at Cap Rouge in 1542, near today's city of Quebec.
1560s–90s	English Protestant and Huguenot fishers in Newfoundland.
1610	Anglican settlement at Cupers Cove, Newfoundland; starting in the 1600s, Lutherans, Presbyterians, Congregationalists, and Quakers in Canada.
1755	British expel Acadian Catholics, import "foreign Protestants."
1750s–90s	Moravians, Methodists, and Baptists, as well as black, Mohawk, and white Protestant Loyalists in Canada.
1763	Treaty of Paris transfers Catholic New France to Protestant British rule.
1793	York (Toronto) founded; origins of the Parish and Cathedral of St. James.
1820s	Black Baptists in York (Toronto); origins of First Baptist Church of Toronto.
1867	Dominion of Canada, known as "His Dominion," is dominated by Protestants.
1925	United Church of Canada merges Methodists, most Presbyterians, Congregationalists, and Local Union Churches.
1944	Canadian Council of Churches founded with Protestants and Orthodox Churches as members; Roman Catholics join in 1977.
1960s–present	Asian, African, Oceanic, Latin-American, and Caribbean Protestants immigrate to Canada in large numbers.

KEY READINGS

Benn, Carl, C.T. McIntire, et al. *The Parish and Cathedral of St. James, Toronto, 1797–1997*. Toronto: University of Toronto Press for St. James' Cathedral, 1998.

Grant, John Webster, John S. Moir, and Henry Horace Walsh. *History of the Christian Church in Canada*. 3 vols. Toronto: Ryerson Press, 1966.

Hayes, Alan L. *Anglicans in Canada: Controversies and Identity in Historical Perspective*. Champaign: University of Illinois Press, 2004.

Hillerbrand, Hans J., ed. *Encyclopedia of Protestantism*. 4 vols. New York: Routledge, 2003.

MacCulloch, Diarmaid. *The Reformation: A History*. New York: Viking Penguin, 2004.

Moir, John S. *Enduring Witness: A History of the Presbyterian Church in Canada.* 2nd ed. Toronto: Presbyterian Church in Canada, 1987.

Murphy, Terrence, and Roberto Perin, eds. *A Concise History of Christianity in Canada.* Toronto: Oxford University Press, 1996.

Schweitzer, Don, ed. *The United Church of Canada: A History.* Waterloo: Wilfrid Laurier University Press, 2011.

Semple, Neil. *The Lord's Dominion: The History of Canadian Methodism.* Montreal: McGill-Queen's University Press, 1996.

Winks, Robin W. *The Blacks in Canada: A History.* 2nd ed. Montreal: McGill-Queen's University Press, 1997.

KEY WEBSITES

http://www.worldchristiandatabase.org/wcd/ [World Christian Database]

http://64.33.81.65/index.htm [Creeds of Christendom]

http://churchhistcan.wordpress.com/ [Canadian Society of Church History]

http://www.councilofchurches.ca/ [Canadian Council of Churches]

http://www.evangelicalfellowship.ca/netcommunity/page.aspx?pid=848 [Evangelical Fellowship of Canada]

http://www.oikoumene.org/ [World Council of Churches]

http://fbctoronto.ca/ [First Baptist Church, Toronto]

http://www.stjamescathedral.on.ca/ [St. James' Cathedral, Toronto]

KEY QUESTIONS FOR CRITICAL REFLECTION

1. What distinguishes Protestants from other kinds of Christians, and do Anglicans, Mennonites, Pentecostals, and twenty-first century Independents fit well under the Protestant canopy?

2. What are the different kinds of ways that there have come to be Protestants in Canada, from the sixteenth century to the present?

3. Why are there so many kinds of Protestants, and are some differences among them more important than others?

4. In what sense has Canada been a Protestant nation and society, and how is that changing?

5. Is it likely that Protestants will wither away, persist, or renew themselves in Canada?

FOUR

Jews

IRA ROBINSON, CONCORDIA UNIVERSITY

J ews constitute the first non-Christian, non-Aboriginal religious group
to come to Canada. As such, their presence opened a debate among
Canadians with respect to the proper place of religious and cultural
diversity in Canada, which persists to this day. Jews have established significant communities in Canada, some of which have a history spanning
two centuries. Today, they are a presence in most major Canadian population centres, but are especially concentrated in Toronto and Montreal,
where the Jewish community is a discernable cultural and social presence.
They number approximately 350,000 and express a wide variety of religious and cultural positions that derive from their historical experience
of some 3,000 years. The author of this article belongs to this group, in
which some adhere faithfully to the practices and beliefs deriving from
premodern times, while others have responded to their perception of
the intellectual and social demands of contemporary life in an attempt to
create a balance between the Jewish heritage and their lives as contemporary Canadians.

THE HERITAGE

Genesis, the first book of the Hebrew Bible (**Tanakh**), begins with the creation of the universe. Every **Sabbath** (*shabbat*), Jews rest from their weekly labours to recall and honour God's act of creation. Creation is further commemorated in the annual holiday of *Rosh ha-Shana*. The Hebrew Bible then goes on to recount the foundation story of the Jewish people. In their historical memory, Jews trace their origins to the family of Abraham, Isaac, and Jacob, the three patriarchs or "fathers" of Jewish tradition. According to the story Genesis tells, Abraham lived in the city of Ur and, with his wife Sarah, journeyed at God's command to the Land of Canaan. Then, in her old age, Sarah bore Abraham a son, Isaac. God tested Abraham's faith by instructing him to sacrifice Isaac. When Abraham stood the test, God sent an angel to prevent the filicide, substituted a ram for the boy, and rewarded him with a covenant (**berith**): if Abraham and his descendants obeyed God's commandments, God would protect and preserve them. As a sign of this covenant, God required Abraham to circumcise himself and all males in his family. At eight days old, every male Jew is circumcised. This ritual act renews the covenant between God and the people of Israel. Circumcision is also a requirement for male converts to Judaism. Though modern academic scholarship does not always accept the biblical narratives as they present themselves, this foundational story is essential for understanding who Jews understand themselves to be. They are the family of the descendants of Abraham, Isaac, and Jacob, either in a literal sense or, in the case of converts, through a process of "adoption" into the group.

The Hebrew Bible goes on to describe how this family ultimately developed into a people called Israel. According to the story, Jacob (who was also called Israel) fathered 12 sons, who founded the 12 tribes of Israel. Settling in Egypt, the Israelites were eventually enslaved. A leader named Moses arose, whom God instructed to guide the Israelites to freedom. God sent ten plagues upon the Egyptians, culminating in the death of the firstborn. The Egyptians then allowed the Israelites to leave. On the yearly festival of **Passover**, Jews retell the story of the **Exodus** from Egypt and the creation of the Jewish nation. God guided the people to Mount Sinai where God revealed to Moses the **Torah**, literally meaning "instruction." Jews celebrate the giving of the Torah in the annual holiday of *Shavuot*. After they wandered in the desert for 40 years, a sojourn commemorated in the holiday of **Sukkot**, the Israelites conquered Canaan, the land promised by God to Abraham.

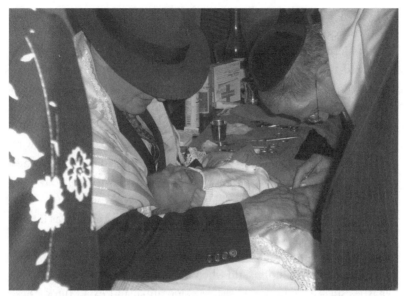

A ritual circumcision (*brit milah*). PHOTO BY YOSEF DOV ROBINSON. REPRINTED WITH PERMISSION.
© YOSEF DOV ROBINSON.

After a succession of charismatic leaders known as judges, the Hebrew
Bible speaks of a monarchy which developed in Israel, ultimately settling in
the city of Jerusalem, which the second king, David (*ca.* 1040–970 BCE),
conquered and established as his capital. Here his son Solomon (*ca.* 1011–
931 BCE) built a magnificent temple, which became the ritual centre of
Israelite life. The biblical narrative emphasizes that there alone was God
to be worshipped, though it is clear, from the biblical narrative itself, that
Israelites had established numerous sanctuaries outside of the Jerusalem
Temple. After Solomon, the monarchy was divided into two kingdoms,
with Israel in the north and Judah in the south. Prophets like Elijah, Elisha,
Hosea, Amos, Micah, and Isaiah spoke to the people of Judah and Israel,
criticizing their deeds and warning of disaster because of their sins.

In 722 BCE, the Assyrian Empire destroyed the northern kingdom of
Israel, and in 586 BCE, the Babylonian king Nebuchadnezzar conquered
Judah, destroyed its temple, and carried off the country's élite into **exile**
(*galut*). Jews commemorate the destruction of Jerusalem and its First
Temple in an annual fast day on the ninth day of the month of Av (*Tisha
B'Av*). Prophets like Jeremiah (*ca.* 655–586 BCE) and Ezekiel (*ca.* 622–
570 BCE) continued the tradition of their predecessors among the exiles
from Judah, and promised a time when God would re-establish the people of Israel in their land under the leadership of a king of the Davidic

line. In 538 BCE, having conquered Babylon, the Persian king, Cyrus the Great (*ca.* 600 BCE or 576 BC–530 BCE), allowed the exiles from Judah to return to Jerusalem. By *ca.* 515 BCE, a Second Temple had been built, and in the mid-fifth century BCE, Nehemiah, the governor of Judah, and the priestly scribe Ezra dedicated the people to Torah. According to biblical tradition, Ezra proclaimed the Torah to the people assembled in Jerusalem and inspired them to renew their religious commitment. At the same time, Babylonia remained a centre of Jewish culture, since not all of the Jewish exiles had returned to Judah. Having no temple, these **diaspora** Jews met in small groups to pray, study Torah, and observe Jewish holy days and festivals, thus originating the religious life of the synagogue.

For a time, Jewish religious life flourished in Judah, which was known to the Persians as Yehud and later to the Greeks and Romans as Judea. In 333 BCE, the Macedonian Alexander the Great (356–23 BCE) conquered the Persian Empire, and when he died ten years later, Hellenistic dynasties succeeded him in Egypt, Mesopotamia, and Asia Minor. These Hellenistic empires posed severe cultural challenges to traditional Jewish religious life. In 167 BCE, the Seleucid King Antiochus IV Epiphanes (215–164 BCE), with the support of some Hellenized elements among the Jews, converted Jerusalem's Second Temple to the worship of the Greek high god Zeus Olympios. The Hasmonean family (the Maccabees) led a revolt against this action, and in 164 BCE rededicated the Second Temple to Judaic worship and, ultimately, established an independent Jewish state. The Jewish festival of **Hanukkah** celebrates this victory. Elsewhere, encounters between Jewish and Hellenistic traditions brought happier results. In Alexandria, Egypt, for example, Jewish scholars produced a Greek translation of the Hebrew Scriptures known as the *Septuagint,* while the philosopher Philo of Alexandria (*ca.* 20 BCE– 50 CE) drew upon Greek methods of philosophical interpretation to explicate the Hebrew biblical tradition.

The Hasmonean Jewish state did not last long. In the last century BCE, it came under Roman domination. In this era, there were many competing schools of thought among Jews. The Sadducees were a group that believed in what was written in the Torah but did not accept ideas, like an afterlife, which did not explicitly appear in the Torah's text. There is evidence that many priests and other upper-class Jews adhered to this group. The Sadducees were opposed by another group, the Pharisees, who are said by some scholars to represent the middle classes among the Jews. The Pharisees argued that there was an ancient ancestral tradition that was to

A place of pilgrimage, the Western Wall is all that remains of Solomon's Jerusalem (Second) Temple, destroyed by the Roman general Titus in 70 CE. PHOTO BY GOLASSO. REPRINTED UNDER THE TERMS OF THE CC-BY-SA LICENSE AGREEMENT.

be considered authoritative, like the written Torah, and which dealt with issues, like the afterlife, which the written Torah did not explicitly address. Two other factions also vied for religious authority. One was the Essenes, a sect in opposition to the established authorities in Jerusalem's Second Temple and living in ascetic expectation of the **messiah**, a descendant of the royal line of David who was to redeem Israel from its oppressors. Another powerful group was the Zealots, who hoped to hasten the arrival of the messiah by driving the Romans from Judea. Another messianic sect that arose in the first century CE was made up of the followers of Jesus of Nazareth (*ca.* 4 BCE–30 CE). In 66 CE, the Zealots launched a rebellion and seized Jerusalem. In 70 CE, the Roman general Titus (39–81 CE) conquered the city and torched the Second Temple, leaving intact only a portion of its outer retaining wall, which Jews came to call the "Western Wall" and which became a place of Jewish pilgrimage. In 135 CE, the Roman emperor Hadrian (76–138 CE) crushed another major Jewish rebellion in Judea that was led by Simon bar Kosiba, who is also known as **bar Kokhba** (died 135 CE), and who was supported by the influential rabbi, Akiva ben Joseph (*ca.* 50–135 CE). In the aftermath of the Bar Kokhba revolt, Rome banned Jews from living in Jerusalem, renamed Judea Palestina, and temporarily outlawed Jewish religious practices and study of the Torah.

The Roman effort to de-Judaize Judea never completely succeeded, though it did serve to relatively increase the influence of diaspora Jewish communities. Unable to worship God through the sacrifice of animals in the now destroyed Second Temple, Jews developed alternative religious practices. Led by rabbis, who were the spiritual heirs of the Pharisees, Jews successfully substituted the synagogue life of prayer and the study of Torah for the sacrificial system, while continuing to look forward to a messianic restoration of the Temple and its worship. A key figure in this process was Rabbi Yohanan ben Zakkai (*ca.* 30–90 CE), who escaped the Roman siege of Jerusalem, founded a rabbinic academy at Yavneh, and there re-established the Sanhedrin, the supreme Jewish religious author-ity which had existed in Jerusalem prior to the destruction of the Second Temple. The Yavneh academy's scholars determined with some finality the canon of the Hebrew Bible and debated the principles of Jewish law (*halakha*) as well as the meaning of the sacred narratives (*midrash*).

The debates within the rabbinic schools culminated in the third century CE in the *Mishnah,* a work created under the leadership of Rabbi Judah ha-Nasi ("The Patriarch") (135–219). Rooted in, but parallel to the written Torah (*Torah she-be-ktav*), *Mishnah* was understood as an expression of an oral Torah (*Torah she-be-'al peh*) based, according to the rabbis, on an authoritative tradition going back to Moses. *Mishnah* served as the basis for future rabbinic scholarly discussions (*Gemarah*). By the end of the fourth century, rabbinic schools in the Galilee had collected the teachings of post-Mishnaic rabbis into a collection known as the Palestinian **Talmud**. By the end of the sixth century, Babylonian rabbis had created a parallel work known as the Babylonian Talmud. An extraordinary compendium of legal, ethical, historical, medical, scientific, and agricultural informa-tion, as well as proverbs, folklore, and rules of etiquette, the Babylonian Talmud remains an established religious authority among rabbinic Jews whose discussions and debates continue to be informed by it to this day.

The development of rabbinic Judaism did not take place in a histori-cal vacuum. The success of the religious traditions of both Christianity and Islam held serious implications for Jews and Judaism. Originally a sect within Judaism, Christians believed Jesus of Nazareth to be the Jewish messiah, and they proclaimed their faith that the Christians were the true heirs to the promises contained in the prophecies of the Hebrew Scriptures, which they called the Old Testament. Several docu-ments included in the Christian New Testament speak derogatorily about Jews and Judaism. Casting Jesus as the fulfillment of biblical prophecy, for instance, the Gospel of Matthew represents the Jews as accepting responsibility for crucifying their own messiah: "His blood be on us and our children!" (27:25). Beginning late in the first century CE, Christians and Jews began an often bitter process of separation. In the fourth century CE, the triumph of Christianity in the Roman Empire cemented this separation. Converting to Judaism and intermarrying with Jews became capital offences, and in 439, Emperor Theodosius II (401–450) enacted other legislation discriminating against Jews, including a law barring them from public offices.

For the next millennium, the Jewish experience in Christian countries expressed the ambiguities of Christian doctrine. Because Jews were understood by Christians to be the bearers of the Old Testament, and because Christians hoped that the conversion of the Jews would come before the Second Coming of Christ, they were allowed to live in Christian lands. In the early ninth century, for example, Holy Roman emperor Louis the Pious (778–840) extended royal protection to Jewish merchants, a privilege enabling the establishment of successful Jewish communities in northern France, the Rhineland and elsewhere. Rabbinic studies flourished in these countries. A most notable example of this scholarship is the work of Rabbi Solomon ben Isaac of Troyes (also known as Rashi; 1040–1105), whose biblical and Talmudic commentaries remain models of clarity and accessibility.

But there were also Christians who opposed such tolerance of Jews on the grounds that God had cursed the Jews because of the crucifixion of Christ. Popular anti-Jewish feelings among Christians sometimes surged out of control in times of economic, social, or political upheaval. In 1096, Christian soldiers of the First Crusade, on their way to take back Jerusalem from the Muslims, massacred Jews in the Rhineland, and, starting in 1144, Jews in Norwich, England, and elsewhere were charged with using the blood of Christian children in unleavened Passover bread (*matza*). In the mid-fourteenth century, Christians in France and across Central Europe blamed Jews for causing the Black Death epidemic by poisoning wells. Jews were expelled from England in 1290, from France in 1306, and from many other parts of Western and Northern Europe by the end of the fifteenth century. Large numbers of these displaced Jews settled in Eastern Europe, especially Poland. These **Ashkenazic** Jews took advantage of protective charters issued in the fourteenth and fifteenth centuries by kings of Poland, who encouraged their aristocracy to employ Jews as fiscal agents, tax collectors, and estate managers. Granted relative autonomy, Ashkenazic

Jews developed a distinct culture of intense piety, as well as their own language, Yiddish, a mixture of Hebrew and German.

In the seventh century, the rise of Islam posed another set of challenges to Jews and Judaism. In 626, Muhammad (*ca.* 610–632), the founder of Islam, killed some of his Jewish opponents and expelled other Jews from Medina for refusing to accept his prophecy, but Muslims were generally tolerant to Jews as well as Christians. By the beginning of the ninth century, Arab Muslim armies controlled an empire stretching from India in the east to the Iberian Peninsula in the west. As fellow monotheists, Jews and Christians were known as *dhimmis* and were permitted to practice their religion in these Islamic lands. They were, however, required to dress in distinctive clothes, to pay an annual poll tax, and to differentiate themselves in other ways from slaves living under Islamic rule on the one hand, and from Muslims on the other.

The impact of the Muslim conquests was soon evident among the Jews living under Islamic rule. In the eighth century, for example, Babylonia's ancient pre-eminence as a centre of rabbinic learning passed naturally to nearby Baghdad, the capital of the Islamic empire, but disputes over the authority of the Talmud led to the founding of a puritanical sect by the respected scholar, Anan ben David (*ca.* 715–795). Known as Karaites, which literally means "readers of scriptures," the members of this sect rejected rabbinical efforts to represent themselves as the authoritative interpreters of Torah and insisted that individuals should interpret the teachings of scripture for themselves. Borrowing ideas from Muslim *Kalam* theology, Saadiah ben Joseph Gaon (882–942) led rabbinic resistance to Karaism, producing the first medieval Jewish attempt at a systematic theology, the *Book of Beliefs and Opinions* (933). A Karaite academy was established in Jerusalem and Karaism gained further adherents throughout the Jewish diaspora, though the ascetic character of Karaite teachings meant that it did not appeal to the majority of Jews. Today several thousand Karaites live in Israel, the United States, and elsewhere.

By the end of the tenth century, the Islamic world had fractured into a number of independent dynasties, but economic interests usually transcended political tensions and trade routes remained open. Accompanying Jewish merchants, rabbinical scholars travelled and settled throughout the Islamic world, and Jewish intellectual life thrived in communities around the Mediterranean, from Palestine and Egypt across North Africa to Muslim Spain. The eleventh to thirteenth centuries saw a golden age of Spanish culture forged out of extraordinarily fertile exchanges between

The Moorish Revival architecture of Franz Josef Jubilee Orthodox Synagogue, built in 1906 on Jerusalem Street, Prague, Czech Republic, hearkens back to the golden age of medieval Spanish culture, when Sephardic Jews enjoyed a fertile exchange of ideas with Muslims and Christians.
PHOTO BY THORSTEN BACHNER. REPRINTED UNDER THE TERMS OF THE CC-BY-SA LICENSE AGREEMENT.

Muslim, Christian, and Jewish thinkers. A number of Spanish cities hosted Jewish schools for the study of Torah and Talmud, most notably Lucena, near Cordova. These **Sephardic** Jews included intellectuals like Moses ben Jacob ibn Ezra (*ca.* 1055–1138), Judah ben Samuel Halevi (1075–1141), and Moses ben Maimon, also known as Moses Maimonides, or in acronym, *Rambam* (1138–1204). In the Sephardic liturgy, ibn Ezra's beautiful hymn, "*El nora 'alilah*" ("O God, awesome in deeds") sets the mood, at once fervent and hopeful, for the closing service of the most solemn day of the Jewish year, Yom Kippur (Day of Atonement). Halevi's exquisite poems express Jewish longing for Zion, while his defence of Judaism, the *Kuzari,* argues for the truth of Judaism based upon the public nature of the revelation of Torah.

The writings of Maimonides represent the most significant legacy of medieval Sephardic Judaism. A philosopher and scholar of *halakha*, Maimonides wished to show the harmony of human reason and biblical revelation. In Judeo-Arabic, his *Guide for the Perplexed* (1190) draws on Aristotle's philosophy, mediated through Muslim thinkers like Ibn Sīnā (also known as Avicenna; *ca.* 980–1137) and Abū Nasr al-Fārābi (*ca.* 872–950), to reveal the ways in which Torah and reason are compatible. In Hebrew, the *Mishneh Torah* (1178) was a monumental digest of *halakha,* and constituted one of the major sources of Rabbi Joseph Caro's

(1488–1575) *Beit Yosef*. This latter work, especially through its abridgement, the *Shulchan Arukh* ("Set Table"; 1565), today forms the basis for both the Sephardic and, with the glosses of Rabbi Moses Isserles (1520–72), the Ashkenazic codes of religious law and practice.

In 1492, the new Christian rulers of Spain, Ferdinand of Aragon (1452–1516) and Isabella of Castile (1451–1504), issued an edict making Judaism illegal in their newly united kingdom, expelling what was perhaps the largest and culturally most creative Jewish community of its era. Some Sephardic Jews made their way to Ashkenazic communities in Central, Northern, and Eastern Europe, but most scattered across North Africa and the Middle East. At a loss for rational explanations for this tragedy, some Jewish thinkers turned to a system of Jewish mysticism called **Kabbalah**, which had developed since the twelfth century and which saw the appearance of its greatest work, the *Zohar* ("*Splendour*"), at the end of the thirteenth century. Kabbalah understands the ultimate divine reality as *Eyn Sof* ("infinite"), unknown and unknowable, whose relationship to the created universe is mediated through ten degrees of manifestation (*sefirot*). Kabbalistic symbolism casts the last of the *sefirot*, *Malkhut* ("Royalty")—also known as *Knesset Yisrael* ("Community of Israel") and the "Divine Presence" (*shekhinah*)—as the feminine link between the *sefirotic* realm and the created universe. Through ritual, meditation, study, and good deeds, kabbalists believed that Jews made a difference in the relationship between God and creation, having the potential to transform the world and repair its defects. For Isaac Luria (1534–72), perhaps the greatest kabbalistic master of the sixteenth century, this *tikkun olam* ("repair of the world") is the essential meaning of Kabbalah's key texts. To different degrees, both Sephardic and Ashkenazic communities had accepted the authority of these ideas by the seventeenth century.

In eighteenth-century Poland, a Jewish pietistic movement based on kabbalistic teachings, whose adherents were called *Hasidim* ("pious ones") grew up around the charismatic figure of Israel ben Eliezer (*ca.* 1700–60), also known as *Baal Shem Tov* ("Master of the Good Name [of God]"). A *zaddik* ("righteous man"), the Baal Shem preached a mystical message of prayer, humility, and joy. He inspired a large group of devoted disciples who began to transform many Jewish communities on the basis of these teachings. This movement aroused opposition as well. Known as *Mitnagdim* ("Opponents"), traditionalist Ashkenazic rabbis like Elijah ben Solomon Zalman of Vilna (1720–97), a distinguished kabbalist himself, feared **Hasidism**, sensing a threat to traditional rabbinic authority even on the part of Hasidic leaders like Shneur Zalman of Lyady (1746–1812), who was a distinguished rabbinic scholar, and who sought to reconcile rabbinic and Hasidic traditions. The tension between the *Hasidim* and their *Mitnagdic* opponents was acute for much of the nineteenth century, and has not completely abated even today.

During the seventeenth and eighteenth centuries, significant changes occurred in the social and political position of Jews and Judaism in Europe. Disillusioned with decades of war between Roman Catholic and Protestant Christians, secular Enlightenment thinkers argued that the universality of human reason obviated social and political inequalities resulting from differences in religion. Human equality included equal citizenship in the modern nation state, as evidenced most dramatically in the French Revolution (1789–93). It seemed reasonable to many to apply these arguments to Jews and Judaism. In 1791, the National Assembly of France granted full citizenship rights to Jews, and in 1807, the French Emperor Napoleon Bonaparte (1769–1821) encouraged Jews living under French imperial authority to establish an authoritative body, called the Sanhedrin, to adjust Judaism to the new demands of emancipation. Hitherto marginalized in ghettos, Jews now enjoyed civil equality and religious freedom throughout Napoleon's empire, and for the most part Jewish emancipation in France survived his defeat at the Battle of Waterloo (1815). Emancipation occurred in other parts of Europe, too. In 1858, Baron Lionel de Rothschild (1808–79) became the first Jew to take a seat in Great Britain's House of Commons; in 1871, a new German constitution lifted all economic, social, and political restrictions on Jews; and in 1917, revolution finally brought emancipation to Russian Jews.

Emancipation did not come without problems, however. Its advocates expected Jews to modify their economic, social, and religious behaviour so as to diminish their separateness from their fellow countrymen. Although restrictive laws were abolished in many parts of Europe, old religious prejudices persisted. While influential German Jewish intellectuals like the poet and essayist Heinrich Heine (1797–1856) considered conversion to Christianity essential for Jews wishing to gain full social and professional acceptance in predominantly Christian countries, this total assimilation threatened Jewish national identity and the integrity of Judaism. From the 1830s on, significant numbers of Central and Eastern European Jews had moved to Western Europe and North America in search of a better life. From the 1880s to the early twentieth century, however, a massive wave of Jewish immigration to North America—with smaller movements to

Israel, South America, South Africa, and Australia—came about in large part as a result of rising anti-Semitism in Central and Eastern Europe and Russia. Originating in the 1870s with publications like the pamphlet "The Victory of Judaism over Germandom, Considered from a Non-Religious Point of View" (1879), written by Wilhelm Marr (1819–1904), modern anti-Semitism combined the age-old Christian antipathy towards Judaism with nineteenth-century racist theories asserting a Jewish threat to European civilization. In this view, by permitting Jews more economic, social, and political influence, emancipation made them that much more dangerous.

The challenges of emancipation spurred Jews to religious and cultural creativity. Premodern Judaism was largely based upon the ancient teachings of the rabbis, but emancipation caused many Jews to rethink this religious orientation. The life and writings of Moses Mendelssohn (1729–86) were indicative of this process. A strictly observant Jew, Mendelssohn is known as the father of the Jewish movement for cultural Westernization referred to as *Haskalah* ("Enlightenment"). He translated Torah into German and published a biblical commentary (the *Biur*), which drew upon both rabbinic teachings and Enlightenment ideas. In an analogous way, his magnum opus, *Jerusalem; or, On Religious Power and Judaism* (1783), mounted a polemical defence of Judaism against both secular rationalists and Christian dogmatists. Part one of *Jerusalem* argues that no religion has the right to coerce adherence; only the state may use force when public security was threatened. Part two identifies the essential elements of all religion worthy of the name—God's existence, divine providence, and the immortality of the soul—and contends that Judaism is a more reasonable religion than Christianity, because Jews have never claimed that the particular forms in which God revealed these truths to them are binding upon the rest of humankind. Freedom of religion, Mendelssohn concluded, permits Jews to practise their religion, but at the same time, thus freed from religious coercion, Jews must adhere fully both to the civil law of the secular nation state and to the ceremonial law of their ancestors.

Mendelssohn's *Jerusalem* helped to establish the terms for nineteenth- and twentieth-century debates about what it meant to be a Jew and on the nature of Judaism, though Jewish immigration to North America eventually shifted the centre of these debates. Today, most Jews in Europe and North America identify with one of the four branches of Judaism—**Orthodox, Reform, Conservative,** or **Reconstructionist.** In different ways, Orthodox and Reform Judaism resulted directly from aspects of Mendelssohn's thought. Reform sought to create a Judaism that was appropriate for Jews who either enjoyed or aspired to achieve equal rights with their non-Jewish countrymen. In 1810, Israel Jacobson (1768–1828) established the first Reform synagogue in Seesen, Germany, and in 1824, the first North American Reform synagogue was set up in Charleston, South Carolina. Liberal rabbinic seminaries were set up to educate a modern rabbinate. Thus in 1854, a moderate Reform rabbinical seminary opened in Breslau and in 1875, Isaac Mayer Wise (1819–1900) founded Hebrew Union College in Cincinnati, Ohio, which taught a more radical Reform. Conferences of Reform rabbis in Germany in the mid-nineteenth century, and, later, in the United States, attempted to define what Reform Judaism meant. In 1885, Rabbi Kaufmann Kohler (1823–1946) presided over the Pittsburgh Platform that focused on the Torah's ethical message of universal justice and denied the divine inspiration of Talmud. The Platform dispensed with most restrictions on diet, purity laws and dress, advocated that men and women worship together using a mixed vernacular and Hebrew liturgy, renounced claims to Palestine, and rejected the doctrine of the messiah. Over the next century, Reform rabbis significantly modified the Pittsburgh Platform to demonstrate a greater appreciation of the richness of the rabbinic tradition as well as Jewish ties to the Land of Israel. Often preferring to call their synagogues temples, Reform congregations comprise the largest Jewish religious movement in contemporary North America.

By contrast, Orthodox Jews sought largely to continue in the path of premodern rabbinic Judaism. Orthodox Jews persisted in their belief that that the divinely revealed status of Torah encompassed not just the Hebrew scriptures but also Talmud, the *Shulhan Arukh*, and the rest of the rabbinic tradition. One of the major figures in nineteenth-century Orthodox Judaism was Samson Raphael Hirsch (1808–88), a rabbi in Frankfurt, Germany. Well aware of the demands of modernity, he argued that Jews needed reforming, not Judaism. In *The Nineteen Letters of Ben Uziel* (1836), he insisted that the first and absolutely binding duty of the Jews lay in obeying the 613 prescriptions (*mitsvot*) of Torah in their entirety, for the Jews were the means by which God had chosen to educate the world ethically and spiritually. Hirsch's message that Jews need not fear contemporary science and culture, his unwavering sense of Jewish mission, and his systematic opposition to the teachings of Reform attracted significant numbers of followers.

Other traditionally minded Jews felt unable to embrace either Orthodoxy or Reform, and ultimately formed two other branches of

Judaism, Conservative and Reconstructionist, which sought to fill a middle ground between Orthodox and Reform Judaism. They did so in different ways. Conservative Judaism originated in Germany under the guidance of moderate reformer Zecharias Frankel (1801–75), founder of the Breslau Seminary, and developed more fully in the United States during the twentieth century. Conservative Judaism accepts the need for change in Judaism, but wishes to do so only in ways that are essentially based on its conception of *halakhic* precedent, whereas for Reform past precedent is rather less influential. The Conservative movement was powerfully influenced by Solomon Schechter (1847–1915), head of the Jewish Theological Seminary in New York. Schechter acknowledged the challenges to traditional Jewish belief posed by modern secular thought, but argued that the true meaning of Judaism lay in the everyday observance of the tradition by Jews down through the ages. Still more pragmatic in outlook, Reconstructionist Judaism, which emerged from the left wing of the Conservative movement, was founded by Mordecai Menahem Kaplan (1881–1983). It values Judaism as the historical embodiment of Jewish culture, and seeks to reconstruct Jewish life on the basis of an all-encompassing Jewish civilization in order to foster Jewish identity. Like Reform Jews, Conservatives and Reconstructionists are egalitarian, provide religious education for girls on the same basis as for boys, celebrate *bat mitzvah* for girls as well as *bar mitzvah* for boys, and ordain women as rabbis as well as men, all of which run contrary to Orthodox practice.

Finally, whatever their differences, Orthodox, Reform, Conservative, and Reconstructionist Jews are generally united in their support of the State of Israel. Modern Jewish nationalism is in many ways the outcome of nineteenth-century anti-Semitism. In response to the rise of anti-Semitism, Theodor Herzl (1860–1904) and other Zionist thinkers argued that policies advocating Jewish acculturation as a *quid pro quo* for emancipation failed to provide Jews with dignity and security, and that ultimately their only hope of survival lay in **Zionism**—the establishment of a Jewish homeland. To advance his agenda, Herzl published *The Jewish State* in 1896 and founded the World Zionist Organization at the first Zionist Congress in Basel, Switzerland, in 1897. In 1917, the Balfour Declaration pledged British support for a Jewish homeland in Palestine, and in 1922, with the collapse of the Muslim Ottoman Empire after World War I, the newly formed League of Nations mandated the British to govern Palestine.

After World War II, Zionists pursued all avenues to push for a Jewish homeland in Palestine. Before the war, anti-Semitism became German public policy under the leadership of Adolf Hitler and his National Socialist (Nazi) government. From 1933 to 1938, a series of laws deprived German Jews of their civil and political rights, culminating in the destruction of Jewish synagogues and property, and the arrest and murder of Jewish men on *Kristallnacht* ("Night of Broken Glass"), 8–9 November 1938. From 1939 to 1945, Jews in Germany and in lands occupied or influenced by Germany during World War II were forcibly separated from the rest of the population, first in ghettos before being shipped to concentration and extermination camps at places such as Belzec, Sobibor, Treblinka, Chelmno, Majdanek, and Auschwitz-Birkenau. On 20 January 1942, at the Wannsee Conference, top Nazi officials and bureaucrats organized the extermination of all Jews under German control. As many as 6,000,000 Jewish men, women, and children perished in this **Holocaust**, which many Jews call the *Shoah*, which literally means "calamity." On 29 November 1947, the United Nations resolved to partition Palestine into Jewish and Arab states, and on 14 May 1948, Jewish leaders in Tel Aviv proclaimed an independent State of Israel. The Nazi Holocaust and the survival of the State of Israel in the face of sustained Arab opposition have constituted the most salient facts of Jewish existence in the last century.

THE MAKING OF A CANADIAN JEWISH COMMUNITY

The Jewish presence in the territories that would become Canada begins with the English and French settlements of Halifax and Quebec. Officially, New France was off limits to all but Roman Catholic immigrants. While individual Jews may have set foot in the French colony, the authorities did not allow an open Jewish presence. But there were Jewish communities in France proper, and in 1748, the mercantile family of Abraham Gradis (*ca.* 1699–1780) became the main supplier of food, munitions, and military reinforcements to New France. At the same time, a small Jewish community thrived in Halifax. The four Hart brothers—Abraham, Isaac, Naphtali, and Samuel—were the most prominent members of this community, and in 1793, Samuel was elected to Nova Scotia's House of Assembly. Although it is likely that he was obliged to swear a Christian oath in order to take his seat in the legislature, Samuel Hart (1747–1810) became the first Jew to assume public office anywhere in the British Empire.

After the British conquest in 1760, the centre of Jewish activity shifted to the former French colony. The Jewish community in Quebec grew slowly in the late eighteenth and early nineteenth centuries, beginning with the arrival of merchants like Samuel Jacobs (died 1786), Lucius Levy Solomons (1730–92), and Jacob Franks (*ca.* 1768–1840). In 1768, the first synagogue, called Shearith Israel ("Remnant of Israel"), was built in Montreal on land owned by David David (1764–1824). The 1831 census lists only 107 Jews in Upper and Lower Canada, but they made their presence known, especially on issues having to do with equal rights in religion and politics. The family of Aaron Hart (1724–1800) was in the forefront of these battles. In 1807, his son, Ezekiel Hart (1770–1843), was elected to the House of Assembly of Lower Canada from a constituency in Trois-Rivières, but he was not allowed to take his seat. The House decided that a Jew could not represent a Christian constituency or take the Christian oath of office as prescribed by law.

Ezekiel Hart lost his seat, but his family continued the struggle for religious and political rights. After the British conquest, only the Anglican Church was able to officially register births, deaths, and marriages. The Quebec Act of 1774 served to protect the religious and political rights of Roman Catholics, but members of other religious communities remained in a kind of legal no man's land. Led by Aaron Hart's brother, Benjamin (1779–1855), Ezekiel Hart's son, Samuel Bécancour Hart (born 1798), and Moses Judah Hayes (1789–1861), Montreal's Jewish community campaigned for the legal clarification of Jewish religious rights. In 1831, Benjamin's petition to Lower Canada's House of Assembly succeeded in securing the right for Jews to register their own births, deaths, and marriages. Buoyed by this success, Samuel Bécancour Hart petitioned the legislature to clarify Jewish political rights. Spurred by the influential house speaker, Louis-Joseph Papineau (1786–1871), in 1831 the legislature passed a bill, entitled "An Act to Declare Persons Professing the Jewish Religion Intitled [*sic*] to All the Rights and Privileges of the Other Subjects of His Majesty in this Province." This legislative landmark made Jews in Lower Canada among the first in the British Empire to enjoy full religious and political emancipation, 25 years before Jews in Great Britain achieved these rights.

The first census after Confederation, taken in 1871, lists 1,115 Jews throughout the new Dominion of Canada. These Jews founded synagogues and charitable associations, acculturated to English Canadian society, and established themselves relatively successfully. In 1838, Moses Judah Hayes and Benjamin Hart oversaw the rebuilding of Shearith Israel, and in 1847, Alexander Abraham de Sola (1825–82) arrived from London to serve as the synagogue's rabbi. A Sephardic Jew, de Sola ministered to

Shearith Israel's largely Ashkenazi congregation for 35 years. Also a prolific scholar and translator, de Sola taught Hebrew and rabbinical studies at McGill University. In 1858, the university made him an honorary doctor of laws, the first such honour to be bestowed upon a rabbi in Great Britain or North America. Montreal's Jewish community thrived in other respects, too. Of mainly English, German, and Polish extraction, some members of Shearith Israel preferred the Ashkenazic liturgy and founded the Sha'ar Hashomayim ("Gate of Heaven") congregation in 1846. They opened Montreal's second synagogue building in 1859, and in 1863, the Young Men's Hebrew Benevolent Society was established to provide assistance to new immigrants and to foster a greater sense of community.

By the 1870s, increasing numbers of Jews were living in the major metropolitan centres of Toronto and Winnipeg, as well. Toronto's first synagogue, Holy Blossom Temple, began in the 1850s. Smaller congregations also developed in Saint John, Quebec City, Kingston, Brantford, Hamilton, and London. In the West, Jews were among the many adventurers attracted by the discovery of gold along British Columbia's Fraser River. Because *halakha* requires that Jews be buried in consecrated ground, cemeteries are often the first sign of a communal Jewish presence. In 1860, Victoria's Jewish community acquired land for a cemetery, now the oldest in Western Canada, and in 1863, they opened Temple Emanu-El, a synagogue which remains in use today. However, Vancouver was chosen as the terminus of the Canadian Pacific Railway and it soon superseded Victoria as the West Coast's most important commercial centre. Spearheaded by the five Oppenheimer brothers—David (1834–97), Charles, Meyer, Isaac, and Godfrey—Jewish settlement shifted there, too. In 1887, part of the public burial grounds now known as Mountain View Cemetery was given over for Jewish interments, and by the early 1890s, Vancouver's Jews had formed two congregations: in 1891, the Orthodox Agudas Achim ("Congregation of Brothers"), led by Zebulon Franks (1864–1926); and in 1894, Reform Temple Emanu-El, presided over by Solomon Philo (1842–1923).

Towards the end of the nineteenth century and in the first few decades of the twentieth century, new waves of immigrants markedly changed the character of the Jewish community and its position in the country as a whole. As part of the massive emigration from Eastern Europe between the early 1880s and the beginning of World War I, more than 100,000 Jews came to Canada, many via the United States. In 1880, there were only a handful of synagogues in Canada; by 1914, there were over 100. This influx brought Jews into the forefront of ongoing public debates about the kind of country Canada should be. In important ways, many Canadians thought that Jews did not seem to fit in to the sort of nation they were creating. Canada's nineteenth-century self-image was of a primarily agricultural country, for example, and most immigration officials considered Jews unlikely to become successful farmers. Nonetheless, Jews did not merely immigrate to the established Jewish communities in Montreal, Toronto, and Winnipeg. In appreciable numbers they began to establish farm colonies in the Canadian Prairies. In 1884, the first colony was settled at Moosomin, Saskatchewan; it was abandoned after several failed seasons. In 1886, a second colony was founded at Wapella, Saskatchewan, that was much more successful. In 1891, the philanthropist Baron Maurice de Hirsch (1831–96) set up the Jewish Colonization Society, which funded the Montreal Young Men's Hebrew Benevolent Society and was later renamed the Baron de Hirsch Institute, in its attempts to establish agricultural colonies. The first of these colonies was named Hirsch in honour of its benefactor. By 1906, about a dozen Jewish farm settlements dotted the prairie landscapes of Manitoba, Saskatchewan, and Alberta. In 1921, there were 2,568 Jews living on farms in the Canadian Prairies and in Quebec as well. After World War II, though, the descendants of these Jewish farmers mostly gravitated to Canada's cities, where the sheer numbers of Eastern European immigrants had already created a new social, cultural, and religious reality.

By the end of the nineteenth century, the older Canadian Jewish communities were relatively acculturated to Anglo Canadian life. At the same time, Jewish charitable organizations, especially women's societies, were unstinting in their efforts to help impoverished Jewish newcomers. Montreal's Ladies' Hebrew Benevolent Society was created in 1877, and in 1878 both Toronto's Ladies' Montefiore Benevolent Society and Hamilton's Temple Anshe Sholom's Deborah Ladies' Aid Society were founded. By the late 1890s, there were Jewish women's associations in cities across Canada, most notably the National Council of Jewish Women, which had been founded in the United States and came to Toronto in 1897. By the mid-1920s, the Council had opened branches in Winnipeg, Calgary, Edmonton, and Vancouver.

Unlike their more established benefactors, though, the newcomers clustered in Jewish immigrant neighbourhoods where Yiddish, not French or English, was the language of everyday life. Along Montreal's Boulevard Saint Laurent, Jews read the Yiddish newspaper, *Der Keneder Odler* (*Canadian Eagle*); in Toronto's St. John's Ward, they read the *Yiddisher*

Zhurnal (*Jewish Journal*); and around Winnipeg's Selkirk Avenue, *Dos Yiddishe Vort* (*The Jewish Word*) was the popular choice. The new immigrants opened libraries of Yiddish and Hebrew books, notably the Jewish Public Library in Montreal, founded in 1914 by Reuben Brainin (1862–1939) and Yehuda Kaufman (1886–1976). Most significantly, however, the newcomers reinvigorated Jewish Orthodox religious life. By 1914, Montreal, Toronto, and Winnipeg alone had become home to dozens of small Orthodox communities from Hungary, Moldavia, Poland, Romania, Russia, and Ukraine. Each of them established their own synagogues, which served as places of worship, schools, and social and cultural centres. In 1907, for example, Toronto's Jewish immigrants from Lithuania opened the Goel Tdedec synagogue. By contrast, there were only three Reform congregations in Canada until the 1950s: Montreal's Temple Emanu-El, erected in 1911 and expanded in 1922; Toronto's Holy Blossom congregation, which moved to its present location on Bathurst Street in 1938; and Hamilton's Anshe Sholom congregation, which incorporated in 1863 and dedicated its first synagogue in 1882. Other nascent Reform congregations did not survive. Thus, in Vancouver in 1921, a new 600-seat Orthodox synagogue, Schara Tzedeck ("Gates of Righteousness") was opened. In this case, the city's Reform Jews had united with this Orthodox congregation, until they parted company to build their own synagogue, Temple Shalom in 1965.

Another debate had to do with whether Canada could or should consider itself to be a Christian country. As the first non-Christian group to immigrate to Canada in significant numbers, the Jews found themselves at the centre of this debate. For many nineteenth- and early twentieth-century Canadians, being civilized meant being Christian, and not to be Christian was to be in need of civilizing. Education lay at the heart of this equation, especially in Quebec, where the British North America Act (1867) guaranteed both Roman Catholic and Protestant Christians their own systems of education, supported by public taxes. A compromise solution was agreed on, which allowed Jewish children to enter the Protestant school system, although their parents were initially not allowed to teach in the schools, to vote in school board elections, or to sit on school boards. By 1916, almost half the students in the Protestant system were Jewish, and English-speaking Christians feared losing control.

In the 1920s, the situation came to a head, leading to tensions at the local and provincial level and to court action, which went as far as the Privy Council in London. The issue was whether Jews should have their own school board, similar in nature to those of the Protestants and Roman Catholics, or remain part of the Protestant system. On this issue the Jewish community was itself divided. For most Orthodox Eastern European traditionalists, a Jewish school system was essential for preserving cultural and religious identity. Many established and acculturated Jews, however, feared that this formal segregation between Jewish and Christian children might portend other measures of discrimination against Jews within Canadian society. While the ultimate solution to this problem saw Jews remain in the Protestant school system, the education issue remained a point of debate within the Canadian Jewish community. In every major Canadian Jewish neighbourhood, major efforts were made to establish schools teaching the Jewish heritage. Beginning with one-room schools modelled on the Eastern European *cheder,* schools that would provide supplementary religious teachings to the public educational systems were founded. These were called "Talmud Torahs." Montreal's first Talmud Torah was founded in 1896 by Rabbi Aaron Mordecai Ashinsky (1867–1954). By some accounts, Winnipeg's Hebrew Free School, founded in 1912, was the best Talmud Torah in Canada, thanks in large part to the efforts of immigrant rabbi Israel Isaac Kahanovich (1872–1945), who led the city's Beth Jacob congregation for almost 40 years. Day schools that taught both the public school curriculum and Judaic studies would be founded somewhat later. By World War II, Montreal and Toronto boasted several day schools, which in different degrees taught Hebrew Bible, Talmud, and Hebrew and Yiddish language and literature, in addition to the standard public school curriculum, helping to ensure the survival of Judaism and Jewish culture across Canada. Today, the Canadian Jewish community has been successful in opening day schools in many communities and in obtaining provincial government subsidies for these schools, with the major exception of those in Ontario. While most of these schools are Orthodox, there are Reform, Conservative, and community-wide day schools available in Toronto and Montreal.

Anti-Semitism was prevalent in Canada during these years. Never tiring of characterizing Jews as an untrustworthy nation within the nation, the prolific nineteenth-century historian and journalist Goldwin Smith (1823–1910) established himself as the ideological father of Canadian anti-Semitism. Smith's intellectual authority swayed powerful figures in both English and French Canada. In 1905, federal Member of Parliament Henri Bourassa (1868–1952) drew extensively on Smith's writings to exhort the House of Commons to curtail Jewish immigration to Canada. Bourassa continued this campaign for decades in the editorial pages of his influential newspaper, *Le Devoir*. In 1910, Quebec City notary, Joseph Edouard Plamendon (1862–1928), peppered an address to L'Association canadienne de la jeunesse catholique with slanders concerning Jewish usury and the ritual murder of Christian children, prompting attacks on Jews and Jewish stores. By the 1930s, anti-Semitism in Quebec was freely expressed in many circles. During the Great Depression, Bourassa's *Le Devoir* joined official Roman Catholic periodicals like *Action Catholique* in supporting the "*Achat chez-nous*" ("Buy from ourselves") boycott of Jewish businesses, and Father Lionel-Adolphe Groulx (1868–1967) fostered the alliance between French Canadian nationalism and Roman Catholic Ultramontanism epitomized in nineteenth-century figures like Jules-Paul Tardivel (1851–1905), for whom Jews represented the twin threats of liberal modernism and secular materialism. The federal government of Prime Minister William Lyon Mackenzie King (1874–1950), who was also heavily influenced by Smith, severely restricted entry to Jews fleeing Nazi-dominated Europe. Anti-Semitism did not prevent Canadian Jews from serving their country, however, and by World War II, the sheer number of Jewish servicemen obliged a reluctant Department of National Defence to appoint S. Gershon Levi (1909–90) as the first official Jewish chaplain to the armed forces.

Levi's appointment took place in large measure due to pressure from the Canadian Jewish Congress, which was founded in 1919 to represent the interests of Canadian Jewry. Great fanfare accompanied the founding of the Congress in Montreal, but the association languished till the 1930s. In 1934, rising anti-Semitism at home and abroad prompted Jewish leaders to reconvene the Congress. With financial support from prominent businessman Samuel Bronfman (1889–1971), the Congress joined in the fight for civil and political equality for Jews in Canada. Activists like Kalmen Kaplansky (1912–97), Sid Blum (born 1925), and Ben G. Kayfetz (1916–2002) were heavily involved in the labour movement of the 1920s and 1930s, and David Lewis (1909–81) drew upon Jewish traditions of social justice to help shape the Co-operative Commonwealth Federation (CCF), later the New Democratic Party.

The Canadian Jewish Congress also joined international calls for the establishment of a Jewish homeland in Palestine. In 1887, a Russian Jewish immigrant, Alexander Harkavy (1863–1939), founded a Montreal branch of Hovevei Zion ("The Lovers of Zion"), an organization devoted to the creation of Jewish agricultural settlements in Palestine. In 1892, Lazarus Cohen (born 1856) founded Shavei Zion ("Return to Zion"), a successor to Hovevei Zion. In 1899, inspired by the publication of Theodore Herzl's *The Jewish State* and the founding of the World Zionist Organization in 1897, Clarence de Sola (1858–1920), son of Abraham de Sola, organized the Canadian Federation of Zionist Societies, which was headquartered in Montreal and had affiliated groups in Quebec, Ottawa, Kingston, Toronto, London, and Winnipeg. Canadian Zionism ranged from secular associations like the socialist Poalei Zion ("Workers of Zion") to the Orthodox Mizrachi organization. Jewish women played a key role in the movement, too. Founded in 1899, Toronto's B'not Zion ("Daughters of Zion"), opened branches across Canada, and in 1917, Hadassah, the Women's Zionist Organization, came to Canada from the United States. In the 1930s, concern with Nazi anti-Semitism and the ever-increasing stream of European Jewish refugees further strengthened the Zionist movement in Canada, though Canadian Jewish leaders were unable to persuade Mackenzie King to loosen immigration restrictions for Jews. Denied a haven in the United States and in Canada in 1939, over 900 Jewish refugees aboard the steamship *St. Louis* were forced to return to an almost certain death in Europe. In a numbing irony, Jews in the Auschwitz death camp named the building holding their confiscated belongings "Kanada"—a place of incomparable comfort into which entrance was strictly forbidden. To commemorate the *St. Louis* tragedy, the steel sculpture *Wheel of Conscience* by American architect Daniel Libeskind (born 1946) was installed on 20 January 2011, at Pier 21, Canada's harbourside National Immigration Museum in Halifax, Nova Scotia.

The atrocities of the Nazi Holocaust and the founding of the state of Israel in 1948 prompted changes in Canadian immigration policy towards Jews. After World War II, some 40,000 Jewish refugees from Nazi Europe were allowed to come to Canada, reinvigorating ties between Canadian Jewry and European Jewish religion and culture. In 1956, a further wave of Jews was admitted after the failure of the Hungarian uprising against the Soviet Union. Also in the 1950s, some 20,000 French-speaking Jewish immigrants began arriving, mainly from Morocco. These Sephardic Jews dramatically changed the predominantly Ashkenazic character of Canadian Jewry, especially in Montreal. Other, more recent waves of Jewish immigration from the former Soviet Union and Israel have begun to make their mark on the Canadian Jewish community. Today, the vast majority of Canadian Jews live in cities, most notably Toronto and Montreal, with the rest located mainly in Vancouver, Winnipeg, Ottawa, Hamilton, Calgary, and Edmonton. Each of these communities hosts a plethora of synagogues, charities, schools, and other organizations. Most of these local institutions are affiliated with a Jewish Community Federation, which coordinates the fundraising efforts required to keep these institutions going. Indeed, the Federations themselves often constitute the major focus and unifying factor in the Canadian Jewish communal endeavour. Communal organizations are often further affiliated with national or international Jewish parent organizations. As the Canadian philosopher Emil Fackenheim (1916–2003) stressed, this sense of Jewish communal and organizational interconnectedness reflects the obligation incumbent upon all Jews to never again allow themselves to become defenceless victims.

Canada's Jews are remarkably diverse in their religious and ideological expressions. Committed to the lifestyle of the premodern rabbinic tradition and to maximal training in the Judaic textual tradition, Orthodox Jews enjoy an importance out of proportion to their minority numbers because of the strong network of religious and communal institutions they have created and maintain. Hasidic Jews are a highly visible presence, especially in Montreal. The first Hasidic Jews came to Canada with the wave of Eastern European immigration early in the twentieth century. Their ongoing organized presence, however, dates from the 1940s. Chabad-Lubavitch *Hasidim* came to Canada in 1941, for example, and established centres in Montreal, Toronto, and other Canadian cities, encouraging members to reclaim less observant Jews for the Orthodox tradition. Charismatic rabbis (*rebbes*) serve as spiritual guides to some Hasidic groups, like the Tasher Hasidim, centred in Boisbriand, Quebec. Other Hasidic congregations look to rabbinic leadership from the United States and Israel. Also, large numbers of Canadian Jews who do not follow the totality of Orthodox teachings in their personal lives nonetheless join and support Orthodox synagogues and other institutions. This trend is especially evident within the Canadian Sephardic community. The relative strength of Orthodox Judaism in Canada tends to steer the community as a whole towards traditionalism.

At the same time, Canadian-born and educated second-generation Jews often demanded a more "modern" congregation, with no segregation of the sexes and with greater English-language content in the services. They were thus prepared to accept the model of American Conservative Judaism, which promised needed changes while respecting the precedents of the Judaic tradition. Across Canada today, a large number of observant Jews identify themselves as Conservative. There are also a few Reconstructionist congregations in Canada, which look more to the fostering of Jewish peoplehood and civilization than to theology per se. Reform temples are also an important component of every major Canadian Jewish community, though Reform does not enjoy as wide support among Canadian Jews as among Jews in the United States. But whatever the differences in their theological understanding of the religious tradition, these non-Orthodox groups invariably share certain key religious practices, most notably a family *seder* at Passover, attending synagogue during the **High Holy Days** (*Rosh ha Shanah* and Yom Kippur), and celebrating *Hanukkah* with the lighting of candles.

Finally, a significant number of Canadian Jews understand their Jewishness less in terms of religious belief and more in terms of a celebration of their ethnic and cultural heritage. These people appreciate the cultural heritage of the Jewish religion, and often attend synagogues to participate in naming ceremonies for newborns, circumcision, **bar mitzvah** and **bat mitzvah**, and remembrance services for the dead. These affirmations do not, however, mean that these Jews agree with all, or even any, of the theological tenets of Judaism, however defined. In the Canadian census, "Jewish" is a possible response to two questions: religion and ethnic origins. Thus, the approximately 350,000 Canadians who today think of themselves as Jews tend to feel that they share more than simply religious beliefs. They also feel that they are members of an ethnic family encompassing Jewish people living in many countries around the world, particularly in the United States and Israel. This identification with Israel is expressed in many ways, most notably political support in Israel's struggles with its Arab neighbours and financial support of its institutions, including personal travel to Israel. Though criticism of some of Israel's policies is certainly a feature of Canadian Jewish communal life, this communal solidarity with Israel reflects an existential feeling within Canada's Jewish community that the State of Israel, founded so soon after the Nazi Holocaust, embodies a major part of the life-force of the Jewish people in contemporary times.

RECENT TRENDS IN THE JEWISH COMMUNTY

It is not possible to present the full diversity of Canadian Jewish belief and behaviour with only two examples of specific communities, of course, but depicting two quite different communities—Montreal's Shearith Israel and Toronto's First Narayever synagogue—does convey a sense of some important recent trends within the Canadian Jewish community. Both communities are urban and middle-class because Canadian Jewry as a whole is urban and middle-class. They are, however, diverse in their institutional structure. One is a long-established large congregation with a large building and paid clergy; the other is a small institution whose services are for the most part conducted by its membership and which at one time chose not to have a full-time professional rabbi. The communities also differ with regard to Jewish religious tradition: one upholds the legacy of Sephardic Orthodoxy, while the other continues with a mix of Sephardic and Ashkenazic traditions, although its members have rejected significant areas of Orthodox doctrine. Finally, the two communities illustrate the ongoing strength of the Judaic tradition in today's Canada, as well as the significance of the question of the place of women within the contemporary synagogue.

Shearith Israel, also known as the Spanish and Portuguese Synagogue, was Canada's first synagogue. Founded in 1768, the congregation is still thriving more than 200 years later. The congregation's original synagogue was built in the 1770s located in what is now called "Old Montreal." In 1838, the congregation moved to Chenneville Street, and in 1890, to Stanley Street. Since 1947, the congregation has gathered at 4894 St. Kevin Avenue, in the Snowdon-Côtes des Neiges district of Montreal. Though no single synagogue or community could be considered as encompassing the entire diversity of the Canadian Jewish community, Shearith Israel harbours within itself a remarkably diverse congregation of over 700 families. Originally founded in the eighteenth century as a Sephardic synagogue, it remained the only Sephardic congregation in Canada till the early 1960s and still retains its Sephardic ritual today. From the very beginning, though, Shearith Israel welcomed Ashkenazic members, as Montreal's Jewish community was not large enough to support another congregation until the 1840s. Even after an Ashkenazic synagogue was founded in the city, many Ashkenazic Jews stayed with Shearith Israel; indeed, there were many times in the history of the Spanish and Portuguese congregation when its Ashkenazic congregants outnumbered its Sephardim. The absolute number of Ashkenazic members has remained relatively constant over the past few decades, however, while the Sephardic element in the congregation has greatly increased. Thus, today the congregation comprises mainly Sephardic Jews with origins in Iraq, Lebanon, Morocco, and several other North Africa countries, many of them French-speaking. Appointed rabbi in 1970, Howard S. Joseph (born 1940) has described his congregation as a mosaic of communities. As such, it reflects both the diversity and the demographic development of Montreal's Jewish community as a whole.

Whereas in previous generations, synagogues tended to be relatively homogeneous in character, with Jews seeking out other Jews of similar origin and background with whom to worship, large synagogues, such as Shearith Israel, increasingly cater to a diverse community of Jews. Seeking to reconcile such a diverse community is not a simple task. An example of the accommodation that takes place is the insertion of certain Ashkenazic prayers into the Sephardic High Holy Day ritual. Orthodox Jews tend to be very cautious when it comes to changes in the liturgy, thus the sort of accommodation which takes place at Shearith Israel is quite remarkable. Another sort of accommodation involves giving a place to French. For most of its history, the congregation was overwhelmingly English-speaking. But changes in the immigration patterns of Jews coming to Canada in the latter half of the twentieth century, specifically the immigration of large numbers of French-speaking Jews to Montreal, and the emigration of significant numbers of English-speaking Jews from Montreal to other parts of Canada and to the United States, resulted in French being the language of a significant number of Shearith Israel's congregants. Also, political and social changes affecting the province of Quebec as a whole during and after the "Quiet Revolution" meant that French became part of a new reality for Montreal's Jews. In 1973, Rabbi Joseph symbolically embodied this change. Though he was born, grew up, and was trained in the English-speaking United States, like most contemporary Canadian Jewish clergy, he determined to master a new language so that he might deliver occasional sermons in French and increase the use of French in his relations with his congregants and in the governance of the synagogue.

The congregation of Shearith Israel is Orthodox, and maintains a full schedule of daily, Sabbath, and holiday services. Daily services attract several dozen worshippers, Sabbath morning services average around 400, and the High Holy Days bring the congregation to nearly 2,000. Both a rabbi and a cantor, who take care that the Sephardic Orthodox traditions are maintained, supervise the synagogue's rituals. Its Orthodoxy, however, is far from insular; it is tempered by openness to the concerns of contemporary Jewish society. The development of the synagogue's choir embodies certain aspects of this openness. Before the 1970s, a handful of adult males accompanied services in a choir loft. In 1972, Shearith Israel started a boys' choir, which sings in the main sanctuary every Sabbath and holiday. Successive directors have expanded the choir's repertory, with new arrangements and melodies, as well as revivals of old tunes found in the synagogue's own archives. Today, the choir numbers over thirty members, ranging in age from seven to twenty-one. Some of them learn more about their faith by helping with other aspects of the liturgy, like reading Torah, or by participating in the annual Youth Sabbath, when choirboys get a chance to be cantor or rabbi for a day.

The best illustration of the synagogue's openness to the concerns of contemporary Jewish society has to do with the position of women in the ritual life of the synagogue. Historically, Orthodox Judaism has maintained synagogue ritual as a "public" (i.e., male) activity, and assumed that women would, by and large, fulfill their religious duties in the "private" sphere of the home. Insofar as women came to the synagogue, they were seated in a separate section and had no active part in the congregational ritual. Whereas a boy's *bar mitzvah* normatively required him to publicly demonstrate his expertise in synagogue ritual, a girl's coming of age (*bat mitzvah*) was not usually celebrated in public. This situation began to change in twentieth-century North America among non-Orthodox Jewish movements, which accorded the *bat mitzvah* a place in the "public" life of the congregation. In an unusual step, Shearith Israel and its rabbinical leadership have included *bat mitzvah* celebrations as part of the congregational life of this Orthodox synagogue. In addition, the rabbi and congregation made the controversial decision to introduce a separate women's prayer service on a monthly basis, at the time of the inauguration of a new month in the Jewish calendar (*rosh hodesh*), which allows women to lead and to participate in synagogue ritual in an entirely new way. The *Beit Hamidrash* ("House of Study") program, begun in 2001, includes morning and occasional evening Torah classes for men and women and a weekly women's study group, as well as Talmud and Modern Hebrew classes. Shearith Israel has revised its by-laws, too, ensuring a significant female presence in its governance structure.

By contrast with Shearith Israel, Toronto's First Narayever synagogue began as a small congregation of Eastern European Jewish immigrants from the town of Narayev in Galicia, the name for those parts of southeast Poland and southwest Russia then controlled by the Austro-Hungarian Empire. As early as 1914, a building at the corner of Huron Street and Bathurst Street served as a meeting-place for this *landsmanschaft* ("mutual association of immigrants"), which received a provincial charter in 1918. A section of the cemetery on Dawes Road was purchased and consecrated.

In 1940, the congregation moved to its present premises at 187 Brunswick Avenue. Built as a Foresters Lodge and later used as a Methodist chapel, the congregation's new building contained seating for slightly more than 100. Immigrant Galician Hasidic rebbe Moshe Langner of Kozowa-Strettin (1878–1945) served as rabbi, although his time was divided between First Narayever and two other Orthodox synagogues, Kiever and Shaarei Tzedec, where he also served as rabbi. Langner did not lead services, but acted as spiritual teacher and authority on the *halakhic* traditions of Torah and Talmud. Moshe Langner's son Shlomo (1900–73) also served the Narayever synagogue, which flourished for most of its life as an Eastern European immigrant Orthodox congregation. By the 1960s and 1970s, however, most of the immigrant generation had died and many of their offspring had moved out of Toronto's downtown neighbourhoods to suburban areas. Inner-city synagogues closed or moved to these new areas, principally along the Bathurst Street corridor.

That this fate did not befall the First Narayever synagogue was due to the presence of a group of young Jewish academics and professionals who had moved into the neighbourhood, which is not far from the University of Toronto. Of varying degrees of religious commitment, these newcomers were looking for a synagogue with which to affiliate, and in which they could express their desire to pray in a small congregation that was conveniently located. For a number of years, the newcomers were able to coexist with the remnant of the original membership of the synagogue. The synagogue thus maintained its existence, but not without significant change. Its new congregants were basically comfortable with the idea of maintaining the synagogue and its traditional service, and they had among them sufficient people with the requisite knowledge to conduct the services themselves, so that they were not obliged to go to the expense of hiring a rabbi or cantor. But they were not ultimately willing to maintain that aspect of the traditional structure of Orthodox ritual that denied women a public voice in the synagogue.

In the early 1980s, the congregation renovated the basement to include a social hall, kitchen, and modern washrooms. In 1982, the newcomers decided to introduce an alternative service downstairs, in which men and women shared synagogue rituals and honours on an equal basis, with no physical demarcation indicating where men and women could sit during the services. Orthodox services continued upstairs, but the alternative gender egalitarian service soon began to attract additional members. Outnumbered, the older members launched a lawsuit in an

In First Narayever synagogue, Brunswick Avenue, Toronto, the Holy Ark (*aron ha-kodesh*), which contains the Torah scrolls, is screened by a tapestry curtain (*parokhet*) depicting the city of Jerusalem, the Jordan River, and the Tree of Knowledge as a symbol of Torah. PHOTO BY JAMIE S. SCOTT. REPRINTED BY PERMISSION OF FIRST NARAYEVER SYNAGOGUE, TORONTO. © JAMIE S. SCOTT/FIRST NARAYEVER SYNAGOGUE.

effort to restore the *status quo ante*. The lawsuit failed and the new leadership group remained in control of the congregation. Without the numbers to sustain a *minyan* (religious quorum of ten), remaining older members dispersed to other Orthodox congregations, and within a few months the egalitarian service moved upstairs. At first, the new leadership of the congregation sought to establish gender egalitarianism within Orthodox liturgical parameters, but it soon became clear that no Orthodox rabbi was willing to countenance such developments. Officially unaffiliated with any Jewish religious denomination, the congregation embarked on a new period in which it was to become the best attended and most active synagogue in downtown Toronto.

Today, the constitution of the First Narayever synagogue states that the services and policies of the congregation are in accordance with *halakha* except insofar as it conflicts with the principle of gender egalitarianism. All food at synagogue functions must be **kosher**, for example, and the congregation stresses the traditional Jewish values of *gemilut hasadim* ("charitable deeds"). At the same time, though, the principle of gender egalitarianism governs many aspects of the synagogue's ritual life. Although the traditional prayer book is largely retained, the liturgy is amended so that when the great patriarchs or "fathers"—Abraham, Isaac, and Jacob—are mentioned, so too are the names of the "mothers"—Sarah, Rebecca, Rachel, and Leah. Women in the congregation wear the same ritual head coverings and prayer shawls as men. First Narayever has also modified the procedures for calling congregants to be honoured during the public reading of the Torah. Whereas a non-egalitarian congregation calls a member by his name and the name of his father, First Narayever calls a person by his or her Jewish name and by the Jewish names of both of the person's parents.

In some ways, Toronto's First Narayever synagogue is *sui generis,* in others it exemplifies seemingly contradictory trends in contemporary Canadian Judaism. On the one hand, many Jews are turning away from large, institutionalized congregations with full-time professional clergy towards smaller, more intimate settings for worship and Judaic study. Often under the leadership of the congregation's own members, this sort of assembly is reminiscent of the small and intimate Orthodox congregations attended by late nineteenth- and early twentieth-century Eastern European Jewish immigrants to Canada. Today, Orthodox Jews tend to call this sort of gathering a *shteibl* (prayer room) or *minyan,* while Reform, Conservative, and Reconstructionist Jews often refer to it as a *havurah* (association). On the other hand, the events at First Narayever synagogue seem to signal gradual changes in the characteristic ethos of Canadian Jewry. This ethos has been fundamentally traditionalist in theological outlook. However, it is significant that, like Toronto's First Narayever, the Shearith Israel leadership, while maintaining continuity with Orthodox Sephardic observance, has affirmed egalitarian efforts to include women to the fullest extent in both the ritual and the liturgical life of the synagogue. Also, for decades, First Narayever resisted affiliating itself formally with any of the non-Orthodox Jewish religious movements that have institutionalized departures from rabbinical tradition. In 2000, however, Edward Elkin

(born 1962), who received his rabbinical ordination from Reform Judaism's
Hebrew Union College, became rabbi of First Narayever congregation.

AFTERWORD

It is clear that Canadian Jews, like all contemporary Jews, live to one extent
or another in two civilizations. They are at one and the same time integral
members of the Canadian polity and sensitive to the many ways in which
Judaism and the religious civilization it has created can connect with their
lives. As Jews, they maintain close ties with the two major centres of Jewish
population and cultural creativity: the United States and Israel. They share
many characteristics with American Jews and participate actively in the
religious and cultural life of American Jewry. Yet in subtle ways they are
different. As a group they seem to be more strongly "Jewishly" identified
and educated and less acculturated than most American Jews. Their religious life seems, relatively speaking, more "traditional." Canadian Jews'
relatively closer ties to Israel, through family connections, travel, and other
forms of support distinguish them as a group from American Jewry. Israel,
its promise and its problems, loom large in the consciousness of Canadian
Jews. As the one country on earth where being Jewish is "normal," Israel is
seen by most Canadian Jews as a country with which they have special ties.
Whatever their interpretation of Judaism, their opinion on specific policies
of the State of Israel, and whether or not they believe in the literality of the
biblical message, for most Canadian Jews, Israel is a "home away from home."

Canadian Jewry is a community that is growing moderately, largely
through immigration, and is undergoing significant demographic change.
Because of the political and social trends in the province of Quebec, the
population of the Jewish community in Montreal, historically the largest
in Canada, has fallen from a high of approximately 110,000 in the 1970s
to approximately 90,000 today. In contrast, the Toronto Jewish community has burgeoned, partly with the help of displaced Montreal Jews, and
has taken Montreal's place as Canada's primary Jewish community. As
a community, Canada's Jews have largely prospered and put down deep
roots in this country. The multicultural mosaic that has evolved in Canada
affords them a secure place in a polity that tends to respect difference. The
essential problem of Canadian Jews, that of achieving a balance between
living in North American society and responding to the Jewish tradition,
remains to be solved by each individual Canadian Jew.

KEY TERMS

Ashkenazic	From *Ashkenaz,* the medieval Hebrew name for Germany, the term refers to Jews with roots in medieval Western Europe.
Bar and Bat Mitzvah	"Son" and "daughter of the law," a term designating the initiation of boys and girls into ritual adulthood, at ages thirteen and twelve, respectively.
Berith	"Covenant," the term applied to the special relationship between Jews and their God.
Conservative	Term used to describe contemporary Jews who desire that change in Judaism be in basic agreement with premodern rabbinic teachings without being fundamentalist.
Diaspora	"Dispersion," a term used to describe the settlement of Jews outside the land of Israel, often associated with exile.
Exile	The deportation of Jews from the land of Israel, especially the deportation of the Israelite élite to Babylon in 586 BCE after the destruction of the First Temple, and in 70 CE after the destruction of the Second Temple, often associated with diaspora.
Exodus	The migration of the Hebrews from Egypt under the leadership of Moses, resulting in the birth of the ancient nation of biblical Israel.
Halakha	The laws of the Torah and their rabbinic interpretation.
Hanukkah	The eight-day winter festival of lights marking the rededication of the Second Temple in 164 BCE.
Hasidism	Jewish pietistic movement originating in eighteenth-century Eastern Europe.
High Holy Days	A term for the major Jewish religious holidays of *Rosh ha Shanah* and *Yom Kippur,* celebrated in the autumn.
Holocaust	During World War II, the systematic murder of Jews by Nazi Germany and its allies, called the *Shoah* by many Jews.
Kabbalah	"Received tradition," the term for Jewish mysticism.
Kosher	Derived mainly from Torah (Leviticus and Deuteronomy), the part of Jewish law (*halakha*) that deals with food regulations.
Messiah	"One anointed by God," the term applied to the expected saviour of the Jews.

Orthodox	Term used to describe contemporary Jews who adhere strictly to premodern rabbinic teachings.
Passover	A festival that commemorates the ancient Israelite Exodus from Egypt.
Rabbi	"My teacher," a term used to describe a spiritual leader and scholarly expert in the interpretation of Torah and Talmud.
Reconstructionist	Term used to describe contemporary Jews who interpret Judaism as a multifaceted civilization.
Reform	Term used to describe contemporary Jews who are willing to liberalize premodern rabbinic teachings to accommodate the demands of the modern age.
Sabbath	The seventh day of the week, which Jews observe as a holy day of rest, prayer, and study.
Sephardic	From *Sepharad,* the medieval Hebrew name for Spain, the term refers to Jews with roots in medieval Islamic countries.
Sukkot	Jewish festival celebrated in the fall by the erecting of temporary shelters (*Sukkot*) commemorating the 40 years the Israelites wandered in the wilderness.
Talmud	The *halakhic* (legal) and *aggadic* (non-legal) religious literature produced by rabbis from approximately the second through the seventh centuries CE.
Tanakh	An acronym for the Hebrew Bible (the Christian Old Testament), *Tanakh* divides into Torah, *Nevi'im* ("prophets"), and *Ketuvim* ("sacred writings").
Torah	"Instruction," in a narrow sense it refers to the *Pentateuch* ("Five Books of Moses"), the first division of *Tanakh*. In a broader sense, Torah encompasses all teachings believed to have emanated from God, and thus includes not only *Tanakh* as a whole but also rabbinic teachings as a whole, especially the Talmud.
Zionism	A movement to create a Jewish homeland in Israel as a solution to the problem of modern anti-Semitism.

KEY DATES

ca. **2000–1500 BCE**	Abraham and the patriarchs, or "fathers," of Jewish tradition.

ca. **1500–1200 BCE**	Egypt, the Exodus, and wandering in the desert.
1200–1050 BCE	Occupation of Canaan.
1050–920 BCE	United kingdom under Saul, David, and Solomon, with its capital at Jerusalem.
920–597 BCE	Divided kingdom of Israel (north) and Judah (south).
586 BCE	Destruction of Jerusalem and the First Temple by the Babylonians.
ca. **515 BCE**	Construction of the Second Temple.
167–164 BCE	Maccabean Revolt.
70 CE	Destruction of Jerusalem and the Second Temple of Jerusalem by the Romans.
ca. **500**	Redaction of the Babylonian Talmud.
1204	Death of Moses Maimonides.
1492	Expulsion of professing Jews from Spain.
1768	Montreal's Shearith Israel consecrated as the first synagogue in Canada.
1786	Death of Moses Mendelssohn.
1832	Jews in Upper and Lower Canada granted equality of rights.
1880s	Beginning of great wave of emigration of Jews from Eastern Europe.
1897	First Zionist Congress, in Basel, Switzerland.
1919	Convening of Canadian Jewish Congress in Montreal.
1938	*Kristallnacht* portends the Nazi Holocaust.
1948	Establishment of the State of Israel.

KEY READINGS

Abella, Irving. *A Coat of Many Colours: Two Centuries of Jewish Life in Canada*. Toronto: Lester and Orpen Denys, 1990.

Brown, Michael. *Jew or Juif? Jews, French Canadians and Anglo Canadians, 1759–1914*. Philadelphia: Jewish Publication Society, 1987.

Brym, Robert J., William Shaffir, and Morton Weinfeld, eds. *The Jews in Canada*. Toronto: Oxford University Press, 1993.

De Lange, Nicholas. *An Introduction to Judaism*. Cambridge: Cambridge University Press, 2000.

Encyclopaedia Judaica. 2nd ed. 22 volumes. New York: Thomson Gale's Macmillan Reference USA, 2007.

Gilbert, Martin. *The Holocaust: The Jewish Tragedy*. London: Fontana Press, 1987.

Pardes, Ilana. *The Biography of Ancient Israel: National Narratives in the Bible*. Berkeley: University of California Press, 2000.

Schneider, Susan Weidman. *Jewish and Female*. New York: Simon and Schuster, 1984.

Seltzer, Robert M. *Jewish People, Jewish Thought: The Jewish Experience in History*. New York: Macmillan, 1980.

Tulchinsky, Gerald. *Canada's Jews: A People's Journey*. Toronto: University of Toronto Press, 2008.

Weinfeld, Morton. *Like Everyone Else . . . But Different: The Paradoxical Success of Canadian Jews*. Toronto: McClelland and Stewart, 2001.

Wertheimer, Jack. *A People Divided: Judaism in Contemporary America*. New York: Basic Books, 1993.

Yerushalmi, Yosef. *Zakhor: Jewish History and Jewish Memory*. Seattle: University of Washington Press, 1982.

KEY WEBSITES

http://www.acjs-aejc.ca/about.html [Association for Canadian Jewish Studies]

http://www.cjc.ca [Centre for Israel and Jewish Affairs]

http://portico.concordia.ca/jchair/index.php [Concordia Institute for Canadian Jewish Studies]

http://www.jhcwc.org/ [Jewish Heritage Centre of Western Canada]

http://www.jewishcanada.org [Jewish Federations of Canada–United Israel Appeal]

KEY QUESTIONS FOR CRITICAL REFLECTION

1. How did the Jewish presence in Canada spur the process of defining what being a Canadian meant?
2. In what sense can it be said that the role of women in the synagogue is a defining issue for contemporary Canadian Judaism?
3. How did immigration patterns affect the development of the Canadian Jewish community in the twentieth century?
4. How are the Ashkenazic and Sephardic traditions reflected in the life of Canadian Jews?
5. What is the interplay between religion and ethnicity in the lives of Canadian Jews?

FIVE

Muslims

AMIR HUSSAIN, LOYOLA MARYMOUNT UNIVERSITY
JAMIE S. SCOTT, YORK UNIVERSITY

||||||||||||||||||||||||||||||||||||||||||||||||||||||||||||||||||||||||||||||||||||||||||||||||||||||||||||||

slam is the second-largest religious tradition in the world. **Sunnis** comprise 80–85 per cent of the community, **Shi'ites** 15–20 per cent. With over 700,000 members, Islam is also the second-largest religious group in Canada. In the late nineteenth century, the handful of Muslims in Canada traced their roots to Scottish ancestors. By the end of the next century, Canada's Muslim population clearly reflected the ethnic variety of the country as a whole. Since World War II, immigration has created large Muslim communities in major urban centres, notably Toronto, Montreal, Vancouver, Ottawa, Calgary, and Edmonton. By some counts, the Toronto region alone is home to almost 250 Islamic organizations. South-Asian and Middle-Eastern Muslims outnumber newcomers from other parts of the world, who include immigrants from Africa, China, Europe, Southeast Asia, Australasia, and the South Pacific. With their numbers supplemented by converts, today Muslims are Canada's fastest-growing religious community. Blending historical and phenomenological approaches, this chapter mixes insider and outsider viewpoints to explore the diverse origins of this community and to capture something of the richness and variety of Muslim religious life in contemporary Canada.

THE HERITAGE

Islam is an Arabic word meaning "engaged surrender to God." Muslims undertake such engaged surrender through *jihad*, a word often narrowly translated as "holy war," particularly against non-Muslims, but which more accurately means "striving for moral and spiritual perfection," especially against one's own inner weaknesses. Islam originated in the Arabian Peninsula in the sixth century. Judaism and Christianity were already known in Arabia at that time, and historians of religion see Islam as another form of ethical monotheism. Muslims associate the origins of the tradition with the historical figure of Muhammad, who was born into the Quraysh tribe of Mecca around 570 CE. Broadly speaking, the history of Islam divides into four periods: the career of Muhammad (*ca.* 610–632); the classical age (632–1258); the imperial age (*ca.* 1258–1800); and the modern age (*ca.* 1800–the present day).

According to tradition, God (**Allah**) summoned Muhammad as a prophet to warn the people of Mecca against polytheism and social injustice. Long the spiritual centre of the Arabian Peninsula, Mecca attracted many pilgrims to the shrines and idols housed in an ancient sanctuary dominated by a sacred black cube, the **Ka'ba**. The city's leaders feared that Muhammad's attacks on idolatry would jeopardize business, a good deal of which catered to the pilgrims. In 622, after an unsuccessful attempt on Muhammad's life, he and his followers migrated from Mecca to neighbouring Medina where they built the first mosque or *masjid*, meaning literally "the place of prostration." Known as the *umma*, the community established a way of life based on Muhammad's revelations. Three times their enemies from Mecca tried to destroy the new Muslim community, and three times they were unsuccessful. This strength of conviction attracted many new converts. In 630, the expanded Muslim community waged a successful campaign to capture the sanctuary of the Ka'ba in Mecca, which they believed the biblical Abraham and his son Ishmael originally built to honour God alone. All other shrines and idols were destroyed and the sanctuary was rededicated to God. Soon, the peoples of Mecca and the Arabian Peninsula converted to Islam.

Muhammad died in 632. Some followers argued that succession in matters of both spiritual and temporal authority should remain in Muhammad's family. This minority believed that the Prophet had so designated his cousin, Ali ibn Abu Talib (599–661), who was also Muhammad's son-in-law by virtue of marriage to his daughter, Fatima al-Zahra (*ca.*

605–633). But the majority of Muhammad's followers argued that the revelation had ended with the Prophet's passing, that he had appointed no spiritual successor, and that the community was now responsible for choosing temporal leaders. Known as Sunnis, this majority turned to the senior members of the community and chose Muhammad's close advisor, Abu Bakr (573–634), as his first successor or caliph (**khalifa**)—a title denoting military and political leadership, but not prophetic authority. Umar ibn al-Khattab (581–644) succeeded Abu Bakr, then Uthman ibn Affan (574–656), and at last Ali himself, to constitute the dynasty of the Rashidun, or "Rightly Guided" caliphs. Under the Rashidun, Islamic rule expanded over much of Egypt, Libya, Syria, and Persia. After a group of political fanatics called Kharijites assassinated Ali in 661, his followers separated from the Sunnis and became known as Shi'ites, or "partisans." Based in Damascus, a second dynasty, the Ummayads (661–750), eliminated Shi'ite competition by killing Ali's son, Husayn, at the Battle of Karbala (680), and then extended the Islamic caliphate east to northern India and west across North Africa into the Iberian Peninsula. Governing from Baghdad, a third dynasty, the Abbasids (750–1258), saw the rise of a Muslim golden age. Although political and religious tensions between Sunnis and Shi'ites and Arabs and non-Arabs weakened the central authority of Abbasid caliphs, Islamic civilization assumed rich local and regional forms, flourishing throughout Iberia, North Africa, the Middle East, and Central Asia. This prosperity continued until the Mongols, under Hulagu Khan (1217–65), sacked Baghdad in 1258, only to withdraw with the death of their leader, Möngke Khan (1208–59).

Muslims consider 622 to be the first year of their calendar, and the migration to Medina, known as the **hijra**, came to symbolize the notion that Islam is transportable, not dependent upon living in a particular place. Wherever Muslims live, however, they base their faith on God's revelations to Muhammad. Muslims believe that God sent the archangel Gabriel to inspire Muhammad with revelations in the year 610. As prophet (*nabi*) or messenger (*rasul*), he recited these revelations to his companions—most notably his beloved first wife, Khadijah bint Khuwaylid (*ca.* 555–619), who often memorized them, sometimes using verses (*ayas*) for prayer. From memorized passages and words written on palm leaves, stones, or other materials, Muhammad's revelations were gathered into a collection known as the **Qur'an**, meaning "recitation." Several variant readings of the Qur'an survived Muhammad, but a canonical text was established during the caliphate of Uthman. It consists of 114 chapters (*suras*), which vary greatly in the number of verses; the longest chapters are first and the shortest are last, though the latter were the earliest revelations Muhammad received. Muslims recognize the Arabic version of the Qur'an as a perfect expression of the infallible word of God because Arabic served as the medium of transmission throughout this process. While the Qur'an has been translated into other languages, Muslims are encouraged to memorize the Arabic text and to conduct prayers in Arabic, regardless of their mother tongue. Reciting and listening to the Qur'an in Arabic remain pre-eminent forms of religious practice, enabling Muslims to cultivate a sacred sense of closeness to God.

Although the Qur'an is the supreme miracle of Islam, Muslims also cherish Muhammad's example as a paradigm for all aspects of daily living. Traditionally, this authoritative way of life, known as the **sunna**, embraces what the Prophet said, what he did, and what he silently approved. Reported in collections of sayings known as the *Hadith*, the *sunna* provides a historical model of appropriate behaviour and exemplary wisdom. An individual saying (**hadith**) is adjudged genuine, good, or weak, depending on how reliably it can be traced to Muhammad's closest companions. Sunni Muslims acknowledge a canon of six major collections of sayings, the most important of which were compiled in the ninth century by Muhammad ibn Ismail al-Bukhari (810–70) and Muslim ibn al-Hajjaj al-Nisaburi (817–75). Shi'ites reject sayings attributed to enemies of Ali and his lineage, preferring instead to refer to collections of their own, like the tenth-century *Usul al-Kafi* (*Sufficient Fundamentals*) of Muhammad ibn Yaqub Kulaini (864–941). Either way, the name of the Prophet prompts believers to utter praises like "May God bless him and give him peace" or "Peace be upon him."

Muslims regard their faith to be as much a matter of religious practice (*din*) as it is of belief. Rooted in the Qur'an, the main duties of every adult Muslim, male or female, are known as **al-Arkan**, or the Five Pillars of Islam, as articulated by Muhammad in a *hadith* recorded in al-Bukhari's collection. The first duty of a believing Muslim is to publicly recite the **shahada** ("witness"). The words of this simple creed capture the essence of Islam: "There is no god but God, and Muhammad is the messenger of God." Fulfillment of the remaining pillars follows from acceptance of the *shahada*. Praying five times a day constitutes the second pillar, known as **salat**. At dawn, noon, mid-afternoon, sunset, and in the evening after dark, a *muezzin* ("herald") summons Muslims to prayer from the tower, called a "minaret," which adjoins almost every mosque. Outside the mosque,

Muslim pilgrims circumambulating the Ka'ba as part of the Hajj, Mecca, Saudi Arabia. PHOTO BY
MUHAMMAD MAHDI KARIM. REPRINTED UNDER THE TERMS OF THE GNU FREE DOCUMENTATION LICENSE.

devotees perform *wudu,* washing their hands, forearms, parts of their
faces, heads, and feet three times in a specified order. Inside, men and
women pray separately. Guided by a marker called the *qibla,* they repeatedly prostrate themselves in the direction of the Ka'ba in Mecca, reciting
the words of the *shahada,* the opening chapter of the Qur'an, and other
prescribed prayers. On Friday, the Muslim holy day, the prayer leader,
known as an *imam,* preaches a sermon (*khutba*) on some pressing social
or political topic at a noon service (*jum'ah*). When no mosque is near,
observant Muslims conduct their prayers in private at the decreed times,
kneeling upon small rugs specially woven for the purpose.

The third pillar of Islam is **zakat**, which literally means "growing in
goodness," and in this context describes the command to give alms. Such
charity reminds more fortunate Muslims of God's munificence, but also of
the transience of worldly pleasures. Fourth, Muslims are required to fast
from sunrise to sunset during **Ramadan**, the ninth month of the Muslim
lunar calendar. As in other religious traditions, such abstention from food,
drink, and sexual relations, known as **sawm**, turns the heart and mind to
spiritual things. Muslims celebrate the end of Ramadan with *Eid al-Fitr,*
or "Feast of [Fast-]Breaking," a time of reconciliation and renewal, when
families don their finest clothes to attend a special service of thanksgiving
at the mosque, then gather at home to share gifts and a feast of traditional
food and drink.

The fifth and final pillar is a pilgrimage to Mecca, known as *hajj*, which takes place during *Dhu al-Hijja,* the last month of the Muslim calendar. Every Muslim must undertake this pilgrimage once in a lifetime, health and means permitting. Within the sacred territory of Mecca, all devotees wear simple white robes to symbolize purity of spirit on the one hand, and the shared humanity of all believers before God on the other. Inside Mecca's Great Mosque, pilgrims walk counter-clockwise seven times around the Ka'ba. They then jog seven times between the hills Safa and Marwa in remembrance of Hagar, who searched high and low for water for her infant son, Abraham's first-born, Ishmael. Next to the Ka'ba, pilgrims pray at the wellspring of Zamzam, miraculously revealed to Hagar by an angel from God. The Great Mosque also contains a shrine dedicated to Abraham. Pilgrims then walk nine miles to Mount Arafat, where an *imam* commemorates Muhammad's last sermon with a homily. Other observances include a symbolic stoning of the devil in the nearby city of Mina, which involves hitting three walls (*jamarat*) with seven pebbles each. Wealthy pilgrims then sacrifice animals to provide a three-day feast for everyone, known as *Eid al-Adha* or "Feast of Sacrifice." This feast commemorates Abraham's readiness to obey God by sacrificing a son, whom Muslims believe to have been Ishmael—not Isaac, as the Hebrew scriptures record. The forefather of the Arabs, Ishmael helped Abraham build the first house of God at Mecca, where pilgrims end the *hajj* with a last walk around the Ka'ba. Though they are not required to do so, many devotees also choose to visit Medina's Mosque of the Prophet, which contains the tombs of Muhammad, Abu Bakr and Umar.

In addition to the festivals of *Eid al-Fitr* and *Eid al-Adha,* both Sunni and Shi'ite Muslims celebrate Muhammad's birthday on *Mawlid al-Nabi,* as well as numerous occasions of national, regional, and local religious significance. For Shi'ites, however, *Ashura,* the tenth day of the first month *Muharram,* is particularly important. Shi'ites believe that the rightful authority in Islam rests not with the caliphate, but with the **Ahl al-Bayt**, a term referring to the family of Muhammad's daughter Fatima, her husband Ali, their sons Hasan (625–69) and Husayn (626–80), and the imamate, an unbroken line of protectors of the faith (*imams*) descended from Husayn. *Ashura* marks the death of Muhammad's grandson Husayn. Shi'ites travel as pilgrims to Karbala, in modern Iraq, to worship at the shrine said to house the martyr's remains. Worldwide, they stage local productions of the *Taziyeh,* a passion play rehearsing Husayn's suffering, with devotees sometimes flagellating themselves with whips or beating their chests in mourning. At the same time, though, Shi'ites disagree on the constitution of the imamate. Named after the fifth *imam*, Husayn's grandson Zayd ibn Ali (695–740), Zaydis or "Fivers" consider themselves a fifth school in addition to the four orthodox Sunni schools. The death of the sixth *imam*, Ja'ffar al-Sadiq (702–765), brought further divisions. Those who believe al-Sadiq's elder son Isma'il bin Jafar (721–55) to have been the last *imam* are called Ismai'ilis or "Seveners."

Further rifts over succession divided the Ismai'ilis. The Nizaris, today's most visible Ismai'ili sect, are named for the *imam* Abu Mansur al-Nizar (1045–97). Known as Ithna Asharis or "Twelvers," devotees of al-Sadiq's younger son, Musa al-Kazim (746–99), believe al-Kazim's descendant Muhammad ibn Hasan ibn Ali (born 868) to have been the twelfth and last *imam*. Twelvers argue that God spirited away the twelfth *imam* to protect him from Sunni persecution, but that he will emerge from hiding as the **Mahdi**, or "Divinely Guided One," to bring divine justice to the world at the end of days. For this largest Shi'ite sect, the observances of *Ashura* thus assume a messianic flavour, as they not only lament Husayn's death but also look forward to the coming of the Mahdi. Until then, charismatic figures known as *ayatollahs*, meaning literally "signs of God," serve as caretakers of God's purpose. By contrast, the Nizari Ismai'ilis believe in an uninterrupted imamate from Muhammad to the Aga Khan IV, Shah Karim al-Husayn (born 1936). In yet another tradition, Alawite Muslims trace their heritage directly to Ali, to whom some attribute almost divine status.

Alongside their ritual undertakings, Muslims are guided by a broad range of legal and ethical precepts known collectively as **shari'a**. During the classical period, a cadre of scholarly jurists called the **ulema** developed guidelines about what is permissible (**halal**) and what is forbidden (**haraam**) in various areas of personal and public Muslim life, including family, business, and civil relations. Islamic dietary laws forbid pork and intoxicants, for example, while other legislation covers everything from marriage, adultery, and divorce to murder, theft, fornication, cheating, and bearing false witness. Another important area covers the status of the **dhimmi**, that is, adult males who are neither slaves nor Muslims living under Muslim rule. Originally designating Jews and Christians, or "People of the Book"—and sometimes extended to include members of other religious communities—the *dhimmi* paid a special tax, known as the *jizya*, in return for freedom of faith and security of person and property. In all such matters, the Qur'an served as the ultimate source of legal authority, followed by the Hadith. Where these sources required interpretation, the *ulema* made rulings by consensus (*ijma*), and failing clear consensus, by analogy (*qiyas*) from one situation to another, producing a legal opinion, or **fatwa**. Differences of opinion resulted in different schools of Islamic jurisprudence (**fiqh**). Among Sunni Muslims, the Hanifi, Maliki, Shafi'i, and Hanbali groups gained pre-eminence, with the Hanifi—named for Abu Hanifa (699–765)—often being considered the most liberal, and the Hanbali—named for Ahmad ibn Hanbal (780–855)—the most conservative. Named for Ja'ffar al-Sadiq (702–68), the sixth *imam*, the Ja'ffari school came to dominate Shi'ite jurisprudence. After the tenth century, jurists were usually trained in educational institutions known as *madrassas*. Sometimes, scholars of the Qur'an and the Hadith developed independent opinions, a process known as *ijtihad*. Though this practice still enjoys respect among many Shi'ites, orthodox Sunnis generally follow the teachings of the celebrated Shafi'i scholar, Abu Hamid Muhammad al-Ghazali (1058–1111), whose *Tahafut al-falasifa* (*Incoherence of the Philosophers*) argues that excessive innovation (*bida*) threatens the well-being of the community, especially in matters of religious belief and practice. Jurists may also serve as judges in courts of Islamic law, as well as teachers of the Qur'an and the Hadith.

But this focus upon religious duty, law, and ethics does not mean that Islam has not developed sophisticated mystical and doctrinal traditions. In matters of doctrine, the Qur'an and the Hadith form the basis of Muslim faith (*iman*), as elaborated by such classical thinkers as Abu al-Hasan al-Ash'ari (873–935), al-Ghazali, and Ibn Rushd (1126–98). Traditionally, Muslim faith involves six areas of belief. First is the doctrine of the transcendent reality of one God. For Muslims, anyone who associates God with any aspect of creation, whether material or spiritual, real or imagined, commits the worst form of heresy, known as *shirk,* for to compromise God's transcendent unity (*tawhid*) is to commit idolatry. Second, Muslims believe that, beginning with Adam, God has revealed the way of salvation to humankind through a line of prophets. The five most important prophets are Noah, Abraham, Moses, Jesus, and Muhammad, who was the last to be so addressed and is therefore called the "seal of the prophets." Third, Muslims believe in the reality of spiritual beings, notably the archangels Gabriel, Michael, Raphael, and Israel, who execute the will of God by serving as emissaries between the visible and invisible realms. Fourth, Muslims recognize that the Torah, the Psalms of David, and the Gospel of Jesus embody earlier revelations to humankind, conveyed by the archangel Gabriel to earlier prophets. The last two aspects of Muslim belief have to do directly with the nature of God: judgment and predestination. On the Day of Resurrection (*Yawm al-Qiyamah*), announced by the prophet Jesus, God will destroy the world and judge the living and the dead according to the degree to which they adhered to the revelation with which they were blessed. For Sunnis and Shi'ites, the Mahdi will play a key role in this judgment, too. The good will enjoy paradise and the bad will suffer a fiery hell, with temporary punishments for weak believers. Finally, Muslims believe in divine destiny (*qadar*). Nothing in the natural world or in human history happens beyond God's omnipotence and omniscience, while God's absolute goodness and perfect unity isolate him from all evil and furnish prophets and revelations to guide those who believe.

Islamic mystics are known as **Sufis**. With the rapid spread of Islam in the seventh and eighth centuries, the faith's leaders accumulated great wealth. Certain Muslims feared that such worldly success would compromise the spiritual purity of the tradition. In the Qur'an and the *sunna*, they found inspiring poetry and a humble lifestyle, not military conquest and personal aggrandizement. Thus begins an interpretation of Islam from a mystical, ascetic point of view. Because they wore simple robes of undyed wool, these ascetic mystics were called Sufis, from the Arabic *suf*, meaning "wool." Early Sufis, like the woman mystic Rabia al-Adawiyah (713–801) and the Egyptian Dhu al-Nun al-Misri (died 859), cultivated an intense interior devotion to God through prayer and meditation upon the Qur'an and the *sunna*. Other mystics pursued spiritual union with the divine, sometimes running afoul of the religious courts of the *ulema*. In 922, for example, Mansur al-Hallaj (858–922) was convicted of the heresy of *shirk* and crucified like Jesus for declaring, "I *am* the real [or the truth]," which seemed to imply a belief in divine incarnation. In *Ihya ulum al-din* (*Revivification of the Religious Sciences*), al-Ghazali resolved some important tensions between Sufis and their persecutors by skilfully blending the inspired mysticism of spiritual "revivification" and the theological legalism of "the religious sciences." Invoking images of ecstatic intoxication, divine illumination, and the ultimate unity of being, later Muslim mystics like Shihab al-Din Suhrawardi (1155–91), Ibn Arabi (1165–1240), and Jalal al-Din Rumi (1207–73) produced a large body of writing, including handbooks on meditation, esoteric philosophy, collections of visionary poetry, and biographies of Sufi holy men and women, called **walis**, or "friends of God." Known as *shaikhs*, Sufi masters developed orders (**tariqas**), devotional centres (*zawiyas*), and networks of Muslim schools (*madrassas*), which often provided employment, health care, and education to the poor and underprivileged. From the ninth century on, mainly Sunni Sufi orders furnished missionaries who followed in the footsteps of Muslim troops, merchants, and diplomats, carrying Islam south and west through sub-Saharan Africa and north across Central Asia and southern Russia.

When the classical age ended with the Mongol sacking of Baghdad, law, commerce, education, political theory, philosophy, mathematics, medicine, and science and technology were all thriving in the "House of Islam" (*dar-al-Islam*). In many cases, Muslim achievements in these fields of knowledge passed to the non-Muslim world, contributing to the resurgence of European culture in the Renaissance. The modern Western university has institutional roots in Islam, too. The centuries following the classical age are often referred to as the imperial age of Islam. Some scholars talk of this period as a dark age; others argue that the tradition developed in more localized ways, free of the centralized authority of the Abbasid caliphate. After the death of Salah al-Din (1138–93), the Kurdish Muslim leader who recaptured Jerusalem from Christian crusaders in 1187, rival factions fought for control of Muslim territories in the Middle East. Egypt, Syria, and Palestine soon came under the sway of the Mamluks. Meaning "owned," a Mamluk was a captive slave who became a Muslim warrior. Known as "sultans," Mamluk leaders defeated the Mongols in 1260 and made Cairo their capital. The Mamluk sultanate (1250–1517) expanded from southeastern Anatolia to the Hejaz, including parts of Libya and Sudan. Disciplined in mind and body, Mamluk élites worked with a conservative Sunni *ulema* to preserve the classical Muslim heritage. Islamic art and culture prospered, epitomized by the unrivalled calligraphy, illuminations, and bindings of Mamluk Qur'ans; highly accomplished metalwork; the flourishing of historiography; and the popular Persian, Arabic, and Indian tales collected in *The Book of One Thousand and One Nights*.

The Mamluk sultanate was overtaken by the Ottoman Empire (1299–1923). This most powerful of Muslim empires traced its own origins to the period before the Mongol invasions, when the Seljuk Turks of Anatolia presided over Abbasid territories from the borders of the Christian Byzantine Empire as far east as China. At its zenith under Malik Shah I (died 1092), the Seljuk capital, Isfahan, thrived as a Sunni Muslim centre of Persian culture, until the invading Mongols made vassal states of Seljuk domains in 1243, including Anatolia. Taking advantage of the Mongol withdrawal, the Ottoman Turk leader, Osman I (1258–1326), declared western Anatolia independent in 1299. Osman and his successors used a standing army of troops known as *janissaries* to control vast territories; unlike their adversaries, these troops possessed guns and artillery. In 1453, Muhammad II (1429–81) took Constantinople and renamed the Byzantine capital Istanbul, turning the Christian Church of Hagia Sophia into the Ayasofya Mosque. He also created the important office of *shaikh al-Islam* to oversee the empire's religious affairs. Though chosen by the sultan, the *shaikh al-Islam* technically possessed the power to issue a *fatwa* dismissing any political officeholder, including the sultan. The most renowned sultan, Suleiman the Magnificent (1494–1566), extended Ottoman rule west over most of North Africa, south through the Levant, and east across Persia, then turned to the Balkans and Central Europe, advancing as far as Vienna, Austria, in 1529. Notable for harmonizing Ottoman civil law with *sharia* throughout the empire, Suleiman also ensured that Jews, Christians, and Muslims enjoyed equal access to the city of Jerusalem. A celebrated poet as well, Suleiman transformed Istanbul into a centre of Islamic culture. In later decades, however, persistent tensions between successive sultans and the *shaikh al-Islam* all but paralyzed the empire, which went into slow decline following a second disastrous siege of Vienna in 1683.

Further east, other Muslim empires warrant attention, notably the Safavids in Persia (1501–1736) and the Mughals in India (1526–1730). A militant Sufi order from west of the Caspian Sea, the Safavids successfully resisted Ottoman power, and under Shah Ismail I (1487–1524) in 1502, they recruited *ayatollahs* from Jabal Amil, Lebanon, to impose Shi'ite Islam upon Persia's mixed population of mainly Sunni Arabs, Turkmens, Kurds, and Baluchis. Pressured by successive Ottoman incursions, Safavid influence tended eastwards, until Shah Abbas I (1571–1629) moved the capital to Isfahan—which quickly became a celebrated centre of Shi'ite Iranian culture, especially painting and such architectural gems as the Masjed-e Shah and the Masjed-e Sheykh Lotfollah mosques. A ruthless ruler, Shah Abbas nonetheless encouraged religious tolerance and attempted to outflank the Ottomans by forging treaties with European nations. Raiding from the north and east, however, Turkmen and Afghani warlords added to continuing Ottoman threats from the west, and the Safavid Empire dissolved into a series of civil wars. In 1742, Agha Mohammad Khan (1742–97) gained control, making Tehran the Shi'ite capital of the new Qajar dynasty in 1796.

Over the same time period, a succession of Mughal emperors strengthened Muslim power in India. In 1526, the Turkmen warlord Zahiruddin Mohammed Babur (1483–1530) and his son Nasiruddin Mohammed

Humayun (1508–56) defeated the Delhi sultan, Ibrahim Lodhi, and founded the Mughal dynasty, establishing Sunni Islam as the official religion of the empire. Their successor, Jalaluddin Muhammad Akbar (1542–1605)—who was remembered for his liberal attitudes towards non-Muslims, especially Hindus, Jains, Parsis, and Christians—expanded Mughal power in India, which was further consolidated by his son, Nuruddin Jahangir (1569–1627). A great patron of garden designers and painters, Jahangir also concluded special trading agreements with Great Britain's East India Company. Shahbuddin Mohammed Shah Jahan (1592–1666) built Agra's inimitable Taj Mahal as a mausoleum for his beloved second wife, Arjumand Bano Begum, who was known as Mumtaz Mahal (1593–1631). He oversaw the construction of other architectural masterpieces, too, like the Red Fort and Jama Masjid in Delhi and the Shalimar Gardens and Moti Masjid in Lahore, Pakistan. In addition to Mughal art and architecture, Sufi orders translated the Qur'an into Persian and Urdu, adapted certain Hindu mystical practices to Islam, and created a vast library of devotional music and hagiographical literature, while Sufi missionaries and Muslim merchants carried the faith from India to Indonesia, Malaysia, and points further east. Under Aurangzeb (1618–1707), Mughal imperial authority extended to all but the southern tip of India. Unlike his more tolerant predecessors, however, this deeply pious emperor cultivated a conservative *ulema*, imposed strict adherence to *shari'a*, replaced several important Hindu temples with mosques, legislated against non-Muslim forms of worship, and restored the *jizya*, which his predecessors had abolished. In the last years of Aurangzeb's reign, the Mughal Empire edged towards decline, fragmenting under his successors into small states ruled by rival Muslim, Hindu, and Sikh leaders.

From the late eighteenth century onward, European colonial expansion and the influence of Western modernity spurred further decline among the empires of Islam. Various reformers argued that only a return to the fundamentals of Islam would halt the faith's inward collapse and capitulation to Western influence. In *Kitab al-Tawhid* (*Book of Monotheism*), the most influential revivalist, Muhammad ibn Abd al-Wahhab (1703–92), draws upon the conservative theology of the Hanbalite scholar Taqi al-Din ibn Taymiya (1263–1328) not only to condemn Shi'ite devotion to Husayn and Sufi veneration of saints as *shirk*, for example, but also to accuse the orthodox *ulema* of too readily conflating the wishes of worldly leaders with the will of God. By contrast, al-Wahhab and his followers called themselves Salafis, meaning "predecessors," in reference to their efforts to emulate Muslim life before the age of empire. Backed by the military muscle of Muhammad ibn Saud (died 1765), the Salafis united Arabia under strict *shari'a*. Invoking the principle of *ijtihad* to authorize literal interpretation of the Qur'an and the *sunna*, they imposed a puritanical regimen of plain clothes and simple houses, banned such pastimes as music and chess (which might distract the believer from prayer and study), and preached the individual Muslim's responsibilities for mission (*da'wa*) and *jihad*. Known to outsiders as Wahhabis, they captured Mecca in 1803 and Medina in 1804, but lost the holy cities to the Ottoman Empire in 1813. After World War I, Great Britain and the United States cemented access to Arabia's vast oil reserves by supporting the Saudi family's reconquest of Mecca and Medina in 1924. Funded by profits from this industry, Salafi missions continue to export al-Wahhab's vision of Islam to the present day.

Although revivalist movements arose elsewhere in the Muslim world, they were generally unable to resist Western encroachment upon the "House of Islam." Three African movements epitomize this trend. In West Africa, the Muslim missionary and scholar Usman Ibn Fodio (1754–1817) led the Fulani people in a holy war against the oppressive regime of Hausa king Yunfa. In 1808, he established the Sokoto caliphate, which remained the largest empire in Africa until its defeat by Frederick Lugard (1858–1945) in 1903. The British brought most Fulani into the protectorate of Nigeria, while the French assumed control of other regions of equatorial and West Africa with significant Muslim populations. A second African revivalist movement, the Sanusi order, was founded in Mecca in 1837 by Mohammed bin Ali al-Sanusi (1787–1860). In 1843, he introduced the nomadic Bedouin of Libya to al-Wahhab's teachings on hard work, ascetic piety, and missionary activity. Maintaining uneasy relations with the orthodox Ottoman *ulema* throughout the nineteenth century, the order proved ineffectual against French expansion in the Sahara in the early twentieth century, as well as the Italians in Libya and the British in Egypt. In 1969, Sanusi influence finally dissolved with Muammar al-Qaddafi's (1942–2011) military coup in Libya, while Egypt, in British hands since 1882, remained so until 1956; Tunisia and Morocco remained in French control until 1956; and Algeria, until 1962. Sudan presents a third variation on this theme. In 1881, Muhammad Ahmad (1844–85) declared himself the Mahdi. He defeated the British under Charles George Gordon (1833–85) at Khartoum in 1885, proclaimed himself an agent of divine purpose, and established a Muslim state under *shari'a*. In 1898, however, Ahmad's successors lost Sudan to combined British and Egyptian forces under

Horatio Herbert Kitchener (1850–1916) at the Battle of Omdurman. Like Egypt, Sudan remained under British control until 1956.

These setbacks typify the often uneasy relationship between the "House of Islam" and the West from the late eighteenth century to the present day. Muslims debate the degree to which they should adopt, adapt, or resist Western influences. At one extreme, secularists identify the decline of Islam with the failure of Muslim leaders to adopt modern ideas and practices. Mustafa Kemal Atatürk (1881–1938) epitomizes this position. Turkey, which was known as the "Sick Man of Europe" in the mid-eighteenth century, endured a debilitating series of wars with Russia and other European powers, culminating in the partitioning of the Ottoman Empire after its defeat in World War I (1914–18). In 1922, Atatürk and a party of secularist reformers known as the "Young Turks" established the new republic of Turkey. In 1923, to break clearly with tradition, they moved the country's capital from Istanbul to Ankara, abolished the offices of sultan and *shaikh al-Islam*, and curtailed the activities of Sufi orders—notably the Mevlevis, founded in 1273 by Rumi's followers and known as "Whirling Dervishes" after their distinctive dance of meditative devotion. The Young Turks set up the Department of Religious Affairs to administer Turkey's mainly Sunni mosques, even permitting women to be *imams*. Religious dress was not allowed in public buildings, including schools and universities, where students used the Latin rather than the Arabic alphabet, and the curriculum included Western science and technology. Liberal laws were introduced to regulate marriage, family life, divorce, and the status of women. In 1982, a new constitution declared Turkey a parliamentary democracy, guaranteeing equality of language, race, colour, sex, political opinion, philosophical convictions, and religious beliefs. More recently, Turkey's rich Sufi heritage has begun to capture the popular imagination, while traditionalist Sunni clerics have pushed the country to reinstate *shari'a*, much to the concern of Muslim minorities like the Alawites.

Elsewhere, identifying too closely with Western ways has led to other outcomes. In Iran, for example, Reza Shah Pahlavi (1878–1944) overthrew the Qajar dynasty in 1921 and introduced policies promoting modernization and closer relations with the West. After World War II, his son Muhammad Reza Pahlavi (1919–80) continued these policies, risking the ire of the Shi'ite clergy. In 1979, a popular uprising ended Pahlavi's rule, and Ayatollah Ruhollah Khomeini (1900–89) returned to Iran from exile in Paris, France, to establish a Shi'ite theocracy rooted in literalist understandings of the Qur'an and the Hadith. Khomeini's *Velayat-e faqih*

(*Guardianship of the Islamic Jurist*, 1963) describes an Islamic republic based on *sharia* and ruled by clerics. Every eight years, 86 jurists known as the *Majles-e-Khobregan* or "Assembly of Experts" elect a *Valiye-faqih* or "Supreme Leader," a fellow jurist who enjoys absolute authority in both secular and religious matters. Shi'ite Islam permeates key aspects of Iranian life; for example, schools follow a traditionalist curriculum that criticizes modern fashions, films, and other forms of Western culture as morally and spiritually decadent. Khomeini hoped to export Islamic revolution as a third ideological option to the West's secular modernism and the Soviet Union's atheistic communism, prompting the United States to support the secular Ba'athist regime of Saddam Hussein (1937–2006) in Iraq's war with Iran (1980–88).

Fundamentalist movements have arisen among Sunni Muslims, too. In 1928, for instance, Hassan al-Banna (1906–49) founded the Muslim Brotherhood to resist Western occupation of Egypt. After World War II, the movement gained fresh impetus in Muslim North Africa and the Middle East from radical intellectuals like Sayyid Qutb (1906–66), whose *Ma'alim fi-l-Tariq* (*Milestones along the Way*, 1964) argues for a universal *jihad* against the non-Muslim world, known as the "House of Persuasion" (*dar-al-Islam*). Chapters of the Muslim Brotherhood now thrive in many Muslim countries, as well as among Muslim immigrant communities in the West. In the mid-1990s, the Taliban, meaning literally "students," imposed strict *sharia* upon Afghanistan after the withdrawal of the Soviet Union, which had occupied the country in 1979. The Taliban required Afghani males to attend conservative Sunni *madrassas*, while women were denied formal education and limited to traditional family roles. Other radical movements have enjoyed varying degrees of support in parts of North Africa, Pakistan, Bangladesh, Malaysia, and Indonesia. Today, the widely dispersed terrorist network known as Al-Qaeda, founded by the Saudi Arabian exile Osama bin Laden (1957–2011), represents the most militant form of resistance to Western ways.

In the late nineteenth and early twentieth centuries, more moderate voices of Islamic revival navigated between the extremes of secularism and fundamentalism, notably the Iranian Shi'ite scholar Jamal al Din al-Afghani (1838–97), his Sunni Egyptian student Muhammad Abduh (1849–1905), and the Indian intellectual Muhammad Iqbal (1877–1938). For all their differences in detail, al-Afghani's *Al-Radd 'ala al-Dahriyyin* (*The Refutation of the Materialists*, 1881), Abduh's *Risālat at-Tawhīd* (*Theology of Unity*, 1897), and Iqbal's *Reconstruction of Religious Thought in Islam* (1930) generally recognize that Europe and North America have made great strides in science and technology. Inspired by the Salafis to engage with Western ways on Islam's own terms, however, they point out that the West's failure to put these advances into proper moral and spiritual perspective has resulted in a hypocritical culture of self-indulgent materialism at home, and colonial and imperial oppression abroad. Addressing both Muslim and non-Muslim readerships, they argue that, by contrast, Islam provides a suitable moral and spiritual context for science and technology in several ways. First, the Qur'an instructs Muslims to appreciate and investigate the wonders of the world as aspects of divine creation; second, Muslims believe only that which can be demonstrated rationally from the Qur'an and the *sunna*; and third, the principle of *ijtihad* obliges Muslims to work out their own peace with God by engaging constructively in all aspects of human endeavours, including Western science and technology. A political activist, al-Afghani ended his days under house arrest in Istanbul, while Abduh used his positions in government to introduce Western science and technology into Egyptian life. As well as being celebrated as a poet in Urdu and Persian, Iqbal is seen by many as the ideological father of modern Pakistan, the Muslim state partitioned from predominantly Hindu India in 1947. Dedicated and influential teachers themselves, all three of these thinkers urged educational reform in Muslim countries in an effort to modernize the "House of Islam." Today, the work of the Algerian intellectual Mohammed Arkoun (1928–2010) epitomizes Muslim efforts to continue this dialogue between Islam and the West, notably in books like *Rethinking Islam* (1994) and *The Unthought in Contemporary Islamic Thought* (2002), which draw upon Western social sciences to explore ways in which Muslims might critically reconstruct Islam to meet the challenges of the modern world.

THE MAKING OF A CANADIAN MUSLIM COMMUNITY

Before World War II, Muslim immigration to Canada was sparse. Ontario records pre-dating Confederation in 1867 mention a few "Mahometans" from Western Europe and the United States, and the federal census of 1871 lists 13 Muslims in the new Dominion of Canada. In the late nineteenth century, a handful of Arab Muslim adventurers came to Canada from the disintegrating Ottoman Empire. Landing in the east and then heading to the north-west frontier, Lebanese and Syrian newcomers settled as fur traders and mink ranchers in Lac La Biche, Alberta, eventually building Al-Kareem Mosque in 1958. Ali Hamdon, also Lebanese, traded furs in Fort Chipewyan, while his countryman Saleem Shaben opened a general store in Endiang. Later, both entrepreneurs moved their families to Edmonton, where Hamdon's wife Hilwie helped raise funds from Muslims in Alberta and Saskatchewan to build Al-Rashid Mosque. In 1938, the renowned Indian scholar, Abdullah Yusuf Ali (1872–1953), presided over opening ceremonies for this Sunni house of worship, which Heritage Canada now preserves at Fort Edmonton Park as Canada's first mosque. In 1975, Saleem Shaben's grandson, Lawrence Shaben (1935–2008), became the first Muslim elected to the Alberta legislature and the first Muslim cabinet minister in Canada. Other Lebanese and Syrian Muslims settled elsewhere in Canada. In 1935, a group established a Muslim cemetery in Bible Hill, near Truro, Nova Scotia. Today, a small mosque stands near the cemetery, built by the Islamic Association of the Atlantic Provinces, which was founded in 1967. Now called the Islamic Association of Nova Scotia, this Sunni organization opened a larger house of worship and community centre in Dartmouth, Nova Scotia, in 1971. Montreal, Ottawa, London, Thunder Bay, and Calgary are home to other Lebanese and Syrian Muslim communities.

Despite their historical importance, the Lebanese and Syrian communities now constitute only a small part of a much larger Canadian Muslim mosaic. In 1962, a federal Immigration Act did away with discrimination

Al-Rashid mosque in Edmonton, Alberta, is Canada's oldest Muslim house of worship. PHOTO BY AMIR HUSSAIN. REPRINTED BY PERMISSION. © AMIR HUSSAIN.

based on race, religion, and country of origin, and a new points system taking account of education and other employment qualifications was introduced in 1967, Canada's centennial year. Following these changes, Muslim immigration increased rapidly. Though significant numbers of Shi'ite Muslims now live in Canada, the majority of these new immigrants were Sunni. In many cases, highly educated professionals or investors and entrepreneurs arrived, settling comfortably into Canadian middle-class life. In other cases, local and regional conflicts brought Muslims to Canada as refugees. Whatever the reasons for these migrations, however, some general patterns emerged. Like other groups of newcomers, Muslims from a wide variety of linguistic and cultural origins often formed ethnic associations. At the same time, brought together by common religious interests, they gathered to pray in private homes and organized events to raise funds for building mosques. Weekend Islamic schools developed, as well as summer camps, where Muslims from around the world shared a new life, hiking, boating, canoeing, and swimming, as they debated different ways of being Muslim in this unfamiliar country. Sunnis, for example, sometimes disagreed as to whether new mosques should func-tion only as prayer halls or as cultural centres, too. Once immigrants built mosques, they looked for *imams* to serve as teachers and guides—ideally leaders trained in the disciplines of Qur'anic interpretation (*tafsir*), Islamic jurisprudence (*fiqh*), theology (*kalam*), and ethics (*akhlaq*). There were also other issues to consider here, however. An *imam* in Canada might be expected to develop new skills, like pastoral counselling or acting as a referral agent for Canadian social services, since wider Canadian society tended to expect Muslim religious leaders to play similar roles to Christian clerics or Jewish rabbis. In later years, an *imam* might serve as a chaplain in a prison, a hospital, the military, or a university.

The more specific stories of Muslims in Canada are as various as their times and places of origin. To begin with, Lebanese and Syrian Arab Muslims have been joined in Canada by Egyptian, Eritrean, Ethiopian, Iraqi, Moroccan, Palestinian, Somali, and Sudanese newcomers. After the expulsion of Asians by the Ugandan dictator Idi Amin Dada (*ca.* 1925–2003) in 1972, some 6,000 Ismai'li Muslims migrated to Canada from East Africa. In 1979, three upheavals spurred Muslim migration: Khomeini's assumption of power in Iran; Saddam Hussein's in Iraq; and the Soviet Union's invasion of Afghanistan. From 1975 to 1989, civil war in Lebanon between Christians and Muslims, exacerbated by the presence of the Palestinian Liberation Organization and Syrian and Israeli armed forces, created large numbers of refugees, the poorest of them Shi'ite Muslims from the south. More Arab Muslims came to Ontario and Quebec after the Iran-Iraq War (1980–88) and the Gulf War (1990–91), especially Palestinians already displaced to Jordan, Lebanon, and countries bordering the Persian Gulf after wars between Arabs and Israelis in 1948, 1967, and 1973. For many, the region's mixed French and British colonial heritage made Montreal as desirable a destination as Toronto. In 1991, a group of Syrian professionals and businessmen bought a Jehovah's Witness church in Dorval and converted it into the Canadian Islamic Centre Al-Jamieh. Outgrowing this building, the Sunni congregation purchased new premises in Dollard des Ormeaux in 2002. With a prayer hall for over 1,000 worshippers, as well as classrooms and other facilities, the new Canadian Islamic Centre Al-Jamieh is Montreal's largest mosque. Religious services are conducted in Arabic, the first language of the vast majority of the congregation, and the centre offers Qur'an recitation, *shari'a* and Arabic-language classes, and religious discussion groups. Committed to maintaining the future vitality of the community, the Centre Al-Jamieh also sponsors a summer camp for Muslim youth, as well as educational, athletic, professional, and social activities, from computer lessons to Islamic movies. Women from the congregation staff many of these activities. Another largely Arab congregation in Montreal, Markaz El-Islam, which openly recognizes the need to cater to the whole Muslim family, has developed the Islamic Community Centre of South Shore in Brossard. This centre includes day-care facilities, an Islamic school, a library, and a gymnasium *cum* multipurpose hall for sports and social activities.

In the 1990s, members of Arab and Arabic-speaking groups like the Jebertis and Oromos came to Canada to escape tribal, racial, or religious persecution in new trouble spots in Ethiopia, Eritrea, Somalia, and Sudan. Often traditional in moral and social outlook, such refugees are gradually establishing their own religious institutions. While the Sudanese-Sufi Tariqa Burhaniya has a devotional centre in Montreal, for example, cattle-raising pastoralists from Somalia have opened *halal* butcher shops in Toronto, where the Somali Islamic Society of Canada (founded in 1994) publishes a monthly newsletter, *Codka Jaaliyadda* (*Community Voice*), and is raising funds to build a mosque, community centre, and Islamic school. The Khalid bin al-Walid mosque, on Bethridge Road in Toronto's north-western suburb of Rexdale, takes care to serve the city's Somali community, often providing services in Somali as well as Arabic and English, including daily prayers, Friday *khutba*, an Islamic bookstore, a

da'wa centre and library, funeral arrangements, Islamic educational programs and discussion groups, youth activities and summer camps, *Eid
al-Fitr* and *Eid al-Adha* festivities, *hajj* travel planning, and regular family
events. Elsewhere in Ontario, smaller Arab Muslim organizations thrive
in Ottawa, Windsor, London and Hamilton, as well as across Canada in
Calgary, Edmonton, Halifax, and Vancouver.

Significant numbers of Muslims have also migrated to Canada from
Turkey and the Balkans. Toronto is home to most Turkish, Albanian,
Albanian Kosovar, and Bosnian Canadians, with smaller communities elsewhere in southern Ontario, Montreal, and other major cities. In the 1960s
and 1970s, Turkish Canadian life revolved around cultural societies like
Toronto's Canadian Turkish Friendship Association, which was founded in
1964, and then after 1976 lost membership to the newly established Turkish
Culture and Folklore Society of Canada. More recent immigrants have
demonstrated a stronger commitment to their faith, increasing demand
for regular Friday prayers and opportunities for communal involvement
in Muslim festivals. The founding of Toronto's Canadian Turkish Islamic
Heritage Association in 1983 exemplifies this trend. Since 1984, the association has published the quarterly newsletter *Haber Bülteni* (*News Bulletin*).
In 1987, the Canadian Turkish Islamic Trust was established to support the
association's Canadian Turkish Islamic Centre on Pape Avenue in Toronto.
Appointed to a four-year term by Turkey's Department of Religious Affairs
and paid by the Turkish government, the *imam* at the centre's mosque
serves the community as prayer leader, spiritual guide, and interpreter of
the Qur'an and Hadith. Similar arrangements support *imams* at mosques
in Windsor, Ontario, and Montreal, while other predominantly Turkish
Canadian institutions, like the Anatolia Islamic Centre in Mississauga,
Ontario, operate independently. Not surprisingly, Turkish Canadian
mosques invoke Turkish names for Muslim festivals: *Eid al-Fitr* becomes
Ramazan Bayramı; *Eid al-Adha* becomes *Kurban Bayramı*; and *Mawlid
al-Nabi* becomes *Mevlid Kandili*. The intellectual and artistic revival of
Turkey's Sufi legacy has spread to Canada, too, especially at the popular
level. In 2006, for example, the Mevlevi "Whirling Dervishes of Rumi" visited Canada from Konya, Turkey, where the Sufi poet's tomb still attracts
large numbers of Muslim pilgrims. The troupe toured Toronto, Calgary,
Vancouver, Montreal, and Ottawa, exposing Canadian audiences for the
first time to the *sema*, a mystical ceremony in seven parts featuring a
ring of dancers, each of whom spins counter-clockwise, ever faster to the
increasing tempo of kettle drums, reed flutes, and strings. The whole ring

whirls faster and faster, too, reflecting the revolving nature of all existence. "Dervish" means "mendicant," and the ritual enacts the mystic's role as link between heaven and earth. The dancers turn their right hands up to receive God's blessings and their left hands down to convey them to creation, their long, white gowns and high-coned hats symbolizing the burial shrouds and gravestones of their egos.

Canada's Balkan Muslims include Albanians, Albanian Kosovars, and Bosnians. Like many newcomers, small groups of Balkan Muslims at first held prayer meetings in one another's homes or attended mosques with Muslims from different ethnic backgrounds. Founded in 1954, the Albanian Muslim Society of Toronto opened a shopfront Islamic centre on Dundas Street. Regep (Rajjab) Assim, an Albanian political exile from the Ottoman Empire, served as *imam*. A learned man, Assim presided over small meetings which included sermons, readings from the Qur'an and prayers, and occasionally conducted funeral services and wedding ceremonies. The centre also held a small library, a Sunday school for children, annual dinners for *Eid al-Fitr*, and biannual *bajram* festivities, where Albanians gather to discuss politics, listen to traditional music, and dance the *dubke,* a Middle Eastern line dance popular with men and women in the Balkans. From the late 1960s to the 1990s, increasing numbers of non-Albanian Muslims bolstered the congregation, including Bosnians and South Asians. In 1969, the society converted a former Presbyterian church on Boustead Avenue into the Jami Mosque, removing pews and a Christian stained-glass window, and installing wall-to-wall carpeting at an angle so that worshippers may pray facing Mecca. The society also purchased a section of Glendale Memorial Gardens for Muslim interments; Assim was among the first buried there. Tensions eventually developed among the different ethnic groups and the community fragmented, although a steady trickle of Albanian immigrants continues to maintain the Albanian Muslim Society of Toronto, which now runs a local mosque on Annette Street. Other cities are home to small communities of Albanian Muslims, notably Hamilton, Kitchener, London, Calgary, and Edmonton. In 1999, Canada participated in United Nations efforts to assist Albanian Kosovar refugees fleeing ethnic conflicts in the Balkans, many of whom eventually settled among Albanian Muslims in Ontario, Alberta, and British Columbia.

A few Bosnian Muslims settled across Canada in the 1940s and 1950s, but the disintegration of Bosnia-Herzegovina in 1992 brought a wave of refugees to Toronto, where they found established Muslim communities in the suburb of Etobicoke. Led by Kerim Reis, who acted as *imam,* some of these earlier immigrants had fled communist Yugoslavia's predominantly Roman Catholic Christian province of Croatia in 1947, eventually founding the Croat Muslim Centre in 1973. Eventually renamed the Bosnian Islamic Centre, this mosque still serves a sizable congregation. In 1977, another group of Bosnian Muslims founded the Association of Islamic Community Gazi Husrev-Beg. Identifying less with Croatian traditions and more with Albanian Muslims, these Bosnian newcomers became affiliated with the Albanian Muslim Society of Toronto in 1982. In 1984, however, differences of opinion about the situation in Yugoslavia led their patron Hasan Karachi, a businessman from Niagara Falls, to end this affiliation. Changing their name to the Bosnian Islamic Association Gazi Husrev-Beg in 1995, the congregation supports a mosque and community centre on North Queen Street in Etobicoke. Their numbers were bolstered by Bosnian victims of ethnic cleansing in the Balkans in the late 1980s and early 1990s, and the association promotes a distinctly Bosnian flavour of Islam in the more liberal Hanafite tradition. As well as classes in the Qur'an, the Hadith, and Islamic jurisprudence, their Etobicoke mosque provides services for arranging marriages; sacrificing animals to celebrate newborns (*aqiqah*); personal and family counselling; preparing wills; and arranging interments, including praying the funeral prayers (*salat al-janazah*). It also sponsors a variety of educational, cultural, creative, and sporting activities for men, women, and children. Throughout the year, the community interweaves social, cultural, and religious traditions in a series of *zabavas*, which are joyous family occasions for music, dancing, and feasting, usually launched by a Bosnian Muslim guest speaker of some eminence, especially for *Eid al-Fitr.* In 1996, the association inaugurated an annual gathering of North American Bosnian Muslims, an event now hosted every year by a different community in Canada or the United States. Other Bosnian Muslim newcomers to Canada have formed communities in Hamilton, Kitchener, London, and Waterloo, with smaller numbers making their homes in Montreal, Sherbrooke, and Quebec.

Small numbers of South-Asian Muslims found a home in Canada early in the twentieth century, but in the 1960s and 1970s, immigration from Pakistan, Bangladesh, and India dramatically increased, the majority settling in Toronto and environs. Other Muslim immigrants of South Asian heritage have come to Canada from diaspora communities in various parts of the world, including Great Britain, the Caribbean, Fiji, South and East Africa, and Southeast Asia. Like other South Asians, Muslims from

Trinidad, Guyana, and Fiji share the legacy of the British indentured labour system, which provided sugar plantation workers after 1833—when the British Parliament legislated against slavery in the empire—until indenture was also abolished in 1917. Caribbean South-Asian Muslims come mainly from Trinidad and Guyana. Like other South-Asian newcomers, these mainly Sunni Muslims benefited from the changes to Canadian immigration policy in the 1960s, settling mostly in Ontario, with smaller communities in other cities—notably Halifax, Montreal, and Vancouver. In the 1980s, Guyanese South-Asian claims for refugee status in Canada accelerated as a result of the perceived prejudice of the government of Linden Forbes Burnham (1923–85). Fijian South-Asian immigration to Canada increased markedly after coups in the late 1980s left militant indigenous nationalists in control of the island's government, police, and military. About one-sixth of these immigrants are Muslims, almost all of whom are Sunnis. Most Muslims from Fiji live in British Columbia, with smaller numbers in the metropolitan centres of Alberta and Ontario.

Islam plays an important role in the life of South-Asian Canadian families, many of whom tend to be conservative in outlook; for example, newcomers attending Boustead Avenue's Jami Mosque objected to some Balkan Muslim practices as "un-Islamic," especially the mixing of the sexes in the *dubke*. In 1969, mainly Pakistani Muslims formed the Islamic Foundation of Toronto, buying a building on Rhodes Avenue in the east end of the city. This Sunni organization purchased a new site on Scarborough's Nugget Avenue in 1984. Court challenges delayed a building permit for over five years, but the new premises were completed in 1992, at a cost of $6,000,000—almost all of which was raised by the local Muslim community. Designed by Khalil A. Syed, the Nugget Avenue mosque is an imposing, three-storey building of white stone. Reminiscent of classical Islamic architecture, its 125-foot high minaret and copper-clad dome bear striking testimony to the Muslim presence in Toronto. An elected committee of seven members, known as the *majlis*, serves as the Foundation's governing body, while an elected Board of Trustees holds the property's title and advises the *majlis*.

The Islamic Foundation offers educational and social facilities as well as religious services. The latter include prayer halls for men and women, and full-time *imams* preside over daily worship and Friday services, spiritual seclusion (*i'tikaf*) for the last ten days of Ramadan, and annual festivals like *Eid al-Fitr* and *Eid al-Adha*. Every year, the Foundation also organizes a *hajj* group and a Qur'an recitation competition. By assisting with introductions, a Matrimonial Services Committee encourages Muslim men and women to fulfill their worldly responsibilities, and a modern mortuary enables ritual washing (*ghusl*) and burial of the deceased in wooden caskets according to *shari'a*. Sunnis and Shi'ites alike believe that the dead should be buried as quickly as possible. Men wash the bodies of men, women of women; and the procedure is the same for everyone, whatever their station in life. Prayers for the dead (*salat al-janazah*) may be performed in the mosque, and the Foundation has access to a Muslim graveyard at Pine Ridge Memorial Garden in Pickering, Ontario. Educational services include a full-time school with over 600 students from junior kindergarten to grade 12, programs for adults in subjects like Arabic and Islamic theology, and classes in memorizing the Qur'an. A library contains books on Islam, a reference collection, and materials related to Ontario's public school curriculum. Social services include a cafeteria, where volunteers prepare and serve dozens of meals for the less fortunate on Hot Soup Days every Saturday; and a gymnasium, where men's and women's teams enjoy various sports and activities. The Foundation regularly oversees fundraising events, especially for natural disasters in overseas regions with large Muslim populations, like the devastating Asian Tsunami on 26 December 2004. At the same time, though, life in Canada has posed challenges to some traditional Muslim practices. In 2005, for example, Husain Patel, the Foundation's *imam,* joined with Haroon Salamat, head of the Toronto and Region Islamic Congregation's Islamic Centre of Toronto; Tarek Fatah (born 1949), host of the weekly television show *Muslim Chronicle*; and Dr. Mohamed Elmasry (born 1943), President of the Canadian Islamic Congress, to protest the Miss Canada Pakistan pageant as an affront to Islamic values. In another vein, Etobicoke's mainly Caribbean United Muslim Association caused controversy in more conservative Muslim circles by inviting Pamela K. Taylor—an American who converted to Islam in 1986 and who is the co-chair of New York's Progressive Muslim Union— to become the first woman to lead Friday prayers and preach a sermon in a Canadian mosque. Before a mixed congregation of men and women on Canada Day, 2005, Taylor spoke about equality between races, genders, sexual orientations, and persons with disabilities, praising Canada for embodying these Muslim ideals.

Sunni Muslim congregations with significant South-Asian memberships thrive elsewhere in the Toronto region, too, notably Brampton, Markham, and Mississauga; as well as in other Ontario cities, including Hamilton, Ottawa, and Windsor. Brampton's Islamic Society of Peel has room for 1,500 worshippers in the Makki Masjid, a large, white stone building crowned by a green dome. Similarly in Mississauga, the Islamic Centre of Canada, which is run by the Islamic Society of North America, Canada, includes a large mosque, a banquet hall, funeral facilities, a bookstore, a high school, travel services, and space for sports and community functions. Citing a Qur'anic prohibition against usury (Qur'an 2:275), this society also affiliates with the Ansar Co-operative Housing Corporation and the Islamic Co-operative Housing Corporation to provide interest-free home loans and investment opportunities for Canadian Muslims. To Toronto's northeast, the Islamic Society of Markham plans a Jame' Masjid complete with *madrassa,* library, *da'wa* centre, mortuarial amenities, and learning facilities for new members of the local Muslim community; and to the west, the Muslim Association of Hamilton has proposed a mosque that will accommodate over 3,000 worshippers. Elsewhere in Ontario, the Ottawa Muslim Association's premises include prayer halls for men and women, a library, and washing facilities for the deceased, while reconstruction of the present Jami Omar Mosque, itself a converted United Church building, will provide a larger *masjid,* gymnasium, library, classrooms, funeral services, community centre, and seniors' residence for Nepean's Muslims. As well as a mosque, a school with an Islamic dress code for boys and girls, and various community services, the Windsor Islamic Association offers burials according to *shari'a,* with the body facing *qibla,* in Essex County's Country Meadows cemetery. Beyond Ontario, smaller numbers of South-Asian Muslims have made homes in the metropolitan regions of Quebec, Montreal, Calgary, Edmonton, and Vancouver, often helping to establish ethnically diverse congregations. As we shall see, the Islamic Centre of Quebec epitomizes this trend.

In addition to these predominantly Sunni communities, significant numbers of Twelver and Ismai'ili Muslims have been coming to Canada since the 1970s. We will discuss a Twelver Shi'ite community later in the chapter. Most Ismai'ilis arrived from East Africa, specifically Kenya, Uganda, and Tanzania. The legacy of Sir Sultan Muhammad Shah (1877–1957), the Aga Khan III, permeates the lives of Ismai'ilis today, including Ismai'ili Canadians. Exposed to Western economic and social values in British Imperial India, the Aga Khan III was determined to modernize Ismai'ili life, in part by urging his followers to seek educational and professional opportunities outside India. British economic development in colonial East Africa provided such opportunities, and like other South Asians in East Africa, Ismai'ilis established thriving communities. By the 1960s, however, this success was beginning to attract discriminatory policies from newly empowered African nationalist governments, culminating in the expulsion of nearly 80,000 South Asians from Uganda by Idi Amin Dada (*ca.* 1925–2003) in 1972. The Aga Khan IV (born 1936), who succeeded his grandfather in 1957, personally approached Prime Minister Pierre Elliot Trudeau (1919–2000) with the situation. Trudeau agreed to accept several thousand refugees—the single largest Ismai'ili influx to Canada in history. Other Ismai'ilis have come to Canada from India, Pakistan, and Bangladesh, as well as central and southern Africa, the Middle East, and more recently Europe. Francophone Ismai'ilis have migrated from west and central Africa and Madagascar, as well. Today, nearly 80,000 Ismai'ilis live in Canada, the largest number in Ontario, with sizeable communities in Vancouver, Edmonton, and Calgary.

After being advised by the Aga Khan IV to settle in Canada permanently, Ismai'ilis quickly established a network of *jamat khanas* or "community houses." Now nearly 80 in number, these premises range from single rooms to architectural masterpieces. As the annual Aga Khan Award for Architecture attests, Ismai'ilis view architecture as a form of religious expression. For example, the Ismai'ili Jamatkhana and Centre, opened in 1985 in Burnaby, British Columbia, attracted international plaudits. A sunken courtyard garden of fountains, trees, and flowers leads to the main building, which is clad in beige sandstone. The work of architect Bruno Freschi (born 1937), the whole design seems a modern Western reimagining of classical Islamic principles of geometric symmetry, enclosure, and layered symbolic decoration. Serving primarily as a prayer hall for over 1,000 faithful, the *jamat khana* includes social facilities, administrative offices, a council chamber, and classrooms. As in all Ismai'ili houses of worship, a man or a woman may lead daily prayers, special meditations, or Friday services, though men and women sit separately, divided by an aisle. Also purpose-built, Calgary's new Jamatkhana and Ismai'ili Centre includes a prayer hall, with committee rooms upstairs, as well as classrooms for a range of educational activities—from children's English lessons to women's courses on reproductive health. Other Ismai'ili communities enjoy similar facilities. Montreal's two-storey Jamatkhana and Ismaili Centre, a converted building, accommodates 1,000 people and maintains regional links with groups in Brossard, Laval, Granby, Sherbrooke, Quebec City, and the Maritimes. Across Canada, Ismai'ilis are raising funds for a grand *jamat khana* at Eglinton Avenue and the Don Valley Parkway in Toronto; it will be the largest in the country. By contrast, at many Canadian universities Ismai'ili student associations gather regularly in improvised campus accommodations to share spiritual, academic, athletic, and social concerns, the first dating to 1972, when young Ismai'ilis from Uganda met on Fridays in the Student Union Building at McGill University in Montreal.

A network of local, regional, and national associations structures Ismai'ili life in Canada. Groups made up of two men and two women, including married couples, administer the religious affairs of every Ismai'ili community, serving for two or three years as representatives of the Aga Khan, the final authority in all things religious and secular. A national council oversees boards for education, health care, and economic planning, while the work of local and regional committees might entail sponsoring, housing and employing Ismai'ili newcomers; organizing fund-raising drives; arbitrating in family disputes, including divorce; and formulating educational agendas and retirement strategies to help the young and old alike negotiate the challenges of modern life in Canada. In Toronto, for example, youngsters attend annual summer camps, while Ismai'ilis help to fund meals-on-wheels programs and a health care centre for seniors at the North York General Hospital. Ultimately coordinated by the Aga Khan's secretariat in Aiglemont, near Paris, France, committees depend on volunteers at every level, while legal, ethical, and theological guidance is always available from the Institute of Ismai'ili Studies, an academic research centre based in London, England.

At the same time, Ismai'ili Canadians participate in the work of the Aga Khan Development Network, headquartered in Geneva, Switzerland. Fostering the social conscience of Muslims, this network coordinates a vast range of education, health care, heritage recovery and preservation, and microfinancing and rural business initiatives, especially in Africa and Asia. For example, Aga Khan University in Karachi, Pakistan, has partnered with the Canadian International Development Agency and McMaster University in Hamilton, Ontario, to train women health care professionals, while the Aga Khan Foundation Canada sponsors an annual Partnership Walk to raise funds for health care programs in developing countries. Published three times a year, the magazine *Ismaili Canada* provides a forum for the discussion of these initiatives, as Ismai'ilis try to acclimatize to life in a new country without compromising their religious identity. The theme for the issue of July 2001, for example, was "Fostering Pluralism"—a sentiment the Aga Khan IV echoed almost five years later in Ottawa when he joined Adrienne Clarkson (born 1939), Governor General of Canada, for the foundation ceremony of the Delegation of the Ismaili Imamat. This facility, opened in 2008, was designed by award-winning architect Fumihiko Maki (born 1928) as a sanctuary for the quiet diplomacy that informs the global vision of the Ismai'ili *imam*. Plans are also underway for a Global Centre for Pluralism in Ottawa, to promote such values in the developing world; and an Aga Khan Museum in Toronto, to house collections of Islamic art and heritage.

Finally, on the academic front, McGill University's Institute of Islamic Studies (established in 1952) has not only developed an international reputation among Muslim scholars and scholars of Islam, but has also played a key role in raising the profile of the Muslim faith and Islamic culture in Canada. The Institute's founding director, Wilfred Cantwell Smith (1916–2000), recruited celebrated Islamic scholars like Fazlur Rahman Malik (1919–88), Ismail al-Faruqi (1921–86), and Muhammad Rasjidi (1915–2001). In turn, these scholars attracted graduate students from around the world. Born in Egypt, Hammudah Abdalati (1928–76) exemplifies this trend. A graduate of Al-Azhar University in Cairo, Sunni Islam's most prestigious institute of higher learning, Abdalati took degrees in Islamic Studies and Sociology from the Institute of Islamic Studies at McGill University in Montreal and from Princeton University in the United States. In 1960, Abdalati became the first full-time *imam* of Edmonton's Al-Rashid mosque, known after 1946 as the Canadian Islamic Centre of Edmonton. Largely in response to the needs of Muslims in Canada, he published *Family Structure in Islam* (1977) and *Islam in Focus* (1978). Locating Muslim beliefs and practices within a Western context, both books reveal the influence of Muhammad Abduh, whose works Abdalati studied at McGill; and Yusuf Ali, whose widely read English translation of and commentary on the Qur'an, in contrast to those of medieval scholars, evoke the scripture's lessons for everyday life rather than its usefulness as a source of proof-texts for judicial problems.

Pioneering *da'wa* in North America, Abdalati encouraged Muslims to develop bonds of mutual understanding with other Canadians in order to dispel the widespread distortion of Islamic teachings. Stressing the core value of peacefulness, *Family Structure in Islam* and *Islam in Focus* explore many delicate issues. The Qur'an indeed permits a man to have up to four wives, for example, but few Muslims are involved in polygamous marriages, since monogamy is the rule if there is any fear of injustice or harm. Similarly, Abdalati notes that the rights and responsibilities of women are equal to those of men, but not necessarily identical to them. The Qur'an provides that sons shall inherit equal amounts from their parents, for instance, but that daughters shall inherit half what their brothers receive, since married men must provide for their wives and children, whereas Muslim women do not bear this financial responsibility. In sum, argues Abdalati, the Qur'an teaches that Muslim piety (*taqwa*) holds in tension both the hope of God's mercy and the fear of God's justice.

RECENT TRENDS IN THE MUSLIM COMMUNITY

In the 1990s, Muslims surpassed Jews to become Canada's second-largest religious grouping. Between the census of 1991 and that of 2001, the number of Canadian residents identifying themselves as Muslims more than doubled to 580,000, a figure expected to double again by 2011. In addition to immigration, several factors may account for this growth: the higher-than-average birthrate of Muslim Canadians; the reversion of lapsed Muslims to the faith in response to *da'wa*; and conversions to Islam, estimated at 3,000 annually. Also, Al-Qaeda's attacks on the World Trade Centre in New York and the Pentagon in Washington on 11 September 2001 resulted in an unprecedented media focus on Muslim life in Canada, spawning a wide range of questionable views—including caricatures of Islam as the faith of terrorists; criticisms of Muslim dress codes for women (*hijab*); and erroneous descriptions of localized ethnic practices, like female circumcision, as characteristically Muslim. Perceived as anti-Islamic prejudice, this scrutiny has sometimes led to public declarations of solidarity among Muslims whose faith might otherwise have remained a private matter.

In recent years, Muslim missionary societies have increased their efforts in the West, partly to minister to Muslim immigrants, partly to preach among non-Muslims. The orthodox Sunni Muslim Brotherhood inspires the Muslim Association of Canada (MAC), for example. Committed to promoting individual, family, and community Muslim life within a contemporary Canadian context, MAC's programs implement the vision of Hassan al-Banna, especially the doctrine of *tarbiyah*, an Arabic term for education that addresses the heart, mind, body, and soul by putting God at the centre of every learning experience. Cultivating a range of educational opportunities that include study networks, overnight programs, outings, summer camps, training courses, conventions, and conferences, MAC strives to develop *da'wa* workers, particularly among younger Muslim Canadians. In 2002, the opening of Masjid Toronto established a visible

MAC presence in the heart of Canada's largest city, and the association runs youth groups in Ottawa, Toronto, London, Winnipeg, and Edmonton. Since the early 1980s, MAC has also organized an annual *Eid al-Fitr* Festival at Toronto's Canadian National Exhibition, the largest such gathering in Canada. The day of prayer ends with fun for the whole family, including a bazaar, children's rides, and sporting events, and organizers are careful to collect *zakat* in adherence to Islamic law.

At the same time, MAC makes pronouncements on public issues deemed to be of importance to Muslim Canadians. In September 2005, for example, the association expressed disapproval over the decision of Premier Dalton McGuinty (born 1955) to end all religious arbitration in Ontario. Pointing out that Aboriginal, Jewish, and Christian communities successfully employed religious tribunals under the provisions of the province's Arbitration Act (1991), MAC argued that McGuinty was reacting specifically to the efforts of the Islamic Institute of Civil Justice, founded in 2003 by Syed Mumtaz Ali (1927–2009), to require Muslims to submit family disputes to legal mediation under *sharia*. Regardless, in February 2006 the Ontario legislature passed amendments to the Arbitration Act excluding all forms of religious arbitration. MAC has spoken out on international issues, too, condemning the terrorist bombings in London in July 2005 as wholly contrary to the fundamental values of Islam, and expressing outrage at the controversial caricaturing of Muhammad in the Danish newspaper *Morgenavisen Jyllands-Posten* in September 2005.

Another orthodox Sunni organization, Tablighi Jama'at—which literally means "preaching community"—enjoys a strong presence in Canada as well. This revivalist organization was founded in 1927 by Maulana Muhammad Ilyas (1885–1944), a puritanical Sufi based at the shrine of the mystic saint Hazrat Khawaja Nizamuddin Auliya (1238–1325), in New Delhi, India. Influenced by radical Wahhabi efforts to recover the lifestyle of Muhammad and his immediate circle, Ilyas taught that God's blessings flowed to every lay Muslim who preached the faith, not just religious professionals. Jama'at's textbook, *Tablighi Nisab*, promotes six fundamentals: confession of faith; prayer; knowledge of Islamic texts; respect for fellow Muslims; sincerity; and spiritual self-renewal through proselytizing. This last doctrine requires Tablighis to evangelize fellow Muslims for one hour a day, or one day a week, or one week every two months, or one month a year, or once in a lifetime for four months. Travelling in groups, Tablighis lecture in local prayer halls, living simply and sleeping in mosques or Muslim homes. Ilyas also advised that Tablighis dress traditionally, that women be secluded, and that children not be taught secular subjects until they have completed religious instruction. The movement grew rapidly and members are now found throughout the South Asian diaspora. Over 1 million adherents from around the world attend their annual conventions in Raiwind, Pakistan, and Tongi, Bangladesh.

In 1952, Tablighi missionaries from Pakistan came to the United States. American membership grew rapidly and the country now holds annual conferences. In 1988, almost 6,000 attended the event in Chicago, at that time the largest single gathering of Muslims in North American history. In 1968, Tablighi missionaries from India appeared unexpectedly at Montreal's Islamic Centre of Quebec (ICQ). On a visit to Hyderabad, India, Bashir Hussain, a member of the centre, had spoken casually with Tablighis about Canada. Some weeks later, a telephone call to ICQ from Dorval airport announced the arrival of 17 persons from India. The group stayed for six months, leaving a following that has been increasing ever since. Elsewhere in Canada, the Jama'at pursues its missionary agenda through education. For example, some scholars have described the curriculum at the Al-Rashid Islamic Institute, in Cornwall, Ontario, as being Tablighi. Set up in 1987 as a traditional *madrassa,* Al-Rashid maintains close links with Toronto's Muslim community. About 50 boys reside at the school; some attend just to memorize the Qur'an, while others undertake basic training for careers as religious scholars, a course of instruction usually requiring further studies abroad in Muslim institutes of higher learning. In both cases, religious education takes precedence over secular subjects. Highly sophisticated in their use of modern media techniques, Tablighi missionaries travel to other Canadian cities from Montreal and Toronto, too, and many Canadian Tablighis attend the American conferences. Although a breakaway Pakistani group began to promote worldwide *jihad* as the seventh doctrine of Jama'at's program in the 1990s, Tablighis do not generally proselytize among non-Muslims.

Generally known as Ahmadis after their founder Mirza Ghulam Ahmad (1835–1908), the Ahmadiyyas are another Muslim missionary movement whose presence in Canada has recently become more visible. Orthodox Muslims view Ahmadis as heterodox, mainly because Ahmad claimed to be the Messiah or Mahdi foretold in Jewish, Christian, and Muslim scriptures. In 1889, he founded a missionary movement in Punjab, India, and adopted the title of *caliph,* which his elected successors inherit. Ahmad taught that God called every Muslim to dedicate resources to at least part-time missionary work. In 1947, the Ahmadis opened the Jamia Ahmadiyah for students of Islam in Rabwah, in newly independent Pakistan. At the invitation of the *caliph,* graduates from this theological academy may become full-time evangelists. In 1920, Mufti Muhammad Sadiq (d. 1957) became the first Ahmadi missionary to the United States. Records indicate that a few Ahmadis had settled in Halifax as early as the 1930s, but immigration from Pakistan increased quickly after 1974, when the National Assembly presided over by Prime Minister Zulfikar Ali Bhutto (1928–79) declared Ahmadis to be non-Muslims. Today, Toronto is home to Canada's largest Ahmadi community, which includes newcomers from East Africa, the Caribbean, the Middle East, and South Asia, as well as converts born in Canada.

The *caliph* appoints the Canadian Ahmadi community's leader, known as the *emir,* who presides over a network of local, regional, and national committees. Staffed by volunteers and funded by donations, this network maintains links with the international Ahmadi community. Paid for by the movement, a satellite dish in every Ahmadi home receives the worldwide, 24-hour learning channel Muslim Television Ahmadiyya, which underlines Islam's ethical superiority over Western materialism and propagates specifically Ahmadi beliefs, from non-violence and religious tolerance to the important role of women in maintaining Ahmadi values at home and in the community. Opening in 1992 with room for 1,200 worshippers, Bai'tul Islam Mosque in Maple, just north of Toronto, serves as headquarters for Canada's Ahmadis. Architect Gulzar Haider (born 1939) used the prayer rug as inspiration for the mosque's construction, from its formal proportions to the placement of doors and windows and the pattern and layout of tiles and carpets. A prayer rug has even been etched into the glass of the doors to twin prayer halls—one for men and one for women. The mosque features a traditional minaret and dome, as well. Television screens show the *caliph*'s Friday sermons, while modern electronics provide instant translations into several languages for attending congregants and for broadcasts relayed to remote locations across Canada. Published monthly, the mosque's *Ahmadiyya Gazette Canada* contains readings from the Qur'an, the Hadith, and the writings of Ahmad and his successors, as well as articles on the Ahmadi way of life. Modelled on the academy in Rabwah, the mosque's Jamia Ahmadiyya Canada trains missionaries, taking advantage of Toronto's multi-ethnic demographics to offer students courses in numerous European and Asian languages, as well as Arabic and Urdu. The congregation supports numerous humanitarian initiatives, too; from local, non-profit housing projects to Humanity First, a non-sectarian charity dedicated to international relief and development. Across Canada, other Ahmadi groups are steadily growing, with mosques or prayer halls in most major urban centres.

While missionary movements like the Muslim Brotherhood, the Tablighis, and even the Ahmadis focus their evangelizing efforts mainly on lapsed Muslim Canadians, non-Muslim Canadians have been drawn into the "House of Islam," too. Although the conversion of Jews, Christians, and the non-religious has been part of Muslim experience for centuries, current systematized missionary efforts probably owe much to the techniques of nineteenth- and early twentieth-century Christian evangelists in the Arab world and South Asia. The Islamic Circle of North America (ICNA), an American missionary organization founded in 1971, exemplifies this phenomenon. It holds a well-attended annual convention and disseminates the Muslim faith across the United States and Canada using various media, including through tracts and the bi-monthly magazine *Message International*; in telephone, radio and television campaigns; and in conventional and electronic mailings. Its Canadian outreach includes support for a *da'wa* centre on Bloor Street in Toronto, which features documents in its windows explaining the superiority of Islam to Christianity. The Internet has also become an effective tool for Muslim missionary organizations. The website *Converts to Islam* offers a free Qur'an, advice on how to become a Muslim, and representative conversion testimonies. Similarly, *DawaNet*, which is affiliated with ICNA, expressly identifies North America as a mission field, and among its guiding principles it includes commitments to cultivate evangelizing methods appropriate to the North American context; to operate democratically; to abide by American and Canadian secular law; to foster gender equality; to further social justice and charity work; to collaborate with other Muslim missionary organizations; and to reflect the ethnic diversity of North American Muslims, from the organization's general membership to its governing board and their professional advisors. Adhering to these guidelines, *DawaNet* intends "to convey the message of Islam with beauty, wisdom and tolerance." Other websites target specific audiences; *Jews for Allah,* for instance, serves Jewish converts to Islam. By contrast, the ICNA website *SoundVision* develops materials for children. Widely used throughout Canada, *SoundVision*'s video and audio tapes dramatize Islamic history, bringing stories of Muslim heroes alive, while a computer game features an action hero named Abu-Saleh who is on a "one-man *dawah* mission to spread the Truth with strength, wisdom and the vigour of youth."

The reasons for which Canadians convert to Islam are as various as missionary techniques, though the proportion of converts making up particular Muslim Canadian congregations is hard to determine. Converts helped to found Montreal's *Centre culturel islamique et mosquée Salahouddine* in 1990, for example, and now number about a tenth of the congregation, a percentage some scholars would generalize to the Muslim Canadian population as a whole. Most women convert with marriage; the case for men is usually different. Some converts are attracted to the moral ethos of Islam, perceiving, for instance, a stronger sense of traditional family values in Muslim critiques of the overt sexuality of Western materialist culture and society. But the mystical traditions of Islam have proven especially appealing to many non-Muslim Canadians. Different aspects of Sufism appeal to different converts: some are drawn to Sufi meditational practices; some to devotional poetry, like *ghazal* and *kafi*; some to esoteric collections of mystical philosophy; some to sacred song and dance, like *qawwali* and *sema*; and some to Sufi notions of universal humanity and community service. Although orders adopt and adapt one another's principles and practices, a particular expression of Sufi devotion is commonly associated with a particular holy man or woman. Usually, converts identify with a Sufi master and join the order to which this master belongs, an approach which suits the individualistic sensibilities of modern Western culture.

Canada is home to branches of several Sufi orders—especially in Toronto and the surrounding region—and, like Sufis everywhere, their members take part in a greater variety of religious practices than is the Muslim norm. The Sufi Study Circle at the University of Toronto, for example, adheres to the Chishtiyya order, named for the medieval Persian saint Hazrat Khwaja Muinuddin Chishti (1138–1236) who taught that the true friend of God shows affection, generosity, and hospitality to all without distinction. This group associates locally with the Canadian Society of Muslims, the International Institute of Islamic Studies and Research, and the Society for Understanding the Finite and the Infinite, all founded in the 1960s by Mirza Qadeer Baig (1931–98) and Syed Mumtaz Ali (1935–2009)—immigrants from India who succeeded one another in serving Toronto's Sufis as their spiritual leader, or *shaikh*. Members of the Sufi Study Circle meet weekly for *hadra*, an Arabic term meaning "presence," which refers to the mutual presence of God and devotee in Sufi worship. In the ritual of **dhikr**, meaning literally "remembrance," devotees praise, thank, and glorify God in rhythmic repetition as they gather together to sing hymns and recite the 99 divine names from the Qur'an. Every year in Toronto, several Sufi groups join the Sufi Study Circle for *dhikr* in the week before Ramadan. Groups also celebrate the festival days of renowned Sufi *walis*. Other orders have chapters in the Toronto region, too—each identifiably Sufi Muslim, yet embodying a distinctive understanding of Islam. Headquartered in Mississauga, for example, the Jerrahi Sufi Order of Canada stresses humanitarian service to vulnerable communities locally, nationally, and internationally.

In Montreal, by contrast, members of *Le centre Soufi* belong to the Naqshbandi order, named for the Baha-ud-Din Naqshband Bukhari (1318–89). Notable for tracing its spiritual lineage through Abu Bakr directly to Muhammad, the Naqshbandi order fragmented into several sub-orders, some maintaining the founder's distinctive ritual practice of silent remembrance, some not. Typically, the Montreal group gathers for *dhikr* twice a week at Masjid al-Iman. Though men and women form two separate circles for observances, a strong sense of unity pervades the group. Led by the resident *shaikh*, individuals in each circle stand and begin to whirl around as if entranced. The service ends with everyone whirling in circles in the Dervish way, offering thanks to God, Muhammad, and the Sufi saints. Also in Montreal, a branch of the Burhaniyya order perpetuates the teachings of their modern Sudanese founder, Muhammad 'Uthman 'Abdu al-Burhani (1902–83), whose collection of ecstatic poetry, *Sharab al-wasl* (*The Drink of Union*, 1993)—miraculously revealed to his followers after his death—draws upon metaphors of intoxication to express personal experience of the divine. Elsewhere in Canada, Vancouver's Rumi Society, which enjoys close ties with the Mevlevi Order of America, gains inspiration from the Sufi poet's classic vision of unity and harmony. Meanwhile, the International Sufi Movement has generated a network of groups in several provinces, each perpetuating the vision of the organization's founder, Inayat Khan (1882–1927), who saw music as a way of bringing together the cultures of East and West.

In addition to the intensifying activity of international missionary organizations, two other factors testify to the consolidation of Muslim identity in Canada: the heightened profiles of a number of individual Muslim Canadians; and increased membership in and importance of national Muslim associations, some with links to American *da'wa* movements. Established in 1963 by members of the Muslim Brotherhood at the University of Illinois at Urbana-Champaign, for example, the Muslim Student Association (MSA) now represents a vibrant Sunni presence on college and university campuses across the United States and Canada. In 2006, the University of Toronto's branch celebrated its 40th anniversary. It has grown from the handful of students who attended the first Friday prayer meeting at Hart House in 1966 into the university's largest student association, with over 1,500 members. Serving both Canadian and international students, the association hosts an annual Islam Awareness Week, with interactive seminars, public lectures, exhibits, *halal* food sales, and information booths designed to educate non-Muslims about Islam and to create dialogue between Muslims and non-Muslims. Several other MSA branches in Ontario sponsor similar events. In the main, however, MSA chapters focus on helping Muslim students live as Muslims in the predominantly secular campus environment. From Memorial University in St. John's, Newfoundland, to the University of Victoria, British Columbia, branches offer various supports, including prayer meetings, Qur'an study groups, Arabic classes, visits to local mosques, potluck dinners and barbeques, accommodation, newsletters, email lists, and websites. Muslim traditions sometimes prompt MSA branches to lobby for special on-campus considerations, like rescheduling an examination that conflicts with *Eid al-Fitr* or *Eid al-Adha,* or providing reserved hours for women in the swimming pool. Other MSA activities fulfill wider ethical responsibilities by serving off-campus community needs. For example, the Queen's University MSA sponsors a blood drive at a clinic in Kingston, Ontario, while students from the McGill University and Université de Montréal chapters collaborate to run a summer camp for young urban Muslims, with classes on Islam, sports, and various outdoor pursuits.

After they have graduated, some members of the MSA have also formed new Muslim organizations, notably the Islamic Society of North America (ISNA). Founded in 1978, ISNA offers various kinds of Islamic assurances, like marriage certificates for Muslim couples and *halal* certificates for Muslim restaurants. The association also holds conferences, such as a regional event at the University of Montreal that was held in October 2002, and attended by roughly 600 persons. Invited to the event as keynote speaker, Tariq Ramadan (born 1962), the Swiss Muslim grandson of Hassan al-Banna, elaborated on the central themes of his book, *Islam, the West and the Challenges of Modernity* (2001). Speaking in both French and English, he argued that Islamic traditions furnish Muslims not only with the tools to discriminate between positive and negative aspects of Western modernity, but also with the resources for developing economic, social, and political frameworks within which Muslims might respond constructively and effectively to the challenges of life in North America without relinquishing their ethical and spiritual values. At the same time, Ramadan called upon non-Muslims to be true to their own pluralistic ideals. In many ways, Ramadan's thinking seems to capture the current ethos of ISNA. In 2006, ISNA members elected the Canadian Ingrid Mattson (born 1963) as president, an appointment notable for two reasons: Mattson is not a member of a conventional Muslim ethnic group, but a convert; and she is not a male member of the North American Muslim establishment, but the female Director of Islamic Chaplaincy and a professor at the Macdonald Center for Islamic Studies and Christian-Muslim Relations, Hartford Seminary, Connecticut. Her research includes publications on the Qur'an, slavery, poverty, and Islamic legal theory, and she has argued equally strongly against Muslim extremist attempts to excuse suicide attacks on civilians, and non-Muslim efforts to justify the torture of suspected terrorists in cases of perceived emergency.

Another Canadian association with American links, the Council of American-Islamic Relations Canada (CAIR-CAN), has also become a leading advocate of Muslim civil liberties. Founded in 2002, CAIR-CAN monitors the stereotyping of Muslims in the Canadian media and in Canadian society generally in the wake of the terrorist attacks of 11 September 2001. Like other Muslim Canadian leaders, CAIR-CAN's board rejected Al-Qaeda's violent tactics and appealed to Muslim Canadians to respond charitably with public statements of sympathy and condolences. In practical terms, they urged Muslim medical professionals to volunteer their expertise, and other Muslims to donate blood and raise funds for relief and recovery efforts. But CAIR-CAN also warned of increased anti-Muslim feelings, advising mosques and Islamic centres to increase security and to report anti-Muslim incidents to the authorities. More recently, CAIR-CAN has published guides to Islam and to Muslim religious practices for journalists, employers, educators, and health care providers, as well as *Know Your Rights,* a handbook of protections afforded by the Charter of Rights and Freedoms and other Canadian human rights legislation.

CAIR-CAN has launched numerous high-profile media campaigns, too. In 2002, the group lobbied strenuously on behalf of Maher Arar (born 1970), whom American authorities illegally deported to Syria, where he was tortured on suspicion of terrorist links. CAIR-CAN also petitioned the Canadian Radio-television and Telecommunications Commission to accept a broadcasting application from Al-Jazeera, a media network headquartered in the Arab Muslim state of Qatar. CAIR-CAN also campaigned to secure Canadian legal representation for Omar Khadr (born 1986), the young Muslim Canadian captured fighting for the Taliban in Afghanistan and detained at Guantanamo Bay, Cuba, on charges of murdering an American military medic. In 2007, CAIR-CAN urged Canada's federal government to scrap the Passenger Protect program, arguing that Transport Canada's "no-fly list" risks systemic profiling of Muslim Canadian travellers. Like CAIR-CAN, the Canadian Islamic Congress (CIC), founded in 1998, keeps a close eye on the Canadian media, reporting annually on the way in which newspapers represent Islam and Muslims. By contrast, progressive groups like the Muslim Canadian Congress, also founded in the aftermath of Al-Qaeda's attacks, advocate the liberal modernization of Muslim Canadian life; for example, the group supports same-sex marriage.

Other Muslim Canadian groups, like the Canadian Council of Muslim Women (CCMW) and Young Muslims Canada (YMC), represent the interests of particular constituencies. Muslim women from across Canada launched the CCMW at a conference in Winnipeg, Manitoba, in 1982. A national board oversees the CCMW, with chapters implementing policies in local communities. These policies include introducing newly arrived Muslim women to Canada's larger Muslim community and helping them to negotiate the challenges of a new way of life in a strange land; educating non-Muslims about Islam and Islamic culture by building bridges between the CCMW and other Canadian women's groups; and promoting human rights by forging links with international women's organizations. In pursuing these goals, the CCMW sometimes has to negotiate difficult terrain. In 2000, for example, the CCMW's newsletter described female circumcision as genital mutilation, although minority interpretations of *sharia* require the practice. Members of chapters in Ontario worked actively with health care providers in an effort to halt the custom among certain African immigrant communities. For similar reasons, the association opposed the efforts of other Muslim Canadian groups to submit family disputes to mediation under *sharia*.

CCMW also hosts a national conference as well as regional workshops, and publishes position papers on topics of importance to Muslim Canadian women. For example, Nevin Reda, a member of CCMW, published a study of the Qur'an, Hadith, and other authoritative texts that found strong support for granting women the right to lead prayers and to deliver sermons at Friday services and Muslim festivals. Another book examines the attitudes of contemporary Muslim Canadian women towards traditional dress codes from various scholarly perspectives, and another provides comparative information on *sharia* and Canadian family law for Muslim women and professionals in the judiciary and social services. In a different vein, *At My Mother's Feet: Stories of Muslim Women* (1999), edited by Sadia Zaman, collects spiritual testimonies from Muslim Canadian women, including a piece by Lila Fahlman (1924–2006), the CCMW's first president. Born into a pioneer Lebanese Muslim family, Fahlman played a key role in the successful campaign to preserve Edmonton's Al-Rashid Mosque as a cultural heritage site. She was a trustee on Edmonton's Public School Board and a chaplain at the University of Alberta, the first Muslim woman in North America to be so appointed. Fahlman also served as Vice-Chair of the interfaith channel Vision-TV, and helped to produce programs giving voice to Muslim Canadian women and youth. In 2001, she was awarded the Order of Canada for service to the Muslim community and to the country as a whole.

In recent years, youth organizations have also assumed an important role in Muslim Canadian life. Formed in 1994, Young Muslims of Canada (YMC) draws inspiration from figures like Sayyid Qutb and Hassan al-Banna and their disciples in an effort to engage Muslim youth in the active cultivation of their Sunni heritage. In 2004, YMC launched *MuslimFest*, a day-long celebration co-sponsored by *DawaNet* and *SoundVision*. Every August, Muslim performers of all kinds are showcased at the Living Arts Centre in Mississauga, Ontario. The festival includes educational workshops, art exhibits, a film competition, and an international bazaar, as well as variety, puppet, and fashion shows. The day ends with a concert featuring spoken-word artists, stand-up comics, and Muslim musicians. Another expression of Muslim youth activity, Toronto's *Reviving the Islamic Spirit* has become the largest annual event of its kind in Canada. Attendance at this year-end holiday event has grown from 3,500 in 2003, its inaugural year, to over 15,000 in 2006. Conference themes have included "Legacy of the Prophet," "Islamic Civilization," and "The Neglected *Sunnah*: Patience in the Face of Rejection." Organizers hope to revive Islamic traditions of education, introspection, and tolerance among Muslim youth in dialogue with broader trends in North American society and culture. Speakers have included Muslim and non-Muslim activists, scholars, journalists, and sports figures, and like *MuslimFest*, the conference culminates in a concert. Featured artists have included the Muslim Danish hip-hop band "Outlandish," whose music adapts traditional forms to explore issues facing young Muslims growing up in contemporary Western urban situations. Muslim youngsters also join organized Internet groups, logging on to websites, chat rooms, and blogs to participate in a range of activities—from Qur'an study workshops to information about social activities, and even links for finding suitable marriage partners. Discussion threads often involve more observers than participants, but individuals may use pseudonyms, which mask age, gender, marital status, or ethnicity, creating virtual Islamic spaces for candid exchanges not risked in real-life encounters, either with fellow Muslims or with non-Muslims.

Just as prominent Muslim individuals and organizations represent a wide array of Muslim identities, so, too, do many mosques and community centres now embrace the faith's contemporary image, which is at once local, national, and international. In different ways, the Islamic Shia Ithna-Asheri Jama'at of Toronto and Montreal's Sunni Islamic Centre of Quebec exemplify this sort of congregation. Like Ismai'ilis, many Twelver Shi'ites came to Canada from East Africa, notably Uganda, where their forebears had migrated from western India and prospered until they were expelled by Idi Amin in 1972. About 3,000 Ugandan Twelvers settled in the Toronto region, retaining strong connections with Shi'ite communities around the world. Largely Urdu- and Gujarati-speaking, the Ithna-Asheri Jama'at community began with about 30 families; by 2000, membership approached 5,000 and included Shi'ite newcomers to Canada from Iran, South Asia, Lebanon, and Iraq.

In 1979, Ithna-Asheri Jama'at opened the Ja'ffari Islamic Centre at Bayview and Steeles Avenues, named in honour of the sixth *imam,* Ja'ffar al-Sadiq. Deliberately designed to blend in with local architecture, the centre lacks a dome or a minaret. Inside, however, Islamic influences predominate. The main floor mostly comprises an assembly hall (*imam-bargah*) and a prayer hall (*masjid*). As in all mosques, a *mihrab* indicates the direction of Mecca and a *minbar* or "pulpit" stands ready for the Friday sermon, decorated with the 99 names of God. Fourteen arched windows feature geometric designs in stained glass, as well as the word "Allah" and verses from the Qur'an in Arabic calligraphy. In addition, countless details reflect Shi'ite spiritual allegiance to the *Ahl al-bayt:* the names of Ali, Fatima, Hasan, and Husayn are inscribed in Arabic on the walls; the assembly room is named Zainabia Hall, after Husayn's sister Zainab; the names of Muhammad, Fatima, and the 12 *imams* cap the arched windows; and two pieces of calligraphy stand on either side of the archway leading from Zainabia Hall to the mosque—one depicting the *hadith* in which Muhammad designated Ali as his successor, the other a verse from the Qur'an assumed to refer to Husayn. Off the main prayer hall, a smaller room decorated with intricate,

During Muharram, Shi'ites in Dar es Salaam, Tanzania, listen to a sermon commemorating the death of Muhammad's grandson Husayn at the Battle of Karbala. PHOTO BY MUHAMMAD MAHDI KARIM. REPRINTED UNDER THE TERMS OF THE GNU FREE DOCUMENTATION LICENSE.

light-reflecting mirrored glass contains silver replicas of the tombs of the *imams*, sacred objects suggestive of the *Ahl al-bayt*, and collection bowls for offerings made in their names. At the JIC, men congregate for worship upstairs in the main hall, while closed-circuit television delivers services to women and children in halls in the basement and on the second floor.

In 2003, Ithna-Asheri Jama'at began raising money for a new Ja'ffari Community Centre (JCC), issuing a bond in compliance not only with *shari'a*, but also with the regulatory requirements of the federally administered Registered Retirement and Savings Plan for Canadian Residents. Located at 9000 Bathurst Street, Richmond Hill, the JCC was completed in 2010. At 161,000 square feet, it ranks among the largest facilities of its kind in the Western world, with prayer halls for men and women, an *imambargah*, the As-Sadiq Islamic School, washing amenities, and offices. The complex also offers a number of social and recreational services, including the Salam Café, banqueting rooms, and a fitness centre and gymnasia for men and women. Mothers and young children may take advantage of a specially designed nursery area, too. In addition, Ithna-Asheri Jama'at completed the Masumeen Islamic Centre in 2003, replacing a smaller facility, and the organization has centres of worship in different stages of planning and development in both Hamilton and London, Ontario.

Throughout the year, Shi'ites acknowledge the same prescribed prayer times and major festivals as Sunnis, but they also participate in a number of observances not recognized by Sunnis, meaning that mosques tend to be more central to their lives. These devotions have mainly to do with the *Ahl al-Bayt,* and Husayn in particular. During *Muharram,* Shi'ites from far and wide join the Ithna-Asheri Jama'at congregation for celebrations honouring Muhammad's grandson, especially *Ashura.* Observances include recitations from the Qur'an, poetry, sermons, and processing around the *imam-bargah* with a coffin draped in white cloth dyed red, as if bloodstained. Other features include the Tanzanian Shi'ite custom of constructing a scale model of the battlefield of Karbala, complete with toy soldiers, signs marking important spots, recorded explanations of events, and a map tracing the route taken by Husayn and his followers from Mecca to Karbala. The model appeals greatly to children. Observances culminate in *gham,* or "lamentation," when Shi'ites mourn Husayn's bloody martyrdom. Shi'ites sometimes express their grief with self-flagellation. In Canada, members of the Ithna-Asheri Jama'at congregation have transformed this form of ritual bloodletting into an annual blood drive for the Red Cross, though congregants debate whether non-Muslims should receive the donated blood. The congregation also organizes a procession in downtown Toronto. Most participants wear black, and some carry banners like "Islam Stands for Peace" and "Every Day is *Ashura,* Everywhere is Karbala." One year, a *da'wa* pamphlet titled *Islam: The Faith that Invites People to Prosperity in both Worlds* drew parallels between Judaism, Christianity, and Islam, but also stressed Shi'ite virtues like the willingness to confront tyranny and injustice with martyrdom when necessary. Sometimes participants share a meal before going home, and collecting food for the needy is also a traditional part of *Ashura* observances.

Ithna-Asheri Jama'at provides a broad range of religious and community services at its various premises. With appropriate legal disclaimers, a sample marriage contract is available through the organization's website, and weddings may be held at the JCC. Signing the marriage contract before witnesses is central to the wedding service, and those present at the service recite the opening *sura* of the Qur'an (*fatihah*). A licensed *imam* records the marriage for the state. The *imam-bargah* is also used for lectures and discussion groups, and the Jaffari Funeral Services Board oversees burial arrangements and facilities for preparing the deceased, including sprinkler hoses for cleaning bodies, a roll of cloth for shrouds, and a stock of simple wooden boxes for coffins. There is a library on the second floor, and the centre publishes a quarterly magazine, *The Ja'ffari News*, in part to ease its members' transitions to Western ways. Sometimes, however, living in Canada accelerates change. Women congregants, for example, question whether separate seating during prayers is a requirement of *shari'a* or a function of South-Asian and East-African patriarchal customs. Other members dislike the use of English in services in place of the traditional Urdu. Different Shi'ite communities acknowledge different *ayatollahs* as their spiritual authorities, and Ithna-Asheri Jama'at seeks opinions from Grand Ayatollah Sayyid Ali Husaini al-Sistani (born 1930) in Iraq. Fully involved in local community affairs, community members also work with several Christian churches to provide shelter to Toronto's homeless.

Lastly, the story of Montreal's ICQ exemplifies the way in which a Sunni congregation has come to epitomize Canada's multicultural environment. In 1958, Habibullah Khan, Mumtazul Haque Rehman, and other South-Asian immigrants founded the Islamic Centre of Montreal, but soon discovered that Quebec's laws only recognized births, marriages, and deaths registered with Christian churches. Renaming their congregation the Islamic Centre of Quebec, they found legislative sponsorship in the National Assembly for a private member's bill granting the association civil status. In 1965, the historic bill passed, effectively recognizing Islam as a minority religion in the province. By 1967, the ICQ had raised funds for a mosque and community centre, purchasing a former World War II army barracks in Ville St. Laurent and appointing Roohi Kurdy as the first *imam* to a mixed congregation of Sunnis and Shi'ites. Members of the congregation renovated the premises on weekends. Muslim immigration from Afghanistan, the Balkans, the Caribbean, India, Indonesia, China, Pakistan, Somalia, Turkey, and various parts of the Arab world, as well as increasing numbers of African and European Canadian converts, multiplied attendance. In 1973 and again in 1985, ICQ expanded the centre's main prayer hall, with an area reserved for women, and added washing amenities, a library, a bookstore, offices, a conference room, and facilities for burial preparations. In 1973, the purchase of 50 plots in Rideau Memorial Gardens, an ecumenical cemetery, satisfied short-term needs for a graveyard within 50 miles of Montreal.

It was not all plain sailing during these years, however. In 1974, Moeen Ghauri became *imam* of ICQ, serving the congregation for 15 years. He was much loved in the community, and was honoured as an *hafiz,* a term which literally means "guardian" and hence describes Muslims who have memorized the whole Qur'an. In the mid-1970s, though, Shi'ites broke with the ICQ and purchased a building in Notre-Dame-de-Grâce to serve as a mosque and *imam-bargah.* Incorporated in 1976, Shiane Haidery International Association, now known as Shiane Haidery Islamic Association, moved into the Haidery Centre in 1982. Relations between the two communities remained amicable until Ghauri's successor fomented tensions over the use of new burial grounds, purchased by ICQ in 1990 from the city of Laval. Appointed shortly afterwards as the centre's first salaried *imam,* Syed Fida Bukhari arrived from Pakistan with credentials from Saudi Arabia's Medina University. His Arabic language skills and Wahhabi training appealed to Arab congregants. In a sermon, Bukhari pronounced that Shi'ite Muslims should be buried in a separate cemetery, a position endorsed by conservative Sunnis in the congregation. Eventually, the new cemetery was divided into two sections, one for Sunnis and one for Shi'ites. Today, tensions have abated, and ICQ administers Muslim funerals for all Muslim congregations in Montreal, irrespective of their sect. These services include removing the deceased to the ICQ for ritual washing and funeral prayers, freezer storage, and conveyance to the Islamic Cemetery of Quebec—*Cimetière Islamique du Québec* in Laval—for burial according to *shari'a.*

In the 1970s, radical Muslim movements caused other concerns at the ICQ. At that time, as we have seen, the MSA enjoyed a good deal of success on several Canadian university campuses. Wary of Wahhabi influences on the MSA, several prominent members of the ICQ, including founding figures like S. Ali Husain, Bashir Hussain, and Mumtaz H. Rehman, wished to maintain some distance between the mosque and student organizations. In a related series of events, increasing visits from Tablighi Jama'at members also began to cause tensions between these groups. Sometimes, as many as 25 Tablighis would use the mosque as a dormitory, disrupting the community's enjoyment of the premises. In 1978, the board of ICQ resolved to ban such uses of the mosque, but the Tablighis enjoyed strong support for their missionary work among the more conservative elements of the association. Encouraged, the Tablighis secured a large number of new memberships in the ICQ, eventually succeeding in securing control of the association's Executive Committee, and hence of the centre itself. Liberal members of the ICQ argued that the Tablighis and their supporters had violated traditional Islamic procedures of *shura,* or "consultation."

Others countered that the Tablighis were acting according to the principles of *shura*, since disagreements were being resolved through democratic process. Either way, the difference of opinion divided the community. Led by Mohamed Amin, several members resigned from the ICQ, founding the Muslim Community of Quebec in Notre-Dame-de-Grâce in 1979.

For a short while, the ICQ played an important part in the story of Islam on the national stage, too. In 1973, several Muslim leaders met in Montreal's ICQ to set up the Council of Muslim Communities of Canada (CMCC), including S. Ali Husain, Bashir Hussain, and Mumtaz Haque Rehman. CMCC attracted representatives from Muslim communities in Cambridge, Hamilton, Ottawa, and Windsor, Ontario, as well as in Edmonton and Montreal. Funding from Saudi Arabia helped to support an office in Ottawa and the publication of a quarterly magazine, *Islam Canada*, which featured liberal Muslim views on politics, religion, education, and the place of Muslims in Canada. Internal disputes led to dissatisfaction within CMCC, and soon funding dried up and the association's activities ceased. Still, the council established an important precedent for Muslim Canadians wishing to engage one with another on a national platform, anticipating the numerous national organizations that are now active in Canada.

Despite these setbacks, the ICQ has blossomed into the first truly multi-ethnic Sunni congregation in Montreal. Painted white and featuring a green, onion-shaped dome, the present mosque is modest and conventional in appearance. Inside, prayer areas are covered with carpets striped in alternating shades of green, clearly demarcating lines for kneeling. In the evening, chandeliers hanging in rows from the ceiling reveal the niche directing devotees to Mecca and the pulpit for the preacher. Phrases from the Qur'an, written in Arabic, decorate the walls. The ICQ now serves about 75,000 people from the Montreal region; on Fridays, conversation among congregants might take place in Afghani, Arabic, English, French, Persian, Turkish, or Urdu. The ICQ is affiliated with about 20 other Sunni mosques, prayer halls, and organizations in and around Montreal, including MSA chapters at Concordia University and McGill University. Licensed to register marriages among Muslims in Quebec, the *imam* performs three or four ceremonies every week in the mosque. Sometimes, he also conducts weddings in private homes. In 1998, about 3,000 weddings took place at the ICQ. Other services offered include Islamic education programs, youth groups, social welfare support, protection for Muslim rights, and coordination with the Canadian

Correctional Services that enables the *imam* to visit Muslim inmates. To encourage exchanges between Muslims and non-Muslims, the mosque regularly welcomes parties of schoolchildren, social workers, government officials, and police. The community also publishes an electronic newsletter, the *Montreal Muslim News,* which provides regular information about events in the community. In November 2002, Bashir Hussain, a member of the Executive Committee who helped to build the original mosque, was presented the Queen's Golden Jubilee award for consistency of service to the community. In the same year, he witnessed the start of work on a third expansion of ICQ. This latest work will allow the main hall to accommodate over 1,000 congregants, as well as expanding the library and office space, and adding a *da'wa* centre, a *madrassa*, a gymnasium, a mini-market, and extra parking.

AFTERWORD

Muslims have come from every region of the world to make a new home in Canada. A sampling of recent public honours exemplifies this diversity. In 1997, Ugandan Canadian Rahim Jaffer (born 1971) became the first Muslim elected to the federal Parliament. In 2001, Lebanese Canadian Lila Fahlman and Indian Canadian Haroon Siddiqui (born 1942), editorial page editor emeritus of the *Toronto Star,* became the first Muslims appointed to the Order of Canada, and Ugandan Canadian Mobina Jaffer (born 1949), the first woman of South-Asian descent to practice law in British Columbia, became the first Muslim to be appointed to the Senate of Canada. In 2003, Shafiq Qaadri (born 1964) became the first Canadian of Pakistani origin to win a seat in Ontario's provincial legislature, and in 2004, Tanzanian Canadian Yasmin Ratansi (born 1951) became the first Muslim woman elected to the Canadian House of Commons. In 2010, an Ismai'ili Muslim, Naheed Nenshi, was elected as the Mayor of Calgary. At the same time, the common bonds of Islam unite Muslim Canadians, a unity only strengthened by the events of 11 September 2001. Some Muslim Canadians may view Islam as an unchanging system of beliefs and practices, but the majority views it as continually evolving to meet the challenges of new situations. A tiny minority of Muslims have embraced extremist views, exemplified by the "Toronto 18," a group charged with plotting terrorist activity in 2006. Seven of the 18 members admitted their guilt, and four others were convicted in 2009 and 2010. Other Muslims

Inaugurated by the British Columbia Muslim Association in 2009, the Masjid al-Salaam and Educational Centre, Burnaby, British Columbia, fuses the local timber and masonry vernacular with an identifiable Islamic expression. PHOTO BY SHARIF SENBEL. REPRINTED BY PERMISSION. © SHARIF SENBEL/ STUDIO SENBEL DESIGN + ARCHITECTURE INC., VANCOUVER, BC.

have resisted official policies on multiculturalism, and have tried to create their own distinctively Islamic communities.

Perhaps nowhere is the flourishing of Islamic heritage and Muslim life in a new Canadian context more vividly celebrated than in the various expressions of cultural creativity, both institutional and popular. As instances of institutional expression, take three mosques designed by the Egyptian-born Vancouver architect Sharif Senbel (born 1966). A skilful fusion of local vernacular and global Islamic influences, Senbel's houses of worship in Burnaby, Port Coquitlam, and Surrey, British Columbia, respond creatively to the natural environment of northwest Canada's ocean, forests, and mountains. On the one hand, Senbel makes pervasive use of materials from the region; on the other, his designs echo traditional Islamic styles without slavishly repeating them. For example, at

Port Coquitlam's Masjid al-Hidayah and Islamic Cultural Centre, which the British Columbia Muslim Association (BCMA) opened in 2003, geometric patterns etched into the glass of the arched windows of the prayer hall refract across the worshippers the Pacific brightness of God's guiding light. At the same time, Senbel's buildings furnish a fitting religious setting for the diverse ethnic cultures of their congregations, epitomized by the membership of Port Coquitlam's sister institution, Masjid al-Salaam and Education Centre. Inaugurated by the BCMA in 2009, this Burnaby mosque welcomes worshippers from Afghanistan, Bosnia, China, Egypt, Fiji, Hong Kong, India, Lebanon, Pakistan, Senegal, Sierra Leone, South Africa, Syria, Turkey, and the United Kingdom.

On a more popular level, the Canadian Broadcasting Corporation's hit television sitcom *Little Mosque on the Prairie* likewise succeeds in capturing something of the diversity of Muslim experience in Canada—reflecting in turn the varied influences upon its creator, media polymath Zarqa Nawaz (born 1968), who is herself of blended English, Pakistani, and Canadian background. Almost a microcosm of the "House of Islam," the fictional town of Mercy, Saskatchewan, includes Muslims from Africa, Lebanon, and South Asia; Muslims born into Muslim families in Canada and Canadian converts to Islam; and Muslims with progressive views as well as Muslims who are more traditional in outlook, both socially and religiously. In the last analysis, though, the homely and familiar ethos of *Little Mosque on the Prairie*, alternately humorous and dramatic, reflects a way of life which may best be described as at once Muslim *and* Canadian.

KEY TERMS

Ahl al-Bayt	Revered by Shi'ite Muslims, the family of Muhammad's daughter Fatima, her husband Ali, and their sons Hasan and Husayn.
Al-Arkan	"Five Pillars of Islam," meaning the required religious duties of *shahada, salat, zakat, sawm,* and *hajj.*
Allah	The Arabic word for God.
Da'wa	Inviting people to Islam, and hence Muslim mission.
Dhikr	The meditative practice of freeing the mind from thoughts of anything other than God, and hence remembering God.
Dhimmi	A protected person, usually Jewish or Christian, living in a Muslim society.
Fatwa	The legal opinion of a qualified scholar on a religious matter.

Fiqh	Islamic jurisprudence.
Hadith	An authoritative saying reporting what Muhammad said, did, or silently approved; and, collectively, the whole corpus of such sayings.
Hajj	The pilgrimage to Mecca which every Muslim must undertake at least once, health and means permitting.
Halal	In Islamic law, what is permissible.
Haraam	In Islamic law, what is forbidden.
Hijra	The migration of Muhammad and his followers from Mecca to Medina in 622, which hence becomes the first year of the Muslim calendar.
Jihad	"Striving," and hence striving for moral and spiritual perfection, especially against one's own inner weaknesses.
Khalifa	"Steward," and hence a title denoting military and political leadership, though not spiritual authority.
Ka'ba	The sacred, cube-shaped shrine in Mecca that serves as the centre of the Muslim world.
Mahdi	The divinely guided messianic figure whom Shi'ites believe will return from hiding to restore justice and order to the world.
Masjid	"Place of prostration," and hence mosque.
Qur'an	"Recitation," and hence God's revelations to Muhammad constituting Muslim sacred scripture.
Ramadan	The month in the Muslim lunar calendar when Muslims are expected to fast and to abstain from all bodily pleasures between dawn and dusk.
Salat	The cycle of five prayers required of Muslims every day.
Sawm	Muslim fasting, especially during Ramadan.
Shahada	Islam's simple creed: "There is no god but God, and Muhammad is the messenger of God."
Shari'a	The various elements of a proper Islamic life, captured in the religious law of Islam developed by jurists in the ninth and tenth centuries.
Shi'ites	The second-largest group of Muslims, comprising about 15–20 per cent of the faithful.
Sufis	Muslims who belong to one of the many mystical and ascetic movements in Islam, which are collectively known as Sufism.
Sunna	The authoritative way of life established by Muhammed.

Sunnis	The majority of Muslims, comprising over 80–85 per cent of the faithful.
Tariqa	"Way" or "path," and hence a Sufi brotherhood or religious order.
Ulema	A collective term for Muslim jurists trained in the scholarly interpretation of the Qur'an, the Hadith, and Islamic jurisprudence.
Umma	The Muslim community.
Wali	"Friend," and hence a Muslim honoured for saintly closeness to God.
Zakat	"Growing in goodness," and hence Muslim almsgiving.

KEY DATES

622 CE	The first year of the Muslim calendar.
632	The death of Muhammad.
650s	A canonical text of the Qur'an is established.
680	The death of Husayn, son of Ali, at the Battle of Karbala.
800–900s	Authoritative editions of the Hadith are composed.
922	Mansur al-Hallaj is crucified for declaring, "I *am* the real [or the truth]."
1058–1111	Abu Hamid Muhammad al-Ghazali, Persian reconciler of Sufism and Sunni orthodoxy.
1187	Salah al-Din recaptures Jerusalem from Christian crusaders.
1207–73	Jalal al-Din Rumi, Persian Sufi poet.
1453	Ottoman Turks take Constantinople and rename the Byzantine capital Istanbul.
1526	Zahiruddin Mohammed Babur founds the Mughal dynasty in India.
1703–92	Muhammad ibn 'Abd al-Wahhab, conservative Muslim revivalist.
1838–97	Jamal al Din al-Afghani, Iranian Shi'ite modernist reformer.
1871	First Canadian census counts 13 Muslims.
1922	Mustafa Kemal Atatürk establishes the new republic of Turkey.
1938	In Edmonton, Alberta, Al-Rashid mosque opens, the first in Canada.
1947	Muslim Pakistan is partitioned from predominantly Hindu India.

1952	Founding of the Institute of Islamic Studies, McGill University, Montreal, Quebec.
1973	Founding of the Council of Muslim Communities of Canada.
1979	Ayatollah Ruhollah Khomeini establishes a Shi'ite theocracy in Iran.
1982	Founding of the Canadian Council of Muslim Women.
1997	Rahim Jaffer, an Ismai'ili, becomes the first Muslim elected to the federal Parliament.
2004	Yasmin Ratansi, an Ismai'ili, becomes the first Muslim woman elected to the federal Parliament.

KEY READINGS

Abu-Laban, Baha. *An Olive Branch on the Family Tree: The Arabs in Canada*. Toronto: McLelland and Stewart, 1980.

Ahmed, Leila. *Women and Gender in Islam*. New Haven: Yale University Press, 1992.

Ayoub, Mahmoud. *Redemptive Suffering in Islam: A Study of Devotional Aspects of 'Ashura in Twelver Shi'ism*. The Hague: Mouton, 1978.

Bakht, Natasha, ed. *Belonging and Banishment: Being Muslim in Canada*. Toronto: TSAR, 2008.

Ernst, Carl. *Sufism: An Essential Introduction to the Philosophy and Practice of the Mystical Tradition of Islam*. Boston: Shambala, 1997.

Esack, Farid. *The Qur'an: A Short Introduction*. Oxford: Oneworld, 2002.

Hussain, Amir. "Muslims in Canada: Opportunities and Challenges." *Studies in Religion / Sciences Religieuses* 33, no. 3–4 (2004): 359–79. doi:10.1177/000842980403300305.

Metcalf, Barbara Daly, ed. *Making Muslim Space in North America and Europe*. Berkeley: University of California Press, 1996.

Ramadan, Tariq. *Western Muslims and the Future of Islam*. New York: Oxford University Press, 2004.

Rippin, Andrew. *Muslims: Their Religious Beliefs and Practices*. 3rd ed. London, New York: Routledge, 2005.

Waugh, Earle, Sharon McIrvin, Baha Abu-Laban, and Regula Qureshi, eds. *Muslim Families in North America*. Edmonton: University of Alberta Press, 1991.

Zine, Jasmin. "Creating a Critical-Faith-Centred Space for Anti-Racist Feminism: Reflections of a Muslim Scholar-Activist." *Journal of Feminist Studies in Religion* 20, no. 2 (2004): 167–87. doi:10.2979/FSR.2004.20.2.167.

KEY WEB SITES

http://www.2muslims.com [Muslims Internet Directory]
http://www.isna.net [Islamic Society of North America]
http://muslimcanada.org [Canadian Society of Muslims]
http://www.canadianislamiccongress.com [Canadian Islamic Congress]
http://www.caircan.ca [Canadian Council on American-Islamic Relations]
http://www.ccmw.com [Canadian Council of Muslim Women]
http://www.macnet.ca [Muslim Association of Canada]
http://www.muslimcanadiancongress.org [Muslim Canadian Congress]

KEY QUESTIONS FOR CRITICAL REFLECTION

1. Some scholars refer to the three religions of Judaism, Christianity, and Islam as religions of Abraham. Why would they make this comparison?
2. Why have Muslim immigrants come to Canada? Where might they have come from, and when?
3. Where was the first mosque built in Canada? Where in Canada do you find Muslim houses of worship today, and what are they like?
4. Why do Shi'ite Muslims often spend more time in their mosques than Sunnis do?
5. What sorts of challenges face Muslim newcomers to Canada, and how do they negotiate them?

SIX

Hindus

PAUL YOUNGER, MCMASTER UNIVERSITY

||||||||||||||||||||||||||||||||||||||||||||||||||||||||||||||||||||||||||||||||||||||||||||||||||||||||||||||

Though Hindus first came to Canada in the early decades of the twentieth century, it is only recently that the Hindu community has become a significant feature of the Canadian religious mosaic. The community began to develop rapidly in the 1960s, almost doubling in size between the 1991 and 2001 census, with new immigration accounting for about half of this increase. By the end of the millennium, nearly 300,000 Canadians were identifying themselves as Hindus, with nearly two-thirds living in Ontario's metropolitan Toronto region. The vitality of Hindu religious life in Canada is reflected in the fact that within this short time hundreds of architecturally interesting temples have been built, representing a wide range of Hindu devotional traditions. I arrived in Canada to teach at McMaster University in 1964 and watched these developments with great excitement. Almost all Hindus in Canada are immigrants, so it is possible for us to go back and examine the heritage out of which they came, and to better understand what parts of that heritage they brought with them to Canada.

THE HERITAGE

The religious practices of the people of India evolved for many centuries in the sheltered environment of the Indian subcontinent. Because that subcontinent is protected on the north by the Himalaya mountains and on the other three sides by a long coastline, the flow of people in and out of the area was relatively modest until recent times. The people within the subcontinent moved about somewhat, but gradually settled down in its mountain regions, river valleys, dry plateaus and fertile plains, and established stable social units and a rich cultural life. India's diverse culture is characterized by a dozen or more distinct language groups, and each language group is made up of a number of units or birth groups (*jatis*). Today, these birth groups determine most aspects of daily life, from the sort of work people may hope to undertake to the kind of person their children might expect to marry. Members of a given birth group tend to share its primary religious rituals, too.

Despite strong attachments to local languages and the religious rituals of the birth group, Hindus have historically found themselves exposed to a variety of religious ideas and practices from further afield as a result of the influence of itinerant spiritual teachers. Among the earliest of the itinerant teachers were those trained in the secret teachings known as the **Vedas**. Some of these Vedic teachers may have come from outside of India, because some of their hymns seem to reflect conditions to the north and west of India, but we know that they made a major impression on thinkers within India as early as the sixth century BCE. Their teachings included hymns (*samhitas*) to male deities such as Indra and Agni and to female deities such as Sarasvati. They also taught rules on ritual called *brahmanas,* magical practices called *aranyakas,* and, most important to later thinkers, meditations on the nature of reality called *upanisads.* This whole body of thought taken together is called the Vedas and is thought of by most Hindus as a kind of sacred revelation. Only much later in the tradition were these oral teachings set down as written texts.

The majority of today's Hindus accept the sacred authority of the Vedas, but there is much more to Hinduism than these ancient teachings. When powerful emperors and kings began to be part of the Indian landscape, from the third century BCE on, many of the itinerant teachers were for a while linked with one or another of the court systems. In this context, systematic treatises on ritual and law were written. Known as the **shastras**, these treatises include the *Dharma-shastra,* one of which—the *Laws of*

Manu (*ca.* 500 BCE)—proposes a universal system of social divisions. Manu called these social divisions *varnas,* which literally means "colours," but which is usually translated into English as "castes." According to Manu there were to be four divisions, each with its own ritual rules, with *brahmins* serving as priests and learned people, *kshatriyas* as warriors, *vaisyas* as merchants, and *sudras* as labourers. The courts also sponsored the scholars who composed the *Ramayana* and *Mahabharata* epics, and the **puranas** ("Old Tales"), which sought to give literary form to the popular religious stories circulating in society. As time went on, the courts also lent their support to local efforts at temple-building, and major temples were established with elaborate ritual traditions. This whole system is in some ways well integrated and internally coherent, but it allows individuals to walk through it in a great variety of ways. Because of this unique structure, Hinduism has been very difficult for people of other religious traditions to understand. Outsiders look in vain for a single focus of religious authority, a single origin story, or a single book or institution that could speak for the whole system. On the other hand, it is a religious tradition that has been able to adapt to changing economic, political, and intellectual situations with remarkable creativity.

Hindu understanding of human life takes full shape in the *Upanishads.* These sacred writings explore the relationship between the individual self or soul (**atman**) and the ultimate reality or the cosmic soul (**brahman**). Hindus believe that all existence is a continuing cycle of birth, death, and rebirth, known as **samsara**. The law of **karma**, which is the cumulative effect of one's intellectual, verbal, and physical actions over a series of lives, determines one's place in the cycle of *samsara.* Though all existence strives for **moksha**, that is, eventual liberation from the ongoing effects of *karma,* at every stage of the cycle, everyone comes to recognize their role in the given order of things as a set of obligations. These obligations constitute one's social, moral, and religious duty (**dharma**), the details of which are specific to the sub-caste into which one is born.

Whatever one's sub-caste, however, Hindu tradition teaches that every individual passes through four stages of life called **ashramas**. For much of life, Hindus define themselves in terms of the *dharma* of *grihasta* ("household life") of a certain caste. During this period, they organize the lives of younger members of the community in the earliest stage of *brahmacarya* ("student life") and respectfully care for their elders, who may be in the stage of retirement known as *vanaprasta* (literally, "forest-dweller," indicating a life of semi-retirement), or, more rarely, in the stage of ascetic renunciation, known as *samnyasa*. Hindu tradition also talks of the four goals of life: *kama* ("pleasure"), *artha* ("wealth"), *dharma* (in this context, "religious duty"), and *moksha* ("liberation"). In a sense, these four goals correspond with the four stages of life.

For an Indian child, religious behaviour starts long before the dawn of consciousness with a series of ritual acts of purification known as the **samskaras**. Quite elaborate, these rituals are associated with the conception, birth, and naming of the child. The ceremonies that accompany the first cutting of the hair, the onset of puberty, and the arrangement of a marriage come during the exciting early phases of one's life. These rituals leave an indelible sense that the initiate belongs to a specific family and caste, and that one's identity is directly related to that group's place in the cosmic order. The fact that a variety of natural and human forces gradually position themselves around a child and impinge on its life is initially accepted as a given.

In the role of householder, Hindus become involved in wider social responsibilities, including helping to support the temples to which the local rulers, caste elders, or more recently, wealthy businessmen have pledged their patronage. For centuries, this aspect of Hindu religious observance has assumed great importance as a popular way of expressing personal piety, known as **bhakti**. The *Bhagavad Gita,* a long devotional poem added to the epic *Mahabharata* in the second century BCE, culminates with **Vishnu**, the Hindu preserver god, teaching the warrior king, Arjuna, how to gain release from the ceaseless effects of *karma* through this sort of personal piety. Starting in sixth-century Tamil-speaking south India, the *bhakti* movement taught intense devotion to the deities Vishnu and **Shiva**. Popular cults developed around the saintly life stories and devotional poetry of the 12 Alvars, who worshipped Vishnu, and a larger group of 63 Nyanmars, who worshipped Shiva. A number of these saintly poets travelled widely, dedicating temples to Vishnu and Shiva wherever they went. By the twelfth century, the *bhakti* movement had spread to western and northern India, where devotional cults thrived, inspired by vernacular poets like Kabir (1440–1518), Caitanya (1486–1583), Tulasidas (1532–1623), and Tukaram (1598–1649). In the nineteenth century, Bhaktivinoda Thakura (born Kedarnatha Datta; 1838–1914) and his son Bhaktisiddhanta (born Bimala Prasada; 1874–1937) revived Caitanya's practice of love for Krishna, known as Gaudiya Vaishnava. The movement spread widely in India, and Bhaktisiddhanta encouraged disciples to carry Caitanya's vision worldwide. Perpetuating this *bhakti* tradition, the International Society for Krishna Consciousness (ISKCON), popularly known as "Hare Krishnas," today runs over 200 centres around the world, with temples, farms, restaurants, and schools practising and propagating Gaudiya Vaishnavite.

Although local rulers, caste elders, or in recent times, wealthy businessmen sometimes bestowed patronage exclusively on Vaishnavite temples, dedicated to Vishnu, and sometimes exclusively on Shaivite temples, dedicated to Shiva, more often than not they chose to support a variety of temples. Significantly, they even encouraged lower sub-castes to develop goddess (*devi*) temples. These places of worship tend to have a very individualized local character. When villagers in the course of everyday life associate a miracle with a nearby tree, say, or a snake-filled anthill, they often establish a simple place of worship there. Usually, as time passes, they come to define the spiritual centre in this sacred place as a goddess, on whom they bestow a local name. Resulting goddess stories can become very elaborate and widely known, and local worshippers are often happy to equate their local goddess with one of the more powerful goddesses. In the southern Indian state of Tamil Nadu, for example, a local goddess is usually linked with Mariyamman, who is known for dealing swiftly with smallpox, drought, or even enemies at work. In other areas, it is more common to make a link with Kali, the naked, black goddess who wears a necklace of skulls, or with Durga, whose ten arms gave her the power to slay demons, which in turn kept changing forms in order to avoid her weapons. In ancient times, rulers and landlord castes seldom lent direct support to these goddess temples, but they too recognized their great popularity and often tried to link some form of goddess worship with the Shaivite and Vaishnavite temples they built. Today, most families worship at several different temples and are familiar with several styles of devotion.

A vast network of pilgrimage sites has grown up across India, since in each case devotees believe that the deity resides in the local temple. Both Vaishnavite and Shaivite temples were often built with support from kings and landlord caste leaders. Such patronage did not mean that the temples were royal temples, because the king had very little influence on the way the worship was carried out. Devotions follow prescribed formulas codified in the *agama* texts of traditional doctrine, and can only be conducted by properly initiated *brahmin* priests, who are usually members of a Vaishnavite or Shaivite family lineage assigned to a given temple for generation after generation. In Saiva temples, worship usually centres on a sacred phallus known as a Shiva *lingam*. Various smaller shrines for other deities are scattered around the temple corridors or the compound out-side the main building. In particular, devotees may conduct preliminary worship to Shiva's elephant-headed son Ganesha, the god who removes obstacles, and Shiva's consort (**shakti**) Parvati, the universal female whose forms include the gentle and maternal Uma, the dominant and dignified Durga, and the violent and horrific Kali. By contrast, Vaishnavite tem-ples enshrine a wide array of primary images, for Vishnu has manifested himself in a number of different forms, notably the ten incarnations (*avataras*), the most celebrated of which are Krishna and Rama. Stories associated with Krishna and Rama and their respective partners Radha and Sita are often incorporated into Vaishnavite worship, too, and some-times an image of one of the couples is made the primary image of worship. In both Vaishnavite and Shaivite temples, ritual actions include feeding, bathing, adorning, and manifesting the deity with camphor lights (*aarati*). The sequence of rituals is followed two, four, or six times a day in accor-dance with a strict schedule, and devotees choose which times they wish to glimpse and be spotted by the deity, an experience known as *darsana,* which expresses the devotee's participation in the cosmic patterns cap-tured and recapitulated in the local temple.

Temple traditions tend to be quite similar within an area defined by language, and Indians are sometimes unaware that the traditions in other language areas are quite different. Temple architecture, for instance, is dif-ferent from region to region. Southern Indian architecture features great stone walls surrounding the temple's sacred centre (*vimana*), while the northern Indian style is reminiscent of towering mountain peaks built over a darkened womb or cave known as the *garbha griha*. In the southern Indian style, worship takes place within the walls after one enters through grand doorways (*gopurams*). Priests greet worshippers in great hallways and carry offerings into the sacred centre, where the laity is strictly for-bidden to go. In the northern Indian style, worship begins as the devotee approaches the temple from afar, and priests are not always involved. In Gujarat and other parts of western India, the worshipper may be able to see a number of deities at one time, and both priests and worshippers go about their worship by making a great variety of offerings and gestures of respect and reverence.

All over India, temple festivals signify special days when the power of the deity is transferred into an image (**murti**) that can be carried into the streets. Most festivals are thought of as unique to a particular temple, though some are widely celebrated, because they mark cosmic events, like the movement of the sun, or an important episode in the life of a major deity. Often, it is not priests who are the central religious figures in a festival but other devotees who have prepared for the occasion by taking a vow (*vrata*). Such vows indicate a devotee's intention to undertake the sort of ascetic behaviour that might culminate in a trance state. As the images of the deities are brought out of the temple to be part of the celebration, thousands swarm into the streets to welcome them into their community. Goddess festivals can be among the most dramatic, as they frequently celebrate the overcoming of disease or the exorcism of evil spirits, while Shaivite and Vaishnavite festivals often centre on the marriage of the god and his consort, which symbolizes harmony and balance in the social order.

A key feature of the Indian religious system that transcends language boundaries is the itinerant religious specialist. Ancient Vedic texts referred to ascetics (*sramanas*) and priestly scholars (*brahmanas*; later *brahmins*) who travelled about the countryside. Mahavira (*ca.* 540–477 BCE), who founded the Jain monastic order, and Siddhartha Gautama (*ca.* 563–483 BCE), who founded the Buddhist tradition, were two famous members of the first group. In the Hindu religious system, *sadhus,* who are lifelong ascetics, and *samnyasins,* in life's fourth stage of renunciation, perpetuate this ascetic tradition. *Sadhus* and *samnyasins* take vows of celibacy, insisting that they have no caste and no ties to society. In turn, they are revered by those living within the social order, and as **gurus** they are expected to have achieved advanced states of spiritual life or yogic power and to be able to teach others. By contrast, the *brahmins* were known more for their ritual knowledge and philosophical wisdom than their asceticism. To this learned group we owe the Vedas themselves. In Vedic times, a family of scholars would memorize a section of this great body of literature and then make themselves available to share their knowledge with a court, a temple, or a wealthy family. While they considered the knowledge of the text itself sacred and secret, they would share the expertise in religious ritual and philosophical wisdom that the text gave them.

In the royal courts, the *brahmins* would sometimes be asked to put their wisdom into forms that were less overtly related to the spiritual goal of liberation. In this context, the great epic stories of the *Mahabharata* and *Ramayana* were gradually put together. Consisting of over 100,000 verses, the *Mahabharata* tells of a legendary internecine struggle between the older Kauravas and their younger cousins, the Pandavas, for the throne of the Kuru king, Bharata, who ruled over Hastinapura, north of modern Delhi, in the third millennium BCE. Along the way, the poem weaves in philosophical teachings and spiritual insights from the Vedas and other Hindu scriptures, as well as dozens of stories about demons, gods, and goddesses from Hindu mythology, all in an effort to dramatize the four goals of life, most importantly *moksha.* The epic ends with the ascent of the victorious Pandava brothers to heaven, as they achieve liberation from the ceaseless cycle of *samsara.* By contrast, the *Ramayana's* 24,000 verses tell of Vishnu's appearance as Lord Rama of Ayodhya, whose wife Sita is abducted by the demon (*rakshasa*) Ravana. Also dating to pre-Vedic times, the epic recounts Rama's noble efforts to overcome the demon and rescue his wife, with the help of a great army of monkeys, led by the popular monkey god Hanuman. As ideal husband and wife, Sita and Rama personify the virtues Hindu tradition associates with the fulfillment of the social, moral, and religious responsibilities of *dharma,* while the demon Ravana serves as a warning against the ill effects of lust and greed. The devotional poet Tulasidas put the story of Rama and Sita into the vernacular Hindi spoken in his region of northern India, and the *Ramacaritamanasa* (*Lake of the Deeds of Rama*) very quickly became the holy book of a large section of the Indian population. Verses were put to memory, chapters were read daily, and the traditional castes of teachers were suddenly turned into expositors of this one text. In addition to these epics, priestly scholars formulated the legal literature of the *Dharmashastra,* including the *Laws of Manu,* to assist rulers in governing fairly and wisely. Lastly, the *brahmins* were responsible for assembling and disseminating the *puranas,* which speak of the abodes of the gods and planes of existence beyond even heaven and hell, to which the soul transmigrates before final release from the law of *karma* and the *samsaric* cycle of birth, death, and rebirth. These stories date from the fifth to the tenth centuries, and in Hindu temples today, *brahmin* priests are frequently asked to recount the adventures of **Brahma**, Vishnu, and Shiva, and the legendary exploits of their saintly devotees.

The early traditions of itinerant ascetics and scholars were brought into a more organized form by Sankaracarya, the greatest scholar of one of the old Vedic lineages. According to tradition, Sankaracarya lived between 788 and 820 CE. He became an ascetic, established monasteries (**maths**), and organized an order of ascetics called the Dasanamis. Sankaracarya was a vigorous opponent of Buddhism, which had thrived since the Emperor Asoka the Great (*ca.* 304–232 BCE) adopted it in the second century BCE as a way of unifying his conquests across India under a non-violent ideology free of caste prejudices. Encouraging Hindus to restore neglected temples and to maintain their domestic ritual duties (*puja*), Sankaracarya argued that ultimate reality is non-dual (*advaita*), without attributes, and that to believe otherwise is to betray one's enthrallment to illusion (*maya*). The spiritual teacher's task is to free his pupils from this illusion through the careful study of the truths of Hindu scripture, especially the *Upanishads*. Sankaracarya introduced the *pancayana-puja*, which brings together Hindus from different sects to simultaneously worship the five deities Vishnu, Shiva, Devi, Ganesha, and Surya. Divided into ten branches, each distinguished by a different surname, the Dasanamis continued Sankaracarya's teaching tradition, known as **Advaita Vedanta**, which quickly became the most prominent body of religious teaching throughout India. To this day, their successors, who call themselves "world-teachers" (*jagad-gurus*), tour their allotted districts, teaching, preaching, and encouraging Hindus to worship in the temples and to practise their religion.

Subsequently, other teachers found that they too were expected to establish *maths* where their teachings could be carried on. Later Vaishnavite figures like Ramanuja (1017–1137) and Madhva (1199–1278), whose views differed markedly from the Advaita Vedanta tradition, and other schools of thought like Shaiva Siddhanta and Vira Shaiva, were all based in *maths*, but their influence tended to be limited to one language area, and their ties to regional temple traditions were closer than Sankaracarya's had been. Even later followers of the charismatic *brahmin* Caitanya, who sang and danced in the streets with members of lower castes and other religions in celebration of Lord Krishna's universal love, found themselves promoting the ascetic *samnyasa* ideal. In 1918, the scholar and teacher Bimal Prasad Dutta, known as Bhaktisiddhanta (1874–1937), took up the life of spiritual renunciation and founded a network of 64 Gaudiya Vaishnava monasteries, with headquarters at Mayapur. And at Vrindavana, generations of Gaudiya Vaishnava devotees have restored ancient holy places associated with Krishna's life in the *Bhagavata-purana* and elaborated the rituals and doctrines of the *bhakti* tradition.

With the arrival of Islam in the tenth century and Western Christianity in the eighteenth century, the ancient traditions of India developed some new forms of religious life. The most dramatic of these new religious forms was the Sikh movement started by Guru Nanak (1469–1539) in the early sixteenth century. An ascetic and a mystic, Nanak was heavily influenced by such northern Indian devotional poets (*sants*) as Kabir. In a manner similar to the way Tulasidas' lyrical epic *Ramacaritamanasa* gained enormous popularity, Sikhism in some ways arose out of long-standing concerns about the way Islam was encroaching upon the spiritual traditions of India, especially after the founding of a Muslim Mughal sultanate in Delhi in 1206. At the same time, though, such phenomena expressed creative adaptations made by Indians to the new religious atmosphere Islam was creating. Both the Sikh and the *bhakti* movements included a critique of priestly ritual and caste divisions. Kabir himself was a weaver of lower-caste status, and like other devotional sects, the followers of Rama came from all levels of society. In addition, both these developments embody a turn towards the veneration of a central theistic being and a strong sense of rectitude. Like the critiques of traditional Hindu social and religious conservatism, these characteristics are central features of Islamic religion.

In 1498, the Portuguese adventurer Vasco da Gama (1469–1524) landed at Calicut, on the west coast of India. His arrival marked the beginning of 450 years of European involvement in the subcontinent. With Muslim rule in decline, the British established colonial control of Calcutta in 1757, primarily to protect trading interests developed by the East India Company. It was some time before India's religious leadership recognized the presence of British imperial administrators and Christian missionaries as a source of intellectual challenge to traditional Hindu beliefs and practices. Supremely confident in the rationalist heritage of the scientific revolution and the Enlightenment, however, the British considered Hindu devotions to be forms of idolatry and the caste system institutionalized injustice, especially with respect to the status of women. Motivated to defend India's spiritual legacy from such wholesale challenges, and sincerely admiring of certain aspects of European religion and culture, several Hindu reformers undertook programs combining what they saw as the best of both worlds. Chief among these reformers was Ram Mohan Roy (1772–1833). Of orthodox *brahmin* birth, Roy was fluent in Sanskrit, Arabic, Persian, and English, as well as his native Bengali. Though rejected by Christian missionaries, his *The Precepts of Jesus* sees similarities between the teachings of Jesus and Hindu moral teachings. In 1828, he founded a reform movement, later called Brahmo Samaj, charged with propagating the eminently reasonable egalitarian message he believed lay at the heart of the *Upanishads*. In an effort to counteract the educational and charitable ventures of Christian missionaries, Roy's colleague Debendranath Tagore (1817–1905) set up Hindu schools and disseminated a modernized form of Hinduism through newspapers and book publications. Debendranath's son Rabindranath (1861–1941) continued his father's work, most notably at the celebrated "forest university" of Shantiniketan, just over 200

A Hindu *brahmin* in Kerala, India, throws offerings into a consecrated fire as part of an ancient Vedic sacrificial ritual (*havan*). PHOTO BY SRKRIS.

kilometres north of Calcutta, which he visualized as a meeting place for the best of Eastern and Western traditions.

Other Indian visionaries responded to the British presence as an opportunity for different kinds of Hindu reform. Maharishi Dayananda Sarasvati (1824–83) liked the critique of temple ritual implicit in Ram Mohan Roy's reform, but he disagreed with Roy's willingness to accommodate Western views of reason. His solution was to return to the fire sacrifices described in the Veda and to re-develop the religious meaning the teachers had found in that ritual form. Dayananda also thought that the strict religious boundaries and missionary techniques used by both Muslims and Christians were part of the new religious structure the colonial era had introduced to India, and Hindus had no choice but to develop a similar attitude. He started a movement called the Arya Samaj, and it developed a strong following in the Punjab area in northwest India. Dayananda introduced the ritual of *suddhi*, a purification ceremony which entitled members of lower castes to be invested with the sacred thread associated with the twice-born castes, and also enabled Muslims and Christians whose forebears had been Hindus to return to the Hindu fold. Later, the Arya Samaj sent missions to Guyana, South Africa, Mauritius,

Fiji, and other regions of the world where Indian workers indentured by the British had settled.

In a third initiative in the late nineteenth century, the aristocratic scholar Narendranath Dutta, known as Swami Vivekananda (1862–1902), undertook to redevelop Sankaracarya's Advaita Vedanta. He grew up in the reform atmosphere of Ram Mohan Roy's Brahmo Samaj, but he had been strongly influenced by the teachings of Ramakrishna Paramahamsa (1836–86), a Vaishnavite devotee whose ascetic experiments with Hindu, Muslim, and Christian meditation convinced him that every religious tradition was true in its own way. Vivekananda saw in Advaita Vedanta a philosophical message capable of transcending all religious paths, a message he put forward most forcefully at the World Parliament of Religions in Chicago in 1893. Returning to India, he founded the Ramakrishna Mission in Calcutta in 1897. While the mission opened Hindu schools and sponsored Hindu charities to balance the influence of similar Muslim and Christian organizations in India, Vivekananda also intended to disseminate his vision of neo-Vedanta Hinduism to the whole world. Disciples continue to set forth Vivekananda's message under the banners of the Ramakrishna Mission and the Vedanta Society, which Vivekananda founded in New York, in 1894. There are now over 20 Vedanta Societies in the United States and Canada, and many more around the world, devoted to promoting the spiritual universalism of Ramakrishna's neo-Vedanta philosophy.

While these reformulated forms of Hinduism have become important components of the modern Hindu sense of identity, few Hindus have felt bound by the critique of traditional ritual that they entail. Mohandas K. Gandhi (1869–1948) spoke for most Hindus when he applied his mind enthusiastically to the social and political reforms needed for life in the new economic order, but just as enthusiastically said he had no intention to question the blessings of childhood *samskaras,* temple visits, and itinerant ascetics and teachers. With the coming of independence from British rule in 1948, the close association between the Hindu religion and other aspects of India's social and cultural heritage carried mixed blessings. Gandhi himself was assassinated by a nationalist fanatic in 1948, and in recent years, Hindu militants have taken to the streets against members of other religious communities. As adopted by nationalist organizations like Vishva Hindu Parishad (VHP), or "World Council of Hindus," the ideology of *Hindutva,* meaning literally "Hindu-ness," argues that the Hindu religion cannot be separated from the Indian national identity, and in fundamentalist hands has led to such acts of terror as the destruction of the Muslim monument at Ayodhya in 1992. At the same time, however, emigrants who have left India during the past two centuries did not do so because of any unease about their religious heritage, and they seem to have quickly taken up the task of finding local equivalents for the *samskara* rituals and temple visits at the heart of that heritage.

THE MAKING OF A CANADIAN HINDU COMMUNITY

Indians began to move out of the subcontinent looking for employment early in the nineteenth century. First, traders from Gujarat followed the Muslim-led coastal trade around the Indian Ocean to Zanzibar and the newly busy ports of East Africa. Later, British colonial authorities developed a system of indentured labour to supply workers for the sugar plantations of the Caribbean, after the British Parliament ordered the abolition of slavery in 1833. By the time this recruitment ended in 1920, significant Indian communities had been established in Guyana, Trinidad, Mauritius, Fiji, South Africa, and East Africa. By the end of World War II, the British Commonwealth tied India and the indentured satellite communities to Great Britain itself, which received most of the migrants from those places. By the mid-1960s, Indian migration to North America started. Many immigrants to Canada had already stopped over in one of the indentured societies or in Britain, and often in both. In the 1980s and 1990s, many Tamil-speaking Sri Lankans began to arrive in Canada, and they now constitute the largest single block of Hindu immigrants.

While Guyanese, East African, and Sri Lankan Tamil Hindus moved to Canada in large numbers in order to escape political crises, most Hindu immigrants from India came as individuals or as members of families seeking better economic opportunities. Religion was not a direct cause of migration; on the contrary, these immigrants often felt a deep reluctance to leave the revered homeland of India, with its ancient mythologies and sanctified social order, myriad temples and pilgrimage shrines. As they start life in Canada, Hindus from India face some puzzling questions. To begin with, they find themselves part of a tiny minority instead of part of an overwhelming majority. In India, Hinduism is a multifaceted way of life that outsiders have labelled a religion. Arriving in Canada in pursuit of economic betterment, Hindus from India may take some time to get used to thinking of themselves as "Hindu" at all. This inversion of status is compounded by the fact that Canada's Sikhs are as numerous as Canada's

Hindus, and they seem to figure more prominently in the Canadian social, cultural, and political consciousness. Also, Canada has welcomed significant numbers of Muslims and Christians from India, and they often feel as loyal to their fellow religionists from other parts of the world as to their fellow Indians. These new realities lead to some very practical questions. How much does being Hindu in Canada have to do with the religious practices of India? Is it important to bring over from India as many architects, priests, and *gurus* as one can afford, or does that not matter? Is it natural to borrow ideas from the Christian churches down the street, or is that something that should be forbidden? Is there any way at this late date to close the doors a little and convince the children to marry within the community? Or will the community thrive if it finds a way of going out and addressing this interfaith situation with courage?

The answers the Hindus of Canada have given to these difficult questions have changed over the years, and the history of the evolving community can be traced in the different ways those answers have been formulated. To begin with, the 5,000 or so Sikh labourers who took up residence in British Columbia between 1904 and 1908 were virtually the only Indians living in Canada until well after World War II. During this period, Vivekananda's dramatic presentation of Advaita Vedanta to the World Parliament of Religions in Chicago in 1893 represented the dominant Hindu voice in Canada. The Vedanta Society founded branches in a number of major American cities, and the movement spread to Toronto, where Vivekananda himself lectured in 1894. Later, *swamis* ("monastics") who spoke on behalf of the Vedanta Society tried to fill out their talks with Western science and philosophy, and implied that the discussion of religion should take place outside the arena of particular ritual practice. At that time, university classes on Hindu themes were packed, and the few Hindus available lectured as if Hindu practice took the form of Advaita philosophy or was a meditation on the nature of absolute reality or *brahman*. A trickle of distinguished Hindu scholars, professionals, and graduate students arrived in Canada over the next few decades. The Indian community began to grow more rapidly in the late 1960s and early 1970s, after changes in the federal Immigration Act began to address discrimination based on race, religion, and country of origin in 1962 and introduced a points system for judging would-be immigrants in 1967. This new system enabled skilled professionals from India to qualify for Canadian residential status, and opened up an opportunity for other English-educated Indians to dream of a future in Canada.

By this time, the attention of Western youth had drifted away from the austere philosophical system of Vivekananda, and new *gurus* were opening **yoga** institutes with a variety of different teachings. *Yoga* literally means "yoke," and it is associated with the *Yoga Sutras* attributed to Patanjali around 2,000 years ago, which refer to various schools of physical and intellectual discipline designed to release the soul from the cycle of birth, death, and rebirth. Two movements had a significant impact in Canada: the Transcendental Meditation (TM) method of Maharishi Mahesh Yogi (1911–2008), and the Hari Krishnas of the International Society for Krishna Consciousness (ISKCON). Ignoring breathing exercises and other traditional yogic practices, participants in TM tried to achieve relief from the stresses of everyday life through short periods of mental concentration every morning and evening. The Maharishi also claimed that dedicated followers would attain supernormal powers (*siddhis*), like levitation and astral travel. During the 1970s, the movement attracted thousands, but later it lost many followers and never became part of the larger Hindu community in Canada.

By contrast, ISKCON has roots in the nineteenth-century revival of the Gaudiya Vaishnava *bhakti* tradition founded by Caitanya. In 1966, Bhaktisiddhanta's disciple Bhaktivedanta (born Abhay Caran De; 1896–1977) legally incorporated ISKCON as a religion in Brooklyn, New York. Attracted by the movement's street-corner chanting, temple devotions, and gospel of Lord Krishna's universal love, converts repeat 16 rounds of the Hare Krishna chant (*mantra*) daily to help them hold fast to ISKCON's standards of personal cleanliness, healthy diet (*prasadam*), moral etiquette, and spiritual growth. In 1968, members of ISKCON from Buffalo, New York, started a branch in Toronto, and in 1976, this group converted a large Baptist church on Avenue Road in Toronto into a temple, where Vaishnavite holy days and festivals are celebrated. An established presence in the Hindu community for Westerners and Indian immigrants alike, with temples in Montreal, Calgary, and Ottawa as well as Toronto, ISKCON now seems to attract married couples with families rather than individual converts to the monastic ideal of *samnyasa*.

Although Western interest veered away from Advaita Vedanta towards more esoteric expressions of Hinduism, Hindus new to Canada were not keen on claiming these less familiar forms as their own. These Indian immigrants turned for leadership to the small numbers of scholarly immigrants who had been in Canada for a few years, many of whom were *brahmin* caste, and some of whom even became licensed to perform marriages and funerals. Becoming a community in Canada often meant families from all corners of India and all kinds of religious backgrounds could gather together and develop activities in which all could participate. Initially, Muslims, Sikhs, Jains, and Christians did not feel uncomfortable joining Hindus with a simple *aarati* in front of a poster of Lakshmi or Rama and Sita. Gradually, however, Muslims, Sikhs, and Christians developed their own worshipping organizations, and by the late 1970s, the large but disparate Hindu community was making its own arrangements for worship. This need was not felt earlier because attending the temple was an optional activity in India, and many people had set up elaborate altars in their homes when they arrived in Canada, and had even arranged for travelling *gurus* to visit these altars. Hindu immigrants were able to perform the *samskaras* under these conditions. Since in India these essential rituals marking the stages of life were also thought of as a family and caste responsibility, living near fellow caste members in Canada was deemed a key consideration. But when increasing numbers of Hindu immigrants began to realize that marriage rituals and death ceremonies were regulated by federal and provincial laws, and must be performed by licensed practitioners in Canada, the need for temples and full-time priests became urgent.

In the United States, some larger early Hindu temples were grand displays that were financed and planned in conjunction with influential temples in India. By contrast, in Canada, almost all such community projects resulted from the efforts of a hundred or more Hindu immigrant families under local leadership. In 1967, the Prarthana Samaj was formed in Brampton, Ontario; in 1974, the Hindu Vishva Parishad in Vancouver; in 1976, the Hindu Samaj in Hamilton, Ontario; in 1984, temples in Ottawa and Montreal, and others in Halifax, Fredericton, St. Catharine's, London, Winnipeg, Saskatoon, Calgary, Edmonton, and Victoria. In each of these situations, the local community spent many hours of debate defining itself and forming a temple constitution. This process was difficult because such procedures do not exist in India, where temples were founded long ago by powerful rulers and caste elders, or more recently, by influential businessmen. When generous benefactors are forthcoming in Canada, Canadian tax laws require that donations be given to religious organizations registered as tax-exempt charities. In any case, Hindu immigrants were soon keen to form such groups for social, cultural, and spiritual reasons.

The boards of these community temples faced three challenging issues: the nature and role of democratic discussion in temple life; the deities the community wanted to worship; and the style of worship they wanted to use in the temple. In the first instance, Canadian law did not exactly dictate the style of management temples should use, but as each community approached lawyers about incorporating as a religious organization, they found themselves writing up elaborate constitutions with large membership lists. Because Hindu practice in India does not emphasize religious ceremonies such as baptism in Christianity or circumcision in Judaism and Islam, which define membership in the community, agreeing to be a member of a temple community in Canada took on new religious meaning. In addition, membership on the board of the temple began to assume the hierarchical features of life in India. Sometimes major donors and founding members, who were usually early immigrant higher-caste professionals, were given permanent membership, while other board members were elected to specific terms. Tensions soon arose between these two classes of board members, and the number of elected members was increased or permanent members were elevated to senior status with a different title. Because temple communities in Canada were made up of Hindus from all corners and castes of India, such differences played a role in elections to the board, too. At first, representatives of every region and caste were enthusiastically elected to the board. Inevitably, however, issues of regional and caste identity seriously complicated subsequent deliberations about which deities to worship and what styles of worship to use.

Choosing deities and agreeing on styles of worship are very involved matters for Hindu immigrants. Most temples in India have a single primary altar (*mulasthana*), and people speak of the temple as belonging to Shiva, Vishnu, or the goddess. Each deity might take one of a number of different forms, and most temples would have subsidiary deities in other shrines within the temple precincts, so that even in India the number of possible arrangements was quite large. Almost all community temples in Canada decided right away to include in their worship some form of the Shaivite, Vaishnavite, and goddess traditions. At Hamilton's Hindu Samaj temple, for example, five deities were arranged in five separate canopied *mulasthana* along the long wall of a rectangular worship hall. Ganesha came first, on the worshipper's left, then Ram/Sita, Krishna/Radha, and Durga, with Shiva Nataraja and Shiva *lingam* together on the right. With nine shrines, the Hindu Temple of Ottawa-Carleton is still more inclusive. The three major deities—Shiva, Vishnu/Laksmi, and Durga—reside in equal-sized *mulasthanas*. Ganesha and Subramanya, the sons of Shiva, and Shiva Nataraja are in the background, as are Vishnu's *avataras*, Rama and Radha/Krishna, and Rama's divine helper, Hanuman, this last largely because of a special donation.

The question of styles of worship has tended to engender even more intense and partisan discussions. In southern India, deities are made of dark granite or of bronze; northern Indian deities are usually made of marble. In Hamilton, a compromise was reached; Ganesha and the Shiva *lingam* were made of granite and the others of marble. In Ottawa, Ganesha, the Shiva *lingam*, Subramanya, and Hanuman are of granite. In addition, southern Indian style requires that the deities be given a full bath (*abhiseka*) during each worship period; northern Indian style does not. Only priests from southern India would know the detailed ritual southern Indians would expect for the *abhiseka*, and especially for the life-giving (*pranapratistha*) and consecration (*kumbhabhiseka*) ceremonies which establish temples. In both Hamilton and Ottawa, southern Indian priests were hired initially to dedicate the temples there, but in Hamilton, the priest was unable to communicate with the Hindi-speaking majority and a northern Indian priest was soon appointed.

On a more intellectual note, the boards of early community temples often debated the deeper theological question of the status of the images that were being installed. In almost every instance, the generation of founders who had come to Canada in the 1950s or 1960s were reluctant to see the *murtis* described as "deities." As higher-caste professionals, they still tended to hold an Advaita Vedanta view of *brahman* as ultimate reality, and they insisted that the literature of the temple describe the *murtis* as "manifestations" of a single deity. In Ottawa, the founders even objected to the *murtis* being dressed in the customary way, and further emphasized their point by enshrining the sacred texts of the *Bhavan Veda* and the *Ramayana* and *Mahabharata* in the way Jewish, Christian, Muslim, and Sikh places of worship honour their scriptures. In the Hindu Mission Temple of Montreal, the Punjabi priest couches Sunday morning worship in terms of Advaita Vedanta and invites professors of Hinduism from the city to give regular lectures on Hindu philosophy. This style of worship continues to be strong in temples in Halifax, Nova Scotia, and Surrey, British Columbia, too. Despite these efforts to introduce and maintain the influence of Advaita Vedanta in Hindu temple worship in Canada, however, most priests and worshippers from India cling closely to the ritual and theological traditions they have brought with them to Canada. These traditions involve treating the *murtis* as living deities who must be honoured with a full round of care at least twice a day.

Hindu immigrants to Canada from the indentured communities of Guyana, Trinidad, and East Africa were for some time almost as numerous as those who came from India. Such immigrants belong to societies that have been reinventing their heritage for three generations or more. The communities from Guyana and Trinidad have had a particularly prominent role in the development of Hindu identity in Canada. Starting in 1838, Guyana received 238,000 indentured labourers from India. This community eventually formed the majority, living and working side by side with the freed slaves of African background who had laboured on the sugar plantations before them. Because they were so far from India and constituted such a significant portion of the local populace, Guyana's Hindu community formed very distinct systems of worship. Two different systems developed, one southern Indian and Tamil-speaking, the other more numerous, northern Indian and Hindi-speaking. The southern Indian "Madrasi" system revolves around temple compounds built to the north of most villages. These temples are dedicated to the goddess Mariyamman, whom devotees sometimes call "Kali" in order to gain wider understanding. Her shrine faces east, with smaller shrines for subsidiary deities nearby. Worship involves the sacrifice of chickens and goats, and is known for its intensity and the frequency with which priests and worshippers go into trance and become skilful in exorcising evil spirits.

By contrast, northern Indian community worship in Guyana centres on devotions to Rama and Krishna, and the exposition of the *Ramacaritamanasa*. This worship is carried on in church-like structures built along main roads, often right beside the small mission churches erected for the Afro-Guyanese Christians living in the village. The main service is on Sunday morning, and involves a great deal of singing and a major sermon. The sermon is sometimes called a *katha* and it is preached by a *pandit* or "wise man," not by a priest, as one might find in an Indian temple. In these temples, the devotees do not move around from shrine to shrine as they might in India; they sit facing the front platform, where images of the deities are grouped closely together on the left. The *pandit* sits in a great pulpit on the right. After the missions of the Arya Samaj arrived in the 1930s, a few villages added Arya Samaj temples with no images, where worship focused on the fire altar (*havan*). Influenced by this new devotional style, many northern Indian Guyanese temples added a short *havan* ritual to the end of their services.

In the early 1960s in Guyana, political tensions grew between the Afro-Guyanese and the Indo-Guyanese. Large numbers from both communities fled to Canada, including 50,000 Guyanese Hindus who arrived in Ontario in the early 1970s. The Guyanese Hindus realized that they had the language skills for easy entry into Canadian society, and for a brief period many started attending Christian churches in their enthusiasm for their new environment. But a second cultural option soon presented itself. They found that they were considered to be part of the larger Caribbean community, which was developing its own role in Canadian society with celebrations like the annual Caribana Festival in Toronto, first held in 1967. Gradually, however, an increase in numbers and financial security made it possible to begin to transplant Guyanese Hindu practices to Canada. This process has been successful, bolstered in part by Hindus from Trinidad, who did not come to Canada in numbers large enough to support independent communities of worship.

Indian immigrants from East Africa comprise a second large block of Hindus with origins in the British indenture system. The Indian community in East Africa was quite diverse, having developed over a century and a half after the British Parliament passed the Slavery Abolition Act in 1833. Though Hindus constituted a distinct majority in this community, they came from different parts of India and from different levels of society. Some Gujarati-speaking Hindus settled in East Africa as businessmen, along with Shia Muslims and Jains from their home districts, while Punjabi-speaking Hindus arrived with their Sikh neighbours as indentured labourers hired to build the railway. Following the example of pioneering Ismaili Muslim traders, who had developed extended kinship networks inland from the coastal cities of Zanzibar, Mombasa, and Dar es Salaam, Indian Muslim, Jain, Sikh, and Hindu communities fostered and maintained their distinct social, cultural, and regional Indian identities. Religious divisions based on caste thus became the norm for Hindus in East Africa, each caste consisting of discrete and diverse communities, each with its own community centre, style of temple, and colourful religious practices.

After World War II, the growth of African movements for independence from Great Britain spelled further fragmentation for several East African Indian communities, even though local Indian leaders actively supported such struggles in Kenya, Uganda, and Tanzania. By the 1960s, many Indian East Africans began to feel uncomfortable with African nationalist movements, especially when they spawned native African dictators like the notorious Idi Amin Dada (*ca.* 1925–2003), who in August 1972 gave 80,000 East Asian citizens with British passports 90 days to leave Uganda.

Forced into a second round of migration, many East African Indians returned to India or moved on to Great Britain. Canada welcomed large numbers of East African Indians, too, and soon became a priority destination for those that remained, especially Gujaratis. Also, the East African Gujaratis had maintained strong family and caste ties to India all along, so that their move to Canada soon brought others directly from India.

Though significant in number and often wealthy, the first East African Indians fleeing to Canada felt like refugees who had lost all sense of community. While Muslims, Jains, and Sikhs have preserved some peculiarly East African traditions in Canada, Hindus have tended to seek out fellow caste members already in the country. At the same time, since they are used to affirming cultural distinctness within caste boundaries, Gujarati immigrants from East Africa tended at first to focus on maintaining their language and keeping up family worship, waiting to see what further initiatives might be taken by their fellow caste members. In 1970, a Gujarat Samaj was formed to represent the Chovis Gam Patidars, a branch of the Patel caste, and in 1973, a closely related caste, the Lohana Hindus, who are traditionally associated with careers in trade and business and who numbered one of the largest Gujarati groups then arriving in Canada from East Africa, formed the Lohana Cultural Association.

But perhaps the Leva Patels offer the most interesting story. In Gujarat, many members of this caste had converted to the sectarian Swaminarayan movement started by the *brahmin* ascetic Sahajanand Swami (1781–1830). Originally from the Hindi-speaking area of northern India, Sahajanand settled in Gujarat in 1802 and began teaching an austere form of Vaishnavite devotion. Titled the *Shikshapatri* (1826), his book of 212 instructions provided a detailed moral code for lay people, and he initiated an order of disciplined ascetics to lead them. Sahajanand founded temples devoted to Vishnu or Narayan, usually with *murtis* of the god's manifestation, or *avatara,* and to Krishna and his consort Radha. He also taught that he himself was the modern manifestation of Vishnu and *purushottam,* or the human form of the highest divine reality. Swaminarayan temples now give Sahajanand's *murti* equal prominence with other statues. Before his death, Sahajanand appointed his nephews to oversee two communities of followers in Gujarat, one in Vadtal and one in Ahmedabad. Finding theological difficulties with this kind of hereditary succession, influential devotees of Sahajanand declared that true spiritual authority lay in ascetic example. In 1905, Shastriji Maharaj (1865–1951) left Vadtal and founded the Bocasanwasi Akshar Purushottam Sanstha (BAPS) in 1907. Then in 1947,

Dedicated primarily to Ranganatha, an *avatar* of Vishnu, and celebrated in medieval Alvar poetry, this temple complex in Tiruchirapalli, Tamil Nadu, India, typifies the highly decorative Dravidian style.

a group called the Swaminarayan Gadi separated from the Ahmedabad foundation. All four associations later opened successful branches in East Africa and in Great Britain, and although each established large temples among East Africa Gujaratis, under Pramukh Swami Maharaj (born 1921), who assumed leadership of the organization in India in 1971, BAPS became the first Swaminarayan congregation to organize in Canada.

Like the Guyanese and East African Hindus, Tamil-speaking immigrants from Sri Lanka enjoyed a distinct social and cultural identity prior to their arrival in Canada. These Hindus have occupied the northern peninsula and parts of the eastern coast of Sri Lanka for centuries and today make up almost 20 per cent of the island's population. In Sri Lanka, they practice a classical form of temple ritual, their larger temples mirroring architectural styles found in Tamil-speaking parts of India. Despite such similarities, however, Indian and Sri Lankan Tamils have remained separate over the centuries, and small differences in language, in social status, and in ritual practice have been magnified between the two immigrant communities in Canada.

The Tamils from India came to Canada largely as doctors, professors, and other professionals in the early 1960s. By caste, these immigrants were often *brahmin* or *vellala,* a higher Tamil sub-caste claiming ancient roots in Dravidian culture. In the southern Indian state of Tamil Nadu, this group normally patronized temples dedicated to Shiva or Vishnu, while the majority of the lower castes attended temples venerating the goddess Mariyamman. In Sri Lanka, social and religious divisions were different. Mariyamman presided over some temples, but devotees of all castes worshipped in the temples dedicated to Shiva and Vishnu. In fact, there were very few *brahmins* in Sri Lanka and they mostly served as priests. Also, Tamil Hindu identity has become intensely political, particularly since Sri Lanka became independent from Great Britain in 1948. In 1978, the separatist Liberation Tigers of Tamil Eelam (LTTE) began fighting for their own country against the Sinhalese-speaking Sri Lankan majority, who practice Theravadan Buddhism. Large numbers of Sri Lankan Tamils then moved to Europe and to Canada as refugees, but their sense of identity is still strongly tied to events in Sri Lanka, and they are not always willing to sacrifice that identity to make common cause with their fellow Hindus in Canada. As with a minority of Canadian Sikhs and the issue of Punjabi nationalism, a few second-generation Tamils chose to support the revolutionary movement that their peers in the LTTE were pursuing in Sri Lanka. For a time the Tamil communities in Toronto and Montreal faced serious problems with the emergence of armed street gangs among some youth, and the community was concerned that these youth would become involved in the drug trade and a life of violent crime.

By the 1970s, Canada's Hindus were beginning to see the breakdown of community temples into regional and sectarian groups based on language and sectarian affiliation. This trend towards "ethnic" temples started in Toronto, and is now evident in Vancouver, Montreal, and Ottawa. As the destination of most Indians coming to Canada in the early years, Toronto spawned aid organizations to help with settlement. As the number of immigrants grew, these organizations identified themselves in terms of the language areas of India. Language-based dance teachers and hymn-singing groups followed throughout the metropolitan region, and separate cultural associations were set up first for Bengalis, then Punjabis, then Tamils, and then Gujaratis. By the mid-1970s, the few *brahmins* with licences to perform marriage ceremonies and other *samskaras* were becoming overwhelmed. Indian community leaders hesitated to think of religion in terms of regional languages, but unintended consequences flowed from various efforts to found temples in which Canadian Hindus from diverse backgrounds might all feel at ease. In 1972, for example, community leaders in Richmond Hill, Toronto, formed the Hindu Temple Society of Canada, intending to represent the best of various worship styles from different regions of India. Familiar with the southern Indian style, the society started work by engaging the revered head of the monastery in Kanchipuram, Tamil Nadu, which according to legend was founded by Sankaracarya himself. Asked to draft plans for devotions under one roof in the Shaivite, Vaishnavite, and goddess traditions, the pontiff recommended that worship start with the veneration of Ganesha, and that the society recruit from India priests expert in the *agama* traditions practised in Tamil Nadu. The society did not intend the temple to serve Tamil-speaking worshippers exclusively, but in attempting to make the worship style authentically Indian, they soon discovered that it appealed primarily to this group. Before long, the flood of Tamils fleeing hostilities in Sri Lanka made the temple their home. It was soon recognized as an ethnic Tamil place of worship, and became known as Ganesha Temple.

Vigorous growth often means large changes, and changes affect different individuals differently. In many Hindu families in Canada, fathers have concentrated on establishing a sound financial basis for the family, and children have been encouraged to excel in their studies, with the expectation that they would earn professional opportunities matching or exceeding the achievements of their fathers. Mothers were frequently left out of this equation. Punjabi women, especially, found that taking jobs in the workplace did not bring personal satisfaction in some respects, while performing traditional duties to three generations at home failed to satisfy in other respects. Increasing attention to vows of fasting has offered some solace for women in this situation. Such fasts have the indirect effect of releasing a woman from routine family obligations like preparing meals and from the need to respond to a husband's sexual demands. All-night worship (*jagran*) is another popular form of ritual practice taken up by Punjabi women in Canada. Groups of women stay awake, sing religious songs (*bhajans*), and listen to the chanting of scriptures. For Gujarati women, the performance of vows provides a natural opportunity for meeting and maintaining ethnic language groups and for establishing networks to discuss problems on a range of subjects from childrearing to business life in the Canadian environment. For southern Indian women, the *jagran* is not common, but developing the home altar has an almost infinite potential to keep one occupied, since vows to the specific deities installed in the home altar can become lifelong obligations. Like their Sikh and Muslim Punjabi peers, Hindu women in Canada also seek out individuals who specialize in reading horoscopes or who are experts in alternative healing practices and exorcisms. Many individuals with these special skills operate from their homes or small shops in the downtown areas of Toronto, Montreal, and Vancouver, although priests in most Hindu temples have won reputations for work in these areas and often travel widely to perform such services.

The well-being of the young and the elderly also poses considerable challenges to the Hindu community in Canada. Most early immigrants came as young married couples, and they would care for their parents at home if they joined them. But this situation has started to change, and most temples now include in their plans housing for the elderly, although none has been built to date. Another concern is the need to develop some form of community care for those who are in hospital and visitation for the sick and elderly, since priests from India are rarely trained in what other religious traditions in Canada call "pastoral care." As for Hindu youth, Canadian society demands certain conformity among young people when it comes to schooling, dressing, and socializing. Some first-generation Indians were alarmed to find their children drawn into this unfamiliar world, and made initial efforts to provide their children with classes in Indian language, music, and dance, and tried to restrict their social behaviour. Most Hindu parents soon recognized the futility of their struggle against the socialization of their children, and in general, the second generation has created its own hybrid Hindu identity.

A key question for Hindus in Canada has to do with whether the second and third generations will follow the lead of the first generation and maintain the home altars their parents have developed and support the many temples that have been built. In many cases, the second generation have alternated between pulling away from the more traditional Hindu identity parents have tried to foster by refusing to go to temple or spending time in the family *puja* room or altar and feeling a sudden need to re-identify with that religious heritage, even undertaking such ascetic practices as vows of fasting. For many Indian families in Canada, marriage has represented a crucial choice. A priest at a Mississauga Hindu temple reported that three of every four weddings he conducted in 2002 were mixed marriages involving Hindus and Christians. In most cases, however, even marriage has not necessitated a final decision about identity, because most non-Indian marriage partners are willing to have a partly Hindu wedding. Even among Indians, fewer betrothals in Canada have involved a parentally arranged marriage within the same-caste community than would have been the case in India. In Canada, parents often suggest "Middle Path Marriages," permitting children to choose their own friends till courtship starts in earnest, at which time parents take a more active role in the vetting of suitable partners, even engaging Hindu marriage consultants.

In general, however, the Indian family has survived the challenges associated with settling into a new social and cultural setting. Later generations seem to be adapting to slightly modified traditional family arrangements, as members of the three generations continue to develop their own cultural niches. Women are gradually finding ways to take advantage of the new opportunities available to them, to the extent that, ironically, the successes of the second generation in various areas of professional life now cause the community some concern about a potential loss in family values. Younger generations born in Canada are beginning to manifest the sort of hybrid identities that result from the imaginative and constructive reworking and blending of traditional Hindu values with the ways of the secular modern West. At the same time, in the public realm, the absence of a single Hindu organization or Hindu voice in Canada causes some frustration. The government tax authorities and the various forums for interfaith discussion about ethical and religious issues such as youth violence and same-sex marriage often report that they do not know who to talk to within the Hindu community. Hindus from other organizations quickly point out that the Hindu Temple Society of Canada and the Federation of Hindu Temples each have links to only a handful of temples. The Canadian Council of Hindus is more widely acknowledged as a proper voice of mainstream Hinduism, but it has no organizational home and the journal it once published has been discontinued.

Hindus are now anxiously aware of this organizational weakness, but the temple tradition of India was part of a different kind of situation altogether, where Hinduism was the dominant religion. If Hindus in Canada are to function as a minority religion in the public realm and lend their voices to wider discussions of social and cultural issues, significant changes will have to be made in the way the Hindu religion is organized. Those changes are only now being thought about, but the colossal figure of Gandhi seems to serve as an inspiration and a rallying point. He was universally admired by the first generation of Indian immigrants to Canada after World War II and Indian independence in 1948, but their initial concerns were with economic betterment, and they were not sure when they would be able to address social and cultural issues. In 1988, a group now known as the Mahatma Gandhi Canadian Foundation for World Peace was founded and began actively promoting awareness of Gandhi's ideas on non-violence and interfaith dialogue in schools and universities, first in Edmonton, Alberta, where the group originated, and subsequently across Canada and internationally. In 1996, members of the Indo Canadian Society endowed a major lecture series in the name of Gandhi at McMaster University. The endowment invites international figures to address issues of war and peace each year. These forums at least give Hindus a recognizable public voice.

RECENT TRENDS IN THE HINDU COMMUNITY

According to the 2001 census, 297,200 Hindus now call Canada home, with a median age of 31.9 years. This figure represents an increase of 89.3 per cent over the 1991 census. Almost one-quarter of this number were born in Canada (76,220), and well over half of those born outside Canada (213,685) immigrated between 1991 and 2001 (118,560). Significant and growing Hindu communities exist in the major urban centres of Quebec, Alberta, and British Columbia, but the majority of Canada's Hindus live in Ontario (216,560), mostly in metropolitan Toronto (191,305). A more detailed look at some temple communities in the Toronto region thus provides a fairly clear impression of recent and current trends in the religious life of large numbers of Hindus in Canada. To begin with, after the mid-1980s almost every temple built in the metropolitan Toronto area was defined at least partly in terms of the language group to which it was intended to appeal. Earlier community temples in Toronto and elsewhere were mostly established in converted churches or industrial buildings and existed on marginal budgets of under $100,000 per annum. However, Hindu communities are now better able to raise larger funds. For example, the Hindu community in Ottawa has invested $2,000,000 in a new building, and Toronto's ethnic congregations are fundraising large sums of money to finance the construction and maintenance of architecturally significant temples.

Built in 1991, the Vaishno Devi Temple in Oakville represents an outstanding individual statement of Hindu elegance. The temple was built on the rural edge of the suburb with the highest average income of any municipality in Canada. The major donor insisted that the temple's central deity be Vaishno Devi, a divinity associated with Kali, Lakshmi, and Sarasvati, three principal forms of *shakti,* Hinduism's mother goddess figure. Especially revered in the state of Punjab, Vaishno Devi presides over a remote temple near Katra, in the Trikuta foothills of the Himalayas, where pilgrims flock to worship at the goddess's shrine in a cave. In keeping with the air of majesty surrounding the goddess, the gardens outside Oakville's Vaishno Devi Temple, its bright and heavily carpeted worship hall, and the full range of carefully dressed deities—five from the Shiva family and five linked with Vishnu, arranged in a neat semicircle around the goddess—all contribute to the elegance of the sacred precincts. The temple offers daily *puja* or prayer services, Mondays to Saturdays, 7:00 a.m. and 7:00 p.m., and special prayer services to Shiva, Mondays, 6:00 p.m. to 8:00 p.m. A knowledgeable congregation takes an active part in community devotions carefully organized by priests and music leaders on Sunday afternoons, 3:00 to 5:30 p.m., somewhat after the manner of Christian evensong services. Everyone is welcome and the temple offers free Hindu vegetarian food at these services. An educated *brahmin* from the Punjab at ease in both Hindi and English acts as the head priest, and uses Hindi in worship and insists that Hindus stand up for their language and their religion. At the same time, his sermons clearly show that he is aware of the need to make Hinduism relevant to the everyday life of his relatively well-heeled Canadian audience. In the background of Vaishno Devi Temple stands an image of a reclusive sage. This *murti* further identifies the religious affiliation of the temple's Oakville donor. It belongs to the Natha ascetic order, an ancient Himalayan tradition of mystical Tantric *yoga* which refuses to acknowledge caste distinctions in its emphasis upon spiritual pursuits. This sense of ascetic spirituality is reflected in Vaishno Devi Temple's social and cultural policies, which permit members of the community to use the hall only for religious functions, discouraging loud music and dancing, and forbidding alcohol and the consumption of fish, meat, and eggs. With special ceremonies on Hindu religious days, Vaishno Devi is gradually becoming the home temple for non-Punjabi Hindus from other parts of northern India, too, and even some Sikhs attend such joyous celebrations as *Diwali,* the pan-Hindu winter solstice festival of lights, and *Holi,* the northern Indian spring festival of colours.

Hindu Sabha is another major temple in the northern Indian style in the Toronto area. In 1975, five founding members of the congregation began to organize weekly prayer meetings in a series of temporary locations, starting with Falling Dale Public School in Brampton. In 1985, Hindu Sabha purchased land near Brampton, and in 1995 inaugurated a new temple, which was finally completed in 2001, with landscaping taking a further two years. A huge monument with three pyramidal towers reminiscent of the peaks of the Himalayas, this temple sits in the midst

The interior of the Hindu Sabha temple in Brampton, Ontario, with Vishnu/Lakshmi at the back, Ram/Sita and Krishna/Radha in the middle, and Shiva *lingam*, Durga and Hanuman in the front.
PHOTO BY PAUL YOUNGER. REPRINTED BY PERMISSION. © PAUL YOUNGER.

of an ambitious suburban development along Gore Road, north and west of Toronto. The deities are massive and seem to fill the well-lit worship hall, with Vishnu/Lakshmi high above at the back, Ram/Sita and Krishna/Radha in the middle tier, and Shiva *lingam*, Durga, and Hanuman in the front at a lower level. The setting of the deities is as far removed as one could imagine from the cave-like *garbha griha* over which the towers of a temple in northern India rise. Nevertheless, the worshippers seem in awe of the large figures, and busily go about their devotional routines in the traditional way. Services are held every Tuesday, 7:00 p.m. to 9:00 p.m., every Saturday, 3:00 p.m. to 5:00 p.m. and 9:00 p.m. to 12:00 a.m., and every Sunday, 11:00 a.m. to 2:30 p.m. Hindu Sabha is publicly committed to the practice and development of the Eternal Law (*sanatana dharma*) contained in Hindu culture, philosophy, and religion. The temple includes a school, where students five years old and over may attend classes in Hindi language and Hindu religion, as well as classical dance and music, *yoga,* and, oddly enough, Korean *Tae-kwon do.* At the same time, this well-managed temple seems very modern. Hindi- and Punjabi-speaking Torontonians find it a convenient place to drop into, as much as to catch up on Indian newspapers as to worship. A group of Hindu Sabha seniors meets regularly, and in 2002, the temple's board of 12 male and 3 female directors initiated "Seniors' Green House," an ambitious project that includes accommodation and specialized recreational facilities for the elderly.

Several Hindu temples in the Toronto region have strong connections with the Caribbean, but perhaps the congregations associated with Guyanese immigrants to Canada rank as the most sociologically interesting. In 1990, one Guyanese congregation moved from the basement of a founding member's home to a renovated church in Cambridge, naming it Radha Krishna Mandir. The temple conducts worship very much in the northern Indian style of *mandirs* in Guyana, with songs in Hindi and sermons based on the *Ramacaritamanasa* in English, even though immigrants more familiar with the southern Indian style of worship are among the temple's keenest supporters. Reminiscent of community life in Guyana, devotions focus upon the goddess, and many older members of the congregation make a point of speaking to one another in the Creole dialect of their Guyanese childhood. By contrast, worship at Toronto Arya Samaj involves devotees sitting around a fire altar or *havan* conducting simple prayer rituals, in accordance with the expectations of this Hindu reform movement. The congregation split when Punjabi devotees, who wanted worship to be conducted in an Indian language, left to form Arya Samaj Toronto, later Arya Samaj Markham. Since 1996, on 15 August, the day of India's independence from British rule, these groups have shared the Vedic Cultural Centre in Markham, which offers a range of activities and services, from classes in *yoga* and meditation to five annual youth scholarships for high school students of South Asian and Indo-Caribbean descent.

Yet another distinct style of Caribbean Hindu worship may be found at the Devi Mandir in Pickering. Inaugurated in March 2000, Devi Mandir advertises a full calendar of Hindu services and festivals, as well as classes in Hindi and traditional Hindu music and dance, like other temples in the Toronto region. But Devi Mandir is characterized by contemporary architecture, its interior highlighted with lots of bright mirror work and sweeping circular stairs. The temple features a richly carpeted worship hall and a very large Durga *murti* on an open platform, with a semicircle of other deities around her. The *murti* is also unusual for its highly modern design, which takes the form of one Durga and lion atop another Durga and lion. All in all, though, the worship hall looks remarkably like that of the Vaishno Devi temple, and may represent the beginnings of a distinctly Canadian Hindu style. An even newer Guyana style temple is the

Ram Mandir in the affluent Toronto suburb of Mississauga. The distinctive feature of this temple is the vibrant community life it encourages with its youth activities, counselling services, and care of the elderly.

No account of Guyanese Hindu life in Toronto can ignore the Vishnu Mandir and the contributions of Dr. Budhendranauth Doobay (born 1940). As a temple *pandit,* Doobay assisted his father, a Hindu priest, with *pujas* and other domestic rituals in Guyana. In 1976, he came to Canada to work as a heart surgeon at McMaster University Hospital, and in 1977, he started a program called *Voice of the Vedas* on Vision Television, both to provide a source of spiritual nourishment for Hindus in the diaspora and to cultivate some understanding of Indian history and Hindu teachings and rituals among non-Hindu viewers. By 1981, Doobay was leading Hindu Sunday worship in a small house in Thornhill, and in 1984, Swami Dayananda Saraswati (born 1930), a popular teacher of Vedanta from Chennai, laid the cornerstone for Vishnu Mandir. Not wishing to limit membership to Guyanese and Trinidadian Hindus, Doobay hired Yogi Raj, a *pandit* from Varanasi, to serve as his assistant. The temple was expanded in 1990, and again in 2002, making room for more than 1,000 devotees. In October 2003, a glorious golden dome was installed on the main tower. Over the years, Guyanese and Trinidadian Hindus have established themselves as the most loyal members of Vishnu Mandir, although the temple makes serious efforts to appeal to other Hindu Canadians. Recent additions to the altar include *murtis* of the popular southern Indian deities, Ayyappa and Balaji Venkateshwara. Providing a comfortable atmosphere not only for devotees who may no longer be familiar with Indian languages but also for second-generation Hindus brought up in a Canadian religious atmosphere strongly influenced by Christian ecclesiastical traditions, Vishnu Mandir offers services in English on Sunday mornings, 8:30 a.m. to noon, with lots of music and readings from Hindu scripture. Doobay usually delivers a homily. In addition to these devotions, the temple holds special prayer services to Shiva on Monday evenings, 6:30 p.m. to 8:30 p.m., to Hanuman on Tuesday evenings, 6:45 p.m. to 7:30 p.m., to Devi on Friday evenings, 6:30 p.m. to 8:00 p.m., and to Navgraha and Ayyappa on Saturday mornings, 10:00 a.m. to 1:00 p.m. On Wednesday evenings, 7:00 p.m. to 7:30 p.m., in rituals known as *aartis,* light from wicks soaked in camphor and purified butter or *ghee,* are offered to the deities, accompanied by devotional songs, and on Thursday evenings, 7:00 p.m. to 8:30 p.m., services are conducted at the temple by followers of the Indian saint, Sai Baba of Shirdi (*ca.* 1838–1918), whose philosophy seeks to reconcile tensions between separate religious communities, including Hindus and Muslims.

Vishnu Mandir also offers numerous other activities of varying degrees of religious significance. For children of all ages, the Bal Vihar Sunday School follows a curriculum designed by the Arsha Vidya Gurukulam in Saylorsburg, Pennsylvania, which was established in 1986 by Swami Dayananda Saraswati. The temple is home to meditation and *hatha yoga* classes, and the Voice of the Vedas Academy of Learning and Montessori School opened in September 2005. A youth group holds seminars and takes part in conferences on a range of topics having to do with the betterment of women and their families, as well as running summer camps for kids and trips for seniors. The library at Vishnu Mandir contains books on a wide array of Indian and Hindu subjects in English, Hindi, and Gujarati, and the temple's community hall is capable of seating about 300 people for weddings, religious festivals, and cultural events. Now titled *The Voice of Hinduism*, Doobay's television program airs not only on Vision Television but also on Crossroads Television Services and by cable and satellite networks on various channels in the United States and Guyana. Vishnu Mandir expresses this sense of outreach in other ways, too. Visionaries in the community felt that Gandhi could serve as an inspiring symbol of Hindu commitment to non-violence and interfaith understanding, and in 1988, a Peace Park was opened on the grounds of the temple, its centrepiece a bronze statue of the Mahatma, 20 feet high. In 1991, Vishnu Mandir temple members collaborated with leaders of Toronto's African Canadian community to host a large conference on Gandhi and the American Civil Rights leader Reverend Martin Luther King Jr. (1929–68). Still under development, the Canadian Museum of Hindu Civilization at Vishnu Mandir boasts 17,000 square feet of space, including permanent exhibits dedicated to the South Asian history and essence of Hinduism as a living tradition, from the Indus valley civilization through the classical and medieval periods to contemporary Hinduism in the diaspora, with a strong focus, of course, on Canada's Hindu community.

As we have seen, Gujarati and Tamil Hindus comprise other important ethnic groups in the Toronto region. The Sanatan Mandir and the Shri Swaminarayan Mandir of Toronto are of particular interest, though the Gujaratis support several other temples. The Gujarati Samaj met for some years as a cultural organization before building the Sanatan Mandir on Woodbine Avenue, northeast of Toronto, in 1995. The temple was initiated by the revered Vaishnava spiritual leader Krishnashankar Shastri (died 2002), who was from the Bhagwat Vidyapith educational institute at Sola, near Ahmedabad, India. The temple is a massive structure of 32,000 square feet, designed to serve as a worship centre on the upper level and a cultural centre on the lower level. The Sanatan Mandir has a busy schedule of specially sponsored worship events to celebrate the seasonal holy days and the birthdays of saints and worshippers. The prayer hall houses numerous *murtis,* including manifestations of the Shakti, Hanuman, Ganesha, and Shiva *lingam,* Radha and Krishna in various forms, as well as such saints as Mahavira and Swaminarayan. Every October, Sanatan Mandir sponsors the important *raas garbha* dances. Originally associated with the story of mischievous Krishna at play with the *gopis* or cowgirls, these dances form part of the Navaratri festival, when for nine nights and ten days Hindus celebrate the goddess as universal mother, notably in the forms of Durga, Lakshmi, and Sarasvati. Nightly at the temple, men and women perform the *raas garbha,* moving in circles and clicking together painted sticks with tinkling bells attached. These joyous celebrations culminate in a grand dance in the arena at the Canadian National Exhibition grounds, with more than 10,000 dancers in attendance. In the Canadian context, Gujarati Hindus have thus transformed this traditional village folk dance, in which girls went to the houses of neighbours with lighted *kumbhas* or pots symbolizing the goddess, into an ethnic celebration of the community's success in establishing itself and prospering in its new environment.

By contrast, the large community of members belonging to the BAPS Swaminarayan focus on the movement's strict moral code of eleven *sadhanas* or spiritual disciplines. These disciplines include proscriptions against violence of any kind, even killing insects; against adultery; against eating meat and taking medicines derived from animal products; against alcohol and medicines containing alcohol; against taking advantage of the less fortunate; against suicide; against theft; against slander; against the vilification of other faiths; against impure foods, including onions and garlic; and against keeping the company of the irreligious. BAPS members associate these proscriptions with the Vedic *yamas* and *niyamas*—principles of restraint and observance—codified in such classic scriptures as the *Shandilya* and *Varuha Upanishads.* BAPS members are also enjoined to respect parents and elders, to donate a proportion of their earnings to the organization, to read the Swaminarayan scriptures daily, to attend temple seminars and spiritual meetings regularly, to fast on the eleventh day of each half of each lunar month, and to cultivate a enlightened spiritual

In 2007, the Bocasanwasi Akshar Purushottam Sanstha (BAPS) Swaminarayan Mandir, in Toronto, became the first traditional stone and marble temple in Canada. PHOTO BY CANDACE IRON. REPRINTED BY PERMISSION. © CANDACE IRON.

sensibility through frequent family prayers and personal thanksgiving, both at home and at the temple, through chanting the sacred Swaminarayan *mantra* and singing devotional hymns and through care of the temple *murtis.* The organization strongly encourages participation in ceremonies marking Hindu festival days, as well as selfless service to BAPS and to the wider community. In these ways, BAPS members pursue liberation from the cycle of birth, death, and rebirth. For many years, Toronto's BAPS Swaminarayan members met in a large hall in an industrial complex, but in July 2004, Pramukh Swami Maharaj presided over the Vedic rituals marking the official opening of Swaminarayan Haveli. In a consecration ritual known as *abhisheka,* purifying water from the Ganges and other sacred rivers in India was sprinkled about the building, which is a traditional Gujarati structure featuring intricate wooden carvings of dancing peacocks, delicate lotus flowers, and royal elephants. In April 2005, BAPS Swaminarayan celebrated the breaking of ground for the first traditional stone and marble *mandir* in Canada with a colourful procession of *murtis,* the performance of *abhisheka,* and the ceremonial laying of sacred bricks. In 2007, the finished marble structure became one of Canada's best-known buildings, just beside one of its busiest highways.

In contrast to the steady development of the large Gujarati community in Canada, the arrival of the Sri Lankan Tamils was sudden, marked by political and social turbulence directly linked with religion. There are now 72,000 Tamil speakers in Toronto, and they already make up nearly one-third of the total Hindu population. The so-called Ganesha Temple, in Richmond Hill, northeast of Toronto, served as the first religious home of the Hindu Sri Lankan Tamil in Canada. As we have seen, this temple was planned by *brahmins* from Tamil Nadu in southern India, who were among the group of professionals that entered Canada in the early 1960s. The worship of the Ganesha *murti* started on the site in 1984 in a building constructed entirely by volunteers. A priest brought from India conducted daily *pujas*. By the time the Sri Lankans began to arrive in large numbers, a dozen priests from southern India were serving this busy temple. Efforts were made to accommodate Sri Lankan ritual needs, and the democratically elected management board of the temple was soon predominately Sri Lankan. A member of a famous southern Indian family of temple architects, V. Janakiramana Sthapathi designed the present structure, which opened in July 1988 with the installation of the god, Murugan, a popular Tamil name for the second son of Shiva and brother of Ganesha. Covered because of the Canadian climate, the temple is otherwise very much in the southern Indian style, a huge enclosed compound with a grand *gopuram* entranceway. Now called the Richmond Hill Hindu Temple and the Ganesha Temple, it houses two families of deities, one on either side of the central Ganesha altar. In the Shiva family on the left, the major deity is Murugan or Subramanya, but there are separate altars for the Shiva *lingam,* Parvati, and Nataraja, with a major Durga altar facing north, and further removed, altars for Murugan's consorts, Valli and Devasena. To the right of the Ganesha altar is the Vishnu family of deities, presided over by Venkateshwara, with the consorts Sridevi and Bhudevi further removed. These two families of deities are positioned around two *vimana* towers, added in 1992, which reach skywards over the altars of Murugan and Venkateshwara. In 2002, *murtis* of Ramanuja and the 12 Alvars were consecrated in the temple, a first in North America, consolidating Richmond Hill's reputation as one of the most distinguished Hindu temples on the continent. The temple offers a busy schedule of over 200 religious services and other events every week. Recent initiatives include workshops in traditional arts, crafts, and Vedic chanting for children and young adults, and the Hindu Temple Youth Corps, to help younger members of the community maintain some balance between traditional Hindu values and the challenges of modern Western life.

As widely respected as the worship in Richmond Hill Hindu Temple is, however, many Sri Lankan immigrants have sought out additional worship opportunities closer to home and closer to their specific religious traditions. In Montreal, a little Durga temple in the industrial area along Jean Talon Avenue appeared very early and had a very orthodox style of worship with a priest from Sri Lanka. More recently, a grand Murukan temple has been built in a wealthy suburb on the West Island of the city, and its wild *kavati* festival is considered the most authentic form of Sri Lankan worship in Canada. This temple is affiliated with the *ashram* in the mountains north of the city in Val Morin, which it is hoped will become the spiritual centre of Sri Lankan Shaivites. In Toronto, over 20 smaller temples have provided Sri Lankan worshippers with alternatives to the Richmond Hill temple. Worship in these temples varies from decidedly orthodox to more populist styles. A Sri Lankan priest, Sivasri Thiagarajahkurukkal Kanaswami, assumed personal responsibility for converting a warehouse in Scarborough to temporary use as a temple. Inaugurated in 1991 and consecrated in 1992, Sri Durka moved to permanent quarters on Carnforth Road in Scarborough in 1994. In 1996, work began on remodelling these new quarters, and on 1 July, 2001, tens of thousands attended the opening of the new temple. Ceremonies took the form of a *maha kumbhabhisekam*, culminating in the priest's pouring holy water (*abhisheka*) from a golden container (*kumbha*) to purify the premises and to consecrate the *murtis*. The statue of the main deity at Sri Durka, the mother goddess (*shakti*) faces east, and her devotees refer to the temple as "the temple of mother," or "the temple of miracles," where it is believed suitable marriage partners are matched, the infertile made fertile, family arguments resolved, and incurable diseases cured. Sri Durka also features a huge flagstaff, and both daily and festival devotions are conducted in strict accordance with the ritual prescriptions revealed in the sacred Agama scriptures.

By contrast, a newer form of southern Indian devotion has become popular with other Sri Lankan immigrants in Toronto. Also in Scarborough, on Middlefield Road, the Canada Sri Ayyappan Hindu Temple is dedicated to a popular deity believed to have been born of the union of Vishnu and Shiva. Devotees make pilgrimages to the mother temple atop Sabarimalai, a sacred hill in Kerala, where they believe Ayyappan appears as a divine light in the night sky. In January 2003, 75 pilgrims journeyed from Toronto, dressed in black, and under strict vows of celibacy. All of the pilgrims were men and they promised to treat one another as Ayyappan incarnate for the 41-day pilgrimage. In 2007, the new temple of Ayyappan was opened and the crowds are now larger and the devotions more intense. In Toronto, devotees often show signs of the trance-like behaviour typical of Ayyappan pilgrims in India. Sri Lankan youth are at the centre of this spiritual adventure, and they particularly like the symbolism of the deity's personality and purpose expressed through the tiger, which serves as Ayyappan's *vahana* or sacred conveyance. Even newer forms of Sri Lankan worship now take place in a significant number of storefront temples dedicated to goddesses. The temple to Ati Para Shakti on Ellesmere Road in Scarborough is typical. Its intense services of worship are led by women and take place every day as dozens of women bring their everyday problems to the altar of the goddess, who is considered profoundly understanding and powerful.

AFTERWORD

It has been about 25 years since Hindu temples first began to take shape in Canada. The story around the development of these temple communities is a story of pride and community solidarity, and they continue to look to the future with confidence. Hindus have felt comfortable in the Canadian environment, especially in comparison with the situations sometimes faced by their peers in Great Britain and the United States. Hindus settling in Great Britain soon after World War II arrived during a period of difficult social change, whereas Hindus coming to Canada were able to define their own social identity in a period of economic expansion and general prosperity. In Great Britain, Hindu immigrants moved into crowded urban areas and developed political solidarity with recent arrivals from the Caribbean. In Canada, stronger economic conditions enabled many Hindu immigrants to move into the suburbs, where they quickly established vibrant temple communities. In the United States, to give them a more militant and defensive posture on university campuses, Hindus often turn to the Vishva Hindu Parishad of America, which is closely allied to India's nationalist VHP. Hindus in Canada, by contrast, seem rarely to feel the need to be apologetic about their religious ideas and practices. While Hindu Americans still detect orientalist descriptions of their spiritual life as idol worship and of Indian culture embodying a pre-rational world view laden with mystery, Canadian commitment to cultural pluralism provides a kind of negative protection against this sort of hegemonic thinking. Hindu immigrants to Canada have frequently experienced the sort of benign indifference which permits the community to grow and prosper.

On the other hand, partly because they were able to establish their temple communities with such ease, Canadian Hindus have been slow to give intellectual form to their own religious practice and to address issues in society at large. There were good reasons for turning away from the style of philosophical teaching associated with Vivekananda and for not introducing the *math* system to Canada; still, it is surprising that there has not been more religious education in the temple life of Canada's Hindus. Many temples offer language classes, but generally, these classes are not very regular, and they rarely equip young people to read Hindu scriptures in Sanskrit and Hindi or to discuss classical Hindu philosophy. A number of temples sponsor classes in Hindu dance and music, but not in Hindu scripture or thought, and except for the efforts of such fringe movements as ISKCON, Arya Samaj, and the followers of Sai Baba (1926–2011), almost no Hindu literature of any kind is produced in Canada. Many temples produce calendars marking Hindu holy days, but nearly always in regional languages, with little or no explanation of the history and significance of such festivals.

The board members of the various temples have debated this lack of religious education a great deal, but efforts to address the need have been for the main part piecemeal. Some community leaders have adopted indirect methods of religious education. Worship at the Vaishno Devi Temple and the Vishnu Mandir assumes a congregational form and includes a sermon at the heart of the service, in the manner of Christian church services. Other Hindu leaders have taken steps to transform the role of priests in Canada. When priests attend the images of the deities in India, for example, they rarely think of themselves as playing an educational role. Most priests brought from India to serve in Canada lack the sort of formal training that would allow them to rethink their traditional functions. Professor Krishna Sivaraman (died 1991) of McMaster University in Hamilton tried to initiate a program for training priests, and, with somewhat the same purpose in mind, Jagdish Chander Sharda (born 1926) founded the Hindu Institute of Learning in 1989 to promote Indian languages, arts and culture in North America. But Canada's Hindu community has yet to commit to religious education in the same way as, for example, the Western convert to Hinduism, Satguru Sivaya Subramuniyaswami (1927–2001), who established the Himalayan Academy, a monastic centre for instruction in Hinduism in Kauai, Hawaii, and who launched the highly respected and widely disseminated newsmagazine *Hinduism Today*, as well as a plethora of other publications and websites. That said, this intellectual quietude may indicate that any anxieties felt by the first generation of Hindu immigrants to Canada have now dissipated. Feeling little need to defend Hindu ways, the second generation will perhaps find intellectual forms for their spiritual experience as and when times require. Classes in Hindu dance and music, for example, do provide popular ways for learning not only specific artistic skills but also Hindu mythology and the cultural history associated with these traditional modes of creative expression. Hindu students approach university courses on Hinduism with a kind of innocent curiosity, too. The generations born in Canada are defining their own identity as Hindus and will soon enough begin more publicly to address issues relevant to their lives as Hindus in Canada.

KEY TERMS

Advaita Vedanta	A school of philosophy developed by Sankaracarya in which *brahman* is understood as the only reality after illusion is removed.
Ashramas	The four stages of human life: the student (*brahmacarya*); the householder (*grihasta*); the forest-dweller (*vanaprasta*); and the renunciant (*sannyasin*).
Atman	The individual self or soul, which is identical with *brahman.*
Bhakti	The idea and practice of loving devotion to a deity.
Brahma	The Hindu creator god.
Brahman	Ultimate reality or the cosmic soul, which has no attributes and is unknowable by humans.
Devi	Goddess.
Dharma	One's social, moral, and religious duty.
Guru	A spiritual teacher.
Karma	"Action," and hence the cumulative effect of one's intellectual, verbal, and physical actions in determining one's place in the cycle of death and rebirth (*samsara*).
Mandir	A temple.
Math	A scholarly monastery.
Moksha	"Release," and hence liberation from the cycle of death and rebirth (*samsara*).
Murti	An image of a deity.
Puja	Ritual offerings made to a deity.

Purana "Old Tale," and hence a story about the gods.

Samsara The continuing cycle of birth, death, and rebirth.

Samskara Rituals of purification to mark major stages in a person's life, like birth, marriage, death, and cremation.

Shakti "Power," and hence the female consort of a Hindu god.

Shastra A systematized Hindu religious text.

Shiva The Hindu god of destruction and rebirth.

Vedas Revealed scriptures, from *veda*, which means "knowledge."

Vishnu The Hindu god of preservation and love.

Yoga "Yoke," and hence a system of physical and intellectual discipline designed to lead to *moksha*.

KEY DATES

3100 BCE	Traditional date of the legendary Bharata War, subject of the *Mahabharata*.
1500 BCE	Aryan influences on the Indus valley civilization of northern India.
600s BCE	Probable age for the compilation of the *Upanishads*; the life of Mahavira, founder of Jainism; and the life of Gautama Siddhartha, founder of Buddhism.
273–232 BCE	Reign of the Emperor Asoka and the beginning of the golden age of Buddhism in India.
788–820 CE	Sankaracarya forms *maths* and the Advaita Vedanta school.
1000	Muslim armies arrive in northern India.
1206	The Muslims found a Mughal sultanate in Delhi.
1757	The British take control of Calcutta.
1838	Indentured workers leave India for Guyana.
1960s (early)	Indian professionals arrive in Canada.
1967	A new federal Immigration Act eliminates discrimination based on race, religion and country of origin, and Punjabis and Guyanese begin to arrive in Canada in large numbers.
1972	Idi Amin expels Asians from Uganda and Gujaratis arrive in Canada in large numbers.
1980s	Sri Lankan Tamils arrive in Canada in large numbers.

KEY READINGS

Babb, Lawrence. *Redemptive Encounters: Three Modern Styles in the Hindu Tradition.* Berkeley: University of California Press, 1986.

Baird, Robert D., ed. *Religion in Modern India.* 3rd ed. New Delhi: Manohar, 1995.

Basham, Arthur Llewellyn. *The Wonder That Was India.* 3rd rev. ed. London: Fontana, 1971.

Coward, Harold, John R. Hinnells, and Raymond Williams. *The South Asian Religious Diaspora in Britain, Canada and the United States.* Albany: SUNY Press, 2000.

Hawley, John, and Mark Jurgensmeyer. *Songs of the Saints of India.* New York: Oxford University Press, 1988.

Hiriyanna, Mysore. *The Essentials of Indian Philosophy.* London: Allen and Unwin, 1985.

Hopkins, Thomas. *The Hindu Religious Tradition.* Belmont, CA: Wadsworth, 1982.

Kinsley, David. *Hindu Goddesses: Visions of the Divine Feminine in the Hindu Religious Tradition.* Berkeley: University of California Press, 1986.

Rukmini, T.S., ed. *Hindu Diaspora: Global Perspectives.* Montreal: Concordia University, 1999.

Waghorne, Joanne P., Norman Cutler, and Vashuda Narayanan, eds. *Gods of Flesh, Gods of Stone: The Embodiment of Divinity in India.* Chambersburg, PA: Anima, 1985.

Williams, Raymond Brady, ed. *A Sacred Thread: Modern Transmission of Hindu Traditions in India and Abroad.* Chambersburg, PA: Anima, 1992.

Younger, Paul. *Playing Host to Deity: Festival Religion in the South Indian Tradition.* New York: Oxford University Press, 2002.

Zimmer, Heinrich. *Myth and Symbols of Indian Art and Civilization.* Princeton: Princeton University Press, 1970.

KEY WEB SITES

http://www.himalayanacademy.com [Kauai's Hindu Monastery, Hawaii]

http://www.thehindutemple.ca [Richmond Hill Hindu Temple, Ontario]

http://www.tamilelibrary.org [list of temples in Canada]

http://www.toronto.baps.org [Bocasanwasi Akshar Purushottam Sanstha (BAPS) Shri Swaminarayan Mandir, Toronto]

http://www.durka.com [Sridurka Hindu Temple, Toronto]

KEY QUESTIONS FOR CRITICAL REFLECTION

1. What are some of the patterns of ethnic identity in the Hindu temples of Canada? Why is the ethnic identity of the temples so prominent in the Canadian setting?

2. What are some of the modifications in Hindu practice which help successive generations of Hindus in Canada adapt to local Canadian religious practices?

3. What kinds of religious festivals and public celebrations do Hindus in Canada enjoy? Why are these practices given such prominence in this setting?

4. Are there changes in the roles of women and youth in the practice of Hinduism in Canada as compared with the practice in India? What are these new roles and are there trends towards greater changes?

5. Is there a need for some central organization in Canadian Hinduism? Why has there been so little central organization? What kind of organization would be appropriate?

SEVEN

Buddhists

JAMIE S. SCOTT, YORK UNIVERSITY
HENRY C.H. SHIU, UNIVERSITY OF TORONTO

C hinese and Japanese immigrant workers brought Buddhism to Canada in the second half of the nineteenth century. In sectors ranging from communications through to natural resources and the hospitality industry, these newcomers were essential to the development of the new province of British Columbia. Chinese and Japanese families migrated eastwards across Canada over the following decades, forming Buddhist communities in most urban centres. By the 1960s, Buddhist temples had become a colourful feature of Canada's religious landscape, counting among their members not just Chinese and Japanese Canadians, but immigrants from elsewhere in East, Southeast, and Central Asia, as well as many Western converts to Buddhism. From the 1970s to the 1990s, Buddhist communities grew at a faster rate than any other religious group in Canada. The 2001 census recorded the Buddhist population of Canada as 300,345. Many Chinese and Japanese, of course, also identify themselves as Confucians or Daoists. However, in the same census, Confucianism and Daoism are lumped together under the category "Eastern Religions," and its population, at 37,550, is only one-eighth of that of the Buddhists.

THE HERITAGE

"Buddhism" is an English word coined by eighteenth-century European philosophers of the Enlightenment and indicating primarily Asian religious traditions that follow the Buddha's teachings. It is an umbrella term denoting a wide range of religious practices and cultures. "Buddha" is a title referring to someone who has fully awakened to the ultimate truth of all things. Buddhists believe that Shakyamuni Siddhartha Gautama is the historical Buddha, the founder of Buddhism. The exact dates of his birth and death are uncertain and are still debated by scholars, but tradition holds that he was born into a Hindu royal family of the *ksatriya*, or warrior class, sometime in the mid-sixth century BCE, in a town called Lumbini in what is now southern Nepal. Discussions of Buddhism usually begin with the life of its spiritual founder, legends about whom are widely known. The most notable of these legends deal with the Buddha's miraculous birth, his luxurious early life as a prince, and the four sights that set him on his spiritual journey beyond the seclusion of the palace walls: the sight of sickness, the sight of old age, the sight of death, and the sight of a monk seeking a path for overcoming suffering.

In addition to these narratives, Buddhists enjoy a vast library of early texts about the founder of the tradition, ranging from legends and myths to collections of sermons and other teachings. For centuries, his followers have loved to tell the story of how the Buddha renounced temporal power and became an ascetic, and how he resisted the temptations of Mara, lord of death, and gained perfect enlightenment beneath the *bodhi* tree at Bodh Gaya, in the modern Indian state of Bihar. Known as the **Jatakas**, accounts of the acts that the Buddha is believed to have performed in previous lives have remained favourites, too—as have stories about his passing into the state of perfect bliss known as *parinirvana*, where all suffering ceases. Though not entirely historical in the modern sense, these traditional narratives have served as powerful pedagogical tools for 2,500 years. Of particular educational importance, however, are the discourses of the Buddha, collectively known as the **Sutra**, which contain his 45 years of ministry; in particular, the Buddha's fundamental teachings, called the **Dharma**, which are expressed in the **Four Noble Truths**, and the idea of a chain of causation leading from rebirth to death, known as the "doctrine of dependent origination" (*pratitya-samutpada*).

The Four Noble Truths constitute the first sermon given to fellow ascetics by the Buddha after his enlightenment. The first noble truth is

Tradition holds that Siddhartha Gautama resisted the temptations of Mara, lord of death, and gained perfect enlightenment beneath the *bodhi* tree at Bodh Gaya, in the modern state of Bihar, India.

the truth of suffering (**dukkha**), which is found in every aspect of life in the continuing cycle of birth, death, and rebirth known as **samsara**. This cycle of existence is characterized by suffering, impermanence (*anitya*), and a delusory sense of self (**anatman**). Buddhists believe that all existence is impermanent. Human existence is filled with attachments to possessions and experiences. Such attachments will only lead to suffering, because everything we are attached to is impermanent. For Buddhists, even human personality is constituted out of sets of shifting elements, known as *skandhas*: the physical body, feelings, perceptions, volitions, and consciousness. No unchanging, permanent substance transcends these shifting components, and attachment to the notion that every individual embodies an everlasting soul or self (*atman*) is delusory. Without the wisdom to see through such delusions, we are trapped in *samsara*, life after life. Whether sentient beings are reborn in favourable realms as heavenly gods or human beings, or in unfavourable realms as animals, hungry ghosts, or demons, depends on the law of **karma**. Literally meaning "actions," *karma* describes the natural law of cause and effect governing every individual's place in *samsara*. This law is not mechanical, however, like rewards and punishments dispensed by a supreme divinity, or like the deterministic fate dramatized in classical Greek tragedy and elsewhere. Rather, Buddhist *karma* functions as a dynamic web of causal relationships, so that good actions lead to good karmic fruit that ripens either in this life or in future lives, while bad actions lead to bad karmic results.

The second, third, and fourth noble truths identify what causes bad *karma* and offer a way to increase karmic merit. In the second noble truth, the Buddha attributes suffering to three types of craving (*tanha*): for pleasure, for existence, and for non-existence. Hence, "craving" here does not just mean "want," but also the deeper, existential sense of attachment that leads to further becoming. This insight is elaborately expressed in the 12 interconnected links in the cycle of dependent origination: ignorance; constructing activities; consciousness; mind and body; the six sense fields; contact; sensation; craving; attachment; becoming; rebirth; and old age and death. This process of conditional attachment does not cease with the twelfth link, for aging and death lead to another rebirth, so that the 12 links can together be pictured as a circular chain without a beginning or an end. Through learning, reflection, and meditation, however, anyone may eliminate one or more links, thus breaking the circular chain of transitoriness and releasing the individual from the conditional realm of *samsara* to the unconditioned sphere of **nirvana**—the ultimate goal of the Buddhist path.

The third and fourth noble truths have to do with the cessation (*nirodha*) of suffering and the path that leads to this cessation in *nirvana*. The cessation of suffering, according to the Buddha, is literally the extinguishing of the fires of greediness, hatred, and ignorance—the so-called three poisons. But Buddhism does not promote a pessimistic view of life. On the contrary, Buddhists understand the Buddha's diagnosis of life to be realistic, and the scriptures of the different communities that follow the Buddha's teachings uniformly represent *nirvana* as a blissful and joyful experience. Accordingly, the fourth truth affirms that there is indeed a path that brings suffering and rebirth to an end. Known as the **Noble Eightfold Path**, this teaching spells out the essentials of Buddhist salvation: right understanding; right thought; right effort; right mindfulness; right concentration; right speech; right action; right livelihood. The last three injunctions involve Buddhism's fundamental moral code, known as the **Five Precepts** (*panca sila*): refraining from killing (*ahimsa*), theft, sexual misconduct, lying, and the taking of intoxicants.

Classically, there were four classes of Buddhist practitioner: monks, nuns, laymen, and laywomen. Together, they comprised the **Sangha**, or Buddhist community, in its fuller sense. Collectively, the Buddha, the *Dharma*, and the *Sangha* are known as the *Triratna* or "**Three Jewels**."

Buddhists are said to seek refuge in the Three Jewels, meaning that Buddhist salvation lies in these three elements. In the fifth century BCE, the Buddha founded monastic orders of monks (*bhiksus*) and nuns (*bhiksunis*). These orders constituted the *Sangha* in a narrower sense. In his lifetime, the Buddha criticized Hindu traditions as overly ritualistic; rituals, he taught, were merely a means to an end, a way of increasing good *karma*. After the Buddha's death, however, disciples erected ten monuments around India, each sanctuary housing a portion of his cremated remains and crowned with a pole symbolizing Mount Meru, the *axis mundi* of Indian mythology. By the first century CE, Buddhists had developed a vast network of local sanctuaries, shrines, temples, and monasteries, many incorporating icons and statues depicting the Buddha in various symbolic postures, or illustrating scenes from the *Jatakas* and the Buddha's life. Dating from the reign of the Mauryan king Ashoka (260–218 BCE), the sacred complex at Sanchi, near Bhopal, exemplifies such developments. Taking part in pilgrimages to these sacred sites, known as *stupas* or *caityas,* became important ways for lay Buddhists to accumulate karmic merit—as did the full-moon festival of **Vaisakha** in early May, when the followers of the Buddha celebrate his birth, enlightenment, and *parinirvana.*

To assume the monastic life itself, of course, was to add to the store of good *karma.* Lay followers entered the monastic order in ordination ceremonies involving the renunciation of secular ways, or *pravrajya,* and consecration into monastic life, or *upasampada.* Monks and nuns must commit to the more stringent moral codes of the Eight Precepts or the Ten Precepts, which include prohibitions against eating after midday and indulging in various kinds of physical luxuries. To ensure harmony in the monastic order, sets of rules known as *pratimoksa,* meaning literally "bond," gradually evolved. At the First Buddhist Council, held in about 543 BCE, shortly after the Buddha's death, these guidelines were gathered together and collectively named the **Vinaya**, or "discipline." The *Vinaya* were much more elaborate than the codes of moral precepts. In the centuries following the *parinirvana* of the Buddha, however, his followers came to differ over doctrinal matters, notably which version of the *Vinaya* should be followed. These tensions led to the Second Buddhist Council, which convened in 383 BCE in Vaisali, not far from Bodh Gaya, the place of the Buddha's enlightenment and the most important pilgrimage site in Buddhism. Some monks insisted that even the slightest infringements of the rules of the *Vinaya* were attributable to the bad karmic effects of the three poisons and warranted immediate expulsion from the community.

Theravadin Buddhist child monks at Wat Khung Taphao (Temple at the Bend in the Sailing Ship Waterway), Mueang Uttaradit, Uttaradit Province, Thailand. PHOTO BY TEVAPRAPAS MAKKLAY. REPRINTED UNDER THE TERMS OF THE CC-BY LICENSE AGREEMENT.

Other monks argued that Buddhist monastic discipline was not designed to impose an overly strict ascetic life upon the ordained and that the rules prescribed in the *Vinaya* possessed no absolute authority. Rather, the Buddha had encouraged his disciples to maintain a "middle way," meaning that Buddhist training should teach practitioners neither to fall into strict asceticism nor to yield to excessive pleasures.

As these disagreements persisted, schisms occurred and various schools of Buddhist thought developed. The **Theravada** school represented a more austere approach to the tradition. Meaning "Teachings of the Elders," Theravada emphasized the division between monastic and lay practitioners, and insisted that the former strictly adhere to the rules of the *Vinaya*. The pursuit of enlightenment, it was assumed, required ascetic withdrawal, while the laity contributed to the general cultivation of good *karma* by gifting monks and nuns the materials of everyday life, a service known as *dana*. Other early Buddhist schools included the Mahasanghika, the Sautrantika, and the Sarvastivada. Some schools incorporated a body of literature known as the **Abhidharma** into their canon of sacred texts. Essentially attempts to classify and explain the *Sutra*, the *Abhidharma* mark points of divergence between the various early Buddhist schools of thought. At one extreme, the Sautrantika school refused to accept such a body of literature as in any way authoritative. At the other extreme, certain schools regarded their own collections of *Abhidharma* so highly that they revered these writings alongside the *Sutra* and the *Vinaya*, and insisted upon including them in collections of sacred texts known as the

Tripitaka, or "Three Baskets." Convened around 250 BCE by Ashoka to establish an orthodox interpretation of the tradition, the Third Buddhist Council standardized the text of the *Tripitaka* in the **Pali** language, and missionaries were dispatched throughout South and South-east Asia to disseminate this canonical version of the Buddha's teachings. Strongly influenced by the Theravada school, the orthodox Buddhism of the Pali canon gradually spread across the region, and by the fifteenth century it had come to dominate the religious landscapes of Sri Lanka, Burma (now Myanmar), Cambodia, Thailand, Laos, and Vietnam, where it remains strong to this day.

More liberal schools of Buddhist thought, like the Mahasanghika and the Sarvastivada, flourished, however—especially in India's north-west where, roughly 150 years after the Third Buddhist Council, the Kushan emperor Kanishka convened another congress. Considered a meeting of heretical monks by Theravadin Buddhists, this Fourth Buddhist Council produced alternative versions of the *Tripitaka* and is often associated with the development of **Mahayana** Buddhism, though the exact origins of this form of the tradition are still obscure. Some scholars closely relate Mahayana, which means "Greater Vehicle," to the activities of the laity; because the Buddha travelled and taught widely throughout India, scholars surmise that at least some of what we now regard as Mahayana *sutras* began life as teachings transmitted only among his lay followers. In any case, the more liberal schools of Buddhist thought disseminated their interpretations of the tradition widely throughout South Asia over the next few centuries, producing such celebrated new *sutras* as the *Lankavatara*, the *Saddharma-pundarika* (*Lotus*), the *Prajnaparamita* (*Perfection of Wisdom*, including the *Heart* and *Diamond*), and the *Vimalakirti-nirdesa* (*Seven Treasures*).

Two teachings in particular distinguish Mahayana from earlier Buddhist thinking: the notion of the "awakening mind" (**bodhicitta**) and the role of **Bodhisattvas**, whose task is to perfect the *bodhicitta*. In Theravada Buddhism, the individual who renounces all other considerations in order to strive for and attain *nirvana* is known as the **Arhat**, or "worthy one." Often translated simply as "sage" or "saint," the *Arhat* is deemed worthy of respect because an ascetic life of "insight meditation" (*vipassana*) has revealed to him or to her that it is delusory to believe in the transcendent self. But Mahayana Buddhists viewed such figures as too self-absorbed, and therefore lacking in the sort of compassion for their fellow human beings that characterizes true enlightenment. By contrast, Mahayana enlightenment, the goal of the awakening mind (*bodhicitta*), can be defined as the union of wisdom and compassion. Pursuing the non-dual wisdom that accepts all things as empty—as is so persuasively articulated in the *Vimalakirti-nirdesa*—Mahayana teaches that the Buddha forgoes personal entry into *nirvana*, and out of compassion vows to help all sentient beings suffering in *samsara* to achieve enlightenment. The *Bodhisattva* perfects the six virtues (*paramitas*) of generosity, patience, morality, diligence, meditation, and wisdom, and the ultimate perfection of *bodhicitta* is the attainment of perfectly enlightened Buddhahood in *nirvana*, beyond all names and forms.

The Mahayana movement gave rise to two major Mahayana schools: **Madhyamaka** and **Yogacara**. Literally "the middle way," Madhyamaka is traditionally linked to the important Buddhist thinker, Nagarjuna (*ca.* 150–250 CE), and his disciple, Aryadeva, who lived during the early third century CE. Elaborated upon by later scholars like Bhavaviveka (*ca.* 490–570) and Candrakirti, who lived in the early seventh century, their writings attempt to systematize and demonstrate the teachings of the *Perfection of Wisdom sutra*, often through subtle, dialectical arguments. Broadly speaking, the central axiom of Madhyamaka is that all existing things are "empty" (**sunya**) of inherent, substantial reality (*svabhava*)—just as the concept "zero," which is also called *sunya* in Sanskrit, symbolizes essentially empty, though functioning, positions in mathematics. According to Madhyamaka teachings, all things originate interdependently; in other words, from the standpoint of the middle way, all antinomies, from the opposition of self and other to the opposition of *samsara* and *nirvana,* are empty of autonomous reality: self exists only in relation to other, *nirvana* only in relation to *samsara,* and vice versa. We cannot, therefore, attain *nirvana* through the eradication of samsaric defilements, since such defilements are also "empty"; they possess no ultimate reality, and consequently there is nothing real to be eradicated. Rather, we attain *nirvana* by uncovering intrinsic wisdom that is in a defiled state because of greediness, hatred, and ignorance.

The difference between Madhyamaka and Yogacara lies mainly in their particular emphases; the former illustrates the ultimate emptiness of all things by dialectical means, while the latter—including the later form of the Vijnanavada or "Way of Consciousness" school—emphasizes the meditative practices that lead the adept towards such awareness. Literally "the practice of yoga," Yogacara is associated with the teachings of Maitreyanatha (*ca.* 270–350), which were transmitted and clarified by

Asanga and his brother, Vasubandhu, in the later fourth century. Taking inspiration from the *Lankavatara sutra* in particular, Yogacara focuses on meditative stages that lead the adept, or *yogin,* to attain ultimate union or "yoking" (*yoga*) with **tathata**—that is, the "suchness" or "thusness" of things, and hence ultimately "reality-as-such," which in the Yogacara tradition holds the same sort of conceptual status as the notion of "emptiness" (*sunyata*) in Madhyamaka Buddhism. Classical Yogacara outlines five paths or stages for attaining *nirvana*: on the path of accumulation, the practitioner acquires merit by cultivating a proper understanding of Buddhist teachings; the path of application leads to a proper awareness of the "thusness" of things; in the third stage, known as the path of seeing, meditation leads to the first *Bodhisattva* level of awareness; on the fourth path, the adept advances through the remaining nine *Bodhisattva* levels; and finally, the path of fulfillment leads to the complete attainment of Buddhahood. The Yogacara tradition also formulated these stages in terms of the "Doctrine of the Three Natures" (*trisvabhava*). The "imagined nature" (*parikalpita-svabhava*) of things is the form in which their "dependent nature" (*paratantra-svabhava*) manifests itself. In other words, we are deluded when we impute reality to objects that seem to exist externally to us. By contrast, the "perfected nature" (*parisnipanna-svabhava*) expresses our direct experience of the way things really are, free of falsely imposed subject-object duality.

Applying this sort of thinking to the person of the Buddha himself, Yogacara developed the Mahayana doctrine of the "Three Bodies" (*trikaya*). While Theravada stressed the Buddha's identity as a historical human being, who struggled to gain perfect enlightenment and demonstrated exemplary willingness to share his insight with his fellow human beings, Mahayana came to speak of his historical "appearance or transformation body" (*nirmanakaya*) as an earthly manifestation of the "truth body" (*dharmakaya*). Dwelling in various heavenly realms as *Bodhisattvas,* other Buddhas have appeared as a perfect manifestation of an "enjoyment or bliss body" (*sambhogakaya*), Mahayana teaches, with each embodying the bliss of exemplary compassion. In turn, these *Bodhisattvas* themselves realize the "*dharma* or truth body" (*dharmakaya*), the ultimate and eternal perfection of wisdom defining *nirvana* as the transcendent reality of the Buddha, beyond all names and forms. In the seventh century CE, a movement known as Yogacara-Madhyamaka revived classical Yogacara teachings, focusing upon the notion of "essence in embryo" (**tathagatagarbha**), which appears in such early Mahayana scriptures as the fourth-century *Srimala sutra*, or *The Lion's Roar of Queen Srimala*. This *sutra* identifies *tathagatagarbha* with the essential nature of the Buddha (*dharmakaya*), and argues that this Buddha-nature dwells hidden within every sentient being, defiled by the moral contaminants of greediness, hatred, and ignorance. True devotion to the celestial Buddhas and *Bodhisattvas,* according to Yogacara-Madhyamaka, helps to purify individuals of these defilements and awaken them to their own essential Buddha-nature.

From the first century CE on, hand in hand with philosophical developments, Mahayana began to cultivate a wide array of devotional practices, each designed to enlist the help of the various Buddhas and *Bodhisattvas* in an effort to hasten enlightenment. The earliest devotional cult revered the *Bodhisattva* Maitreya, who holds sway in his heavenly realm, waiting to descend to earth as the next Buddha, at which time his devotees hope to be reborn fully enlightened. Other Buddhists venerated Manjushri, a *Bodhisattva* of meditation, who brandishes the sword of incisive logic in his right hand and the *Perfection of Wisdom sutra* in his left. Statues of Manjushri are often found in Buddhist monasteries. By far the most popular figure, however, was Avalokitesvara, the *Bodhisattva* of infinite compassion. Looking down from his heavenly paradise, known in the *Amitabha sutra* and other Mahayana writings as the Pure Land of the West, this *Bodhisattva* sees the world's suffering with a thousand eyes and comes to the world's aid with a thousand arms. In his celestial form, Avalokitesvara is associated with the Buddha Amitabha. Worshippers draw upon the Buddha's infinite store of merit by meditating upon his sacred name—or more likely by repeatedly chanting the simple *mantra*, "*Namo Amitabha Buddha* (Homage to Amitabha Buddha)," especially with their dying breaths. Even lay petitioners who in good faith invoke the powers of Amitabha Buddha embodied in this formula may look forward to being reborn in the Pure Land, free of suffering, old age, and death. Devotees might then profit from the Buddha's perfected wisdom in their efforts to eventually realize *nirvana*.

Like Theravada, Mahayana Buddhism spread well beyond India. Traders carried the tradition to China in the first century CE, thence to Korea by the late second century, and thence to Japan in the fifth century. By the middle of the second century, missionaries were translating Buddhist scriptures into Chinese. At that time, the indigenous philosophies in China were already fully established; important works such as the *Laozi* and the *Zhuangzi* from philosophical Daoism, and the *Analects* from Confucianism, were also well-known to the Chinese literati, who were proud of them as symbolic of the apex of Chinese civilization. As a result, the "foreign" Buddhist texts from India were initially interpreted and translated in the light of heavy Chinese philosophical influence. This continued until the arrival of Kumarajiva (344–413), who set a new standard for the translation of Buddhist texts in China and eventually established the Chinese branch of Madhyamaka, known as the Sanlun or Three Treatises school. The translation of Buddhist scriptures carried on until the tenth century, allowing Chinese Buddhists to enjoy a rich canon of inherited texts—including such classic Mahayana texts as the *Lotus*, *Perfection of Wisdom*, *Seven Treasures*, and *Amitabha sutras*—and also to compose new works, most notably the *Platform Sutra of the Sixth Patriarch*. The first Chinese schools of Buddhist thought reflected the tradition's South Asian beginnings, with the Sanlun school recapitulating Indian Madhyamaka and the Faxiang school perpetuating Indian Yogacara. Later, more distinctively Chinese movements appeared, including the Tiantai school, the Huayan or Flower Garland school, Chan Buddhism, and Chinese Pure Land Buddhism.

Named for a mountain in Zhejiang, China, and associated with the philosopher Zhikai (538–597), the Tiantai school drew inspiration from the *Lotus sutra*; stressed the importance of meditation; and argued for the comprehensive integration of all forms of Buddhist teaching. Through the work of scholars like Ch'egwan (died 971), Uich'on (1054–1101), and Chinul (1158–1210), Tiantai also enjoyed a renaissance in Korea, where it had been known as Ch'ont'ae since the fourth century. After being promoted by the monk Saicho (766–822), Tiantai became the Tendai school in Japan, based at the Enryakuji temple complex on Mount Hiei, near Kyoto, where it is still headquartered. Tendai differs from Chinese Tiantai, however, in its willing embrace of other modes of religious expression— in particular indigenous Japanese Shinto, and certain forms of tantric Buddhism that centre on initiation rites and the role of personal *gurus*. Esoteric **mantras** and **mandalas** play an important part here, too, for tantric Buddhists believe that engaging the mysterious powers embodied in such secret words and images through various forms of yogic meditation and bodily posture leads to higher levels of spiritual awareness on the path to *nirvana*. Ironically, however, this tolerance in Tendai eventually led to disputes within the movement over religious leadership and the status of the *Lotus sutra* itself. The most notable outcome of these disputes was the founding of the distinctively Japanese school of Nichiren Buddhism by the nationalist monk Nichiren Daishonin (1222–82), who asserted his version of Buddhism alone to be true and tried to convince the Japanese state to adopt it. Followers of this fundamentalist sect, which is based at the temple of Taisekiji, near Mount Fuji, believe that to simply invoke the *Lotus sutra* in the chant "*Namu myoho renge kyo* (Homage to the *Lotus sutra*)" speeds the processes of enlightenment.

Like Tiantai, the Huayan school travelled from China to Korea and Japan. Named for the *Avatamsaka* (Flower Garland) *sutra,* Huayan owed a good deal to the work of the Chinese translator and philosopher Fazang (643–712), who wrote over 60 books exploring the paradoxical implication of the doctrine of dependent origination that everything is at once the cause and the effect of everything else. Led by monks like Wonhyo (617–686) and Uisang (625–702), Huayan became the Hwaeom school in Korea and the Kegon school in Japan, which was founded in 736 CE by the monk Rōben (689–773) and headquartered at the temple of Todaiji, near Nara. This temple houses a giant statue of Buddha Vairocana, an embodiment of *dharmakaya,* in one of the largest wooden buildings in the world. Interestingly, this Buddha also inspired another important Japanese Buddhist school known as Shingon, the Japanese transliteration of the Sanskrit *mantra,* or "sacred word." Based on Mount Koya near Osaka, and founded by the monk Kukai (774–835), the Shingon school domesticated South Asian tantric Buddhist teachings still more profoundly than Tendai, even at times incorporating *anuttarayoga tantra*—that is, "supreme yoga tantra," which symbolizes enlightenment as a sexual union between the female principle of wisdom (*prajna*) and the male principle of effective techniques (*upaya*). Unique in its use of calligraphy, Shingon also encourages devotees to meditate upon certain sacred letters, believing that such practices may lead to enlightenment in the here and now. Also like Tendai, Shingon Buddhism melded with Japanese Shinto traditions, to the extent that shrines dedicated to various Buddhas and *Bodhisattvas* will be found in the temples of both schools alongside altars honouring indigenous gods, known as *kami.*

Likely developing as a grass-roots movement, Chan differs from other Chinese schools in placing less emphasis upon intellectual and ritual formality, and in requiring monks to be self-supporting through hard work in the everyday world. A transliteration of the word *dhyana,* which in Sanskrit means "meditation," Chan claimed the legendary sixth-century Indian monk Bodhidharma as its founder. Bodhidharma's authority passed down through a line of Chinese patriarchs, culminating in Huineng (638–713), the author of the celebrated Chinese Mahayana scripture, the *Platform Sutra of the Sixth Patriarch*. The Chan Buddhist emphasis on simplicity, naturalness, and spontaneity, cultivated through the practice of *dhyana*, gives the school a unique status in China, capturing an aspect of Indian Mahayana teachings in ways no other Chinese Buddhist school does. Chan stressed the possibility of enlightenment in this life even more enthusiastically than Shingon—though some, like the ninth-century Caodong sect, argued that enlightenment required many years of meditation; and others, like the Linji sect, also in the ninth century, claimed that enlightenment came in a sudden moment of insight. By the end of the ninth century, the Vo Ngon Thong school was practising Chinese Chan in Vietnam, where it was known as Thien, as were the Nine Mountain schools in Korea, where it was called Seon Buddhism. By the twelfth century, Chan had gained followers in Japan, where it was known as Zen. Over the centuries, Seon merged with other forms of Mahayana Buddhism, resulting in the Chogye school, which now predominates in Korea. Thien has also tended to be syncretistic, but in key respects, Japanese Zen has recapitulated the different approaches found in Chan. Founded by Eisai (1141–1215), the Japanese Rinzai sect follows Linji in its stress on sudden awakening, while the Soto sect, founded by Dogen (1200–53), emphasizes the more meditative approach of the Caodong sect. Less élitist, the Rinzai school has become well-known outside Japan for the Chan technique of *gongan*, or Zen **koan**. This technique confronts the adept with paradoxical riddles, like the sound of one hand clapping, in an effort to break through everyday consciousness to some deeper level of clarity, like the sun appearing from behind clouds.

Like Chan Buddhism, Chinese Pure Land developed as a popular form of devotion in reaction to the formalities of more philosophical kinds of Chinese Buddhism. The *bhiksus* An Shih Kao and Lokaksema brought the Pure Land *sutras* to China in the second century CE. In 402, Huiyuan (334–416) founded a monastery on Mount Lushan, and by the end of the seventh century—thanks in large part to the proselytizing efforts of another monk, Shan-tao (613–681)—Pure Land had found numerous adherents at all levels of Chinese society. Though less prevalent than other strains of Buddhism in medieval Korea, Pure Land slowly grew in importance in Japan, most notably through the Jodo-shu school, founded by Honen Shonin (1133–1212) and later revitalized as Jodo-shinshu, or "True Pure Land," by his disciple, Shinran Shonin (1173–1262). Twirling rosaries, Chinese and Japanese worshippers address Amitabha as Amida Buddha by chanting "*Namu* Amida (Amitabha) *Butsu.*" The repetitious chanting is called *nianfo* in China and *nembutsu* in Japan. In his conventional male form, Amida Buddha has been associated with benevolent government throughout East and South-east Asia, but in a fascinating Chinese Pure Land variation, Amida Buddha's helper, Avalokitesvara, became the female *Bodhisattva* Guanyin, known as Kannon in Japan. Guanyin is a nurturing mother figure, often dressed in white and revered for the gift of children. In related developments, other local *Bodhisattvas* came to enjoy large followings, too. In fifteenth-century China, for example, the heroic Maitreya became the carefree Milo, a scruffy, pot-bellied figure with a hemp sack full of candies and toys for children; and in Japan, worshippers turn to the *Bodhisattva* Jizo, the protector of firemen, travellers, pilgrims, expectant mothers, and especially sick and dying children (his statue can often be found standing guard over the graves of the young.) Elsewhere, Pure Land frequently flourishes alongside other forms of Buddhism, too. In Vietnam, for instance, Thien and Theravadin Buddhism are also widely practised, and in Korea, the non-sectarian ways of the Chogye monks include veneration of Amida Buddha. At the popular level, Pure Land is currently the dominant form of Buddhism in China, Japan, North and South Korea, Taiwan, and Vietnam.

Interestingly, certain aspects of the Buddhist traditions that originated in China and then travelled to other parts of East and Southeast Asia sound superficially similar to earlier Confucian and Daoist teachings, as found in the *Four Books* and *Five Classics* attributed to or inspired by Confucius (551–478 BCE), and in the *Dao de jing* and the *Zhuangzi*, composed respectively by the revered sages Lao Tzu and Zhuangzi in the sixth and fourth centuries BCE. The Buddhist concept of *Dharma* resonates with the notion of *Dao*, or "the Way," for example, while the Buddhist term *sunyata* and the Daoist term *taixu* may both be translated as "emptiness." The popularity of Chan Buddhism may also be explained by similarities between the school's meditative focus on simplicity, naturalness, and spontaneity and Daoist themes like "self-so-ness" (*ziran*), "actionless-action" (*wuwei*), freedom from contrivance, fasting, holism, and skepticism about language. Indeed, during the initial phase of the transmission of Buddhism to China, Buddhist texts were sometimes translated into Chinese using Daoist terminology, leading the Chinese to interpret these scriptures from a Daoist perspective.

On the other hand, Confucianism also helped to shape the development of Buddhism in China, though in a rather different way. In many respects the direct opposite of Daoism, Confucianism stresses the importance of a social order and emphasizes the establishment of harmony between humans and nature. The Confucian thus cultivates filial piety; fosters education in the classics, history, poetry, and music; and observes religious rituals (*li*) as a way of developing goodness or benevolence (*ren*). Maintaining the so-called Five Cardinal Relationships (*wulun*) helps to cultivate the ideal social order according to the Confucian vision, which prescribes specific duties for each member of the pairs of ruler and subject, husband and wife, father and son, elder brother and younger brother, and friend and friend. This grand vision of order and harmony inspired such apocryphal Buddhist texts as the *Renwang huguo bore boluomi jing* (*Perfection of Wisdom Sutra for Benevolent Kings to Protect the Country*) and the *Fumu enzhong jing* (*Sutra of Filial Piety*). These texts were composed in China in a style that mimics the style of Buddhist *sutras,* their intention being the imposition of Confucian ideals over Buddhist practice. Eventually, for these reasons and in other ways, there appeared in China—as well as in other parts of East and South-east Asia influenced by Chinese beliefs and practices—the lively development of three religious traditions, all influencing one another in complex and sometimes surprising ways. Daoists fell under the influence of Buddhist beliefs in *karma* and rebirth, for example, while the teachings of the Confucian classics blended with the Buddhist ideal of compassion to bring about such fascinating practices as the ceremonial purchase and release of animals that are due to be slaughtered (*fang sheng*).

Finally, we must say a few words about **Vajrayana** Buddhism. Often referred to as the third turn of the wheel of *Dharma* after Theravada and Mahayana, Vajrayana means "diamond" or "thunderbolt vehicle," which is a term symbolizing the indestructible nature of emptiness as well as the wisdom that realizes it. Vajrayana elaborates certain Mahayana Buddhist techniques, or *upaya*, associated with third-century esoteric Buddhist texts known as *tantras*. The four forms of tantric Buddhism are *kriya-tantra*, which considers ritual practices; *yoga-tantra*, which deals with meditation; *carya-tantra*, which blends ritual practices with meditation; and *anuttarayoga-tantra*, which is widely, if prejudicially, recognized in the West for offering adherents an expedient way to attain Buddhahood in their lifetimes and for the way in which its complementary principles are symbolized in terms of sexual union, as certain Japanese Shingon Buddhists taught. The first three forms were transmitted to China, and from there to Korea and Japan, but the fourth form is otherwise almost exclusive to Tibet.

The eighth-century *bhiksu* Padmasambhava is credited with bringing Vajrayana to the "Land of Snow." Like other kinds of Buddhism, Vajrayana aims to liberate sentient beings from *samsara*, and like all forms of *tantra*, Tibetan Buddhism makes use of various meditative and ritual practices to accelerate the passage to enlightenment. Meditative practices include the cultivation of *sadhana*, or blissful communion with the Buddha, by focusing the mind's eye intently upon *mandalas* representing celestial figures; and incantation, most notably the *mantra* invoking Avalokitesvara, "*Om mani padme hum* (O, the jewel in the lotus)," chanted or written on strings of small flags hanging in trees, or on pieces of paper spun around and around in prayer wheels. Significantly, Tibetan Buddhists believe that Avalokitesvara is incarnated in His Holiness the fourteenth Dalai Lama, Tenzin Gyatso (born 1935), the spiritual and political leader of Tibet, who since 1959 has led his people from exile in Dharamsala, India, following the communist Chinese invasion of Tibet in 1950. Other Tibetan Buddhist traditions include **mudras**, or ritual hand-gestures, and the *Bardo thodol*, or *Tibetan Book of the Dead*, which monks read aloud to the dying to help them negotiate the three stages of the *bardo* state that exists between death and rebirth. Tibetan Buddhism also incorporates practices inherited from pre-Buddhist Bon traditions of magic and shamanism, as well as sand-painting and folk singing and dancing. Its esoteric ethos has meant that Tibetan Buddhism has been transmitted mainly through orders of *gurus*, known as *lamas*. The Nyingma order traditionally traces its lineage to Padmasambhava himself, whose followers laud him as the second Buddha. The other major monastic orders are the Kagyu, the Sakya, and the Gelug, the latter of which was founded by Tsongkhapa (1357–1419) at Ganden. The Dalai Lama belongs to the Gelug order, whose monks are distinguished by their yellow hats and for their profound understanding of Madhyamaka.

While the political relationship between Tibet and China remains fraught with tension, some scholars have perceived a different, if equally ambiguous, relationship between the religious traditions of these Asian neighbours. Some Vajrayana Buddhists occasionally employ sexuality as one dimension of the spiritual path towards enlightenment. This practice has led to comparisons with a form of Chinese Daoism known as "religious Daoism" (*daojiao*). Distinct from more purely philosophical Daoism (*daojia*), religious Daoism encourages a range of physical, mental, and spiritual techniques, including breathing exercises, fasting, and Tai Chi (*taiji*) exercises, in an attempt to replenish the vital energy (*qi*) that naturally invigorates a person at birth, but dissipates with aging.

Sometimes these techniques include specified sexual practices. Followers of religious Daoism believe that these practices, known collectively as "internal alchemy" (*neidan*), cultivate bodily health, longevity, and ultimately immortality. Confucians find the Daoist employment of sexual practices deeply offensive, and in periods when Confucian values dominate Chinese society, this form of religious Daoism becomes all the more controversial. Similarly, Chinese Confucians remain suspicious of the tantric sexual practices of Vajrayana Buddhism, even though Vajrayana Buddhists themselves recognize that this esoteric form of the tradition is not suitable for all practitioners. A historical argument lies behind the Confucian prejudice. Confucians blame Mongolian Buddhist monks for introducing sexual tantra to the Song Dynasty (960–1279), resulting in sensual indulgence, moral decline, and ultimately the loss of the empire to the Mongolians. The Mongolians then established the Yuan Dynasty (1271–1368), which marks the first time that China was not under the rulership of Han Chinese.

THE MAKING OF A CANADIAN BUDDHIST COMMUNITY

Scholars have recently been studying fascinating stories of Chinese Buddhist monks sailing to North America in 458 CE and settling on the west coast of Canada in 499 CE. There is also an account of a voyage from China reaching what is now British Columbia in 594 CE. These studies suggest that such an early arrival of Chinese Buddhist monks in North America is not improbable. Such speculations aside, however, the formal history of Buddhism in Canada can be traced back to the nineteenth century. In 1858, Chinese labourers travelled from California to work in gold mines in the new province of British Columbia, so named by Great Britain's Queen Victoria (1819–1901) in that same year. These labourers became the first Buddhists to settle in modern Canada. Over the next three decades, they were joined by immigrants coming directly from China, many of whom took jobs in British Columbia's fish canneries or helping to build the province's infrastructure of telegraph lines, roads, and railways. Japanese newcomers also worked in these fields, as well as in farming and the lumber and hospitality industries. Gradually, Chinese and Japanese Buddhists moving into central and eastern Canada were joined by immigrants from elsewhere in East and Southeast Asia. By the 1960s, Buddhism had a significant presence upon the Canadian religious landscape, and it now makes up both the largest and the fastest-developing group of non-Western religious communities in Canada. According to Statistics Canada, the country's Buddhist population grew most rapidly between 1971 and 1981, a decade that saw an increase of 227 per cent, although this growth rate declined to 215 per cent in the 1980s, and then to 83.8 per cent in the 1990s. In the 2001 census, the Buddhist population of Canada was reported as 300,345.

Japanese Jodo-shinshu is the strain of organized Buddhism boasting the longest history in Canada. Invited from the Honpa Honganji temple in Kyoto, Japan, the Jodo-shinshu minister Senju Sasaki led Canada's first formal Buddhist congregation in October 1905, in a rented room at the Ishikawa Hotel on Vancouver's Powell Street. By the start of World War II, there were several Jodo-shinshu temples in Vancouver, as well as in New Westminster, Marpole, Steveston, Mission, Royston, Maple Ridge, Okanagan, Chemainus, Victoria, Skeena, Ocean Falls, and Whonnock. In 1930, Raymond, Alberta, became the site of the first Buddhist temple outside British Columbia, and others followed in Lethridge, Picture Butte, Coaldale, Taber, and Rosemary, mainly to serve the needs of Japanese Canadians resettled from British Columbia. A key figure in this missionary activity, the Jodo-shinshu minister Takashi Tsuji (1919–2004), moved to Toronto where he helped found the Toronto Buddhist Church in 1945. Later, he also established temples in Hamilton and Montreal.

The Toronto Buddhist congregation became the largest in Canada. In 1955, its members built their own temple at 918 Bathurst Street, employing triangles as a structural motif to reflect Buddhist notions of harmony between humankind and nature. The temple's interior featured a hand-crafted shrine (onaijin), which contained a statue of Amida Buddha. In 1955, the temple also hosted a national conference of Japanese Buddhists and formed the Buddhist Churches of Canada (BCC). By the late 1990s, this organization embraced 20 congregations across Canada, mainly in the Toronto region, southern Alberta, and British Columbia. In 2005, Gomonshu Koshin Ohtani (born 1945), the spiritual head of Jodo-shinshu Buddhism, travelled from Japan to visit several of these congregations in celebration of the tradition's Canadian centenary. To commemorate his visit, the Toronto Buddhist Church, which by then was sharing new modern facilities with the BCC Dharma Centre at 1011 Sheppard Avenue West, replaced the statue of Amida Buddha with a scroll on which Gomonshu had written the six characters of "Namu Amida Butsu" in classical calligraphy.

Despite its longevity, however, the Jodo-shinshu community has earned criticism from other Canadian Buddhists, who worry that the sect emulates the rituals, forms, and terminology of the Christian churches at the expense of traditional Buddhist meditation and philosophy. There are good historical reasons for this tendency. The first generations of Chinese and Japanese immigrants to Canada keenly felt the pressure to convert to Christianity—the country's principal form of institutionalized religion—in order to gain access to and acceptance in mainstream society. World War II animosities cemented this phenomenon among many Japanese Canadians; according to one calculation, the number self-identifying as Christian rose from less than a third to well over half between 1941 and 1951. Perhaps reflecting this influence, Canadian Jodo-shinshu Buddhists sometimes try to draw parallels between the figures of Amida Buddha and Christ, or between the Buddhist philosophy of compassion and the Christian theology of grace, or between the Pure Land and the heavenly Zion of biblical teaching. A Protestant Christian social and cultural ethos permeates many Jodo-shinshu congregations, as well. Today, in addition to such events as "Guiding Light" *Dharma* talks and a calendar of religious services and festivals, a Jodo-shinshu "church" in Canada might offer a range of more secular services. In August 2005, for example, opening ceremonies for the Toronto Buddhist Church's new Sheppard Avenue premises featured talks on the tradition's history, rituals, and philosophy, as well as demonstrations of various sacred arts, including Tai Chi, rosary-making (*nenju*), paper-folding (*origami*), flower-arranging (*ikebana*), calligraphy (*shodo* and *sumie*), and sacred dance and music (*odori, gagaku,* and *sakuhachi*). But other activities at Jodo-shinshu temples in Canada might now include courses in English as a second language, employment counselling, citizenship classes, youth groups, day-care facilities, support for senior citizens, and Japanese folk-dancing lessons. The Calgary Buddhist Temple has also sponsored youth tours of Japan, for example.

Since the 1950s, however, several waves of immigration have helped to strengthen and enrich the Canadian Buddhist community in more conventional ways. Chinese newcomers have continued to arrive from Hong Kong, Taiwan, and mainland China, as well as from less traditional places of origin such as South Africa, the Caribbean, and Peru. In the late 1960s, large numbers of new immigrants came from Japan. Vietnamese, Cambodians, and Laotians escaped to Canada after the Communists took over Saigon in 1975, as did refugees from domestic conflicts resulting from Burma's long struggle for stability in the wake of its independence from British colonial rule. The 1980s also saw significant immigration from Singapore. More recently, Koreans, Thais, and Sinhalese have settled in Canada, as have Punjabi-speaking Buddhists fleeing persecution in India. Ironically, though profoundly shaped by the social and cultural traditions of Buddhism, many of these newcomers have been unfamiliar with the tradition's religious teachings. And yet, perhaps as a way of maintaining identity in a strange environment, many have turned to the moral values and spiritual ways of their forebears with renewed vigour. At the same time, the ethnic diversity of these immigrant groups means that Theravada, Mahayana, and Vajrayana Buddhist congregations can all be found in Canada in a variety of lineages, teachings, ritual forms, and meditative practices. Indeed, such sectarian distinctions likely make Buddhist schools appeal to a more diverse range of Canadians.

If, in their efforts to adapt to life in Canada, Jodo-shinshu Buddhists have tended to emulate the ways of non-Buddhist religious organizations to some degree, other Buddhist groups have adopted different approaches. Formed in 1973, the Canadian Buddhist Vihara Society established Canada's first Theravadin temple in Scarborough in 1978. Bolstered by immigration from Burma, India, and Sri Lanka, the Toronto Mahavihara moved to a more rural site in Scarborough, on the edge of the peaceful Rouge River valley. Partly funded by the Sri Lankan government, the new quarters serve as residence for three monks, with Ahangama Rathanasiri Mahathera (born 1950) presiding as abbot. Capturing the legacy of Theravadin Buddhism associated with the ancient Singhalese kingdom of Anuradhapura, Toronto Mahavihara stresses the importance of *vipassana*, with weekly meditation classes and regular meditation retreats. The temple houses a shrine room and a library for the study of the *Abhidharma*, and the monks also offer counselling, run a children's Sunday school, publish Buddhist literature, and give public lectures on Buddhism at local academic and religious institutions. At full and new moons (**poya**), especially during the celebrations of the Buddha's birth, enlightenment, and *parinirvana* in May, lay devotees gather at Toronto Mahavihara to add to the store of good *karma* by meditating and adhering for a day to the stricter monastic codes of moral precepts. Elsewhere in Canada, the Sri Lankan community provides strong support for Theravadin groups like the Buddhist Vihara Society in Surrey, British Columbia, the Alberta Buddhist Vihara Association in Edmonton, the Sri Lankan Buddhist Society of Calgary, the West End Buddhist Centre in Mississauga, the Hilda Jayewardenaramaya Vihara in Ottawa, the First

Theravadin abbot Ajahn Sona shares insights about Buddhist teaching (*dharma*) with "Bruce,"
a carpenter and lay meditator, at Birken Forest Monastery, Kamloops, British Columbia.
PHOTO BY AJAHN SONA. REPRINTED BY PERMISSION. © AJAHN SONA/BIRKEN FOREST MONASTERY.

Sri Lankan Buddhist Temple in Montreal, and the Buddhist Society of
Newfoundland and Labrador in St. John's.

Other ethnic immigrant groups have developed Theravadin congregations in various parts of Canada, too. Perhaps not surprisingly, newcomers
from regions with historical links to France naturally gravitate to Quebec.
Cambodian and Laotian Theravadin Buddhist congregations have found
homes in the province, including the Ottawa-Hull Cambodian Buddhist
Association, Ste-Julienne's Centre communautaire et culturel boud-
dhiste Laotien, and Montreal's Pagode Khmere du Canada. In 1997, the
monk Aggasami (Khanh Hy) founded the Centre de méditation Agga
Pannarama, the first Vietnamese Theravada temple in Montreal. South-
east Asian Theravadin congregations form part of the religious landscape
of Canada's anglophone cities, too. In Toronto, for example, you will find
the Burma Buddhist Association of Ontario's Mahadhammika Buddhist
Vihara; the Vietnamese Linh-Son Buddhist Association; the Cambodian
Khmer Buddhist Temple of Ontario; and the Lao Buddhists of Toronto.
Whether located in francophone or anglophone Canada, however, these
ethnic Theravadin congregations rarely conduct services in English or
French alone, preferring the vernacular or some mixture of the vernacular with English or French.

Theravadin Buddhism has also inspired occidental Canadians to
form congregations, most notably in the monastic forest traditions of
Sri Lankan, Thai, and Myanmarese Buddhism. Located near Kamloops,

British Columbia, and associated with the Theravada Buddhist Community of Vancouver, Birken Forest Buddhist Monastery exemplifies this trend. Ajahn Sona (born 1954), who was raised in British Columbia, serves as abbot of the monastery and as spiritual guide to the community—a tradition that follows the lineage of Ajahn Chah (1918–92), an austere monk who spent many years wandering the rainforests of Thailand in meditation. In 1975, Ajahn Chah founded Wat Pah Nanachat ("International Forest Monastery"), the first monastery in Thailand to be run by and for English-speaking monks, and in 2003, Ajahn Sona, who trained in part at Wat Pah Nanachat, presided over the first *upasampada* ceremonies that were held by Canadians, in Canada, for Canadian-born Theravadin Buddhist ordinands. Birken Forest Buddhist Monastery hosts various kinds of meditation retreats and welcomes visitors who are interested in chanting, in discussions about *Dharma,* and in learning about the forest traditions. It enjoys ties with the Arrow River Forest Hermitage, a monastery and meditation centre nestled in a peaceful woodland setting 50 miles south-west of Thunder Bay, Ontario, with links to the Theravada Buddhist Community of Toronto. Founded in 1975 by Kema Ananda, formerly Eric James Bell (died 1996), Arrow River is now run by his disciple, Ajahn Punnadhammo. Born Michael Dominskyj in Toronto in 1955, Ajahn Punnadhammo was ordained in 1990 at Wat Pah Nanachat, where he studied until he assumed the position of resident *bhiksu* at Arrow River in 1995.

Other Canadian monasteries identify with other Theravadin lineages. The Manamaya Theravada Buddhist Monastery in Surrey, British Columbia, for example, represents the Myanmarese revival movement inspired by Mahasi Sayadaw (1904–82), whose disciple, Sayadaw U Pandita, trained U Pannobatha, the Surrey monastery's resident *bhiksu* since 1991. Regardless of lineage, however, monks at Canadian Theravadin monasteries follow traditional ascetic routines, which in many ways run counter to the typical lifestyle in modern Western societies like Canada. The guidelines of the *Vinaya* counsel monks against storing food overnight or handling money, for example. Western forest monasteries therefore invite laypeople to serve as monastic stewards who stay for an agreed period of several months, coupling such chores as grocery shopping, cooking for the monks, and general maintenance with lessons in *vipassana* and *Dharma.* Sometimes, studying the Pali canon under such conditions appeals to those interested in the notion of the "original" or "fundamental" teachings of the Buddha, but this group of intellectuals remains small in number. In any event, monks and laypeople alike believe that they bring great benefit to Canada by increasing the country's store of good merit.

Arguably, it is *vipassana* meditation that really appeals to occidental Canadians, and it is debatable whether or not this appeal always represents a full interest in Buddhist religion. Widely taught on university campuses as well as in hospitals and prisons, the "*vipassana* movement" or "insight meditation movement" arose as an American form of Theravadin practice, independently of the traditional religious context of Buddhism. The movement's founders, Joseph Goldstein (born 1940), Jack Kornfield (born 1945), and Sharon Salzberg (born 1952), were inspired by ancient Theravadin traditions and studied Buddhist teachings in South-east Asia. But the *vipassana* movement has often tended to be more secular in spirit, translating traditional rituals and symbols into Western psychological theory and therapeutic methods, and tolerating closer relationships between masters and disciples. Goldstein and Kornfield have published several books on *vipassana*, notably their co-authored *Seeking the Heart of Wisdom: The Path of Insight Meditation* (1987). The movement has spawned a network of over 200 retreats and affiliated groups in the United States, as well as a periodical, *Inquiring Mind*, that was launched in 1984.

Introduced into Canada from the United States, the *vipassana* movement enjoys a wide following, with meditation groups in major cities and many smaller communities. The Vipassana B[ritish] C[olumbia] network, for example, includes several teachers trained at Kornfield's Spirit Rock Meditation Center in California, and Goldstein and Salzberg's Barre Center for Buddhist Studies in Massachusetts. Based in Vancouver, with sitting groups throughout British Columbia, Vipassana BC offers residential and non-residential meditation classes and retreats of various lengths, focusing on a range of issues from sexual identity to human mortality, with many emphasizing so-called mindfulness-based stress reduction. At its most superficial, Western *vipassana* practice does not aim at achieving the Theravadin notion of enlightenment, offering instead remedial techniques to cope with pain, illness, and the emotional stress and anxiety of daily life in modern Western society—much in the way that yoga, which was originally a major system of orthodox Hindu philosophy, has become a form of physical exercise that is widely taught in fitness clubs, clinics, and commercial videos. Over the years, however, the movement's awareness of the fuller meaning of *vipassana* has deepened. Instead of advocating the personal benefits that flow from following ethical precepts (*sila*), teachers try to awaken students to the logic defining Buddhist compassion in

terms of the interconnectedness of all things; the cycle of dependent origination characterizes our relations with ourselves, with other people, and
with the environment.

Since the 1980s, the *vipassana* movement has flourished as one of the
two fastest-growing Buddhist movements in North America; the other
is Soka Gakkai International (SGI). This movement developed out of
Japanese Nichiren Buddhism. In 1930, Tsunesaburo Makiguchi (1871–
1944) founded the Soka Kyoiku Gakkai, or Value Creation Society, to
reform Japanese education, and then to promote Nichiren's Buddhist
teachings starting in the 1940s. Under the leadership of Josei Toda
(1900–58), the movement grew as Japanese tried to come to grips with
the aftermath of their defeat in World War II. In the early 1950s, Japanese
wives of American servicemen brought Soka Gakkai to the United States,
where the organization's third leader, Daisaku Ikeda (born 1928), began
an ambitious missionary campaign—first among Japanese Americans,
then among non-Japanese, aggressively proselytizing in a practice known
as *shakubuku,* or "break and subdue." This highly successful method
transformed the movement. The proportion of ethnic Japanese members dropped from almost 100 per cent to just over 30 per cent between
1960 and 1970. At the same time, Soka Gakkai began to mature as an
organization, replacing *shakubuku* with a less confrontational recruiting
style known as *shoju,* or "gradual leading." In 1975, Ikeda founded SGI
to cement the movement's worldwide membership and to further promote its ideas. Today, the organization claims over 12 million members
in more than 190 countries. While *vipassana* Buddhist groups function
as more or less independent associations in loose affiliation, SGI mirrors
Jodo-shinshu, operating as a structured organization somewhat like the
Roman Catholic or mainline Protestant churches. It funds proselytizing and scholarly publishing; an educational network centred on Soka
University in Aliso Viejo, California; and numerous cultural institutions,
including the Tokyo Fuji Art Museum.

Ikeda visited Toronto in 1960, and the first Canadian branch of SGI
was established in 1976. The promotion of peace, culture, and education
is central to SGI's activities. During the 1980s and 1990s, the Canadian
branch participated in SGI's Peace Movement, joining centres around
the world in monthly prayer services for peace. In 1986, major Canadian
universities in Montreal and Toronto cooperated with SGI Canada to
mount the touring exhibition, "Nuclear Arms: Threat to Our World,"
and in 1993, a second exhibition, "Toward a Century of Humanity: An

Overview of Human Rights in Today's World." In terms of personal faith, chanting, rather than meditation, lies at the heart of Soka Gakkai practice, especially the *Lotus sutra* and prayers for world peace. Unlike other Buddhists, though, Soka Gakkai sees chanting as more than just a means to spiritual development, claiming that its power to bring about personal happiness includes material benefits. Today, SGI Canada runs centres in Vancouver, Calgary, Edmonton, Winnipeg, Toronto, Ottawa, Montreal, and Quebec. Canadian members based at these centres practise *kosen-rufu*, a term from the *Lotus sutra*, which translates literally as "to declare and spread widely." Joining their colleagues around the world in the effort to realize SGI's vision of global peace, SGI Canada publishes selections from *The Writings of Nichiren Daishonin* and *SGI Canada News* online, as well as a booklet introducing Nichiren Buddhism, and the magazines *New Century* and *Ere Nouvelle* in hard copy. These three periodicals contain news of local SGI Canada activities, submissions from members, and study materials for discussion groups, which generally meet in members' homes. As with the *vipassana* movement, SGI Canada comprises mainly educated, middle-class, non-Asian men and women, with women assuming an increasing number of leadership roles.

Zen is another form of Japanese Buddhism that is popular in Canada, the country's first Zen centre having opened in Montreal as early as 1968. If, in their different ways, Jodo-shinshu and SGI have acclimatized to the new environment by imitating certain characteristics of Western institutional life, Zen Buddhists have domesticated the tradition by shedding overly ritualistic or ethnically obscure elements. Both major Japanese Zen schools, Soto and Rinzai, enjoy adherents in Canada; however, some associations, like the Montreal Zen Center and its affiliates in Quebec City, Rimouski, Granby, and Kingston, Ontario, blend the former's belief in gradual enlightenment with the latter's preference for the sort of sudden insight that the *koan* makes possible. Both schools practise *zazen*, that is, "seated meditation," and some Canadian teachers encourage secular disciplines, from calligraphy to martial arts, as ways of achieving enlightenment. Many Canadian Zen centres follow patterns of organization and practice developed in the United States, where Japanese masters have authorized occidental *roshis*, or "old teachers," to head Western Zen groups and to guide Western students. The Zen Centre of Vancouver, founded in 1970, exemplifies this trend. The Centre's abbot, Eshin John Gregory, studied at the temple of Rinzai-ji in Los Angeles under Joshu Sasaki Roshi (born 1907), who himself trained at Myoshin-ji, one of the most respected Rinzai temples in Japan. By contrast, Ottawa's White Wind Zen Community, founded in 1985, identifies with the lineage of Dogen. Embodying a more direct link between Canada and Japan, White Wind is led by Anzan Hoshin, who trained at Hakukaze-ji, a small Zen monastery near Hamilton, Ontario, established by Yasuda Joshu Dainen Hakukaze (1895–1979), a Zen master who left Japan to protest his superior's refusal to accept women as Zen teachers. Chinese Chan, Vietnam Thien, and Korean Seon centres may also be found in Canada; there are at least ten in the Toronto area alone. But whatever their lineage, most Zen groups offer seven-day, two-day, all-night, and occasional meditation sittings, as well as talks and workshops on different aspects of *Dharma*. Like other Buddhist associations, they publish religious materials and celebrate the birth, enlightenment, and *parinirvana* of the Buddha. Some Zen temples also arrange Buddhist weddings and memorials.

Since the 1980s, Chinese Buddhism has also come to play a significant role upon the Canadian religious stage. By 2002, Chinese immigrants numbered over one million, and Chinese adherents represent more than half of Canada's Buddhists today. Wealthier groups have built temples and monasteries in the style of traditional *pagodas*, most notably the International Buddhist Society's magnificent complex, the first phase of which opened in Richmond, British Columbia, in 1984. The premises include manicured gardens with fish ponds and fountains in the form of leaping carp, statues of the Buddha, stone carvings of lions and dragons, incense burners, and huge bells. Inside, worship halls and memorial rooms are adorned with golden Buddhas and colourful *Bodhisattvas*, altars, images and other ritual objects, banners proclaiming passages of scripture, silk paintings, ceramic murals, and intricately carved wooden furnishings. Offerings of fruit and flowers are placed before the Buddha, while the smell of incense and the music of drums, bells, and chants complete the synaesthetic experience of worship. Other associations have transformed existing buildings by adding traditional architectural elements, such as the red entrance gates into the forecourt of the Cham Shan Temple in Thornhill, Ontario, or the red-tiled portico fronting the Fo Guang Shan temple in Mississauga, Ontario. As well as providing shelter for monks and nuns, these larger facilities also house meditation rooms and auditoriums for public lectures and social functions. By contrast, smaller groups might simply adapt rented premises to their purposes. Founded in 1990, for example, the Montreal Chinese Buddhist Society occupies four rooms on the third floor of a building owned by *La Société des Francs-Maçon Chinois* in the

This marble Buddha Amitabha sits at the entrance to Cham Shan Temple in Thornhill, Ontario, a Chinese Mahayana house of worship and monastery that serves as the headquarters for the Buddhist Association of Canada. PHOTO BY CANDACE IRON. REPRINTED BY PERMISSION. © CANDACE IRON.

city's Chinatown. The largest room contains three large, golden figures at one end: to the left, Amida Buddha, who presides over the Pure Land of the West; in the centre, Shakyamuni, who represents Siddhartha Gautama in perfect Buddha form; and on the right, Bhaisajya, the healing Buddha who reigns over the Pure Lapis Lazuli Paradise of the East. Whether lavish or unassuming, however, Chinese Buddhist temples invariably include kitchens and dining areas for preparing and eating vegetarian meals, at once a sign of Chinese community spirit and of Buddhist compassion for other living creatures.

While earlier generations maintained ritual and doctrinal distinctions between traditional Buddhist schools like Tiantai, Huayan, Chan, and Pure Land, Chinese Buddhists in today's Canada rarely do so. This innovation is partly because the community hails not only from mainland China, but also from Taiwan, Hong Kong, and elsewhere. Most Chinese Buddhists do not practise meditation to seek enlightenment; instead, they identify with one form or another of Pure Land devotion. Founded in 1975, Cham Shan Temple, which serves as headquarters for the Buddhist Association of Canada, prepared an English translation of Pure Land liturgy to serve the needs of both English- and Chinese-speaking Buddhists as the tradition puts down roots in North America. Published in 1983, this liturgy typifies orders of service used in temples across Canada; it includes morning and evening devotions, chanting the names of Buddhas and *Bodhisattvas,* and reciting Buddhist scriptures, particularly the Pure

Land *sutra* and the *Heart Sutra*. By calling upon Amida Buddha and the *Bodhisattva,* Avalokitesvara—especially in his female form, Guanyin—Chinese Buddhists hope to accumulate merit to ensure an auspicious future and, upon death, a better rebirth or even rebirth into the Pure Land. Copying Buddhist scriptures in brush calligraphy and printing them for dissemination earns merit, too; as a result, free copies of popular Pure Land *sutras* are usually available to the wider public. Merit may also be gained by restoring freedom to animals specially captured for this ritual purpose; by building temples and giving alms to monks and nuns; and by performing charity work. A "merit box" for donations can be found in every temple, and on Sundays, larger associations offer a free vegetarian lunch buffet, since becoming a vegetarian also earns merit—as the plethora of vegetarian Chinese restaurants across Canada can testify.

Many Chinese Buddhist groups begin as Canadian branches of Asian organizations. For example, Fo Guang Shan temples in Montreal, Ottawa, Mississauga, and Richmond, British Columbia, are affiliated with the Buddha's Light International Association, Taiwan's largest Buddhist association. Occasionally, however, Chinese Buddhist congregations develop from associations with no active Asian links. Vancouver's Gold Buddha Monastery, for instance, originated with the Dharma Realm Buddhist Association (DRBA). DRBA was founded by Hsuan Hua (1918–95), a disciple of Hsu Yun (1840–1959), whose extraordinary prowess as a modern master of Chan Buddhism earned him the status of a *Bodhisattva* in Pure Land devotions. In 1970, in San Francisco, California, Hsuan Hua opened Gold Mountain Monastery, DRBA's first institute. Now headquartered in Burlingame, California, DRBA set up Gold Buddha Monastery in 1984, later adding retreat facilities in Golden, British Columbia. In 1987, the organization also established the Avatamsaka Monastery in Calgary. DRBA advocates a non-sectarian approach to Mahayana traditions. Drawing upon practices and teachings from all the main Chinese Buddhist schools, the monks and nuns at Gold Buddha engage in a full range of Mahayana activities, including morning, noon, and evening services every day, as well as weekly sessions for meditation, the recitation of scriptures, the chanting of *mantras*, and discussions of *Dharma*. The temple caters free vegetarian meals on weekends and important Buddhist holidays, and oversees the ritual release of animals on the last Sunday of every month. Every spring, Gold Buddha holds a festival to celebrate youth, and another every fall to honour the elderly. The temple also sponsors Sunday school and youth programs, as well as classes for studying Chinese languages, classical Buddhist texts, music, folk dancing, martial arts, and calligraphy. Meanwhile, DRBA's smaller Avatamsaka Monastery is developing ambitious plans to expand its programs along similar lines.

Often, Chinese Buddhists in Canada enjoy close relationships with Vietnamese Pure Land Buddhists. Vietnamese Buddha and *Bodhisattva* statues are similar to Chinese figures, and Chinese protector deities may frequently be found in Vietnamese Buddhist temples. At the same time, Vietnamese Buddhism has developed its own contemporary leadership. In Canada, Thich Thien Nghi (born 1933) has attracted a wide following. He founded Montreal's Pagode Tam Bao and Toronto's Chùa Hoa Nghiem in the 1980s, and then established the Union of Vietnamese Buddhist Churches in Canada, a national Vietnamese Buddhist association with other branches in Victoria, Nanaimo, Vancouver, Regina, Saskatoon, Winnipeg, and London. The Tam Bao temple's Dai Tòng Lâm ("Great Pine Forest") monastery, in Harrington, Quebec, epitomizes Thich Thien Nghi's ministry. Inaugurated in 1991, the retreat houses the Institute of Buddhist Teachings, and its extensive gardens feature several magnificent statues, including a bronze female *Bodhisattva,* seven metres high on a base in the form of a lotus flower with 49 petals; and a figure of Buddha the Enlightened standing at the foot of a silver birch with seven trunks towering 30 metres into the air. Generally, Quebec's French language and culture provide more familiar surroundings for many Vietnamese newcomers than the rest of Canada, and the Dai Tòng Lâm monastery is only one of many Buddhist institutions scattered across the province. As well as Pagode Tam Bao, Montreal's Vietnamese temples alone include To Dinh Tu Quang, Pagode Quan Am, and Pagode Thuyên Tôn. Some Vietnamese groups are also affiliated with French Buddhist organizations. In Montreal, for example, Thien Vien Linh Son's Centre de Méditation Sommet du Vautour looks for leadership to the Congrégation bouddhique mondiale Linh Son in Joinville-le-Pont, France.

Perhaps the most influential Vietnamese Buddhist leader in Canada is Thich Nhat Hanh (born 1926), who heads the celebrated Plum Village Buddhist *Sangha* in Meyrac, located in France's Dordogne region. Ordained in 1949 as a Thien (Zen) master in the Rinzai tradition at the Tu Hieu temple near Hue, Vietnam, in 1964 he founded the Unified Buddhist Church of Vietnam and the School of Youth for Social Service, whose members worked to rebuild health and educational facilities in rural areas devastated during the Vietnam War. An outspoken peace activist, Thich

Nhat Hanh was declared *persona non grata* by both the communist and the republican sides. He was exiled from Vietnam in 1966, and was nominated for the Nobel Peace Prize by Martin Luther King Jr. (1929–68) in 1967. After being granted asylum in France, Thich Nhat Hanh founded the Unified Buddhist Church in 1969. The small Buddhist community of Sweet Potatoes, named for a staple food of Vietnamese peasants, followed in 1975, and that was followed in turn by Plum Village in 1982, which now serves as headquarters for Thich Nhat Hanh's Order of Interbeing.

A community of monks, nuns, and lay practitioners, the Order of Interbeing promotes Engaged Buddhism. Using "mindfulness training," this modernizing blend of Mahayana meditation and Western psychology suggests Zen approaches to contemporary life, from issues of social injustice, environmental degradation, and sexual misconduct, to the proper use of electronic devices like computers, cellphones, and video games. In the 1990s, the movement's particular appeal to non-Asians encouraged Thich Nhat Hanh to open Maple Forest Monastery and Green Mountain Dharma Center, both located within Vermont in the United States, and in 2000, Deer Park Monastery in Escondido, California. Based in Berkeley, California, the Order's Parallax Press publishes Thich Nhat Hanh's writings as well as a journal, *The Mindfulness Bell*. In Canada, most Engaged Buddhism affiliates are located in the more populous areas of British Columbia, Ontario, and Quebec, though you will find a Yukon Mindfulness Centre in Whitehorse. Some congregations, like the Pagode Bô-Dê in Beauport, Quebec, maintain dedicated permanent premises; other groups, like the Mindfulness Meditation Centre in Pointe-Claire, Quebec, meet in private homes, or in rented halls, like Toronto's Mindfulness Practice West End, who gather weekly in the Fellowship Room of Emmanuel Howard Park United Church. Community activities include Zen training sessions of various lengths and intensities, walking meditations, the study of Buddhist scriptures, and various social and cultural events. Directly or indirectly, Thich Nhat Hanh maintains links with his affiliates. He visits groups to lead retreats, and his writings provide inspiration to their members. Ottawa's Pine Gate meditation hall, for example, is named for Thich Nhat Hanh's tale about an ambitious warrior who leaves home through the pine gate to fight demons in the world. After many years, he returns but cannot open the gate. Purer in spirit, a younger brother lets him in. The parable teaches that often the fiercest demons dwell in the heart, and that the *Sangha* is our refuge from them, too.

RECENT TRENDS IN BUDDHIST COMMUNITIES

When writing of Buddhism in North America, many scholars have dis-tinguished ethnic Asian immigrant communities from Euro American Buddhists. This contrast helps us to understand how migrating Asians brought Buddhism to North America, as well as tensions between tradi-tional Buddhist ideas and practices and the modernizing efforts of some converts. On the other hand, recent studies have shown that this distinction only really applies to the first generation of North American Buddhists, since the children of Asian immigrants were born and raised in North America, and the children of non-Asian converts were raised as Buddhists. The picture is especially complex in Canada, where official multicultur-alism fosters social and cultural variety. As well, some scholars like to differentiate between refugee and immigrant Buddhists. Often suffering from physical and psychological trauma, refugees face greater difficulties in recovering their cultural and religious identities, while immigrants are frequently wealthier and able to maintain closer connections with their countries of origin. The fact that many Canadian Buddhist organizations started in the United States before establishing themselves in Canada has further complicated things. In this section, we will focus on two young Canadian Buddhist organizations that ring changes on such complexities. Associated at first with a tiny group of Asian refugees, Canada's Tibetan Buddhist community now appeals to large numbers of Chinese Canadian adherents, while Toronto's Zen Buddhist Temple headquarters a Korean Canadian Buddhist organization with a strong non-Asian following. For all their differences, these small ethnic Buddhist groups have thrived by attracting adherents from unexpected quarters, both within Canada and beyond the country's borders.

Given the Dalai Lama's status as the spiritual and political leader of Tibet, Buddhism symbolizes many aspects of personal and collec-tive identity for Canada's small Tibetan refugee community. Founded in 1979, Ontario's Lindsay Tibetan Community—now known as Tibet's Independence Movement, Lindsay Chapter—was among the first groups to raise funds for refugees and to publicly protest against the Chinese occupation of Tibet. Every year in Toronto, Ottawa, and Vancouver, exiled Tibetans and non-Asian sympathizers affiliated with the Canada Tibet Committee demonstrate for the freedom of Tibet on Tibetan National Day, 10 March. Tibetans in Canada also meet regularly to recite prescribed prayers for Tibet, its people, and their leader, and they usually maintain

Buddhist shrines in their homes. On these shrines, an image of Buddha Shakyamuni symbolizes enlightened body; a short passage of scripture symbolizes enlightened speech; and a small *chorten* or *stupa* symbolizes enlightened mind. These objects also represent the Three Jewels of refuge, and sometimes adherents surround them with images of personal deities, known as *yidams*, and other celestial beings, known as *dakinis*. Chosen for their synaesthetic appeal, offerings to these blessed figures include flowers, candles or butter lamps, and incense, as well as tea and a part of every meal. Transforming selfish tendencies into feelings of generosity, such offerings accumulate merit. At the same time, however, Tibetan immigrants rarely engage in intensive meditative practices or attend lectures by Tibetan *lamas*. Ironically, these aspects of Vajrayana Buddhism appeal more to non-Asian Canadians, even if this appeal sometimes originates in the sentimentalized *shangri-la* image of Tibet often portrayed in Western fiction and Hollywood movies.

Meditation centres, *Dharma* courses, and retreat facilities representing all four Tibetan Buddhist monastic orders may be found across Canada. In Alberta, for example, you will find Edmonton's Gaden Samten Ling Tibetan Buddhist Society, established in 1986 by Geshe Ngawang Kaldan (1930–98), who, like the Dalai Lama, trained in the Gelug lineage of Vajrayana Buddhism. Alberta also holds Calgary's Marpa Gompa Meditation Society, a branch of Dechen, an international Tibetan Buddhist association based in the United Kingdom and founded by Karma Thinley Rinpoche (born 1931), a master of the Kagyu and Sakya traditions. Gampo Abbey, in Pleasant Bay, Cape Breton, Nova Scotia, is perhaps Canada's best-known Tibetan Buddhist site. The first Tibetan monastery for Westerners, the abbey was founded in 1984 by the Tibetan-born monk Chögyam Trungpa Rinpoche (1939–87). It was established as the headquarters for Shambhala International, a North American Buddhist organization originally based in Boulder, Colorado, and now led by Sakyong Mipham Rinpoche (born 1962), eldest son of Chögyam Trungpa Rinpoche. Believed to be the ninth incarnation of Sherap Gyaltsen, a fifteenth-century abbot of the historic Thrangu monastery, the Tibetan-born monk Khenchen Thrangu Rinpoche (born 1933) presides as Gampo's abbot; and the *bhiksuni* Pema Chödrön (born 1936), once known as Deirdre Blomfield-Brown, serves as Gampo's resident teacher of Kagyu and Nyingma meditative traditions. On 26 August 2001, Nova Scotia's first *stupa* was consecrated at the abbey; dedicated to world peace, it contains relics of Chögyam Trungpa Rinpoche. Gampo is affiliated with Shambhala centres and branches of the Vajradhatu Buddhist Church of Canada located across the country, while other Shambhala centres may be found in the United States, Europe, South America, Asia, and New Zealand. Wishing to attract Tibetans and non-Tibetans alike, Shambhala centres also offer such traditional ethnic disciplines as archery, visual arts, flower arranging, and tea ceremonies.

Like Shambhala International, the Vajrayana Buddhism Association (VBA) originated outside of Canada, and then moved to Canada before expanding internationally. Significantly, however, the VBA's origins lie in Hong Kong. Well-educated in traditional Chinese arts and letters, the association's spiritual leader, Tam Shek-wing (born 1935), hails from a long line of distinguished *literati* and public officials. In 1962, before Mao Zedong (1893–1976) launched the Cultural Revolution in China (1966–76), Tam Shek-wing settled in Hong Kong where he gained prominence writing for newspapers on Chinese painting and calligraphy, politics, literature, astrology, and Buddhism. At the same time, he became a disciple of Dudjom Rinpoche (1904–88), the supreme head of the Nyingma order of Vajrayana Buddhism. In 1972, after many years of study, Tam Shek-wing received from Dudjom Rinpoche the title *vajracarya*, which denotes mastery of the theory and practice of Buddhist meditation. Dudjom Rinpoche also bestowed upon his disciple the *Dharma* name Dorje Jidral, as well as the Nyingma "Seminal Heart" (*snying thig*) teachings of the Great Perfection (*rdzogs chen*). In 1993, after a seven-year retreat in Hawaii, Tam Shek-wing returned to Hong Kong to found the VBA. Soon afterwards, Hong Kong's *Ming Pao* newspapers, which are published in Toronto and Vancouver, arranged for him to travel to Toronto to lecture on Buddhism and to lead introductory classes in seated meditation. Recalling Dudjom Rinpoche's hope that Nyingma teachings would spread to North America, Tam Shek-wing moved to Toronto in 1994 to establish a branch of the VBA. This branch now serves as headquarters for VBA affiliates in Hong Kong, Hawaii, Vancouver, and San Francisco.

Tam Shek-wing's Vajrayana Buddhist mission has taken several forms. Most importantly, the translation and publication of the key writings of Tibetan masters into Chinese is exposing Canada's Chinese community to authentic Vajrayana Buddhist teachings. The VBA's Chinese publications include the *Reading Guides to Buddhist Scriptures*, a 26-volume scholarly study of a selection of important Buddhist *sutras* and *sastras* aimed at university and college students, and Tam Shek-wing has organized a panel of scholars and translators to produce a *Nyingmapa Series* in 16 volumes. He himself has translated the *Natural Liberation Teachings on the*

Six Bardos into Chinese, and the VBA has provided funds for New York's Tibetan Buddhist Resource Center to scan rare Bhutanese Nyingma teachings on different forms of meditation. Another project, launched jointly with Beijing University, involves comparative studies of Chinese and Tibetan translations of the entire *Ratnakuta sutra*. This corpus of ancient texts contains the *Prajnaparamita sutra* and the longer *Amitabha sutra*, which in turn form the basis of Nagarjuna's Madhyamaka philosophy and the Mahayana doctrine of the Pure Land. Scholars from China, Japan, the United States, and Germany are making use of recent research on the late nineteenth- and early twentieth-century archaeological discoveries made at Dunhuang Library Cave and other sites along the ancient Silk Road through the Taklamakan and Gobi deserts. These discoveries include thousands of Buddhist manuscripts in Tibetan, Chinese, and other languages, as well as innumerable religious artifacts; and the research sheds light on the similarities and differences between Tibetan Vajrayana and Chinese Mahayana teachings and their relationship to Buddhist ritual life.

Through his work, Tam Shek-wing emphasizes the importance of meditative practices as well as doctrinal learning. The VBA's centre in Scarborough, Ontario, offers introductory workshops and regular classes in visualization meditation, usually in the evenings and on weekends, since most disciples work on weekdays. Tam Shek-wing divides classes into small groups, so that students may enjoy the master's personal attention. Groups engage in preliminary meditative practices, known as Vajrasattva purification, which is designed to help students rid themselves of obstacles to enlightenment posed by accumulated negative *karma*. To help them express remorse, make confessions, and compensate for bad actions, students chant prescribed *mantras* as they seek the support of Vajrasattva, the supreme *Bodhisattva* of Vajrayana Buddhism. They visualize Vajrasattva above their heads, as it were, seated cross-legged upon a white lotus and a moon disc, smiling, serene, and dazzling white, like a snowy mountain illuminated by the rays of countless suns. In everyday terms, this technique helps to calm the mind, enhance understanding and conviction of Buddhist teachings, and improve stamina, concentration, and the quality of sleep. After years of such practices, senior disciples receive more intensive meditative and doctrinal training on Thursday and Saturday evenings, usually from 9:00 p.m. to 1:00 a.m.; and all disciples gather at the centre every Sunday from 2:30 p.m. to 6:30 p.m. to hear Tam Shek-wing's public teachings on *Dharma*. Topics range from the examination of early Buddhist *sutras* to explanations of *tantras* important to the Nyingma school, which Tam Shek-wing links to different kinds of meditation in terms of the Nyingma tradition's hermeneutics of "outer," "inner," and "innermost" or "secret" meanings. On occasion, disciples from the VBA's overseas branches join the Toronto community, and from time to time Tam Shek-wing visits affiliated associations and conducts sessions there. He always teaches in Cantonese, his mother language, although on some Friday evenings and Saturday mornings the VBA sponsors other scholars of Buddhism to lecture in English, for the benefit of non-Asians and children of Asian disciples who were raised in Canada.

Although the VBA is essentially a Chinese Canadian community, the training in Vajrayana Buddhism remains fundamentally Tibetan. The group maintains traditional *poya* day meditative practices on the 10th and 25th of the lunar month, and no hymns are sung and no coffee is offered after rituals. The VBA differs from other Chinese Buddhist communities in not offering incense and not permitting casual visitors to worship. Also, the centre does not open during the Chinese New Year for the public to request blessings. Instead, Tam Shek-wing goes on retreat during the New Year, either by himself or with disciples. On the other hand, the VBA has instituted some changes in the practice and teaching of Vajrayana Buddhism. Although *mantras* retain a phoneticized form of Tibetan, chants are not recited in Tibetan, since Tam Shek-wing uses meditation manuals translated into Chinese and English. The group does not sing traditional *vajra* songs, either. Associated with such celebrated figures as the Kagyu poet and master of tantric meditation Jetsun Milarepa (1052–1135), these traditional odes of enlightened experience reflect doctrinal teachings in deeply inspirational, intensely lyrical verses. Instead of using these verses, Tam Shek-wing's understanding of Chinese literature enables him to present his own meditative experience in rhymed, easily memorized, rhythmical verses—not sung, but recited in the style of Chinese poems as another aspect of the training of his disciples. In 2005, this intercultural dimension of Tam Shek-wing's ministry eventuated in the VBA teaming up with Toronto's Nalanda College of Buddhist Studies—which was founded in 2000 with seed money from Cham Shan Temple, and which publishes the *Canadian Journal of Buddhist Studies*—to offer a six-week meditation workshop as part of the wider Buddhist community's celebration of 100 years of Buddhism in Canada. In late 2007, the VBA launched an academic publication series in English, the *Monograph Series in Sino-Tibetan Buddhist Studies,* jointly published by the Renmin University of China and the China Tibetology Publishing House.

If the VBA is unusual for succeeding in cultivating Vajrayana Buddhism among Canada's Chinese community, Toronto's Zen Buddhist Temple is a rare instance of a Korean Buddhist association with a large number of non-Asian adherents. Samu Sunim (born 1941) founded the temple in 1979 and remains its spiritual head. The title "*sunim*" combines "*sung*," which transliterates the Sanskrit *Sangha* into Korean, with the honorific suffix, "*nim*." Koreans refer to all Buddhist monks and nuns as *sunim*. Born in Chinju City, South Korea, raised on a farm by his widowed mother, and orphaned at the age of ten amidst the terrors of the Korean War (1950–53), Samu Sunim spent more than three years in poverty on the streets of Pusan and Seoul. Drawn to the red-tiled roof of an old Buddhist temple in Seoul, Samu Sunim felt a surge of recognition and was determined to become a monk. Entering the Chogye order at Pomosa monastery in Pusan, he became a disciple of the Seon (Zen) masters Tongsan Sunim (1890–1965) and Seolbong Sunim (1890–1969). Reluctant to obey the South Korean government's dictate that monks join the armed forces, Samu Sunim fled first to Japan in 1966, then to New York in 1967, where he founded the Zen Lotus Society. In 1968, he moved to Canada, settling first in Montreal and then relocating to Toronto in 1971, where he went into solitary retreat for three years. In 1974, Samu Sunim revived the Zen Lotus Society and started to offer Seon meditation classes to the Korean Canadian community.

By his own admission, Samu Sunim disdained physical work when he first entered the Chogye order, believing that any involvement in the material world was a waste of time and effort that would be better spent in meditation and retreat. In 1977, however, he purchased an old flophouse in Parkdale, Toronto, and for three years supervised a small group of lay followers in extensive renovation work. Realizing that physical labour may be an important part of Seon training, Samu Sunim awakened to a fuller understanding of the meaning of compassionate service, and the master and his disciples toiled together to foster a community of living *Bodhisattvas* in deep devotion to *Dharma* practice. In 1979, the Zen Lotus Society moved into their new premises, and in 1981, pursuing a similar strategy of direct involvement, Samu Sunim opened a branch in Ann Arbor, Michigan, in the United States. Other centres were established in 1984 in Mexico City, as well as in 1992 in Chicago, Illinois, in the United States. Collectively, these centres are no longer known as the Zen Lotus Society but as the Buddhist Society for Compassionate Wisdom. The change of name mirrors the group's shift of focus from meditation in isolation to a form of engaged Seon Buddhism that balances reflective learning with a selfless commitment to the problems of everyday life.

Like the VBA, the Zen Buddhist Temple is active on many fronts in its efforts to further Samu Sunim's mission to cultivate a community of living *Bodhisattvas*. In 1981, as a way of publicizing this mission, the temple launched a newsletter, *Spring Wind*. In 2001, the newsletter was renamed *Spring Wind: Buddhist Cultural Forum*, a non-sectarian quarterly exploring the role of Buddhist culture and thought in the contemporary Western world. From 1984 to 1986, the temple organized annual exhibitions of Seon painting and calligraphy to promote Buddhist culture and to raise funds for the construction of future temples. In 1986, Samu Sunim founded the Buddhist Institute of Canada, which continues to engage scholars from the University of Toronto and York University; and in 1989, shortly after the Dalai Lama received the Nobel Peace Prize, the Institute held an inter-religious service and a seminar on non-violent social action in his honour. These activities culminated in the week-long "First Conference on Buddhism in Canada," convened in 1990, which brought together for the first time a majority of the clergy and lay leaders involved in establishing and maintaining over 100 Buddhist temples, churches, centres, and monasteries across Canada. Scholars from a number of Canadian universities also attended the conference, which aimed to promote greater understanding among different Buddhist traditions, to strengthen relations among Canada's various Buddhist communities, and to foster better understanding of Buddhism in the academic sphere.

In addition to these scholarly initiatives, the Zen Buddhist Temple oversees a wide range of services, including Buddhist teacher training, meditation classes, retreats, ritual ceremonies, and Buddhist holiday celebrations. The temple's Maitreya Buddhist Seminary provides novitiate training for those who wish to take monastic vows, as well as instruction for lay *Dharma* teachers. Samu Sunim prefers that prospective students be practising Buddhists who have attended meditation classes and committed themselves in formal ceremonies to the Three Jewels of refuge and the Five Precepts. The training programs involve three to five years of tutoring in Seon meditation practice and the study of Buddhist scriptures. Described as "Liberation Gates," courses of instruction cover all aspects of Buddhist doctrine and practice. Under ritual and ceremonial topics, for example, students learn how to lead different forms of chanting and meditation; how to use various ritual objects and musical instruments;

how to direct wedding, funeral, and memorial services; how to perform purification, repentance, and forgiveness ceremonies; and how to conduct a wide range of Buddhist community functions, from home visits to holiday celebrations. Students pay significant fees and are expected to write essays and take examinations. They must also follow a rigorous meditation schedule, both at home and at the temple, and keep a detailed journal of their practices. They are advised to set up an altar at home, with a small desk for studying the scriptures, and to make regular offerings to Buddha Shakyamuni. Once every lunar month, they are required to come to the temple for devotions on Friday evening, stay overnight, and spend Saturday in *Dharma* study. Samu Sunim insists that students not attending the temple meetings must email or fax him their journals and conduct meetings by telephone. Because his disciples are mostly non-Asians, Samu Sunim teaches entirely in English.

Lastly, the Zen Buddhist Temple also serves the wider public in a number of ways. Public meditations are held from 9:30 a.m. to 11:00 a.m. and from 4:00 p.m. to 5:30 p.m. on Sunday, and the temple offers introductory meditation courses, Tibetan breathing classes, and Seon retreats for beginners. Samu Sunim also presides over weddings, funerals, and memorial services. Celebrations for the birthday of the Buddha include ceremonies to bless children in honour of the baby Siddhartha Gautama. These celebrations close with a Lotus Lantern Lighting and Chanting Service, when adherents renew their commitments to the *Dharma* with prayers written on slips of paper and attached to lanterns. Participants may dedicate these prayers to themselves, family members, the sick and the disadvantaged, those suffering hardship or languishing in hatred or in jail, or even to pets and the dead. Other public celebrations include festivals honouring the Buddha's enlightenment and *parinirvana* as well as the Buddhist day of the dead, known as *ullambana*. Meaning "the agony of hanging upside down," *ullambana* symbolizes the utter helplessness of the dead, which may be relieved with special prayers from an ancient *sutra* originating in sixth-century China. Such public services, Samu Sunim argues, indicate that Buddhist engagement in the world need not mean simply imitating the sort of aid programs that Christian churches run. While larger, wealthier Christian organizations provide more material sustenance to people in need, Buddhist groups may teach Westerners that meditation and prayer serve as antidotes to the moral contaminants of greediness, hatred, and ignorance—partly by the spiritual work of monks and nuns, whose "high Buddhism" entails pursuing enlightenment in isolation from the world, and partly by the engagement of living *Bodhisattvas*, whose "folk Buddhism" embodies Buddhist compassion in its selfless service to the world. Samu Sunim encourages his disciples to take Buddhism out of the more intellectual sphere of the monastery and into the marketplace, to counterbalance the stress and agitation of workaday life in North America with the peace and tranquility that comes from meditative practice.

AFTERWORD

Several factors have contributed to the growth of Buddhism in Canada. To begin with, this story shares a good deal with the story of Buddhism in the United States. Since the 1960s and 1970s, many Americans have harboured an increasing fascination with different aspects of the tradition. In recent years, this interest has manifested itself in various areas of popular culture. The writings of figures like Daisetz Teitaro Suzuki (1870–1966), Alan Watts (1915–73), and the Dalai Lama fill shelves in bookshops devoted to "Spirituality," while the self-immolation of Buddhist monks protesting the Vietnam War, the plight of Tibet, and the house arrest of Aung San Suu Kyi (born 1945)—a devout, Myanmarese (Burmese) Buddhist, non-violent political activist—have at different times become Western *causes célèbres.* Hollywood studios have funded the production of pictures like Martin Scorcese's *Kundun* (1997) and Jean-Jacques Annaud's *Seven Years in Tibet* (1997), as well as the distribution of such widely admired art-house films as Ang Lee's *Crouching Tiger, Hidden Dragon* (2000) and Kim Ki-Duk's *Spring, Summer, Fall, Winter ... and Spring* (2003). And the media never seem to lack for stories about the ways in which Buddhism has transformed the lives of celebrities like Tina Turner (born 1939), Harrison Ford (born 1942), and Richard Gere (born 1949). In turn, this American phenomenon has spread northwards to become partly responsible for increased curiosity about Buddhism in Canada, especially among non-Asian Canadians.

Second, the academic field of Buddhist Studies has benefited from changes in Canadian educational policy. Before the 1960s, the field of Buddhist Studies was considered peripheral to the Canadian scholarly enterprise. The study of religion was more or less confined to divinity schools and theological colleges, where it mostly involved the study of Christianity. During the 1960s, however, the federal and provincial governments in Canada provided generous funding to develop tertiary education in response to demands from the "baby boomer" generation of the years following World War II. These demands coincided with the loosening of restrictions against Asian immigration to Canada from countries with significant Buddhist populations, as well as the development of the social and cultural agenda of multiculturalism. In this more relaxed and expansive atmosphere, the study of Buddhism entered the standard curriculum of most undergraduate programs, either through East Asian Studies or through Religious Studies. Since then, a growing number of prominent scholars at Canadian universities have developed valuable programs in Buddhist Studies at both the undergraduate and graduate levels. In 2006, the University of British Columbia launched North America's first program in Buddhism and Contemporary Society, thanks to a 4-million-dollar gift from the Tung Lin Kok Yuen Canada Foundation. The foundation donated another 4 million dollars to the University of Toronto Scarborough in the same year in order to foster Buddhist studies.

Finally, the sort of interaction we see in Canada among Buddhist groups of different ethnic and cultural backgrounds is virtually unknown elsewhere. Japanese, Chinese, Vietnamese, Cambodian, Laotian, Myanmarese (Burmese), Thai, Korean, Sinhalese, and other East Asian, South Asian, and South-east Asian Buddhists for the most part mix freely and easily with increasing numbers of non-Asian adherents—and they do so in temples, centres, and other venues claiming allegiance to various Theravadin, Mahayanin, and Vajrayanin lineages and espousing diverse forms of Buddhist teaching, ritual, and meditative practice. In this context, most Canadian Buddhists feel the freedom to seek out spiritual fulfillment from a comfortable style of religious observance, rather than pressure to recover ethnic security or cultural identity. That said, attempts to present Buddhism as a non-partisan religion with diverse forms of thought and practice have not completely succeeded. In 1980, for example, the Buddhist Federation of Toronto was founded to represent 16 Buddhist groups. This umbrella organization gathered more than 1,500 adherents to celebrate the Buddha's birth, enlightenment, and *parinirvana*, but in later years failed to overcome differences of opinion among participating members, particularly over issues of what constitutes authentic Buddhist practice.

Inevitably, the social, cultural, psychological, and spiritual conditions of life in Canada require transformations in such things as the format of services, the choice of language used in *Dharma* instruction, and even the conduct of rituals, ceremonies, festivals, and meditation practices. At the same time, however, Canadian Buddhists take care to see that the processes of cultural translation do not distort or undermine such essential Buddhist teachings as the Three Jewels of refuge and the Five Precepts. It is too soon to talk about "Canadian Buddhism," or even "North American Buddhism," in the same way that we talk about Chinese Buddhism or Japanese Buddhism or Tibetan Buddhism as distinct forms of the tradition's heritage. Buddhist ideas and practices have not yet integrated seamlessly into Canadian culture; for example, Zen practitioners still use English translations of age-old Asian *koans*, rather than contemporary Canadian *koans*. But Canada's multicultural policies do provide a framework for distinctive developments in Buddhism's steady evolution into a truly global religious tradition.

KEY TERMS

Abhidharma	"Higher teaching," and hence a body of literature that classifies and explains the *Sutras* in a systematic fashion.
Anatman	"Not-self," and hence the denial of the belief that all phenomena, including oneself, have an independent, transcendent identity.
Arhat	"Worthy one," and hence a sage or saint in Theravada Buddhism.
Bodhicitta	"Awakening mind," and hence the aspiration to perfect the wisdom and compassion of the *Bodhisattva* in Mahayana Buddhism.
Bodhisattva	"Wisdom being," and hence, in Mahayana Buddhism, figures who have achieved the perfect union of wisdom and compassion.
Dharma	First and foremost, the teachings of the Buddha, and hence essential truths implied in that teaching, including the nature of ultimate reality, the path leading to it, and the various qualities associated with it.
Dukkha	"Suffering," which is characteristic of all forms of life within the cycle of *samsara* as a result of craving, ignorance, and attachment.
Five Precepts	Contained in the last three injunctions of the Noble Eightfold Path, the moral code that applies to all Buddhists: refraining from killing, theft, sexual misconduct, lying, and the taking of intoxicants.

Four Noble Truths   The essential teachings of the Buddha's first sermon: life means suffering; suffering originates in attachment; the cessation of suffering is attainable; and following the Noble Eightfold Path leads to the cessation of suffering.

Jatakas   Stories of the Buddha's exploits in previous lives, used to delight and teach.

Karma   "Action," and hence the impersonal moral law determining one's place in the cycle of *samsara*.

Koan   Paradoxical notions, like the sound of one hand clapping, used in Zen Buddhism to push consciousness beyond everyday ways of thinking.

Madhyamaka   "The Middle Way," the school of Mahayana Buddhist thought traditionally associated with Nagarjuna and his disciple, Aryadeva.

Mahayana   "Great Vehicle," and hence the later, first-century CE Buddhist movement that spread from India to China, Korea, Japan, and elsewhere.

Mandala   "Circle," and hence geometric designs believed by Tibetan Buddhists to embody secret powers associated with Buddhahood.

Mantra   "Sacred word," and hence chants or incantations believed by Buddhists to embody secret powers associated with Buddhahood.

Mudra   Symbolic hand gestures believed by Tibetan Buddhists to embody secret powers associated with Buddhahood.

Nirvana   The ultimate goal of the Buddhist path, in which attainment of perfect knowledge frees the individual from *samsara*.

Noble Eightfold Path   The moral and spiritual path leading to the cessation of suffering: right understanding; right thought; right effort; right mindfulness; right concentration; right speech; right action; right livelihood.

Pali   An ancient literary language of India in which the Theravadin canon, or *Tripitaka*, is written.

Poya   The sacred days of the full and new moons, when the most important Buddhist rituals, festivals, and other religious activities are performed.

Samsara   "Passing through," and hence the continuing cycle of birth, death, and rebirth.

Sangha	The Buddhist community in two senses: more narrowly, the orders of Buddhist monks and nuns; and more widely, all followers of Buddhism, including both the laity and the ordained.
Sunya	"Empty," and hence the notion that all existing things possess no inherent, substantial reality.
Sutra	A discourse attributed to the Buddha.
Tathagatagarbha	"Essence of the Tathagata," and hence the innate potential of all sentient beings for attaining Buddhahood.
Tathata	"Suchness or thusness," and hence the focus in Yogacara Buddhist thought on the ultimate object of consciousness, "reality-as-such."
Theravada	"The way of the elders," and hence the longest-surviving form of Buddhist thought and practice.
Three Jewels	The Buddha, the *Dharma*, and the *Sangha*.
Tripitaka	"Three Baskets," and hence the collection of early Buddhist writings comprising the Pali canon of *Sutras, Vinaya*, and *Abhidharma*.
Vaisakha	The second month of the Hindu calendar, associated with Theravada full-moon festivals in early May, which celebrate the Buddha's birth, enlightenment, and *parinirvana*.
Vajrayana	"Thunderbolt or diamond vehicle," referring to Mahayana tantric practices and Tibetan Buddhism in particular.
Vinaya	The rules of monastic discipline for monks and nuns.
Yogacara	"The practice of yoga," the school of Mahayana Buddhist thought associated with Maitreyanatha and later clarified by Asanga and Vasubandhu.

KEY DATES

566–486 BCE	Traditionally, the life of Shakyamuni Siddhartha Gautama.
486 BCE	First Buddhist Council at Rajagaha.
383 BCE	Second Buddhist Council at Vaisali.
272–231 BCE	Reign of the emperor Ashoka, who convened the Third Buddhist Council at Pataliputra (250 BCE) to establish the Pali canon and to send Buddhist missionaries to Sri Lanka.
200s BCE	Rise of the Mahayana movement.

68 CE	The first Buddhist missionaries arrive in China from India.
200s	Nagarjuna founds the Madhyamaka school.
300s	Maitreyanatha founds the Yogacara school.
372	Introduction of Buddhism to Korea from China.
538	Introduction of Buddhism to Japan from Korea.
550s	Introduction of Buddhism to Vietnam from China.
750s	Introduction of Buddhism to Tibet from India.
1193	Muslim Mughals virtually wipe out Buddhism in India.
1700s	British, French, and Dutch powers occupy South and Southeast Asia.
1905	Japanese immigrants build Canada's first Buddhist temple in Vancouver.
1909	The provincial government of British Columbia grants official recognition to Buddhism.
1930	The first Buddhist temple outside British Columbia is built in Raymond, Alberta.
1955	The Buddhist Churches of Canada organization is formed by Jodo-shinshu in Toronto.
1967	A new federal Immigration Act paves the way for large numbers of newcomers from East, South, and South-east Asia.
1968	Canada's first Zen centre opens in Montreal.
1976	Soka Gakkai International opens its first Canadian branch in Toronto.
1978	Canada's first Theravadin temple opens in Scarborough, Ontario.
1979	Ontario's Lindsay Tibetan Community is founded (now known as Tibet's Independence Movement, Lindsay Chapter).
1984	The International Buddhist Society opens a traditional Chinese Buddhist complex in Richmond, British Columbia.
1989	The Buddhist Council of Canada is formed.
1990	Canada's first national conference on Buddhism takes place in Toronto.
2000	The Nalanda College of Buddhist Studies is founded in Toronto.

KEY READINGS

Batchelor, Stephen. *The Awakening of the West: The Encounter of Buddhism and Western Culture*. Berkeley: Parallax Press, 1994.

Fields, Rick. *How the Swans Came to the Lake: A Narrative History of Buddhism in America*. Boulder, CO: Shambhala, 1981.

Gross, Rita M. *Buddhism after Patriarchy: A Feminist History, Analysis, and Reconstruction of Buddhism*. Albany: State University of New York Press, 1993.

Harding, John S., Victor Sogen Hori, and Alexander Soucy, eds. *Wild Geese: Buddhism in Canada*. Montreal: McGill-Queen's University Press, 2010.

Harvey, Peter. *An Introduction to Buddhist Ethics*. Cambridge: Cambridge University Press, 2000.

Matthews, Bruce. *Buddhism in Canada*. New York: Routledge, 2006.

McLellan, Janet. *Many Petals of the Lotus: Five Asian Buddhist Communities in Toronto*. Toronto: University of Toronto Press, 1999.

Prebish, Charles S., and Martin Baumann, eds. *Westward Dharma: Buddhism beyond Asia*. Berkeley: University of California Press, 2002.

Queen, Christopher S., ed. *Engaged Buddhism in the West*. Boston: Wisdom Publications, 2000.

Rahula, Walpola Sri. *What the Buddha Taught*. New York: Grove Press, 1959.

Robinson, Richard H., and Willard L. Johnson. *The Buddhist Religion: A Historical Introduction*. Belmont: Wadsworth, 1997.

Seager, Richard Hughes. *Buddhism in America*. New York: Columbia University Press, 1999.

KEY WEB SITES

http://www.sacred-texts.com/bud/index.htm [Buddhist scriptures]

http://www.ciolek.com/WWWVL-Buddhism.html [Buddhist resources online]

http://online.sfsu.edu/~rone/Buddhism/BuddhistDict/BDIntro.htm [Buddhism A to Z]

http://www.buddhanet.net/ [Buddha Dharma Education Association's database]

http://blogs.dickinson.edu/buddhistethics/ [*Journal of Buddhist Ethics*]

http://www.bcc.ca/ [Buddhist temples in Canada]

http://www.sumeru-books.com/ [An internet guide to Buddhism in Canada]

KEY QUESTIONS FOR CRITICAL REFLECTION

1. In what ways does Mahayana Buddhism differ from earlier Buddhist traditions?
2. What elements are common to the various Buddhist traditions?
3. How can there be rebirth without a soul?
4. How does the teaching of *karma* differ from the notion of fatality?
5. In what ways should Buddhist traditions change, and in what ways should they not, in order to make Buddhism a strong and lively religious tradition in Canada?

EIGHT

Sikhs

PASHAURA SINGH, UNIVERSITY OF CALIFORNIA, RIVERSIDE

P unjabi immigrant workers brought Sikhism to Canada from India at the beginning of the twentieth century. Resolute, resilient, and resourceful, these pioneers played a significant role in the development of the province of British Columbia, quickly establishing a reputation as dependable and diligent employees at logging camps and lumber mills, tobacco plantations and farms. Members of the community were soon prosperous enough to start their own businesses, and by the 1920s these new settlers had established a network of Sikh places of worship, known as *gurdwaras*—a term that literally means "doors of the Guru" and invokes Guru Nanak (1469–1539), the founder of the tradition. Brought together under the umbrella of the Khalsa Diwan Society, the *gurdwaras* added a new dimension to Canada's religious landscape and provided an organizational base for collective action on several issues facing the community. By the 1960s, Sikh professionals were beginning to arrive in Canada in response to the liberalization of Canadian immigration policy. From the 1970s to the 1990s, Sikh communities grew rapidly in most urban centres throughout Canada. The 2001 census recorded the Sikh population of Canada as 278,415, though some scholars argue that the current estimate of the total number of Sikhs may be closer to the half-million mark. This chapter tells the story of Sikhs in Canada. In what follows, I approach the study of the Sikh faith from an insider's perspective, at the same time maintaining scholarly objectivity in the analysis of documents, historical events, and other aspects of the tradition. A practising Sikh, I am at once an academic researcher and a faithful member of the Sikh community (**Panth**).[1]

THE HERITAGE

The Sikh religion began in the region of the Punjab in north-west India some 500 years ago. Sikhs make up less than two per cent (1.8 per cent) of India's one billion people, and theirs is the youngest of the subcontinent's independent religious traditions. Sikh contributions to the realms of politics and economics are especially notable. Worldwide, Sikhs total around 25 million, which is a little higher than the global figure for the Jewish people. Roughly 20 million Sikhs call the state of Punjab home, while the rest have settled in other parts of India and elsewhere. Successive waves of emigration have established substantial communities of Sikhs in Southeast Asia, Australia, New Zealand, East Africa, the United Kingdom, the United States, and Canada.

The origins of Sikh piety and culture lie in the unique spiritual revelations experienced by the tradition's founder, Guru Nanak. Announcing his autonomy from contemporary expressions of religious thought and practice, Guru Nanak was determined to awaken a resolute sense of independence in those who stepped forward as his disciples, or *Sikhs*, which literally means "learners." At the same time, he absorbed influences from the religious environment of his day, in particular the thoughts and ideals of medieval North Indian poet-saints known as Sants, like Kabir (*ca.* 1398–1448), with whom he shared such traits as iconoclasm and mystical

---

1   Some of the material in this chapter is adapted from works I have previously published, notably "Sikh Traditions," in *World Religions: Eastern Traditions*, ed. Willard G. Oxtoby and Roy C. Amore, 3rd ed. (Don Mills, ON: Oxford University Press, 2010), 106–43; "Sikhism," in *Worldmark Encyclopedia of Religious Practices*, vol. 1: *Religions and Denominations*, ed. Thomas Riggs (Detroit: Gale, 2006), http://www.omnilogos.com/2011/07/21/sikhism; "Sikhism in Punjab and Beyond," in *The World's Religions: Continuities and Transformations*, ed. Peter Clarke and Peter Beyer (New York: Routledge, 2009), 638–51; "Scripture as Guru in the Sikh Tradition," *Religion Compass* 2, no. 4 (2008): 659–73; "Sikh Dharam," in *Religions of South Asia: An Introduction*, ed. Sushil Mittal and Gene Thursby (London: Routledge, 2006), 130–48; with Norman Gerald Barrier, *The Transmission of the Sikh Heritage in the Diaspora* (Delhi: Manohar, 1996); "Sikh Traditions in Ontario," *Polyphony: The Bulletin of the Multicultural History Society of Ontario*, 12 (1 January & 1 December 1990): 130–36.

contemplation. But it was essentially his own ideals that propelled Guru Nanak to lay the foundation of a new religious tradition, especially the special sense of mission he felt compared with other religious figures in North India at the time. This sense of mission is associated with a particular set of events in 1499, when Guru Nanak experienced a mystical call to awaken people to the presence of God. He felt that this experience of enlightenment compelled him to proclaim his message for the ultimate benefit of contemporary society, especially his convictions about socially responsible living.

Guru Nanak was born on 15 April 1469 to a professional, upper-caste Hindu family in the village of Rai-Bhoi-Di-Talwandi—known today as Nankana Sahib—in Pakistan's province of Punjab. Much of the material concerning his life comes from hagiographical birth narratives (*janam-sakhis*). His life may be divided into three distinct phases: his early contemplative years; his enlightenment experience, accompanied by extensive travels; and a climactic period that resulted in the establishment of the first Sikh community in West Punjab. In one of his own hymns, Guru Nanak proclaimed:

> I was a minstrel out of work; the Lord assigned me the task of singing the Divine Word. He summoned me to his Court and bestowed on me the robe of honor for singing his praises. On me he bestowed the Divine Nectar (*amrit*) in a cup, the nectar of his true and holy Name.[2]

Profoundly autobiographical, these words unambiguously testify to Guru Nanak's own understanding of his divine mission, and they indicate the beginning of his ministry. At the time of the hymn's writing, he was 30 years old, had been married to Mata Sulakhni (1473–1545) for more than a decade, and was the father of two young sons, Sri Chand (1494–1592) and Lakhmi Das (1497–1555). Still, he initiated a series of pilgrimages to both Hindu and Muslim sacred sites in India and elsewhere. During his travels he met with the leading proponents of various religious views and tested the authenticity of his own ideas in debate and dialogue with them.

Guru Nanak ended his travels in the 1520s, bought property on the right bank of the Ravi River in West Punjab, and founded the village of Kartarpur, which means "Creator's Abode." He remained in Kartarpur

---

2 M1, *Var Majh* 27, AG, 150. The reference here means that the passage quoted comes from the 27th stanza of the ballad (*Var*) in the musical measure *Majh*, by Guru Nanak (M1), on page 150 of the *Adi Granth* (AG).

for the rest of his life, serving as the spiritual guide to a newly emerging religious community. Stories from this time reveal that his charismatic personality and persuasive teaching won over numerous disciples, who were convinced that they were hearing a fresh message of liberation in their master's uniquely insightful words and beautifully crafted hymns. These disciples took to using Guru Nanak's hymns in devotional singing (*kirtan*) as part of worship services, and thus the families who first gathered around Guru Nanak in the early decades of the sixteenth century at Kartarpur would form the nucleus of a religious congregation. This rudimentary organization became known as the *Nanak-panth* (the "Path of Nanak"), and this term specifically identifies the community constituted by those early Sikhs who followed Guru Nanak's path to liberation. In his role as what the German sociologist Max Weber (1864–1920) called an "ethical prophet"—that is, a charismatic messenger who understands his teaching as an expression of the will of God—Guru Nanak advocated important departures from the day's dominant understandings of moral and social life and proposed a new, rational model of normative behaviour founded on divine authority.[3] It was his immediate inner realization of the reality of God, and not his relationship with the inherited traditions of the time, that informed the power and veracity of his spiritual message. This direct access to the divine constituted the ultimate strength of his message and furnished him with a firm conviction, upon the basis of which he could more fully comprehend, interpret, and adjudicate the various elements of received religious traditions. Guru Nanak's writings reveal that he always conceived of his work as divinely commissioned, and in terms of this conviction he required obedience from his followers as an ethical duty.

Guru Nanak prescribed a daily routine for the Kartarpur community, along with agricultural activity for sustenance. He defined the ideal person as a Gurmukh ("one oriented towards the Guru") who practised the threefold discipline of "the divine Name, charity, and purity" (***namdan-ishnan***). Indeed, these three features—***nam***, or the believer's relation with the divine as represented in the divine name; *dan,* or the believer's relation with society; and *ishnan,* or the believer's relation with the self—provide a balanced approach for the development of the individual and the society. They capture the cognitive, the communal, and the personal

---

3   Max Weber, *Economy and Society: An Outline of Interpretive Sociology,* ed. Guenther Roth and Claus Wittich (1922; reprint, Berkeley: University of California Press, 1968), 447–50.

aspects of developing Sikh identity. For Guru Nanak, authentic spiritual life required that "one should live on what one has earned through hard work and that one should share with others the fruit of one's exertion."[4] In addition, he taught that the individual's pursuit of spiritual liberation involved cultivating the ethical virtues of service (*seva*), self-respect (*pati*), truthful living (*sach achar*), humility, mellifluence of tongue, and taking only your rightful share (*haq halal*). At Kartarpur, Guru Nanak combined disciplined spiritual devotion with the sort of worldly commitments demanded by everyday family responsibilities, thus exemplifying in his own life the moral and social principles that had come to intellectual fruition during his travels. His own devotional practices made their way into Sikh liturgy: in the early hours of the morning, devotees recite Guru Nanak's "Meditation" (*Japji*), while "That Door" (*So Dar*) and "Adoration" (*Arti*) are sung in the evening.

The spiritual message of Guru Nanak found various forms of institutional expression at Kartarpur. The most important forms are the sacred fellowship known as the *sangat*, which expresses the sense that devotees share membership in a common spiritual fraternity; the original form of the *gurdwara*, called the *dharamsala*, which literally means "holy refuge"; and the dining practice of the **langar**, in which people of all castes sit down in status-free lines (*pangat*) to enjoy a shared meal. By encouraging a mutual spirit of belonging and community, the institution of the *langar* in particular called into question a major characteristic of traditional Indian caste practice; and, in so doing, significantly helped to distinguish Sikh identity from other forms of Indian social and religious expression. Finally, Guru Nanak created the institution of the **guru**, a notion that expresses the idea of a teacher or enlightener who brings his followers from spiritual darkness to light. Often translated simply as "teacher," the *guru* became the central authority in Sikh community life. Before he passed away in 1539, Guru Nanak bestowed upon his disciple Lehna the new name Angad, meaning "my own limb." In so doing, he determined legitimate succession and founded a lineage that remained unbroken from the appointment of Guru Angad (1504–52) to the death of Guru Gobind Singh (1666–1708), the tenth and the last human *guru* of the Sikhs.

During the period of Guru Nanak's nine successors, three important events took place. First, in 1604, the fifth Guru, Arjan (1563–1606),

---

4   M1, AG, 1245.

sponsored the initial compilation of the canonical scripture: the **Adi granth**, which literally means "original book." As canonical scripture, this text provided an authoritative context within which the Sikh community could take shape. The second key event was Guru Arjan's execution by the Muslim Mughal authorities at Lahore in 1606, a tragedy that became a turning point in the history of the Sikh *Panth*. Following Arjan's martyrdom, much of the seventeenth century was marked by political and military conflict with the Mughals, culminating in the execution of the ninth Guru, Tegh Bahadur (1621–75), on 11 November 1675 in Delhi. Tegh Bahadur was put to death by the Mughal emperor Aurangzeb (1618–1707) for refusing to renounce his faith in favour of Islam. The third important event was the founding of the institution of the **Khalsa** by Guru Gobind Singh. Literally meaning "pure," the Khalsa is an order of loyal Sikhs bound by common identity and discipline, understood in terms of a code of conduct or *rahit-nama*, several of which were written by various Sikh scholars and theologians over the next two centuries. Guru Gobind Singh formed the nucleus of the new order of the Khalsa by initiating the "Cherished Five" (*panj piare*) on **Baisakhi** Day 1699, at Anandpur, in the state of Punjab, India. These five willing respondents to the Guru's call for loyalty came from different castes and regions of India. The Guru Gobind Singh conducted a formal ceremony of initiation, using a two-edged sword to stir sweetened water (*amrit*), and reciting five liturgical prayers to sanctify the ceremony. In turn, he asked the five volunteers to initiate him, after which he initiated many more men and women into the Khalsa order in the same way.

The creation of the Khalsa consummated the canonical period in the history of Sikhism. Visible symbols known as the **Five Ks** are mandatory for members of the Khalsa: uncut hair (*kes*); a comb for one's topknot (*kangha*); a short sword (*kirpan*); a wrist ring (*kara*); and breeches (*kachh*). Guru Gobind Singh also added a collection of the writings of his father, the martyred Guru Tegh Bahadur, to the original compilation of the *Adi granth*, and in so doing closed the canon of Sikh scripture. Tradition holds that before he passed away in 1708, Guru Gobind Singh brought an end to the succession of personal *gurus* and installed the *Adi granth* as the scriptural *guru*, giving it the new title of "Guru granth sahib." In this way, the *Adi granth* became an eternal source of divine guidance for Sikhs. Indeed, as a mark of respect for the scripture's revered status, Sikhs never open it without first ceremonially waving over it a whisk (**chauri**) made of yak hair or man-made fibre, fixed in metal, and attached to a wooden handle.

Along with uncut hair (*kes*) and breeches (*kachh*), a comb for a topknot (*kangha*), a wrist ring (*kara*), and a short sword (*kirpan*) are mandatory visible symbols of faith for members of the Khalsa.

The authority of the *guru* is therefore invested together in the scripture (Guru Granth) and in the corporate community of Sikhs (Guru Panth), epitomized by the Khalsa.

Sikh traditions went on to evolve in terms of four principal factors. The first factor has to do with a set of principles based on the religious and cultural innovations of Guru Nanak and his nine successors. Known as **miri-piri**, this ideology is at once political, military, and religious. It was the principal motivating factor in the evolution of the Sikh *Panth*, as expressed in the motto, "The Khalsa Shall Rule" (*Raj karega khalsa*). The second factor has to do with the rural base of Punjabi society. During the period of Guru Arjan, the founding of the villages of Tarn Taran, Sri Hargobindpur, and Kartarpur in the Punjabi countryside became occasions for large numbers of converts to the new faith from local Jat peasantry. Further, Guru Tegh Bahadur's influence in the rural areas of the Punjab attracted more Jats from the Malwa region, and most of these new believers became Khalsa during Guru Gobind Singh's period. It may have been the militant traditions of the Jats that brought the Sikh *Panth* increasingly into confrontation with the Muslim Mughals in a series of encounters that greatly influenced the later development of the Sikh movement. Third, dissidents within the Sikh community created

The Golden Temple in Amritsar, Punjab, India, is the most important Sikh house of worship.
PHOTO BY RAJINDER BANGA. http://picasaweb.google.com/rsbanga. REPRINTED BY PERMISSION.
© 2004, RAJINDER BANGA.

disharmonies within the movement—although, paradoxically, internal conflicts which at first worked against the evolution of Sikh tradition would later enrich the process. And fourth, uneasy relations between Sikhs and the Mughals and Afghans among whom they lived had important effects upon the development of the Sikh *Panth* in the period of Punjab history from the seventeenth to the eighteenth centuries.

The career of Ranjit Singh (1780–1839), the celebrated Sikh *maharaja*, or "great king," illustrates these third and fourth factors. During the eighteenth century, the Sikhs formed 12 hereditary militias called *misals*. Decades of rivalry between these militias threatened to destroy the Sikh community. In 1799, Ranjit Singh, who was also known as the "Lion of the Punjab," seized control of the Sukerchakkia *misal*, disbanded the rest, and established sovereign Sikh rule in the Punjab. His subsequent achievements included military victories against the Afghans and the gilding of the dome of the *Darbar Sahib*. Meaning "Divine Court," the *Darbar Sahib* is known today as the Golden Temple in Amritsar, the most important Sikh house of worship. But this golden age in Sikh history was short-lived. In 1849, ten years after Ranjit Singh's death, Great Britain annexed the Punjab. Protestant Christian missionaries followed, and Sikh traditions once again came under threat, this time from Western colonial and imperial influences. Several reform movements attempted to revive the faith, culminating in the founding of the "Society of Sikhs" (**Singh Sabha**) in Amritsar on 30 July 1873. Led by Baba Khem Singh Bedi (1832–1905), Kanvar Bikrama Singh (1835–87), and Sardar Thakur Singh Sandhanvalia

(1837–87), Singh Sabha embarked upon a comprehensive program of cultural and religious revival. Carefully avoiding open confrontation with Christian missionaries, the reformers gained the support of influential colonial administrators for literacy and educational projects, and published large numbers of books on Sikh history, sacred texts, and doctrine in the Punjabi language. The society succeeded not only in consolidating Sikh orthodoxy and orthopraxy, but also in bringing Sikhs who had converted to Christianity back into the community.

Founded in 1902 by élite Sikhs with a more politicized agenda, the Chief Khalsa Diwan institutionalized the religious and cultural reforms initiated by Singh Sabha. The organization advocated the education of Sikh men and women, and expanded Singh Sabha's publication program, translating literary and religious texts from other languages into Punjabi. It also instituted community welfare projects, opened orphanages, and founded schools and colleges. Initiated in 1907, the association's Sikh Educational Conference promoted Western-style education among Sikhs. To this day, the annual gathering rotates from town to town in the Punjab, and its well-attended meetings include discussions on Sikh education, politics, and religion, as well as competitions for singing *kirtans* and reciting Sikh poetry. In 1910, the Chief Khalsa Diwan also formed a committee to oversee the codifying of Sikh ritual and rules of conduct. Led by Bhai Kahn Singh Nabha (1861–1938), the committee consulted with branches of Singh Sabha and other Sikh societies, as well as with individual Sikh scholars and theologians. In March 1915, it published the *Gurmat Sanskar Bhag,* a code of conduct that forms the bridge between traditional *rahit-namas* and the current **Sikh Rahit Maryada**, published in 1950 by the Shiromani Gurdwara Prabandhak Committee (SGPC; "Chief Management Committee of Sikh Shrines"). Eventually, the Chief Khalsa Diwan's élitist ethos caused the association to lose influence to more populist organizations, especially the SGPC and the Shiromani Akali Dal (SAD; "Chief Army of the Followers of the Timeless One"), the main political party of the Sikhs. The SGPC came into being as the result of the Gurdwara Reform Movement (1920–25), which was started by the SAD. This movement began as a non-violent agitation demanding control of Sikh shrines, in opposition to British-supported "Custodians" (*Mahants*), who did not follow the Khalsa code of conduct. The Sikh Gurdwaras Act finally brought an end to the SAD campaign in 1925.

Let us now turn to Sikh doctrines and religious practices. The *Mul Mantar,* or "seed formula," concisely communicates the Sikh understanding of the nature of ultimate reality. Serving as a preamble to the *Guru granth sahib*, this text contains a series of fundamental theological assertions:

> There is One Supreme Being [*Ek Oankar*], the Eternal Reality, the Creator, without fear and devoid of enmity, immortal, never incarnated, self-existent, known by grace through the Guru. The Eternal One, from the beginning, through all time, present now, the Everlasting Reality.[5]

The numeral "1" (*Ek*) at the beginning of the original Punjabi text represents the unity of **Akal Purakh**—that is, the "one beyond time," or God—a concept that Guru Nanak interpreted in monotheistic terms. It affirms that God is one without a second, the source as well as the goal of all that exists. Paradoxically, he is both transcendent, "without attributes" (*nirguna*), and immanent, "with attributes" (*saguna*). Only in personal experience can he be truly known. Although Sikh tradition emphasizes *nirguna* discourse, which directs devotees to worship a non-incarnate, universal God, Sikh doctrine also teaches that *Akal Purakh* is in part embodied in the divine name (*nam*), as well as in the collective words (*bani*) and persons of the *gurus* and the saints. He is the source of love and grace, and the creation of the universe expresses this divine benevolence. In the *Guru granth sahib*, Guru Nanak asserts that the universe "comes into being by the divine order."[6] Invoking the traditional Indic association of creation with the five basic elements of air, water, ether, fire, and earth, he further affirms: "From the True One came air and from air came water; from water he created the three worlds and infused in every heart his own light."[7] As the creation of *Akal Purakh*, the physical universe is real, but subject to perpetual change; as creator of the physical universe, God lovingly sustains and watches over his creation. The physical universe offers humankind opportunities to perform their duties and to achieve union with *Akal Purakh*, while the actions we perform during our time on earth gain significance from the fact that God responds to the faithfulness of even the humblest devotee, for as Sikh scripture says, "all of us carry the fruits of our deeds."[8]

Indeed, the principles of *karma* ("actions") and *sansar* ("rebirth" or "transmigration") are basic to all religious traditions originating in India.

---

5   M1, AG, 1.
6   M1, AG, 2.
7   M1, AG, 19.
8   M1, AG, 4.

The idea of *karma* is popularly understood in classical Indian thought as the principle of cause and effect. A kind of moral law of gravity, this reality of cause and effect is logical and irresistible, even as traditional teachings about *karma* preserve the notion of free choice. Sikh doctrine, however, rethinks the idea of *karma* in a radical way. For the Sikh *gurus,* the law of *karma* is not irresistible. In Guru Nanak's theology, *karma* is subject to the higher principle of the "divine order" (*hukam*), an all-encompassing principle that embraces the sum total of all divinely instituted laws in the cosmos. The immutable divine order of *Akal Purakh* transcends the law of *karma,* which thus loses its traditional aura of impersonal inevitability, since it falls within the sphere of a loving God's absolute omnipotence and ultimate justice. In other words, Sikh doctrine asserts the primacy of divine grace over the law of *karma,* and suggests that divine grace may break the chain of adverse *karma.*

Guru Nanak uses several important terms to describe the nature of divine revelation in its fullness: *nam* ("divine name"), *shabad* ("divine word"), and *guru* ("divine teacher"). The *nam* reflects the way God manifests himself everywhere around us and within us. We fail to perceive the ubiquity of the divine presence because of our *haumai* or self-centredness. The Punjabi word *haumai* ("I, I") signifies the often irresistible urge to yield to personal gratification, which inevitably results in our separation from *Akal Purakh* on the one hand, and our continued subjection to the effects of *karma* within the cycle of rebirth (*samsara*) on the other. Sikh doctrine, however, teaches that *Akal Purakh* looks graciously upon the suffering of humankind; he reveals himself through the *guru* who utters the *shabad* ("divine word") that conveys abundant understanding of the *nam* ("divine Name") to those who are able to hear it. Sikhs believe that the *shabad* is God's actual utterance, and that those who hear it awaken to the reality of the divine name, which is immanent in all that lies around and within.

In the Sikh tradition, the institution of the *guru* also bears profound spiritual authority. The majority of South Asian religious traditions teach that the term *guru* indicates a human teacher who communicates divine knowledge and furnishes his disciples with a cognitive map for spiritual liberation. Sikh doctrine, however, has developed the meaning of the term *guru* in a number of ways over its existence. In the main, Sikh doctrine invokes the notion of *guru* in four contexts of spiritual authority: the doctrine of eternal *guru*; the doctrine of personal *guru*; the doctrine of Guru Granth; and the doctrine of Guru Panth. In the case of the doctrine of eternal *guru,* Guru Nanak uses the term *guru* in three essential ways: the *guru* is *Akal Purakh*; the *guru* is the voice of *Akal Purakh*; and the *guru* is the word—that is, the truth—of *Akal Purakh*. For Guru Nanak, to experience the eternal *guru* is to enjoy the guidance of God. In Sikh understanding, therefore, the *guru* is the voice of God, mystically uttered within the human heart, mind, and soul (*man*).

Second, the notion of the personal *guru* indicates the human vehicle by means of whom the voice of God becomes audible. Only when Nanak received the divine word and conveyed it to his disciples did he come to embody the eternal *guru*. Subsequently, the same spirit manifested itself in the unbroken line of nine succeeding *gurus*—beginning with Guru Angad, on whom Guru Nanak personally bestowed his authority; and ending with Guru Gobind Singh, who in turn imputed spiritual authority to the *Adi granth*. Sikh doctrine thus elaborates a theory of spiritual succession that not only asserts the unity of the office of the *guru*, but also denies any difference in authority between founder and successors: the ten personal *gurus* from Guru Nanak through Guru Gobind Singh all manifest one and the same light (*jot*), as a single flame lights a series of lamps.

Third, Sikhs habitually refer to the *Adi granth* as *Guru granth sahib*. The use of this honorific clearly attests to a confession of faith in the scripture as *guru*, which in turn indicates that for Sikhs, the *Guru granth sahib* enjoys the same moral status and spiritual authority as the ten personal *gurus*. In other words, Sikhs look to the *Guru granth sahib* as a living source of divine guidance within the Sikh *Panth*, and in actual practice the scripture functions as *guru* in matters of personal piety and serves to ground the corporate identity of the Sikh community. This brings us to the fourth and final sense in which Sikh doctrine invokes the notion of *guru*: the doctrine of Guru Panth. Sikhs normally employ the phrase Guru Panth in two senses: first, they speak of the *Panth* of the *guru*, by which they mean the Sikh community; and second, they speak of the *Panth* as the *guru*, by which they mean the doctrine of Guru Panth. This doctrine evolved from earlier notions about the mystical presence of the Guru in the congregation associated with the inauguration of the Khalsa in 1699, when Guru Gobind Singh ritually transferred his authority to the "Cherished Five" and in turn received initiation from their hands. For this reason, the élite corps of the Khalsa has invariably asserted the right to speak authoritatively on behalf of the whole Sikh *Panth,* although at times Sikhs who do not belong to the Khalsa interpret the doctrine of Guru Panth as imputing spiritual authority to a more broadly defined community. In practice, Sikh congregations prefer to achieve consensus through democratic means.

As we have seen, Sikhs associate the unregenerate life with the influence of *haumai* and believe that achieving a state of spiritual liberation means transcending this influence. Sikh doctrine speaks of *haumai* as the source of five evil impulses: lust (*kam*), anger (*krodh*), greed (*lobh*), attachment to worldly things (*moh*), and pride (*hankar*). Under the sway of *haumai,* individuals become "self-willed" (*manmukh*); enslaved to worldly pleasures, they waste their lives in wrongdoing and suffer the inevitable karmic effects, oblivious to the divine name. According to Sikh teaching, however, cultivating the interior discipline of **nam-simaran**, or "remembering the divine Name," helps the unregenerate to transcend their corrupt condition. A three-stage process, this strict regimen includes the repetition of a sacred word, usually *vahiguru*, meaning "praise to the eternal *guru*"; participation in public worship, especially singing hymns; and sophisticated meditation on the nature of *Akal Purakh*. The first and the third levels of *nam-simaran* are matters of private observance, while the second involves the repentant in congregational observances. In the last analysis, participants in the discipline of *nam-simaran* hope to achieve some sort of harmony with the divine order (*hukam*). Repentants gradually develop a sense of spiritual wonder (*vismad*), eventually achieving blissful equanimity (*sahaj*). In this ultimate condition, the spirit ascends to the "realm of truth" (*sach khand*), the fifth and final spiritual stage of *nam-simaran,* in which the soul finds mystical union with God.

Although personal effort is always subject to divine grace in Guru Nanak's theology, his view of life yields neither to fatalism nor to the passive acceptance of some predestined future. After all, it was he who proclaimed, "With your own hands carve out your own destiny."[9] Guru Nanak's thinking includes personal effort in the form of good actions, and his notion of "divine free choice" on the one hand, and his understanding of human freedom as the basis for a "life of activism" on the other, together reflect an ability to hold apparently antithetical positions in tension. Openly recognizing the need to maintain a dialectical tension between opposing tendencies, Guru Nanak rejects unforgiving theories of predestination and yet encourages devotees to understand the privilege of human freedom in the context of the divine will. This vision permits Sikhs opportunities to create their own destinies, a characteristic

---

9   M1, AG, 474.

stereotypically associated with Sikh ingenuity and enterprise through-out the world. Properly understood, Sikh teaching and tradition stress the dignity of everyday labour as an integral part of spiritual discipline. A triple commandment encapsulates this conviction: undertake honest labour (*kirat karani*) in order to earn a living; honour and adore the divine name (*nam japana*); and share the fruits of your labours with others, espe-cially the less fortunate (*vand chhakana*). In turn, this formula places a premium on the importance of meditative worship and the necessity of righteous living in the world.

In practical terms, the Sikh path towards spiritual liberation has come to mean abiding by a modern code of conduct. In 1926, Sikh scholars and theologians formed the Shiromani Gurdwara Prabandhak Committee (SGPC) to administer Sikh education and publication programs, and to oversee various Sikh historical sites in Punjab, which at that time included the states of Haryana and Himachal Pradesh. In 1931, the SGPC was charged with developing a standardized Sikh code of conduct for the Khalsa, and in 1945, consultation among more than 70 of the most respected Sikh scholars and theologians produced the current *Sikh Rahit Maryada*. Based on the *Guru granth sahib* and supplemented with teach-ings from revered Sikh leaders, this manual guides Sikhs in the moral, social, and religious aspects of everyday life. It enjoins Sikhs to cultivate a pure and pious inner spirituality (*bani*), symbolized by the adoption of the Five Ks as outwardly visible signs of virtuous conduct (*bana*). The *Sikh Rahit Maryada* forbids hair-cutting, adultery, the use of intoxicants, and the eating of *kutha* meat—that is, Muslim *halal* or Jewish *kosher* meat, obtained through the slow bleeding or religious sacrifice of animals. Upholding belief in one God, the *Guru granth sahib,* and the teachings and lifestyle examples of the ten Gurus, the *Sikh Rahit Maryada* encour-ages Sikhs to undergo Khalsa initiation, to attend divine services, and to mediate on the divine name. It calls upon Sikhs to earn a living hon-estly and truthfully; to share selflessly with the needy and less fortunate in order to further the well-being of all; to nurture such virtues as com-passion, honesty, generosity, patience, perseverance, and humility; and to avoid superstitions, idols, and images. Not punitive in intent or effect, the *Sikh Rahit Maryada* urges devotees to regulate their daily lives to the will of God, just as the discipline of *nam-simaran* is designed to attune Sikhs to the divine order (*hukam*). It calls for tolerance of those who stray or who are slow developers, suggesting that these **sahaj-dharis** ("gradual-ists"), who follow the teachings of Guru Granth Sahib without accepting the full discipline of the code of conduct, will slowly progress towards becoming the Khalsa. The only code of conduct now sanctioned by the *Akal Takht,* which is the highest seat of religious and temporal authority among Sikhs, the *Sikh Rahit Maryada* serves to unify the religious and social practices of Sikhism around the world. Distributed free of charge by the SGPC, the *Sikh Rahit Maryada* has been translated from Punjabi into Hindi and English, in acknowledgement of the needs of Sikhs living outside their historical homeland.

THE MAKING OF A CANADIAN SIKH COMMUNITY

In 1897, after parading in London for Queen Victoria's Golden Jubilee celebration, a Sikh regiment passed through British Columbia on their way home to India. Sikh immigration to Canada began within a few years. The history of Sikh immigration may be divided into two broad periods, each about half a century long and each further divisible into a briefer, turbulent phase and a longer, calm phase. In 1903, ten Sikh members of a Hong Kong military contingent, who a year earlier had travelled to London for the coronation of Edward VII, returned to establish themselves in British Columbia. They wrote optimistic letters about the opportunities for work and better pay to their friends and relatives in India, stimulating a chain of migration that pushed the Sikh population of British Columbia beyond 5,000 by 1908. With the establishment of the Khalsa Diwan Society in Vancouver in 1907, these pioneer Sikhs laid the foundations of organized community life. In 1908, the Khalsa Diwan Society opened the first *gurdwara* in North America at 1866 Second Avenue, West Vancouver. In the same year, however, the British Columbia government took certain discriminatory legislative measures that virtually eliminated further migration from the Indian subcontinent by the end of the decade. Indian immigrants were deprived of their right to vote—a right that ought to have been guaranteed by their status as British subjects, as with all other Canadians. In addition, the discriminatory measures required immigrants from India to bring an unrealistically high minimum personal capital, and demanded that prospective immigrants travel by "continuous journey" from their place of birth to their intended final destination. In fact, these measures became powerful weapons for Canadians who sought to defend their country from non-European immigrants. Described in such racist terms as "Asian peril" and "brown invasion," Punjabi immigrants were required to have $200 in their possession on arrival, while immigrants of European extraction needed only $25. In addition, the stipulation by British Columbia's provincial government that Sikhs come by continuous journey from India was impossible to meet, because steamship companies did not provide that service.

In 1914, Canadian hostility towards Punjabi Sikhs reached its high point with the notorious expulsion of the Japanese steamship *Komagata Maru* from the Vancouver harbour. Chartered and renamed *Guru Nanak Jahaj* by the wealthy Punjabi businessman Gurdit Singh, the steamship carried 376 would-be immigrants from India, of whom 351 were Sikhs. A direct challenge to Canada's discriminatory immigration laws, the *Komagata Maru / Guru Nanak Jahaj* arrived in Vancouver harbour on 23 May and was denied landing rights. Having collected money and supplies to help the ship's passengers once they landed in Vancouver, the Indian community in Canada came together to protest the situation. Their efforts were to no avail: the *Komagata Maru / Guru Nanak Jahaj* was forced to return to Calcutta two months later, on 23 July. Following these disappointments, the Sikh population in British Columbia declined to fewer than 2,000, as many Sikhs either migrated to the United States or returned home to India. There was very little new immigration until after the end of World War II, as those early Sikhs who remained in Canada struggled to bring their wives from India and to establish a small but enduring Canadian Sikh community. During that same time, the Khalsa Diwan Society would organize its meetings at the Vancouver *gurdwara* to fight the discriminatory policies of the Canadian government. Indeed, this Sikh house of worship served as a rallying point for all Indians to discuss their grievances and mutual problems. By 1920, more *gurdwaras* had been established in British Columbia at New Westminster, Victoria, Nanaimo, Paldi, Abbotsford, Fraser Mills, and Golden. As a premier institution, the Khalsa Diwan Society in Vancouver played a central role in holding together these *gurdwaras* and the Punjabi community in British Columbia.

After World War II, the Canadian government changed its policy of excluding and disenfranchising Asian immigrants, and in 1951, a new federal Immigration Act liberalized the laws to some extent by introducing a quota system for applicants from different parts of the world. For most of the 1950s, the majority of new immigrants from South Asia were Sikhs, generally relatives of earlier settlers. In addition, a small number of Sikh students and professionals arrived in Toronto from India, East Africa, and the United Kingdom. In 1967, Canada's centennial year, a federal

Immigration Act eliminated discrimination based on race, religion, and country of origin, and further relaxed the rules to favour highly skilled professionals under a new points system of qualification. Throughout the 1960s, about half of the new Indian immigrants were Punjabi Sikhs who landed at Montreal, Toronto, and Vancouver, the three main ports of entry into Canada. As the criteria for migration shifted to semi-skilled workers in the 1970s, Sikhs still accounted for nearly half of the immigrants from India as a result of chain-migration process. At this time, anti-Asian prejudice and hostility sprang up again due to economic slowdown and unemployment. Being among the most visible of "visible minorities," Sikhs became the primary target of racist abuse.

In the early 1980s, overt hostility to South-Asian immigrants abated, owing to the prominence of human rights on government agendas, and specifically to the Canadian federal government's policy of "multiculturalism." The policy was officially adopted in 1971 and was later enshrined in the Canadian Multiculturalism Act, which was passed into law on 21 July 1988. These new policies seemed to receive at least the tacit approval of the bulk of Canadian population. For Sikhs, however, the year 1984 became a historical watershed because of the protracted conflict between the government of India and the main Sikh political party, the Shiromani Akali Dal. This conflict revolved around the issue of increased autonomy for individual states in India. Long controlled by the Congress Party, the Indian federal government evidently sought to provoke disruption within the ranks of Shiromani Akali Dal by promoting the interests of a young, charismatic preacher, Jarnail Singh Bhindranwale (1947–84), who followed a fundamentalist approach to Sikh religion and Punjabi self-determination. He proved more radical than the moderate Shiromani Akali Dal leadership, and to instigate militancy, he and his followers occupied the building of the Akal Takhat ("Throne of the Timeless One") in the Golden Temple complex of Amritsar. This occupation led to Operation Blue Star, an assault on the sacred precincts conducted by the Indian army over two days, from 5–6 June 1984. Directly ordered by India's Prime Minister Indira Gandhi (1917–84), this attack resulted in the death of Bhindranwale along with many other Sikhs. In turn, Gandhi was assassinated on 31 October 1984 by her own Sikh bodyguards.

For several days, unchecked Hindu mobs in India's national capital, Delhi, and elsewhere throughout the country killed thousands of Sikhs. But tensions were not limited to the subcontinent; the assault on the Golden Temple outraged Sikhs around the globe. Canadian Sikhs saw this as an act of sacrilege, brutality, and contempt, a sign that the government of India was poised to destroy the Sikhs and their religious and cultural heritage. The events in Punjab created a worldwide identity crisis within the *Panth*. Sikhs were divided into liberal and conservative camps, the former wishing to pursue a path of religious and political reconciliation with non-Sikhs, both in India and among Indian diaspora communities around the world; and the latter adopting a harder line of religious militancy and Punjabi nationalism. No account of the activities of the Sikh community in Canada, or of the individual members of that community, can hope to be understood without some appreciation of the profound impact that these events had upon the *Panth*. There are indications that the Sikh extremists responsible for the bombing of Air India Flight 182 on 23 June 1985, killing 329 passengers, committed this infamous act as part of a continuing response to the attack on the Golden Temple just over a year earlier. To draw historical parallels is risky, but perhaps the impact upon Sikhs of the desecration of their most sacred religious site is somewhat analogous to the status in Jewish history of the destruction of the Temple of Solomon, carried out by troops under orders from the Babylonian King Nebuchadnezzar in 586 BCE. At any rate, the assault on the Golden Temple in 1984 remains a powerful factor in the lives of Sikhs everywhere, and plays a large role in determining the way Canadian Sikhs continue to identify with the cause of their fellow Sikhs in India.

More specifically, the great influx of new Sikh immigrants to Canada in the 1980s and 1990s took place as a result of the Indian army's assault on the Golden Temple in 1984 and the subsequent persecution of Sikhs in India. These tragic events provided many Sikhs with a potent incentive to seek new lives elsewhere, resulting in a spate of Sikh emigration from India. This phenomenon marks the beginning of the third phase of Sikh migration to Canada—and, perhaps not surprisingly, some of it was unconventional. In the early hours of the morning on Sunday, 12 July 1987, for example, the crew of a Chilean ship, *Amelie*, disembarked 173 men and one woman onto a rocky beach at Charlesville, Nova Scotia. Sometimes compared with the unfortunates aboard the *Komagata Maru / Guru Nanak Jahaj,* these illegal immigrants were taken into custody by the Canadian authorities. Most of the refugees were young Sikhs fleeing the Punjab to escape police brutality. The Maritime Sikh Society in Halifax took the case to court and succeeded in gaining the group's release on bail. Subsequent immigration hearings resulted in the migrants being granted refugee status in Canada. In the 1990s, however, Sikh militancy in the Punjab declined and Sikh politics shifted more in the direction of Indian constitutional democracy. Canadian Sikhs underwent a corresponding change in their overall approach to migration and settlement. They became more concerned with building up the economic, social, and political bases of the community in a conscious effort to provide secure futures for their children in Canada. With changing immigration patterns in the last decades of twentieth century, the Sikh population rose 89 per cent to 278,415. New *gurdwaras* have continued to proliferate, with increasing demands for Sikh missionaries (*parcharaks*) to visit from India and preach the religion of their forebears among Canadian Sikhs.

Personal piety is important to Canadian Sikhs. Ideally, the devout begin their daily routine by meditating upon the divine name. They conduct these observances during the *amritvela,* the "ambrosial hours"—that is, the last watch of the night, between three and six in the morning—immediately after rising and bathing. After meditating, pious Sikhs recite five liturgical prayers, which include the *Japji* of Guru Nanak. Usually, these early morning devotions conclude in the presence of the *Guru granth sahib.* In a ritual known as *vak laina,* or "taking God's word," the whole family gathers to seek the guidance of scripture. It is traditional that a passage from *Guru granth sahib* be selected at random. Male or female Sikhs may read aloud from the sacred text, but non-Sikhs may read only to themselves. Similarly, tradition stipulates that for the evening prayers pious Sikhs recite from a collection of hymns known as the *Sodar rahiras* ("Supplication at that Door"). Often, they sing these hymns before their evening meal. Finally, before retiring for the night, they recite passages from another text known as the *Kirtan sohila* ("Song of Praise"). Like the *Japji* of Guru Nanak, these two sets of daily devotions form part of the prologue of the *Guru granth sahib.*

In the Canadian environment, Khalsa Sikhs—men as well as women—faithfully observe the daily routine of morning and evening prayers. Many Sikhs are able to recite these prayers from memory because they learned them in their childhood in Punjab before immigrating to Canada. In a Canadian Sikh household, it would not be unusual to see a mother reciting Guru Nanak's *Japji* while preparing breakfast for the children, and a father doing so while getting ready for work. Sometimes, grandparents help the children by praying with them on weekends. Other Sikhs may just listen to these prayers from recorded tapes and CDs while driving to work. Canada's Sikh community faces challenges when it comes to maintaining these observances among the young, however. Without a working familiarity with Punjabi, the language of the *Guru granth sahib,* second- and third-generation Canadian Sikhs risk becoming theologically illiterate and losing touch with daily liturgical routines. The sacred language of scripture has helped to shape the consciousness of previous generations of Sikhs starting from their childhood, furnishing a cognitive framework for the way they perceive and understand the meaning, value, and purpose of life. It is quite likely that the *Guru granth sahib* no longer serves this key role in the lives of many young Canadian Sikhs. Increasing numbers of Sikhs in Canada may well come to experience their faith only in nominal ways, as little more than a point of reference for important life-cycle rituals like naming, marriage, initiation, and death.

Visits to the *gurdwara* sometimes serve to keep young Canadian Sikhs in touch with the traditions of their forebears, even if such visits are infrequent and as much for social as for religious reasons. As an institution, the *gurdwara* has played a pivotal role in changing the terms of reference for Canadian Sikh self-understanding. Migration tends to turn people who think of themselves in religious and nationalistic terms into people whom others think of in ethnic terms, and who therefore also begin to think of themselves in ethnic terms. This shift in self-perception entrenches ethnic identity in a situation of contrast with mainstream society, drawing attention to difference and engendering a sense of life on the margins of society as a minority immigrant group. Historically, Sikhs have always thought of themselves in more or less exclusively religious and nationalistic terms; in Canada, they are just as likely to add the notion of ethnicity to the mix of self-referents. The ethnic identity of Canadian Sikhs is by and large a distinctly Punjabi Sikh identity, although in more recent years significant numbers of Sikh immigrants have come to Canada from localities outside the Punjab, and even from places outside India; notably, East Africa, South Africa, South-east Asia, and the United Kingdom. The social and religious activities of the *gurdwara* serve as a bulwark against the assimilative pressures exerted by the apparently exotic ways of Western culture. Indeed, the *gurdwara* plays a central role in Sikh community life by making it more religiously and culturally homogenous. Sikh worship and all the key life-cycle rituals for members of the Sikh community take place at the *gurdwara.*

In Canada, Sikhs celebrate congregational worship in all *gurdwaras* on every Sunday—not because Sunday is a holy day, but because most Canadians do not work on Sundays, making it a day when Canadian Sikhs are free to worship. This practice is certainly different from the major historical *gurdwaras* in the Punjab, where worship takes place every day. During congregational worship, the main focus is upon the *Guru granth sahib*, which is installed with great ceremony every morning. Worship consists mainly of the singing of scriptural passages set to music, with the accompaniment of instruments. Amateur and professional Sikh musicians, known as *ragis,* lead the congregation in devotional singing. Indeed, the singing of hymns in a congregational setting lies at the heart of the Sikh devotional experience. Known as *kirtan,* this liturgical practice enables worshippers to attune themselves to the divine word, which has the power to transform and unify the consciousness of the practitioner. This singing of hymns also fosters a sense of harmony, which helps devout Sikhs to cope with the challenges and obstructions that modern technological society puts in the way of their spiritual life.

At an appropriate time during the service, either an appointed *granthi* ("reader") of the *gurdwara* or a traditional Sikh scholar (*giani*) delivers an exposition of the scriptures known as *katha* ("homily"). At the conclusion of the service, all who are present join together in reciting the Sikh prayer. Known as *Ardas* ("petition"), this prayer invokes the grace of *Akal Purakh* and recalls the rich heritage shared by the Sikh community. This is followed by the reading of the *vak* ("divine command") from a passage of the *Guru granth sahib,* selected at random, and the distribution to everyone present of **karah prashad** ("sanctified food"), a cooked, sweet porridge made of flour, sugar, and clarified butter. Larger *gurdwaras* offer a free community meal (*langar*) after the service, or sometimes at the same time in a basement hall. The meal usually consists of such traditional Indian vegetarian foods as flatbread, bean stew, and curry. Sikhs and non-Sikhs sit together to share the meal, and a powerful egalitarian spirit infuses the *langar* and the way it is served.

The *Guru granth sahib* is always the central feature of key life-cycle rituals like naming, initiation, marriage, and death. When a child is to be named, the family takes the baby to the *gurdwara* and offers *karah prashad* for welcoming into the *Pranth.* After offering thanks and prayers through *Ardas,* the *Guru granth sahib* is opened at random, and a name is chosen beginning with the same letter as the first composition on the left-hand page. In this way, every Sikh child's chosen name results from the deliberate seeking of guidance from sacred scripture (*vak laina*). Underlying this practice is the belief that every Sikh child thus derives his or her identity from the *Guru granth sahib* and begins life as a Sikh. It is a tradition that the common surname Singh ("Lion") is added to the name chosen for boys, and the common surname Kaur ("Princess") for girls. In some cases, however, particularly in North America, Sikhs use caste identifiers as the last elements of their names, like Grewal, Sethi, Kalsi, or Ahluwalia. For such Sikhs, Singh and Kaur become middle names. Finally, infants are administered sweetened water (*amrit*), stirred with a double-edged sword, and the first five stanzas of Guru Nanak's *Japji* are recited.

Known as *Anand karaj* ("bliss event"), a Sikh wedding also takes place in the presence of the *Guru granth sahib* in the *gurdwara*. The couple is required to circumambulate the sacred scripture four times clockwise, and to take four vows. Before the bridegroom and the bride make each round, they listen to a verse of the *Lavan*, or "wedding hymn"—composed by the fourth Guru, Ram Das (1534–81)—as recited from the *Guru granth sahib* by a scriptural reader. The couple bows before the *Guru granth sahib* and then stands up to make their round while professional musicians sing the same verse with the congregation. As they circumambulate the sacred text, they swear four vows: (1) to lead a life of active righteousness and never to shun the obligations of family and society; (2) to maintain bonds of reverence and dignity between them; (3) to keep enthusiasm for life alive in the face of adverse circumstances and to spurn worldly attachments; and (4) to cultivate a "balanced approach" (*sahaj*) in life, avoiding all extremes. Sikhs believe that the repeated circumambulation performed in the *Anand karaj* recaptures the primordial movement of life, in which there is no beginning and no end. Every couple's married life will remain blissful as long as they remember and abide by the four marital vows.

Sikh tradition dictates that initiation ceremonies (**amrit sanskar**) must take place in the presence of the *Guru granth sahib,* too. Individuals may undergo initiation whenever they are willing to accept the Khalsa discipline; there is no fixed age for the ceremony. Representing the original "Cherished Five," five Khalsa Sikhs officiate at every initiation. Each officiate recites one of the five liturgical prayers from memory while stirring sweetened water (*amrit*) with a double-edged sword. To purify his/her body of the evil impulses of lust, anger, greed, pride, and attachment to worldly things, the initiate drinks the *amrit* five times. The sweetened water is also sprinkled on his/her eyes five times in order to transform his/her outlook on life. Lastly, the officiates pour *amrit* on the initiate's head five times to sanctify his/her hair, so that he/she will preserve his/her natural form and listen to the voice of conscience. At each stage of the ceremony, the initiate vows a formal oath: *Vahiguru Ji Ka Khalsa! Vahiguru Ji Ki Fateh!*

("Khalsa belongs to the wonderful Lord! Victory belongs to the wonderful Lord!"). In this way, the power of the sacred word transforms the initiate into a Khalsa Sikh. To conclude proceedings, the officiates read aloud a *vak* and distribute *karah prashad*.

The tradition of giving *amrit* was quite alive among the pioneer Sikhs. The Punjabi Sikh missionary and activist, Sant Teja Singh (1877–1965), regularly toured British Columbia and California during the period of his stay between 1908 and 1911, exhorting all who called themselves Sikhs to take *amrit* and administering to those who responded. In his autobiography, he claimed to have initiated hundreds of Sikhs in Vancouver, Victoria, Seattle, Portland, and California. Evidently, there was a significant number of Khalsa Sikhs in the early phase of migration. They were certainly influenced by two important factors. First, it was the peak of the Singh Sabha period; and second, the hostility many Canadians directed against them made them more firm in their commitment to the Khalsa ideal and to earlier versions of the code of conduct later standardized in the *Sikh Rahit Maryada*. More recently, Canadian Sikhs, particularly young adults, have begun to recognize the significance of and need for full commitment to the Khalsa discipline, especially since the Indian army's attack on the Golden Temple in 1984. This new trend is quite evident from the frequent arrangements made by *gurdwara* committees for the *amrit* ceremony, which was once a rare occurrence. Concerned about discrimination by prospective employers, many Sikhs abandoned their turbans and beards; today, however, many are returning to traditional ways.

Finally, it will come as no surprise that Sikhs turn to the *Guru granth sahib* at times of death. Funeral ceremonies divide into two sets of rituals: *Sanskar* ("ritual"), which includes cremation; and *Antim ardas* ("final prayer"), which includes the optional *Bhog* (literally, "delight") ceremony, when the *Guru granth sahib* is recited in its entirety. For cremation, the body of the deceased is washed and dressed in clean clothes, complete with the Five Ks in the case of Khalsa Sikhs. Unlike in India, where the body is cremated on a funeral pyre, in Canada the deceased may lie in a casket at a funeral home with the necessary facilities for cremation. Bereaved family and friends then gather around to pay final respects, perhaps scattering flower petals as a tribute to the deceased. Following devotional singing and a eulogy, *Ardas* is offered by a *granthi* from a local *gurdwara*. Then the casket is pushed on a trolley to the cremation furnace, usually accompanied by family and friends. While the casket is burning inside the high-technology furnace, the congregation recites the late-evening prayer, *Kirtan sohila*. The rituals of *Antim ardas* and *Bhog* take place at the home of the deceased or in a *gurdwara*. Members of the family of the deceased are required to take turns reading the entire *Guru granth sahib*, and if they cannot, they are expected to sit and listen to a *granthi* engaged from a local *gurdwara* so that they may receive the support and consolation of the sacred words. The reading of the *Guru granth sahib* must be completed on the tenth day after cremation. Sikhs do not erect monuments to the dead: traditionally, the ashes of the deceased are collected and committed to the nearest river or sea. Some Canadian Sikh families like to take the ashes of the deceased to Punjab.

In Canada, Sikh houses of worship also provide a number of non-liturgical services. Most *gurdwaras* offer educational and cultural programs, such as propagation, perpetuation, and preservation of the Punjabi language and Sikh music and song among younger generations of Sikhs. Some Sikh organizations operate Sikh versions of Sunday school, where children are given formal instruction in the tenets of Sikhism, while others support charitable and political causes. The libraries in *gurdwaras* provide educational resources to rising generations of Canadian-born Sikhs who want to learn more about their religious and cultural heritage. In addition, *gurdwaras* offer rare opportunities for socializing beyond the home and for sharing news and views about Sikhs and Sikhism elsewhere in Canada and abroad. On the other hand, tensions can arise over the proper use of these facilities, especially if more traditional members of a diaspora congregation feel that Western customs are gaining too strong a hold on time-honoured practices. In 1998, for example, a fierce controversy erupted over the use of tables and chairs for the *langar* in the basement halls of *gurdwaras* in British Columbia. This custom dated to the early days of Canada's pioneer Sikh community. A committee of the SGPC, which, it will be recalled, was formed as the result of the Gurdwara Reform Movement (1920–25), passed a resolution on 20 February 1934 in Amritsar, Punjab:

> In Europe and America, there is a tradition to sit on chairs in places of worship. As long as the *Guru granth sahib* can be put for public display at an elevated place, there is no harm in sitting on chairs below.[10]

---

10   Cited in Gurinder Singh Mann, "Making Homes Abroad: Sikhs in the United States," in *Nation of Religions*, ed. Steven Prothero (Chapel Hill: University of North Carolina Press, 2006), 160–77.

Clearly, at that time the Sikh leadership in Amritsar found no theological basis for denying the use of furniture at communal meals put on by diaspora Sikh congregations. On the contrary, the authoritative SGPC committee affirmed that the key egalitarian principle of the *langar* is maintained as long as everyone at the meal is equally able to bathe in the blessings flowing from the elevated *Guru granth sahib*. Still, a dissenting group lost control of a *gurdwara* in Surrey, British Columbia, and approached the governing Akal Takhat in Amritsar in an effort to secure a verdict against their opponents, apparently intent on transforming factional politics into a theological dispute within the Sikh community.

In addition to such internal tensions, the Sikh community in Canada has also been faced with external challenges to certain aspects of their religious identities, most notably misunderstandings arising from the wearing of the turban and the ceremonial *kirpan* ("sword"). Although in principle the Canadian Charter of Rights supports the Sikh right to wear religious symbols, there have been several controversial incidents involving these Sikh ceremonial items in recent years. In 1988, for example, the Royal Canadian Mounted Police (RCMP) would not permit Baltej Singh Dhillon, a Canadian Sikh born in Malaysia in 1966, to wear his turban in uniform. On 15 March 1990, the Solicitor General of Canada announced that the RCMP code of dress would be amended to allow turbaned Sikhs to serve in the force, and Dhillon became the first initiated Sikh to join the RCMP. Bearing the signatures of over 195,000 Canadians, petitions objecting to this change in the code of dress launched a long judicial process. On 8 July 1994, a federal Supreme Court of Appeal judge, Barbara Reed (born 1950), at last ruled that Sikhs in the RCMP would be allowed to wear turbans. In 1993, in an analogous case, four turbaned Sikh veterans were denied entry to the Newton Royal Canadian Legion (RCL) in Surrey, British Columbia, which exercised a policy forbidding headgear of any kind as a sign of respect for fallen comrades. On 31 May 1994, delegates to the RCL's national convention voted down a bylaw that required all 1,700 branches to admit those wearing religious headgear into public areas of RCL halls. The issue is still debated across the country and numerous RCL halls persist with such headgear policies, although the Newton branch revoked theirs and invited turbaned Sikh veterans to a special Remembrance Day ceremony on 11 November 2001.

The wearing of the *kirpan*, which translates literally as "kindness and honour," has also resulted in unfortunate misunderstandings. In 1986, Suneet Singh Tuli, a student at Paul Kane High School in St. Albert,

Nanaksar Gurdwara Gursikh, Edmonton, Alberta. PHOTO BY WINTERFORCE MEDIA.

Alberta, was suspended from school because he refused to stop wearing his *kirpan* to class. The St. Albert Protestant Separate School Board claimed that the ceremonial sword could be used as a weapon. Tuli lodged a complaint with the Alberta Human Rights Commission and filed a lawsuit in the court against the school board's decision. Eventually, the Alberta Human Rights Commission ruled that a ban on the *kirpan* violated the rights of Sikhs to practise their religion. In a similar case, Sukhdev Singh Hundal was suspended from Brampton's Central Secondary School in May 1988 because he insisted on wearing his *kirpan* to class. Ontario's Peel Board of Education ratified the suspension, citing its no-weapons policy. When Hundal tried to obtain a court order against the decision of the school board, he was barred from a Peel District courtroom because the judge refused to let him wear his *kirpan* there, as well. Judge John Goodearle asked the Supreme Court of Ontario to decide whether a board of education may prevent a Sikh teenager from wearing a *kirpan* to school, even though schools in the Etobicoke and North York districts did allow the practice, as long as it was not abused. Meanwhile, Sikh leaders changed their strategy and took the *kirpan* case to the Human Rights Commission of Ontario, a move opposed by the Peel Board of Education. The Supreme Court sided with the Ontario Human Rights Commission, whose adjudicator, W. Gunther Plaut (born 1912), ruled that a ban on *kirpans* violated Ontario's human rights legislation and that the Peel Board of Education must allow Sikh students and teachers to wear the ceremonial sword. In such cases, courts and commissions have accepted the opinions of Sikh and non-Sikh experts that the *kirpan* is not a weapon, but a sacred symbol of dignity and devotion.

Different school boards have recognized this religious reality in different ways, however. The Toronto District School Board has a religious accommodation document, for example, that only permits Sikh children to wear *kirpans* in class if the swords are no longer than six inches, tightly secured, and registered with the school administration. Both the Toronto and Vancouver school boards require Sikh students to keep the *kirpan* under their clothing, though in Vancouver there are no other restrictions. At the same time, misunderstandings have arisen elsewhere. In 2001, Gurbaj Singh Multani (born 1996) accidentally dropped his *kirpan* in the playground of his Montreal elementary school. Pressured by non-Sikh parents, the School Board banned the 12-year-old from wearing the ceremonial sword, claiming that it posed a danger to others. The Multanis prevailed in court against the school board, and their son returned to school wearing his *kirpan,* but the Quebec Court of Appeal reversed this decision on 7 March 2004, arguing that the ban on the *kirpan* was a reasonable limit to the freedom of religion guaranteed to all Canadians in the Charter of Rights and Freedoms. Supported by the Canadian Human Rights Commission, the Multanis appealed this decision to the Supreme Court of Canada, which on 2 March 2006 unanimously upheld the right of the Sikh student to wear the ceremonial dagger at school, sealed in its sheath and kept under his clothing. In effect, the court recognized definitively that, like the turban, the *kirpan* enjoys the same sort of sacred status among initiated Khalsa Sikhs as does the *menorah* among practising Jews or the crucifix among faithful Christians.

RECENT TRENDS IN THE SIKH COMMUNITY

In the census of 2001, the number of people designated as Sikh by religion in Canada was 278,415, with concentrations in British Columbia (135,310), Alberta (23,470), Saskatchewan (500), Manitoba (5,485), Ontario (104,785), Quebec (8,220), and Nova Scotia (270). By far the largest number of Canadian Sikhs may thus be found in the three provinces of British Columbia, Alberta, and Ontario, and within those provinces in the cities of Vancouver, Calgary, and Toronto. In this section of the chapter, let us explore what life in recent years has been like for the Sikhs living in two of these urban environments—Calgary and Toronto.

The Sikh community in Calgary is the youngest of these three communities, though its origins may be traced to the early twentieth century and the figure of Harnam Singh Hari. After living in Vancouver for two years, Hari made Calgary his home in 1910, thus becoming the first Sikh to move to the Prairies. His wife, Khem Kaur, joined him later when wives and children of immigrants were allowed into Canada in 1919. The family of Berama Singh and Dhun Kaur became the second Sikh family to make Calgary their home in 1931. These two pioneer families were the only Sikhs living in Calgary for a long period. In the early 1960s, several Sikh families migrated to Calgary because there was a high demand in the Prairies for professionals such as teachers, professors, and doctors. In November 1966, the first religious gathering (*diwan*) was held at the house of Gurbachan Singh and Madan Kaur Paul, where a cassette tape of devotional hymns (*shabad kirtan*) was played. This occasion, held in a family setting, marked the beginning of Sikh communal worship in Calgary.

Meanwhile, several East-African Sikh families migrated from Kenya and Tanzania in the late 1960s and early 1970s. In a symbolic way, the Gurdwara Singh Sabha of Nairobi (Kenya) donated the first set of a *chanani* ("canopy"), *romalas* ("ornate clothes"), and a *chauri* for the *Guru granth sahib* in Calgary, as well as utensils for the community kitchen. The first formal *diwan* in a public setting was held in November 1967, in the Jubilee Auditorium complex, to celebrate the birth anniversary (*gurpurb*) of Guru Nanak. About 20 Sikh families participated in the celebration, bringing vegetarian food prepared in their homes for serving in the *langar*, and *karah prashad*, the sanctified food made from flour, sugar, and clarified butter, which is placed in the presence of the Sikh scripture during worship and then distributed among the congregation. Soon it became a monthly event to fulfill the social and religious needs of the evolving Sikh community, and the group decided that a non-profit organization should be registered with the goal of building a permanent *gurdwara* in Calgary within a decade. After seeking guidance about the details of the constitution from such Sikh scholars as Harbans Singh (1940–2011), Khushwant Singh (born 1915), and Pamela M. Wylam, the organization was registered as the Singh Society on 18 March 1968. The society's founding executive committee consisted of Gurcharanjit Singh Attariwala (President), Sundar Kaur Grewal (Vice-President), Teja Singh (Secretary), Gulzar Singh Sihota (Joint Secretary), and Ranjit Singh Dhaliwal (Treasurer). Initially, the name Singh Society was chosen for practical purposes, so that a new Sikh immigrant could easily locate the *gurdwara* in the telephone directory. Later on, its name was changed to Sikh Society, Calgary, to make it more inclusive.

Sikh devotional singing (*kirtan*) in Calgary gurdwara, Alberta. PHOTO BY PASHAURA SINGH. REPRINTED BY PERMISSION. © PASHAURA SINGH.

In 1972, the Calgary Sikh community bought a parcel of land outside the city limit at a cost of $18,594. Fundraising and planning activities continued for the next four years. Dozens of volunteers organized a number of fundraising trips to various parts of Alberta, British Columbia, and California. Meanwhile, local residents expressed strong opposition to the local authority's issuing of a building permit for the space, on the grounds that building the Sikh house of worship at the proposed location would create parking and traffic problems. Eventually, a building permit was granted, but not before the Sikh Society was required to make elaborate presentations to demonstrate to the authorities that appropriate architectural controls and provisions for parking had been incorporated into the construction plans. All in all, the building of a permanent *gurdwara* in Calgary required much more detailed planning and much more complex social and political negotiations—both within the Sikh community and with local public authorities—than usually governs the activities of religious institutions.

In 1975, the constitution of the Sikh Society was amended to include a Board of Trustees to advise and oversee the working of the Executive Committee. The Board consists of five trustees, with one new member being elected every year for a five-year term. The trustees do not interfere in the day-to-day working of the society, but participate only to if there is a need to arbitrate major conflicts. With its administrative structure firmly in place, the Sikh Society pushed ahead with plans for the new house of worship. At its first meeting, held in March 1976, the Gurdwara Construction Committee raised $66,000. At the sod-turning ceremony on Baisakhi Day, 13 April 1976, the Sikh community invited Rabbi Lewis N. Ginsberg to break the soil five times at the site. At no cost to the Sikh Society, professional members of the community furnished civil, structural, and electrical design, project engineering and management, accounting, construction material, interior framing, carpentry, cedar for the interior ceiling, a *palki* ("palanquin") for the *Guru granth sahib*, a sound system, chandeliers, electrical fixtures, painting, and numerous other components and assistance. It is estimated that the labour and materials thus volunteered were worth $200,000. The Sikh ideal of *seva* ("service") became the motivating factor for these contributions to the collective good of the local community. In addition, families took turns in providing *langar* and refreshments for the volunteers. In this way, the process of building a new *gurdwara* was simultaneously the process of building a new Sikh community. The Calgary Sikh community named its first *gurdwara* the Guru Nanak Centre. It was built at a cost of $600,000, not counting the value of the additional volunteer labour and services. Its completion further strengthened the nascent community's solidarity and vitality.

On Baisakhi Day, 13 April 1979, the Calgary Sikh Society invited the academic W.H. McLeod to inaugurate the *gurdwara*. Their aim in inviting a Western scholar of Sikh Studies from New Zealand was to build a positive image of Sikhs in their host society. McLeod inspired the Sikh community to work for the establishment of a Chair of Sikh Studies at a Canadian university. He assured them that this kind of program would give academic respectability to the Sikh tradition within the academy and remove prevailing ignorance about Sikhs in the larger society. In 1987, the Sikh Society contributed a significant portion of the funds towards the establishment of a Chair of Sikh and Punjabi Studies at the University of British Columbia, Vancouver. In this spirit, the Calgary Sikh Society has led the way in helping Sikhs to build new lives in Canada without sacrificing their faith and their traditions. In the realm of worship, the society pioneered the concept of an educated Sikh *granthi*, who was expected not only to be an expert in the interpretation of Sikh scriptures and the study of Sikh traditions, but also to be qualified academically in the comparative study of religion. The society also introduced the use of English translations of the hymns being sung in the congregation (*sangat*). Originally, handouts of these translations were distributed to the *sangat*, but now the translations are projected on a screen through the use of computers and digital technology. The sermon (*vakhian*) by the *granthi* has become a regular feature of worship, too.

In addition to these initiatives in Sikh scholarship and worship, Calgary's Sikh Society places a great deal of emphasis on educational programs in a wide range of subjects for new generations of young Sikhs. Guru Nanak Sikh School offers classes in the Punjabi language, in Sikh music, and in the Sikh religion. The Canadian Sikh classical violinist, Parmela Attariwala, has produced a CD of music inspired by the *Guru granth sahib*, drawing upon both Eastern and Western sources. The society maintains a well-equipped library at the Guru Nanak Centre as part of the Sikh Learning Resource Centre, which has been described as "one of the most organized and best stocked facilities on literature relating to the Sikhs in Canada."[11] In 1981, the society organized and hosted the All Canada Sikh Convention, in which more than 30 Sikh organizations participated. This convention resulted in the formation of the Federation of Sikh Societies of Canada, a national organization of Sikhs active across Canada for many years. Since 1983, Calgary's Sikh Society has regularly organized Sikh youth camps in the summer. Over the years, the society has participated in charity work; it has donated cash, food, and goods to the Interfaith Food Bank, soup kitchens, shelter houses, the Alberta Children's Hospital, and the Canadian Red Cross, as well as the Rick Hansen, Steve Fonyo, and Terry Fox runs. Most importantly, the society responded to the Punjab crisis by adopting 100 Sikh children whose parents were killed in the November riots of 1984. Finally, Calgary's Sikh Society sponsors an active outreach program. This program has involved more than 300 presentations to schools, teachers, churches, politicians, and police staff in an effort to familiarize them with Sikh religious and cultural traditions.

In sum, the Calgary Sikh Society's approach to maintaining Sikh cultural and religious identity is sophisticated and has been successful. In large part, this success has to do with the unusual make-up of the society's leadership. The efforts of Sikh professionals from an urban background in the Punjab have been boosted by a significant number of pioneer families from East Africa, whose reasonable fluency in English has enabled them to move quite quickly into a wide range of technical, clerical, and professional occupations. These double migrants tend to be much more

---

11 Manmohan S. Minhas, *Sikh Society, Calgary—The First 25 Years* (Calgary: Sikh Society, 1993), n.p.

religiously active, and hence far more likely to sustain the external symbols of their faith.

By contrast with Calgary, the presence of the Sikhs in Toronto only first came to be felt in the mid-1950s. In 1954, the birthday of Guru Nanak was celebrated for the first time in Toronto, at the home of Kuldeep Singh Chhatwal. By 1965, there were about 400 Sikhs in the Greater Toronto Area, and they began to gather at a community centre on Eglinton Avenue for a monthly religious service. In 1969, on the quincentenary of the birth of Guru Nanak, the community converted a warehouse at 269 Pape Avenue into the first permanent *gurdwara*. Since the large influx of new immigrants in the 1970s, Sikh houses of worship have continued to proliferate in Toronto. Most of the early *gurdwaras* were established in older buildings or in large warehouses. At present, there are 20 permanent *gurdwaras* in the Greater Toronto Area, serving the religious and cultural needs of more than 100,000 Sikhs, most of whom have roots in India, East Africa, or the United Kingdom.

In some instances, the principal cause for the proliferation of *gurdwaras* in the Greater Toronto Area has had to do with factionalism in the community. Although the institution of the *gurdwara* serves as a rallying point and integrative force for the Sikh community, the management of its affairs sometimes becomes a bone of contention between different groups. Such difficulties arise when members of the *gurdwara* committee use their positions to enhance their own images in wider Sikh society. Usually based on personalities, rather than on substantive theological or moral issues, these factional politics in the affairs of the *gurdwara* can have a divisive effect in the community. In the absence of an external threat, this factionalism seriously weakens the community's ability to work towards a unified goal. Paradoxically, however, factionalism may easily result in greater long-term solidarity, because eventually it draws people's attention to more important community issues. Happily, the Sikh community in the Greater Toronto Area has steadily become more mature in organizational matters—notwithstanding the fact that some *gurdwaras* have been embroiled in bloody factionalism in the past, resulting from political and personal intrigues. On 25 June 1989, the inauguration of a new building housing the *gurdwara* of the Ontario Khalsa Darbar at 7080 Dixie Road, Mississauga, marked the beginning of a new phase of development for the Greater Toronto Area's Sikhs. This house of worship was the second-largest *gurdwara* in Canada, seating 4,000 people. In November 1990, Sri Guru Singh Sabha inaugurated Canada's largest *gurdwara* at 7280 Airport

Road, Mississauga, with the capacity to seat more than 5,000 Sikhs at a time. It was followed in January 1991 by the inauguration of the golden-domed Gursikh Sabha Gurdwara at 905 Middlefield Road, Scarborough. Demographic pressure and geographic convenience have since led to the construction of additional *gurdwaras*. In particular, two houses of worship reflect the caste (*zat*) orientation of particular Sikh groups, catering to the needs of *ramgarhia* ("artisan") Sikhs, who traditionally comprise such trades as carpenters, masons, blacksmiths, and barbers, and who have come to Canada mostly from East Africa.

Living in the Greater Toronto Area has not brought a significant change to Sikh religious practices. Sikh worship in the *gurdwara* continues to follow tradition, and a Sikh *granthi* still comes from India. Not surprisingly, the traumatic events of 1984 in the Punjab and Delhi have had a powerful impact on the Sikhs of the Greater Toronto Area. Pictures of Sikh martyrs and banners advocating the creation of a Sikh homeland, known as Khalistan ("Country of the Pure"), are prominently displayed in some *gurdwaras*. In fact, the Sikh congregational prayer (*Ardas*) itself includes references to Sikh martyrs and exhortations to Sikh victory, especially the rallying cry of *Raj karega Khalsa* ("The Khalsa shall rule"). Recovering the blended political and military spirit of Guru Gobind Singh, this rallying cry continues to provide a sacral context for fighting against tyranny and establishing the rule of truth and justice on earth.

In the middle of April, the Sikhs of the Greater Toronto Area celebrate the annual *Baisakhi* festival, marking the anniversary of the founding of the Khalsa with much dedication, pomp, and pageantry. All the *gurdwara* committees collaborate in organizing a colourful march through the streets of downtown Toronto to the provincial legislature at Queen's Park. The procession is always led by the "Cherished Five," followed by a float carrying the *Guru granth sahib*. Every year, thousands of Sikhs from across the province participate in this procession. In 1997, the Greater Toronto Area's Sikh community put on a particularly spectacular parade, joining Sikhs across the country to celebrate "A Century in Canada, 1897–1997." Special features included historical exhibits of Sikh pioneer towns in Canada, traditional dancing, and a performance of a play called *The Komagata Maru Incident*, dramatizing the British Columbian government's abandonment of mainly Punjabi would-be immigrants in 1914. The *Baisakhi* festival is also an occasion for the Sikhs of the Greater Toronto Area to give something back to the wider community. On one occasion, the celebration committee donated a wheelchair and a heart monitor to

Sick Children's Hospital on behalf of the Sikh community. The committee has also made generous donations to food banks and the United Way. The Sikhs also responded to the call of the Red Cross Society to donate blood on a number of occasions, and they participated in the Terry Fox Run to raise funds for the Cancer Society. In the centennial year, award ceremonies honoured both Sikhs and non-Sikhs who had made outstanding contributions to Canada.

Recent years have also witnessed a revived interest in inherited traditions and identities among the Sikhs of the Greater Toronto Area. This re-awakened consciousness has produced a flurry of activities in children's education. Sikh parents realize that worship in the *gurdwara* is conducted in Punjabi, which scarcely responds to the needs of children born in Canada. At school, these children are being trained to think critically and rationally, and they are therefore questioning the meaning of traditional rituals and practices. Traditional Sikh *granthis* and *gyanis* in the Greater Toronto Area's *gurdwaras* are unable to answer these queries. In addition, second- and third-generation Sikhs are steadily being assimilated into the ways of wider Canadian society and culture. In response to these issues, a group of concerned parents has started home-based Sikh worship, which is conducted in both Punjabi and English, so that children may participate in the recitation of prayers and follow their meaning. Notably, a group of second-generation Sikh musicians, led by Onkar Singh, has offered a creative response to the problems of assimilation and loss of language and tradition by producing two CDs under the title "*Shabad Kirtan* with English Discourse." These albums feature traditional *kirtans* from the *Guru granth sahib*, with easy-to-follow explanations in English.

Another innovation has seen the formation of Sikh youth camps to train Canadian-born children in the teachings of the *gurus*. These camps last one or two weeks. Through them, a spiritual environment is created that provides the children with continuous exposure to Sikh values and traditions. Similarly, in 1994, the Greater Toronto Area Sikh community celebrated the opening of the Khalsa Community School in Mississauga. Established and operated in accordance with the provisions of provincial law and the Ontario Ministry of Education regarding independent religious denominational schools, this Sikh institution offers the standard Ontario academic curriculum in addition to Sikh religious and language instruction. At the beginning of the second millennium, the school enjoyed an enrollment of about 200 students, though it did not receive full public funding. In 2005, citing the Supreme Court of Canada's acknowledgement in 1996 that "the Jewish community's survival as an identifiable and practising religious community depends upon broad access for Jewish children to Jewish day schools," Ripsodhak Singh Grewal, a member of the Khalsa Community School, joined voices with Metropolitan Archbishop Sotirios (Multi-faith Coalition for Equal Funding of Religious Schools), Aaron Blumenfeld (Ontario Association of Jewish Day Schools) and M.D. Khalid (Islamic Society of North America, Canada) to argue that the Ontario government should provide equal funding to all faith-based schools.[12] In a poignant reference, they asserted that such a move was necessary if youngsters from other minority traditions were to avoid the fate of Aboriginal children, so many of whom lost their religious and cultural identities in the federally funded residential school system run by the Christian churches.

There are certain Sikh organizations outside the *gurdwaras* in the Greater Toronto Area that have made concerted efforts to address the educational, social, cultural, and ethnic concerns of the community. Their members organize conferences, seminars, community dinners, and inter-faith dialogues that provide a forum for serious intellectual exchange, both among Sikhs and between Sikhs and non-Sikhs. These events offer an excellent opportunity for lobbying efforts in front of government representatives. Perhaps not surprisingly, these organizations have produced an array of Sikh leaders who do not necessarily represent large sections of their apparent constituencies, with the result that these élite efforts have tended for the most part to have little impact at the popular level. In sum, the management of *gurdwaras* in the Greater Toronto Area is largely in the hands of Punjabi Sikhs from rural backgrounds. From a social scientific perspective, Sikhs from urban backgrounds tend to stress the importance of devotional activity, while those from rural backgrounds are highly politically motivated. This phenomenon helps to explain why factionalism pervades the management of *gurdwaras* in the Greater Toronto Area. That said, throughout its history in Canada, the Sikh community has always been involved in the process of renewal and redefinition. In fact, the question, "Who is a Sikh?" occupies much of the attention in the online discussions among various Sikh networks. Each generation of Sikhs has to respond to this question in the light of a new set of historical and geographical circumstances. In turn, these new circumstances

---

12 "Our Kids Deserve Equality," *Toronto Star,* 31 January 2005, accessed 27 June 2011, http://www. canadiancrc.com/Newspaper_Articles/Tor_Star_Our_kids_deserve_equality_31JAN05.aspx.

require Sikhs to address larger issues of orthodoxy and orthopraxy, particularly in the areas of identity, gender, and authority.

These challenges have resulted in a variety of responses to the conventions of religious and cultural tradition among Sikhs in Canada. Among Canadian Sikhs, 15–20 per cent are **amrit-dharis** ("initiated")—that is, those who represent the orthodox ideology and practice of the Khalsa embodied in the *Sikh Rahit Maryada*. They control the *gurdwaras* and dominate the public discourse. Another 30 per cent are **kes-dharis**—that is, those who "retain their hair" and thus maintain a visible Sikh identity. These Sikhs follow most of the *Sikh Rahit Maryada* without having gone through the formal initiation ceremony (*amrit sanskar*). The number of Sikhs who have shorn their hair, and are thus less conspicuous, is quite large in Canada. Popularly known as *mona* ("clean-shaven") Sikhs, they retain their Khalsa affiliation by using the surnames "Singh" and "Kaur." These Sikhs are also called **ichha-dharis** because they "desire" to keep their hair but cut it under some form of compulsion. They are frequently confused with *sahaj-dhari* ("gradualist") Sikhs, who have never accepted the Khalsa discipline. Although *sahaj-dharis* follow the teachings of the *Guru granth sahib*, they do not observe the Khalsa *Sikh Rahit Maryada*, and in particular because they cut their hair. The number of *sahaj-dharis* in Canada declined during the last few decades of the twentieth century, although they have not disappeared completely from the Sikh *Panth*. Finally, there are those who violate the Khalsa *Sikh Rahit Maryada* after initiation by committing any one of the four prohibitions: cutting the hair; committing adultery; using intoxicants; and eating meat that has not come from an animal killed with a single blow. These lapsed *amrit-dharis* are variously known as **bikh-dhari** or *patit* ("apostate") Sikhs. There is thus no single way of being a Canadian Sikh, and the five categories of Sikhs are not permanently fixed. Punjabi Sikhs frequently move between them according to their situations in life. There are some Western Sikh converts in Canada, popularly known as *gora* ("white") Sikhs, for whom being Sikh does not imply an ethnic identity. The Sikh community at large is, however, fairly homogenous, in the sense that Sikhs can freely enter any *gurdwara* and feel spiritually at home. Indeed, Canadian Sikhs vehemently assert their distinctiveness in public discourse. The ideal before them is integration into the Canadian mosaic without the loss of their cultural and religious identity. Symbolic of this process, in 1999 the Canada Post Corporation released the postal stamp, "Sikh Canadians," to mark the tricentenary celebration of the Khalsa.

AFTERWORD

Several factors have contributed to the growth of Sikhism in Canada. First of all, the Sikhs have always adopted a proactive approach in addressing significant issues confronting the community to ensure its survival at various points in time. The early Punjabi immigrants, for instance, organized farm workers into a union to ensure the improvement of their working conditions and wages. Fighting systematically against racial discrimination, they eventually won equal rights to vote as Canadian citizens as well as the right to bring their families to Canada. More recently, Sikhs have achieved tremendous success in Canadian politics by participating at various levels. On 11 June 1997, Liberal Prime Minister Jean Chrétien appointed Sikh Herb Dhaliwal (born 1952) Member of Parliament (MP) for Vancouver South-Burnaby, as Revenue Minister of Canada. At the time of writing, there are six Sikh MPs in Canada: Gurbax Singh Malhi (born 1949); Navdeep Singh Bains (born 1977); Ruby Dhalla (born 1974); Ujjal Dosanjh (born 1947); Nina Grewal (born 1958); and Sukh Dhaliwal (born 1960). All belong to the Liberal Party except Grewal, who is a Conservative. It should also be noted that Dosanjh was appointed federal Minister of Health on 20 July 2004, having previously served as the 33rd premier of British Columbia. All these political achievements speak volumes about a highly motivated ethnic group in Canada. In addition, Sikh organizations have equally participated in charitable projects in Canada. Through the active motivation of the Guru Nanak Shrine Fellowship, for instance, the Canadian Sikh community raised 2.2 million dollars for the Guru Nanak Dev Healing Garden at the Mazankowski Alberta Heart Institute. The Guru Nanak Dev Healing Garden will take up over 4,000 square feet in the $196-million heart institute, which is located in Edmonton. A healing garden is one of the newest innovations in modern care. This indoor garden will be located on the fourth floor of the heart institute, and will include a balcony providing a two-storey environment for quiet conversation, time with family members, and personal reflection. The Guru Nanak Dev Garden will be enriched with natural elements and will create an atmosphere to assist patients and families in healing.

Second, there is an urgent issue related to the public visibility of Sikhs across North America, particularly in Canada. In the last few decades, Sikhs have received a great deal of media attention. Much of this attention has been negative and stereotypical, and a great deal of ignorance still persists in the Western world about the Sikhs and their religious traditions.

Not surprisingly, the first victim of racial backlash during the recent crisis after the terrorist attacks of 11 September 2001 was a Sikh, Balbir Singh Sodhi of Arizona, who was shot dead by an angry gunman calling himself a patriot. Mr. Sodhi was targeted because of a mistaken identity, and this tragedy made it clear that many people simply do not know who Sikhs are. Particular issues stand out: turbaned Sikhs in the workplace; *kirpans* in public schools; the impact of the Indian army's assault on the Golden Temple Complex (1984) on Canadian Sikhs; and the Air India tragedy (1985) and subsequent trial in Vancouver (2005), when the British Columbia Supreme Court acquitted Ripudaman Singh Malik and Ajaib Singh Bagri. More generally, instances of racial and religious discrimination, as well as the frequent inability of the public to discern Sikhs from other religious and ethnic groups, remain pervasive and conspicuous in the news. The growing interest in and attention to Sikh issues in the public sphere has created the need for a forum to reflect upon and to discuss these public issues. The participation of Sikh media groups in this endeavour has been quite remarkable in providing a corrective to public misunderstandings. Indeed, Sikhs form a singular group that has struggled enormously to shape their community as separate from other South Asians as well as from Hindu traditions, while dealing with widespread antipathy to articles of their attire from the Canadian public. Also, Sikhs seem to find themselves more rigorously affected by events "back home" than other religious groups in Canada.

A third factor affecting Sikhs in Canada was brought forth in the first North American conference on Sikh Studies, held in 1976 at the University of California, Berkeley. Among the attendants at the conference it was generally felt that the Sikh tradition was indeed "the forgotten tradition" in scholarly circles in North America. In particular, American academic Mark Juergensmeyer (born 1940) argued that in the textbooks of world religions courses, the study of Sikhism was either completely ignored or misrepresented. He examined the various reasons for this treatment and suggested that there are two prejudices in the academic study of Indian culture and society that work against the study of the Sikh tradition. The first prejudice concerns suspicion of all things modern. Many scholars following the orientalist perspective have been more interested in classical texts on Indian philosophy than in a medieval devotional tradition. Since Sikh traditions are barely 500 years old, the religion has been completely ignored in Indian studies. The other prejudice that affects the serious study of Sikhism has to do with the notion of regionalism. Sikhism is not only relatively modern but it is also almost exclusively Punjabi. In his arguments, Juergensmeyer made the case for the utility of Sikhism in the study of religion.

Since then, the study of the Sikh tradition and culture has received some cautious scholarly attention, and the mistaken notion that Sikhism offers a synthesis of Hindu and Muslim ideals has been completely abandoned in most of the recent scholarly works. The latter decades of the twentieth century saw a steady growth of scholarly literature on Sikhism, and there are now seven programs of Sikh and Punjab Studies that have been established in North America with the active financial support of the Sikh community. In fact, a landmark event in this context occurred when the first endowed Chair of Punjabi and Sikh Studies was established at the University of British Columbia, Vancouver, in 1987. The increasing scholarly attention that Sikhs and Sikhism are beginning to receive is a new phenomenon in the academy. Indeed, Sikh Studies is now moving away from being "the forgotten tradition" and is becoming increasingly recognized in undergraduate programs, as well as being the benefactor of a growing number of endowed chairs in universities across North America. At last count, these included the University of Michigan; Hofstra University; three campuses of the University of California at Santa Barbara, Riverside, and Santa Cruz; and California State University, East Bay. In addition to these academic programs, there are a growing number of scholars in the United States, Canada, the United Kingdom, and Europe whose teaching and research interests are related in some way to the study of Sikhs and Sikhism. Most instructively, the Program of Punjabi and Sikh Studies at the University of British Columbia, Vancouver, was partly funded by the Canadian government as a result of the multiculturalist policy to support the projects of various ethnic groups.

Finally, religious freedom in Canada is a constitutionally protected right, allowing the right of assembly and the right to worship without limitation or interference. In this context, Sikhism is a mouthpiece for mutual coexistence and understanding. It emphasizes tolerance and argues for the acceptance of diversity in religious faith and practice. It projects an existential commitment towards ideals of universal brotherhood and universal sisterhood and an altruistic concern for humanity as a whole (*sarbat da bhala*). In Canada's pluralistic and multicultural context, where official policy places a premium upon liberty, diversity, tolerance, and the equality of race and gender, Sikh ideals are thoroughly in place and congenial to the developing values of society as a whole.

KEY TERMS

Adi granth	"Original book," first compiled by Guru Arjan in 1604 and subsequently invested with supreme authority as the *Guru granth sahib*.
Akal Purakh	"The One beyond Time"—that is, God.
Amrit-dhari	"Nectar-bearer," and hence an initiated member of the Khalsa.
Amrit sanskar	The formal ceremony initiating Sikhs into the Khalsa.
Baisakhi	An Indian New Year's Day, observed by Sikhs annually around 13 April to mark the birthday of the Khalsa.
Bikh-dhari	"Poison-bearer," and hence a lapsed *amrit-dhari*.
Chauri	A whisk, made of yak hair or man-made fibre, fixed in metal, and attached to a wooden handle, and ceremonially waved over *Guru granth sahib* as a mark of respect.
Five Ks	The five marks of Khalsa identity, whose Punjabi names are *kes* (unshorn hair), *kangha* (wooden comb), *kirpan* (sword), *kara* (wrist ring), and *kachh* (short breeches).
Gurdwara	"Door of the Guru," and hence a Sikh place of worship.
Guru	"Teacher," meaning either a spiritual person or the divine inner voice.
Ichha-dhari	A Sikh who "desires" to keep his/her hair, but cuts it under some form of compulsion.
Karah prashad	Sanctified food made from flour, sugar, and clarified butter, placed in the presence of the Sikh scripture during worship and then distributed in the congregation.
Kes-dhari	"Hair-bearer"—that is, a Sikh who maintains the visible mark of identity by wearing unshorn hair.
Khalsa	"Pure" or "crown estate," and hence an order of Sikhs bound by common identity and discipline.
Kirtan	The singing of hymns from the scriptures in worship.
Langar	The community kitchen serving meals to all present in the congregation.
Miri-piri	Doctrine which maintains that the Guru possesses temporal (*miri*) as well as spiritual (*piri*) authority.
Nam	"The divine name."
Nam-dan-ishnan	The Sikh's threefold discipline of "the divine name, charity, and purity."

Nam-simaran	"Remembrance of the divine name," especially the devotional practice of meditating on the divine name.
Panth	"Path," and hence the Sikh community.
Sahaj-dhari	"Gradualist," and hence a Sikh who follows the teachings of the *gurus* without accepting the discipline of the Khalsa code of conduct.
Sikh Rahit Maryada	The code of conduct for the Khalsa.
Singh Sabha	"Society of Singhs," a revival movement initiated in 1873 that redefined the norms of Sikh orthodoxy and orthopraxy.

KEY DATES

1499	Guru Nanak's mystical call to a spiritual mission.
1519	Guru Nanak founds the village of Kartarpur.
1604	The fifth *guru*, Arjan, oversees the compilation of the *Adi granth*.
1699	On *Baisakhi* Day, the tenth *guru*, Gobind Singh, founds the Khalsa at Anandpur.
1799	Maharaja Ranjit Singh accedes to power in the Punjab.
1849	Great Britain annexes the Punjab.
1873	The founding of the Singh Sabha reform association.
1903	Ten Sikh members of a Hong Kong military contingent settle in British Columbia.
1907	The Khalsa Diwan Society is established in Vancouver.
1908	First *gurdwara* is inaugurated in Vancouver. In the same year, an Order in Council is promulgated with the "continuous journey" clause for new immigrants.
1910	First Sikh moves to Calgary.
1914	On 23 May, the ship *Komagata Maru / Guru Nanak Jahaj* arrives in Vancouver with 376 passengers, and is ordered back to Calcutta, India on 23 July.
1919	Spouses and children of Sikh immigrants are allowed into Canada.
1945	Consultation among more than 70 of the most respected Sikh scholars and theologians over 14 years produces the authoritative Khalsa code of conduct, the *Sikh Rahit Maryada*.
1951	A new federal Immigration Act establishes national quotas.

1967	In Canada's centennial year, a new federal Immigration Act formally eliminates discrimination based on race, religion, and country of origin by introducing a points system.
1969	The first *gurdwara* is established in Toronto.
1979	The first *gurdwara* is inaugurated in Calgary.
1981	The constitution of an active national organization, the Federation of Sikh Societies of Canada, is adopted in Calgary.
1984	The Indian army assaults the Golden Temple in Amritsar, resulting in strong Sikh protests in Canada.
1994	On 8 July 1994, a federal Supreme Court of Appeal judge, Barbara Reed, rules that Sikhs in the RCMP would be allowed to wear turbans.
1997	Sikh Canadians celebrate "A Century in Canada" (1897–1997).
1999	The Canadian federal government releases the postal stamp "Sikh Canadians" to mark the tricentenary celebration of the Khalsa.

KEY READINGS

Buchignani, Norman, and Doreen M. Indra, with Ram Srivastava. *Continuous Journey: A Social History of South Asians in Canada.* Toronto: McClelland and Stewart, 1985.

Johnston, Hugh J.M. *The Voyage of the Komagata Maru: The Sikh Challenge to Canada's Colour Bar.* Delhi: Oxford University Press, 1979.

McLeod, Hew. *Sikhism.* London: Penguin Books, 1997.

Minhas, Manmohan S. *Sikh Society, Calgary—The First 25 Years.* Calgary: Sikh Society, 1993.

Nayar, Kamala Elizabeth. *The Sikh Diaspora in Vancouver: Three Generations Amid Tradition, Modernity, and Multiculturalism.* Toronto: University of Toronto Press, 2004.

O'Connell, Joseph T. "Sikh Religio-Ethnic Experience in Canada." In *The South Asian Religious Diaspora in Britain, Canada, and the United States*, ed. Harold Coward, John R. Hinnels, and Raymond Brady Williams, 191–209. Albany: State University of New York Press, 2000.

Singh, Narinder. *Canadian Sikhs: History, Religion, and Culture of Sikhs in North America.* Ottawa: Canadian Sikhs' Studies Institute, 1994.

Singh, Pashaura. "Sikh Traditions in Ontario." *Polyphony: The Bulletin of the Multicultural History Society of Ontario* 12 (1990): 130–35.

Singh, Pashaura. *The Guru Granth Sahib: Canon, Meaning and Authority.* Oxford, New Delhi: Oxford University Press, 2000.

Singh, Pashaura. *Life and Work of Guru Arjan: History, Memory and Biography in the Sikh Tradition*. Oxford, New Delhi: Oxford University Press, 2006.

Singh, Pashaura. "Sikh Traditions." In *World Religions: Eastern Traditions*, 3rd ed., ed. Willard G. Oxtoby and Roy C. Amore, 106–43. Don Mills, ON: Oxford University Press, 2010.

Tatla, Darshan Singh. *The Sikh Diaspora: The Search for Statehood*. London: University College London Press, 1999.

KEY WEBSITES

http://www.sikhs.org [The Sikhism Home Page, Brampton, Ontario, Canada]

http://www.sikhnet.com [SikhNet, Espanola, New Mexico, USA]

http://www.akalsangat.com [Akal Publications, Ann Arbor, Michigan, USA]

http://www.sgpc.net [Shiromani Gurdwara Parbandhak Committee, Amritsar, Punjab, India]

http://www.sikhnn.com [Sikh News Network]

http://www.sikhcoalition.org [The Sikh Coalition, New York, USA]

http://www.sikhchic.com [The Art and Culture of the Diaspora]

KEY QUESTIONS FOR CRITICAL REFLECTION

1. Do you think Guru Nanak intended to found an independent religion in the last phase of his life? If so, what is the evidence in his works? Describe the Kartarpur period of his life in detail.

2. How did Sikhism evolve in response to the changing historical situation during the canonical period of the ten *gurus*?

3. Do you think the rural base of Punjabi society played a major role in the evolution of militant traditions within the *Panth*? What role did the martyrdoms of Guru Arjan and Guru Tegh Bahadur play in this direction? Is there any relationship between the rural background of Punjabi Sikhs and the spirit of factionalism in the *gurdwaras* in Canada?

4. How did modern Sikhism come into being? What role did the Singh Sabha reform movement play in defining Sikh orthodoxy and orthopraxy in the colonial period? Was the Khalsa Diwan Society of Vancouver following the example of Singh Sabha and the Chief Khalsa Diwan at Amritsar?

5. How would you describe the Canadian experience of the pioneer Sikhs? Do you think the institution of the *gurdwara* played a major role in the survival of the Sikh traditions in Canada? How will the second and third generations of Canadian Sikhs redefine Sikhism? Will they provoke new responses to the notions of identity, gender, and authority in the postmodern world?

NINE

Bahá'is

WILL C. VAN DEN HOONAARD, UNIVERSITY OF NEW BRUNSWICK
AND ST. THOMAS UNIVERSITY

The Bahá'ís in Canada form part of the worldwide Bahá'í community. The religion originated in nineteenth-century Persia (now called Iran) when **Bahá'u'lláh** (1817–92) proclaimed to be a Messenger of God and announced the fulfillment of the millennial visions of previously revealed religions. The Bahá'í tenets address matters related to both personal conduct and social issues. While mystical in nature, the tenets include a system calling for the structural reorganization of human society. This system envisions a planetary society with a common script and language, universal education, the elimination of racial discrimination, the equality of women and men, the harmony between science and religion, the establishment of a world tribunal, and a democratically elected parliamentary form of world government. Worldwide, over 80 per cent of adherents of the Bahá'í Faith are found in developing countries. Numerically, the largest Bahá'í communities are found in India, Iran, East Africa, parts of South-east Asia, and the Andes. In some South Pacific locations, Bahá'ís constitute as much as one-fourth of the whole population. The Bahá'í community of Canada has played a significant role in the worldwide Bahá'í community. The 1910s saw the establishment of the first Canadian organized communities in Quebec, Ontario, and New

Brunswick. The 2001 federal census enumerated 37,931 Bahá'ís in Canada, and they are to be found in every corner of the country, in rural, suburban and urban locales, from sea to sea to sea.

Blending scholarly sources with personal insights, this chapter falls into three main sections. The first offers a general survey of the Bahá'í heritage and history, highlights its central message along with its scripture and its administrative system, addresses the idea of Bahá'í consultation, and speaks about membership qualifications and how the Bahá'í Faith is spread. The second section presents a detailed account of the Bahá'í Faith in Canada: its history, its social and demographic composition, and its involvement in social and economic development. A third section discusses recent trends, focusing upon the workings of a typical Canadian Bahá'í community. In the light of these observations, the afterword reflects upon prospects for the Bahá'í community in relation to Canada as a whole.

THE HERITAGE

What is one to make of a religion that seeks converts and yet affirms the right of every person to shape his/her religious and spiritual beliefs? What if that religion promotes a strict personal moral code while advocating progressive social teachings? What can one say about a religious community in which mothers are seen as the primary educators of children and in which the equality of women and men is at the forefront of its teachings and activities? What about that religion's premise that science and religion can go hand in hand and yet in its roots sees itself as mystical? What about its sacred scriptures that affirm evolution and creation at the same time? These seeming contradictions, however, exemplify the dynamic nature of the Bahá'í Faith, an independently revealed religion of more than nearly 170 years. Other perplexities abound. A relatively young tradition, the Bahá'í Faith in Canada is spread across 2,342 localities, but it is not concentrated in large urban centres as new religions tend to be. Despite its multifarious activities, newspapers and magazines do not report much on Bahá'í events. And the Bahá'í Faith has no initiation ceremonies or other rites of passage, no sacraments and no clergy—institutions which in other religions promote the aims of the religious tradition and play a significant part in its infrastructure.

The history of the Bahá'í Faith helps to clarify some of these issues. The tradition originated in Iran. In 1844, a young merchant in Persia named

Siyyid 'Alí-Muhammad took the title of the **Báb** ("The Gate"; 1819–50) and declared himself to be the spiritual reformer long-awaited by Shi'ite Muslims—the "Mahdi" or "Hidden Imam." His teachings and his challenge to Shi'ite secular and clerical authorities led to his execution in Tabriz in 1850. These same authorities persecuted and jailed or put to death many thousands of his followers, who were called Bábis. The remains of the Báb were eventually buried in what was then Palestine. The brief life of the Báb and the history of his followers claim the steady attentive devotion of contemporary Bahá'ís and form an important part of their religious identity. For Bahá'ís, the Báb retains a special status as the precursor of Bahá'u'lláh. Bahá'ís make pilgrimages to Haifa and Akka (Acre) in today's Israel, where they visit the shrine of the Báb on Mount Carmel as well as the shrine and other holy places associated with Bahá'u'lláh.

Assuming the title Bahá'u'lláh ("Glory of God"), Mirza Husayn Ali (1817–92) declared himself to be the "Manifestation of God" anticipated by the Báb. From his earliest life, he seemed to possess charismatic qualities. At the age of 25, for example, he was known as the "Father of the Poor" because of his generosity and compassion to society's less fortunate. He became a follower of the Báb, and like many other Bábis, he was jailed by the Shi'ite authorities. Incarcerated in an underground dungeon in Tehran, Iran, Bahá'u'lláh first received an intimation of his mission in 1853. In his own words:

> During the days I lay in prison of Tihran [Tehran], though the galling weight of the chains and the stench-filled air allowed Me but little sleep, still in those infrequent moments of slumber I felt as if something flowed from the crown of My head over My breast, even as a mighty torrent that precipitateth itself upon the earth from the summit of a lofty mountain. Every limb of My body would, as a result, be set afire.[1]

After three months, the authorities released Bahá'u'lláh from the dungeon, but exiled him to Iraq with his family and some 70 of his followers. In April 1863, Bahá'u'lláh openly announced his mission in the Garden of Ridván, outside the city of Baghdad. Around the world today Bahá'ís mark that occasion as the "Most Great Festival," which also includes the election of Bahá'í local governing councils ("**Spiritual Assemblies**").

---

1 Office of Public Information, *Bahá'u'lláh: A Statement Prepared by the Bahá'í International Community* (Toronto: National Spiritual Assembly of the Bahá'ís of Canada, 1991), 7.

According to Bahá'ís, Bahá'u'lláh occupies the same status as the prophets of the earlier revealed religions such as Noah, Abraham, Moses, Jesus, and Mohammad. As well as fulfilling Muslim messianic expectations, Bahá'u'lláh professed to be the second coming of Christ for Christians, the future Buddha Maitreya, and the living Krishna for Hindus. After a succession of other exiles throughout the Ottomon Empire that lasted 39 years, Bahá'u'lláh passed away in Palestine, in 1892.

After the passing of Bahá'u'lláh, and according to his explicit wishes, his oldest son, **'Abdu'l-Bahá** ("Servant of Bahá"; 1844–1921), assumed leadership of the Bahá'í Faith. Born in Iran, 'Abdu'l-Bahá became known as the "Centre of the Covenant" and sole authoritative interpreter of Bahá'u'lláh's teachings. At this time, there were practising Bahá'ís in five countries in the Middle East and in India. Under the guidance of 'Abdu'l-Bahá, the Bahá'í Faith spread to other lands, including South America, South Africa, Australia, Japan, and Hawaii. 'Abdu'l-Bahá himself endured some 55 years of formal imprisonment and exile under the Muslim Turks of the Ottoman Empire. It was the 1908 revolution led by Kemal Ataturk that resulted in 'Abdu'l-Bahá's release from restricted personal circumstances. From 1911 to 1913, 'Abdu'l-Bahá undertook voyages to Egypt, Europe, and North America to spread the new religion. His travels received wide publicity. He was also recognized for saving thousands in Palestine from famine. As part of his goal of establishing the Bahá'í Faith around the world, 'Abdu'l-Bahá issued 14 letters to the Bahá'ís in North America. Composed during World War I (1914–18), these letters asserted the spiritual and administrative significance of the Bahá'í communities in the United States and Canada. He also left some 16,000 letters in addition to records of his talks in the Western hemisphere. These documents constitute the substance of his authoritative interpretations and explanations of the teachings of Bahá'u'lláh and how the Bahá'í community is to be organized.

In 1921, 'Abdul-Bahá died in Palestine, as had his father. His last will and testament appointed his grandson, **Shoghi Effendi** (1897–1957), as leader of the Bahá'í Faith under the title of Guardian. 'Abdu'l-Bahá also designated him as the sole interpreter of the Bahá'í teachings. Under Shoghi Effendi, the Bahá'í Faith spread from 35 countries to 257. He clarified the nature of the Bahá'í administrative order and assisted Bahá'í communities around the world in laying the foundation of such an order by mapping out specific goals for spreading the Bahá'í Faith. Before his death in 1957, Shoghi Effendi appointed a group of men and women, known as the "Hands of the Cause of God," to act as "Chief Stewards" of the Bahá'í Faith with the mandate of encouraging believers to fulfill the goals of the Ten-Year Plan (1953–63) that their leader had laid out. They also prepared the worldwide Bahá'í community for the election of the **Universal House of Justice** in 1963, whose formation and function had been anticipated by Bahá'u'lláh. Situated on Mount Carmel in Haifa, Israel, near the shrines of the Báb and Bahá'u'lláh, the Universal House of Justice serves as the supreme governing body of the Bahá'í Faith, possessing the administrative authority to legislate to the faithful on matters not expressly revealed in the writings of Bahá'u'lláh. Every five years members of all National Spiritual Assemblies around the world elect the nine members of the Universal House of Justice. The Bahá'í Writings expressly prohibit canvassing and electioneering; votes are by secret ballot and they exempt women from serving on the Universal House of Justice, though women have served on the Institution of the Hands of the Cause of God, where individual membership constitutes a higher rank than that of a member of the House of Justice. The first election took place in 1963, and the first Universal House of Justice was comprised of Bahá'ís from four continents and various ethnic backgrounds.

Turning to scripture and Bahá'í beliefs, we find that Bahá'ís do not possess a narrow canon of sacred texts. The religious teachings of the faith derive from the writings of the Báb and Bahá'u'lláh, and interpretations by 'Abdu'l-Bahá and Shoghi Effendi. A central message of the writings of the Báb and Bahá'u'lláh announces that working towards world unity as a prerequisite to peace offers the best means to achieve a new society—a truly global society. Calling for one standard of moral measurement to be used around the world, Bahá'u'lláh's teachings articulate a progressive set of social doctrines, including a call for universal disarmament and peace. Numbering some 5,000 letters and over 100 major texts, Bahá'u'lláh's Writings amplify these views, as well as other pronouncements on matters of personal morality. Bahá'ís are enjoined to pray daily, to abstain completely from narcotics, alcohol and other psychotropic substances, to obtain parental consent before marrying, and to be monogamous. The writings of the Universal House of Justice also constitute part of the **Bahá'í Writings** although they are not considered to be sacred or to be interpretations of the core of the Bahá'í Writings. Moreover, adherents to the faith continue to produce commentaries on these texts.

At the heart of the Bahá'í Faith lies the belief in the existence of one God, although this divinity is known by different names by virtue of the many languages in the world. They believe that knowing and loving God is the core of humanity's goal. To bring about this goal, they believe, God periodically provides divine messengers not only to reaffirm this spiritual purpose, of which all past messengers have spoken, but also to bring about the means to achieve a renewed vision of society based on new social teachings. For Baháʼís, God is unknowable, but His attributes can be known through these messengers ("Manifestations"), who include Zoroaster, Moses, Jesus, and Mohammad. These Manifestations of God are responsible for the spiritual renewal of humanity. This belief entails the idea of **progressive revelation,** where every messenger builds upon the teachings of his predecessor and prepares humanity for the next divine teacher. Baháʼís do not rank revealed religions; rather, they believe that respective divine messengers emphasize particular religious teachings.

For Baháʼís, individuals are not only personally responsible for coming to know and to love God but also for sharing a responsibility towards humanity as a whole. Baháʼuʼlláh states that all humans have been created "to carry forward an ever-advancing civilization."[2] The Baháʼí Writings stipulate daily prayer and regard service to humanity as the practical means by which the soul develops its spiritual strength. The Baháʼí Writings speak of good works and prayers as equally efficacious, as long as the former are performed in the spirit of service to humanity.

Baháʼís do not believe in reincarnation. Rather, each human soul starts its journey on this earthly plane of existence and continues to progress after physical death, moving towards the Creator. The terms "heaven" and "hell" are understood by Baháʼís to be metaphorical in nature and to refer to the degree to which a person's thoughts and deeds enable (or hinder) his/her spiritual essence to approach the Creator. While Baháʼís must work actively for the betterment of society by diminishing or eliminating human suffering or injustice, the Baháʼí Writings also recognize the special place of unintended suffering as a means for the soul to become purified and the character to become strengthened.

The Baháʼí Writings embody a vision of society that acknowledges the ultimate unity of the human race. This vision is also derived from the teachings of past messengers who spoke of the "kingdom of God" on earth. For Baháʼís, there is no greater cause for individuals to follow than the spiritualization and unification of the planet. The dispensations of past messengers inspired individuals to become personally more spiritual

---

2   Baháʼuʼlláh, *Gleanings from the Writings of Baháʼuʼlláh,* trans. Shoghi Effendi (Wilmette, IL: Baháʼí Publishing Trust, 1971), 215.

or fostered spiritual unity within one's immediate group, and neither of these achievements is lost. But today, Bahá'ís believe that nothing short of a major restructuring of the world is necessary to realize the vision of human unity.

Rather than relying exclusively on a code of laws to bring about the dream of global unity, the Bahá'í Faith sets before humanity standards of thought, behaviour, and morality in the form of general principles that embody a distinctive vision of a new society. In addition to the principles already referred to, the idea of the oneness of humanity implies the elimination of the extremes of poverty and wealth and the eradication of racism and religious fanaticism. At the same time, the Bahá'í vision of a new society is not monolithic. Rather, Bahá'ís advocate unity in essentials and diversity in secondary matters. Freedom of expression is important, for example, but so is the elimination of untrammelled individualism and materialism. Such a global society will therefore, in the Bahá'í view, value those occupations that most obviously serve the general good, like education, agriculture, and health. But the Bahá'í Writings advocate that people who possess any kind of talent and use it for the public benefit should be honoured, whether in the arts or trades.

Underscoring the newness of the religion, the Bahá'í Faith introduced a new calendar starting with the declaration of the Báb in 1844. The year consists of 19 months of 19 days each. The **Nineteen-Day Feast** is held on the first day of each month. The Bahá'í year starts 21 March, preceded by a fast starting 2 March, from sunrise to sunset each day, to be observed by those between the ages of 15 and 70. A number of exceptions do apply. Work is suspended on Bahá'í Holy Days, of which there are 9: **Naw-Rúz** (the Bahá'í New Year, 21 March); the first, ninth, and twelfth days of the Ridván Festival, Bahá'ís holiest festival, which marks the start of Bahá'u'lláh's mission (21 and 28 April, and 2 May); the Declaration of the Báb (23 May; the Passing of Bahá'u'lláh, 29 May); the Martyrdom of the Báb (9 July); the Birth of the Báb (20 October); the Birth of Bahá'u'lláh (12 November); the Day of Covenant (26 November); and the Passing of 'Abdu'l-Bahá (28 November). Normally, the program for each occasion consists of a formal part explaining to non-Bahá'í guests the nature of the holy day, often followed by a potluck meal.

The social organization of the Bahá'í community is known as the Administrative Order and is another distinguishing feature of the Bahá'í Faith. The Administrative Order makes it possible for the Bahá'í Faith to express itself in the world. The earliest revealed writings of Bahá'u'lláh already offer clear guidance about how local and international Bahá'í governing institutions should run the affairs of the Bahá'í community. At the local level, whenever there are nine or more adult Bahá'ís, they are to elect each year, by democratic and secret ballot, nine members to a Spiritual Assembly. These members are to be elected on the basis of spiritual qualification, irrespective of material considerations. Some 30,000 such bodies exist around the world, of which 239 are in Canada. At the international level, the Universal House of Justice oversees the development and evolution of the international Bahá'í community. At the national level, annually elected National Spiritual Assemblies, also comprising nine members, govern the affairs of their respective national communities. In all of these elections, as mentioned earlier, electioneering or calling for nominations are not allowed. There are currently over 180 national bodies.

What is noteworthy about the running of Bahá'í communities is the principle of consultation. The Bahá'í Writings attach great importance to this principle. In small or large groups, individuals are free to contribute their ideas to the process of decision-making, while the group retains collective ownership of the deliberations. By such means, no individual feels slighted if an idea is rejected in whole or in part. Similarly, this process is designed to ensure that no individual ego dominates, even if his/her idea gains favour with the group. According to the Bahá'í Writings, the principles of the Bahá'í Administrative Order rest on a spiritual basis defined by the importance of unity. The principles of consultation and non-participation in partisan politics contribute to this goal of unity. The Bahá'í Writings, however, do exhort adherents to follow the secular laws of the country they reside in, to abstain, individually and collectively, from partisan political behaviour, and to be the well-wishers of those in authority. At the same time, Bahá'ís do take their citizenship responsibilities seriously by voting in general elections and by their general interest in the welfare of society. They do not isolate themselves from society.

Membership in the Bahá'í community is open to all who profess faith in Bahá'u'lláh and accept his teachings. It should also be stressed that Bahá'u'lláh expressly prohibited proselytizing, but at the same time he actively encouraged new members to join the Faith. The means by which Bahá'ís spread their message mainly involve **pioneers**, the term that Bahá'ís have coined for volunteers who move to another locale to establish or strengthen a Bahá'í community. Such a move might be local, national, or even international. At the local level, Bahá'ís hold **firesides**, a concept that refers to informal gatherings, usually in one's home, to explain the Bahá'í

Often referred to as the "Lotus Temple," the Bahá'í House of Worship, in New Delhi, India, is one of the most frequently visited sacred sites in the world. PHOTO BY THE BAHÁ'Í MEDIA BANK. REPRINTED BY PERMISSION. © THE BAHÁ'Í MEDIA BANK.

message to "seekers." More recently, devotional meetings have become the means to attract others to the faith. These meetings incorporate prayers and meditations from many other sources of sacred scripture. The method of teaching the Bahá'í Faith is gradually shifting its focus by finding others to help build a new civilization, whether or not they choose to become Bahá'ís. The Bahá'í community is entering a new era of learning in which it wishes to engage in social discourse with the larger society.

At the international level, in 1996 the Universal House of Justice asked all national Bahá'í communities to establish "training institutes." These institutes were intended to oversee decentralized networks of locally based "study circles," where interested seekers could learn about the Bahá'í Faith in a more structured setting. Led by a trained tutor, these study circles used the "Ruhi" books as a curriculum. Developed by the Ruhi Institute in Cali, Colombia, this curriculum presently contains a number of texts and commentaries with such titles or topics as *Reflections on the Life of the Spirit, Arising to Serve, Teaching Children, History, Teaching the Bahá'í Faith*, and *Service*. These texts offer a series of discussions about the Bahá'í Writings, and believers are encouraged to move through the series consecutively as they endeavour to develop the spiritual insights and moral awareness needed if the Baha'i community is to continue to grow and flourish.

In all these aspects—the religious teachings, the vision of society, the calendar of festivals, the social organization, and the means used to spread the faith—there is little or no variation in the worldwide Bahá'í community. A Bahá'í from Canada will feel quite at home in a Bahá'í community in another country, and vice versa. At the same time, though, regional cultures, local traditions, and even personal interests are welcome. Known as Houses of Worship, Bahá'í temples provide a very good example of the way in which the Bahá'í Faith accommodates its vision of global peace and unity to particular social and cultural environments. Located in every continent—in Sydney, Australia; Frankfurt, Germany; New Delhi, India; Panama City, Panama; Kampala, Uganda; Chicago, United States; Apia, Western Samoa; and Santiago, Chile, this last still under construction at time of writing—these temples vary a good deal in their architectural details and building materials. One similarity, though, is that every temple is nine-sided, with nine entrances and a dome, set within a peaceful and meditative ambience of pathways and gardens. Although Bahá'í teachings encourage cultural richness and diversity, there are no variations in the formal aspects and spiritual inspiration of the overall design of the Houses of Worship. The nine sides of every temple represent the world's nine living religions. Exquisitely beautiful structures, Baha'i Houses of Worship are open to all as places to commune with God, usually in silence and reverence, but sometimes with recitations of poetry and sacred writings; only a capella choir music is allowed. The Arabic name for such an occasion, **Mashriqu'l-Adhkar**, means "Dawning-Point of God's Remembrance." Bahá'ís have plans for each House of Worship to serve as a focal point for a variety of humanitarian, educational, social, cultural, and scientific pursuits.

THE MAKING OF A CANADIAN BAHA'I COMMUNITY

It was a group of expatriate Canadians in Chicago during the 1890s who first became attracted to the Baha'i religion. These Canadians first heard mention of Bahá'í during a presentation on the new religion at the World Columbian Exposition in 1893. These and other early adherents were, for the most part, vitally concerned with social reform and social change. Honoré Jaxon (1861–1952), former secretary to the Canadian rebel Louis Riel (1844–85), became the first Canadian to join the Bahá'í community in Chicago in 1897, followed soon after by his French Canadian wife,

In 1912, May and Sutherland Maxwell, around whom the Bahá'í community in Canada developed, welcomed 'Abdu'l-Bahá, the son of Baha'u'lláh, to their home, located on Avenue des Pines in Montreal, Quebec. PHOTO BY EM DASH DESIGN.

Aimée Montfort (1867–1932), a school teacher. In Canada itself, Rose Henderson (1871–1937) was another such early convert, known for her work in education and social justice to improve the fate of children, youth, and mothers. Paul K. Dealy (died 1935), a railroad engineer and inventor originally from Saint John, New Brunswick, was another early adherent. Eventually, the women members of one family, the Magees, established the initial Canadian base in London, Ontario, in 1898.

The first stage (1897–1912) of the Bahá'í Faith in Canada featured members with diverse ideologies and mixed commitments. This period seems chaotic, with new converts having little or no sustained contact with one another. The beliefs of these Bahá'ís were not yet clearly formulated as so few of the Bahá'í Writings were then available. They came into the new religion with an admixture of liberal Protestantism, New Thought, higher biblical criticism, Theosophy, Rosicrucianism, occultism, and spiritualism. Such a medley of beliefs was not enough to sustain a body of committed adherents organized around Bahá'í principles and discourse. However, without much social contact, many of these early believers eventually went their own way. A few remained committed, however, though it was left to an American Bahá'í, May Ellis Maxwell (1870–1940), arriving in Montreal from France in 1902, to become the driving force behind the Bahá'í Faith in Canada during these early years. She articulated a clear sense of Bahá'í mission, directly inspired by 'Abdu'l-Bahá. Maxwell reached across various social strata and managed to gather together a small group of believers in Montreal. Through her, their loyalty in the person of 'Abdu'l-Bahá crystallized; in him they saw a Christ-like character, whose selfless life and work towards the betterment of humankind assumed, in the hearts and minds of those early adherents, an enormous influence. In 1912, 'Abdu'l-Bahá's sojourn in North America, including his nine-day visit to Montreal, reinforced the individual loyalty and personal faith of these early believers, enabling the emergence of a Bahá'í community, however rudimentary.

His visit launched the second stage (1912–37) of the Bahá'í Faith in Canada, shaping community identity and changing styles of boundary maintenance and organization. The Bahá'ís in Canada increasingly began to envision the development of Bahá'í institutions and collective action as an integral part of being Bahá'í. In 1927, the legal incorporation of the National Spiritual Assembly of the Bahá'ís of the United States and Canada, a joint organization, created new and more stringent criteria for Bahá'í membership. Previously porous membership boundaries became firmer, and as the need arose to develop a Bahá'í administrative framework among what was initially a loose-knit gathering of individuals, there developed a perceptible pattern of Bahá'í community.

Propagation of the new religion also began to assume a different character. A quiet change began to take effect among the Bahá'ís when Maxwell joined forces with Marion Jack (1866–1954), an artist and prominent Canadian believer nicknamed "General Jack" for her indomitable pioneering spirit. Jack had also helped found the Bahá'í Faith in the Balkans and France, and she and Maxwell undertook long trips together as travelling teachers, with Jack venturing as far north as the Yukon and as far east as Newfoundland, speaking of the Bahá'í Faith to those whom they met along the way. Persian Bahá'ís and their American colleagues also responded to 'Abdu'l-Bahá's call to spread the Bahá'í Faith through travels in Canada. Significantly, a number of Bahá'ís seized upon the vision of Shoghi Effendi, Guardian of the Bahá'í Faith since 1921. He taught that the fundamental aim of the religion of Bahá'u'lláh was to transform society so as to bring about an emerging new world order. With this vision, Bahá'í teaching work gained momentum, as new topics and ideas became vehicles for attracting new believers from wider social strata. In 1922, the Montreal Bahá'ís formed the first modern Spiritual Assembly in Canada.

The great transformation of the Bahá'í community in Canada occurred during the third stage (1937–44). When Shoghi Effendi considered the

Bahá'í administrative framework sufficiently ready in 1937, he called upon the North American Bahá'í community to organize a systematic teaching campaign and to establish new Spiritual Assemblies across the continent. Whereas previously the Bahá'í teaching work had been left in the hands of a few believers, the new directives specifically involved Bahá'í governing councils, that is, "Spiritual Assemblies." In Canada, the Bahá'ís had the goal of forming a Spiritual Assembly in at least one city in each province by 1944. The task was immense, for there were only 90 Bahá'ís in the whole country—barely enough members to establish nine-member Spiritual Assemblies in each of the provinces and territories. This period saw an efflorescence of approaches in spreading the Bahá'í Faith that were well suited to the cultural milieu of Bahá'ís whose previous religion was mainly Protestant Christianity. These adherents developed Bahá'í fireside gatherings in private homes, public meetings, systematic teaching campaigns, and both home-front and long-distance pioneering. Shoghi Effendi encouraged the use of all of these methods for propagating the Bahá'í Faith in North America and even internationally, and they found a positive response in Canada. The individual fate of these early Bahá'í communities in Canada varied. Once established, some experienced rapid growth, some little or no growth, and some even declined. Maintaining a diverse approach to the propagation of the newly established religion and fostering linkages with the wider society usually meant the community flourished. The community that came to rely too much on other communities for its teaching work, or on the occasional visits of transient pioneers, had a short life. Gender imbalance was also higher in these latter communities than in the more successful ones.

Either way, by the fourth period (1944–48) Bahá'ís in Canada began to develop a distinctly national identity. By way of external influence, World War II had already helped to create this identity among the Bahá'ís through currency regulations as they were forced to establish a Canadian Bahá'í Fund. These regulations also obliged the Bahá'ís of Canada to hold their own Bahá'í schools and conferences, independently of their American colleagues. Moreover, Bahá'ís were also obliged to articulate their convictions concerning non-involvement in partisan politics in general and in World War II, in particular. In this fourth period, the travelling teacher campaigns initiated in earlier years were maintained with considerable vigour. The teaching campaigns and the summer schools had, however, an intrinsic value beyond the fact that they propagated the Bahá'í Faith; they educated a body of new believers across Canada about the Bahá'í systems of beliefs and administration. For the first time, too, Baháʾís were in touch on a national scale with their most active organizers and teachers. The process of developing travelling teachers, schools, and conferences allowed Baháʾís to experience firsthand the array of personal abilities that existed in the Canadian Baháʾí national community. These developments culminated in 1948 with the formation of Canada's own national governing council, the National Spiritual Assembly of the Baháʾís of Canada, as a separate entity from the United States Baháʾí community. By now, there were 263 Baháʾís in Canada living in 41 localities, including 16 Spiritual Assemblies.

The fifth stage (1948–63) saw the community beginning to make serious plans for mounting its own international work. The Guardian of the Baháʾí Faith issued Canada's first set of international goals (1948–53) and when those goals were achieved, he launched a Ten-Year Plan (1953–63) that involved all national Baháʾí communities, including Canada. The Baháʾís of Canada attached spiritual and material significance to the pursuit of this plan and their part in it. The challenges seemed large, as the resources of this community were so few. In April 1953, there were 554 Baháʾís in 102 localities, with 30 local Spiritual Assemblies, scattered across a land which is the second largest in the world. In a message to the Canadian Baháʾís, the Guardian typified them as "progressive, youthful and dynamic."[3] The main thrust of Canada's mission concentrated on pushing the frontiers of the Baháʾí Faith into the more remote northern areas of Canada and establishing the faith in the Pacific regions. There were other goals as well that were no less significant. By 1963, 2,500 Baháʾís could be found in 290 locales, with 68 Spiritual Assemblies spread across Canada.

These developments mark the beginning of the sixth period of the Baháʾí Faith in Canada (1963–79), which saw a vast increase in the enrollment of new believers, especially from the peoples of the Arctic north and other Aboriginal Canadians. In the late 1960s and 1970s, considerable numbers of youth entered the Baháʾí community, reflecting the optimism and enthusiasm of the day. At this time, perhaps one-third of the membership consisted of new members between 15 and 20 years of age. As the 1970s came to a close, enrollments reached a plateau, with the Baháʾí community now totalling 12,591 members in 1,550 localities with 315 Spiritual Assemblies.

---

3   Shoghi Effendi, *Messages to Canada* (Toronto: National Spiritual Assembly of the Baháʾí s of Canada, 1965), 60.

The seventh stage in the growth of the Bahá'í Faith in Canada (1979–present) marks an entirely different period in the evolution of the community. In 1979, Ayotollah Ruhollah Khomeini (1902–89) and other Shi'ite Muslim clerics spearheaded a revolution in Iran that succeeded in overthrowing the regime of Mohammad Reza Shah Pahlavi (1919–80). Facing persecution from the new theocratic government, many Iranians fled their homeland, and Canada opened its doors to thousands of these refugees, some 1,500 of whom were Bahá'ís. Many of these Bahá'ís had been spreading the Bahá'í message in countries outside of Iran, but Khomeini's revolution made it virtually impossible to have their passports renewed. Stateless, they arrived to settle in Canada during the early 1980s, strengthening the Canadian-born Bahá'í communities in 150 different localities across the country. Many of the newcomers joined smaller Bahá'í communities in suburban and rural areas, adding further to the expanding diversity of the Bahá'í Faith in Canada. These episodic changes in the Canadian Bahá'í community hinged on several social factors, of which social class, Aboriginal and ethnic composition, and the participation of women played vital roles.

In terms of social composition, we find that the nature and extent of the engagement of the community with the Arctic north, with Aboriginal peoples, and with French-speaking Canadians and Quebecois have also contributed to the profile of the Bahá'í community in Canada. While a liberal Protestant outlook of the early converts dominated their approach to the Bahá'í Faith, with its emphasis on individualism and personal salvation, the use of fireside meetings in the home and public meetings in hotels allowed the Bahá'í community to attract both those who favoured home life and those who favoured neutral settings, respectively. Later, as other social groups—women, Aboriginal peoples, and French Canadians—entered into the Bahá'í community, the methods of teaching the new religion began to vary.

Women were a significant factor in shaping the dynamics of the Bahá'í community's life and expansion. The Bahá'í Faith initially attracted a large proportion of women; they comprised 70 per cent of new believers. In the earlier periods, the Bahá'í Faith was a magnet for suffragists and women social reformers like May Maxwell's colleagues, Edith Magee (born 1880) and Rose Henderson, who campaigned tirelessly for the advancement of women, the eradication of poverty, and the elimination of prejudice. Increasingly, the faith began to attract single, urban women, many of whom served with distinction in the teaching and administrative fields.

Between 1942 and 1947, for example, the number of women members in Vancouver's Bahá'í community rose from 56 per cent to 84 per cent, while Hamilton's women members in the Spiritual Assembly reached 74 per cent. Given the social contexts in the mid-twentieth century, this feature meant that the Bahá'í Faith primarily reached other single women, and that the strategy of holding public meetings, rather than home firesides by single women, provided the most appropriate and usually the only means for propagating the new faith. Without the ties of marriage of many of their peers, these women became the primary means by which the Bahá'í Faith spread across Canada, particularly among the growing numbers of women trained in technical and professional occupations. Today, the proportion of new Bahá'ís who are women is still larger than that of men, but the differences are narrowing. Currently, 53 per cent of all Bahá'ís are women. At the 1998 National Convention, the Bahá'í community of Canada enjoyed an equal representation of women and men delegates for the first time.

Class and occupation have contributed to the shifting social composition of the Bahá'í community, too. While initially the community attracted members from the upper classes, particularly the leisured intelligentsia, it successively moved to attract people from the managerial class and from lower middle-class occupations. Gradually, the class composition of the Bahá'í community has come more closely to resemble that of the larger Canadian population. This shift has had a bearing on the ability of the Bahá'í community to propagate the Bahá'í Faith. The occupational skills of the lower middle-class have afforded them freedom to move around the country and to settle in those locales where the need for new Bahá'ís was the greatest. That said, the Bahá'ís of Canada do not constitute a wealthy group of individuals. In 1985, for example, only 40 per cent of the 10,000 adult Bahá'ís with known addresses were estimated to be wage earners, contributing an average of $790 per year to the Canadian Bahá'í Fund. By the end of the 1980s, it was estimated that 60 per cent of adult Bahá'ís were wage earners, with an average contribution of $332 to Bahá'í work at the national level. Still, the annual budget of the national Bahá'í governing body was around $8 million in 2010–11.

Deeply intertwined with gender and social class, ethnic composition is another factor affecting the way the Bahá'í community of Canada has evolved. During its early years, Bahá'í membership retained its British basis. Catholic Christian and francophone Canadians, for example, found an unfamiliar landscape in the lack of ritual and congregational prayer, the large number of single people and couples without children, and the absence of extended family and social ties. Such a social landscape lacked recognizable landmarks for new Bahá'ís from other cultural and religious backgrounds. Nonetheless, 'Abdu'l-Bahá's *Tablets of the Divine Plan,* authored in 1916–17, explicitly called for taking Bahá'í teachings to francophones, and Shoghi Effendi confirmed the necessity of spreading the faith among this group. The work was initially slow, even though the new religion had established an early Canadian stronghold in Montreal. The Bahá'ís in that city, however, were English-speaking, and the long-standing traditions of Catholic Christianity in Quebec may also have contributed to such slow progress. Progress has been made, though, and today the 500 or so French-speaking Bahá'ís assume an important role in promoting the Bahá'í Faith in Canada and elsewhere.

Jewish Canadians and African Canadians also joined the Bahá'í community in its early days, though their experiences must have been markedly different. The Jewish element in the Bahá'í community has become quite apparent. Already in 1921, Bahá'ís of Jewish heritage were among the first to respond with clarity and understanding to Shoghi Effendi's vision of the faith of Bahá'u'lláh as one that encompasses a world order of unity and peace. The Jewish contribution helped to transform a Canadian Bahá'í community that was inner-directed to one that opened up to the world. The vigour and erudition of certain Bahá'ís of Jewish descent resulted in a new orientation of the faith's teaching work. Emeric Sala (1906–90), for example, became the most prolific writer among Canadian Bahá'ís. Published in 1945, his book, *This Earth, One Country,* led the way among Western Bahá'ís in its advocacy of religious internationalism and global peace and unity.

At the same time, as a religion of the private home and of public meetings, the Bahá'í community must have been a new and challenging experience for its few African Canadian members. The first Bahá'ís had limited social knowledge of each other, for although they shared Bahá'í membership, they maintained extensive ties to their own circles, often keeping them separate from the Bahá'í community. Instead of finding a social group that engaged all aspects of individual life, African Canadians initially found a community that favoured individualism. Again, the Bahá'í community lacked familiar cultural and religious landmarks to ease the transition to a new spiritual community. Edward Elliott (no dates), whose mother worked as a maid in the Maxwell household, proved a rare exception. Recognized as an important bridge between Montreal's African Canadian and white communities, he represented the Canadian National Spiritual Assembly at the African Intercontinental Teaching Conference, in Kampala, Uganda, in 1953. Currently, racial and ethnic diversity is a very striking feature of Baháʾí community life.

The participation of Aboriginal Canadian peoples in the national Baháʾí community has been of deep interest to the National Spiritual Assembly. More than 29 per cent of all new adherents to the faith fall into these two groups. To a large extent, this interest may be traced to statements by ʾAbduʾl-Bahá himself, who wrote that if "the fragrances of God be diffused amongst the Eskimos [Inuit], its effect will be very great and far-reaching."[4] Shoghi Effendi also encouraged the settlement of the North. "Earthly symbols of Baháʾuʾlláhʾs unearthly Sovereignty," he wrote, "must needs ... be raised as far north as Franklin beyond the Arctic Circle. ..."[5] He also described the Baháʾí work in the North as a "strenuous yet highly meritorious obligation."[6] Indeed, the "ultimate triumph" of Canadaʾs "collective and historic task" depends, in Shoghi Effendiʾs words, upon the work carried out in the Arctic.[7] According to him, work "on the northern fringes of the Western Hemisphere" holds serious consequences for work among peoples in other lands.[8] In an address to the first Alaskan Baháʾí Convention, he stated that "the region ... must needs play a prominent part in the shaping of the destinies of mankind."[9]

Planting the Baháʾí Faith in these regions mainly calls for long-term pioneering and teaching during the summer, a rather lonely work with sometimes painfully slow progress. On average, Baháʾí teaching work in the Arctic has entailed a 14-year lapse between the first teacher to visit the area and the settlement of the first pioneer; a 13-year lapse between the first pioneer and the first northern believer; and another 8 years before the first local Spiritual Assembly is formed. Under these conditions, virtually all pioneers had to possess exceptional resourcefulness, a good deal of humility, and a profound reliance on prayer and faith. The physical isolation of northern communities, along with the entrenched strengths of some Christian denominations, required the sort of self-sacrifice hardly necessary in other situations. Begun in earnest in 1950, this work has

---

4   ʾAbduʾl-Bahá, *Tablets of the Divine Plan*, rev. ed. (Wilmette, IL: Baháʾí Publishing Trust, 1977), 523.

5   Shoghi Effendi, *Messages to the Baháʾí World, 1950–1957* (Wilmette, IL: Baháʾí Publishing Trust, 1958), 57.

6   Shoghi Effendi, *Messages to Canada* (Toronto: National Spiritual Assembly of the Baháʾís of Canada, 1965), 61.

7   Ibid., 61.

8   Shoghi Effendi, *High Endeavours: Messages to Alaska* (Anchorage, AK: National Spiritual Assembly of the Baháʾís of Alaska, 1976), 32.

9   Ibid.

born some fruit. By 1988, the number of Inuit Bahá'ís had grown to 30, and today there are 71 Bahá'ís of Inuit background.

Similarly, in 1916 'Abdu'l-Bahá repeatedly emphasized the importance of reaching the Aboriginal populations of Canada. He stated that North American Bahá'ís "must attach great importance to the Indians, the original inhabitants of America," and that "there can be no doubt that through the Divine teachings they will become so enlightened that the whole earth will be illumined."[10] Thirty-two years after 'Abdu'l-Bahá's appeal, the Bahá'í community embarked on the work of teaching the Bahá'í Faith to First Nations peoples. When the Canadian Bahá'í community formed its own administrative body in 1948, its goals included a call for the participation of Aboriginal peoples in the membership "to share administrative privileges in local institutions of the Faith in Canada."[11] At that time, there were only three Aboriginal Canadian believers in the country—Mohawk Alfred James Loft (1908–73) and his wife Chippewa Melba Whetung Loft (1912–81), who lived in Tyendinaga Mohawk Territory in Ontario, and Cree Noel Wuttunee (no dates) in Calgary. Between 1948 and 1960, however, the Canadian Bahá'í community laid the practical foundation for work among the Aboriginal Canadians, although very few Bahá'ís thought of undertaking this work until the start of the international Ten-Year Plan (1953–63). By the mid-1950s, many more Bahá'ís had become active in bringing their message, both by direct contact on reserves and through Aboriginal Canadian organizations. Bahá'í efforts to be of service to Aboriginal peoples often took the form of joint projects with non-Bahá'ís, like the Yukon Indian Advancement Association, founded in the late 1960s. As another example, in the fall of 1960, Calgary Bahá'ís Mr. and Mrs. Arthur B. Irwin (no dates) formed a social club where Aboriginal and non-Aboriginal peoples could come together. By early 1961, the club had become the foundation of what later became known as the Native Friendship Centre, attracting gatherings of 50 to 150 people, more or less equally divided between Aboriginal and non-Aboriginal Canadians.

Between 1960 and 1963, the first surge of Aboriginal Canadian enrollment in Bahá'í communities took place. In 1960, there were 19 adult Aboriginal Canadian believers in Canada, nine of whom were in Alberta. In July that year, Ben and Louise Whitecow (no dates), who lived on Alberta's Peigan Reserve, became the first Bahá'ís in Canada to have an

---

10 'Abdu'l-Bahá, *Tablets of the Divine Plan*, 32–33.
11 Effendi, *Messages to Canada*, 104.

actual Bahá'í wedding legally accepted by secular authorities, though British Columbia had recognized the legitimacy of Bahá'í marriage two years earlier. By 1963, 20 of the 68 Spiritual Assemblies in Canada were Aboriginal Canadian Assemblies and almost one-third of the 2,000 Bahá'ís in Canada were Aboriginal Canadians. By 1989, 4,305 Aboriginals formed one-fifth of the Bahá'í community of Canada. As we begin the twenty-first century, some 9 of the 247 Spiritual Assemblies in Canada are found on reserves and about one-quarter of Canadian Bahá'ís are Aboriginal peoples. The overwhelming majority of Aboriginal Canadian Bahá'ís live in Alberta, Saskatchewan, and the Yukon, and had entered the Bahá'í Faith in the 1960s and late 1970s.

The theology and administrative structure of the Bahá'í Faith may help to explain why Aboriginal Canadians continue to form such a large percentage of the Bahá'í community. The Bahá'í concept of one creator and its central teaching of the oneness of humanity resonate comfortably with traditional Aboriginal spirituality. As Canadian Broadcasting Corporation commentator Dan David (no dates) noted in 1989, the Bahá'ís "do not try to wipe out Native religion."[12] The Bahá'í prohibition on prosletyzing underscores this basic position to other religions as well. There is also a Bahá'í administrative principle that recognizes the position of minorities. In this case, the Bahá'í Writings make a clear point of according elected office to a member of a minority group when there is a tie of votes between him/her and someone from the dominant group. According to Dan David, such theological and administrative factors mean that Aboriginal Canadians feel "a sense of belonging" in the Bahá'í community, especially because they do not have to renounce traditional Aboriginal spirituality if they become members of the Bahá'í community and find meaning in the Bahá'í understanding of life.

At the same time, as ways have been found to recognize and integrate Aboriginal Canadians into the national Bahá'í community, it has also sought more generally to enrich its social, intellectual, and cultural life in an effort to realize the moral and spiritual goals of the faith. These pursuits have taken many forms, including education, and social and economic development programs in Canada and overseas. In the 1980s, when national Bahá'í communities around the world began to use

---

12   Dan David, interviewed on *Main Street*, CBC Radio Fredericton, May 1989. Quoted in Will C. van den Hoonaard, "Socio-demographic Characteristics of the Canadian Baha'i Community, 1991–06," *Baha'i Library Online*, http://bahai-library.com/ hoonaard_socio-demographics_canadian_bahais.

the Ruhi study courses developed in South America, Canadian Bahá'ís increasingly encouraged attendance at special gatherings purely devoted to the contemplation of the Bahá'í Writings. In 1988, Canadian Bahá'ís also established the Maxwell International Bahá'í School, at Shawnigan Lake, British Columbia. Named in honour of May Maxwell and her husband William Sutherland Maxwell (1874–1952), the school was a non-denominational institution geared towards the International Baccalaureate degree program. Sadly, after many years of operation, it was closed down in 2008. Other independent schools have been inspired by Bahá'í principles, notably the Nancy Campbell Collegiate Institute, founded in 1994 in Stratford and now located in London, Ontario, and the Roger White Academy, in Newmarket, Ontario. Named for Roger White (1929–93), the "poet laureate" of the Canadian Baha'i community, the Newmarket school offers classes from kindergarten to Grade 8.

In the area of social and economic development, the Bahá'í community of Canada has asked for and has received funding from the Canadian International Development Agency (CIDA) for the establishment of nondenominational projects overseas. The Canadian Bahá'í International Development Services (CBIDS) runs a number of these projects. Incorporated in 1981, CBIDS has worked with CIDA to assist with development programs initiated by Bahá'í communities in other parts of the world. These programs have ranged from primary health care in Kenya, Zambia, and Uganda to radio broadcasting in Bolivia and Ecuador, rural development in Haiti, and literacy and vocational training in India. On the domestic front, the Office of External Affairs of the Canadian Bahá'í community has issued a number of trenchant statements on social issues in Canada, several of them at the invitation of the Canadian government, and in 2003, the Bahá'í community of Canada established the Canadian Bahá'í Development Agency (CBDA). This organization helps local Bahá'í groups in Canada with modest grass-roots projects, from environmental activities like clean-ups and tree-planting, to health camps and workshops on issues like race relations, the status of women, and job opportunities.

Whether social and economic development assistance involves basic health care and substance abuse, child care and immunization, agriculture and the environment, race and gender equality, or literacy and setting up modest grass-roots enterprises, CBDA tries to put into practice the principles of the Bahá'í Faith. At the heart of this faith is the conviction that the practical and spiritual aspects of daily life should not be separated. Economic and material improvements, Bahá'ís believe, go hand in hand with moral and spiritual progress. Nor are individual achievements to be valued in terms of personal gain. Engagement in social and economic development projects seem a natural extension to what Bahá'ís believe about service, not just to fellow Bahá'ís but also to the wider community. At the heart of this process is the Bahá'í principle of consultation spoken of earlier. Just as this principle is central to the running of Bahá'í communities, so Bahá'í social and economic initiatives stress collective decision-making and collective action. The use of such methods often gives rise to imaginative new solutions to community problems, as well as greater fairness in the way the resources of the community are distributed, especially among parties who historically have been excluded from decision-making processes. In this way, Bahá'í social and economic initiatives help to realize the greater goal of a global community of peace and unity.

BAHÁ'ÍS IN TODAY'S CANADA

According to the Department of Statistics of the National Bahá'í Office, in Thornhill, Ontario, there were 37,791 Bahá'ís in Canada in 2011. Their distribution is mixed, with 39 per cent living in large urban areas, 27 per cent in small towns, 16 per cent in rural communities, and 17 per cent in Aboriginal settlements or on reserves. The geographical distribution of Bahá'ís thus differs markedly from the Canadian norm, where over 75 per cent of the population live in large urban areas. The three areas with the highest ratio of Bahá'ís are the Yukon, the Northwest Territories, and Saskatchewan. A high proportion of Aboriginal Bahá'ís live in those areas. British Columbia also has a higher rate due to high enrollments among recent migrants to the province. On the whole, the ratio of Bahá'ís to the general population increases as one travels west, except for Quebec, where the ratio is rather low. Bahá'ís in the Atlantic provinces also have a low ratio to the general population. Bahá'ís are more mobile than the general Canadian population. Almost 36 per cent of the whole Bahá'í population moves each year. By contrast, about 10 per cent of Canadians in the general population change their addresses each year. One administrative result of such mobility is the rate of old addresses lost, which sometimes outpaces the rate of new addresses recovered.

While the overall rate of growth of the Bahá'í community in Canada has not been spectacular, it has been steady, marked by occasional peaks of immense growth. In the peak years of 1963, 1971, and 1979, these growth spurts climbed as high as 200 new believers per month. At the other end of the scale, the enrollment rate for January 1989, for example, was 54 new members, while it had been 49 per month during the whole of the previous year. Of these new Bahá'ís, 41 per cent were new adherents from outside Bahá'í families, while 59 per cent came from Bahá'í families. There are both advantages and disadvantages to periods of rapid expansion. Such spurts add immensely to the diversity and resources of the community in the short term, but they are also marked by poor consolidation, perhaps because of excessive demands on existing resources. The rate of enrollment seems to depend to a large extent on a particular group's sense of unity. Such feelings of unity appear to have the best possible chance in small cities and small towns. Finally, resignation, relocation, and death affect the number of Bahá'ís in Canada. Between April 1987 and April 1988, for example, the community grew by 5 per cent, but an equal proportion resigned, transferred, or died, leaving zero growth. Taken together, these trends mean that the Bahá'í community in Canada has maintained an average annual growth rate of 1.2 per cent, with a membership of up to 50,000 predicted by 2025.

What does everyday life look like for a typical Bahá'í community in Canada today? To begin with, we need to recognize that many Bahá'í communities are relatively small. So to protect the identity and privacy of its members, let us imagine that the very real Bahá'í community described here exists in the fictionally named Canadian town of Elmsford. Located outside a city, Elmsford has some 1,500 homes with 6,500 people who principally work in that city. The Bahá'í community was started in 1987 when the *first* family (a couple and their children) moved out of the city to "open" Elmsford to the Bahá'í Faith. Since then, seven other families settled there. However, due to change in jobs, 3 families moved away, leaving 5 families, currently totalling 11 adults, 5 youth (aged 15 to 21), 7 children and pre-youth (aged under 15). This community is typical of many others in Canada in that it has a local governing council, holds Nineteen-Day Feasts, and celebrates the nine Bahá'í holy days, the organization of which alternates with the Spiritual Assembly in the nearby city. The *second* family that has remained in Elmsford consists of a Canadian woman who married someone from the Middle East who comes from a long Bahá'í family line; they have four children. The wife is a teacher and the husband is a technician in a print shop. More recently, the wife's mother (also a Baha'i) has moved into that household. The *third* family has two children. The parents are naturopathic doctors. The wife lived for the good part of her life as part of a Bahá'í pioneering family in a Saharan country; her extended

A small group of Canadian Bahá'ís gather to explore ways of applying spiritual principles to their lives and communities. PHOTO BY BAHÁ'Í CANADA. REPRINTED BY PERMISSION. © BAHÁ'Í CANADA.

family is originally from Iran and India and includes Zoroastrians, Jews, and Muslims. Her husband's family was originally from New York and New Jersey, and includes Bahá'is and Christians. His Bahá'í parents were part of the back-to-the-land movement in the 1970s and settled in Cape Breton. The *fourth* family constitutes another household that represents an intercultural marriage; the wife is a second-generation Bahá'í and white, married to an Aboriginal Canadian Baha'i. She is a teacher and he is a member of a national police force. They have three children. The *fifth* household consists of a Nova Scotian, a musician and composer of Aboriginal and African Canadian background, who is widely known and very popular in the larger region. He has three teen-aged boys. The community is diverse in all respects, in terms of age, ethnicity, and religious heritage.

What has been the impact of this diversity—which Bahá'ís prize so highly—on the character of Bahá'í activities in Elmsford? Both inwardly and outwardly the diversity has worked to the advantage of the Bahá'ís. The Bahá'ís have been able to pool their diverse resources. For example, when the women in two households decided to go to university, they arranged their class schedules in such a way as to alternate taking care of their children. Moreover, other households made similar arrangements for the purposes of work. Given the abundance of new musical talent, community gatherings have become more festive. Moreover, the Bahá'í children and youth have become close friends, which has allowed them to nurture courtesy in each other; some take responsibility for the care and education of the younger children during some Bahá'í gatherings.

While its aims and organizational make-up is typical of Bahá'í communities, the Elmsford Bahá'ís are unique in other aspects as they try to exemplify the Bahá'í approach by developing the community in a spiritual, social, intellectual, and economic sense. The 11 adults have succeeded in maintaining a local Spiritual Assembly for more than 12 years (with a hiatus of one year), and this fact alone gives them a spiritual boost. The holding of in-depth studies of particular segments of the sacred Bahá'í Writings, as well as following the Ruhi curriculum, is understood by the community as a positive spiritual development. The community also sees the completion of the annual Canadian Bahá'í Fund goal as an expression of spiritual vitality in the community. Occasional devotional gatherings that sometimes draw in a neighbour or two reinforce that vitality.

The social aspects of the Elmsford Bahá'í community cannot be divorced from its spiritual thrust. The nature and extent of Bahá'í community life are shaped by the interests of each person and, indeed, of each household. There is considerable interfamily visiting and stay-overs by children and youth, which builds social bonds between the young and other household members. Given the ethnic and racial diversity of the households, a visitor would have difficulty noting what child or youth belonged to what household. With the guidance of the local Spiritual Assembly, three of the households with children have taken upon themselves sharing responsibility for children's education, which take place in conjunction with the larger nearby Bahá'í community. One household takes particular interest in holding gatherings for youth. Social interaction also occurs elsewhere in the community. The wife in another household is known to engage in book exchanges with a few pre-youth. Because that household seems to be more widely known in the general community of Elmsford and beyond, their work and professional activities are regularly reported in newspapers, on radio, and sometimes on television. They see their visibility as "credible" people as one of the contributions they can make to the Bahá'í community, which is just emerging from obscurity in small towns like Elmsford. They also frequently appear as speakers at Bahá'í and non-Bahá'í religious gatherings. Yet another family makes their sizeable shed available every few months for "family-fun" gatherings for all of Elmsford, providing music and potluck food; some 60–70 people attend. Most recently, the local Bahá'ís have organized a craft fair, open to the whole community.

The Nineteen-Day Feast constitutes the cornerstone of Bahá'í community life and is universally attended with the exception of those who are out of town or ill. Held on the first day of each Bahá'í month, the Nineteen-Day

Feast consists of three consecutive sets of activities: readings from the Bahá'í Writings; consultation about community affairs; and socializing and renewing fellowship. As the structure of the Feast is the same the world over, a Bahá'í from Elmsford would feel quite at home attending the Feast in another Bahá'í community, whether in Canada or elsewhere. While adults engage in consultation during the central part of the Feast, a member of the community (often an older youth) takes younger children into a separate part of the house for a children's activity. When children reach eight or nine years of age, their parents begin to encourage them to remain during the consultative part of the Feast and even to offer suggestions to the community as a whole. In this way, children and youth begin to assume fuller roles themselves in the consultative process. According to visitors, the children in the Elmsford community seem exceptionally courteous, a reflection of the value Bahá'ís place upon good manners as an aspect of the global peace and unity for which they strive. One hears the children recite prayers in Arabic, English, French, and Persian. The Bahá'ís in the Elmsford community highly value spending time together and they do their best to turn their Nineteen-Day Feasts into attractive events. If the Feast falls on a school day, it starts earlier in the evening, so that the children will have less trouble getting up for school the following day.

The Elmsford Bahá'ís take advantage of the period known as Ayyam-i-Há at the end of February, representing four or five additional dates in the Bahá'í calendar. Bahá'ís use the added time for hospitality and charity, involving modest gift exchanges with children and among the households, potluck dinners, outdoor activities, and informal gatherings open to the wider community. Given their small number, however, the Elmsford Bahá'ís must manage their time and material resources carefully. First, the Canadian Bahá'í Fund requires sufficient attention. Donations are always voluntary and anonymous, and when participation falls between 98 and 100 per cent of its members, the community is pleased. These donations are used to help sustain local, national, and international plans. Bahá'ís have also set up Canadian Bahá'í Fund goals for children and youth, who decide at the end of the year how the monies should be allocated to various causes, both Bahá'í and otherwise. For example, the local food bank usually gets a fair share of these donations. Second, the Bahá'ís are finding new ways of internally raising monies for the Canadian Bahá'í Fund: some have chickens producing eggs that are sold within the Bahá'í community; another has a well-stocked video collection, where voluntary "rents" go towards the Fund; and another one does yard work, the payment of which helps the Fund. The Bahá'í women have set up a craft group and create items of interest, the proceeds of which go to the Fund.

Social cohesion is apparent in other ways, such as when someone needs an impromptu ride into town. A special relationship is developing between and among the youth and children of these families. A high school student interested in philosophy or another one in DJ-ing will find someone else among the Bahá'ís who shares these interests. A local youth with a penchant for writing poetry will find ample support and encouragement, as does the pre-youth with an interest in reading fantasy books. When Bahá'ís aged 15 to 70 are fasting from sunrise to sunset, 2–20 March, before Naw-Rúz, the Elmsford community holds a special dawn breakfast on 2 March to celebrate the first fast of any youth who has reached the age of 15 in the last year. As with other Bahá'í Holy Day gatherings, the Elmsford Bahá'ís organize Naw-Rúz festivities in conjunction with the larger Bahá'í community in the nearby city. This New Year's celebration draws a particularly large crowd of 150 to 200 people, most of whom are friends of the Bahá'ís in the whole area. As with every Bahá'í Holy Day, few rules are stipulated for observing Naw-Rúz, although some Bahá'ís like to mark the occasion by buying new clothes. Old and young alike, Bahá'ís and their guests dance until late into the night or early morning.

Two or three times a year, the Elmsford Bahá'í community organized open meetings with featured speakers in the local school, believing not only that the topics proposed for discussion might be of interest to the larger community but also that the events provided a kind of public service. The subjects of these meetings varied, ranging from marriage and raising children, to education and gossip in the workplace. Normally, Bahá'ís who are professionals in various fields gave informal presentations, but on occasion non-Bahá'ís were invited to participate as panel members. The Elmsford Bahá'í community advertised these meetings by mailing flyers to each home. Some of the meetings drew four or five interested people who are not Bahá'ís, sometimes as many as a dozen. Once, though, no one showed up. On a brighter note, the community has chosen to participate as a collective activity in the local highway clean-up campaign. As it turns out, the Elmsford Bahá'í community was one of the first communities in the province to offer to do this work. Twice a year, five or six adults and the youth clean up the litter on the highway. Two large government-sponsored signs at each end of the five-kilometre stretch of road make local people aware of the contributions to the public good made by this small Bahá'í community.

In terms of fostering relations with the wider community, the Elmsford Bahá'ís have experienced varying degrees of success and disappointment. On the one hand, notices of the public meetings sent to all households received approving comments from those who personally knew the Bahá'ís, even if such approval often did not translate into attendance or participation. In addition, in the past the Bahá'ís embarked on a once-a-week after-school program on a nearby Aboriginal reserve, using whatever suitable talents were available among the Bahá'ís. Most of all, the highway clean-up campaign has been seen in a positive way, as have the family-fun gatherings and the growing popularity of the craft sale. On the other hand, occasional mailings directly inviting people to investigate the Bahá'í Faith have been greeted with silence. Attempts by the Bahá'í community to foster links with one of the local churches have fallen on deaf ears as well, and sometimes they have even been greeted with hostility or indifference. Not even a suggestion by the Bahá'ís for organizing prayers for world peace was welcomed. Occasionally, the local school put up obstacles to hinder the Bahá'ís from holding their public meetings on the premises. A principal familiar with the Bahá'í Faith might have been sympathetic, but a principal uncomfortable with the unknown was less so. Sometimes, the Elmsford Bahá'ís sense a micro-climate of fear among their neighbours, although in various aspects of their daily lives they enjoy many personal non-Bahá'í friends who do not seem to share that fear. At the same time, these same friends rarely show any interest in the new religion. The local telephone book includes a Bahá'í listing that enquirers may use if they wish to obtain information about the new religion while remaining anonymous. At a display in a local restaurant to celebrate the tenth anniversary of the Spiritual Assembly, three non-Bahá'ís showed up.

AFTERWORD

Today, the Bahá'í Faith enjoys a secure place among the many spiritual traditions constituting the Canadian religious landscape, and Canadian Bahá'ís occupy a favoured position in the Bahá'í world. Legal recognition of the Bahá'í Community in Canada is extensive. In 1935, the Government of Quebec granted such recognition to the Spiritual Assembly of the Bahá'ís of Montreal, the first of its kind for Bahá'ís in Canada. An Act of Parliament incorporated the National Spiritual Assembly of the Bahá'ís of Canada in April 1949. In February 1958, an important victory was achieved

The ceremony marking the opening of the "Terraces of Light," at the Bahá'í World Centre, in Haifa, Israel, May 2001. PHOTO BY THE BAHÁ'Í MEDIA BANK. REPRINTED BY PERMISSION. © THE BAHÁ'Í MEDIA BANK.

for the Bahá'ís when the Superior Court in Montreal ruled in their favour against the City of Montreal, binding it to recognize the Bahá'í Faith as an independent religion and to exempt it from municipal taxes. In 1961, the Department of National Defence recognized an application from the National Spiritual Assembly of the Bahá'ís of Canada to be placed on the list of religious denominations represented in the armed services. In another context, as noted earlier, Bahá'í marriage was first legalized in British Columbia in December 1958. Other jurisdictions eventually followed, but so far only Newfoundland, in 1983, has granted such a right to Bahá'í Spiritual Assemblies rather than to a "marriage officer," a term more familiar to Christians than to Bahá'ís. Bahá'í Holy Days are now accepted in all provincial and territorial jurisdictions, too, which is a boon to Bahá'í students attending school. And in the world of contemporary entertainment, Bahá'ís played a significant role in the work of Vision TV, an interdenominational television channel premised on mutual respect.

Overseas, Canadian Bahá'ís are recognized by their fellow believers for numerous achievements in many areas of the Bahá'í Faith, not least their administrative knowledge and experience, which they frequently offer to other Bahá'í communities attempting to fulfill their own moral and spiritual goals, including in *la francophonie*. But perhaps the most visible signs of the faith among their fellow believers come in the concrete form of their contributions to the shape and substance of Bahá'í administrative and sacred space. The French Canadian architect Jean-Baptiste Louis Bourgeois (1856–1930) designed the Bahá'í temple in the Chicago suburb of Wilmette, Illinois, a House of Worship of remarkable beauty and grandeur, sometimes called the "Taj Mahal" of the West. Still more significantly, Canadian Bahá'ís have provided the designs for many of the buildings at the Bahá'í World Centre on Mount Carmel in Haifa, Israel, as well as the Monument Gardens nearby, commissioned from Bourgeois by Shoghi Effendi in 1932 as the resting place for Bahá'u'lláh's daughter, Bahíyyih Khánum (1846–1932). Born in Iran and now a Canadian citizen living in Vancouver, Hussein Amanat (born 1942) designed the Universal House of Justice, and more recently, additional administrative buildings on Mount Carmel, including the Centre for the Study of the Texts.

Another Canadian architect of Iranian background, Sahba Fariborz (born 1948) designed 18 terraces of gardens, 9 above and 9 below, as magnificent approaches to the Shrine of the Báb, decades after William Sutherland Maxwell, himself a Montreal-born architect, had conceived the building. Fariborz also designed the Bahá'í House of Worship in New Delhi, India. Shaped like a lotus flower about to open to the sun, Fariborz's creation is frequently referred to as the "Lotus of Bahapur." Among the most visited sites in the world, New Delhi's Bahá'í House of Worship has been dubbed the "Taj Mahal" of the twentieth century and seems destined to be recognized as one of the architectural and construction masterpieces of our time. More recently, the Universal House of Justice commissioned Toronto's Siamak Hariri (born 1958) as architect of the Baha'i House of Worship to be built near Santiago, Chile, as part of the 2001–2006 Five Year Plan. Hariri feels a strong personal connection to his task: "I'm Baha'i, too, my parents were persecuted as a result of it, and so you can imagine what this commission means. Things are unadorned in Baha'i. Music can only be *a capella*, and no icons can line the walls. So you need to embed a sacred feeling in the building itself."[13] Construction started in November 2010.

---

13   Alec Scott, "Higher Power: Toronto Architect Siamak Hariri Ascends to Architectural Greatness," *CBC.ca, Arts, Art & Design*, 13 July 2006, http://www.cbc.ca/arts/artdesign/hariri.html.

In many ways, the experience of the Elmsford community reflects the situation for Bahá'ís across Canada, whether they belong to a rural, suburban, or urban Spiritual Assembly. The country presents a geographical challenge to any religious group that is trying to administer to needs of members scattered widely across small communities. These logistical problems present a particular challenge to the far-flung Bahá'ís, whose numbers of nearly 38,000 believers appear as relatively few in comparison with other religious groups in Canada. The community has grown steadily, however, even if not spectacularly. The number of believers grew very slowly at first, and the cost of communication and travel presented genuine difficulties. Religious indifference in urban areas and religious conservativism in rural areas are some of the other difficulties faced by this new religion in its efforts to find a place in society and to flourish. After all, as recently as 1991, only 0.1 per cent of the population of Canada identified itself with a new religion; and in the most recent long-form census of 2001, the Bahá'í Faith, Eckankar, Jainism, Shinto, Taoism, and Zoroastrianism together accounted for only 0.13 per cent of those identifying themselves as practising and believing members of an "Eastern Religion" other than Hinduism, Buddhism, and Sikhism. If the evolution of the Bahá'í community in the United States is any indication, we might assume that people look to alternative religions when more traditional options are languishing.

Although there are large concentrations of Bahá'ís in some cities, it is striking that the Bahá'í community in Canada is found mainly in small towns. It is also notable that despite its small size, the Bahá'í community seems to enjoy a higher public profile and a more positive influence on public affairs than is the case with some religious groups of comparable size. Even though Bahá'í doctrine insists that its members should not be involved in partisan politics, Bahá'ís are not isolated from the rest of society. In addition, they stress serving humanity as an integral part of being Bahá'í, as expressed through various social and economic development projects undertaken for the common good. Finally, the Bahá'í tradition of not aggressively seeking converts, while welcoming new members with open arms, continues to render the Bahá'í community an appealing way of life within the broader Canadian religious landscape. Today, the Bahá'í community is characterized by higher levels of education than the Canadian population in general, and a higher proportion of youthful to older members. These demographics alone should ensure that the Bahá'í community will continue to grow, developing even deeper roots in Canada.

KEY TERMS

'Abdu'l-Bahá	"Servant of Bahá," the son of Bahá'u'lláh, the founder of the Bahá'í faith, who was appointed sole authoritative interpreter of his father's teachings.
Báb	"The Gate," the founder of Babism and the precursor to Bahá'u'lláh, the founder of the Bahá'í faith.
Bahá'í Writings	The Bahá'í sacred scriptures, in particular the writings of the Báb, of Bahá'u'lláh, of 'Abdu'l-Bahá, and of Shoghi Effendi. Also refers to the writings of the Universal House of Justice.
Bahá'u'lláh	"The Glory of God," the founder of the Bahá'í faith.
Firesides	Informal gatherings, usually in private homes, to explain the Bahá'í message to "seekers."
Mashriqu'l-Adhkar	"Dawning-Point of God's Remembrance," the Bahá'í House of Worship, of which there are presently seven worldwide, with an eighth under construction in Santiago, Chile.
Naw-Rúz	"New Day," the Bahá'í New Year, celebrated at the vernal equinox on or about 21 March.
Nineteen-Day Feast	Held on the first day of each Bahá'í month, the Nineteen-Day Feast consists of devotions, consultations, and social gatherings.
Pioneer	A Bahá'í who moves voluntarily to another locale to establish or strengthen a Bahá'í community, locally, nationally, or internationally.
Progressive Revelation	The dynamic unveiling of divine truth through successive Manifestations of God (such as Moses, Christ, Muhammad, Baha'u'llah), who at once reaffirm eternal truths and provide laws and tenets appropriate to the society in which they appear.
Shoghi Effendi	Grandson of 'Abdu'l-Bahá and Guardian of the Bahá'í faith, 1921–57.
Spiritual Assembly	The Local and National Spiritual Assemblies are the Bahá'í governing bodies, elected by adult believers annually and democratically without nominations or platforms and by secret ballot. Whether local or national, an assembly consists of nine members.
Universal House of Justice	The supreme international governing body of the Bahá'í faith.

KEY DATES

1844   The Báb (the "Gate") declared himself the spiritual reformer long-awaited by Muslims, the "Mahdi" or "Hidden Imam."

1850   The martyrdom of the Báb in Tabriz, Iran.

1853   Bahá'u'lláh received intimation in Tehran of his station as "Manifestation of God."

1863   Bahá'u'lláh publicly declares his mission in Baghdad, Iraq.

1892   Bahá'u'lláh passes away in Akka, still formally a prisoner.

1893   First mention of the Bahá'í faith in North America, at the World Columbian Exposition in Chicago.

1897   In Chicago, Honouré Jaxon and Aimée Montfort become the first Canadian Bahá'ís.

1898   In London, Ontario, the women in the Magee household become the first Canadian Bahá'ís in Canada.

1902   May Maxwell arrives in Montreal and establishes the first permanent Bahá'í presence in Canada.

1912   Bahá'u'lláh's son, 'Abdu'l-Bahá spends nine days in Montreal.

1921   'Abdu'l-Bahá dies and Shoghi Effendi assumes the role of Guardian of the Bahá'í faith.

1922   The Montreal Spiritual Assembly becomes the first modern Assembly in Canada.

1948   The National Spiritual Assembly of the Bahá'ís in Canada is constituted.

1949   An Act of Parliament legally incorporates the National Spiritual Assembly of the Bahá'ís in Canada.

1957   Shoghi Effendi dies.

1963   The Universal House of Justice, the supreme body in the Bahá'í faith, is elected.

1973   A Spiritual Assembly is established in every provincial and territorial capital city in Canada.

KEY READINGS

Effendi, Shoghi. *Messages to Canada*. Thornhill, ON: Bahá'í Canada Publications, 1958.

Gaustad, Edwin Scott, and Philip L. Barlow. "Bahá'ís." In *New Historical Atlas of Religion in America*, 278–81. Oxford: Oxford University Press, 2001.

Hatcher, William S., and J. Douglas Martin. *The Bahá'í Faith: The Emerging Global Religion*. San Francisco: Harper and Row, 1984.

Jasion, Jan Teofil. *Never Be Afraid to Dare: The Story of "General Jack."* Oxford: George Ronald, 2001.

Smith, Peter. *The Bábí and Bahá'í Religions: From Messianic Shi'ism to a World Religion*. Cambridge: Cambridge University Press, 1987.

Universal House of Justice. *The Bahá'í World: An International Record*. Haifa, Israel: Baha'i World Center, 1925–present.

van den Hoonaard, Deborah K., and Will C. van den Hoonaard. *The Equality of Women and Men: The Experience of the Bahá'í Community of Canada*. Douglas, NB: Deborah and Will van den Hoonaard, 2006.

van den Hoonaard, Will C. *The Origins of the Bahá'í Community of Canada, 1898–1948*. Waterloo: Wilfrid Laurier University Press, 1996.

van den Hoonaard, Will C. "Biographical Zoning and Baha'i Biographical Writing: The Case of Rose Henderson." *Bahá'í Studies Review* 12 (2004): 50–66.

van den Hoonaard, Will C. "Social Activism among Some Early 20th-Century Bahá'ís in Canada." *Social Studies* 2, no. 1 (2006): 77–97.

van den Hoonaard, Will C., and Lynn Echevarria. "Black Roses in Canada's Mosaic: Three Decades of Canadian Black History." In *Lights of the Spirit: Historical Portraits of Black Bahá'ís in North America*, ed. Richard Thomas and Gwen Etter-Lewis, 143–66. Wilmette, IL: Baha'i Publishing Trust, 2006.

van den Hoonaard, Will C., and Deborah K. van den Hoonaard. "Creative Integration: Persian Baha'i Newcomers in New Brunswick." *Journal of New Brunswick Studies* (2010). http://journals.hil.unb.ca/index.php/JNBS/article/view/18197.

KEY WEBSITES

http://www.bahai.org [official international website of the Bahá'í World Centre, Haifa, Israel]

http://www.bahai-encyclopedia-project.org/ [Bahá'í Encyclopedia Project]

http://bahai-library.com/ [online library of Bahá'í materials]

http://ca.bahai.org/ [Bahá'í Community of Canada]

http://www.sacred-texts.com/bhi/index.htm [Bahá'í sacred texts]

http://www.bahaindex.com/ [index of online sources for Bahá'í materials]

http://www.sahbaarchitect.com [architecture of Bahá'í Fariborz Sabha]

KEY QUESTIONS FOR CRITICAL REFLECTION

1. What beliefs does the Bahá'í Faith share with other religions, and how do they differ?
2. Why do you suppose that members of the Bahá'í Faith do not live in communities separate from the wider society?
3. If the Bahá'í Faith has no clergy, how is the community administered and provided with guidance?
4. What is the Bahá'í concept of God, and how do Bahá'ís come to know and worship God?
5. What is the Bahá'í attitude towards contemporary events and contemporary social problems?

New Religious Movements and the Religions of Canadians Going Forward

JAMIE S. SCOTT, YORK UNIVERSITY
WITH CONTRIBUTIONS FROM IRVING HEXHAM
AND KARLA POEWE, UNIVERSITY OF CALGARY

|||||||||||||||||||||||||||||||||||||||||||||||||||||||||||||||||||||||||||||||||||||||||||||||||||||||||||||||||||||||||

I n many respects, the chapters in *The Religions of Canadians* represent fresh research on the history and current status of world religions domesticated within Canada's social and cultural landscape. We close each chapter with an afterword in an effort to offer summary insights into the present situation of each religious community we have visited, and to suggest some of the opportunities and challenges facing its adherents going forward. In many instances, the decades since World War II have proved pivotal for particular communities, leading variously to expressions of religious resurgence, reform, or retrenchment. In some cases, these trends result more or less directly from the liberalization of Canada's immigration policy noted by several contributors to *The Religions of Canadians*. On a wider scale, the same decades have witnessed the effects on religious communities of primarily Western, though increasingly worldwide developments in economic, social, and political activism, most notably the demands for equal rights associated with Aboriginal, black, gay, and women's liberation agendas. Also on a worldwide scale, from one tradition to another, local religious identity has metamorphosed under the influence of late-twentieth-century processes of decolonization and the development of a wired post-colonial world of transnational migration, intercultural exchange, and globalized corporatism. Examples include the effects of the American Indian Movement upon Aboriginal spirituality, the influence of liberation theology and the strengthening of Pentecostal churches among Christians, the rise of Reconstructionist Judaism and the founding of the Nation of Islam in the United States, the global dispersion of the Hindu International Society for Krishna Consciousness, or "Hare Krishnas," and the migration westwards from Japan of Soka Gakkai Buddhism. As the twenty-first century proceeds, we can see that sometimes these movements are enjoying a profound and lasting effect on the collective life of a religious tradition; in other instances, their influence has been marginal or short-lived. Going forward, future editions of *The Religions of Canadians* will need to take continuing account of these and similar developments.

At the same time, it would be misleading to claim that *The Religions of Canadians* offers a comprehensive account of the variety of religious traditions that have found a home in Canada. In several cases, the lack of scholarly research on smaller religious communities leaves them under-represented or not represented at all. Perhaps the most glaring omission is Orthodox Christians, who numbered just short of half a million in the last long Canadian federal census of 2001, or 1.6 per cent of all Christians in Canada. A range of ethnicities and liturgical variations constitute this community, including the Byzantine confessions of Antiochian, Bulgarian, Byelorussian, Estonian, Greek, Macedonian, Serbian, Romanian, Russian, and Ukrainian Orthodox Christians on the one hand, and on the other, the oriental or "non-Chalcedonian" churches, whose members are for the most part of Armenian, Coptic, Ethiopian, South Indian, and Syrian origin. We shall look briefly at the Church of Jesus Christ of Latter-day Saints, commonly known as Mormons, and the Jehovah's Witnesses: the last long Canadian census of 2001 counts 101,805 of the former and 154,750 of the latter. Both groups merit further discussion, as do Christadelphians, Christian Scientists, and the Church of Scientology, which we do discuss briefly. The 2001 census also identifies 2,450 Jains, 4,955 Parsees, and 1,130 Rastafarians in Canada, though such figures are likely on the low side. *The Religions of Canadians* does not include studies of these groups, nor do we discuss Daoists and Unitarian Universalists. Like several of the communities we have visited, these groups for the most part begin to flourish in Canada as a result of changes to the country's immigration policy after World War II. Going forward, we hope that future editions of *The Religions of Canadians* will include significant discussions of such communities, as scholarly research expands and advances.

The Religions of Canadians does not take account of those less familiar expressions of religiosity scholars variously refer to as New Religions or New Religious Movements. A New Religion (NR) usually means a group created by a leader or leaders who combine elements from one or more established religious traditions but do not identify in any significant way with any particular established religious tradition. A New Religious Movement (NRM), by contrast, refers to a cult or a sect that grows out of a long-established religious tradition or traditions, to which the group remains attached in clearly identifiable ways. Careful and sustained research into these phenomena progresses well, and in the last pages of *The Religions of Canadians* we would like to identify some of these groups and sketch a few of their characteristics. To begin with, though, a caveat: the popular media and a number of well-respected scholars have tended to report unfavourably on NRs, NRMs, and other less familiar or unconventional religious groups. This negativity begins in earnest in North America with the publication of *The Kingdom of the Cults* (1965), by Walter R. Martin (1928–89). A Christian, Martin echoes the British psychiatrist William Sargant (1907–88), whose *Battle for the Mind* (1957) raises concerns about conversions associated with the Harringay Crusade (1954) of the American Christian evangelist Billy Graham (born 1918). Later, Americans Flo Conway and Jim Siegelman expressed analogous criticisms of the Holy Spirit Association for the Unification of World Christianity and its leader Sun Myung Moon (born 1920) in *SNAPPING: America's Epidemic of Sudden Personality Change* (1978), and then about fundamentalist Christian proselytizing techniques in *Holy Terror: The Fundamentalist War on America's Freedoms in Religion, Politics and Our Private Lives* (1984). Designating innovative expressions of religiosity willy-nilly as "cults," these writers assert that religious conversion is really psychological manipulation or "brainwashing," and that victims of brainwashing need to be deprogrammed to enable them to rejoin normal society, even against their own expressed desires.

Such negativity stems in large part from a series of tragedies involving NRMs in the later decades of the twentieth century, beginning with the horrors of Jonestown, Guyana, where over 900 followers of the Reverend James Warren "Jim" Jones (1931–78) perished. Jones started out as a preacher at the Laurel Street Tabernacle in Indianapolis, Indiana, leaving this Pentecostal Assemblies of God ministry to found the Wings of Deliverance on 4 April 1955. His new church blended Pentecostal and secular leftist influences to preach and practise freedom, equality, and love in a social gospel that transcended differences of race, gender, age, and physical and mental ability. Renamed the Peoples Temple the following year, the church moved several times within the United States, and eventually established the utopian Peoples Temple Agricultural Project (PTAP) on 4,000 acres of jungle leased for development from the Guyanese government in 1974. By the end of 1977, PTAP numbered over 1,000 members. Under investigation by the American government, Jones' mental health deteriorated, a condition exacerbated by his increasingly heavy use of prescription drugs. Retaining a radical communitarian ideology, Jones developed a doctrine of "translation," teaching that he and his followers would die together and be reborn to a life of bliss on another planet. On 18 November 1978, PTAP gunmen killed California congressman Leo J. Ryan (1925–78) and three journalists who were visiting the settlement, as well as a group member who was defecting with the visitors. Other defectors, journalists, and congressional staffers were wounded. Shortly afterwards, Jones convinced the community that an American government attack on PTAP was imminent and presided over the deaths of 638 adults and 276 children, most of whom drank grape juice heavily laced with barbiturates and potassium cyanide in an act of "revolutionary suicide."

Subsequent tragedies involving NRMs perpetuated the furor aroused by Jonestown, notably the events involving the Students of the Seven Seals, more commonly referred to as the Branch Davidians, and the Heaven's Gate cult, both in the United States, and Aum Shinrikyo in Japan. Originating in 1942 as a breakaway Seventh Day Adventist group, the Branch Davidians believed themselves subject to the fifth chapter of the New Testament's Book of Revelation, which talks of a scroll, protected by seven seals, containing the secret details of events surrounding the second coming of Christ at the end of days. After a seven-week siege by agents of the Federal Bureau of Alcohol, Tobacco and Firearms and the Federal Bureau of Investigation, fire swept through "Ranch Apocalypse," the Branch Davidian compound near Waco, Texas, on 19 April 1993. The cult's leader, David Koresh (1959–93), and at least 75 of his followers perished, though it is unclear whether by their own hands or because of the fire.

There is no doubt about the mass suicide of the Heaven's Gate cult, though, which combined belief in UFOs with elements of Christianity, notably a passage in Revelation about two martyred Christians who are revived and taken up into the clouds after three-and-a-half days. Led by Marshall Herff Applewhite (1931–97), who taught that our bodies are merely a temporary set of clothes for our souls, 21 women and 18 men took their own lives in three groups over three days, 23–25 March 1997, in San Diego, California. The suicides believed that their souls would be transported to the "Next Evolutionary Level above Human" by a spaceship travelling in the wake of the Hale-Bopp comet, which passed closest to earth on 22 March. Unlike Branch Davidian and the Heaven's Gate members, Aum Shinrikyo ("Supreme Truth") planned and executed a terrorist attack on innocent civilians. The group's leader, Shoko Asahara (born 1955), blended Christian apocalyptic beliefs with distorted interpretations of the Tibetan Buddhist doctrine of *poa,* including the notion that adepts may help lesser mortals trapped in a decadent world achieve rebirth in the Pure Land of Amitabha Buddha by murdering them. Implicated in a series of suspicious deaths, Aum Shinrikyo launched a sarin poison gas attack on the Tokyo underground on 20 March 1995. Twelve died and over 5,000 were injured. Convicted of murder on 27 February 2004, Asahara awaits the outcome of legal manoeuvrings over his death sentence. Now led by his third daughter, Rika Matsumoto (born 1965), Aum Shinrikyo has been known as Aleph since 18 January 2000.

Canada has not been immune to scandal, either. In the late 1920s, the British expatriate sea captain Edward Arthur Wilson (1878–1934) declared himself the twelfth "Master of Wisdom," or "Brother XII," a self-styled theosophical prophet responsible for preparing the way for an imminent messiah who would shepherd humankind through the "Day of Adjustment" into a new age. Outlining his vision in publications like *Foundation Letters and Teachings* (1927), Wilson founded an agricultural settlement at Cedar-on-Sea, just outside Nanaimo, British Columbia, and on 25 July 1927, he presided over the first annual general meeting of the Aquarian Foundation, the public face of the community. Over the next six years, Wilson attracted wealthy backers and some 2,000 followers, as well as legal attention for sexual improprieties and misappropriation of the foundation's funds. In 1928, he established new settlements on the nearby islands of Valdes and DeCourcy, where Wilson and his paramour Mabel Skottowe (born 1890), whom he called "Madame Z," used their followers as forced labour to build a fortified "City of Refuge" in which to survive the coming apocalypse. On 28 April 1933, a court returned in favour of the victims suing Wilson to recover their investments in the organization; he retaliated by vandalizing the settlement and disappearing, allegedly fleeing to Switzerland with Skottowe and the foundation's reserves of cash and gold.

The most tragic instance of cult violence in Canada concerns the Order of the Solar Temple. Founded by Joseph DiMambro (1926–95) and Luc

Jouret (1947–94) in 1984 in Geneva, Switzerland, Solar Temple attracted a number of members from Quebec Hydro. The cult blends elements of Christian millennialism, Rosicrucian philosophy, and New Age teachings in an apocalyptic vision of environmental catastrophe. Casting Christ as the solar king, Jouret and DiMambro taught that the world would end in fire and that dying in fire gave followers life after death on a planet revolving around the star Sirius. On 4 October 1994, authorities were alerted to fires at properties owned by the cult in Morin Heights, Quebec, and in the villages of Salvan and Cheiry, Switzerland. Either murdered or convinced to commit mass suicide, 23 members of the cult died at Morin Heights, while five more later took their own lives in Saint-Casimir, Quebec, on 23 March 1997. In every case, pre-set timers ignited fires that incinerated the templars.

In other instances, accusations of child abuse and sexual immorality dog new religious groups in Canada, notably the Society of Kabalarians, the Apostles of Infinite Love, and the Children of God. Founded by Alfred J. Parker (1897–1964) in 1930 in Vancouver, British Columbia, Kabalarian philosophy blends Eastern ascetic disciplines, Western pragmatism, and the numerological analysis of names in an effort to calibrate and hence predict quality of life. In 1997, however, Parker's successor, Ivon Shearing (born 1928), was convicted of several serious sexual offences, temporarily casting a shadow over the movement. Less esoteric, the Apostles were founded in 1962 by Jean-Gaston Tremblay (born 1928), a visionary priest who broke with the Catholic Community of the Brothers of Saint John of God, known as the Hospitalers. Tremblay built a monastery in Saint Jovite, Quebec, attracting a mixed following of single men and women, married couples, and families. In 1966, suggestions of abuse caused authorities to remove 17 minors from the monastery and to order the Apostles to release over 50 more. Tremblay refused and went into hiding with the children. In 1968, Quebec's Superior Court reversed the initial order of seizure and the children all returned to the monastery. On 10 September 1968, the Apostles proclaimed Tremblay the true Pope, Jean Grégoire XVII, and in 1975, he issued an encyclical, *Peter Speaks to the World*, denouncing Rome as the seat of the antichrist, condemning the ecumenism of the Second Vatican Council, and declaring the imminent end of days and the authentic Catholicism of the Apostles. The authorities maintained their vigilance, however, and Tremblay was sentenced to six months in jail in 1978 and a further two years in 1979 for the illegal containment of minors and contempt of court. In 1999, 20 children were removed from the monastery and Tremblay and three other members of the community were arrested on numerous charges of physical and sexual abuse carried out between 1965 and 1985, though these charges were stayed in 2001 after prosecution files went missing. Traditionalist in many respects, the Apostles are progressive in ordaining married men and single and married women, in conducting the mass in French and English, not Latin, and in their public declarations on a range of secular issues, from workers' rights to banning anti-personnel mines. A millenarian community, they have published a great tome of almost 1,000 pages entitled *Thou Art Peter* (1994), which claims to prove Tremblay's status as the Pope of the end of times. Self-identifying as the Order of the Magnificat of the Mother of God or the Catholic Church of the Apostles of the Latter Times, the group's 200 or so full-time monastics have also established missions elsewhere in Canada, as well as in the Caribbean, Central America, Europe, South Africa, and the United States.

Similar allegations haunt the Children of God, founded in 1968 in Huntington Beach, California, by David Brandt Berg (1919–94). Associated with the "Jesus People Movement," Berg blended elements of Pentecostal Christianity with aspects of the era's countercultural rejection of "the system." By the mid-1970s, his charisma and the Children of God's communitarian "hippie" ideology had attracted adherents in over 30 countries around the world. Missionaries were sent to Canada as early as 1968, and Berg and his common-law wife Karen Zerby (born 1946) ran the organization from headquarters just outside Vancouver, British Columbia, between 1988 and 1993. During this period, Berg changed his name to Moses David as a result of "revelations" he claimed to receive from God. He promulgated his teachings in "Mo letters," which were circulated among his followers and used in missionary outreach. Berg's assumption of millenarian prophetic status alienated other Jesus People leaders, as did the suggestion that he communicated with the spirits of the dead. His views on sexuality were even more worrisome. Seeing the love of God in sex, Berg reckoned sexual encounters as missionary opportunities. He encouraged a kind of ritual prostitution called "flirty fishing," by which female followers might bring new members to Jesus. Berg even wrote of rape, incest, and sex with minors as potential opportunities for proselytizing as well, though not male homosexuality, which he denounced as ungodly sodomy. He also criticized Jews and Christians for institutionalizing moral restrictions on the "natural sexual freedom of God's love." In 1987, Berg renamed the organization the Family, and a new constitution officially banned incest and sexual relations with anyone under 21; it also discontinued flirty fishing, ostensibly because of the risk of HIV infection and AIDS. Authorities in several countries have investigated branches of Berg's organization for child abuse, but no case has ever been proved. Led by Zerby since Berg's death, the movement runs numerous outreach programs for the disadvantaged. Known as the Family International since 2004, the organization claims over 12,000 members worldwide, though the exact number in Canada is unclear.

For the most part, however, NRMs and other forms of alternative religiosity have enjoyed healthier, less disturbing histories in Canada. Some small groups survive as branches of movements started in the nineteenth century. Founded by Joseph Smith (1805–44) in the United States in 1830, the Church of Jesus Christ of Latter-day Saints, commonly known as the Mormons, is by far the largest NRM in Canada, numbering well over 100,000 in the 2001 census. According to Mormon teachings, Smith restored true Christianity after centuries of apostasy. Adopting a doctrine of continuous revelation, Mormons believe that *The Book of Mormon* (1830), *Doctrine and Covenants of the Church of the Latter Day Saints: Carefully Selected from the Revelations of God* (1835), and *The Pearl of Great Price* (1851) supplement the Bible as sources of prophecy. For Mormons, the law of eternal progression states that believers eventually become gods. The church is well-known for its energetic efforts to assemble a comprehensive genealogy of humankind, as well as its conservatively dressed young missionaries, who work either as married couples or in pairs of single men and women. There are Mormon congregations across Canada, with the largest concentration in southern Alberta, especially Cardston, which was settled in 1887 by Charles Ora Card (1839–1906) and a group of eight families fleeing opposition in the United States to the Mormon practice of polygamy.

Christadelphians, Jehovah's Witnesses, and Christian Scientists are other interesting examples of NRMs surviving from the nineteenth century. The English immigrant preacher John Thomas (1805–71) coined the name "Christadelphian" in 1864 to describe his conviction that the true Christian life means recovering the first-century understanding of Christ as the fulfillment of a succession of covenants between God and humankind revealed in scripture. *Elpis Israel: An Exposition of the Kingdom of God* (1849) sets forth Thomas' beliefs, which include the imminent return of Christ, denial of his divinity, and rejection of the doctrine of the Trinity. Totalling about 3,500 members, according to the 2001 census, around

50 Christadelphian congregations are scattered across Canada, with the largest concentrations in British Columbia's lower mainland and in south-eastern Ontario. Similar to the Christadelphians in beliefs, the much larger Jehovah's Witnesses developed in 1931 under the leadership of Joseph Franklin Rutherford (1869–1942) out of the Watchtower Bible and Tract Society, founded by Charles Taze Russell (1852–1916) in the late nineteenth century in Pittsburgh, Pennsylvania. This rationalist, pacifist organization blends interpretation of biblical prophecy with various forms of esoteric pre-millennialism. Jehovah's Witnesses are well-known for their prosely-tizing from door to door, and they reject orthodox Christian beliefs like the Trinity, which are thought to contravene biblical teachings. For similar reasons, they also reject a range of modern scientific ideas and practices, from evolution to blood transfusions, which sometimes leads to conflict with educational and health authorities. Numbering over 150,000 in the 2001 census, Jehovah's Witnesses may be found across Canada, from major metropolitan centres to small rural communities.

Like Christadelphians and Jehovah's Witnesses, Christian Scientists are committed to reinstating what they call the "primitive Christianity" of the early church. Formerly known as the Church of Christ Scientist, Christian Science was founded by Mary Baker Eddy (1821–1910) in 1879 in Boston, Massachusetts. Eddy was convinced she had been supernaturally healed after a severe injury in 1866. Christian Scientists stress Christianity's "lost element of healing," arguing that misperception of God's essential good-ness causes physical and material ills, which will therefore disappear with a clear understanding of the spiritual nature of the word of God. Church life revolves around prayer, study of the Bible, and Eddy's *Science and Health with Key to the Scriptures* (1875), which contains her inter-pretations of the ways transcendent reality infuses biblical texts, as well as testimonies to the therapeutic efficacy of her ideas. Like the Jehovah's Witnesses, Christian Science has been involved in controversy over con-flicts between modern medicine and the church's belief in faith healing. In Canada, Christian Science has a few thousand members in about 60 congre-gations, with churches and reading rooms in larger cities, where the public may obtain Eddy's writings and the organization's publications, includ-ing the highly respected daily newspaper the *Christian Science Monitor*.

In the middle decades of the twentieth century, several new religious communities of note found homes in Canada, some of local origin, others branches of movements originating elsewhere. Latter Rain represents the most influential expression of local Canadian religiosity. The phrase "latter rain" refers to a final outpouring of the Holy Spirit in various divine manifestations associated with the imminent return of Christ. The Canadian movement began with a Pentecostal revival at Sharon Bible College in North Battleford, Saskatchewan, in 1948, a year significant for the millenarian meanings attached to the founding of Israel and the establishment of the United Nations. Latter Rain leaders like George R. Hawtin (1909–94), Ernest H. Hawtin (1911–2006), Herrick Holt (1908–87), Percy G. Hunt, and George H. Warnock (born 1917) were soon invited to preach the revival to churches in Western Canada and the United States. Other evangelical pastors carried Latter Rain to congregations elsewhere in North America, having made pilgrimages to North Battleford to experience the revival firsthand. Latter Rain beliefs and practices are detailed in publications like Warnock's *Feast of Tabernacles* (1951) and the 32 booklets of Hawtin's "Treasures of Truth Series," compiled from pieces he wrote for the periodical *The Page* between 1960 and 1983. Though theologically suspect to the Pentecostal Assemblies of Canada, singing in tongues, laying on of hands, personal prophecy, typological hermeneutics, eschatological confidence, the fivefold ministry of apostles, prophets, evangelists, pastors, and teachers described in the New Testament book *Ephesians* (4:11), and other aspects of Latter Rain variously characterize the charismatic Christianity of many independent evangelical churches, including other groups originating in Canada. For example, fivefold ministry is a central plank in the evangelizing platform of Victory Churches International, the worldwide charismatic conglomerate, based in Calgary, Alberta, that began with the Victory Church founded in 1979 in Lethbridge, Alberta, by George and Hazel Hill. In another vein, since an outburst of "holy laughter" visited the congregation on 20 January 1994, tens of thousands of charismatic devotees have travelled from around the world to attend services at Toronto's Airport Vineyard Church in the hope of "soaking" the "Toronto Blessing" and carrying home this gift of the spirit to their own congregations. Founding pastors John and Carol Arnott set up and oversee Catch the Fire ministries and missions to help fulfill these hopes.

Canada is also home to branches of NRMs originating elsewhere. Some of these organizations claim Christian identity, like Moon's Holy Spirit Association for the Unification of World Christianity, often simply referred to as the Unification Church; others, like the Emissaries of Divine Light, the Church of Scientology, and the International Raëlian Movement, draw inspiration from elsewhere. Moon founded the Unification Church in 1954 in Seoul, South Korea, then renamed it the Family Federation for World

Peace and Unification (FFWPU) in 1994. An ambitious agenda propels Moon's re-envisioning of Christian teachings. In *Divine Principle* (1957), he elaborates in detail his belief in divine love as a governing principle of cosmic unity, which alone is capable of achieving peace and harmony among all peoples, races, and religions. Some scholars describe Moon's vision as "orientialized Christianity," finding elements of Buddhist, Confucian, Daoist, and Korean shamanistic ideas in his interpretations of Christian scripture and tradition. Understood as a paradigm of living for others, the human family embodies the sacred power of God's love in Moon's vision. Jesus fulfilled the spiritual promise of biblical revelation, but was crucified before he could marry and have a family in fulfillment of the physical promise. This task remains for Moon and his followers, who prepare the way for the "Lord of the Second Advent" and the universal unification of mind and body, self and others, heaven and earth. The FFWPU's "Holy Marriage Blessing" expresses this conviction, often in the form of multiple weddings, the first of which Moon performed for thirty-six couples in Seoul in 1961. Since 1982, when Moon presided over the wedding of some 2,000 couples in New York's Madison Square Garden, these ceremonies have become a defining characteristic of the organization's international image, too. In the minds of many followers, the disestablishment of the Soviet Union in 1991 seemed to confirm Moon's prophecies about universal unification. The FFWPU's worldwide membership numbers several hundred thousand; and congregations in Montreal, Toronto, and Vancouver total about 300 adherents.

By contrast, the Emissaries of Divine Light (EDL) reflects an essentially yogic vision of the cosmos and the place of humankind within it. Based at the Sunrise Ranch, near Loveland, Colorado, EDL was founded in 1932 by Lloyd Arthur Meeker (1907–54), known as "Uranda." In 1945, Uranda joined with Lord Martin Cecil (1909–88) to establish a Canadian branch at One Hundred Mile House, British Columbia. Meeker's teaching revolves around the theory and practice of "attunement," a form of spiritual healing designed to help the initiate recall his/her hidden divine nature: passing hands over the initiate, the adept radiates energy in an attempt to align both adept and initiate in heart, mind, and body with the transcendent powers of creation. Practitioners recognize "Universal Spirit" as the essence of humankind, so worship, prayer, and meditation play important parts in EDL, too. After Meeker's tragic death in an airplane crash, leadership passed to Cecil. The principal teachings of Uranda and Cecil are collected in the 18 volumes of *The Third Sacred School*. In

1988, Cecil's son Michael (born 1935) assumed leadership, but resigned it to a board of trustees in 1996 after failing to persuade followers to become more engaged with the world at large. That said, sustainability now registers as a key issue with EDL. A dozen or so communities in Australia, South Africa, South Korea, the United Kingdom, and the United States represent the movement, as well as several small groups in Canada, mainly in British Columbia, headquartered at a retreat and conference centre in One Hundred Mile House.

Likely more familiar than EDL, the Church of Scientology was founded in 1953 by L. Ron Hubbard (1911–86). A prolific writer of science fiction, Hubbard travelled widely, especially in Asia. In a number of writings, most notably *Dianetics: The Modern Science of Mental Health* (1950) and *Scientology: The Fundamentals of Thought* (1956), he developed a technology of self-help and applied religious metaphysics. For Hubbard, humans are basically good and over many lifetimes capable of spiritual immortality. He coined the term "thetan" for this sense of infinitely potential personhood that characterizes every individual, like a soul, independent of mind and body. Scientology provides rational techniques, known collectively as "auditing" and "training," for assessing, understanding, and removing the effects of traumatic or otherwise inhibiting experiences that temporarily impede individuals from realizing their limitless capabilities. Detailed auditing menus provide therapeutic training in eight interpenetrating fields of human motivation, or "dynamics": self; sex and family; larger groups, like friends, colleagues, and fellow citizens; all humankind; other living things, that is, plants and animals; the material universe; spirits; and infinity, or the supreme being. For Hubbard, spiritual growth in these areas involves cultivating interdependent qualities: "affinity," "reality"—that is, what we agree to be the case—and "communication" on the one hand; and on the other, "knowledge," "responsibility," and "control." Administered by trained "auditors" belonging to a branch of the movement called the Religious Technology Center, the various clarifying therapies constitute Scientology's "Bridge to Total Freedom." Auditors or "volunteer ministers" of the church also run numerous public programs, some with fairly specific mandates, like Narconon for drug addicts and Criminon for rehabilitating felons, while others are more expansive, like Applied Scholastics and the Way to Happiness Foundation International. Worldwide membership figures vary from around 400,000 to nearly 10,000,000 in more than 160 countries, depending on methods of assessment. With churches or missions in most major cities across the country, Scientology has been embroiled in several controversies in Canada, including convictions and a $250,000 fine for breach of trust in Toronto in 1996. Construed by many scholars as in essence Westernized Indian philosophical ideas coupled with the rich mythology found in Hubbard's science fiction novels, Scientology's official status as a religion remains ambiguous in Canada; under the category "para-religion," the 2001 federal census shows 1,525 adherents.

Different again, the International Raëlian Movement, or simply Raëlians, is an atheist movement that claims to have superseded all established religions, great and small. The movement's roots lie in the personal experience of former crooner and motor racing journalist, Claude Vorilhon (born 1946). In *Le Livre qui dit la vérité* (*The Book Which Tells the Truth*) (1974), Vorilhon reports that on 13 December 1973, he encountered a child-size extraterrestrial called Yahweh inside the crater of Puy de Lassolas, an extinct volcano in central France. In six meetings over six days aboard a spaceship, Yahweh revealed the true meaning of the Bible to Vorilhon, beginning with the fact that the Elohim of Torah refers to his own people, a race of humans living on another world in the centre of the universe. These superscientists, or "fathers in space," used DNA to create earth's humans in their own image, who in their innocence mistook their creators for gods. Now the Elohim want Vorilhon to carry messages to their creatures, fulfilling the work of previous messengers like Moses, Gautama Siddartha, Jesus, Muhammad, and others, and preparing for the return of the Elohim by building a grand Embassy of Welcome near Jerusalem, the "Third Temple" of biblical prophecy. Accepting the mission, Vorilhon changed his name to Raël, meaning "bearer of light," founded MADECH (Mouvement pour l'acceuil des Elohims, créateurs de l'humanité [Movement for Welcoming the Elohims, Creators of Humanity]) in Paris in 1974, and published his prophecies in books like *La livre que dit la verité* and *Acceuillirs les extraterrestres* (*Let's Welcome Our Fathers from Space*) (1979). After internal divisions threatened to destroy the movement, Raël reported a further encounter with Yahweh and reformed MADECH as the Raëlians in 1976. Determined to demystify religion and spiritualize science, Raëlians describe themselves as atheist advocates of peace, sexual liberation, and human rights. Headquartered at UFOland, an estate near Valcourt, northeast of Montreal, the organization runs a number of scientific campaigns. Two of these are Clonaid, which promotes human cloning and genetically modified foods, and Clitoraid, which supports the surgical restoration of sexual enjoyment to circumcised women. Quebec's

Catholic Church has heavily criticized the Raëlians for encouraging condoms in schools and supporting women's right to abortion. The Raëlians now count over 70,000 members in 104 countries, with a core of around 170 "guides," who administer the movement under Raël's personal direction. Raël's principal writings have been gathered into a single publication, *Intelligent Design: Message from the Designers* (2006). He leads monthly gatherings of several hundred followers in Montreal and spends the rest of his time proselytizing abroad.

Finally, we should say a few words about an extraordinary array of interlacing and overlapping expressions of contemporary religiosity that includes New Age, Neo-Pagan, Wicca, and a host of other cognate movements. Research into the life of these Canadian religious communities is in its infancy, and it would be totally misleading to suggest that they share common origins and histories, still less a single world view, code of ethics, or calendar of rituals. We can, however, make a few introductory observations. Innovative religious movements draw variously upon a wide range of practices, including channelling and spiritism; divination through astrology or the oracular reading of *I Ching,* runes, and tarot cards; scrying with auras, bio-rhythms, dowsing rods, dream interpretation, handwriting analysis, ouija boards, pendulum movements, and tea leaves; and spiritual healing by crystal energy treatments, holistic medicines, human potential therapies, laying on of hands, meditation, and naturopathy. In addition to the innumerable textual resources associated with these practices, New Age, Neo-Pagan, Wicca, and related groups find inspiration in a variety of other literary, historical, philosophical, and theological materials, including Indic systems of *yoga* and the principles of *karma, samsara*, and rebirth or reincarnation; the lives and writings of mystics, East and West; alternative contemporary cosmologies, from modern theoretical physics to the doctrines associated with ecological, panentheist, and "Gaia" theories; and the mythologies of pre-modern traditions, some living, like Aboriginal American and indigenous African spiritualities, others reconstructed through the careful study of ancient sources, like the epic narratives recounting the myths of Celtic, Druid, and Nordic polytheistic cultures.

The members of these innovative spiritual communities vary hugely in the degree and nature of their allegiances, too. Some adhere strictly to one movement, while others belong to several at once or move serially from one to another. Personally concerned to shape new ways of life for a new world, most practitioners of these marginal forms of contemporary spirituality shy away from the formalities of organized religion, which many identify with globalized corporatism and the pillaging of planet earth for short-term material gain. Some condemn institutional religion outright, often taking advantage of the Internet to form fluid associations across the boundaries of time and space, or participating in informal networks whose members meet in private homes, coffee shops, and specialty bookstores, as well as outdoors for festivals like the four major Wicca *sabbats* of Samhain (31 October), Imbolc (2 February), Beltane (30 April), and Lammas (1 August). Others work as religious reformers, blending New Age, Neo-Pagan, Wicca, and other innovative beliefs and practices with the established doctrinal and ritual conventions of church, mosque, synagogue, or temple. In a few cases, we find spiritual innovators beginning to build new communities along recognizable institutional lines as viable alternatives to established religious organizations: the Hamilton and Toronto temples of the Wiccan Church of Canada are good examples. Because the development of these various spiritually innovative movements is a relatively new phenomenon, it is too early to tell whether they represent a lasting trend, and therefore a change in Canadian religious consciousness, or simply a temporary aberration from historical norms. Either way, in the 2001 census, 1,525 people identified with the New Age movement, while another 850 declared that they were Satanists. Gnostics numbered 1,165, and Unity, New Thought, and Pantheist practitioners together totalled 4,000. At 21,080, only "Pagan" registered a significant numbers of adherents, and this category included Wicca.

Today, even taken all together, NRMs and related forms of spiritual expression occupy very little space on Canada's social and cultural landscape. Unlike most established mainstream religions in Canada, though, these groups have often received quite an antagonistic press. Before World War II, Jan Karel van Baalen (1890–1968), a Christian Reformed pastor in Edmonton, Alberta, criticized Mormons and Jehovah's Witnesses for trying to recruit converts in his best-selling *The Chaos of the Cults: A Study in Present-day Isms* (1938) and *The Gist of the Cults: Christianity versus False Religion* (1944). Van Baalen describes such groups as "the unpaid bills of the Church," since their success marked the failure of established Christian organizations. Ranging more widely, William E. Mann's *Sect, Cult and Church in Alberta* (1955) raises suspicions about evangelical Christian groups in the 1930s. Later, Canadian critics of NRMs helped to popularize the Cold War terms "brainwashing" and "deprogramming." In the movie *Moonwebs: Journey into the Mind of a Cult* (1980) and the

Canadian Broadcasting Corporation's associated film *Ticket to Heaven* (1981), Josh Freed dramatizes the case of Benji Carroll, a Jewish convert whom he helped in 1978 to deprogram from brainwashing by the "Moonies," as the Montreal journalist calls the Unification Church. In 1979, Colin Clay, the University of Saskatchewan's ecumenical chaplain, wrote a report for the provincial government condemning NRMs, but the minister of education refused funding for the deprogramming centre Clay recommended. In the same year, Ian Howarth established Toronto's Council on Mind Abuse, which dissolved in 1992, bankrupted by lawsuits with the Church of Scientology and EST. Other anti-cult groups continue, though, notably Montreal's Cult Project and Calgary's Christian Research Institute (CRI). Founded in 1980 and funded in part by Quebec's Ministry of Health and Social Services, the Cult Project became Info-Cult (Infosecte) in 1990 and distinguishes between "cults" and "destructive cults." Canada's only organization working full-time in the field, Info-Cult maintains a large, important collection of materials about cults and related groups. A branch of an American evangelical group based in Charlotte, North Carolina, Calgary's CRI subscribes to the parent office's "Bible Answer Man Program," which raises funds to defend "biblical truth" from cults, errant theologians, and atheists.

A few commentators have been less antagonistic towards NRMs, especially in more recent years. In a 5 April 1975 article in the *Toronto Star,* the respected popular commentator on religion Tom Harpur (born 1929) discusses and rejects deprogramming. Newspapers across Canada reproduced the piece, including Saskatoon's *Star-Phoenix,* which ran several informative items on NRMs, especially the Hare Krishnas. In 1976, James Penton published *Jehovah's Witnesses in Canada: Champions of Freedom of Speech and Worship,* exposing systematic prejudice against Jehovah's Witnesses in Canada, and in 1977, the University of Toronto's Herbert Richardson and others founded the academic pressure group, Canadians for the Protection of Religious Liberty, with Mennonite scholar R.J. Sawatsky as president. Richardson produced a sourcebook on deprogramming and in 1978 launched the Edwin Mellen Press with the publication of *A Time for Consideration: A Scholarly Appraisal of the Unification Church,* co-edited with M. Darrol Bryant. That year, he also organized a panel on NRMs at the annual conference of the American Academy of Religion in New Orleans. During the conference, news broke about the events at Jonestown. Overnight, cults became a cause for public concern. The Government of Ontario set up a commission on NRMs, led by the civil libertarian Daniel G. Hill (1923–2003). Tabled in 1980, the commission's report confounded anti-cult activists, however, concluding that NRMs posed no significant threat to the public good and arguing that legislation aimed at such groups might well jeopardize civil liberties. Four years later, Saul Levine, a psychiatrist working at Toronto's Hospital for Sick Children, published a study revealing the scientific baselessness of brainwashing and the potentially harmful effects of deprogramming. In 1985, Diane Choquette's *New Religious Movements in the United States and Canada: A Critical Assessment and Annotated Bibliography* provided useful information about scholarly and other resources on innovative forms of Canadian spirituality, while more recently, studies like *Moon Sisters, Krishna Mothers, Rajneesh Lovers: Women's Roles in New Religions* (1994), by Susan J. Palmer at Montreal's Dawson College, and *Comprehending Cults: The Sociology of New Religious Movements* (2nd edition, 2006), by the University of Waterloo's Lorne L. Dawson, have offered balanced assessments of NRMs and related groups. Other scholars working in the field in Canada include Chris Klassen at Wilfrid Laurier University, Douglas E. Cowan at the University of Waterloo, the University of Ottawa's Lucie DuFresne, and Carleton University's Síân Reid.

As various commentators have noted, contemporary forms of novel religiosity rarely attract large numbers of followers, and the membership of an NRM often peaks and fades quickly. Few NRMs outlive their founders, let alone flourish after the founder's death, and fewer still become global religions. That said, NRMs and other kinds of innovative religious communities do not spring forth fully formed, like Athena from the forehead of Zeus or Brahma from Vishnu's golden egg. Nor do their founders and followers live in a historical and geographical vacuum. Complex combinations of social and cultural factors give shape to NRMs, including religious factors. In the globalized ethos of our age of information, even the most localized efflorescence of fresh spiritual enthusiasm will reflect influences from different Abrahamic, Asian, or indigenous traditions in sometimes dizzying reconfigurations of myths, doctrines, ethics, rituals, institutions, and material resources in nature and culture. Reconstituting religious heritage, NRMs reflect the state of play in contemporary society and culture, while their novelty, marginality, and often heterodox character occasionally offer a window onto the future of established traditions, or even the established traditions of the future: Jews made the first practising Christians, for example, Hindus the first Buddhists, and polytheistic goddess worshippers the first Muslims. In this sense, our glance at NRMs

in Canada quite possibly reflects in miniature the sort of issues scholars need to take into account as we conduct research into the continuing
development of the more familiar, established religions of Canadians.

Going forward, therefore, *The Religions of Canadians* remains an evolving project in at least three respects. First, the chapters that constitute the
bulk of this book identify numerous instances of the transformation and
resurgence of established religions, and in so doing indicate future directions in which Canadian adherents to many of these traditions seem to
be moving. We shall need to take careful notice of fresh developments in
mainstream religions, great and small. Second, as we indicated at the start
of this chapter, a number of Canada's smaller established religious communities await scholarly consideration, including Orthodox Christians,
Jains, Rastafarians, Unitarian Universalists, Zoroastrians, and others. We
shall need to encourage groundbreaking research on such traditions where
such work has yet to begin, and to take note of the published results of initiatives already under way. And third, though we have introduced in this
chapter a variety of NRMs and other innovative expressions of Canadian
spirituality, a good deal of research and analysis remains to be done on these
important religious communities and the individuals who originate and
lead them. We shall need to expand our knowledge of NRMs and cognate
forms of religiosity, and cultivate a deeper understanding of such phenomena in Canada. Nor, finally, may we predict what the shock of the new might
require of scholars and students working in any and all of these fields: particular events like 11 September 2001; global problems like climate change;
fresh archaeological and archival discoveries; desecularization and the re-
enchantment of the world; and shifts in research methodologies, modes of
analysis, and theoretical paradigms all demand that we constantly rework
our appreciation of the religious. Such are the challenges facing us as we
begin to prepare future editions of *The Religions of Canadians*.

FURTHER READINGS

Adler, Margot. *Drawing Down the Moon: Witches, Druids, Goddess-Worshippers,
and Other Pagans in America Today*. New York: Penguin/Arkana, 1997.

Choquette, Diane. *New Religious Movements in the United States and Canada: A
Critical Assessment and Annotated Bibliography*. Westport, CT: Greenwood
Press, 1985.

Clark, Samuel D. *Church and Sect in Canada*. Toronto: Toronto University Press,
1948.

Clarke, Peter B. *New Religions in Global Perspective: A Study of Religious Change in the Modern World*. New York: Routledge, 2006.

Côté, Pauline. "From Status Politics to Technocratic Pluralism: Toleration of Religious Minorities in Canada." *Social Justice Research* 12, no. 4 (1999): 253–82. doi:10.1023/A:1022060806920.

Cowan, Douglas E. *Cyberhenge: Modern Pagans on the Internet*. New York: Routledge, 2005. doi:10.4324/9780203313459.

Daschke, Dereck. *New Religious Movements: A Documentary Reader*. New York: New York University Press, 2005.

Dawson, Lorne L. *Comprehending Cults: The Sociology of New Religious Movements*. 2nd ed. Toronto: Oxford University Press, 2006.

Hill, Daniel. *Study of Mind Development Groups, Sects and Cults in Ontario*. Toronto: Government Printer, 1980.

Mann, W.E. *Sect, Cult and Church in Alberta*. Toronto: University of Toronto Press, 1955.

Palmer, Susan J. *Moon Sisters, Krishna Mothers, Rajneesh Lovers: Women's Roles in New Religions*. Syracuse, NY: Syracuse University Press, 1994.

Palmer, Susan J., and Charlotte E. Hardman, eds. *Children in New Religions*. New Brunswick, NJ: Rutgers University Press, 1999.

Partridge, Christopher H. *Alternative Spiritualities, Sacralization, Popular Culture and Occulture*. Vol. 1. *The Re-Enchantment of the West*. London: T & T Clark, 2004.

Partridge, Christopher H. *Alternative Spiritualities, Sacralization, Popular Culture and Occulture*. Vol. 2. *The Re-Enchantment of the West*. London: T & T Clark, 2006.

Penton, M. James. *Jehovah's Witnesses in Canada: Champions of Freedom of Speech and Worship*. Toronto: University of Toronto Press, 1976.

Pike, Sarah. *New Age and Neopagan Religions in America*. New York: Columbia University Press, 2004.

Reid, Siân, ed. *Between the Worlds: Readings in Contemporary Neopaganism*. Toronto: Canadian Scholars' Press, 2006.

2001 Census Tables:
Selected Religions

Selected Religions, 2001 Counts: Canada (20 Per Cent Sample Data)

Religion*	Selected Religions			
	2001	Percentage distribution (2001)	Percentage change (1991–2001)	Median age
Canada				
Total population	29,639,030	100.0%	9.8%	37.3
Roman Catholic	12,793,125	43.2%	4.8%	37.8
No religion	4,796,325	16.2%	43.9%	31.1
United Church	2,839,125	9.6%	−8.2%	44.1
Anglican	2,035,500	6.9%	−7.0%	43.8
Christian not included elsewhere[1]	780,450	2.6%	121.1%	30.2
Baptist	729,470	2.5%	10.0%	39.3
Lutheran	606,590	2.0%	−4.7%	43.3
Muslim	579,640	2.0%	128.9%	28.1
Protestant not included elsewhere[2]	549,205	1.9%	−12.7%	40.4
Presbyterian	409,830	1.4%	−35.6%	46.0
Pentecostal	369,475	1.2%	−15.3%	33.5
Jewish	329,995	1.1%	3.7%	41.5
Buddhist	300,345	1.0%	83.8%	38.0
Hindu	297,200	1.0%	89.3%	31.9
Sikh	278,410	0.9%	88.8%	29.7
Greek Orthodox[3]	215,175	0.7%	−7.1%	40.7
Mennonite	191,465	0.6%	−7.9%	32.0
Orthodox not included elsewhere[4]	165,420	0.6%	79.9%	35.4
Jehovah's Witnesses	154,750	0.5%	−8.1%	38.7
Ukrainian Catholic	126,200	0.4%	−1.7%	45.0
Church of Jesus Christ of Latter-day Saints (Mormons)	101,805	0.3%	8.4%	28.7
Salvation Army	87,790	0.3%	−21.9%	39.3
Christian Reformed Church	76,670	0.3%	−9.5%	32.3
Evangelical Missionary Church	66,705	0.2%	48.4%	35.2
Christian and Missionary Alliance	66,285	0.2%	11.9%	34.5
Adventist	62,880	0.2%	20.1%	35.5
Non-denominational[5]	40,545	0.1%	26.7%	33.0
Ukrainian Orthodox	32,720	0.1%	−5.1%	45.8
Aboriginal spirituality	29,820	0.1%	175.1%	25.0
Hutterite	26,295	0.1%	22.3%	22.2
Methodist[6]	25,730	0.1%	6.1%	43.9
Pagan[7]	21,080	0.1%	281.2%	30.4
Brethren in Christ	20,590	0.1%	−22.0%	38.2
Serbian Orthodox	20,520	0.1%	109.5%	34.8

*Religions selected for this table represent counts of 20,000 or more for Canada.

Source: Statistics Canada publication *Religions in Canada: Highlight Tables, 2001 Census*, Catalogue 97F0024XIE2001015, http://www.statcan.gc.ca/bsolc/olc-cel/olc-cel?catno=97F0024XIE2001015&lang=eng.

Selected Religions, 2001 Counts: Ontario (20 Per Cent Sample Data)

Religion*	2001	Percentage distribution (2001)	Percentage change (1991–2001)	Median age
Ontario				
Total population	**11,285,550**	**100.0%**	**13.1%**	**37.0**
Roman Catholic	3,866,350	34.3%	10.3%	36.4
No religion	1,809,535	16.0%	47.6%	31.4
United Church	1,334,570	11.8%	−5.4%	43.5
Anglican	985,110	8.7%	−7.1%	44.3
Christian not included elsewhere[1]	301,935	2.7%	121.2%	30.9
Baptist	289,455	2.6%	9.4%	39.8
Lutheran	210,090	1.9%	−7.8%	45.2
Muslim	352,525	3.1%	142.2%	27.5
Protestant not included elsewhere[2]	263,000	2.3%	−18.7%	40.5
Presbyterian	279,195	2.5%	−33.9%	45.4
Pentecostal	158,590	1.4%	−5.1%	33.4
Jewish	190,800	1.7%	8.6%	40.5
Buddhist	128,320	1.1%	96.4%	37.6
Hindu	217,560	1.9%	103.9%	31.9
Sikh	104,790	0.9%	109.2%	29.7
Greek Orthodox[3]	113,440	1.0%	3.6%	39.1
Mennonite	60,595	0.5%	15.1%	26.8
Orthodox not included elsewhere[4]	98,785	0.9%	91.2%	35.1
Jehovah's Witnesses	54,935	0.5%	−2.8%	38.3
Ukrainian Catholic	38,440	0.3%	5.2%	44.7
Church of Jesus Christ of Latter-day Saints (Mormons)	20,355	0.2%	9.1%	30.6
Salvation Army	27,560	0.2%	−29.0%	41.4
Christian Reformed Church	48,795	0.4%	−10.2%	32.6
Evangelical Missionary Church	21,480	0.2%	28.7%	37.1
Christian and Missionary Alliance	14,590	0.1%	14.3%	34.8
Adventist	30,870	0.3%	38.9%	33.8
Non-denominational[5]	16,035	0.1%	36.7%	33.3
Ukrainian Orthodox	9,050	0.1%	−3.8%	46.4
Aboriginal spirituality	7,265	0.1%	161.3%	28.7
Hutterite	55	0.0%	. . .	6.8
Methodist[6]	16,615	0.1%	4.0%	43.3
Pagan[7]	7,565	0.1%	231.8%	30.7
Brethren in Christ	15,265	0.1%	−19.6%	37.9
Serbian Orthodox	15,845	0.1%	89.3%	35.0

*Religions selected for this table represent counts of 20,000 or more for Canada.

Source: Statistics Canada publication *Religions in Canada: Highlight Tables, 2001 Census*, Catalogue 97F0024XIE2001015, http://www.statcan.gc.ca/bsolc/olc-cel/olc-cel?catno=97F0024XIE2001015&lang=eng.

Selected Religions, 2001 Counts: Alberta (20 Per Cent Sample Data)

| Religion* | 2001 | Selected Religions | | Median age |
		Percentage distribution (2001)	Percentage change (1991–2001)	
Alberta				
Total population	**2,941,150**	**100.0%**	**16.8%**	**34.7**
Roman Catholic	756,005	25.7%	18.0%	34.0
No religion	678,875	23.1%	38.7%	29.6
United Church	396,065	13.5%	−5.6%	42.4
Anglican	172,430	5.9%	−0.4%	41.9
Christian not included elsewhere[1]	123,145	4.2%	156.9%	28.2
Baptist	73,640	2.5%	15.5%	37.4
Lutheran	142,530	4.8%	3.9%	39.6
Muslim	49,045	1.7%	58.2%	27.8
Protestant not included elsewhere[2]	78,370	2.7%	−3.9%	39.3
Presbyterian	29,200	1.0%	−39.6%	44.1
Pentecostal	42,615	1.4%	−19.6%	31.2
Jewish	11,090	0.4%	11.2%	41.5
Buddhist	33,410	1.1%	61.1%	36.7
Hindu	15,970	0.5%	48.3%	32.5
Sikh	23,470	0.8%	73.2%	29.5
Greek Orthodox[3]	20,495	0.7%	−22.0%	46.1
Mennonite	22,785	0.8%	2.0%	28.1
Orthodox not included elsewhere[4]	9,985	0.3%	163.1%	36.0
Jehovah's Witnesses	18,830	0.6%	2.5%	35.7
Ukrainian Catholic	28,750	1.0%	9.8%	43.0
Church of Jesus Christ of Latter-day Saints (Mormons)	50,580	1.7%	10.4%	27.1
Salvation Army	5,050	0.2%	−12.6%	33.5
Christian Reformed Church	12,980	0.4%	−13.4%	32.3
Evangelical Missionary Church	17,640	0.6%	47.2%	32.9
Christian and Missionary Alliance	23,715	0.8%	40.4%	32.8
Adventist	8,140	0.3%	1.1%	37.1
Non-denominational[5]	5,965	0.2%	12.1%	32.3
Ukrainian Orthodox	9,865	0.3%	2.2%	41.9
Aboriginal spirituality	5,860	0.2%	189.4%	22.9
Hutterite	12,330	0.4%	23.5%	21.5
Methodist[6]	1,895	0.1%	4.7%	45.6
Pagan[7]	3,035	0.1%	462.0%	29.2
Brethren in Christ	995	0.0%	−23.2%	31.8
Serbian Orthodox	960	0.0%	137.0%	33.8

*Religions selected for this table represent counts of 20,000 or more for Canada.

Source: Statistics Canada publication *Religions in Canada: Highlight Tables, 2001 Census*, Catalogue 97F0024XIE2001015, http://www.statcan.gc.ca/bsolc/olc-cel/olc-cel?catno=97F0024XIE2001015&lang=eng.

Selected Religions, 2001 Counts: British Columbia (20 Per Cent Sample Data)

Religion*	2001	Percentage distribution (2001)	Percentage change (1991–2001)	Median age
British Columbia				
Total population	**3,868,875**	**100.0%**	**19.1%**	**38.2**
Roman Catholic	666,905	17.2%	12.0%	39.1
No religion	1,356,600	35.1%	39.2%	33.1
United Church	361,840	9.4%	−14.0%	49.9
Anglican	298,375	7.7%	−9.2%	49.4
Christian not included elsewhere[1]	200,340	5.2%	131.2%	31.0
Baptist	107,465	2.8%	27.8%	40.0
Lutheran	101,145	2.6%	−6.5%	48.4
Muslim	56,215	1.5%	125.5%	32.2
Protestant not included elsewhere[2]	76,100	2.0%	−15.1%	45.7
Presbyterian	37,115	1.0%	−42.0%	52.3
Pentecostal	47,420	1.2%	−32.9%	36.5
Jewish	21,230	0.5%	27.6%	42.7
Buddhist	85,540	2.2%	134.8%	40.4
Hindu	31,495	0.8%	73.6%	31.3
Sikh	135,310	3.5%	81.5%	29.7
Greek Orthodox[3]	15,490	0.4%	3.1%	44.5
Mennonite	35,490	0.9%	−9.1%	36.5
Orthodox not included elsewhere[4]	11,595	0.3%	222.1%	35.4
Jehovah's Witnesses	31,960	0.8%	−5.1%	40.3
Ukrainian Catholic	7,780	0.2%	3.3%	48.0
Church of Jesus Christ of Latter-day Saints (Mormons)	17,590	0.5%	1.6%	32.9
Salvation Army	5,945	0.2%	−41.3%	43.3
Christian Reformed Church	11,810	0.3%	−0.3%	31.8
Evangelical Missionary Church	9,245	0.2%	59.4%	36.6
Christian and Missionary Alliance	15,155	0.4%	1.7%	36.9
Adventist	11,070	0.3%	8.1%	41.0
Non-denominational[5]	7,055	0.2%	2.9%	33.0
Ukrainian Orthodox	3,020	0.1%	2.2%	47.5
Aboriginal spirituality	5,475	0.1%	136.5%	28.2
Hutterite	220	0.0%	131.6%	15.5
Methodist[6]	4,200	0.1%	24.1%	44.3
Pagan[7]	6,105	0.2%	228.2%	32.5
Brethren in Christ	1,695	0.0%	−30.4%	44.9
Serbian Orthodox	2,495	0.1%	312.4%	34.8

*Religions selected for this table represent counts of 20,000 or more for Canada.

Source: Statistics Canada publication *Religions in Canada: Highlight Tables, 2001 Census*, Catalogue 97F0024XIE2001015, http://www.statcan.gc.ca/bsolc/olc-cel/olc-cel?catno=97F0024XIE2001015&lang=eng.

Selected Religions, 2001 Counts: Manitoba (20 Per Cent Sample Data)

Religion*	2001	Selected Religions		
		Percentage distribution (2001)	Percentage change (1991–2001)	Median age
Manitoba				
Total population	**1,103,700**	**100.0%**	**2.3%**	**36.4**
Roman Catholic	292,970	26.5%	−0.3%	35.8
No religion	201,835	18.3%	38.3%	29.4
United Church	176,820	16.0%	−11.8%	42.8
Anglican	85,890	7.8%	−8.8%	41.2
Christian not included elsewhere[1]	44,540	4.0%	175.3%	27.0
Baptist	22,505	2.0%	11.5%	36.3
Lutheran	50,335	4.6%	−8.7%	41.9
Muslim	5,095	0.5%	44.7%	28.3
Protestant not included elsewhere[2]	20,655	1.9%	−7.8%	43.7
Presbyterian	9,365	0.8%	−41.7%	46.0
Pentecostal	16,565	1.5%	−21.9%	30.3
Jewish	13,040	1.2%	−4.6%	46.3
Buddhist	5,745	0.5%	9.3%	35.6
Hindu	3,840	0.3%	10.7%	35.8
Sikh	5,485	0.5%	57.2%	29.1
Greek Orthodox[3]	6,875	0.6%	−46.1%	50.6
Mennonite	51,540	4.7%	−21.9%	34.6
Orthodox not included elsewhere[4]	3,425	0.3%	83.2%	38.2
Jehovah's Witnesses	4,240	0.4%	−25.9%	40.6
Ukrainian Catholic	29,740	2.7%	−11.0%	46.5
Church of Jesus Christ of Latter-day Saints (Mormons)	1,700	0.2%	−4.8%	30.8
Salvation Army	1,490	0.1%	−47.4%	41.4
Christian Reformed Church	1,335	0.1%	−11.3%	31.1
Evangelical Missionary Church	6,025	0.5%	123.1%	31.2
Christian and Missionary Alliance	3,085	0.3%	−2.4%	35.3
Adventist	1,415	0.1%	3.3%	39.5
Non-denominational[5]	4,945	0.4%	76.0%	31.6
Ukrainian Orthodox	4,640	0.4%	−13.8%	48.5
Aboriginal spirituality	3,415	0.3%	190.6%	23.0
Hutterite	8,795	0.8%	18.1%	22.8
Methodist[6]	540	0.0%	−14.3%	48.8
Pagan[7]	995	0.1%	290.2%	30.6
Brethren in Christ	295	0.0%	−28.0%	42.6
Serbian Orthodox	165	0.0%	371.4%	35.1

*Religions selected for this table represent counts of 20,000 or more for Canada.

Source: Statistics Canada publication *Religions in Canada: Highlight Tables, 2001 Census*, Catalogue 97F0024XIE2001015, http://www.statcan.gc.ca/bsolc/olc-cel/olc-cel?catno=97F0024XIE2001015&lang=eng.

Selected Religions, 2001 Counts: New Brunswick (20 Per Cent Sample Data)

Religion*	2001	Selected Religions		Median age
		Percentage distribution (2001)	Percentage change (1991–2001)	
New Brunswick				
Total population	**719,715**	**100.0%**	**0.4%**	**38.2**
Roman Catholic	385,985	53.6%	−0.1%	37.9
No religion	56,440	7.8%	47.8%	29.5
United Church	69,235	9.6%	−8.4%	43.3
Anglican	58,210	8.1%	−5.0%	42.1
Christian not included elsewhere[1]	8,120	1.1%	69.7%	31.5
Baptist	80,490	11.2%	−0.6%	39.8
Lutheran	1,510	0.2%	−4.7%	47.4
Muslim	1,275	0.2%	410.0%	22.6
Protestant not included elsewhere[2]	9,525	1.3%	−21.7%	43.3
Presbyterian	6,900	1.0%	−31.9%	44.9
Pentecostal	20,150	2.8%	−11.5%	35.1
Jewish	670	0.1%	−23.9%	49.3
Buddhist	545	0.1%	49.3%	31.7
Hindu	475	0.1%	−21.5%	37.1
Sikh	90	0.0%	125.0%	32.2
Greek Orthodox[3]	320	0.0%	−29.7%	42.0
Mennonite	155	0.0%	−35.4%	54.9
Orthodox not included elsewhere[4]	185	0.0%	15.6%	35.2
Jehovah's Witnesses	2,430	0.3%	−31.4%	42.3
Ukrainian Catholic	50	0.0%	−47.4%	41.5
Church of Jesus Christ of Latter-day Saints (Mormons)	1,105	0.2%	20.1%	28.6
Salvation Army	1,195	0.2%	−16.4%	39.0
Christian Reformed Church	230	0.0%	21.1%	29.4
Evangelical Missionary Church	85	0.0%	88.9%	32.6
Christian and Missionary Alliance	115	0.0%	−25.8%	26.7
Adventist	975	0.1%	−19.1%	42.7
Non-denominational[5]	1,550	0.2%	66.7%	32.8
Ukrainian Orthodox	45	0.0%	200.0%	47.4
Aboriginal spirituality	360	0.1%	380.0%	24.3
Hutterite	0	0.0%	. . .	0.0
Methodist[6]	160	0.0%	−45.8%	56.7
Pagan[7]	330	0.0%	187.0%	28.8
Brethren in Christ	105	0.0%	−50.0%	48.1
Serbian Orthodox	15	0.0%	. . .	41.4

*Religions selected for this table represent counts of 20,000 or more for Canada.

Source: Statistics Canada publication *Religions in Canada: Highlight Tables, 2001 Census*, Catalogue 97F0024XIE2001015, http://www.statcan.gc.ca/bsolc/olc-cel/olc-cel?catno=97F0024XIE2001015&lang=eng.

Selected Religions, 2001 Counts: Newfoundland and Labrador (20 Per Cent Sample Data)

Religion*	2001	Selected Religions Percentage distribution (2001)	Percentage change (1991–2001)	Median age
Newfoundland and Labrador				
Total population	**508,075**	**100.0%**	**−9.9%**	**38.1**
Roman Catholic	187,405	36.9%	−10.3%	35.8
No religion	12,455	2.5%	37.2%	36.2
United Church	86,420	17.0%	−11.3%	41.9
Anglican	132,680	26.1%	−10.1%	39.5
Christian not included elsewhere[1]	2,480	0.5%	57.0%	35.8
Baptist	1,155	0.2%	−15.1%	39.7
Lutheran	510	0.1%	22.9%	50.3
Muslim	630	0.1%	110.0%	28.9
Protestant not included elsewhere[2]	725	0.1%	−27.9%	45.6
Presbyterian	1,540	0.3%	−28.5%	43.4
Pentecostal	33,840	6.7%	−15.7%	36.3
Jewish	140	0.0%	7.7%	35.6
Buddhist	185	0.0%	76.2%	41.2
Hindu	405	0.1%	−9.0%	47.3
Sikh	130	0.0%	4.0%	34.9
Greek Orthodox[3]	125	0.0%	−39.0%	35.3
Mennonite	10	0.0%	−66.7%	33.0
Orthodox not included elsewhere[4]	105	0.0%	−4.5%	26.4
Jehovah's Witnesses	1,520	0.3%	−37.1%	42.4
Ukrainian Catholic	15	0.0%	−62.5%	51.2
Church of Jesus Christ of Latter-day Saints (Mormons)	195	0.0%	−2.5%	32.0
Salvation Army	39,955	7.9%	−10.2%	38.3
Christian Reformed Church	0	0.0%	...	0.0
Evangelical Missionary Church	45	0.0%	350.0%	36.1
Christian and Missionary Alliance	30	0.0%	...	16.8
Adventist	580	0.1%	−18.3%	39.7
Non-denominational[5]	395	0.1%	−16.0%	43.4
Ukrainian Orthodox	0	0.0%	...	0.0
Aboriginal spirituality	50	0.0%	...	20.0
Hutterite	0	0.0%	...	0.0
Methodist[6]	45	0.0%	−52.6%	50.0
Pagan[7]	65	0.0%	116.7%	27.0
Brethren in Christ	460	0.1%	−10.7%	30.8
Serbian Orthodox	0	0.0%	...	0.0

*Religions selected for this table represent counts of 20,000 or more for Canada.

Source: Statistics Canada publication *Religions in Canada: Highlight Tables, 2001 Census*, Catalogue 97F0024XIE2001015, http://www.statcan.gc.ca/bsolc/olc-cel/olc-cel?catno=97F0024XIE2001015&lang=eng.

Selected Religions, 2001 Counts: Nova Scotia (20 Per Cent Sample Data)

Religion*	2001	Percentage distribution (2001)	Percentage change (1991–2001)	Median age
Nova Scotia				
Total population	**897,570**	**100.0%**	**0.7%**	**38.5**
Roman Catholic	327,940	36.5%	−0.9%	37.5
No religion	104,275	11.6%	56.0%	29.6
United Church	142,520	15.9%	−6.9%	42.3
Anglican	120,315	13.4%	−6.3%	42.2
Christian not included elsewhere[1]	10,105	1.1%	76.4%	32.9
Baptist	94,990	10.6%	−3.6%	41.0
Lutheran	11,080	1.2%	−3.4%	43.5
Muslim	3,550	0.4%	147.4%	25.0
Protestant not included elsewhere[2]	15,065	1.7%	−15.8%	39.4
Presbyterian	22,450	2.5%	−28.1%	44.8
Pentecostal	9,200	1.0%	−14.3%	35.9
Jewish	2,120	0.2%	8.7%	47.0
Buddhist	1,735	0.2%	16.8%	38.6
Hindu	1,235	0.1%	28.0%	37.7
Sikh	270	0.0%	−18.2%	29.9
Greek Orthodox[3]	2,090	0.2%	38.0%	37.1
Mennonite	790	0.1%	41.1%	23.6
Orthodox not included elsewhere[4]	890	0.1%	60.4%	33.1
Jehovah's Witnesses	4,495	0.5%	−20.2%	40.3
Ukrainian Catholic	280	0.0%	−12.5%	51.2
Church of Jesus Christ of Latter-day Saints (Mormons)	2,530	0.3%	−11.8%	29.4
Salvation Army	3,940	0.4%	−19.9%	36.0
Christian Reformed Church	715	0.1%	−14.9%	32.8
Evangelical Missionary Church	175	0.0%	191.7%	45.3
Christian and Missionary Alliance	180	0.0%	80.0%	34.6
Adventist	1,420	0.2%	−9.8%	42.4
Non-denominational[5]	1,175	0.1%	45.1%	39.8
Ukrainian Orthodox	45	0.0%	125.0%	57.6
Aboriginal spirituality	270	0.0%	500.0%	28.8
Hutterite	0	0.0%	. . .	0.0
Methodist[6]	250	0.0%	−46.8%	53.1
Pagan[7]	775	0.1%	604.5%	28.2
Brethren in Christ	335	0.0%	−43.2%	28.8
Serbian Orthodox	30	0.0%	. . .	24.9

*Religions selected for this table represent counts of 20,000 or more for Canada.

Source: Statistics Canada publication *Religions in Canada: Highlight Tables, 2001 Census*, Catalogue 97F0024XIE2001015, http://www.statcan.gc.ca/bsolc/olc-cel/olc-cel?catno=97F0024XIE2001015&lang=eng.

Selected Religions, 2001 Counts: Nunavut (20 Per Cent Sample Data)

	Selected Religions			
Religion*	2001	Percentage distribution (2001)	Percentage change (1991–2001)	Median age
Nunavut				
Total population	**26,665**	**100.0%**	**25.8%**	**22.0**
Roman Catholic	6,205	23.3%	22.9%	22.0
No religion	1,610	6.0%	111.8%	27.1
United Church	355	1.3%	−5.3%	36.2
Anglican	15,440	57.9%	21.9%	20.2
Christian not included elsewhere[1]	840	3.2%	52.7%	22.6
Baptist	85	0.3%	−5.6%	31.8
Lutheran	70	0.3%	−17.6%	40.5
Muslim	25	0.1%	150.0%	37.5
Protestant not included elsewhere[2]	390	1.5%	136.4%	34.5
Presbyterian	65	0.2%	−13.3%	39.0
Pentecostal	1,175	4.4%	20.5%	19.3
Jewish	10	0.0%	0.0%	39.0
Buddhist	15	0.1%	50.0%	33.5
Hindu	0	0.0%	−100.0%	48.0
Sikh	0	0.0%	. . .	39.5
Greek Orthodox[3]	10	0.0%	−33.3%	32.0
Mennonite	10	0.0%	−33.3%	32.5
Orthodox not included elsewhere[4]	10	0.0%	0.0%	30.0
Jehovah's Witnesses	10	0.0%	0.0%	56.5
Ukrainian Catholic	0	0.0%	−100.0%	48.5
Church of Jesus Christ of Latter-day Saints (Mormons)	10	0.0%	0.0%	46.5
Salvation Army	35	0.1%	0.0%	35.0
Christian Reformed Church	0	0.0%	−100.0%	32.5
Evangelical Missionary Church	15	0.1%	50.0%	14.0
Christian and Missionary Alliance	95	0.4%	−13.6%	19.0
Adventist	0	0.0%	−100.0%	0.0
Non-denominational[5]	15	0.1%	50.0%	19.5
Ukrainian Orthodox	0	0.0%	. . .	45.5
Aboriginal spirituality	25	0.1%	150.0%	25.5
Hutterite	0	0.0%	. . .	0.0
Methodist[6]	0	0.0%	−100.0%	27.5
Pagan[7]	15	0.1%	. . .	30.5
Brethren in Christ	0	0.0%	. . .	26.5
Serbian Orthodox	0	0.0%	. . .	0.0

*Religions selected for this table represent counts of 20,000 or more for Canada.

Source: Statistics Canada publication *Religions in Canada: Highlight Tables, 2001 Census*, Catalogue 97F0024XIE2001015, http://www.statcan.gc.ca/bsolc/olc-cel/olc-cel?catno=97F0024XIE2001015&lang=eng.

Selected Religions, 2001 Counts: Northwest Territories (20 Per Cent Sample Data)

Religion*	Selected Religions			
	2001	Percentage distribution (2001)	Percentage change (1991–2001)	Median age
Northwest Territories				
Total population	**37,100**	**100.0%**	**2.4%**	**30.0**
Roman Catholic	16,940	45.7%	0.9%	28.8
No religion	6,465	17.4%	26.4%	27.9
United Church	2,230	6.0%	−23.8%	36.7
Anglican	5,510	14.9%	−3.0%	31.4
Christian not included elsewhere[1]	920	2.5%	135.9%	26.9
Baptist	650	1.8%	4.0%	27.7
Lutheran	425	1.1%	−32.5%	37.5
Muslim	180	0.5%	300.0%	30.4
Protestant not included elsewhere[2]	675	1.8%	−6.9%	34.7
Presbyterian	150	0.4%	−54.5%	41.5
Pentecostal	1,050	2.8%	−15.7%	27.5
Jewish	30	0.1%	−40.0%	32.5
Buddhist	155	0.4%	121.4%	36.8
Hindu	70	0.2%	7.7%	36.5
Sikh	45	0.1%	−18.2%	29.5
Greek Orthodox[3]	65	0.2%	−35.0%	48.5
Mennonite	50	0.1%	−23.1%	37.9
Orthodox not included elsewhere[4]	40	0.1%	300.0%	41.5
Jehovah's Witnesses	135	0.4%	−30.8%	32.7
Ukrainian Catholic	50	0.1%	−33.3%	37.6
Church of Jesus Christ of Latter-day Saints (Mormons)	95	0.3%	−17.4%	26.8
Salvation Army	205	0.6%	36.7%	29.8
Christian Reformed Church	20	0.1%	−33.3%	49.5
Evangelical Missionary Church	20	0.1%	−50.0%	37.5
Christian and Missionary Alliance	60	0.2%	−20.0%	30.0
Adventist	90	0.2%	125.0%	31.8
Non-denominational[5]	55	0.1%	37.5%	32.5
Ukrainian Orthodox	20	0.1%	0.0%	34.0
Aboriginal spirituality	235	0.6%	422.2%	29.6
Hutterite	0	0.0%	. . .	0.0
Methodist[6]	35	0.1%	133.3%	50.0
Pagan[7]	35	0.1%	. . .	34.2
Brethren in Christ	0	0.0%	−100.0%	0.0
Serbian Orthodox	0	0.0%	. . .	55.5

*Religions selected for this table represent counts of 20,000 or more for Canada.

Source: Statistics Canada publication *Religions in Canada: Highlight Tables, 2001 Census*, Catalogue 97F0024XIE2001015, http://www.statcan.gc.ca/bsolc/olc-cel/olc-cel?catno=97F0024XIE2001015&lang=eng.

Selected Religions, 2001 Counts: Prince Edward Island (20 Per Cent Sample Data)

Religion*	Selected Religions			
	2001	Percentage distribution (2001)	Percentage change (1991–2001)	Median age
Prince Edward Island				
Total population	**133,385**	**100.0%**	**4.1%**	**37.3**
Roman Catholic	63,240	47.4%	4.3%	36.0
No religion	8,705	6.5%	81.9%	28.7
United Church	26,570	19.9%	2.2%	40.0
Anglican	6,525	4.9%	−2.5%	42.4
Christian not included elsewhere[1]	3,210	2.4%	103.8%	28.2
Baptist	5,950	4.5%	11.8%	38.4
Lutheran	160	0.1%	39.1%	53.9
Muslim	195	0.1%	225.0%	26.2
Protestant not included elsewhere[2]	5,105	3.8%	−1.5%	37.7
Presbyterian	7,885	5.9%	−28.3%	43.6
Pentecostal	975	0.7%	−26.4%	35.0
Jewish	55	0.0%	−35.3%	46.5
Buddhist	140	0.1%	133.3%	33.3
Hindu	35	0.0%	40.0%	53.3
Sikh	0	0.0%	−100.0%	0.0
Greek Orthodox[3]	110	0.1%	69.2%	24.8
Mennonite	10	0.0%	−50.0%	43.5
Orthodox not included elsewhere[4]	70	0.1%	100.0%	33.1
Jehovah's Witnesses	475	0.4%	2.2%	42.3
Ukrainian Catholic	15	0.0%	0.0%	53.2
Church of Jesus Christ of Latter-day Saints (Mormons)	215	0.2%	−6.5%	22.4
Salvation Army	340	0.3%	19.3%	42.6
Christian Reformed Church	205	0.2%	−37.9%	27.6
Evangelical Missionary Church	10	0.0%	−89.5%	43.5
Christian and Missionary Alliance	0	0.0%	. . .	0.0
Adventist	35	0.0%	−65.0%	37.7
Non-denominational[5]	165	0.1%	3.1%	38.2
Ukrainian Orthodox	0	0.0%	. . .	0.0
Aboriginal spirituality	50	0.0%	150.0%	20.5
Hutterite	0	0.0%	. . .	0.0
Methodist[6]	10	0.0%	. . .	49.8
Pagan[7]	45	0.0%	. . .	24.7
Brethren in Christ	165	0.1%	−38.9%	34.6
Serbian Orthodox	0	0.0%	. . .	0.0

*Religions selected for this table represent counts of 20,000 or more for Canada.

Source: Statistics Canada publication *Religions in Canada: Highlight Tables, 2001 Census*, Catalogue 97F0024XIE2001015, http://www.statcan.gc.ca/bsolc/olc-cel/olc-cel?catno=97F0024XIE2001015&lang=eng.

Selected Religions, 2001 Counts: Quebec (20 Per Cent Sample Data)

Religion*	2001	Selected Religions Percentage distribution (2001)	Percentage change (1991–2001)	Median age
Quebec				
Total population	7,125,580	100.0%	4.6%	38.4
Roman Catholic	5,930,380	83.2%	1.3%	39.4
No religion	400,325	5.6%	55.6%	28.9
United Church	52,950	0.7%	−14.6%	46.7
Anglican	85,475	1.2%	−11.0%	41.5
Christian not included elsewhere[1]	56,750	0.8%	45.6%	31.9
Baptist	35,455	0.5%	28.9%	33.1
Lutheran	9,635	0.1%	−10.0%	51.1
Muslim	108,620	1.5%	141.8%	28.2
Protestant not included elsewhere[2]	64,040	0.9%	13.3%	34.6
Presbyterian	8,770	0.1%	−53.5%	49.7
Pentecostal	22,675	0.3%	−21.7%	30.7
Jewish	89,915	1.3%	−8.0%	42.5
Buddhist	41,375	0.6%	30.8%	36.2
Hindu	24,530	0.3%	73.7%	30.7
Sikh	8,220	0.1%	81.7%	30.8
Greek Orthodox[3]	50,020	0.7%	−7.3%	38.2
Mennonite	425	0.0%	−74.3%	37.1
Orthodox not included elsewhere[4]	37,600	0.5%	31.0%	35.8
Jehovah's Witnesses	29,040	0.4%	−13.1%	37.6
Ukrainian Catholic	3,430	0.0%	−14.0%	49.7
Church of Jesus Christ of Latter-day Saints (Mormons)	4,420	0.1%	26.8%	25.7
Salvation Army	420	0.0%	−65.6%	37.1
Christian Reformed Church	115	0.0%	−20.7%	45.7
Evangelical Missionary Church	7,575	0.1%	87.3%	34.4
Christian and Missionary Alliance	315	0.0%	−37.6%	42.2
Adventist	6,690	0.1%	40.0%	28.7
Non-denominational[5]	475	0.0%	75.9%	29.4
Ukrainian Orthodox	985	0.0%	−25.1%	45.4
Aboriginal spirituality	735	0.0%	332.4%	31.2
Hutterite	0	0.0%	−100.0%	47.5
Methodist[6]	1,060	0.0%	7.1%	50.2
Pagan[7]	1,330	0.0%	533.3%	27.2
Brethren in Christ	590	0.0%	−36.2%	38.0
Serbian Orthodox	920	0.0%	152.1%	33.6

*Religions selected for this table represent counts of 20,000 or more for Canada.

Source: Statistics Canada publication *Religions in Canada: Highlight Tables, 2001 Census*, Catalogue 97F0024XIE2001015, http://www.statcan.gc.ca/bsolc/olc-cel/olc-cel?catno=97F0024XIE2001015&lang=eng.

Selected Religions, 2001 Counts: Saskatchewan (20 Per Cent Sample Data)

Religion*	2001	Percentage distribution (2001)	Percentage change (1991–2001)	Median age
Selected Religions				
Saskatchewan				
Total population	**963,150**	**100.0%**	**−1.3%**	**36.3**
Roman Catholic	286,815	29.8%	−3.3%	33.9
No religion	148,535	15.4%	40.5%	27.7
United Church	187,450	19.5%	−15.6%	43.7
Anglican	65,740	6.8%	−6.0%	38.7
Christian not included elsewhere[1]	27,075	2.8%	137.4%	27.3
Baptist	16,725	1.7%	8.5%	38.6
Lutheran	78,520	8.2%	−4.4%	39.6
Muslim	2,230	0.2%	88.2%	28.7
Protestant not included elsewhere[2]	14,910	1.5%	−13.3%	41.7
Presbyterian	7,010	0.7%	−39.4%	46.9
Pentecostal	14,605	1.5%	−17.5%	30.0
Jewish	865	0.1%	−37.1%	43.5
Buddhist	3,050	0.3%	61.8%	35.1
Hindu	1,585	0.2%	−5.7%	35.4
Sikh	500	0.1%	−11.5%	31.2
Greek Orthodox[3]	6,040	0.6%	−48.7%	51.1
Mennonite	19,570	2.0%	−22.5%	38.0
Orthodox not included elsewhere[4]	2,695	0.3%	85.9%	43.1
Jehovah's Witnesses	6,565	0.7%	−19.2%	42.3
Ukrainian Catholic	17,615	1.8%	−12.6%	44.7
Church of Jesus Christ of Latter-day Saints (Mormons)	2,885	0.3%	24.1%	24.9
Salvation Army	1,650	0.2%	−24.5%	41.3
Christian Reformed Church	460	0.0%	2.2%	23.5
Evangelical Missionary Church	4,320	0.4%	25.6%	36.7
Christian and Missionary Alliance	8,940	0.9%	−15.4%	34.7
Adventist	1,540	0.2%	−19.8%	43.3
Non-denominational[5]	2,595	0.3%	3.6%	32.8
Ukrainian Orthodox	5,050	0.5%	−11.0%	49.4
Aboriginal spirituality	5,885	0.6%	195.0%	19.8
Hutterite	4,895	0.5%	23.8%	22.8
Methodist[6]	910	0.1%	70.1%	33.7
Pagan[7]	670	0.1%	538.1%	28.7
Brethren in Christ	695	0.1%	−11.5%	36.8
Serbian Orthodox	80	0.0%	433.3%	32.2

*Religions selected for this table represent counts of 20,000 or more for Canada.

Source: Statistics Canada publication *Religions in Canada: Highlight Tables, 2001 Census*, Catalogue 97F0024XIE2001015, http://www.statcan.gc.ca/bsolc/olc-cel/olc-cel?catno=97F0024XIE2001015&lang=eng.

Selected Religions, 2001 Counts: Yukon Territory (20 Per Cent Sample Data)

Religion*	2001	Percentage distribution (2001)	Percentage change (1991–2001)	Median age
Yukon Territory				
Total population	**28,520**	**100.0%**	**3.1%**	**35.8**
Roman Catholic	5,985	21.0%	8.1%	36.3
No religion	10,665	37.4%	14.6%	31.1
United Church	2,105	7.4%	−12.3%	42.0
Anglican	3,795	13.3%	−7.3%	39.3
Christian not included elsewhere[1]	1,010	3.5%	33.8%	29.9
Baptist	905	3.2%	−8.6%	39.2
Lutheran	580	2.0%	−12.8%	46.0
Muslim	60	0.2%	100.0%	37.4
Protestant not included elsewhere[2]	640	2.2%	−33.0%	40.6
Presbyterian	190	0.7%	−47.9%	51.4
Pentecostal	610	2.1%	1.7%	35.2
Jewish	35	0.1%	−22.2%	35.8
Buddhist	130	0.5%	188.9%	42.5
Hindu	10	0.0%	0.0%	59.1
Sikh	105	0.4%	162.5%	32.8
Greek Orthodox[3]	100	0.4%	81.8%	44.6
Mennonite	40	0.1%	−63.6%	35.8
Orthodox not included elsewhere[4]	20	0.1%	100.0%	58.5
Jehovah's Witnesses	130	0.5%	−55.2%	42.2
Ukrainian Catholic	30	0.1%	−33.3%	43.2
Church of Jesus Christ of Latter-day Saints (Mormons)	115	0.4%	−28.1%	29.0
Salvation Army	15	0.1%	−82.4%	48.8
Christian Reformed Church	0	0.0%	−100.0%	49.5
Evangelical Missionary Church	80	0.3%	128.6%	29.7
Christian and Missionary Alliance	10	0.0%	0.0%	46.6
Adventist	55	0.2%	−57.7%	39.7
Non-denominational[5]	125	0.4%	25.0%	14.8
Ukrainian Orthodox	15	0.1%	0.0%	56.8
Aboriginal spirituality	185	0.6%	2.8%	36.2
Hutterite	0	0.0%	. . .	0.0
Methodist[6]	10	0.0%	−75.0%	39.8
Pagan[7]	125	0.4%	1150.0%	29.7
Brethren in Christ	10	0.0%	. . .	53.5
Serbian Orthodox	15	0.1%	. . .	24.0

*Religions selected for this table represent counts of 20,000 or more for Canada.

Source: Statistics Canada publication *Religions in Canada: Highlight Tables, 2001 Census*, Catalogue 97F0024XIE2001015, http://www.statcan.gc.ca/bsolc/olc-cel/olc-cel?catno=97F0024XIE2001015&lang=eng.

NOTES

1. Includes persons who report "Christian," as well as those who report "Apostolic," "Born-again Christian," and "Evangelical."

2. Includes persons who report only "Protestant."

3. In 1991, included counts for Greek Catholic.

4. Includes persons who report "Orthodox." Also includes Armenian Apostolic, Bulgarian Orthodox, Ethiopian Orthodox, and Macedonian Orthodox.

5. Includes persons who report only "Non-denominational."

6. Includes persons who report "Methodist." Excludes Free Methodist and Evangelical Missionary Church.

7. Includes persons who report "Wicca."

2001 Census Tables: Selected Religions by Immigrant Status and Immigration Period

Selected Religions by Immigration Status and Immigration Period, 2001 Counts: Canada (20 Per Cent Sample Data)

Religion*	Total population[a]	Canadian-born population[b]	Foreign-born population[c]	Immigrated before 1991	Immigrated between 1991 and 2001[d]
Canada					
Total population	29,639,030	23,991,910	5,448,480	3,617,800	1,830,680
Roman Catholic	12,793,125	10,983,375	1,757,665	1,335,220	422,440
No religion	4,796,325	3,826,480	924,590	533,810	390,775
United Church	2,839,125	2,684,040	152,540	134,950	17,590
Anglican	2,035,500	1,750,620	279,340	248,010	31,325
Christian not included elsewhere[1]	780,450	556,605	211,660	114,455	97,205
Baptist	729,470	612,075	112,760	76,805	35,955
Lutheran	606,590	475,205	128,580	119,320	9,260
Muslim	579,640	137,835	415,835	139,975	275,860
Protestant not included elsewhere[2]	549,205	457,455	88,200	70,845	17,355
Presbyterian	409,830	334,450	72,675	61,100	11,570
Pentecostal	369,475	304,480	62,740	41,540	21,205
Jewish	329,995	225,795	101,370	79,010	22,360
Buddhist	300,345	74,065	217,780	133,270	84,510
Hindu	297,200	76,220	213,685	95,125	118,560
Sikh	278,410	98,650	176,045	90,695	85,345
Greek Orthodox	215,175	117,100	96,960	81,160	15,805
Mennonite	191,465	160,930	29,550	21,985	7,560
Orthodox not included elsewhere[3]	165,420	47,715	113,880	44,845	69,035
Jehovah's Witnesses	154,750	125,040	28,965	21,975	6,990
Ukrainian Catholic	126,200	104,155	21,825	16,110	5,715
Church of Jesus Christ of Latter-day Saints (Mormons)	101,805	88,370	12,095	8,425	3,670
Salvation Army	87,790	84,805	2,890	2,495	395
Christian Reformed Church	76,670	56,835	19,680	18,105	1,575
Evangelical Missionary Church	66,705	55,280	10,975	7,190	3,785
Christian and Missionary Alliance	66,285	56,585	9,415	6,280	3,130
Adventist	62,880	34,745	27,045	17,305	9,740
Non-denominational[4]	40,545	36,635	3,730	2,865	870
Ukrainian Orthodox	32,720	27,005	5,525	3,185	2,340
Aboriginal spirituality	29,820	28,760	1,015	675	335
Hutterite	26,295	25,860	410	315	100
Methodist[5]	25,730	10,580	13,940	9,370	4,570
Pagan[6]	21,080	19,180	1,815	1,560	255
Brethren in Christ	20,590	18,365	2,160	1,790	365
Serbian Orthodox	20,520	5,200	15,130	4,975	10,155

*Religions selected for this table represent counts of 20,000 or more for Canada.

[a] Includes non-permanent residents (not shown as a separate column in this table), as well as the sum of the counts for the Canadian-born and foreign-born population.

[b] Includes persons born in Canada as well as a small number of persons born outside Canada who are Canadian citizens by birth.

[c] This population is also referred to as the "immigrant population," which is defined as persons who are, or have ever been, landed immigrants in Canada.

[d] Includes data up to Census Day, May 15, 2001.

Source: Statistics Canada publication *Religions in Canada: Highlight Tables, 2001 Census*, Catalogue 97F0024XIE2001015, http://www.statcan.gc.ca/bsolc/olc-cel/olc-cel?catno=97F0024XIE2001015&lang=eng.

Selected Religions by Immigration Status and Immigration Period, 2001 Counts: Alberta (20 Per Cent Sample Data)

Religion*	Total population[a]	Canadian-born population[b]	Foreign-born population[c]	Immigrated before 1991	Immigrated between 1991 and 2001[d]
Alberta					
Total population	**2,941,150**	**2,485,540**	**438,335**	**308,415**	**129,920**
Roman Catholic	756,005	632,650	119,420	86,605	32,820
No religion	678,875	590,725	83,930	57,150	26,780
United Church	396,065	378,415	17,370	15,465	1,905
Anglican	172,430	148,255	23,495	20,170	3,320
Christian not included elsewhere[1]	123,145	102,540	19,235	11,605	7,630
Baptist	73,640	63,220	9,845	7,105	2,740
Lutheran	142,530	123,500	18,580	17,285	1,290
Muslim	49,045	16,125	31,650	16,265	15,385
Protestant not included elsewhere[2]	78,370	69,780	8,245	6,695	1,555
Presbyterian	29,200	23,065	5,690	4,760	930
Pentecostal	42,615	37,805	4,555	3,105	1,445
Jewish	11,090	7,535	3,340	2,585	755
Buddhist	33,410	10,685	22,060	16,030	6,035
Hindu	15,970	4,245	11,185	6,360	4,830
Sikh	23,470	8,030	15,165	7,495	7,670
Greek Orthodox	20,495	16,425	4,025	3,110	910
Mennonite	22,785	19,645	3,085	2,025	1,055
Orthodox not included elsewhere[3]	9,985	4,095	5,665	1,520	4,140
Jehovah's Witnesses	18,830	16,495	2,290	1,915	375
Ukrainian Catholic	28,750	26,120	2,605	1,810	790
Church of Jesus Christ of Latter-day Saints (Mormons)	50,580	46,500	3,740	2,890	845
Salvation Army	5,050	4,855	195	165	30
Christian Reformed Church	12,980	9,950	2,990	2,540	445
Evangelical Missionary Church	17,640	15,915	1,685	1,080	605
Christian and Missionary Alliance	23,715	21,320	2,315	1,845	475
Adventist	8,140	6,120	1,915	1,310	605
Non-denominational[4]	5,965	5,415	490	380	110
Ukrainian Orthodox	9,865	9,060	760	470	290
Aboriginal spirituality	5,860	5,705	155	95	60
Hutterite	12,330	12,110	205	180	25
Methodist[5]	1,895	530	1,200	785	415
Pagan[6]	3,035	2,750	280	230	45
Brethren in Christ	995	910	90	60	25
Serbian Orthodox	960	220	730	195	530

*Religions selected for this table represent counts of 20,000 or more for Canada.

[a] Includes non-permanent residents (not shown as a separate column in this table), as well as the sum of the counts for the Canadian-born and foreign-born population.

[b] Includes persons born in Canada as well as a small number of persons born outside Canada who are Canadian citizens by birth.

[c] This population is also referred to as the "immigrant population," which is defined as persons who are, or have ever been, landed immigrants in Canada.

[d] Includes data up to Census Day, May 15, 2001.

Source: Statistics Canada publication *Religions in Canada: Highlight Tables, 2001 Census*, Catalogue 97F0024XIE2001015, http://www.statcan.gc.ca/bsolc/olc-cel/olc-cel?catno=97F0024XIE2001015&lang=eng.

Selected Religions by Immigration Status and Immigration Period, 2001 Counts: British Columbia (20 Per Cent Sample Data)

Religion*	Total population[a]	Canadian-born population[b]	Foreign-born population[c]	Immigrated before 1991	Immigrated between 1991 and 2001[d]
British Columbia					
Total population	**3,868,875**	**2,821,870**	**1,009,815**	**639,200**	**370,615**
Roman Catholic	666,905	457,370	202,860	143,330	59,530
No religion	1,356,600	1,049,240	293,390	162,365	131,020
United Church	361,840	330,545	30,685	26,255	4,430
Anglican	298,375	236,645	60,750	54,010	6,740
Christian not included elsewhere[1]	200,340	146,350	50,700	27,305	23,395
Baptist	107,465	83,015	23,550	15,460	8,085
Lutheran	101,145	69,160	31,440	28,875	2,560
Muslim	56,215	11,980	42,405	18,965	23,440
Protestant not included elsewhere[2]	76,100	60,655	15,055	12,360	2,700
Presbyterian	37,115	25,510	11,075	8,915	2,160
Pentecostal	47,420	39,945	7,290	5,150	2,140
Jewish	21,230	14,135	6,800	4,970	1,830
Buddhist	85,540	18,420	64,340	30,485	33,855
Hindu	31,495	10,050	20,745	11,315	9,435
Sikh	135,310	53,115	81,080	45,260	35,825
Greek Orthodox	15,490	9,125	6,280	4,840	1,445
Mennonite	35,490	29,525	5,790	4,900	890
Orthodox not included elsewhere[3]	11,595	2,885	8,475	2,225	6,255
Jehovah's Witnesses	31,960	26,795	5,035	3,810	1,230
Ukrainian Catholic	7,780	6,900	860	625	240
Church of Jesus Christ of Latter-day Saints (Mormons)	17,590	14,525	2,740	1,945	800
Salvation Army	5,945	5,535	410	360	50
Christian Reformed Church	11,810	8,710	3,070	2,760	310
Evangelical Missionary Church	9,245	7,265	1,935	1,380	555
Christian and Missionary Alliance	15,155	12,430	2,645	1,695	955
Adventist	11,070	7,940	2,970	2,150	825
Non-denominational[4]	7,055	5,975	1,040	735	300
Ukrainian Orthodox	3,020	2,515	465	125	345
Aboriginal spirituality	5,475	5,225	230	150	85
Hutterite	220	220	0	0	0
Methodist[5]	4,200	960	3,055	1,790	1,270
Pagan[6]	6,105	5,435	650	605	45
Brethren in Christ	1,695	1,370	320	270	45
Serbian Orthodox	2,495	425	2,010	305	1,710

*Religions selected for this table represent counts of 20,000 or more for Canada.

[a] Includes non-permanent residents (not shown as a separate column in this table), as well as the sum of the counts for the Canadian-born and foreign-born population.

[b] Includes persons born in Canada as well as a small number of persons born outside Canada who are Canadian citizens by birth.

[c] This population is also referred to as the "immigrant population," which is defined as persons who are, or have ever been, landed immigrants in Canada.

[d] Includes data up to Census Day, May 15, 2001.

Source: Statistics Canada publication *Religions in Canada: Highlight Tables, 2001 Census*, Catalogue 97F0024XIE2001015, http://www.statcan.gc.ca/bsolc/olc-cel/olc-cel?catno=97F0024XIE2001015&lang=eng.

Selected Religions by Immigration Status and Immigration Period, 2001 Counts: Manitoba (20 Per Cent Sample Data)

Religion*	Total population[a]	Canadian-born population[b]	Foreign-born population[c]	Immigrated before 1991	Immigrated between 1991 and 2001[d]
Manitoba					
Total population	**1,103,700**	**965,515**	**133,660**	**101,310**	**32,345**
Roman Catholic	292,970	243,030	49,020	38,630	10,395
No religion	201,835	184,445	16,590	12,025	4,565
United Church	176,820	171,185	5,495	5,010	485
Anglican	85,890	78,550	7,225	6,070	1,155
Christian not included elsewhere[1]	44,540	37,420	6,700	4,095	2,610
Baptist	22,505	18,885	3,435	2,405	1,025
Lutheran	50,335	44,515	5,700	5,400	290
Muslim	5,095	1,370	3,340	1,260	2,080
Protestant not included elsewhere[2]	20,655	18,360	2,215	1,750	470
Presbyterian	9,365	8,220	1,105	960	150
Pentecostal	16,565	15,120	1,355	1,050	305
Jewish	13,040	10,955	2,020	1,660	355
Buddhist	5,745	1,915	3,645	2,615	1,025
Hindu	3,840	1,230	2,500	1,920	585
Sikh	5,485	1,935	3,500	1,920	1,580
Greek Orthodox	6,875	5,235	1,605	1,255	350
Mennonite	51,540	43,865	7,485	6,140	1,345
Orthodox not included elsewhere[3]	3,425	1,730	1,585	720	870
Jehovah's Witnesses	4,240	3,500	735	515	210
Ukrainian Catholic	29,740	27,890	1,830	1,650	175
Church of Jesus Christ of Latter-day Saints (Mormons)	1,700	1,405	245	160	85
Salvation Army	1,490	1,415	75	70	10
Christian Reformed Church	1,335	980	340	265	75
Evangelical Missionary Church	6,025	4,955	995	525	470
Christian and Missionary Alliance	3,085	2,805	255	150	100
Adventist	1,415	735	675	515	160
Non-denominational[4]	4,945	4,730	215	115	90
Ukrainian Orthodox	4,640	4,180	460	295	155
Aboriginal spirituality	3,415	3,355	55	30	25
Hutterite	8,795	8,680	110	65	45
Methodist[5]	540	145	325	250	80
Pagan[6]	995	940	55	50	0
Brethren in Christ	295	260	30	30	0
Serbian Orthodox	165	35	130	60	75

*Religions selected for this table represent counts of 20,000 or more for Canada.

[a] Includes non-permanent residents (not shown as a separate column in this table), as well as the sum of the counts for the Canadian-born and foreign-born population.

[b] Includes persons born in Canada as well as a small number of persons born outside Canada who are Canadian citizens by birth.

[c] This population is also referred to as the "immigrant population," which is defined as persons who are, or have ever been, landed immigrants in Canada.

[d] Includes data up to Census Day, May 15, 2001.

Source: Statistics Canada publication *Religions in Canada: Highlight Tables, 2001 Census*, Catalogue 97F0024XIE2001015, http://www.statcan.gc.ca/bsolc/olc-cel/olc-cel?catno=97F0024XIE2001015&lang=eng.

Selected Religions by Immigration Status and Immigration Period, 2001 Counts: New Brunswick (20 Per Cent Sample Data)

Religion*	Total population[a]	Canadian-born population[b]	Foreign-born population[c]	Immigrated before 1991	Immigrated between 1991 and 2001[d]
New Brunswick					
Total population	719,715	695,555	22,465	18,070	4,400
Roman Catholic	385,985	377,610	7,850	6,585	1,265
No religion	56,440	53,365	2,670	1,955	710
United Church	69,235	67,535	1,685	1,570	115
Anglican	58,210	55,460	2,670	2,405	270
Christian not included elsewhere[1]	8,120	7,570	510	300	215
Baptist	80,490	78,290	2,060	1,665	395
Lutheran	1,510	960	525	450	75
Muslim	1,275	375	715	195	525
Protestant not included elsewhere[2]	9,525	8,880	590	525	60
Presbyterian	6,900	6,420	465	450	15
Pentecostal	20,150	19,645	490	380	105
Jewish	670	595	75	70	10
Buddhist	545	290	225	150	70
Hindu	475	115	335	220	115
Sikh	90	20	35	15	15
Greek Orthodox	320	185	135	105	30
Mennonite	155	140	15	15	0
Orthodox not included elsewhere[3]	185	35	140	40	105
Jehovah's Witnesses	2,430	2,220	205	155	55
Ukrainian Catholic	50	45	0	10	0
Church of Jesus Christ of Latter-day Saints (Mormons)	1,105	1,025	75	55	20
Salvation Army	1,195	1,190	10	10	0
Christian Reformed Church	230	185	45	40	0
Evangelical Missionary Church	85	75	10	10	0
Christian and Missionary Alliance	115	115	0	0	0
Adventist	975	910	65	45	20
Non-denominational[4]	1,550	1,480	70	55	15
Ukrainian Orthodox	45	40	0	0	0
Aboriginal spirituality	360	315	40	35	0
Hutterite	0	0	0	0	0
Methodist[5]	160	60	95	85	10
Pagan[6]	330	310	20	15	0
Brethren in Christ	105	105	0	0	0
Serbian Orthodox	15	0	10	0	10

*Religions selected for this table represent counts of 20,000 or more for Canada.

[a] Includes non-permanent residents (not shown as a separate column in this table), as well as the sum of the counts for the Canadian-born and foreign-born population.

[b] Includes persons born in Canada as well as a small number of persons born outside Canada who are Canadian citizens by birth.

[c] This population is also referred to as the "immigrant population," which is defined as persons who are, or have ever been, landed immigrants in Canada.

[d] Includes data up to Census Day, May 15, 2001.

Source: Statistics Canada publication *Religions in Canada: Highlight Tables, 2001 Census*, Catalogue 97F0024XIE2001015, http://www.statcan.gc.ca/bsolc/olc-cel/olc-cel?catno=97F0024XIE2001015&lang=eng.

Selected Religions by Immigration Status and Immigration Period, 2001 Counts: Newfoundland and Labrador (20 Per Cent Sample Data)

Religion*	Total population[a]	Canadian-born population[b]	Foreign-born population[c]	Immigrated before 1991	Immigrated between 1991 and 2001[d]
Newfoundland and Labrador					
Total population	**508,075**	**499,095**	**8,030**	**6,015**	**2,015**
Roman Catholic	187,405	185,080	2,060	1,770	295
No religion	12,455	11,105	1,090	800	285
United Church	86,420	85,670	705	645	65
Anglican	132,680	131,215	1,380	1,155	225
Christian not included elsewhere[1]	2,480	2,330	145	70	80
Baptist	1,155	980	100	85	15
Lutheran	510	235	260	230	20
Muslim	630	145	445	105	345
Protestant not included elsewhere[2]	725	615	105	70	35
Presbyterian	1,540	1,165	320	275	50
Pentecostal	33,840	33,690	145	115	30
Jewish	140	80	50	40	10
Buddhist	185	75	105	40	65
Hindu	405	65	335	185	155
Sikh	130	50	80	50	30
Greek Orthodox	125	35	75	35	40
Mennonite	10	10	0	0	0
Orthodox not included elsewhere[3]	105	30	65	15	55
Jehovah's Witnesses	1,520	1,450	70	50	10
Ukrainian Catholic	15	10	10	0	0
Church of Jesus Christ of Latter-day Saints (Mormons)	195	180	0	10	10
Salvation Army	39,955	39,785	170	150	15
Christian Reformed Church	0	0	0	0	0
Evangelical Missionary Church	45	40	0	0	0
Christian and Missionary Alliance	30	25	0	0	0
Adventist	580	555	20	10	10
Non-denominational[4]	395	385	10	10	0
Ukrainian Orthodox	0	0	0	0	0
Aboriginal spirituality	50	55	0	0	0
Hutterite	0	0	0	0	0
Methodist[5]	45	10	25	15	10
Pagan[6]	65	60	10	0	0
Brethren in Christ	460	405	55	0	55
Serbian Orthodox	0	0	0	0	0

*Religions selected for this table represent counts of 20,000 or more for Canada.

[a] Includes non-permanent residents (not shown as a separate column in this table), as well as the sum of the counts for the Canadian-born and foreign-born population.

[b] Includes persons born in Canada as well as a small number of persons born outside Canada who are Canadian citizens by birth.

[c] This population is also referred to as the "immigrant population," which is defined as persons who are, or have ever been, landed immigrants in Canada.

[d] Includes data up to Census Day, May 15, 2001.

Source: Statistics Canada publication *Religions in Canada: Highlight Tables, 2001 Census*, Catalogue 97F0024XIE2001015, http://www.statcan.gc.ca/bsolc/olc-cel/olc-cel?catno=97F0024XIE2001015&lang=eng.

Selected Religions by Immigration Status and Immigration Period, 2001 Counts: Northwest Territories (20 Per Cent Sample Data)

Religion*	Total population[a]	Canadian-born population[b]	Foreign-born population[c]	Immigrated before 1991	Immigrated between 1991 and 2001[d]
Northwest Territories					
Total population	**37,100**	**34,600**	**2,385**	**1,610**	**770**
Roman Catholic	16,940	16,115	785	490	295
No religion	6,465	5,960	480	365	115
United Church	2,230	2,150	70	55	15
Anglican	5,510	5,285	225	180	45
Christian not included elsewhere[1]	920	815	85	45	40
Baptist	650	575	70	35	35
Lutheran	425	360	65	60	10
Muslim	180	60	115	50	65
Protestant not included elsewhere[2]	675	615	55	45	15
Presbyterian	150	120	30	25	0
Pentecostal	1,050	1,015	35	30	10
Jewish	30	20	0	10	0
Buddhist	155	55	95	55	40
Hindu	70	15	50	35	15
Sikh	45	20	25	25	0
Greek Orthodox	65	45	20	15	0
Mennonite	50	45	0	10	0
Orthodox not included elsewhere[3]	40	10	35	15	15
Jehovah's Witnesses	135	130	10	10	0
Ukrainian Catholic	50	50	0	0	0
Church of Jesus Christ of Latter-day Saints (Mormons)	95	85	10	0	10
Salvation Army	205	205	0	0	0
Christian Reformed Church	20	10	10	10	0
Evangelical Missionary Church	20	20	0	0	0
Christian and Missionary Alliance	60	55	0	0	0
Adventist	90	55	35	15	20
Non-denominational[4]	55	50	0	0	0
Ukrainian Orthodox	20	15	0	0	0
Aboriginal spirituality	235	235	0	0	0
Hutterite	0	0	0	0	0
Methodist[5]	35	20	15	0	10
Pagan[6]	35	35	0	0	0
Brethren in Christ	0	0	0	0	0
Serbian Orthodox	0	0	0	0	0

*Religions selected for this table represent counts of 20,000 or more for Canada.

[a] Includes non-permanent residents (not shown as a separate column in this table), as well as the sum of the counts for the Canadian-born and foreign-born population.

[b] Includes persons born in Canada as well as a small number of persons born outside Canada who are Canadian citizens by birth.

[c] This population is also referred to as the "immigrant population," which is defined as persons who are, or have ever been, landed immigrants in Canada.

[d] Includes data up to Census Day, May 15, 2001.

Source: Statistics Canada publication *Religions in Canada: Highlight Tables, 2001 Census*, Catalogue 97F0024XIE2001015, http://www.statcan.gc.ca/bsolc/olc-cel/olc-cel?catno=97F0024XIE2001015&lang=eng.

Selected Religions by Immigration Status and Immigration Period, 2001 Counts: Nova Scotia (20 Per Cent Sample Data)

Religion*	Total population[a]	Canadian-born population[b]	Foreign-born population[c]	Immigrated before 1991	Immigrated between 1991 and 2001[d]
Nova Scotia					
Total population	**897,570**	**853,660**	**41,315**	**31,030**	**10,290**
Roman Catholic	327,940	316,125	11,195	8,725	2,470
No religion	104,275	96,985	6,705	4,985	1,725
United Church	142,520	139,230	3,235	2,985	255
Anglican	120,315	114,935	5,190	4,710	485
Christian not included elsewhere[1]	10,105	8,945	1,050	650	400
Baptist	94,990	92,770	2,090	1,695	390
Lutheran	11,080	10,105	930	795	130
Muslim	3,550	450	2,770	330	2,440
Protestant not included elsewhere[2]	15,065	14,155	865	665	200
Presbyterian	22,450	21,295	1,115	955	160
Pentecostal	9,200	8,945	235	155	85
Jewish	2,120	1,670	415	380	45
Buddhist	1,735	640	945	660	285
Hindu	1,235	380	840	570	275
Sikh	270	125	150	125	20
Greek Orthodox	2,090	1,150	925	750	175
Mennonite	790	690	105	65	35
Orthodox not included elsewhere[3]	890	410	485	200	285
Jehovah's Witnesses	4,495	4,255	235	190	35
Ukrainian Catholic	280	255	25	25	0
Church of Jesus Christ of Latter-day Saints (Mormons)	2,530	2,395	90	90	0
Salvation Army	3,940	3,895	40	35	0
Christian Reformed Church	715	545	175	170	0
Evangelical Missionary Church	175	130	40	10	25
Christian and Missionary Alliance	180	155	20	0	20
Adventist	1,420	1,320	80	65	15
Non-denominational[4]	1,175	1,140	45	35	10
Ukrainian Orthodox	45	40	10	0	0
Aboriginal spirituality	270	245	25	25	10
Hutterite	0	0	0	0	0
Methodist[5]	250	150	75	60	20
Pagan[6]	775	715	50	50	0
Brethren in Christ	335	320	15	15	0
Serbian Orthodox	30	0	30	0	25

*Religions selected for this table represent counts of 20,000 or more for Canada.

[a] Includes non-permanent residents (not shown as a separate column in this table), as well as the sum of the counts for the Canadian-born and foreign-born population.

[b] Includes persons born in Canada as well as a small number of persons born outside Canada who are Canadian citizens by birth.

[c] This population is also referred to as the "immigrant population," which is defined as persons who are, or have ever been, landed immigrants in Canada.

[d] Includes data up to Census Day, May 15, 2001.

Source: Statistics Canada publication *Religions in Canada: Highlight Tables, 2001 Census*, Catalogue 97F0024XIE2001015, http://www.statcan.gc.ca/bsolc/olc-cel/olc-cel?catno=97F0024XIE2001015&lang=eng.

Selected Religions by Immigration Status and Immigration Period, 2001 Counts: Nunavut (20 Per Cent Sample Data)

Religion*	Total population[a]	Canadian-born population[b]	Foreign-born population[c]	Immigrated before 1991	Immigrated between 1991 and 2001[d]
Nunavut					
Total population	**26,665**	**26,195**	**445**	**340**	**110**
Roman Catholic	6,205	6,080	120	85	35
No religion	1,610	1,485	110	90	15
United Church	355	350	10	0	0
Anglican	15,440	15,375	65	55	10
Christian not included elsewhere[1]	840	815	15	10	10
Baptist	85	85	10	0	0
Lutheran	70	55	15	15	0
Muslim	25	0	25	15	10
Protestant not included elsewhere[2]	390	360	30	25	0
Presbyterian	65	55	10	10	0
Pentecostal	1,175	1,170	10	0	0
Jewish	10	0	0	0	0
Buddhist	15	0	10	0	10
Hindu	0	10	0	0	0
Sikh	0	0	0	0	0
Greek Orthodox	10	0	0	10	10
Mennonite	10	10	0	0	0
Orthodox not included elsewhere[3]	10	10	0	10	0
Jehovah's Witnesses	10	0	0	0	0
Ukrainian Catholic	0	10	0	0	0
Church of Jesus Christ of Latter-day Saints (Mormons)	10	0	0	0	0
Salvation Army	35	35	0	0	0
Christian Reformed Church	0	0	0	0	0
Evangelical Missionary Church	15	15	0	0	0
Christian and Missionary Alliance	95	95	0	0	0
Adventist	0	0	0	0	0
Non-denominational[4]	15	15	0	0	0
Ukrainian Orthodox	0	0	0	0	0
Aboriginal spirituality	25	30	0	0	0
Hutterite	0	0	0	0	0
Methodist[5]	0	0	10	0	10
Pagan[6]	15	10	0	0	0
Brethren in Christ	0	0	0	0	0
Serbian Orthodox	0	0	0	0	0

*Religions selected for this table represent counts of 20,000 or more for Canada.

[a] Includes non-permanent residents (not shown as a separate column in this table), as well as the sum of the counts for the Canadian-born and foreign-born population.

[b] Includes persons born in Canada as well as a small number of persons born outside Canada who are Canadian citizens by birth.

[c] This population is also referred to as the "immigrant population," which is defined as persons who are, or have ever been, landed immigrants in Canada.

[d] Includes data up to Census Day, May 15, 2001.

Source: Statistics Canada publication *Religions in Canada: Highlight Tables, 2001 Census*, Catalogue 97F0024XIE2001015, http://www.statcan.gc.ca/bsolc/olc-cel/olc-cel?catno=97F0024XIE2001015&lang=eng.

Selected Religions by Immigration Status and Immigration Period, 2001 Counts: Ontario (20 Per Cent Sample Data)

Religion*	Total population[a]	Canadian-born population[b]	Foreign-born population[c]	Immigrated before 1991	Immigrated between 1991 and 2001[d]
Ontario					
Total population	**11,285,550**	**8,164,855**	**3,030,075**	**2,007,705**	**1,022,375**
Roman Catholic	3,866,350	2,810,255	1,030,850	797,020	233,830
No religion	1,809,535	1,354,325	437,115	248,505	188,610
United Church	1,334,570	1,251,200	82,290	73,365	8,925
Anglican	985,110	819,955	162,520	145,465	17,055
Christian not included elsewhere[1]	301,935	181,785	114,795	60,355	54,440
Baptist	289,455	227,500	60,095	41,590	18,505
Lutheran	210,090	147,090	61,865	57,830	4,040
Muslim	352,525	82,535	257,375	82,160	175,220
Protestant not included elsewhere[2]	263,000	220,725	41,020	35,390	5,635
Presbyterian	279,195	228,040	49,835	42,485	7,350
Pentecostal	158,590	114,725	42,780	27,900	14,875
Jewish	190,800	129,750	59,435	44,415	15,020
Buddhist	128,320	29,845	94,770	59,590	35,185
Hindu	217,560	52,760	160,180	67,130	93,050
Sikh	104,790	33,340	70,315	33,795	36,525
Greek Orthodox	113,440	54,905	57,920	48,160	9,755
Mennonite	60,595	47,940	12,130	8,000	4,130
Orthodox not included elsewhere[3]	98,785	26,180	70,525	27,135	43,390
Jehovah's Witnesses	54,935	39,750	14,840	11,160	3,675
Ukrainian Catholic	38,440	23,810	14,485	10,435	4,050
Church of Jesus Christ of Latter-day Saints (Mormons)	20,355	16,115	3,795	2,510	1,285
Salvation Army	27,560	25,590	1,885	1,615	270
Christian Reformed Church	48,795	35,880	12,850	12,140	710
Evangelical Missionary Church	21,480	16,700	4,605	3,390	1,215
Christian and Missionary Alliance	14,590	10,975	3,525	2,115	1,415
Adventist	30,870	12,925	17,370	10,990	6,375
Non-denominational[4]	16,035	14,255	1,715	1,395	315
Ukrainian Orthodox	9,050	5,765	3,200	1,915	1,280
Aboriginal spirituality	7,265	6,825	425	280	145
Hutterite	55	40	10	0	15
Methodist[5]	16,615	7,780	8,260	5,740	2,525
Pagan[6]	7,565	6,895	665	550	115
Brethren in Christ	15,265	13,785	1,465	1,295	170
Serbian Orthodox	15,845	4,350	11,395	4,140	7,250

*Religions selected for this table represent counts of 20,000 or more for Canada.

[a] Includes non-permanent residents (not shown as a separate column in this table), as well as the sum of the counts for the Canadian-born and foreign-born population.

[b] Includes persons born in Canada as well as a small number of persons born outside Canada who are Canadian citizens by birth.

[c] This population is also referred to as the "immigrant population," which is defined as persons who are, or have ever been, landed immigrants in Canada.

[d] Includes data up to Census Day, May 15, 2001.

Source: Statistics Canada publication *Religions in Canada: Highlight Tables, 2001 Census*, Catalogue 97F0024XIE2001015, http://www.statcan.gc.ca/bsolc/olc-cel/olc-cel?catno=97F0024XIE2001015&lang=eng.

Selected Religions by Immigration Status and Immigration Period, 2001 Counts: Prince Edward Island (20 Per Cent Sample Data)

Religion*	Total population[a]	Canadian-born population[b]	Foreign-born population[c]	Immigrated before 1991	Immigrated between 1991 and 2001[d]
Prince Edward Island					
Total population	**133,385**	**128,935**	**4,140**	**3,350**	**790**
Roman Catholic	63,240	61,955	1,150	1,005	150
No religion	8,705	8,045	630	485	140
United Church	26,570	26,085	465	440	30
Anglican	6,525	6,110	410	380	30
Christian not included elsewhere[1]	3,210	3,020	170	80	80
Baptist	5,950	5,865	80	75	0
Lutheran	160	80	75	70	0
Muslim	195	30	165	35	130
Protestant not included elsewhere[2]	5,105	4,875	185	160	30
Presbyterian	7,885	7,605	275	220	55
Pentecostal	975	955	20	20	0
Jewish	55	30	15	15	0
Buddhist	140	45	95	45	45
Hindu	35	20	20	15	0
Sikh	0	0	0	0	0
Greek Orthodox	110	30	80	25	55
Mennonite	10	10	0	0	0
Orthodox not included elsewhere[3]	70	50	20	15	0
Jehovah's Witnesses	475	445	25	25	0
Ukrainian Catholic	15	20	0	0	0
Church of Jesus Christ of Latter-day Saints (Mormons)	215	195	15	15	0
Salvation Army	340	330	10	10	0
Christian Reformed Church	205	125	75	70	10
Evangelical Missionary Church	10	10	0	0	0
Christian and Missionary Alliance	0	0	0	0	0
Adventist	35	40	0	0	0
Non-denominational[4]	165	155	10	10	0
Ukrainian Orthodox	0	0	0	0	0
Aboriginal spirituality	50	50	10	0	0
Hutterite	0	0	0	0	0
Methodist[5]	10	0	10	10	0
Pagan[6]	45	45	0	0	0
Brethren in Christ	165	160	10	0	0
Serbian Orthodox	0	0	0	0	0

*Religions selected for this table represent counts of 20,000 or more for Canada.

[a] Includes non-permanent residents (not shown as a separate column in this table), as well as the sum of the counts for the Canadian-born and foreign-born population.

[b] Includes persons born in Canada as well as a small number of persons born outside Canada who are Canadian citizens by birth.

[c] This population is also referred to as the "immigrant population," which is defined as persons who are, or have ever been, landed immigrants in Canada.

[d] Includes data up to Census Day, May 15, 2001.

Source: Statistics Canada publication *Religions in Canada: Highlight Tables, 2001 Census*, Catalogue 97F0024XIE2001015, http://www.statcan.gc.ca/bsolc/olc-cel/olc-cel?catno=97F0024XIE2001015&lang=eng.

Selected Religions by Immigration Status and Immigration Period, 2001 Counts: Quebec (20 Per Cent Sample Data)

Religion*	Total population[a]	Canadian-born population[b]	Foreign-born population[c]	Immigrated before 1991	Immigrated between 1991 and 2001[d]
Quebec					
Total population	7,125,580	6,378,420	706,965	462,055	244,910
Roman Catholic	5,930,380	5,597,980	319,160	240,855	78,305
No religion	400,325	321,410	73,020	38,880	34,140
United Church	52,950	46,485	6,240	5,280	955
Anglican	85,475	73,145	11,665	10,055	1,605
Christian not included elsewhere[1]	56,750	38,880	16,490	8,770	7,720
Baptist	35,455	24,470	10,315	5,895	4,420
Lutheran	9,635	4,000	5,260	4,790	470
Muslim	108,620	24,320	75,280	20,080	55,205
Protestant not included elsewhere[2]	64,040	43,700	19,045	12,510	6,530
Presbyterian	8,770	6,540	2,015	1,515	500
Pentecostal	22,675	17,060	5,095	3,170	1,925
Jewish	89,915	60,285	29,040	24,720	4,325
Buddhist	41,375	10,915	29,605	22,230	7,370
Hindu	24,530	6,970	16,480	6,620	9,860
Sikh	8,220	1,825	5,315	1,785	3,535
Greek Orthodox	50,020	24,705	25,005	22,065	2,940
Mennonite	425	365	50	45	0
Orthodox not included elsewhere[3]	37,600	10,425	26,085	12,545	13,535
Jehovah's Witnesses	29,040	23,680	5,170	3,830	1,345
Ukrainian Catholic	3,430	1,945	1,475	1,100	370
Church of Jesus Christ of Latter-day Saints (Mormons)	4,420	3,130	1,185	640	540
Salvation Army	420	370	50	30	15
Christian Reformed Church	115	50	65	55	10
Evangelical Missionary Church	7,575	5,980	1,500	660	845
Christian and Missionary Alliance	315	170	135	100	30
Adventist	6,690	2,685	3,795	2,130	1,665
Non-denominational[4]	475	425	50	45	0
Ukrainian Orthodox	985	625	360	165	195
Aboriginal spirituality	735	700	40	30	10
Hutterite	0	0	0	0	0
Methodist[5]	1,060	180	725	525	200
Pagan[6]	1,330	1,240	55	30	25
Brethren in Christ	590	455	95	75	15
Serbian Orthodox	920	155	740	230	505

*Religions selected for this table represent counts of 20,000 or more for Canada.

[a] Includes non-permanent residents (not shown as a separate column in this table), as well as the sum of the counts for the Canadian-born and foreign-born population.

[b] Includes persons born in Canada as well as a small number of persons born outside Canada who are Canadian citizens by birth.

[c] This population is also referred to as the "immigrant population," which is defined as persons who are, or have ever been, landed immigrants in Canada.

[d] Includes data up to Census Day, May 15, 2001.

Source: Statistics Canada publication *Religions in Canada: Highlight Tables, 2001 Census*, Catalogue 97F0024XIE2001015, http://www.statcan.gc.ca/bsolc/olc-cel/olc-cel?catno=97F0024XIE2001015&lang=eng.

Selected Religions by Immigration Status and Immigration Period, 2001 Counts: Saskatchewan (20 Per Cent Sample Data)

Religion*	Total population[a]	Canadian-born population[b]	Foreign-born population[c]	Immigrated before 1991	Immigrated between 1991 and 2001[d]
Saskatchewan					
Total population	963,150	912,220	47,825	36,460	11,365
Roman Catholic	286,815	273,825	12,515	9,645	2,870
No religion	148,535	139,750	7,870	5,465	2,400
United Church	187,450	183,190	4,195	3,795	405
Anglican	65,740	62,150	3,495	3,135	360
Christian not included elsewhere[1]	27,075	25,280	1,600	1,050	550
Baptist	16,725	15,595	1,030	745	280
Lutheran	78,520	74,700	3,725	3,375	345
Muslim	2,230	420	1,505	495	1,010
Protestant not included elsewhere[2]	14,910	14,185	705	600	110
Presbyterian	7,010	6,265	700	495	200
Pentecostal	14,605	13,910	620	380	245
Jewish	865	705	155	145	15
Buddhist	3,050	1,105	1,845	1,335	510
Hindu	1,585	365	995	745	250
Sikh	500	180	300	185	120
Greek Orthodox	6,040	5,170	855	780	80
Mennonite	19,570	18,645	885	795	90
Orthodox not included elsewhere[3]	2,695	1,850	805	420	385
Jehovah's Witnesses	6,565	6,200	345	300	45
Ukrainian Catholic	17,615	17,075	535	455	85
Church of Jesus Christ of Latter-day Saints (Mormons)	2,885	2,690	180	110	70
Salvation Army	1,650	1,595	55	50	0
Christian Reformed Church	460	400	60	50	10
Evangelical Missionary Church	4,320	4,110	205	140	70
Christian and Missionary Alliance	8,940	8,430	510	370	135
Adventist	1,540	1,420	115	70	45
Non-denominational[4]	2,595	2,490	95	80	20
Ukrainian Orthodox	5,050	4,740	275	200	80
Aboriginal spirituality	5,885	5,835	40	25	10
Hutterite	4,895	4,805	90	70	15
Methodist[5]	910	750	140	100	45
Pagan[6]	670	655	15	0	10
Brethren in Christ	695	605	90	45	50
Serbian Orthodox	80	0	75	30	45

*Religions selected for this table represent counts of 20,000 or more for Canada.

[a] Includes non-permanent residents (not shown as a separate column in this table), as well as the sum of the counts for the Canadian-born and foreign-born population.

[b] Includes persons born in Canada as well as a small number of persons born outside Canada who are Canadian citizens by birth.

[c] This population is also referred to as the "immigrant population," which is defined as persons who are, or have ever been, landed immigrants in Canada.

[d] Includes data up to Census Day, May 15, 2001.

Source: Statistics Canada publication *Religions in Canada: Highlight Tables, 2001 Census*, Catalogue 97F0024XIE2001015, http://www.statcan.gc.ca/bsolc/olc-cel/olc-cel?catno=97F0024XIE2001015&lang=eng.

Selected Religions by Immigration Status and Immigration Period, 2001 Counts: Yukon Territory (20 Per Cent Sample Data)

Religion*	Total population[a]	Canadian-born population[b]	Foreign-born population[c]	Immigrated before 1991	Immigrated between 1991 and 2001[d]
Yukon Territory					
Total population	**28,520**	**25,445**	**3,025**	**2,245**	**780**
Roman Catholic	5,985	5,300	670	480	195
No religion	10,665	9,645	1,000	740	265
United Church	2,105	1,995	105	90	10
Anglican	3,795	3,545	250	220	30
Christian not included elsewhere[1]	1,010	845	155	105	45
Baptist	905	815	95	45	50
Lutheran	580	435	145	130	15
Muslim	60	15	45	30	15
Protestant not included elsewhere[2]	640	550	80	55	20
Presbyterian	190	155	35	35	0
Pentecostal	610	490	115	80	30
Jewish	35	30	10	0	10
Buddhist	130	75	50	30	25
Hindu	10	0	0	0	0
Sikh	105	20	85	45	35
Greek Orthodox	100	70	35	15	15
Mennonite	40	35	10	0	0
Orthodox not included elsewhere[3]	20	0	10	0	10
Jehovah's Witnesses	130	125	10	0	0
Ukrainian Catholic	30	35	0	0	0
Church of Jesus Christ of Latter-day Saints (Mormons)	115	115	10	10	0
Salvation Army	15	20	0	0	0
Christian Reformed Church	0	0	0	0	0
Evangelical Missionary Church	80	70	10	0	0
Christian and Missionary Alliance	10	10	0	0	0
Adventist	55	50	0	10	0
Non-denominational[4]	125	125	0	10	0
Ukrainian Orthodox	15	15	0	0	0
Aboriginal spirituality	185	180	0	0	0
Hutterite	0	0	0	0	0
Methodist[5]	10	0	10	10	0
Pagan[6]	125	95	25	20	0
Brethren in Christ	10	0	0	0	0
Serbian Orthodox	15	10	10	10	0

*Religions selected for this table represent counts of 20,000 or more for Canada.

[a] Includes non-permanent residents (not shown as a separate column in this table), as well as the sum of the counts for the Canadian-born and foreign-born population.

[b] Includes persons born in Canada as well as a small number of persons born outside Canada who are Canadian citizens by birth.

[c] This population is also referred to as the "immigrant population," which is defined as persons who are, or have ever been, landed immigrants in Canada.

[d] Includes data up to Census Day, May 15, 2001.

Source: Statistics Canada publication *Religions in Canada: Highlight Tables, 2001 Census*, Catalogue 97F0024XIE2001015, http://www.statcan.gc.ca/bsolc/olc-cel/olc-cel?catno=97F0024XIE2001015&lang=eng.

NOTES

1. Includes persons who report "Christian," as well as those who report "Apostolic," "Born-again Christian," and "Evangelical."

2. Includes persons who report only "Protestant."

3. Includes persons who report "Orthodox." Also includes Armenian Apostolic, Bulgarian Orthodox, Ethiopian Orthodox and Macedonian Orthodox.

4. Includes persons who report only "Non-denominational."

5. Includes persons who report "Methodist." Excludes Free Methodist and Evangelical Missionary Church.

6. Includes persons who report "Wicca."

Contributors

Terence J. Fay is a member of the Toronto School of Theology and teaches the history of religion at St. Augustine's Seminary and the University of St. Michael's College at the University of Toronto. He co-edited *Spiritual Roots: The Roman Catholic Archdiocese of Toronto at 150 Years of Age* (1991) and was research director of the *Dictionary of Jesuit Biography: Ministry to English Canada, 1842–1987* (1991). He is the author of *A History of Canadian Catholics: Gallicanism, Romanism, and Canadianism* (2002).

Irving Hexham is Professor of Religious Studies at the University of Calgary and a Fellow of both the Royal Anthropological Institute and the Royal Historical Society. He has published 25 books and numerous articles. His latest book is *Understanding World Religions* (2011). He is conducting research on the religious aspects of Nazi ideology.

Amir Hussain is Professor of Theological Studies at Loyola Marymount University, the Jesuit university in Los Angeles. He teaches courses on world religions, and specializes in the study of Islam. His academic degrees are all from the University of Toronto, where he received a number of awards, including the university's highest award for alumni service. From 2011 until 2015, he is the editor of the *Journal of the American Academy of Religion,* the premier scholarly journal for the study of religion. In 2008, he was appointed a Fellow of the Los Angeles Institute for the Humanities. Since 2005, he has written over 25 book chapters or scholarly articles about Islam and Muslims.

C.T. McIntire teaches history and religion at the University of Toronto, and he is a Fellow of Victoria College, Toronto. His publications include *The Parish and Cathedral of St. James, Toronto, 1797–1997: A Collaborative History* (edited by William Cooke, 1998), *Dissenting History, Dissenting Religion: The Unsettling Thought of Herbert Butterfield* (2003), and *The United Church of Canada: A History* (2011).

Jordan Paper is Professor Emeritus in the Religious Studies program at York University, Toronto, Ontario, and a Fellow of the Centre for Studies in Religion and Society at the University of Victoria, British Columbia. His publications include *Offering Smoke: The Sacred Pipe in Native American Religion* (1988), *Through the Earth Darkly: Female Spirituality in Comparative Perspective* (1997), *The Deities are Many: A Polytheistic Theology* (2005), and *Native North American Religious Traditions: Dancing for Life* (2007).

Karla Poewe is Professor Emerita in the Department of Anthropology at the University of Calgary and Adjunct Research Professor at Liverpool Hope University. Her numerous publications include *New Religions as Global Cultures: Making the Human Sacred* (with Irving Hexham, 1997), and *New Religions and the Nazis* (2006).

Ira Robinson is Professor of Judaic Studies in the Department of Religion at Concordia University. He edited *Cyrus Adler: Selected Letters* (2 volumes, 1985), which won the Kenneth Smilen Award for Judaica non-fiction. Among his recent books are *Rabbis and Their Community: Studies in the Eastern European Orthodox Rabbinate in Montreal, 1896–1930* (2007), *Translating a Tradition: Studies in*

American Jewish History (2008), a translation of Joseph Margoshes' memoir *A World Apart* (2008), and *Les Communautés juives de Montréal: histoire et enjeux contemporains* (co-editor, 2010). He is president of the Canadian Society for Jewish Studies, and is past president of the Association for Canadian Jewish Studies (formerly the Canadian Jewish Historical Society) as well as the Jewish Public Library of Montreal.

Jamie S. Scott teaches courses in religion and culture at York University, where he serves as Director of the Graduate Program in Interdisciplinary Studies, and Professor in the Department of Humanities and the Graduate Programs in English, Geography, Humanities and Interdisciplinary Studies. His most recent contributions to research include books and essays on religion and postcolonial literature, pilgrimage and literature, missions and film, and missions and fiction.

Henry C.H. Shiu teaches in the Department of Humanities at the University of Toronto Scarborough. His research focuses on the doctrinal and historical aspects of Mahayana Buddhism in India, China, and Tibet, particularly *tathagatagarbha* theory, as well as the history of Buddhism in Canada and various forms of Socially Engaged Buddhism in the contemporary world. He serves as Co-Editor-in-Chief of The Monograph Series in Sino-Tibetan Buddhist Studies, published jointly by Renmin University of China, China Tibetology Publishing House, and the Sino-Tibetan Buddhist Studies Association in North America.

Pashaura Singh is Dr. Jasbir Singh Saini Endowed Chair in Sikh and Punjabi Studies and Professor of Religious Studies in the College of Humanities, Arts, and Social Sciences at the University of California Riverside. His many publications include *The Guru Granth Sahib: Canon, Meaning, and Authority* (2000), *The Bhagats of the Guru Granth Sahib: Sikh Self-Definition and the Bhagat Bani* (2003), *The Life and Work of Guru Arjan: History, Memory and Biography in the Sikh Tradition* (2006), and *Sikhism in Global Context* (2011).

Will C. van den Hoonaard is Professor Emeritus of Sociology at the University of New Brunswick. His current research covers qualitative and ethnographic research, research ethics, the Baháʼí community of Canada, and the world of cartographers. He has authored eight books, including *The Origins of the Baháʼí Community of Canada, 1898–1948* (1996), *The Equality of Women and Men: The Experience of the Baháʼí Community of Canada* (with Deborah van den Hoonaard, 2006), and most recently, *The Seduction of Ethics: Transforming the Social Sciences* (2011). He is a founding member of the (Canadian) Interagency Advisory Panel on Research Ethics.

Paul Younger studied at Banaras Hindu University and Princeton University. Since 1964, he has taught at McMaster University, where he is now Professor Emeritus. His current research interest is in the Hindu communities formed in Canada and in other diasporic locations. His most recent books are *The Home of Dancing Śivan: The Traditions of the Hindu Temple in Citamparam* (1995), *Playing Host to Deity: Festival Religion in the South Indian Tradition* (2002), and *New Homelands: Hindu Communities in Mauritius, Guyana, Trinidad, South Africa, Fiji, and East Africa* (2010).

Index